Language Policy

Volume 36

Series Editors
Joseph Lo Bianco, University of Melbourne, Melbourne, Australia
Terrence G. Wiley, Professor Emeritus, Arizona State University, Tempe, USA

Editorial Board Members
Claire Kramsch, University of California, Berkeley, USA
Georges Lüdi, University of Basel, Basel, Switzerland
Normand Labrie, University of Toronto, Toronto, Canada
Anne Pakir, National University of Singapore, Singapore, Singapore
Guadalupe Valdes, Stanford University, California, USA

The last half century has witnessed an explosive shift in language diversity involving a rapid spread of global languages and an associated threat to small languages. The diffusion of global languages, the stampede towards English, the counter-pressures in the form of ethnic efforts to reverse or slow the process, the continued determination of nation-states to assert national identity through language, and, in an opposite direction, the greater tolerance shown to multilingualism and the increasing concern for language rights, all these are working to make the study of the nature and possibilities of language policy and planning a field of swift growth.

The series publishes empirical studies of general language policy or of language education policy, or monographs dealing with the theory and general nature of the field. We welcome detailed accounts of language policy-making - who is involved, what is done, how it develops, why it is attempted. We will publish research dealing with the development of policy under different conditions and the effect of implementation. We will be interested in accounts of policy development by governments and governmental agencies, by large international companies, foundations, and organizations, as well as the efforts of groups attempting to resist or modify governmental policies. We are interested in work that explores new sites of language policy development, new approaches to its analysis and effects, and while critique is important we are also interested in documentation of its intentions and practices, including historical examinations and contemporary analyses. We will also consider empirical studies that are relevant to policy of a general nature, e.g. the local effects of the developing European policy of starting language teaching earlier, issues to do with global languages, language and power and resistance, developments in post-colonial settings, de-colonial thinking and practice, all the way to programmatic issues such as the numbers of hours of instruction needed to achieve competence, selection and training of language teachers, the language effects of the Internet. Other possible topics include the legal basis for language policy, the role of social identity in policy development, the influence of political ideology on language policy, the role of economic factors, policy as a reflection of social change.

The series is intended for scholars in the field of language policy and others interested in the topic, including sociolinguists, educational and applied linguists, language planners, language educators, sociologists, political scientists, and comparative educationalists.

Book proposals for this series may be submitted to the Publishing Editor:

Amy Taylor-Snyman, Publishing Editor, Springer, Van Godewijckstraat 30, 3300 AA Dordrecht, The Netherlands Email: amy.taylor-snyman@springernature.com

All proposals and manuscripts submitted to the Series will undergo at least two rounds of external peer review.

This series is indexed in Scopus.

Joseph Lo Bianco • Elizabeth Ka Yee Loh
Mark Shiu-kee Shum
Editors

Supporting the Learning of Chinese as a Second Language: Implications for Language Education Policy

Editors
Joseph Lo Bianco
Faculty of Education
University of Melbourne
Parkville, VIC, Australia

Elizabeth Ka Yee Loh
Faculty of Education
The University of Hong Kong
Hong Kong SAR, China

Mark Shiu-kee Shum
Faculty of Education
The University of Hong Kong
Hong Kong SAR, China

ISSN 1571-5361   ISSN 2452-1027 (electronic)
Language Policy
ISBN 978-3-031-66134-1   ISBN 978-3-031-66135-8 (eBook)
https://doi.org/10.1007/978-3-031-66135-8

© The Editor(s) (if applicable) and The Author(s), under exclusive license to Springer Nature Switzerland AG 2024

This work is subject to copyright. All rights are solely and exclusively licensed by the Publisher, whether the whole or part of the material is concerned, specifically the rights of translation, reprinting, reuse of illustrations, recitation, broadcasting, reproduction on microfilms or in any other physical way, and transmission or information storage and retrieval, electronic adaptation, computer software, or by similar or dissimilar methodology now known or hereafter developed.
The use of general descriptive names, registered names, trademarks, service marks, etc. in this publication does not imply, even in the absence of a specific statement, that such names are exempt from the relevant protective laws and regulations and therefore free for general use.
The publisher, the authors and the editors are safe to assume that the advice and information in this book are believed to be true and accurate at the date of publication. Neither the publisher nor the authors or the editors give a warranty, expressed or implied, with respect to the material contained herein or for any errors or omissions that may have been made. The publisher remains neutral with regard to jurisdictional claims in published maps and institutional affiliations.

This Springer imprint is published by the registered company Springer Nature Switzerland AG
The registered company address is: Gewerbestrasse 11, 6330 Cham, Switzerland

If disposing of this product, please recycle the paper.

Our volume is dedicated to the memory of Kathy Purvis, a committed educator and Chinese language specialist, whose contribution to this volume is greatly appreciated.

Introducing Supporting the Learning of Chinese as a Second Language: Implications for Language Education Policy

The essential aim of our volume is concerned with how to make Chinese language learning more effective, for larger numbers of students, and in the typical conditions in which the language is studied. These "typical conditions" vary greatly, from complete foreign language immersion to the study of the language in formal settings when it is spoken in the wider environment of the learners. It might seem that these settings are so diverse that the term "typical conditions" could not sensibly apply to them all. However, although the differentiation among learners is possibly endless if we include individual and small group characteristics, the conditions of teaching and learning do fit into broader categories shaped by the relevant public policy settings and the sociolinguistic and demographic contexts in which programming occurs.

The volume focuses on language education planning, which is the public policy process applied to educational settings and draws links between such educational policies and student needs in Chinese as a second language (CSL) learning. Related themes extend from policy linked to different pedagogical affordances and their effectiveness in supporting students studying the language, strategies to stimulate their learning motivation, advice to CSL curriculum development, and the perceptual change of CSL teachers' approach to and preparation for teaching. As editors of the book, we have ourselves contributed chapters and participated in the research on which several of the chapters are based, and this, we trust, lends the volume a coherence despite the wide range of specific topics covered. The first word of the title, "Supporting" of the book lends coherence to the content. In their distinctive ways, all chapters are organized by and respond to this key notion, of how research can lead to practical changes that support learners to achieve success in mastering Chinese, as a second or foreign language, in the settings in which they reside. Given the many challenges involved in learning Chinese, the idea of research-informed support sustains the entire volume. In this respect, we believe the volume fills a gap in the literature at a time of surging interest in Chinese language study for second language learners across the globe, a surging interest that is, however, accompanied by concern about the effectiveness and practical outcomes of the programs they are offered.

The volume is divided into thematic parts, and although these are of uneven length, each one offers a distinctive focus in the chapters they contain, and all respond to this overarching focus of support.

Part I: Language Policy

The first part reviews and discusses the policy settings in which Chinese as a second/foreign language (CSL/CFL) programs exist. Although Part I mostly deals with various English-speaking settings and Hong Kong, reference is made to a wider range of global settings. The essential question of this first part is to probe how students' learning is shaped by the policy environment in which school programming occurs, what specific aims are established by authorities, how these are implemented, and the prospects of feedback from the realm of implementation and practice back onto the policy-determining settings of government, administration, and policy. In effect, the key question posed in Part I is how policy supports student learning, to what extent it currently does, and how shortfalls in policy support can be redressed by focused research. Two chapters comprise this first part.

The first chapter is by Lo Bianco and is entitled "Contexts of Learning, Priorities for Research". Lo Bianco examines the ways in which the settings in which teaching and learning of Chinese can be conceptualized as "acquisition planning," a theory positions from classical language policy studies informed by relevant issues of geo-strategic concern and diaspora studies. These sources of knowledge form a coherent base of identifying the characteristics of CSL within public policy across English-speaking settings, with some reference to the policy determinations for Chinese within other geographic areas. The first of these is the continual focus in public media as to the expansion of CSL teaching, with new evidence of decline in some settings, and continued rapid expansion in others. The chapter discusses some of the ways these shifts have been labelled, and how these constitute the context of expectations for achievement in CSL. The chapter reports the wider/longer history of favored second languages and theoretical positions about extant language hierarchies. Finally, some research agendas, relevant to the current volume and discussed in subsequent chapters, are set out, including what impact research might be said to have on public policy.

The second chapter in Part I is titled "Chinese Language Learning by Ethnic Minority Students in Hong Kong: Policy and Support" and addresses the central question of Chinese language learning by ethnic minority students. Like the first chapter in this part, it too seeks to link policy settings with the thematic key of the overall volume: *support*. The authors Ki, Tse, Ho, and Shum provide an overview on how the problem of Chinese language education and social integration of ethnic minority students in Hong Kong has been addressed by the Government in terms of education and language policy. They discuss how ethnic minority students, parents, and teachers have perceived and adapted to the situation as shown by academic research in the field. The chapter also reviews what innovative practices have been tried out by Chinese language education researchers and teachers together to explore new possibilities. The authors discuss a period of about 20 years, from 1997, coinciding with the political handover of Hong Kong, to 2018/2019. In the initial 10 years, the government seemed to subscribe to the idea that a pluralist Hong Kong would be beneficial and was quite responsive to the ethnic minority community demands for education reform. However, an assimilative policy stance has asserted itself in the second 10-year phase of the period under review. Nonetheless, the authors show that some advancement in teacher development and culturally responsive teaching of Chinese for ethnic minority students have been achieved.

Having established the framing effects of policy, the focus on mechanisms for supporting students learning Chinese as a second/foreign language shifts in Part II, which looks in close detail at the trajectory of learning that students undergo in their acquisition of Chinese as a second/foreign language.

Part II: The Learning Trajectory

A trajectory refers to the path followed by an entity, or a person, through the time and space of its development. It is an appropriate metaphor for learners and learning since the time involved is extensive, the duration of their schooling is long, and the space can refer to the settings in which their learning occurs. As learners proceed through the spaces that language policy creates to foster their acquisition of Chinese language, they are subjected to demands of growing complexity, to curriculums designed according to varying theoretical design principles, and to various practical, pedagogical, and material constraints. This part of *Supporting the Learning of Chinese as a Second Language: Implications for Language Education Policy* reports a great deal of research organized in ten chapters, divided into three parts:

Part A: Literacy Development: Character Learning and Reading Comprehension
Part B: Reading and Writing Development
Part C: Integrated Language Learning

Part A is titled *Literacy Development: Character Learning and Reading Comprehension* and contains four chapters. This component of the learning trajectory focuses on the critical domain of the acquisition and mastery of the written form of Chinese, the characters. The learning of characters is a clearly distinctive and central objective of the acquisition of Chinese in any setting by any group of learners and is often considered a demanding and difficult task. The challenge represented by characters, how characters are learned, and how reading comprehension can be best supported as learners acquire characters are all discussed in research-based chapters that respond directly to the central theme of our volume, how to support learners to achieve success in Chinese. Collectively, character learning and reading comprehension constitute the wider task of literacy attainment in the unique writing system of Chinese. There are four chapters in Part A.

Chapter is titled "Cognitive Processing Based Curriculum for the Facilitation of Chinese as a Second Language Young Learners' Chinese Character Learning", by Loh, Chan, Fung, and Fung. The authors report on a three-year longitudinal study, which investigated the developmental orthographic awareness of Chinese characters among K1 to K3 CSL kindergarteners. Their research revealed that single character reading is a significant longitudinal predictor of their radical awareness development. The authors also found that single character reading laid a foundation for the learning of Chinese character meanings. On the basis of these findings, Loh, Chan, Fung, and Fung designed a cognitive processing-based curriculum aimed at strengthening orthographic awareness to facilitate children's Chinese character learning. The theme of supporting is represented in this chapter in the close link between the longitudinal research and the rationale the authors offer for the curriculum design to bolster single character reading, the learning objectives, teaching materials, as well as various pedagogies and learning activities of the curriculum, and how they help to facilitate the development of CSL kindergarteners' orthographic awareness.

Chapter is titled "Comparing the Effects of Inhibitory Control on Chinese Reading Comprehension Between Learners of Chinese as a First and Second Language", by Sun, Loh, and Liao. Taking up the volume theme of *Supporting the Learning of Chinese as a Second Language: Implications for Language Education Policy*, the authors report that Chinese reading comprehension is vital for both native speakers and CSL learners and note that this applies equally to ethnic minority (EM) students from China's Autonomous Regions. These students, such as Uighurs, Kazakhs, Mongolians, and Tibetans, often learn Chinese after acquiring their own language and may attend prestigious universities in major cities, and hence reading comprehension is essential for their academic success. The authors note that executive function (EF), which comprises inhibitory control, cognitive flexibility, and working memory, plays a significant role in reading comprehension and that inhibitory control positively impacts primary school students' second language reading performance, while its effects on senior secondary school native Chinese and CSL students remain unclear. The authors report a study involving 107 CSL students and 142 native Chinese students, in which participants were assessed using Chinese literacy, inhibitory control, and non-verbal intelligence instruments. They found no correlation between reading and inhibitory control in native students, while a negative relation was observed in CSL students and speculate that these findings may offer new insights into inhibitory control's role in reading comprehension for both Chinese and CSL adolescent learners.

Chapter is titled "Space of Learning: The Application of Phenomenography and Drama in Chinese as a Second Language Learning", by Loh, Winston, and Ki, and addresses the theme of research-based support for learners of Chinese during their learning trajectory in relation to drama and phenomenography. The authors note that during the past decade, "drama in education" pedagogy has been widely used to facilitate students' learning of CSL in Hong Kong. Research has found that this pedagogy helps to enhance students' language proficiency and learning motivation. The authors apply phenomenography to examine why "drama in education" pedagogy is effective and how it develops and transforms the students' way of seeing the language and the learning content. They also study these phenomena and approaches to discern how variant and invariant processes work during the learning process. The playfulness and increased freedom of choice provided by "drama in education" pedagogy have been seen to open spaces for learning and thinking, extend the imagination, and stimulate higher levels of text, sentence, and question generation that stretch beyond a straightforward learning of vocabulary. In keeping with the aim of support for learners, the authors develop a series of suggestions for teachers and practitioners to help them apply the pedagogy as part of their daily CSL classroom teaching.

Chapter, the final one in Part A of Part II, is titled, "Song-Stuck-In-My-Head: Acquisition on Adjectival Predicates for Secondary School Students in Hong Kong Learning Chinese as a Second Language Through Mandarin Songs", by Kan. The research reported by Kan also focuses on the necessity of learning CSL in Hong Kong noting that this is increasing as the population growth of ethnic minority students in Hong Kong continues. The lack of a centralized curriculum for students is noted as an obstacle to systematic improvement, as noted even by the examiner report of International General Certificate of Secondary Education (0547), which points out that platitudinous use of the character 是 (is) is one of the most frequently made grammatical mistakes by candidates. Kan applies hypotheses from the research of Krashen, Song-Stuck-In-My-Head Phenomenon, as well as VanPatten's (1996) input processing theory, to generate a distinctive theoretical framework to test whether students who learn CSL could acquire the target grammar point (i.e., the adjectival predicate) by listening to Mandarin songs with input processing activities conducted in classes. Kan used a quasi-experimental design and multiple case study in research with 69 Hong Kong secondary school participants. After a four-week intervention, it was found that students who listened to Mandarin pop songs with input processing activities showed improvement in the usage of the target grammar point and outperformed the control group and the other experimental group without input processing activities.

Part B, *Reading and Writing Development* of Part II, the learning trajectory consists of five chapters, responding to the critical need for better support for learners of Chinese.

Chapter, titled "Learning Chinese as a Second Language in Hong Kong: The Needs of the Learners in Writing", by Shum and Shi. The authors note the heightened status of Chinese language in Hong Kong (a clear connection between policy as discussed in Part I and educational programming) is key to the upward mobility prospects of ethnic minority students from low socioeconomic backgrounds. Because these non-Chinese speaking (NCS) students constitute a disadvantaged group of second language learners, they tend to lack pedagogical support in Chinese language learning in Hong Kong. Shum and Shi conducted research to understand the writing difficulties and learning needs of these students in order to prepare them for targeted pedagogic intervention for better Chinese language acquisition. Based on the students' pre-tests and interview data, genre-based "Reading to Learn, Learning to Write" (R2L) assessment criteria were used to evaluate and identify the deficiencies in the students' writings. The findings lay a solid foundation for teaching that would be specific to the needs of language learning of South Asian ethnic minority students in Hong Kong and constitute a clear line of research-based support for these students.

Chapter, titled "Using 'Reading to Learn, Learning to Write' (R2L) Pedagogy to Teach Explanation Genre to Non-Chinese Speaking Students in Hong Kong", is by Shum, Yung, and Shi. This chapter is linked to chapter seven through the specific focus on the writing needs of non-Chinese speaking (NCS) students learning CSL. In order to provide pedagogical support to cope with the students' learning needs, the authors introduce the "Reading to Learn, Learning to Write" (R2L) Pedagogy, explaining its theoretical underpinning, and illustrating how R2L Pedagogy can be applied in daily CSL classroom teaching. The authors report a case study, which involves classroom observation, interviews, and text analysis, to describe how R2L Pedagogy can provide students with all-round support, illustrated in the specific context of a CSL writing class dealing with the explanation genre. Shum, Yung, and Shi evaluate the effectiveness of the R2L pedagogy on enhancing the writing ability of NCS students through integration of reading and writing. They found that the R2L Pedagogy provided students with abundant support in language input and output and note that the research results indicated that NCS students showed great improvements in writing after R2L teaching.

Chapter titled "When Stanislavski Met Halliday: A Case Study" by Woo. Also occurring in the context of an increasing number of ethnic minority students in Hong Kong. Woo notes that since the 1997 handover, this cohort of students has grown and its Chinese language learning needs have deepened. How to provide effective support to such learners? The chapter poses this question in an innovative way, by looking to ease the Chinese writing difficulties of such students by adopting Stanislavski's system in the learning Chinese narrative writing as a second language. Located in one of Hong Kong secondary schools, the study and innovation reported in the chapter use a three-part theoretical framework. First, second language acquisition theories and specifically the Input Hypothesis Model of Krashen and the Interactive Hypothesis of Long. Second, Woo uses Stanislavski's system, and third, Woo adopts genre theories of narrative writing based on Halliday's Systemic Functional Grammar. The research participants are two Chinese language teachers and two classes of Form 1 and Form 2 ethnic minority students. The research was conducted over a one-year period, based on a researcher-as-practitioner collaboration with the teachers by using Stanislavski's system in the Chinese narrative writing classes. Student writings was analyzed using Halliday's Systemic Functional Grammar, and the pre-experimental research design was used to evaluate Stanislavski's System in the learning Chinese narrative writing. Results showed improvements in the overall writing performance of both low and high achievers. Their ability of expressing feelings through Chinese writing was also improved as more emotive lexicons were found.

Chapter, titled "A Multiple Case Study of 1.5 Chinese Students' Writing Strategies", by Feng directly focused on writing, which has always been recognized as the most difficult and challenging part of language learning. Feng reports a multiple case study of Chinese students' strategies in writing, filling a gap between writing research in other languages and its counterpart effort in relation to Chinese. The term "Generation 1.5" refers to students whose family language differs from the dominant language in education and society, and the author reports that there is a rapidly growing number of Gen 1.5 Chinese students, but that little is known about their writing abilities and strategies. This study adopts target sampling and a differentiated sample of Chinese language Gen 1.5 students of varying language abilities. The researcher used think-aloud protocols and stimulated recall with the students, supplemented by observations on a form and process log, triangulating the data collection in various way, and ultimately identifying 32 types of writing strategy. More skilled students used writing strategies more frequently and effectively in various writing stages than their less skilled counterparts. The more skilled students also deployed more interactive writing strategies which in turn made their writing more effective, while the writing strategies of less skilled students often lacked correlation and were even contradictory with each other, thus negatively impacting their writing performance. Based on these research findings, Feng makes both theoretical and pedagogical contributions to Gen 1.5 Chinese writing strategy research and teaching.

Chapter, titled "Enhancing the Liberal Studies Writing Skills of Non-Chinese Speaking Students Through Genre-based Teaching", is by Shum, Loh, and Chan. The final chapter in Part B of the Learning Trajectory part focuses on Liberal Studies (LS), one of the four compulsory subjects in the Hong Kong Senior Secondary curriculum; at the time of the research, LS was a requirement for tertiary entrance or admission. However, by its very nature, this subject was extremely challenging for NCS students to use Chinese as the medium of instruction for Liberal Studies, especially when writing their answers in Chinese in public examination. In response to their learning needs, a research team at The University of Hong Kong (HKU) launched a pilot study using genre-based teaching to enhance the writing skills of NCS students. Based on MAK Halliday's Functional Linguistics and Genre Theory by James Martin, one of the authors, Mark Shum at HKU, had previously identified the genres of LS. The authors of this chapter used the genres identified by Shum to conduct genre teaching in a class of NCS students to enhance their writing skills with the factorial explanation genre, one of the important genres within the LS subject. In this chapter, the authors report the strategies of the genre-based pedagogy and the outcomes of the genre-based teaching by class observations, interviews, and text analyses of students' scripts of pre-test and post-test. The results indicated that after genre teaching, the written performance of NCS students improved in terms of genre identification, sentence patterns, and overall construction of the texts. The interviews reflected that the students welcomed this kind of learning and teaching model, and they felt more confidence in writing LS essays in Chinese.

Part C of the Learning Trajectory is *Integrated Language Learning* and consists of one chapter, the 12th in the volume, titled *The Sharing Economy in CSL Classroom: mLang – a New Approach of Using IT to Assist Second Language Learning*, by Elizabeth Loh. Second language learners mainly rely on their teachers and the pre-designed textbooks to facilitate their learning. However, due to the diversity of language proficiency and the diverse interests of students, teachers always find that such learning materials cannot address individual student's learning needs. Inspired by the idea of sharing economy, and the application of information technology, teachers and students can create personalized learning materials and then share among the group. Such collectively developed learning materials are then being used to support peer-to-peer learning through a self-developed online platform named "mLang." Results of pre-test and post-test and student questionnaire found that students' learning motivation and second language proficiency have significant improvement after using mLang and related pedagogies supported by second language learning theories for one year. In this chapter, Loh reports the design of mLang, the online learning platform, how it works, the implementation of related pedagogies, and how this constitutes an effective mode of support for Chinese language learners.

Part III: Learning Motivation

It is widely acknowledged that fostering a positive and engaged learning motivation can be critical to language learning success. In this part of *Supporting the Learning of Chinese as a Second Language: Implications for Language Education Policy*, we include two research chapters that address the question of motivation.

Chapter, titled "Developing Strategies for Motivating Australian Secondary Students to Learn Chinese", is by Sit, Sun, Chen, Thomas, and Perterson. This chapter reports a case study conducted by an Australian University, at a mainstream school in the state of New South Wales, and a community language school in the state of Victoria, on developing effective strategies for teaching Chinese to native English-speaking secondary school students. With the regular calls in Australia to improve and extend Asian language study, particularly Chinese, it is crucial to address questions regarding student motivation and effective teaching practices. This study aimed to understand how to promote non-Chinese heritage-background learners' interest in the Chinese language. The research employed a mixed qualitative method, including classroom observations, in-depth interviews, and student focus groups. Three main findings emerged: intrinsic and extrinsic factors to motivation, the effectiveness of various pedagogies, and the relations between using effective pedagogies and maintaining motivation for learning Chinese. Practical recommendations for motivating secondary students to learn Chinese are proposed and discussed. The study fills a gap in understanding how to motivate monolingual English-speaking Australian secondary students to learn Chinese and has wide implications for teaching and learning Chinese across all levels of educational institutions.

Chapter, titled ""We Are Here to Learn Something Useful": Contextualization of Adult Learners' Motivation", is by Bo. In the context of the increasing interest to understand students' achievement motivation in foreign language learning, the chapter notes that previous studies primarily relied on quantitative data of questionnaires to generalize students' learning orientations without considering contextual factors. Considering the context-dependent nature of learning motivation, the author argues that it is critical to obtain a deeper understanding of motivational developments under various learning contexts. However, the study being reported shifts the "research target," usually younger students in K-12 to adults and examines adult learners' motivational changes under different contexts in a foreign language classroom. An ethnographic multi-case study was adopted, focusing on six students. Bo reports findings that all the students demonstrated an extrinsic-oriented motivation in the foreign language course that focused primarily on the utility of learning. Reasons shaping such a motivational orientation were observed to be stable among high-achieving students, while fluctuating among low-achieving students due to the change of learning contexts in the classroom, such as the context of peer comparison and the context of high-stake exam. Bo argues that context-dependent changes across time could provide pedagogical insights to instructors with adult learners.

Part IV: Curriculum Design and Learners' Life Worlds

The fourth part shifts the focus of the ways to support learners of Chinese, and to understand the dynamics of learning and its outcomes, onto the questions of the life worlds of learners and the shape, design, content, and nature of curriculum. Two chapters comprise this part.

Chapter, titled "Planning with Concepts: Creating Opportunities for Rich, Meaningful Language Learning in the Design of Curriculum for the Teaching and Learning of Chinese", is by Purvis. The author notes that an important element of an intercultural approach to teaching and learning languages in the current Australian context is the central role of concepts in curriculum design. She further notes that there has been an identifiable shift from a purely descriptive approach to concepts in curriculum to one in which learning is situated within a broader and deeper conceptual exploration. Concepts such as identity, family, friendship, sustainability, harmony, belonging, celebration not only provide a framework for rich and meaningful language learning within an intercultural orientation, but, the author argues, also connect language learning with learning across curriculum, including Humanities and Social Science, English, and the Arts. By reflecting on her own experience of developing Chinese language learning modules for the learning of Chinese both as an additional language and for a bilingual program, her chapter explores and analyses the value, processes, and challenges of working with concepts through a discussion of particular modules written for the project.

Chapter, "Chinese Language Education in Australia: Attending to the Lifeworlds of Learners", is by Scarino and Kohler. This chapter is also located within the context of Australia and begins by noting the extended and deep history of the presence of Chinese in the social and cultural landscape in Australia. The authors note that because of this extended presence Chinese is now one of the languages that presents the greatest variation in learner background in languages education. This diversity of backgrounds is generally understood as a structural and pedagogical challenge, which impacts on Chinese language learning in schools. However, the authors argue, it is less evident that there is a fundamental difference that pertains to the learners' life worlds and their affiliation with Chinese; their perceptions of its value, nature, and the purpose for learning it; and the different personal meaning that Chinese language learning can hold for different learners of the language in Australia. The authors provide a case study with a single teacher of Chinese, working with a range of learners of senior secondary Chinese, enacting a curricular intervention designed within a multilingual and intercultural orientation. They illustrate the ways in which the teacher of Chinese addresses the nature and purpose for learning for diverse learners within the class group. In this exploration of the teacher's curricular intervention, Scarino and Kohler consider themes related to the students' life worlds, their affiliation and identity, and the multilingual and intercultural nature and purpose of learning for the diverse learners of this language.

Part V: Teachers as the Change Agents

The volume commenced with the context of policy, a collective and public activity that results in the distribution of funding and other resources to the priorities identified in various policy processes. We conclude the volume by a focus on the critical implementer of the policy decisions, the teacher, and specifically on the question of teachers as change agents. In this respect, as agents who foster change, teachers are also a kind of policy maker, if we imagine an expansive notion of policy as activity at local, regional, and national levels.

In this final part, there is one chapter, authored by Loh and Tam. Chapter is titled, "Success or Failure: The Important Role of Emotionality for CSL Teachers' Professional Development". The authors note that over the past decade, many Chinese language teachers in Hong Kong have experienced many new challenges. They are expected to design and implement their own school-based curricula and adopt innovative pedagogies and customized materials for students learning CSL. The current literature suggests that some teachers are not ready for or even resist changes, amid new challenges and paradigm shifts. The authors draw on several theoretical models and frameworks (Guskey's Model of Teacher Change, Hall et al.'s Concerns-Based Adoption Model, and Bennett's Developmental Model of Intercultural Sensitivity) to conduct a multifaceted case study highlighting the role of emotionality as a key factor for successful teacher change. In addition, they revisit the sequences of the progressive stages of teachers facing change or innovations. They report research findings suggesting that an integrated model with inclusive support of collective lesson preparation and teaching demonstrations/practical sessions in professional development programs is a key element that helps the facilitation of CSL teachers' change and provides them with experiential learning opportunities for the enhancement of their confidence and reduction of anxiety, leading to their voluntary adoption of the new pedagogical approach, and gradual change in their beliefs and attitudes after witnessing the feasibility and effectiveness of the newly introduced concepts. Taking reference from such findings, the adaptation and modification of these three classical models is then proposed. Finally, they reveal some implications and suggestions for the design of CSL teachers' professional development programs and demonstrate the ways in which teachers can become change agents in the support of student learning.

In Conclusion

The research, reflections, case studies, and discussion in *Supporting the Learning of Chinese as a Second Language: Implications for Language Education Policy* are all directed at the central question of mobilizing knowledge to make Chinese language learning more effective. The settings in which this task is applied can be extremely varied, as the chapters show, and the participants (students, teachers, and officials) who are of course also highly diverse are tied to the writers in this book by the same ultimate objective, the contribution that researched knowledge can make to improving outcomes in Chinese language education. Unlike the other great languages of public education across the world, Chinese is a relative latecomer to mass global teaching. Yet, no one can doubt that its explosive recent growth is likely to continue for a long period into the future, and hence the urgent need for more and deeper research into the knowledge base for improving, making more effective, and deepening its learning. This is the overarching objective within which the chapters in this volume have been assembled, the research produced, and the volume completed.

Faculty of Education, University of Melbourne, Parkville, VIC, Australia	Joseph Lo Bianco
Faculty of Education, The University of Hong Kong, Hong Kong SAR, China	Elizabeth Ka Yee Loh
Faculty of Education, The University of Hong Kong, Hong Kong SAR, China	Mark Shiu-kee Shum

Contents

Part I Language Policy

Contexts of Learning, Priorities for Research.................... 3
Joseph Lo Bianco

Chinese Language Learning by Ethnic Minority Students
in Hong Kong: Policy and Support............................ 15
Wing-Wah Ki, Shek Kam Tse, Elizabeth Kam-Kau Ho,
and Mark Shiu-Kee Shum

Part II The Language Trajectory: Literacy Development—Character Learning and Reading Comprehension

Cognitive Processing Based Curriculum for the Facilitation
of Chinese as a Second Language Young Learners' Chinese
Character Learning.. 55
Elizabeth Ka Yee Loh, Tikky Sing Pui Chan, Renee Wei Yan Fung,
and Stephanie Mei Lok Fung

Comparing the Effects of Inhibitory Control on Chinese Reading
Comprehension Between Learners of Chinese as a First
and Second Language...................................... 77
Nissom Zheng Liang Sun, Elizabeth Ka Yee Loh, and Xian Liao

Space of Learning: The Application of Phenomenography
and Drama in Chinese as a Second Language Learning............ 99
Elizabeth Ka Yee Loh, Joe Winston, and Wing-Wah Ki

Song-Stuck-In-My-Head: Acquisition on Adjectival Predicates
for Secondary School Students in Hong Kong Learning Chinese
as a Second Language Through Mandarin Songs................. 125
Ziv Wang Ngai Kan

Part III The Language Trajectory: Reading and Writing Development

Learning Chinese as a Second Language in Hong Kong: The Needs of the Learners in Writing 163
Mark Shiu-kee Shum and Dan Shi

Using 'Reading to Learn, Learning to Write' (R2L) Pedagogy to Teach Explanation Genre to Non-Chinese Speaking Students in Hong Kong 179
Mark Shiu-kee Shum, Jojo Wan Shan Yung, and Dan Shi

When Stanislavski Met Halliday: A Case Study 201
Justine Po-Sau Woo

A Multiple-Case Study of 1.5 Chinese Students' Writing Strategies 225
Feifei Feng

Enhancing the Liberal Studies Writing Skills of Non-Chinese Speaking Students Through Genre-Based Teaching 239
Mark Shiu-kee Shum, Elizabeth Ka Yee Loh, and Hiu Ching Chan

Part IV The Language Trajectory: Integrated Language Learning

Sharing Economy in the CSL Classroom: mLang—A New Approach of Using IT to Assist Second Language Learning 271
Elizabeth Ka Yee Loh

Part V The Language Trajectory: Learning Motivation

Developing Strategies for Motivating Australian Secondary Students to Learn Chinese 313
Helena Sit, Haoliang Sun, Shen Chen, Erica Thomas, and Lisa Peterson

"We Are Here to Learn Something Useful": Contextualization of Adult Learners' Motivation 337
Wenjin Vikki Bo

Part VI Curriculum Design and Learners' Lifeworlds

Planning with Concepts: Creating Opportunities for Rich, Meaningful Language Learning in the Design of Curriculum for the Teaching and Learning of Chinese 357
Kathy Purvis

Chinese Language Education in Australia: Attending to the Lifeworlds of Learners 379
Angela Scarino and Michelle Kohler

Part VII Teachers as the Changing Agents

Success or Failure: The Important Role of Emotionality for CSL Teachers' Professional Development 399
Elizabeth Ka Yee Loh and Loretta Chung Wing Tam

Index 421

Editors and Contributors

About the Editors

Joseph Lo Bianco is professor emeritus in the Faculty of Education at the University of Melbourne, former president of the Australian Academy of the Humanities and a specialist language policy and planning analyst. He was author of Australia's National Policy on Languages in 1987, widely cited as a rare example of explicit language policy for multilingualism. He was chief executive and founder of the National Languages and Literacy Institute of Australia until 2002, and professor of language and literacy education at the University of Melbourne until his retirement in 2020. He has more than 140 publications in journals and academic volumes, and 25 books and major reports, and many years of international consulting experience on language policy, multilingualism and peace, and conflict mitigation in Southeast Asia.

Elizabeth Ka Yee Loh is an assistant professor, director of Double Degree programs and assistant dean (Knowledge Exchange) in the Faculty of Education at The University of Hong Kong and an adjunct professor of the Indonesian University of Education. Her research centers on teaching Chinese as both L1 and L2 to learners in K-12 education, particularly on innovative pedagogy. Her most recent research investigates multilingual and multimodal practices to facilitate multilingual children's learning across content. His work has been published in reputable journals across language education and education policy such as *Learning and Instruction*, *System*, *Current Psychology*, *Frontiers in Psychology*, *Language Policy*, and *Asia-Pacific Education Research*. She has received over US$13M in funding support from organizations, including University Grant Council, Language Fund of SCOLAR, Education Bureau, and SIE Fund of Hong Kong SAR Government. She also serves on the editorial boards of *Learning and Instruction* and *CASLAR* journals. She regularly facilitates professional development with in-service teachers and currently teaches pre- and in-service Chinese language teachers preparing to work with multilingual learners.

Mark Shiu-kee Shum received his PhD at the University of Melbourne. He is an honorary associate professor at the Faculty of Education at The University of Hong Kong. He was the founding head of Division of Chinese Language and Literature (2009–2015) at the Faculty of Education. He is also an adjunct associate professor in the Melbourne Graduate School of Education in the University of Melbourne and an adjunct professor of the Indonesian University of Education. He attracted four General Research Funds (GRF) from the Research Grant Council of Hong Kong. His research areas include Chinese language (in) education, text analysis, and second language Chinese pedagogy. His major writings include *The Functions of Language and the Teaching of Chinese* (published by the HKU Press), *Teaching Writing in Chinese Speaking Areas* (Springer), *Integrating IB Philosophy and Pedagogy into Chinese Language Teaching* (John Catt), *Researching Chinese Language Education: From Functional Linguistic Perspective* (Routledge), and *Appliable Linguistics Across Chinese Speaking Regions: Language (in) Education in Mainland China, Hong Kong and Singapore* (Springer).

Contributors

Wenjin Vikki Bo is senior lecturer in the College of Interdisciplinary and Experiential Learning at Singapore University of Social Sciences. Her research interests include language learning, achievement motivation, academic performance, and technology-enhanced learning. Her most recent research focuses on the predictive validity of various language assessments and explores the utility of academic literacy support upon university students' academic achievement. Dr Bo's work has appeared in refereed journals across the fields of language assessment, educational psychology, and higher education. She has received funding support from Singapore Ministry of Education to evaluate university programs to shape university policies.

Hiu Ching Chan is senior lecturer (acting) and programme leader of Special Child Care and Inclusive Education Higher Diploma programme at the Hong Kong Institute of Vocational Education. She received her MPhil in Education at the University of Cambridge. Her research areas include special and inclusion education and second language Chinese pedagogy. She worked closely with Dr. Mark Shiu-kee SHUM and Dr. Elizabeth Ka Yee LOH at the Faculty of Education in The University of Hong Kong as a teacher researcher to design and deliver the genre-based pedagogy to support the subject learning of non-Chinese speaking students in Hong Kong.

Tikky Sing Pui Chan is an adjunct assistant professor at the Centre for Child and Family Science of the Education University of Hong Kong (HKIEd). She has been a teacher educator supporting the professional development of pre-school teachers in HKIEd for more than thirty years. Her research work is focused on early childhood education, with special interests in language and literacy, and curriculum and pedagogy. Her recent research effort is devoted to teaching Chinese as a second language to young children. Collaborating with other academics, Dr Chan has successfully received research grants and project funding from the government and non-profit organizations, such as Oxfam Hong Kong and the Hong Kong Jockey Club Charities Trust.

Shen Chen is an honorary professor in the School of Education at the University of Newcastle, Australia. He is a multilingual teacher educator with nearly 30 years of teaching experience. He taught at Melbourne University, Deakin University in Australia before he moved to the University of Newcastle in 1993. He was invited as a visiting scholar or professor in the University of Cambridge, University of California, Berkeley, University of British Columbia, and the University of Hong Kong. He has published widely including 11 books and numerous articles in high profile academic journals and well-known international publishers.

Feifei Feng is the head of Chinese department in Singapore International School (Hong Kong). She obtained her master's degree from the Chinese University of Hong Kong in 2009, and the degree of Doctor of Education from the University of Hong Kong in 2018. Dr Feng is familiar with a variety of Chinese courses of Cambridge IGCSE and IBDP, and her current job focuses on curriculum mapping and school-based curriculum development.

Renee Wei Yan Fung is a project manager of a project supporting the learning and teaching of Chinese as a second language for preschoolers at the Faculty of Education, the University of Hong Kong. She is currently involved in the management, strategic planning, and curriculum development for the project. Having earned a double degree in BA and BEd in Language Education and an MPhil in Linguistics from HKU, she has contributed her expertise in language teaching and acquisition to projects covering a spectrum of aspects, including Chinese processing in typically and atypically developing children, second language acquisition, and neuroscience for education.

Stephanie Mei Lok Fung is a senior research assistant at the Faculty of Education, the University of Hong Kong. Prior to joining HKU, she obtained her MPhil degree in Theoretical and Applied Linguistics from the University of Cambridge. Her research interests lie in second language acquisition, bilingual development, sociolinguistics, and Chinese language education for non-Chinese speakers in Hong Kong.

Elizabeth Kam-kau Ho is a retired secondary school teacher. Her main job in secondary school was teaching ethnic minority learning Chinese. Her focus on teaching was both verbal and written communication in Chinese. Providing the ethnic minority with the skill in acquiring Chinese vocabulary in a more palatable way and mastering the skill in comprehending Chinese passages. Helping ethnic minority to perform plays in Chinese, publish storybooks written by them in the University of Hong Kong and produce animated video clips in Chinese. Besides, she had helped the University of Hong Kong in setting up a question bank for GCSE Chinese and written paper on autoethnography.

Ziv Wang Ngai Kan With over 14 years of experience in teaching Chinese as a second language, Ziv is familiar with education systems such as GCSE, IGCSE, GCE AS/A Level, and IB. He obtained his doctoral degree at the University of Hong Kong. His research centered on using music in acquiring Chinese grammar acquisition.

Wing-wah Ki is a retired associate professor of Faculty of Education, University of Hong Kong. His works cover teaching and learning of mathematics, computer studies, liberal studies, and second languages. His special interests are in the areas of phenomenographic learning theory of variation, amplification and reduction effects of technologies, designs of computer networks for teacher development, interest/strength-based education, and transformational pedagogies for ethnic minorities students and students with special education needs.

Michelle Kohler is senior research fellow at the Research Centre for Languages and Cultures, University of South Australia. Her research areas include second language teaching and learning, interculturality and mediation, languages curriculum design and assessment, and languages policy and planning. Michelle has led and collaborated on numerous state and national projects in languages education, working extensively with educators from early years to tertiary levels through a praxis-oriented approach. She is the author of *Developing Intercultural Language Learning* (Palgrave) and *Teachers as Mediators in the Foreign Language Classroom* (Multilingual Matters). Michelle is the immediate past president of the Applied Linguistics Association of Australia and a member of the Intercultural Mediation Research Network, International Association of Applied Linguistics.

Xian Liao is an assistant professor at the Department of Chinese Language Studies, Education University of Hong Kong. He obtained his PhD degree at the Hong Kong Polytechnic University. His research interests include the reading process, integrated writing, executive function, and translanguaging. His research has appeared in a series of international peer-review journals, such as *Reading and Writing*, *System*, and *Language Awareness*.

Lisa Peterson is currently the acting deputy head of Newcastle Grammar School. For the past ten years, she has been the director of Learning and Teaching, a role that has allowed her to guide the school to design and implement innovative and engaging learning experiences to improve student outcomes. Lisa has over 25 years of experience in teaching. She holds a Bachelor of Education (University of Sydney) and attained a Masters of Education in pedagogy from the University of Newcastle in 2015. She has worked with AITSL, ISTAA, and NESA on the teacher accreditation process in NSW. She has also received an Outstanding Professional Service Award. Lisa is a dedicated educator who is committed to ensuring students have access to outstanding learning experiences.

Kathy Purvis originally trained as a teacher of German and French but was given the opportunity to go back to university and study Chinese for 3 years in the 1990s and since then has been gradually teaching more and more Chinese. She has been the Languages Coordinator at several government high schools in Adelaide over the last 10 years and in each of these schools has been successful in increasing the numbers of students studying Chinese. She has worked with teams of language teachers in collaboration with university researchers on a number of school based research projects, including Teaching Literacy Through Language, Interaction in the Classroom, and Incorporating Higher-Order Thinking Skills into Teaching and Learning. She has also provided PD to language teachers on the use of iPads in the classroom and on Australian Curriculum through the CLTASA and AFMLTA.

Angela Scarino is associate professor in Applied Linguistics and director of the Research Centre for Languages and Cultures, in Justice and Society at the University of South Australia. Her research expertise is in languages education in linguistically and culturally diverse societies, multilingualism and interculturality in education, and learning-oriented assessment. She has been a chief investigator on numerous research grants in these areas. One of her major publications is *Intercultural Language Learning* (with Liddicoat (2013), Wiley-Blackwell). Her body of research has yielded significant impact on policy and practice. She is currently coeditor of the *Modern Language Journal*.

Dan Shi received her PhD from the University of Hong Kong. After her graduation, she was a post-doctoral fellow in language education research in the Faculty of Education at the University of Hong Kong. She is currently an assistant professor in the School of Education and English at the University of Nottingham Ningbo China. She is working with systemic functional linguistics, multimodality, discourse analysis, and sociological theory of education in her research. Her research interests also include learning style and scaffolding within L2 contexts and exploring learners' engagements with texts.

Helena Sit is a senior lecturer and PhD supervisor in the School of Education at the University of Newcastle, Australia. Her research expertise includes second language education, international education, higher education, and teacher education. She speaks and publishes widely on internationalization, transformative learning, and innovative language education programs. Her research has been nationally and internationally recognized in her discipline. She is an invited visiting scholar to the University of Hong Kong and the University of Cambridge. She has been selected as the recipient of the 2022 College Excellence Award for Research Supervision.

Haoliang Sun is the founder and principal of Xin Jin Shan Chinese Language and Culture School in Melbourne, Victoria, which is the largest community school in the Southern Hemisphere. He was awarded Masters' degree in Fudan University, Shanghai, China, and appointed as the Vice President of the China's Central Institute of Fine Arts in Beijing. He has published extensively regarding Chinese language teaching including his well-known monograph "Teaching Chinese Overseas." As the Chair of the Foundation of Chinese Education, he has supported and cooperated many joint research projects with Monash University and the University of Newcastle.

Nissom Zheng Liang Sun is a doctoral candidate in the Graduate School of Human and Environmental Studies at Kyoto University. His research interests include second language learning, early childhood education, and cognitive development. His most recent research focuses on the predictive role of executive function in learning Chinese as a second language. He also graduated and worked as a research assistant at the University of Hong Kong to enhance the second language learning of ethic minority students.

Loretta Chung Wing Tam is research manager at the Faculty of Education, the University of Hong Kong. After finishing her BA in English and Linguistics at the University of Hong Kong, she received her TCSL training at the International Chinese Language Program, National Taiwan University. She subsequently completed her MAppLing (LangProgMgt) at Macquarie University and her PhD in Anthropology at the Chinese University of Hong Kong. Loretta specializes in Teaching Chinese as a Second/Foreign Language with an emphasis on intercultural pedagogy, teacher professional development, and educational technology. She is also an experienced curriculum developer and published translator.

Erica Thomas is now the principal of Kincoppal-Rose Bay. From 2014 to 2022, she was the principal of Newcastle Grammar School, where she oversaw a significant transformation of the school and leading them through the shift to online learning through the COVID pandemic. A highly experienced and passionate educator with a strong focus on academic excellence and student well-being, Erica is an advocate for the positive influence of modern education. With a career in education spanning over 30 years, Erica has held a number of senior leadership positions in independent schools across NSW, including acting principal, deputy principal and head of Senior School at Queenwood, and director of Teaching and Learning and Director of Boarding at Kincoppal-Rose Bay. Erica holds a Bachelor of Education (Macquarie University), a Masters of Education (University of New England) and a Graduate Diploma in History (Monash University). She is an active member of the Association of Independent Schools Advisory Council.

Shek Kam Tse was former associate dean and director of the Centre for the Advancement of Chinese Language Education and Research in the Faculty of Education at the University of Hong Kong. He is now the consultant of two academic organizations. For many years, he has provided a consultancy service to a number of organizations, including the Chinese Education Centre of the

Netherlands Government, the Ministry of Education in Singapore, the Education Bureau of the Hong Kong Government, the Education and Youth Affairs Bureau of the Macao Government, and five international universities. He was bestowed the Eminent Scholars Award in 2018 by SCCL and the Dick Wolf Memorial Award by IEA in 2007. His research interests include the learning and teaching of Chinese as a first or second language, early childhood Chinese language education, bilingual reading, and ways of assessing and monitoring language learning. He has published more than 60 books, 300 book chapters, and research articles.

Joe Winston is emeritus professor of Drama and Theatre Education at the University of Warwick, UK. He has a particular interest in the use of drama to support second language learning. His many publications include the edited volume *Second Language Learning Through Drama* (Routledge, 2012) and *Performative Language Teaching in Early Education* (Bloomsbury, 2022). For many years, he was the co-editor of the leading academic journal *Research in Drama Education: the Journal of Applied Theatre and Performance*. He continues to train teachers and artists in the educational uses of drama in China and Hong Kong.

Justine Po-Sau Woo is a part-time lecturer in the Faculty of Education at the University of Hong Kong and a research fellow at m-Chinese Solution Limited. Her research focuses on multimodality, drama in education, and teaching Chinese as a second language. She is skilled in applying drama, music, and multimedia in teaching to enhance students' learning motivation and attitude, as well as promoting the professional development of in-service teachers.

Jojo Wan Shan Yung received her PhD at the University of Hong Kong in 2015. She is a lecturer at the School of Education and Languages at Hong Kong Metropolitan University. Her research areas include teaching Chinese as a second language, Chinese language education, text analysis, pedagogy for teaching Chinese to ethic minority students, etc. She has published papers in academic journals in Hong Kong, Mainland China, Singapore, Korea, etc. Her main writings include teaching reading and writing in Hong Kong, reading to learn pedagogy in Chinese language teaching, using social media to teach Chinese language to ethic minority students in Hong Kong, etc.

Part I
Language Policy

Contexts of Learning, Priorities for Research

Joseph Lo Bianco

Abstract This chapter provides a theoretical yet practical grounding for the book by exploring language education policy and planning addressed to Chinese as a second language. The focus is acquisition planning theory from classical language policy studies informed by relevant issues of geo-strategic concern and diaspora studies. These three sources of knowledge will form a coherent base of identifying the characteristics of Chinese as a second language within public policy across English speaking settings in particular, with some reference to the policy determinations for Chinese within other geographic areas, and taking into consideration the vast expanse of the Belt and Road Initiative of the People's Republic of China and the language spread repercussions, both intended and not intended, of the BRI. These lead to the question of the global status of Chinese and its relation to global English, examined using language spread theory. The role of Chinese the various jurisdictions that are linked culturally, strategically and in large population to the PRC are also discussed (Hong Kong, Taiwan, Malaysia, and Singapore).

1 Setting the Scene

Learners of Chinese (Modern Standard Chinese or Putonghua,[1] also Hanyu, the spoken form and Zhongwen, its standard written form, both simplified and traditional, but also Pinyin romanisation) can be represented on a long continuum.

At one end of the range of contexts and circumstances (social, linguistic, and cultural), are learners completely new to the language and whose own languages are totally unrelated to Chinese, and who live in environments where Chinese is to all

---

[1] China's quest for a standard official literary form of its language is a heavily researched question of historical linguistics, but also a question of considerable public interest, exemplified by David Moser's paperback A Million Voices (May 2016, Penguin).

J. Lo Bianco (✉)
University of Melbourne, Melbourne, VIC, Australia
e-mail: j.lobianco@unimelb.edu.au

© The Author(s), under exclusive license to Springer Nature Switzerland AG 2024
J. Lo Bianco et al. (eds.), *Supporting the Learning of Chinese as a Second Language: Implications for Language Education Policy*, Language Policy 36,
https://doi.org/10.1007/978-3-031-66135-8_1

intents and purposes a foreign language. For these learners there is little possibility of inductive learning or local immersion, and hence the school, and explicit language teaching, are the sole source of acquisition. At the other extreme are learners with close familiarity with one or more varieties of Chinese, or even with familiarity with Putonghua itself, but who at school are engaged in learning educated and literate registers of the standard language, and who reside in environments in which a variety of Chinese and its standard form are either dominant or at least available for inductive acquisition.

In between these two ends of the spectrum (from complete beginners in non-Chinese settings to young speakers in Chinese settings) is a Third Space, in which there is a complex array of variables which complicate the prospects for successful acquisition, use and development of the language. For the sake of argument, these can be collectively described as the socio-cultural environment, which I call the 'social envelope', in which the learning occurs. My sense of the impact of the wider socio-cultural environment of the Third Space on the prospects for successful learning of Chinese is influenced by the two functional levels of context identified in systemic functional linguistics, SFL (Halliday, 1973; Halliday & Hasan, 1989). In SFL the communicative environment focuses on texts, both the specific texts produced in and for communication and their component parts, and these are described as the context of situation and the context of culture, constituted by the environment of language itself as a system, referencing its lexis and grammar. Situation and culture contextually frame processes and prospects for learning a language and can be helpful in accounting for the appropriate or most effective pedagogies.

Within this broad intermediary category, the Third Space, learning Chinese involves learning a language that is not wholly new to its learners and yet not familiar to them, in which dialects of Chinese, the other languages of the learner and teacher, and the status of the learners and the settings in which they learn the language can be highly relevant. Some of these factors are whether the students are the children of the majority local community enrolled in regular education and whose identification with Chinese is not ethnicity-based. Also relevant is the question of whether the learners are of Chinese ethnicity residing in a diasporic community, whether long established or recent, and therefore for whom questions of familial and regional Chinese identity become pertinent to questions of learning. Another Third Space variable is whether the learners are completely new to the language, lacking even listening and basic interpersonal comprehension, and who are either speakers of the official or dominant language of their society enrolled in Chinese as a foreign language, or who may themselves belong to an ethnic minority population, but not one of Chinese background.

To make this discussion more concrete we can refer to the related way Australian curriculum planners have classified learners. While the Australian case is only one of many possible environments it can serve as an illustrative case of the two ends of the continuum and the Third Space between. Over recent years extensive effort has been put into national curriculum processes to identify the most effective ways for students to learn Chinese and to be grouped into broad categories. From the research and consultations that informed this question it was determined that three broad 'pathways' best respond to and cater for the cohorts of learners of Chinese present in the education system (Scarino, 2019). Before describing these, it is useful to say that while it would be possible to differentiate other groups, in fact to proceed along an almost indefinite differentiation, these three broad groupings were agreed as sufficiently coherent and robust to allow both responsiveness to student need, and administrative feasibility.

The first is the Second Language Learner Pathway designed to cater for students who are learning Chinese as a second language, in effect adding Chinese as an additional language to their English or in many cases in Australia to their already existing bilingualism. The second category is titled the Background Language Learner Pathway, and this has been devised or rather identified for students who already have "exposure to Chinese language and culture, and who may engage in some active but predominantly receptive use of Chinese at home" (ACARA, 2018). The third grouping is the First Language Learner Pathway, and this is designed for students whose primary linguistic socialisation and initial literacy development (including therefore their primary schooling) is via the medium of Chinese. These learners are likely to use Chinese at home.

As stated, these categories can be further differentiated, and curriculum implementation practices allow for this to occur the three pathways represent a broadly accepted classification that addresses both context and situation variables. Individual schools and teachers are provided with materials and resources enabling them to select which pathway aligns most closely and productively with the learning needs of their students and allowing them to make modifications to suit specific pedagogical objects, phases of teaching or the needs and experiences of students.

Partly influenced by this experience of curriculum innovation for second language learners, but also drawn from the authors' long interest in effective teaching and learning of Chinese, Orton and Scrimgeour (2019) posit 'the way of the learner'. Their 2019 book Teaching Chinese as a Second Language aims to guide effective pedagogy for new learners of the language, referencing Daoist precepts and a deeply intercultural understanding of what this involves. The authors note that many learners do not achieve high levels of language skill and call for refinement and new research in three broad areas to generate long term improved outcomes: first, to extend and deepen descriptive accounts of the language in use, in particular Chinese in its dynamic contemporary forms, second, for more research to be devoted to the dynamics of Chinese language acquisition by new learners and third, a focus on teacher capability, including a diverse teacher workforce of 'native' and 'non-native' speakers. In this identification of the learning challenges of Chinese language for native English speakers 'the way of the learner' overlaps with the present volume, though our focus is not restricted to English speaking learners.

Orton and Scrimgeour point to a large gap in knowledge and skills between learners' initial and future proficiency levels as L2 Chinese speakers, and this too is pertinent to the research reported in the present volume, drawn from different education systems, different groups of learners and different curriculum and pedagogical contexts.

In summary, we can depict specifically the linguistic form that Chinese as a Second Language programs aim to generate, we can depict the learner population along a continuum with two extremes of cultural insider/outsider, or, to use older terminology, native/non-native learners, separated by a Third Space that is heterogeneous but sufficiently coherent from the perspective of learner characteristics, social settings, and educational environments (Lo Bianco, 2014).

2 Chinese Fever, or Peak and Decline?

The Economist magazine, often touted often as the world's premier business analysis and news outlet, headlined an online article as follows *"Why fewer university students are studying Mandarin"* with the subheading *"Learning the difficult language does not seem as worthwhile as it once did"* (*The Economist*, August 2023). The article argues that in the United Kingdom and the United States Chinese language higher education enrolments peaked a decade ago and have steadily declined since then.

The article is striking because it represents a marked departure from the usual tone and character of urgent China study themes. After all, only a decade ago it was possible to describe language learning trends as follows: *"This is the age of 'Chinese fever' (中文热 zhōngwénrè) and 'Asia literacy' has become a national priority'* (Scrimgeour, 2014). If The Economist is correct then the general atmosphere around Chinese language education is in sharp contrast to when it was touted as the '*gigantic up and comer'* (Lo Bianco, 2010) of world language education. Specifically in the UK students were enjoined to *"never mind French and Spanish…Mandarin is the language of the moment in primaries, secondary schools and universities up and down the country"* (Ward, 2007).

Yet, we must be very cautious in endorsing or even believing the claim that the growth of Chinese language education enrolments has peaked and is in decline. The data reported in The Economist do show a reduction in demand, but this may be a contingent and short-lived interruption to what is a longer-term process of growth, which ultimately represents a rectification of the great neglect of Chinese teaching that has persisted for many years.

In any case the data reductions reported do represent challenges that language planners and Chinese language specialists in English speaking countries, will need to tackle. However, Mandarin education continues to expand rapidly in other parts of the world. Saudi Arabia is the latest country to *"mandate Chinese language education in schools as the region embraces Beijing links"* (Zhou & Ziwen, 2023), a trend now apparent also in Egypt, the United Arab Emirates and in many other societies across Africa, Asia, and Latin America. Since the mid 1990s the overwhelming preference for English in South American education systems has been supplemented by many 'early Mandarin' programs, and in Argentina, Chile and Paraguay, these are complemented by teacher support and development programs that suggest a multi-pronged approach of high level of institutional commitment and community-driven demand (Romano et al., 2021).

A recent systematic documentation of higher education 'China studies' in Australia (AAH,[2] 2023), has mapped Australia's research and training capabilities in disciplines that produce knowledge of and skills in Chinese related areas. One outcome of this research, which now appears to be influencing national policy discussions, is a map of current and emerging knowledge requirements for various groups with a direct interest in "China knowledge", including mastery of Modern Standard Chinese language, and a picture of the capabilities needed "*to support informed and effective engagement with China*" (p. v). The research informing this report was based on direct consultations and interviews with more than 100 senior stakeholders (academics, senior business leaders, emerging China scholars, and public servants) to ascertain their understanding of what China capability means, their assessment of Australia's level of preparation to engage effectively with China without having to rely exclusively on the knowledge of English of their Chinese counterparts, and what these individuals propose to overcome perceived shortfalls. The interview results were then set against a dataset of 41,292 Australian research outputs which originated in funded projects from the Australian Research Council national competitive grants, and survey data of course coordinators and teachers of advanced China studies programs.

Australia now produces the fourth-highest volume of English-language research on China after the PRC, the US, and the UK. Enrolments in translation and interpreting courses are soaring, but this growth is a result of international student demand and a function of China's emergence as global research hub. The conclusion of the report however is that Australia's China knowledge 'ecosystem' in universities still falls short of assessed needs, that it tends to favour breadth over depth, research over teaching, technical skills over longer-term capability. All of these shortfalls are linked to language capability, so that the upper end of the knowledge usability spectrum is tied to language skill and therefore despite strong performance in China studies and research across many disciplines, the nation appears to be losing its depth of cultural, social, and political expertise, and this puts at risk the "knowledge pipelines" so that education programs are less likely to interact with employment pathways. Considering the 'peak and decline' conclusion by The Economist the AAH report refines approach that policy makers must follow, to support China capability in education, employment, and effectiveness in language teaching, and point towards the research studies reported in the present volume, whose principal aim is to focus attention on supporting students to achieve better results in Chinese as a Second Language programs, in Third Space settings.

Only time will confirm the accuracy or durability of the calculation by The Economist, though partially corroborated in the AAH study, however what is significant to note in both is the critical question of high level competence in

---

[2] The author served as chair of the advisory committee for the research and publication by the AAH, Australian Academy of the Humanities.

language study, and the utilisation of skills and capabilities gained in education, whether at school or higher education, in professional careers of individuals and business or trade efforts of the private sector or policy and diplomacy activities of government. The base, however, of Chinese language education is high. Speaking at the International Chinese Language Education week in 2020, Tian Xuejun, China's Vice Minister of Education and Chairperson of the National Commission of the People's Republic of China for UNESCO, stated that more than 4000 programs of Chinese language courses to their curriculums and suggested that 25 million people were currently learning Chinese as a second language, added to the 200 million people outside China who had learned Chinese (Language Magazine, 2021). Similarly, HolonIQ another online data source, in March 2023 calculated the financial return of extensive Chinese study, both within the diaspora and outside of it, at $7.4billion and claimed this is "set to double in the next five years" (Holon, 2023) and that of China's "60 million strong diaspora, more than 4 million are seeking to achieve or reconfirm proficiency in the language".

It is my contention, that sustained improvement in the learning and teaching of Chinese language, and the related and equally important objective of building more in-depth China studies (research higher degree level), cannot rely on public policy alone. As the research reported in this volume shows current levels of teaching Chinese may be faltering and difficult to sustain, and at the same time there is an erosion in the number and scope of in-depth research-based scholarship on China topics. These both point to looming shortcomings in the immediate future and can only be redressed through enhancing the effectiveness of current effort, mostly through research and professional development to build Chinese-appropriate pedagogies for new learners. This kind of language policy innovation, starting with teachers and teaching, might be called a bottom-up practice, and if this is not achieved soon, the long lead times inherent in policy-directed (top down) action will mean significant erosion in the total effort of Chinese language teaching. This change corresponds to the third of the three improvements identified by Orton and Scrimgeour (2019) (first, better descriptive accounts of contemporary Chinese language in use, second, more research on the dynamics of Chinese language acquisition by new learners and third, issues of teacher capability including a diverse teacher workforce).

In devolved education systems, such as Australia's, a claim that holds true in many other settings is that educational improvement cannot be produced without robust linkages between targeted research endeavours, public policy writing, consultation and feedback loops between academics and policy makers, and, importantly learners and teachers, curriculum writers, and school and education officials. It is important to note here that what is implemented, and therefore what is 'experienced' by learners is in effect a kind of public policy and language planning if we understand language policy and planning as a continuum of actions.

In reviewing the teaching of Japanese and Italian in Australian schools with a view to placing the experiences of learners within the framework of public policy Lo Bianco and Aliani (2013) argued, building on prior work by Kathleen Davis, that we should consider policy as having three realities which interact with each other, reinforcing or undermining their respective effects. These are the *intended policy*, which refers to the aims formal policy declarations make as they announce action and funding to tackle a perceived problem. Allied to this but significantly different to warrant separate specification is policy as what is *implemented*. The implemented moves our focus from policy texts which are usually legalistic or administrative, and tend to be expressed in general terms, but from which only some components are implemented. This might be because the intended policy is not well conceived, or not sufficiently based on research to be accurate in its aims, or because of resource limitations. The *experienced* policy refers to students' encounter with the policy in its practice, so that we have a sequence of what is stipulated in the law or by official mandate, what bureaucracies actually implement and support and what students encounter, how the implanted policy 'feels' or 'looks' like when it is converted into programmes in classrooms.

Under the experienced policy it is important not to neglect any aspect of the classroom programme, such as the pedagogical activities, materials and resources, timetabling and scheduling of the teaching, and frequency and intensity with which the teaching occurs. Any innovation requires space in curriculum and hence the question of what the innovation might displace, how it is promoted, and what benefits are promised, or penalties announced, form part of how it is experienced. All these layers interact because a poor implementation, or a controversial experience can by feedback loop re-shape or modify the intended policy, and research is the critical mediator in these processes and how research is fed into the decision-making process of policy formulation, especially through programme evaluation.

These considerations of course are true for any language teaching, but in relation to Chinese the question of the public esteem of the language, the hyper-instrumental demand for its teaching, and the existence of an extensive diaspora able to mount programs for teaching and maintenance add specific dimensions to the policy conversations that are conducted for its teaching. The shared responsibility to achieve more and better learning of Chinese, through more effective, theory and research-informed teaching, requires as a primary task a clear account of the socio-demographic contexts in which projects of Chinese teaching take place and an awareness that policy making involves teachers and communities and researchers as an integral, if often neglected, component.

3 Chinese in World Language Education

The presence of languages within curriculum is the result of decisions made by education authorities. Considering the dynamic framework how language policy is made, as sketched out above, relevant questions which arise are: what motivates and justifies the decisions these authorities take, the languages they select for inclusion, the ones which are excluded, and the seriousness of commitment they display? The interplay between communities requesting or organising systems to teach their languages, and systems mandating those or different languages, however, can obscure the fact that over the longer-term language choices reflect what can be called 'world events', or, perhaps more accurately, geopolitical power. In a comprehensive analysis of foreign language study over 150 years, Cha and Ham (2008) track the links between these wider forces and language choices in the following way. The authors distinguish between the category of foreign language (FFL) in the curricula of primary and secondary schools across the world over the past 155 years.

Analysing historical documents to produce data on the FFL, they reveal dramatic redistribution of the languages selected for teaching in schools, premised on the assumption that these would be used in communicating beyond national frontiers. Cha and Ham divide the period 1850–2005 into seven periods of time and across this time scale compare the fate of the five dominant languages—English, French, German, Russian and Spanish—as FFL. The number of countries involved was initially 15 and 12 respectively for the primary and secondary levels in the period 1850–1874 but grew to 151 and 154 for primary and secondary respectively in the 1990–2005 period. The shifts revealed (collapse of German, transition to French and English, emergence of Russian, collapse of Russian, transfer to English) correlate closely with key historical patterns of political, military, technological and economic predominance.

In Asia, English was represented in only 33 per cent of primary curricula during 1945–1969, growing to 83 per cent in primary and 100 per cent for secondary by 2005. By 2006 practically all instances in which foreign languages were employed to teach mainstream subject matter in Asian universities involved English. In the latter two periods, Russian had achieved a presence of up to 5 per cent in curricula as first foreign language; it was the preferred foreign language in many Soviet Bloc states in Eastern Europe and among the ideological allies of the then USSR in central Asia, plus China, Vietnam, and some other states. However, after the fall of the Berlin Wall in 1989 and the collapse of communism in Eastern Europe, the bulk of Russian's enrolment numbers transferred, not to German in Eastern Europe, a traditional zone of strong German language and culture presence, but to English, and progressively in Asia English has consolidated its position.

It is in this light that we can read the growth of Chinese, at least in regard to the 'intended' language policy, as a reflection of the emergence (in truth the restoration) to prominence of China, its economic, technological and geopolitical presence, and the subsequent cultural politics of 'soft power'. Any future macro survey of the First Foreign Language taught in curriculums across the world is likely to feature Chinese, and possibly Japanese as well, but for reasons that combine 'world events' and the shift in education systems across the world that today aim to respond to local cultural conditions as well as global affairs or perceived cultural hierarchies.

4 Research

The studies reported in this volume are of intrinsic interest for the information they supply on learning achievements in response to teaching inputs, but they also represent a category of policy experimentation as well.

It is one thing for top-down mandates to select languages and promote their teaching, it is altogether a different, and in some ways more complex thing, to produce programs of teaching languages that are effective. The aim of most language education is never simply the gaining of proficiency in the language, given the importance of intercultural goals, identity maintenance and general intellectual development which are nearly always cited among the purposes for language teaching. Nevertheless, proficiency aims are central to public mandates for languages. The question arises: what would it be possible to predict about language learning achievements under the typical teaching and learning conditions in schools in a given system, for the 'typical' cohorts of learners, in the Third Space identified above? This is a critical, but often ignored, question of language education policy. To cite the Australian experience with promotion of Asian languages over the past 40 years, during which Asian languages have been allocated funding priority, we in fact find haphazard provision, uneven quality, short duration and, regrettably, scarce evidence of learning (Scarino et al., 2011).

Since the inauguration of the National Asian Languages and Studies of Asia in Australian Schools (NALSAS) program in 1995 Australian public investment in four Asian languages, Chinese, Indonesian, Japanese, and Korean, has been extensive and repeated, and is likely to be extended again following the AAH (2023) study of China capability. The intended policy is often linked to economic relations and specifically to the facilitation of trade and diplomacy, and geo-political security, and as noted above the generality of such a remit involves a large gap between concept and aspiration for policy, and actual delivery. The research conducted on the proficiency gains has revealed large gaps between what is learned in the typical programs provided and what policy aspires to produce (Scarino & Elder, 2012).

Scholarship on how to determine the demand or value of a language in a globalised market is controversial. A widely cited approach and concept is De Swaan's (1993, 2013) Q-value method, which assesses relative power of different languages (their communicative value) and from which he produces a 'global language system'. De Swaan describes his calculation as aligned with 'realist thinking' such that Q-value finds economic principles in marketplaces of exchange govern which languages are preferred by systems which provide for their teaching, or by learners who choose to enrol in courses they judge will bring a return for the effort they expend in acquiring the language (and the opportunity cost of not pursuing an alternative activity or language). A valid criticism of Q-value calculations would argue that the underlying method assumes that language arrangements in the world are neutral in a cultural and political sense, when in fact they reflect state and economic hard power, and histories of linguistic imposition by dominant powers on dominated groups. If this is accepted, then it is reasonable to claim that by ignoring these realities Q value reflects an unjust linguistic order of the world and if no reference is made to these realities this reflection can become complicit in sustaining an unjust order of communication. However, De Swaan (1993, 2013) considers his method a factual depiction of what occurs in practice and therefore a realistic account of the actual world arrangements in language and communication, thereby repudiating critical perspectives or at least relegating them to a different conversation from his concerns to map the power of languages as they exist. In this global system, Chinese is ranked as a supercentral language, alongside 12 other languages that are very widely spoken and which connect large numbers of people and places in the world. However, these are ranked below the hypercentral language, English, which itself connects speakers of the supercentral languages and all other categories, and represents the standard for contemporary science, business, and law, as well as having the widest speaker numbers when second language speakers are included.

5 Diaspora Learners and Transnational Contexts

What is certainly true is that demand for Chinese, even if its rate of expansion has slowed, is now truly global, and the Third Space sector is increasingly complex. Within this the large diasporic presence of Chinese, which appears to enjoy a particularly strong intergenerational retention (Zhu & Li, 2014) of the language, imposes on researchers a requirement to study and theorise pathways to proficiency and pedagogies of effectiveness. Within the diaspora of Chinese are diasporas within China, of ethnic minorities, such as several studied in this volume within Hong Kong.

Almost 20 years ago when the upsurge in demand for Chinese was consolidating itself, Liu and Lo Bianco (2007) identified three broad characteristics involved in this, which they labelled "Teaching Chinese, Teaching in Chinese, and Teaching the Chinese", essentially combining the language as object of instruction, the language as a medium of teaching, and the language as a medium of learning.

The problematisation of diaspora identity and, more practically, their pathways to learning new languages and retaining their existing ones have recently become a significant issue within Australia. A study of Asian-Australian 'business diasporas', focusing on Chinese and Indian communities in Australia, conducted by and for the Australian Academy of the Humanities concluded that governments should see diasporas not as populations to assimilate, but as important source of innovation and commercial enterprise in bilateral and even in multilateral industry and commerce (Rizvi et al., 2016). This discourse of 'leveraging' diasporas for their international facilitative role is significantly hampered if they lose their language skills over the generations and their contacts and cultural knowledge fades. Hence, the public ideology behind this thinking is for commercial advantage, linking diaspora learning to transnational connections. This kind of thinking is now routinely described as 'smart engagement' (Ang et al., 2015) and is promoted to governments by academic scholars as a way to influence and shape public policy.

6 Concluding Remarks

The overriding objective of applied language learning research in the context of a burgeoning growth of Chinese language education, both at the two ends of the continuum of provision, and in the Third Space between them, at this critical juncture in language policy and planning should explicitly prioritise learner support.

This is how this volume has been conceived, and the research reported in the chapters unfolds a large number of studies that demonstrate the practical need and benefit of evidence-based modes of supporting successful acquisition of Chinese, from the multiple pathways that characterise its learning today.

References

AAH, Australian Academy of the Humanities. (2023). *Australia's China knowledge capability*. Canberra.
ACARA, Australian Curriculum and Assessment and Reporting Authority. (2018). *Chinese context statement*. https://www.australiancurriculum.edu.au/f-10-curriculum/languages/chinese/context-statement/. Accessed 18 Sept 2023.
Ang, I., Tambiah, Y., & Mar, P. (2015). *Smart engagement with Asia: Leveraging language, research and culture*. Australian Council of Learned Academies.
Cha, Y.-K., & Ham, S.-H. (2008). The impact of English on the school curriculum. In B. Spolsky & F. M. Hult (Eds.), *The handbook of educational linguistics* (pp. 317–327). Blackwell Publishing. https://doi.org/10.1002/9780470694138.ch22
De Swaan, A. (1993). The evolving European language system. *International Political Science Review, 14*, 241–255.
De Swaan, A. (2013). *Words of the world: The global language system*. Polity Press.
Halliday, M. A. K. (1973). *Explorations in the functions of language*. Edward Arnold.
Halliday, M. A. K., & Hasan, R. (1989). *Language, context and text: Aspects of language in a social-semiotic perspective*. Oxford University Press.
Holon, I. Q. (2023). *Chinese language learning*. https://www.holoniq.com/notes/chinese-language-learning-a-7-4b-market-powered-by-over-6-million-learners-set-to-double-in-the-next-five-years#:~:text=Chinese%20language%20learning%20is%20a,K12%20and%20Higher%20Education%20combined. Accessed 2 Oct 2023.
Language Magazine. (2021, January 6). *Chinese progresses as a world language*. https://www.languagemagazine.com/2021/01/06/chinese-progresses-as-a-world-language/. Accessed 2 Oct 2023.
Liu, G.-Q., & Lo Bianco, J. (2007). Teaching Chinese, teaching in Chinese, and teaching the Chinese. *Language Policy, 6*, 95–117. https://doi.org/10.1007/s10993-006-9041-4
Lo Bianco, J. (2010). Chinese: The gigantic up-and-comer. In I. L. Tsung & K. Cruickshank (Eds.), *Teaching and learning Chinese in global contexts* (pp. xiii–xxiv). Continuum International Publishing.
Lo Bianco, J. (2014). Domesticating the foreign: Globalization's effects on the place/s of languages. *The Modern Language Journal, 98*(1), 312–325.
Lo Bianco, J., & Aliani, R. (2013). *Language planning and student experiences: Intention, rhetoric and implementation*. Multilingual Matters.
Orton, J., & Scrimgeour, A. (2019). *Teaching Chinese as a second language: The way of the learner*. Routledge.
Rizvi, F., Louie, K., & Evans, J. (2016). *Australia's diaspora advantage: Realising the potential for building transnational business networks with Asia*. Australian Council of Learned Academies.

Romano, E., Wu, Y.-H., & Liu, H. (2021). Early Mandarin learning in South America: Present and future directions. In S. Zein & M. Coady (Eds.), *Early language learning policy in the 21st century: An international perspective* (pp. 255–273). Springer.

Scarino, A. (2019). The Australian Curriculum and its conceptual bases: A critical analysis. *Curriculum Perspectives, 39*, 59–65. https://doi.org/10.1007/s41297-019-00066-4

Scarino, A., & Elder, C. (2012). Describing school achievement in Asian languages for diverse learner groups. *Australian Review of Applied Linguistics, 35*(3), 357–361. https://doi.org/10.1075/aral.35.3.07lob

Scarino, A., Elder, C., Iwashita, N., Kohler, M., & Scrimgeour, A. (2011). *Student achievement in Asian languages education*. Report to Department of Education, Employment & Workplace Relations.

Scrimgeour, A. (2014). Dealing with "Chinese fever": The challenge of Chinese teaching in the Australian classroom. In N. Murray & A. Scarino (Eds.), *Dynamic ecologies: A relational perspective on languages education in the Asia-Pacific region* (Vol. 9, pp. 151–168). Springer.

The Economist. (2023). *Why fewer university students are studying Mandarin*. https://www.economist.com/china/2023/08/24/why-fewer-university-students-are-studying-mandarin

Ward, L. (2007, February 4). Never mind French and Spanish. *Education Guardian*. https://www.theguardian.com/education/2007/apr/02/schools.uk. Accessed 20 Sept 2023.

Zhou, L., & Ziwen, Z. (2023). Mandarin learning boom as China extends its soft power in Middle East. *South China Morning Post*. https://www.scmp.com/news/china/diplomacy/article/3233421/mandarin-learning-boom-china-extends-its-soft-power-middle-east. Accessed 20 Sept 2023.

Zhu, H., & Li, W. (2014). Geopolitics and the changing hierarchies of the Chinese language: Implications for policy and practice of Chinese language teaching in Britain. *The Modern Language Journal, 98*(1), 326–339.

Chinese Language Learning by Ethnic Minority Students in Hong Kong: Policy and Support

Wing-Wah Ki ⓘ, **Shek Kam Tse** ⓘ, **Elizabeth Kam-Kau Ho** ⓘ, **and Mark Shiu-Kee Shum** ⓘ

Abstract Chapter "Contexts of Learning, Priorities for Research" has charted the broad international situation of Chinese second language (CSL) learning and the need to provide different learning pathways to cater for the needs of learners with diverse familial and language learning backgrounds. The present Chapter will zoom in to the Hong Kong situation and the education of its non-Chinese ethnic minority learners, to provide the local context for what readers will see in the later Chapters of the book.

The Chapter will briefly review the situation, covering (a) how the problem of Chinese language education and integration of ethnic minority students in Hong Kong has been addressed by the Government in terms of education and language policy (Parts I and II of the chapter); (b) how some of the ethnic minority students and parents have perceived their situation and needs (Part III); and (c) how some teachers and researchers have attempted to face the CSL challenge and improve the learning of these students (Part IV).

The review mainly focuses on the period from 1997 to 2018, the initial 20 years of Hong Kong after its political handover, when it become a Special Administration Region (SAR) of The People's Republic of China. In the first 10 years, the SAR Government seemed to be quite accommodating to the ethnic minority's demands about education. However, its assimilative policy stance became clearer in the second 10 years. Nonetheless, the review indicates that some innovative pedagogical experimentation has happened at the school and classroom level over these 20 years, through the collaborative efforts of teachers and researchers, which could be useful in informing possible CSL policy and practice improvements in the future. The Chapter will only provide a glimpse of such pedagogical innovations, while more of the details will be presented in the later chapters of the book.

W.-W. Ki (✉) · S. K. Tse · E. K.-K. Ho · M. S.-K. Shum
The University of Hong Kong, Pok Fu Lam, Hong Kong
e-mail: hraskww@hku.hk

© The Author(s), under exclusive license to Springer Nature Switzerland AG 2024
J. Lo Bianco et al. (eds.), *Supporting the Learning of Chinese as a Second Language: Implications for Language Education Policy*, Language Policy 36,
https://doi.org/10.1007/978-3-031-66135-8_2

1 Ethnic Minorities in Hong Kong

Hong Kong has a predominately Chinese society. Around 92% of the population is Chinese (Census and Statistics Department, 2021). But there have long been people of other ethnicities living in the place since colonial times. In colonial times, while the British (and some other Westerners) were a minority in number, they were the majority in terms of power. They also brought in some South and South East Asians to work in Hong Kong as businessmen, professionals, civil servants, police, army, and workers under the British colonial reign. Many of these peoples and their descendants have been part of the historical development of the place. When the sovereignty of Hong Kong was returned to China in 1997, most of these South and Southeast Asian peoples stayed in Hong Kong, instead of moving to Britain or their homelands. The South and South East Asian population has grown rapidly after 1997. These ethnic groups are often referred to collectively as the 'ethnic minorities' (EM) of Hong Kong. According to the audit report of expenditure in the year 2015–2016 (Document number EDB219), EM students amounted, at that time, to 6.8% of the students studying in kindergarten, and 3.1% and 2.3% respectively at the primary and secondary levels.

As this term of 'ethnic minorities' (EM) carries a minorizing or devaluing connotation, it has not generally been welcomed by the people for whom this term is used as a label. They preferred to be called Hong-Kong-er, or called Hong Kong Pakistani, or Hong Kong Nepali and so on, which reflect the fact that these groups of people have been associated with the place for a long time and have taken it as their home. (Kapai & Singh, 2018) However, the term 'ethnic minorities' to a large extent reflects truly the situation that these people are indeed in a minority position in Hong Kong, in terms both of numbers and of economic power. (*Poverty Situation Report on Ethnic Minorities 2016*, by Census and Statistics Department, 2018). Hence, the term is still used quite often by equity advocates who are fighting for the welfare of these peoples.

2 Change in Educational Policy on Ethnic Minority Students in Hong Kong Since 1997

2.1 Change in EM Language and Education Policy Right after Political Handover

In colonial Hong Kong before 1997, there was little mentioning about the integration of EM students with the Chinese population in government education policy documents. The EM students were educated in a few special primary and secondary schools, segregated from the majority Chinese student population (Lau, 2015). They had English as the medium of instruction and they also took their heritage language subjects. Or, they could apply for admission to other English-medium schools in Hong Kong. In general, the Chinese language knowledge of the EM people has been weak. They mostly speak heritage languages or a mix of heritage languages and English at home. The EM students have found learning Chinese difficult, not to mention the learning of other subjects using Chinese as the medium of instruction.

However, the situation for them changed drastically around 1997, the time of the political handover of Hong Kong to China. The "Biliterate and Trilingual (liangwen sanyu)" (BLTL) language policy was declared in 1997 by the new Hong Kong Special Administration Region (SAR) government, with 'biliterate' referring to written Chinese and English, and 'trilingual' referring to spoken English, Cantonese, and Putonghua. Though the policy highlights Chinese (including Cantonese, the local version of Chinese language used by most people in Hong Kong) and English as in the past, the importance of Chinese becomes much more emphasized since 1997. According to the BLTL policy, Hong Kong education shall produce citizens who should be able to handle BOTH Chinese and English, and hence, even for the EM students, Chinese language competence would be indispensable for the completion of school education, and entrance to university education and government jobs.

The other major blow to the EM community was the Government's 1998 reform to use mother-tongue as medium of instruction (MOI) in schools, grounded on its educational benefits. (Education Commission, 1996). Logically, to realize the benefits, "mother-tongue" should be understood with reference to the learners, but the Government took it to mean simply Chinese. A "Firm Guidance" (Education Department, 1997) was issued that all secondary schools in Hong Kong should use Chinese, the students' mother tongue as MOI, except a quarter of them which could catch those primary school leavers with the highest academic performance. Before that, most secondary schools in Hong Kong had been using English as the MOI, or a combination of written English (textbook and examination) together with spoken Chinese (classroom explanation and discussion). This change in MOI policy made the EM students, who were relatively more competent in English but very weak in Chinese even more difficult to join the mainstream schools.

This change supports the sociology theory of Bourdieu (1991) that the language of the dominant group defines the linguistic habitus in society, and linguistic capital is gauged based on the ability to use the language habitus so defined. Under the colonial rule, English was the dominant official and working language. Lacking the ability to speak and write Chinese at that time did not deprive EM from getting a job in civil service or entering universities in Hong Kong. However, under the new SAR Government, qualification in Chinese and English is mandatory. Furthermore, while the status of Chinese and English is affirmed, the heritage languages of the EM are marginalized. Before 1997, in the few special schools, EM students could take Urdu or Hindu besides English, but it is no longer the case now if they decide to enter mainstream schools to get a better mastery of Chinese.

2.2 Support Measures Began in the 2000s: Designated Schools, University School Partnership

It was not until the 2000s that the new SAR Government was pushed to attend to the educational problems of EM students. The adverse situations of EM students had led to a rise in advocacy for their education and integration in society. Unison, a vocal non-government organization (NGO) was formed in the early 2000s by some lawmakers, social workers, politicians and EM leaders to promote racial equity. It was also the period when Hong Kong had to legislate the anti-racial discrimination laws as its responsibility to the United Nation (UN) International Convention on the Elimination of All Forms of Racial Discrimination (ICERD). Besides working locally, Unison also sent representatives to speak at the UN International Convention committee meetings to report the economic and educational disparity between EM and the majority in Hong Kong, as evidence of racial discrimination at the system level, and exerted pressure for improvements.

On the education aspect, Unison pressed for several quite focused goals: (1) the Government should support more EM students to be educated in mainstream schools, so that their education would not be limited to the few special schools which were deemed to be less well staffed and equipped; (2) the Government should pay due respect to the current inadequate support to EM students in learning Chinese language learning and should not make Chinese language requirement a bar against their access to higher education, as most higher education teaching was in fact done in English. (3) the Government should provide effective Chinese language education for EM students to improve their social integration, education and career development prospects.

In response to the first request, the education authority began to allow "non-Chinese speaking (NCS) students" to apply for places in all schools from 2004. "NCS students" is the official term used by the education authority in referring to EM students. The "NCS students" could take equal part in the central allocation system for primary education places at age six, like all children of that age in Hong Kong. Their parents could submit their choices of schools just like any others into the pool, and then school places would be assigned through a random process. But, as most primary schools used Chinese as MOI, if EM parents made special indication that their children did not want that, they could be sent to the few special schools for EM students as before.

However, the actual response of EM parents was not forthcoming. They mostly opted for the special schools. To address the problem, in the year 2006–2007, the education authority selected 10 primary schools and 5 secondary schools and provided them with more subsidy to support the learning needs of EM students. These schools were referred by the education authority as "designated schools". Most of them were originally mainstream schools. They would continue to accept Chinese students. At the same time, with the additional subsidy, they would develop school-based Chinese Language curriculum and English medium teaching in content subjects to better serve the needs of the EM students. From then on, the enrolment of EM students in these "designated schools" increased. But, those schools with large numbers of minority students were soon seen as second tier by many Chinese parents and they moved their children out. As the result, many designated schools became overcrowded with EM students, and the originally intended intercultural interaction between EM and Chinese students in these schools diminished.

In response to the second challenge that the high Chinese language requirement bared EM students' access to higher education, the Government began to sponsor EM students to sit the British GCSE Chinese Second Language examination from 2007 and got agreement from the universities in Hong Kong that a grade 'D' or above in the British GCSE examination would be accepted as satisfactorily meeting the basic admission requirement of Chinese language for these EM students.

In response to the third request, for effective Chinese language curriculum and teaching, in 2007, the government began to allocate resource to sponsor university academics to organize afterschool Chinese language programmes for EM students, and to implement university-school partnership for school-based Chinese language curriculum and teacher development (locally known locally as the USP project).

The Government seemed quite responsive in this period to the requests and the measures had been successful in making some practical improvements in the general situation of EM education. In the designated schools, they could still continue to learn content subjects through English, and fortunately the long-standing bilingual public examination practice of Hong Kong remained unchanged. There are separate versions of examination papers in Chinese and English for almost all content subjects, and students can choose which to take in the examination. Chinese language teachers in the designated schools created school-based Chinese teaching materials for EM students to start from the very basic. Having 'GCSE Chinese second language examination' as a goal post, they began to construct their own Chinese curriculum, to move towards that goal step-by-step. There was also an awareness among these teachers that, to teach Chinese as second language (CSL), one cannot just follow the same method for native learners. These teachers had never been trained for teaching CSL before, but after a few years of university-school partnership, some of them got their CSL teaching efficacy improved and began to share their experiences with each other.

In the few years after, improvements of Chinese learning of the EM students could be seen in terms of both the increasing number of EM students taking GCSE Chinese examination and the passing rate of the students. Some schools also developed a series of higher goal posts, for example, to prepare their EM students to take GCSE Chinese earlier at Secondary 3 or 4 and then encouraged them to take the more demanding GCE AS level Chinese in the later years of their secondary education.

2.3 Policy Towards Homogenization from 2010s: No CSL Curriculum for Hong Kong

As more and more EM students passed the GCSE, there was increasing voice in society that the GCSE Chinese examination was too simple and could not meet the demand for real life applications in society. There was strong demand from EM community as well as other sectors in society that the government should develop a second language Chinese (CSL) curriculum for Hong Kong, which had a standard falling in-between the Hong Kong Diploma of Secondary Education (DSE) Chinese curriculum for mainstream Chinese students and the British GCSE curriculum. However, this idea was firmly rejected by the education authority in every public occasion.

The firm stance of the government against creating an alternative Chinese language curriculum for EM students could be seen in the education authority's "Supplementary Curriculum Guide" (Curriculum Development Council, 2008). The document explained that the original Chinese curriculum was based on "a general and comprehensive learning framework for Chinese Language in Hong Kong" which should be sufficiently flexible to be adapted for all students, including the "NCS students". Chinese as a second language (CSL) learning should only be intended for students who would want to have their future life and career elsewhere other than Hong Kong, and these students could sit oversea CSL examinations.

What announced in this Guide was a 'multi-exit' approach. There would be no examination created targeted to a proficiency level between the existing Hong Kong DSE exam (generally regarded to be too demanding and not totally relevant for EM students) and overseas CSL exam (generally regarded to be too simple for effective living in Hong Kong). There would only be supports provided for different exits at the end of secondary education (DSE exam being the exit for students wanting to study and work locally, and overseas CSL exams for students wanting to go abroad). Some officials also explained that they did not want to pre-empt that EM students would not be able to learn well and create a water-downed Chinese curriculum and examination for them. In respond to this, some academic said if it was to encourage more EM students to learn better Chinese and stay, why could it not be a 'multi-level ladder' approach instead, and students could move up the ladder, just like what they do in learning musical instruments. Providing such immediate levels would not go against reaching higher and higher levels in the end.

Irrespective of the 2008 "Supplementary Curriculum Guide", the pressure for a CSL curriculum for Hong Kong remained strong in society. In 2009, a resolution was passed unanimously by the Legislative Council of Hong Kong, and part of which requested the government to create a local Chinese language benchmarking test for EM and other non-native Chinese learners, with due consideration of the learning difference of these people and the need of Chinese for their work and living in Hong Kong. (Legislative Council Secretary, 2009). The law makers envisaged that this would provide the reference standards for schools and public to promote EM's Chinese learning. However, in the executive-lead governing system of Hong

Kong SAR, all binding motions must first be moved by the SAR Government. As this was not the case, and the Government has made no response to this up to date.

In response to the continuous pressure from EM and NGOs for a CSL curriculum for Hong Kong, the education authority finally announced a "Chinese as second language learning framework" (LF) in 2014, and the education authority clarified that the LF should NOT be regarded as an alternative Chinese curriculum. (Education Bureau, 2014). It was a framework to help the second language learners to follow the same one mainstream Chinese language curriculum.

In the LF, one can see a finer breakdown of the original mainstream Chinese language curriculum. The mainstream curriculum originally consists of 4 key learning stages, and in the LF, each original key stage was subdivided into two smaller stages, each with slightly different descriptors of the objectives on the 4 skills (reading, writing, speaking and listening). The assumption was that by making the steps smaller, teachers would then be better equipped to identify the current level of a student and help them to catch up from there in finer steps. Yet, how the overall curriculum goals and objectives in the end remained unchanged.

The campaign for a CSL curriculum continued (Wong & Yip, 2014). Because, there is clear disparity here. What is obvious to everybody is that Hong Kong has long been offering English as second language (ESL) teaching and examination to its Chinese students, and hence, to be fair, offering something similar in nature in for Chinese language does not demand too much imagination.

In the Hong Kong DSE English language curriculum guide, the rationale for English being a mandatory subject is clearly spelt out: English is a global language, and an essential tool for communication, learning and business. And the English curriculum and assessment is designed accordingly. (CDC & HKEAA, 2007a, p. 2) But for Chinese language, the rationale given for making it mandatory is: Chinese is the mother tongue of most students in Hong Kong, and learning of Chinese allow them to understand the heritage culture (CDC & HKEAA, 2007b, p. 1). Hence, Obviously the two are difference in nature. The former is second language curriculum and the latter first language. Although most EM students also want to understand the Chinese culture, but the purpose is mainly for intercultural understanding rather than enculturation. Hence, the EM students would ask: if the Chinese students are given the opportunity to have a L2 curriculum when learning English, why cannot the EM students be offered a L2 curriculum in Chinese?

When the education authority said there would be no CSL curriculum, it announced a pilot programme called "Applied Learning (Chinese)" as an elective subject at the senior secondary level from 2015. It would be solely for EM students, with a total enrolment quota of 200. This measure seemed to offer a safety valve at the end point, while the Government pushed the EM students to follow the same first-language (L1) Chinese curriculum of the mainstream all along from primary to junior secondary.

EM students who reached the senior secondary education level and found unable to cope with the DSE Chinese language examination could apply to study this subject "Applied Learning (Chinese)". If the EM students got an overall pass in it, the result would appear in their DSE certificate, and could be recognized for entering universities or work. The content would focus on the use of Chinese in working situations, such as in hospitality or customer services. The EM student needed to take 270 lesson-hours over 2.5 years beyond normal school time-table. The admission required that the EM students should have Chinese proficiency equivalent to a normal Chinese primary school graduate.

Applied Learning (Chinese) programme was created like one of the many other Applied Learning programmes at the senior secondary level on different vocational skills. These programmes were career-oriented and the teaching was done by outside vocational institutions, instead of school teachers. The outside institutions submitted tenders to run the programme and design its teaching and assessment. Up to the present, different Applied Learning programmes are still running, and so is the Applied Learning (Chinese). The Applied Learning (Chinese) content is usually related to concrete service situations and hence more comprehensible to the students. The method of continuous course-based assessment is also much more welcome by the EM students, as compared to Chinese public examination.

However, the programme demands huge amount of after-school lesson hours (270 hours over the 3-year senior secondary years), as compared to that of other Applied learning programme (180 hours over 2 years). Hence, student attendance level is not easy to maintain, and especially in the later part of the programme, when the students are facing also the pressure of senior secondary school DSE public examination on other subjects. Many EM students who want to enter universities would invest their time in their DSE content subject study (with English as the medium) to get higher grades in the public examination, rather than Applied Learning (Chinese). They choose to sit GCSE second-language Chinese examination to meet the admission requirement of universities.

The more serious problem lies in the ad hoc nature of the Applied Learning programmes. It is different from normal school subjects in the sense that the provision of Applied Learning programmes in different special areas is normally something quite variable from year to year. Hence, unlike a DSE subject, there is no guarantee that Applied Learning (Chinese) will continue. As a result, the outside institutions find it very difficult to recruit and keep experienced CSL teachers to provide quality teaching, as the teachers cannot see their long-term prospect. The institutions also feel insecure and cannot invest too much in improving the programme, because they can only get the contract year-by-year, and in the end the number of students to each institution may be limited.

2.4 Abolishment of the 'Designated Schools' Scheme

There were voices from society that the improvement in EM students' Chinese language ability was slow. One attribution was that EM students did not have much opportunity to use Chinese in their schools. Unison and some lawyers criticized that the "designated schools" had caused de facto racial segregation. This criticism also got the support of Equal Opportunity Commissioner (EOC).

Then the education authority decided to put an end to the "designated schools" scheme in 2014. It was replaced by another scheme: EM students could go to any schools, and the schools would get per-head subsidy for supporting these students, once they have 10 or more EM students. With 10–25 EM students, the total subsidy for a school is 0.8 million HKD per year; and with 91 or more students, the total annual subsidy is 1.5 million, which would be the ceiling; and there were several steps in between.

The government also encouraged EM parents to put their children to mainstream kindergartens, so that EM students could begin to interact with Chinese students from very young age, and then could adapt more easily to the mainstream primary schools. With this early onset of acquisition and assumed effectiveness of LF, it was hoped that more EM students would be able to follow on and sit the same DSE Chinese language examination that Chinese students would do at the end of their secondary education. And it was made clear that the subsidy and recognition for the EM students to sit for the British GCSE CSL examination as substitute would not be a lasting policy.

2.5 Effectiveness of the Policy Remains Unclear

The effectiveness of the LF and the new EM student subsidy scheme for schools was questioned by the UN ICERD Committee when they met in Geneva in August 2018. The committee asked the Hong Kong government to show proof how its schemes had helped ethnic minority pupils learn Chinese and integrate into society better. Although Hong Kong government officer reported that with its new desegregation policy, two-thirds of the city's public schools now have NCS students, Unison pointed out that in fact 60 per cent of these NCS students were concentrated in only 30 primary or secondary schools, out of all 870 local schools. The government was also criticized by UN ICERD Committee that limited guidance has been provided to schools on pedagogical principles, and teachers were not required to train professionally before teaching Chinese as a second language—so, the LF could not be a proof of impact. (SCMP, 2018).

Since the implementation of the new funding scheme from 2015, schools that received the funding had to administer pre and post tests on the Chinese competency of their EM students. However, no reports on their learning growth have ever been released, and that reasonably have made people speculate that the effects have not been too encouraging. As a matter of fact, Applied Learning (Chinese) programme and GCSE Chinese examination still remain to be the important mitigative measures for most EM students at the end of secondary education to date.

2.6 Rethinking About the EM Education and Language Policy: Assimilative vs. Integrative

There are many academics (e.g. Erni & Leung, 2014; Shum et al., 2016) questioning whether the Hong Kong government is encouraging integrative or assimilative acculturation of the EM students. According to John Berry (1997), a renowned cultural psychologist, when people from two different cultural groups come into contact with each other, they will undergo acculturation (i.e. they will adjust their cultural behavior) to cope with the situation, and their acculturation strategies can be classified into 4 kinds, depending on the joint variation of attitudes in two basic dimensions: (1) how much one values the culture of his/her own group and (2) how much one values the culture of the other group.

When the 2-dimensional model is applied to a non-dominant ethnocultural group member, in relation to the dominant ethnocultural group, there are four possible kinds of acculturation strategies: (a) integration—maintaining home culture but also relating to the dominant culture; (b) assimilation—giving up home culture and embracing the dominant culture; (c) separation—maintaining home culture and isolating from the dominant culture; (d) marginalization—giving up home culture and failing to relate properly to the dominant culture.

Numerous studies with immigrant, indigenous and ethnos cultural populations in different places have shown these four orientations are present in individuals in non-dominant groups, and integration is the kind with which the person can experience the least psychological stress, and yet the integrative acculturation can only be successfully pursued when the dominant society is open and inclusive towards cultural diversity (Berry et al., 2006).

Furthermore, according to the observation of John Berry (2011) on cultural development in many places in the recent century, the assumption that cultural homogenization will eventually happen though increasing intercultural contact clearly does not stand up to scrutiny in most parts of the world. The society remains plural. The reason is that more contact can also stimulate resistance and agony rather than cultural acceptance, domination or homogenization. The interaction between cultures is also creative and reactive process. It can generate new customs and values, which have not been prevalent in either of the original groups.

Applying this theoretical lens of Berry, the present education policy of Hong Kong government encourages assimilation rather than integration of ethnic minorities, towards a kind of homogenization close to the Chinese. (Erni & Leung, 2014; Shum et al., 2016) The steadfast rejection of the creation of a CSL curriculum in Hong Kong schools reflects such policy orientation. The education authority wants to merge the second language learners into the same dominant education system with as little deviation as possible.

Such assimilation policy orientation is also evident in many exemption clauses added into the Hong Kong Anti-racial Discrimination Ordinance (RDO). About education, there is the following exemption clause:

> *Nothing in subsection (1) [which protects equal rights of EM to be admitted to educational establishments and to use their facilities] is to be construed as requiring the responsible body for an educational establishment – (a) to modify for persons of any racial group arrangements of the establishment regarding holidays or medium of instruction; or (b) to make different arrangements on those matters for persons of any racial group persons.*

When the Ordinance was moved as a bill by the government to the Legislative Council, the exemption was under strong criticism from many academics. For example, a petition letter was written by 15 teachers of the University of Hong Kong (Ki et al., 2006). The petition reminded the government that the ICERD UN Convention prohibits all forms of racial discrimination, including "direct discrimination" as well as "indirect discrimination", and the exemption can lead to "indirect discrimination", because by imposing the same treatment to all groups, some groups are being victimized while there is little justifiable reasons why such victimization cannot not be mitigated by modifying the treatment.

However, the government held steadfast to the exemption, and threatened that should the exemption be removed from the Bill by amendments passed in the Legislative Council, the government would withdraw the Bill altogether. As all binding laws of Hong Kong have to be moved by the government, if the government withdrew the Bill, society would not have such the anti-racial discrimination laws, at least for some years, before the government would come back with a newer version.

Eventually, the law makers and NGOs backed down, and the exemption became part of the Ordinance. It is important to note that the what made the liberal law makers and NGOs back down was largely because of the silence of the educational institutions about the exemptions. Most Hong Kong schools are governed by non-profit making religious or community organizations. Most of them had never experienced handling EM students and worried about their legal responsibilities if the exemptions were removed. Most local Chinese teachers also shared that fear.

3 Understanding the Perspectives of EM Parents and Students

This part of the chapter will provide a review on some academics' studies on the perceptions of EM parents, students, through different theoretical lenses to reveal some more about the actual context surrounding the question of Chinese language teaching and learning of EM students in Hong Kong, and hence the complexity involved in facing it.

3.1 Language Ideologies

The concepts of language ideology and language identity have been used by some local researchers (Gu et al., 2017a, b) in their studies. The concept of language ideology originates from the fields of linguistic anthropology, social linguistics and cross-cultural studies. It focuses mainly on the beliefs and attitudes of people towards language and language practices (Kroskrity, 2010). In contrast to seeing language just as objective and neutral set of codes and rules for representation and communication of information, it focuses on language as a human activity with a broad and bi-directional connection to their social and historical values and interests. The term ideology is used here to indicate that such connections concerned can be mutually reinforcing and hence robust in determining one's practice and perception of the language. Furthermore, when there is status differentiation in languages and some languages (or versions of a language) are given higher value than others, language ideology also reflects power and identity struggles among social groups, and language purism and authenticity can be ideological weapons used by certain groups for such courses (Irvine & Gal, 2000).

Chinese language has been the government's focus of attention in EM education improvement since early 2000s. It is assumed that once the Chinese language barrier is removed, integration and social condition of the EM will greatly improve. Yet, it is more an ideology than reality which is much more multifaceted. For example, in the LF provided by the government, Chinese language is depicted as a body of technical knowledge and skill—If teachers can correctly identify what is missing, and provide the knowledge and skill to the learners systematically step-by-step, then the learners will learn the language effectively. What not considered is often the learners' and the teachers' motivation and perceptions, that rest upon their personal values and feelings about the language and its meaning in the social context. In other words, the language ideologies that the learners and the teachers carry into the teaching and learning situation are very much ignored, yet such ideologies can greatly affect the motivation and manners they teach and learn.

While the government is focusing solely on EM's learning of just one language, Chinese, with little attention to their English, the EM students are actually facing a much more complex social and linguistic reality in society. As Li (2017), a local professor in multilingual studies points out, English and Chinese are both dominant languages in Hong Kong. As census statistics indicate, many more EM parents can use English than Chinese. Hence, it is likely that Chinese is the third rather than second language to the EM students, after their acquisition of mother tongue and then English. Furthermore, as Dornyei, a world-renowned psychologist in second language learning motivation points out, in this age of globalization, the motivation of learning one second/foreign language cannot be isolated from that of another, and the global value of English is imparting influence on the learning of other second/foreign languages worldwide (Dornyei & Ryan, 2015; Dornyei & Al-Hoorie, 2017). As English and Chinese are both dominant languages in Hong Kong, how the EM student sees the relative values of Chinese and English will have an impact on the investment into learning these two languages.

Many EM students reported in the study of Tsung et al. (2012) that they preferred using English to communicate with strangers in the street. The reason was that they would then be perceived as having a higher social status, because they could use a global language that most ordinary Chinese people in Hong Kong were not fluent in. Furthermore, the EM parents can easily feel the superior value of English assumed by most Hong Kong people. Local news always indicates that Chinese parents are keen in putting their children into EMI school places. It was especially visible when the Chinese parents came to the street to protest against the MOI reform that changed most secondary school into Chinese-medium schools. The high status of English in business and professional sectors is also visible. There are native English-speaking teachers in schools, professors at universities and expatriate managers of companies, who do not know Chinese. That seems to indicate, once you get up to a certain level of professional or job status, you will be able to survive well in Hong Kong with just English. Knowing spoken and written Chinese is advantage, as Chinese is a common language in Hong Kong, but English is also common, and many Chinese people also know English. It is only when you need to serve ordinary populace or bosses who have not been well educated and know only Chinese, then you must use Chinese as the sole medium of communication. This perception has been reflected in some EM students in the study of Hue et al. (2015) when they talked about Chinese assessment standards. They questioned the necessity and fairness that they are required to be tested to high standard of Chinese as native speakers.

Of course, there are also EM students feeling the learning of Chinese more important than English for survival. More recent research indicates that (Chou, 2016; Lau, 2015), EM students born and brought up in areas of Hong Kong with a lot of grassroot Chinese neighbors and playmates are readier to use Cantonese to communicate with others. They regard themselves to be very much a member of that local social populace. Nonetheless, even if the children feel so, their parents are mostly still very concerned about the children's English proficiency. Sharma (2012) interviewed EM students and parents from low-income families and discovered their ambivalent attitude on learning Chinese. They all wanted their children to learn Chinese well, as it is the more common language used in Hong Kong. But they also worried that even if the children learned the language, their Chinese would likely be not as good as the native Chinese, and they might still not be able to get a job of good prospect in the competitive job market of Hong Kong just with their Chinese language. Most importantly, they worried that in case their children could not find a good living in Hong Kong, they would have to move to other places or their home countries. Hence, English and their mother tongue would be their essential safety net not to be missed.

Ideally, the EM parents would hope that their children can learn both English and Chinese well, but the bifurcation of English and Chinese MOI schools in HK has made the choice of school difficult to EM parents. If they send their children to designated or English-medium schools, they will be able to learn content subjects more easily and develop better English, but their command of Chinese would be weak. But if their children go to Chinese-medium schools, their Chinese will likely be fluent for basic social interaction, but their ability of using it for academic purposes may take longer time to emerge and their subject learning likely will suffer, and chance of entering university will be hampered. Furthermore, their English will be weak. One strategy of parents was hence to send the children to mainstream CMI primary school first to learn the basic Chinese, and then change to designated or EMI mainstream secondary school. This has shown to be a more realistic way for getting into universities. And eventually university teaching is mainly in English.

As Li (2017) points out, even if the EM are willing to put their emphasis on Chinese, there are still variations of Chinese which can appear to them almost like totally different languages: Cantonese (the version of Chinese used by many in Hong Kong and South China) and Putonghua (the national language of Chinese, also called Modern Standard Chinese) have many differences. The two Chinese languages often use slightly different words to represent the same thing; and even if they use the same word for the thing, the pronunciation is different. There are also difference between the two languages in terms of word order and grammatical rules. Furthermore, in schools using Cantonese, while Cantonese is used for speaking, all writing of students must be done using Modern Standard Chinese words and grammar.

Loh et al. (2019) further reveals that the change of school and switch in MOI is often imposed onto the EM students, and causes them negative emotions. For example, in changing from Chinese MOI primary school to an English MOI designated secondary school, the student needs to work extra hard to catch up with the English in content subjects. If the EM student changes from a Cantonese school o Mandarin MOI school (or in the opposite way) when they go from primary to secondary school, they can feel very frustrated for not being allowed to express what they know in the previous version of Chinese language, which they have spent great effort to learn but no longer valued in the new environment.

Some scholars also look at the language value issue in relation to the EM students' heritage language and its connection to their cultural identity development (Gu & Patkin, 2013; Gu et al., 2017a). The difference in view of the EM students with their parents and elder generations about the value of learning heritage language literacy can be a source of family conflict. As a lot of EM parents and elderly do not know Chinese or English, ethnic language is essential for family and ethnic community solidarity. Yet, a lot of EM students know only how to speak their own ethnic language but not how to write it, and this make it difficult to claim that their ethnicity is really 'authentic'. Besides, the situation can be particularly sad for many EM students, as their literacy knowledge in Chinese and English is not strong either.

Most teachers in the study of Gu et al. (2017a) agreed that parents must see the value of EM students' literacy in their own ethnic languages. However, the teachers varied when they came to talk about the use ethnic languages in their own Chinese language teaching lessons. Only minority of the teachers in the study saw the facilitative role of ethnic languages in learning and allowed the use of that in students' group discussion; the majority teachers saw the use of ethnic languages a potential threat to classroom management and teacher's authority. A teacher said, "Because I need to understand what you are saying, so you can only speak the three languages that I can understand, English, Cantonese or Putonghua." Unlike the special schools for EM in colonial times, most schools that accept EM students now do not have ethnic language subjects. With the advent of the value of English and Chinese, their mother tongues are further marginalized. Many teachers thought, staying at school after class for Chinese tutorials is of more urgent need to the EM students, as compared to their going to mosque to learn Urdu or Arabic, and this can sometimes become a point of conflict with EM students or parents.

3.2 Chinese Language Proficiency and the Hong-Konger Identity

It is widely accepted that there is certain relationship between language and identity. Obviously, language connects people who know it and excludes other people who do not. So, the languages you use can affects which groups of people you can communicate with and what social identities you can claim. This is the reason why Chinese language learning has been such a strong focus of attention when law-makers, government, and society think about what needs to be done with for the EM. Many Chinese people in HK regard Chinese language proficiency to be an essential criterion for being a 'standard or normal' Hongkonger. Hence, learning Chinese is a necessary condition to bring these EM students the identity of being a Hong Konger. However, how strong the relationship between language and identity really is when applying to Chinese language and a feeling of being a Hong-Konger the case of EM students is quite contestable.

The longitudinal study of Chou (2016) with EM primary school students indicates that as most of the EM students are born in Hong Kong and has grown up locally, and they think Hong Kong is the place they know best in life, as compared to any other places in the world, and it is their home. Hence, they are locals, and naturally they have the right to stand as Hong-Kongers, irrespective of their ability level of mastery of Chinese. And just like many Chinese people in Hong Kong, while they take HK as their home, the EM students may also have different aspirations for studying or living elsewhere in the future. Similarly they also need to know Chinese and English.

Chou (2016) found that Norton's theory of language and power, and her concepts of language identity and investment (Norton, 2006) are useful in explaining the students' variable Chinese language development. According to Norton, in any eco-social system, individuals naturally will look for power, namely the ability to influence the environment to his/her favor, and acquiring a desirable identity or position is a very important way to gain the power. Whether one would invest the huge effort in learning a new language would depend on the desirable identity one wants to gain with the language, and whether the identity can be affirmed by one's significant others who can provide acceptance and support to one's learning and use of the language while the ability is still emerging with a lot of imperfection.

However, Norton clarifies that forming the identity being a learner or user of the target language does not imply one must align with the majority stance of the group that speak the target language. In Norton's own studies, there were cases where the language learner-and-user identity was about using the target language of the dominant group to voice against the domination. In the study of Chou (2016), there is also a EM student who labels herself as 'Pakistani' instead of 'Hong-Konger', and wishes to become a Chinese language teachers one day to help their EM community to mitigate their conditions. This again contrives the assumption that EM must be assimilative (identify themselves with the Chinese mainstream stereotypical 'Hongkonger') in order that he or she can learn Chinese well. What she needs is significant others like parents, teachers and classmates who can accept the reason she sees as legitimate that motivates her to the learning and using of the language and provide her with the encouragement and support.

As the study is about primary school EM students who are at a relatively young age, Chou (2016) discovers some of them are like nomads, taking on different language learner-and-user identities at different times or with different people. This may also be compared with the research on the two kinds of bicultural orientations (compartmentalized and harmonious) identified in the study by Gao and Lai (2017), with the findings that most of the students considered their own ethnic and the dominant cultures different and followed a compartmentalised bicultural orientation, by behaving differently in home and school contexts. Chou (2016) find that at times, the students may look for ways of reconciling conflicts that might arise. They need someone to whom they feel safe to acknowledge their experiences and questions. Chou (2016) also shows that, school examination results affect strongly the EM students' self-evaluation and motivation in learning Chinese, and senior primary level is a particularly challenging stage for them. The Chinese learning text becomes more complex and the cultural proverbs also come into the curriculum, and the EM students at that grade level can become more aware of the big gap in learning progress between them and the Chinese students.

The study of Chou (2016) includes the case of a child from Chinese and Pakistani mixed family. Although she had plenty of exposure to English, Chinese, and heritage language at home and in schools, the unhappy experience in the family and schools brought her difficulty in identifying with any of the ethnic groups, and her proper learning of the languages suffered. This interestingly provide a mirror-image to the results in a slightly earlier study by Lau (2015) that looks at the learning history of some relatively more successful Chinese language learners among EM students.

Lau (2015) tries to understand the relation between Chinese language learning and identity development of EM students. He concludes that the Chinese language learner identity of an individual is formed ecologically and progressively integrated into his or her overall identity, and hence the language identity carries characteristics of the individual and his or her eco-social environment, and the synergetic relationship found. For example, one EM student's parent had been operating a restaurant of ethnic cuisine. The student's basic literacy in Chinese learnt from school was helpful in the business and got the praise by the family as well the Chinese customers. Hence her identity as a Chinese language learner (and user) is reinforced both by Chinese and his ethnic people.

In another case, an EM student learnt Chinese significantly outside the school, from friends while they played football together. When the boy grew older, he joined an EM assistant police programme. He found that his knowledge in ethnic language and English gave him a special role when he patrolled with Chinese constables. He could better handle non-Chinese speakers on the streets, and at the same time, his Chinese language allowed him to cooperate well with the Chinese constables. When he entered university, he also saw his niche in his study groups. The Chinese peers could help him understand local colloquial expressions used by the lecturer while he could help others in reading the English reference text.

There is also a EM student who was born and grew up in HK. She studied in mainstream primary school, had a happy and sociable temperament, and identified herself with her classmates from the working class. When she changed to a designated secondary school, she chose to study the mainstream Chinese curriculum. With her good spoken interaction skill but relatively poor literacy skill, she was not able to get a pass in DSE, but she eventually got a job as an English language teacher in a kindergarten. She only spoke English to the kids, but she could understand well what the kids said no matter they use Chinese, English or South Asian ethnic languages. She found her niche in the kindergarten.

In each of the six cases of Lau (2015), the Chinese language learner-and-user identity carries unique characteristics of the individual and his or her eco-social environment. However, a general trend can be explained in terms of Dornyei's theory of second language learning motivation and Deci & Ryan's Self-Determination Theory of learning motivation (Dornyei & Ryan, 2015).

In Dornyei's theory, motivation in learning a second language can come from a combination of (1) the language learning environment that is motivating; and (2) an 'ought-to language self' in the learner that originates from the external expectations of others in learning the target language; and (3) an 'ideal language self' in the learner, which is a combination of the target language with personal goals he or she finds attractive and realistic for the future. The theory also proposes that 'ideal language self' is the kind of motivation that leads to the highest learning outcome.

Self-Determination Theory (SDT) of learning motivation by Deci and Ryan (1985) suggested that intrinsic motivation and extrinsic motivations often operate at the same time. Furthermore, if three basic human needs are satisfied, the external motivation in doing the thing will gradually become internalized and become an integrative part of one's own identity. The three basic needs are: the increased experiencing of competence (seeing that one is actually able to do the thing), autonomy (seeing that one is given certain freedom of choice in doing the thing and hence feel ownership in the outcome), and relatedness (seeing that the thing they do help them being accepted or appreciated by others).

In the cases of Lau (2015), successful learning paths usually begin with parents' decision and encouragement, and teachers' care and support (learning situation and ought-to self), followed by certain struggle and success over time, and then the students gradually develop their own life goals and personal identities which in turn drive their further learning of Chinese (ideal self). In the end, the learner not just learn a language, but also develop their social identity. And the ideal language self consists of a combination of the various languages one knows, which are creatively used in the niche identity one found.

4 Pedagogical Innovations and Personal Growth of Teachers and Researchers

This part of the Chapter will report some of the innovative CSL pedagogical practices developed since the various USP projects up to the present. The earlier ones focus comparatively more on the 'objective' aspects of the language to be learnt, while the later ones are more about the 'subjective' aspects of the learning, namely more about engaging the learners to make the language their own tool for expressing and capturing what they concern in their multilingual and multicultural life-world. The process of entering into this new space of Chinese teaching has been quite emotionally and intellectually taxing for most of these teachers and researchers, and as a result their growth can be deep and transformative.

4.1 Teaching to Discern Structures in the Chinese Language

In the past decade, some advancement has been made in CSL pedagogy through the university-school collaborative projects. One part of it is about helping EM students to cope with the special structural features of the Chinese language. As Chinese has an ideographic script, its literacy learning can hence be quite different from alphabetic phonetic languages. There is no direct script-sound relationship in Chinese characters and words. And there are numerous strokes in each Chinese character. The learning of characters has traditionally been a painful task even for native Chinese children. Though they can naturally acquire the spoken Chinese and the meaning of spoken words, they generally need to go through painful drilling to learn the characters.

Tse reviewed the many approaches to initial Chinese literacy learning in China and invented the Integrative Perceptual Approach (IPA) based on the Variation Theory of Learning. IPA was first used for native Chinese-speaking children and later used also with EM learners (Tse et al., 2007). The Variation Theory of Learning (Marton & Booth, 1997) originates from the finding of phenomenographic research that people generally see the same phenomenon in different ways, and powerful ways of acting often spring from powerful way of seeing.

According to the IPA, when a teacher teaches learners Chinese characters, he or she should also teach them powerful ways of perceiving them, and one of which is to discern the components that form the Chinese characters. While initial literacy may demand the knowledge of a thousand characters, these characters are likely made up of about 80 recurring components, and each character is likely made up of just a few components. Hence developing the structural awareness of learners towards components can be one way of making their character learning more effectively.

According to the Theory of Variation, IPA suggests that such structural discernment can be stimulated quite naturally when related characters are learnt in clusters, in which the characters are partly the same and partly different in terms of the components they use. The variation (sameness-and-difference) will stimulate the learners to do comparison and contrast on the characters, and they will be able to discern the components that sit within the characters and develop a sense of the components and how can be fit together to form the characters and contribute to the meanings and sounds of the characters.

However, IPA does not suggest teaching these components first in isolation. First of all, before learning to discern the components, the learners need first to learn the characters as wholes. For example, the teacher can first prepare a short rhyme in connection to a group-play and teach students to play the activity and read the text. This will help the students build up some preliminary connection between the sound, shape and meaning of the characters in relation to the play. After that, the teacher can focus the class on the certain small set of characters in the text, which bear structural similarity and differences, and let the students discern the components. Then the teacher can elaborate and use those components discerned as springboard to introduce or help recalling other related characters and words commonly used.

Another key point of IPA is to put the training of character recognition much earlier before the training of character writing. When the harsh conventional requirement on simultaneous mastery of reading and writing is removed, the teacher can scaffold the students to be exposed to more meaningful and interesting reading first. When students are asked to practice writing later, they will not write one character repeatedly to learn the strokes by heart; instead, they will write several related characters in the same task for a few times, to reinforce the variation. Tse et al. (2007) reports that this method with Grade 1 native Chinese students could lead to astounding effect and they significantly outperformed the previous cohort who were taught with the conventional approaches.

IPA had already been widely adopted in primary schools of Hong Kong to speed up native speaker's character/word learning and independent reading, at the time when USP began to come into place for EM students. The pedagogy is then successfully used with EM students, and the approach has then been expanded through such application (Tse et al., 2012). As the EM learners include learners of different age, learning texts in the form of picture book are used, which are simple in language but deep in meaning. As there can be great diversity of Chinese language ability in the class, teaching with differentiated learning materials and learning tasks on the same story line can be used. While individuals or groups may work at different levels of language challenge, there is still the common theme and context for whole-class exchanges.

As Chinese people, including teachers are too familiar with their own language, they may easily take many structural features of their language for granted and hence unable to see how such features are seen (or not seen or mis-seen) by the students. These can include, for example the invisible word boundaries between characters, words or phrases in Chinese text, the implicit rules in the formation of words from characters, and the formation of sentence from words, and so on. Some phenomenographic analysis of errors, interlanguage, or alternative conceptions of EM students in reading and writing Chinese has been carried out to raise teachers' awareness. (Marton et al., 2010).

Another programme of research has been on enhancing EM students' structural awareness at the text level. Shum (2019) adapts Reading to Learn (R2L) pedagogy (Rose & Martin, 2012) from English to Chinese. The pedagogy brings students a strong connection between perception and production of genres. It begins with a pre-reading phase to provide students with a general background understanding of the learning text, and then supports students to gain an understanding of how the text makes specific meanings through detailed reading (collaborative deconstruction), followed by a collaborative reconstruction of a paraphrase of the text in simpler words and sentences, which are closer to the students' own level of mastery in production. The prompting and elaborating strategies developed in R2L were found to be particularly useful to provide EM students. The strategies can provide a lot of opportunity for students to contribute even though their CSL is still emerging, and to feel a sense of self-achievement in the reading. The teacher and students then undergo group co-construction and individual construction of new texts using the same structure (genre) on some other slightly varied topics. Lesson studies have been carried out with Chinese picture book, narrative and explanatory texts, and students' ability and confidence in subsequent writing of the same genres significantly improved.

Shum also makes use of the Variation Theory of Learning. While the same genre is followed and reinforced in the subsequent writing (in the co-construction and individual construction), Shum also emphasizes designing interesting variation in the content of such writing. In some lesson studies, EM students have been successfully guided to do R2L even with classical Chinese text. In one case, EM students were first supported to study a classical text (愛蓮說) which used different flowers as analogies to people's different value-orientations, and then to turned to use analogies in their own writings to describe diverse dispositions of their friends/ family members. In another case, the teacher connected reading of a classical Chinese text (桃花源記) which talked about an incidental entrance into a lost paradise to the subsequent writing about the students' own dream worlds. Such connection between reading and writing with variation, not only could enhance the students' interest in the reading, but also empowered them with a way of organizing and expressing their own thinking. Evaluation results indicated that such genre-based pedagogy could help EM students to write richer and better-structured text in Chinese.

4.2 Culturally Responsive Teaching

Another advancement that has come through university-school collaborative projects is related to Culturally Responsive Teaching (CRT). CRT is a term first used in the educational sector of USA, when the persistent disparity in academic performance between learners from different cultures became a concern. CRT is defined as a pedagogy that recognizes the importance of empowering students by including their cultural references in all aspects of learning (Ladson-Billings, 1994) and by so doing unleash their academic potential and expectation (García, 2000). Imagine that you were stuck to a place where people there told you all your previous knowledge and experiences were useless or even harmful here, and you needed to forget all that and start anew with what you were told. Obviously, you would feel devalued and depowered. In opposition to this, CRT proposes to make reference to the learner's diverse background cultures and their personal experiences as resource, on which new knowledge and understanding can build upon. Furthermore, CRT proposes education should aim at providing an academically enriching environment based on such diverse resource to inspire high expectation of intellectual development of students of all ethnicities, races, beliefs, and creeds.

The practice-based pedagogical research of Loh et al. (2019) with the EM students of Hong Kong can be subsumed under this concept of CRT. It advocates the approach of 'culturally mediated instruction', which is to incorporate and integrate diverse ways of knowing, understanding and representing the cultural experiences of the EM students. The use of multiple ways is emphasized in response to the often-observed depressing situations of EM learners in CSL classrooms: As the learners are weak in the target language, they are made simply to parrot the content given by the teacher and often criticized for being wrong. Their need to use the target language to express their own creative thoughts and personal feelings while learning the language can be totally ignored.

In the work of Loh et al. (2019), CSL pedagogies are developed to elicit and capitalize on the cultural experiences of EM students. Here, "cultural experiences" refers to something authentic to the specific students, fresh and yet to be discovered, rather than the stereotypical images that one may easily assume, such as things in their traditional ethnic cultures. Teachers have found that some of them admire sport and pop-culture stars in Hong Kong and places beyond. These youngsters also have their own lived experience in Hong Kong, and their own personal views about their own ethnic cultures as well as prevalent mindsets in Hong Kong.

The pedagogies are also designed such that it can be flexibly adapted into the different CSL learning texts that schools have already created, as well as the variable levels of mastery among students in the same class. The basic idea is to (1) enrich the existing school-based teaching by providing a simple vehicle for students to express; (2) identify a generative theme related to the school-based learning text that can open a shared space of creative responses; (3) support students to use the vehicle to express their diverse cultural experiences and personal views on the theme; (4) use the students responses as additional collective learning resources to carry out further activities and language work. The idea is partly similar to the model suggested in the critical multicultural pedagogy suggested by Soto Pineda (2016) for EM students in Hong Kong for English as second language learning.

Some common vehicles can be art-jamming, poster design that combine picture and text, formulas for producing short poems, picture books, etc. Students can view examples of such works and use their forms and structures and replace it with their own content. For example, after reading with the class a picture book, the teacher can support students to do their own picture books. Drafts can be made first with sketches, in Chinese or English, and then improved. Suppose the school-based learning text is about school learning, one generative theme arising could be about something that the student has learnt / overcome. Students can create their own story, real or fictious, or a mix; the class can read that picture book first, and then the students can borrow the forms and structures for their own use. The creative works of the students can then be the displayed and presented among classmates, or with an extended audience. No matter the story is true or fictitious, it can be seen as a projection of the authentic cultural experiences and thoughts of the students. The idea is partly similar to that of "identity text" suggested by Cummins and Early (2011).

One special vehicle developed by Loh et al. (2019) is a kind of electronic do-it-yourself flash card called 'mLang'. Unlike conventional flash card software which try to spoon-feed students, 'mLang' is a cloud-based system for students to create what they are interested and contribute them as shared learning content. Teacher can set up projects in which students can create cards anytime anywhere, and thus use the tool as a seamless platform that connect their life situations and classroom learning. Each card must have a photo, a voice recording, and some text. It is multilingual and multimodal. Students can use Chinese sentences or simply words depending on their knowledge; they can also use other languages they know. They are also encouraged to use web resource and multilingual assisting technologies. Teacher can provide individuals with spoken and written feedback over the network on the students' card for improvement if necessary before they are put into a pool for sharing. Once cards are in the pool, classmates can refer to it anytime anywhere. The cards can become resources for further activities, like gaming activities or writing, pretty much up to the imagination of the teachers and students.

Results indicate the activity can quickly expand the vocabulary of the students and develop their reading and writing capability. Analysis of the student-cards indicates that majority of the cards contain new words that are beyond the original CSL learning texts (which are typically short and simple), and the amount of such words brought in by the student-cards is comparable to those from the learning text. Besides, it is noticed that words like 'unemployed' and 'fired' appear in the student-cards on family. Such words would never appear in the original CSL learning text designed by the schools, but can readily be included for the subsequent learning. Usually the school-based learning texts for EM students are short, simple and general. Through the use of 'mlang' pedagogy, learning is deepened to connect the specific lived experiences and feelings of the students.

The creation / reading of cards among students is also found to be an authentic experience of communication for meanings. Students find it highly satisfying when others can understand what they say or write in Chinese. Students are amused in hearing the other classmates' trying to speak the words. Students usually want to do something different, and at the same time inquisitive to know what others have possibly presented or said on the same themes / questions given. As the student's language improves, he or she will naturally try to use phrases or sentences (beyond single words) to express their creative messages more fully. It is observed that beginning from using single words, a student can progress to write sentences or even paragraphs within half year.

Loh et al. (2019) explain how activity design has been inspired by the Self-Determination Theory (SDT) by Deci and Ryan (1985). SDT points out that the relation between intrinsic motivation (e.g. the excitement in the creative process) and extrinsic motivations (e.g. being praised by teachers and peers and improving in examination) can be dynamic. SDT also points out that through experiencing of competence, autonomy, and relatedness in doing something, the external motivation in doing the thing will gradually become internalized and become their own self-motivation. In 'mLang' card, the linguistic requirement is flexible, and learners can work according to their ability and feel competent. As for autonomy, first, students can choose the specific things they like to put into the cards, and second, when students are asked to learn from the cards created by other students for gaming or writing, they are also given the freedom to choose which they feel most close to themselves, e.g. to pick the best 5 or 10 cards by others, instead of being forced to learn all cards in the pool. The students also feel relatedness when their works are appreciated and used by others.

'Drama convention' (DC) is another kind of vehicle used in Loh et al. (2019). Each DC is a simple drama act which can be done within like 10 minutes. It is used in connection to reading and writing activities. The reading and writing can happen before, within or after the act. Students and/or teachers act in roles in the DC. Some commonly used DC include Conscience Alley (a character walks through an alley form by two rows of students, and as he or she pass by, the students on the two sides of the alley persuade him/her to accept or reject a choice), Hot Seating (a character is seated and students can ask him or her questions), Still Image (students are asked to imagine a scene and show it with their body gesture, and they may then be enchanted one by one to speak what the characters they play feel in the scene).

In the DC, students use their imagination to act in roles. Results indicates that although students are often unable to accurately imagine the roles (because they simply lack the actual knowledge and experience in the roles), what interesting is that they often make it an opportunity to project their own thinking, which come from their own real experience. For example, in one DC activity with Conscience Alley, when a girl acted as a parent of the main character to comment whether he should take or leave the working holiday, she made herself the father and gave a firm supportive voice. This reflected her own experience in a patriarchal culture and how strongly she would wish herself to be encouraged by her father to explore more of the world.

To design the learning activities effectively, the teacher needs to learn to (1) find a gap in the learning text, which can provide a situation that allows some space of imagination, and (2) find a generative theme in that gap which may connect to / reflect the personal experiences of the students, (3) make use of the conflict or tension in the situation to intensify the thinking and the need of language in making meaning, and (4) relate the activity to certain specific part of language learning and use.

One example reported was a DC activity related to a learning text about Qu-yuan, who was a patriotic poet in one of the kingdoms of ancient China. He drowned himself in the river to warn his king about his wrong doing. Since then, people commemorated him with the Dragon Boat Festival. There seems to be no way that the EM students can imagine the real situation of Qu-yuan. But the ingenious teacher puts in an interesting generative theme: he asks the EM students to imagine what Qu-yuan will say last (in one minute) to the king before he left, with the additional background information that they have long been very good friends and have worked closely together before to make the kingdom strong. Here friendship and betrayal between friends can become an entry point that the student can connect Qu-yuan's situation to their own.

Even though CRT has earned good learning responses in some CSL classrooms, Loh et al. (2019) points out that the general situations are still challenging. Facing cultural differences and trying out unconventional strategies are emotionally taxing for most teachers (Loh & Tam, 2017). Both 'mLang" and the DC pedagogy are risky in the eyes of many teachers. Hence such research and teacher development need to be done through close collaboration and mutual empowerment of experts and teachers at the front line of practice, and such work must be done in a sustained manner to grow the curriculum leadership and professional network concerned. CSL should be taken to be a discipline with rising importance rather than simply for a transitional period, and teachers in CSL should deserve proper recognition and further study opportunities.

4.3 Teacher's Intercultural Development and Emotional Challenge

In the past two decades, intercultural awareness had increased generally among teachers and educators. Some Chinese teachers find they need to contest their own taken-for-granted cultural ideas when they come to work with EM students. One strong idea among teachers is about 'uniformity / conformity': Individuals should show respect to the community by following common codes and not to be eccentric. And this is anchored on another idea about 'fairness/ justice': to be 'fair/just' within a group, all members of it have to share equal condition, labor, and be examined, rewarded or penalized according to the same criteria.

According to that cultural belief, many teachers feel uncertain when they want to provide additional support to the EM students in the class, or to implement alternative assessment tasks for these students (Hue & Kennedy, 2012). They need to look for justifying reasons and confirming evidence to support that such actions in catering for diversity are morally right and can be beneficial collectively to the whole group of students. It is not just for convincing themselves; they also need to convince other teachers, students and their parents for the alternative treatments.

In their encounter with cultural diversity learners, the teachers also need to be sensitive to the EM learners' alternative way of seeing reality. Westrick and Yuen (2007) has carried out research of such development of intercultural sensitivity among teachers in Hong Kong. The research used the Intercultural Development Inventory (IDI) developed by Hammer and Bennett (1998) based on the theoretical model of Milton Bennett (1993). According to the model, the development goes through two phases:

1. First, the Ethnocentric Phase: one's own culture is experienced as central to reality and difference is perceived as threatening. This phase consists of a few stages:

   (1a) Denial—do not want to know the other culture;
   (1b) Defence/reversal—defend the superiority of one's own culture, or reject one's own culture and embrace the other; and
   (1c) minimization—trivialize the difference and emphasize the similarities between the cultures.

2. Second, the Ethno-Relative Phase: one's own culture is experienced in the context of other cultures; and each culture has a valid and viable construction of the world and differences exist legitimately in our views of the world. This phase also consists of a few stages:

   (2a) Acceptance/adaptation—can respect and internalise two or more different sets of cultural frames of references and regard their own culture as just one of a number of equally complex worldviews;
   (2b) Constructive or Encapsulated Marginality—By marginality, it means that the person can see oneself being at the margins of different cultures. In the case of Constructive Marginality, one can selectively agree with some but not necessarily all elements that represent each culture and is able to move in and out between cultures and perceive such experience positively. But in the case of Encapsulated Marginality, the person feels wondering between the different cultures. He or she can fit in with many cultures but feel 'being at home in none' (Webpage of ICI, 2006).

Westrick and Yuen (2007) did the IDI survey with 160 secondary school teachers in 4 schools with varying degree of cultural diversity in the schools. The results indicate that the average Overall Development Score lied in the Minimization Stage in the Ethnocentric Phase. And further break down of the responses of the teachers indicates that for 'issues' in the different Stages, there was the highest percentage of teachers with the 'issues' unresolved in the Minimization Stage (48.8% unresolved, 46.3% in transition, and 5% resolved), where the term 'issues' referred to questions that the teacher felt uncertain or unsettled in choosing their stance. Such findings indicate that many teachers were still struggling with the question whether they should see the EM students as essentially the same or different. Another finding was that the Overall Development Score generally increased (i.e. becomes closer to the Ethno-Relative Phase of the model) with the increase of cultural diversity in the schools, confirming the importance of direct experience for intercultural sensitivity development.

Teacher research also indicates that teaching EM students has also been felt emotionally challenging by Chinese teachers of Hong Kong. As indicated by numerous studies elsewhere, in the intercultural encounters, many concepts and norms one assumes to be right can be upset, such as in judging friendship, authority, values, fairness, personal space, time, future, motivation, self and social etiquette, ways of verbal and non-verbal communication, and so on. And upsetting these may easily be felt as a challenge to the teacher's dignity.

In Hong Kong, as a matter of fact, many of the Chinese teachers deployed to take such hard job of teaching EM students are often young and junior members of the school teaching staff. The un-cooperation of the EM students can bring these teachers fear about losing their job. Although eventually, many Chinese teachers may learn to become more reflective on their own taken-to-granted beliefs, be able to understand more about students' life and topics of interest, and feel more able in conversing with the students with a mix of authority, friendship and humour, the teachers' learning journeys are often full of emotional fluctuations.

Ho (2013) provides an in-depth auto-ethnography of such an emotional journey taken by a teacher who began to teach ethnic minority students Chinese. In the end, one striking conclusion of the teacher was that she and her students would probably never be able to totally understand the other side. Students walked in with their beliefs and feelings, and so did the teacher. Through interactions, they knew each other more. But to be honest, the two sides had great difference in their background experiences and social situations. How can they be able to feel what the other side feel?

For example, the teacher in the study knew many students had strong bonding to their relatives and could take long holidays back to their homeland to join extended family activities at their homeland, even to the extent of taking extended leave from school and sacrificing their study. But there is no way that she could feel like what the students felt.

From the opposite side, the students also appeared unable to feel the special effort that the teacher had put into her CSL teaching (which is a totally new thing for her). This is one excerpt in the auto ethnography:

> In this term I had fewer lessons (with these students), only 2 lessons per 10-day cycle. Yet, I would have to finish three volumes of the textbook in two years. . . . I also learnt from GCSE examination authority that they had changed the format of the assessment . . . I felt panic. I decided not to follow the textbook page by page. On the unit of clothing, in the first lesson, I showed them PowerPoint slides with different kinds of clothing items including my own wedding dresses. I also created simple dialogues for them to design their own school summer and winter uniforms. Then I told them to bring some of their own dolls together with some clothes for their dolls for the next lesson, so that apart from learning vocabulary, they could have fun. When the lesson came, they were eager in changing clothes for their dolls, and they gave mini presentations on the dresses. All went well until I announced at the end of the lesson that they would need to study the unit and be tested on the unit. Immediately they changed faces. . .

The students then grumbled collectively. There were no signs of any gratefulness to the teacher's earlier work and efforts. Following that were weeks of unhappy tug of war which even included parent's rude phone complaint that made the teacher feel undignified and anxious. A student said "Ms, you haven't taught us page by page. My mum said it was not right. You taught too fast . . ." The teacher, having been hurt, then decided to revert to the boring page-by-page textbook teaching.

Eventually, a critical moment came. Some students signalled to the teacher that they wanted the more interesting way of learning. The teacher asked herself: should I forgive them? The teacher took the students' friendly gesture and chose to forgive. A positive cycle of healing then began. The teacher in the auto ethnographic study went through repeated cycles of such conflict, communication and reconciliation afterwards. In the reconciliation, students were given a chance to voice, but the teacher also let the students know what a person she was, and what the things were that she would not compromise. In these cycles of conflict, communication and reconciliation with the students, the teacher had to handle the conflicts in her inner self. And eventually one striking conclusion of the autobiographic research is that she will never be able to feel what her students feel and vice versa, and what needed is a continuous need of growth in one's emotional, intellectual, and moral self, through the ebb and flow of the journey.

It is useful to notice a special message here from the story. Intercultural growth is not just about knowledge, like knowing the objective knowledge of the EM people's traditional festivals, customs etc., but fundamentally about relationship, the forming of trustful and productive relationship with the students over numerous ebbs and flow, conflicts, and emotional challenges that can come up unexpectedly, and the increasing capacity to embrace and live through all these. It is the bigger heart, quite like what Parker Palmer describe as "The Courage to Teach" in his book first published in 1998 (Palmer, 1998).

5 Discussion and Conclusion

On the whole, the scene described above seems to be quite common in today's world, with its many uncertainties, misgivings and gloominess; but life has to go on. And coming off and on, or sporadically here and there, are some moments of sweetness or light that give us hope and fuel. Such moments can be transient, sporadic, or even weak. Interestingly, however, they can sometimes be even more sharply felt and heart-capturing, even amidst the general gloominess.

In this part of the chapter, the authors will discuss two major drawbacks in the current EM language education policy. They will argue that the problems have been essentially quite similar to those of the mainstream Chinese students (Sects. 5.1 and 5.2). They have tried to understand why the government has been so firmly holding on to its 'non-ideal' policies (Sect. 5.3) They will encourage readers to treasure the important experience, knowledge, and spiritual growth that teachers and researchers have gained over the initial 20 years of Hong Kong SAR, in responding to the needs of the EM learners, and such revelations may have great potential value when some future moments will come that the wind may return to blow towards a certain direction (Sect. 5.3).

5.1 The EM's Capability in and Need for English Learning Has Been Much Neglected

Chapter "Contexts of Learning, Priorities for Research" has mapped out the broad situation about CSL learning internationally, through hot and cool times, and has asserted that it will remain, in any case, an important second language for the world, because of its indispensable value in helping anybody to engage with such a great part of the world's population, who currently live in China or in other parts of the world where they find home. The EM parents and students of Hong Kong would likely be highly agreeable to this view. A good command of Chinese is of great immediate relevance for their better living condition in Hong Kong. Hence, they definitely would like to learn Chinese and be supported to learn it effectively.

However, the review of the government's policy (Parts I and II of this chapter) and the considerations of EM parents and students (Part III of the chapter) reveals some difference in perception between the two sides. Learning English is also close to the hearts of the EM, at the same time when they explain that they want better learning of Chinese. But this desire for English learning or learning through English has not been taken notice of by the Government.

Although the focus of this book is on CSL, the authors think it is important for CSL teachers to understand the EM students' holistic feeling about different languages. Often, English is the EM students' second language, while Chinese is actually the third. Hence, many EM parents and students think English is their stronger language, and using English as the medium can help them learn subject matters more easily, and they know English remains very important for further studies, as well as in professions and business in Hong Kong. They also see that living in Hong Kong can be fine if one knows English. Hong Kong is quite a bilingual city; most educated people in Hong Kong know English; and many public services provide information in both English and Chinese. They can also imagine that if they do not further strengthen their English, and focus only on their Chinese, there will be problems in this highly competitive place of Hong Kong. Many EM students think that no matter how hard they study, their Chinese is unlikely to be as strong as that of the native Chinese speakers. Hence, in order to remain competitive, they must not lose their advantage in English. Furthermore, in the event that they cannot find a satisfactory living in Hong Kong and eventually want to go elsewhere for work or study, English will be their safety net.

It may be of interest to the reader to know that such strong desire to be strong in both English and Chinese does not only exist among EM students. It is largely shared by most Chinese people in Hong Kong. The idea of "Dominant Language Constellation" (Lo Bianco & Aronin, 2020) seems to provide a highly inspiring metaphor for understanding the situation in many places in this global era, including the multilingual needs of the EM as well as Chinese students in Hong Kong. In fact, there has been a long and painful history of debate and struggle in Hong Kong as to whether Chinese or English should be the major medium of instruction (MOI) for the majority Chinese students. Without going into its long history, we can just name the

1998 MOI reform of the SAR government as an example. Tse et al. (2021) has provided an in-depth analysis and reflection of the resistance against the government's initiative and the serious debate and policy adjustment over a period of 20 years from 1997 to around 2018, which is contemporaneous with the period reviewed in this chapter.

Using mother-tongue's educational benefits as the reason, the new SAR government wanted to change about three quarters of all secondary schools into Chinese medium schools in 1998, soon after the 1997 political handover. Before that, most secondary schools were English medium schools. In fact, the real practice in a lot of these schools was to use English learning texts and examination papers, but use predominantly Cantonese for classroom explanation and discussion. This indigenous kind of translanguaging practice had been quite common in many Hong Kong schools for many decades after WWII, but was condemned by the new SAR government as deception, and the practice harmed students' language acquisition and contributed to the undesirable phenomenon of code-mixing in the language commonly used by Hong Kong people.

From 1998, language bifurcation and purism were upheld. Education Inspectors visited schools to ensure that subject classrooms would be either totally in English or totally in Chinese. The government's reform did have some reason, and the increased use of mother-tongue did encourage more active participation from the students, but the whole reform seemed to have gone too far; it seemed to lack a true understanding of the fundamental reasons that such "peculiar" or "deceptive" MOI practice had been judged acceptable and so commonly adopted by parents and students in Hong Kong. Resistance and criticism from parents and society against the 1998 MOI reform were strong and persistent, and the tension only became a little relaxed after the Government announced the tuning down of such MOI policy in 2008, and re-emphasized the importance of English medium teaching, and faded out the clear bifurcations of secondary schools into Chinese and English medium schools.

Through this long debate and struggle, most educators in Hong Kong came to subscribe to an inclusive rather than exclusive mindset regarding languages, and preferred additive and inclusive bilingual education of Chinese and English rather than language bifurcation. Translanguaging within the same classroom is not wrong, but professional development would be needed so that switching and connecting between different languages should be done in a more thoughtful rather than haphazard way (Cummins, 2007; Lo & Lin, 2015).

Given the experience the government has had with the mainstream Chinese population of Hong Kong, the desire of the EM students for better learning of both English and Chinese, and the opportunity of learning (at least partly) through English, should not be too difficult for the government to understand. However, the government did not pay attention to it and tried, as much as possible, to focus singly upon the learning of Chinese. Obviously, this could cause some resentment among the EM students, and such resentment grew even stronger in 2013, when the government decided to abolish the designated school scheme, because before that, many designated schools had given EM students the opportunity of having English medium instruction.

5.2 No Alternative CSL Learning Pathway Has Been Created for the EM Learners

Chapter "Contexts of Learning, Priorities for Research" has shown examples of how CSL teaching and learning can be designed to cater for the diverse needs of students with different familial and language learning history, from those of non-Chinese origins with no knowledge of Chinese, to those young speakers in Chinese diasporas who already have many varying degrees of familiarity with the language or with the purpose of learning it further. The diverse needs can be broadly categorized into several different learning pathways with varied curriculum content and processes, providing the basis for even more finely differentiated teaching to be decided by front-line teachers depending on the actual characteristics of their students.

However, the review in this Chapter clearly indicates that the EM students in Hong Kong do not have such differential pathways. There is only one major pathway for all, the same pathway as that of the native Chinese learners. All students, native Chinese or not, are supposed to take the same DSE Chinese examination when they reach the end of their secondary education. The exam is claimed to be a criterion-reference test that can map out the differential levels of attainment from the emergent to the advanced, and it follows a general and comprehensive learning framework for Chinese learning in Hong Kong that is intended for all learners. Even though there was a unanimous urge from the Legislative Council that the government should set up some Chinese language benchmarking test, especially for the non-native speakers, which is relevant to common local jobs and social functioning, nothing of the sort has been done by the government.

The authors want to point out that, irrespective of the government's claim just mentioned above, the fact is: The DSE Chinese language exam is a serious hurdle even for native learners. In the year 2022, only 59.8% of all Secondary School leavers could get grade 3 or above in DSE Chinese Language (HKEAA, 2022), and that grade is taken as the minimum requirement for tertiary education admission. So about 40% of the students failed to meet such standard. No distinction was made in ethnicity in the Hong Kong Examination and Assessment Authority (HKEAA) report, with the reason being that HKEAA does not have the power to gather candidates' ethnic / linguistic background. But one can make a reasonable guess: about 35% of the native Chinese students could not reach that standard, as EM students could at most be 5% among all students taking this examination.

Hence, even Chinese students have a high percentage of failure (and at least 35% of them are barred from university entrance because their Chinese is regarded as inadequate). In view of this, how could EM students have the confidence that they will survive the system in the end and be eligible for university admission? And as the curriculum is so demanding, one can imagine that these EM students would likely be at the bottom of their classes in their Chinese language attainment throughout the different stages of their education, with the expectation of failure looming over them during their whole course of Chinese language learning.

Currently, there is still the special concession for EM students to use their GCSE-CSL exam results as substitute to DSE Chinese examination results for university admission. At first this concession was intended to be a transitional measure, but it still remains. And that is because the government knows that it is still essential for most EM students. Taking it away would likely lead to another undesirable uproar from the EM population. Thus, the likely present situation is that even though the one-pathway-for-all policy might have pushed some of the EM students up and able to pass the DSE hurdle, its effectiveness over all EM students has been unsatisfactory.

It may also be useful here to mention a little more about the extremely heavy demand in language learning for students in Hong Kong. Both Chinese and English in DSE exam results must reach grade 3 or above for university admission. In 2022, only 59.8% and 53.2% of students could pass those Chinese and English language hurdles respectively (HKEAA, 2022). How many of them could pass both? There was no information in the HKEAA report, but a reasonable estimation would 45–50% at most. In other words, more than half of the Hong Kong students are barred from universities because they are seen as inadequate in their languages, irrespective of their abilities in other aspects. In schools, Chinese and English language subject teaching also can take up nearly half of the teaching time. People may come to ask: What kinds of talent are we looking for here? Are we facing a language era or a knowledge era? Do we need to reset the balance? Clearly, the extremely strong emphasis on language is a problem. And it is a problem for the whole population, including both EM and the mainstream Chinese students.

There is thus a need to revisit the interpretation of the language policy of "Biliterate and Trilingual (liangwen sanyu)" (BLTL policy). Should the policy be interpreted in a more plurilinguistic sense? In this multi-lingual world, people generally have differential strengths in different languages and would collectively make use of all the different relevant language resources they have (or with technologies or people around) to work out their situations. Does upholding the BLTL policy necessarily mean that one should rule out the provision of alternative pathways, or multi-level ladders in these languages? This is not only about the welfare of the EM students, but also the welfare of all students in Hong Kong.

5.3 How Language Education Policy Planning Might Be Seen by the SAR Government

It might be quite puzzling to many people, why the SAR government could have adopted an EM language education policy with two such non-ideal characteristics as outlined in the titles of Sects. 5.1 and 5.2. above. First, such characteristics are quite at odds with the general second language education policy trend in developed places worldwide. Second, the actual local experience in Hong Kong (including that with the mainstream Chinese students and parents), as laid out above, shows that the grievances of the EM parents and students are largely similar to those of majority Chinese students, and thus should not be hard for the government to understand.

It is actually very difficult to guess what the thinking behind the SAR government was. But, some co-incidence of timing may be useful to note. It was in year 2008 when the Government announced its 'multi-exit' approach, asserting that the existent Chinese language curriculum was actually "a general and comprehensive learning framework for Chinese Language in Hong Kong" and should be sufficiently flexible to be adapted for all students, including the EM students, and firmly posited that there would be no alternative CSL curriculum and examination in Hong Kong for the EM students. (The subsequent announcement of the LF in 2014 was just an implementation of that policy decision). Year 2008 was also the year when the Anti-Racial Discrimination Bill was finally passed in the Legislative Council after a 2-year long debate since the draft was put forward by the government, and hence the Government might think it has already fulfilled its obligation to the UN in relation to the International Convention on the Elimination of All Forms of Racial Discrimination (ICERD). The government demonstrated its extremely firm position in this legislation process. As pointed out in Sect. 2.6, the government was especially steadfast in keeping the exemption clause against responsibility of schools to accommodate to the special needs of EM students, to the extent that the government threatened that it would withdraw the Bill altogether if the Legislative Council were to delete the exemption clause from the Bill.

The most interesting co-incidence in timing was the following: it was also the year 2008 when the Government announced the "fine-tuning" of its 1998 MOI reform to calm down the strong and persistent criticism and resistance among the population against the reform. One speculation can be: It was highly likely that the 1998 MOI reform had made the SAR government aware that language policy changes could be a highly thorny issue. The Chines/English MOI controversy had already been a major headache in education for the government for 10 years. Understandably, the government might not want to open yet another controversy for the government to settle. The government seems to have learnt from the 1998 MOI reform that interests of powerful groups and prevalent mindsets in society are the most important things to be considered in its policy planning.

A consistent strategy of the government became evident at the time, in how it dealt with many of its social and economic policies. As the government was quite well off, it could be relatively easy for the government to provide money for schools, universities, NGOs and other community and professional bodies to research or carry out some supportive measures to alleviate the problems. This could bring good rapport with the organizations, and show the government's sympathy to the EM or other grieving communities. But the government would want to stay very cautious from committing anything that could cause changes to the system or the market that may potentially inflict new burdens or loss on the powerful groups of the place, which formed the real "sponsors" or "social base" of its governance, whose endorsement and cooperation is vital for maintaining the government's legitimacy and operation, and its stable ruling of the place.

For example, before moving the Anti-Racial Discrimination Bill, the government officials concerned did a tremendous amount of work in connecting with academic, social, religious, and ethnic bodies which had been promoting the education and welfare of the EM, and responded to them by providing various support for their work. And at the same time, the officials were also in close communication with influential bodies that operated school and teaching and prominent chambers of employers or business (note: It is has been a long tradition to date that most Hong Kong schools are subsidized by the government for its student enrolment, but established and managed by religious, charity, commercial or fraternity organizations.) to make sure that their interests were protected and that this "social base" would not come out to oppose the Bill. Then eventually, when the government threatened that it could withdraw the Bill from the Legislative Council if the exemption clauses were amended or removed, and have a holistic review on the existing plans of the government in helping the EM, those who had all been fighting for the benefits of the EM needed to back down, because a lot of them were already engaged in government-funded projects to serve the EM, and they did not want to lose such benefits for the EM and for their own organizations.

Similarly, in handling the EM students' Chinese language problems, the government was willing to spend a hundred million dollars to subsidize pedagogical research or teaching support over the years, but highly reluctant to move a single inch in revising its BLTL policy and overall curriculum and assessment system. Probably this is because opening a public discussion about the interpretation of the BLTL policy might be seen as potentially too thorny an issue to deal with. As governments are powerful instruments in shaping societies, they are the central point of contest between different interest parties. It seems that the Hong Kong SAR Government therefore must respond to the pressures from those parties in power, and steer their way dynamically to maintain their stable rule.

5.4 *Nonetheless, We Must Not Overlook the Seams of Exciting Possibilities that Have Come to Light*

Nonetheless, there happened to be a true aspiration for developing a pluralist / multicultural society for Hong Kong among its residents over this initial 20 years of the SAR. The university-school collaborative research about more effective teaching of CSL to EM began with the government subsidy. But, when that government subsidy began to shrink in the late 2010s, the research and development seemed to persist up to date, though being sporadic instead of system wide, with various support from charities and philanthropies, and from local social enterprises. The pedagogical research and development survives because of the valuable experiences that teachers and researchers can earn in the process, and the actual changes they witness in the EM learners.

In exploring CSL, the teachers and researchers go beyond the conventional methods for the native learners and look for new ways. Some of the pedagogical innovations have turned out to be quite successful in helping to transform the attitude and achievement of the learners. The learners begin to feel competence and interest in the learning, and take an active and creative part in it. After all, successful practice cannot be directly derived from theories, especially when the situation is new. It is often at the educational frontline, as the actual human interaction unfolded, and through the success and failure experiences in numerous variable trials, that one can really get to learn some new possibilities and understand more of the nature of such CSL teaching and learning for EM learners in Hong Kong. This is a fundamental reason behind the claim in Chapter "Contexts of Learning, Priorities for Research" that,

> [E]ducational improvement cannot be produced without robust linkages between targeted research endeavours, public policy writing, consultation and feedback loops between academics and policy makers, and, importantly learners and teachers, curriculum writers, and school and education officials. It is important to note here that what is implemented, and therefore what is 'experienced' by learners is in effect a kind of public policy and language planning if we understand language policy and planning as a continuum of actions.

In other words, the deliberation of language policy planning must take seriously into account what actually comes up and is experienced in the teaching and learning practice. While the pedagogical practices and the inspiration we can get so far probably cannot be directly translated into a system-wide teaching model or CSL education policy, they can offer an important knowledge base for such purposes. Though the government does not at present have an immediate tendency to modify its EM language education policy, the time for that will eventually come. Because, the gap, contradiction, and grievances reported in the previous sections are not imagination, they will come back as problems, and society or some powerful groups may take them up and want to attend to the issues again, and such cumulated knowledge on the "continuum of actions" concerned will be able to provide great assistance. For this reason, we feel what the teachers and researchers have written in the following chapters in the book is highly valuable, and it is indeed an honour for us to have the opportunity of writing this introductory chapter.

In addition, we also hope that our readers can feel and share the excitement of these teachers and researchers directly as they read the chapters. This is because, in the exploration of these teachers and researchers into CSL, they often have to go beyond their original remits, and try to get inspirations from studies on the fundamental nature of language and its acquisition, and pedagogical theories and practices developed in other second language teaching (as there has already been quite a long history of English as a second language teaching and learning), and the associated discussion about the socio-psychological aspect of learning, including intercultural sensitivity, identity and empowerment. Some even begin to study a bit about the students' own languages and develop some awareness about what the Chinese language might look like in their eyes.

All these are quite novel and pioneering exercises for these Chinese teachers and researchers. It demands courage and open-mindedness. The teachers and researchers involved often experience difficulties, anxieties, and emotions. Yet there are also moments of revelation and joy for them. Sometimes, the experiences with these non-native learners can also inspire them to see some old problems they have come across in teaching native Chinese students. As Sect. 4.3 shows, the process can lead to both intellectual and spiritual growth for the teachers themselves. They can feel their new role, as educators working in a bigger context, serving the needs of increasing numbers of transnational people in this new era, similar to the second language teachers in many other parts of the world. (Here, we feel 'transnationals' can be a much better label than "ethnic minorities", because these groups of people are in fact special in the sense that they have their simultaneous connections to other nations in the world in addition to the connection to the local nation. This is a matter of fact, and whether it is a good or bad thing to the local nation would very much depends on our imagination and actions.)

References

Bennett, M. J. (1993). Towards a developmental model of interculturla sensitivity. In R. M. Paige (Ed.), *Education for the interculturla experience* (pp. 21–71). Intercultural Press.
Berry, J. (1997). Immigration, acculturation, and adaptation. *Applied Psychology: An International Review, 46*(1), 5–68.
Berry, J. (2011). Integration and multiculturalism: Ways towards social solidarity. *Papers on Social Representations, 20*, 2.1–2.21. Retrieved from http://www.psych.lse.ac.uk/psr/
Berry, J., Phinney, J., Sam, D., & Vedder, P. (2006). Immigrant youth: Acculturation, identity, and adaptation. *Applied Psychology: An International Review, 55*(3), 303–332.
Bourdieu, P. (1991). *Language and symbolic power*. Cambridge University Press.
CDC, & HKEAA [Curriculum Development Council and the Hong Kong Examinations and Assessment Authority]. (2007a). *English language curriculum and assessment guide (Secondary 4–6)*. Retrieved from http://www.hkeaa.edu.hk/DocLibrary/SBA/HKDSE/Eng_DVD/doc/HKEAA_eng_lang_final.pdf
CDC & HKEAA [Curriculum Development Council and the Hong Kong Examinations and Assessment Authority]. (2007b). *Chinese Language Curriculum and Assessment Guide (Secondary 4–6)*. Retrieved from https://www.edb.gov.hk/attachment/tc/curriculum-development/kla/chi-edu/chi_lang_final.pdf
Census and Statistics Department. (2018). *Poverty situation report on ethnic minorities 2016*. Hong Kong Government Printer.
Census and Statistics Department. (2021). *Thematic report: Ethnic minorities*. Hong Kong Websites of the Census and Statistics Department.
Chou, W. Y. (2016). *Chinese language learning and identity of ethnic minority students in Hong Kong : Multiple case study of Pakistani and Filipino elementary students* [中文學習與身份認同：香港巴裔及菲裔小學生多個案研究]. Unpublished PhD thesis in Chinese, The University of Hong Kong, Hong Kong.
Cummins, J. (2007). Rethinking monolingual instructional strategies in multilingual classrooms. *Canadian Journal of Applied Linguistics, 10*(2), 221–240.
Cummins, J., & Early, M. (2011). *Identity text: The collaborative creation of power in multilingual schools*. Trentham Books.
Curriculum Development Council. (2008). *Supplementary guide to the Chinese language curriculum for Non-Chinese speaking students*. Retrieved from https://www.edb.gov.hk/tc/curriculum-development/kla/chi-edu/ncs-curriculum-documents.html

Deci, E. L., & Ryan, R. M. (1985). *Intrinsic motivation and self-determination in human behavior.* Plenum Press.

Dornyei, Z., & Al-Hoorie, A. (2017). The motivational foundation of learning languages other than global English: Theoretical issues and research directions. *The Modern Language Journal, 101*, 455–468.

Dornyei, Z., & Ryan, S. (2015). *The psychology of the language learner revisited.* Routledge.

Education Bureau. (2014). *Second language learning framework of Chinese language curriculum* [中國語文課程第二語言學習架構專頁]. Retrieved from https://www.edb.gov.hk/tc/curriculum-development/kla/chi-edu/second-lang.html

Education Commission. (1996). *Education commission report 6. Enhancing language proficiency: A comprehensive strategy.* Hong Kong Government Printer. Retrieved from https://www.edb.gov.hk/attachment/en/about-edb/publications-stat/major-reports/ecr6_e_2.pdf

Education Department. (1997). *Medium of instruction—Guidance for secondary schools.* Hong Kong Government Printer.

Erni, J., & Leung, L. (2014). *Understanding South Asian minority in Hong Kong.* Hong Kong University Press.

Gao, F., & Lai, C. (2017). Biculturalism and segregated schooling in Hong Kong. *Journal of Multilingual and Multicultural Development, 39*(4), 301–312. https://doi.org/10.1080/01434632.1383995

García, E. (2000). *Student cultural diversity: Understanding and meeting the challenge* (3rd ed.). Houghton Mifflin.

Gu, M., & Patkin, J. (2013). Heritage and identity: Ethnic minority students from South Asia in Hong Kong. *Linguistics and Education, 24*, 131–141.

Gu, M., Kou, Z., & Guo, X. (2017a). Understanding Chinese language teachers' language ideologies in teaching South Asian students in Hong Kong. *International Journal of Bilingual Education and Bilingualism, 22*(8), 1030–1047. https://doi.org/10.1080/13670050.2017.1332000

Gu, M., Mak, B., & Qu, X. (2017b). Ethnic minority students from South Asia in Hong Kong: Language ideologies and discursive identity construction. *Asia-Pacific Journal of Education, 37*(3), 360–374.

Hammer, M. R., & Bennett, M. J. (1998). *The intercultural development inventory (IDI) manual.* Intercultural Communication Institute.

Ho, K. K. E. (2013). *Teacher emotions: Autoethnography of a Hong Kong teacher who begins to teach ethnic minority students Chinese.* Unpublished doctoral thesis. The University of Hong Kong.

Hong Kong Examination and Assessment Authority. (2022). *2022 diploma of education analysis of results of candidates in each subject.* Retrieved from https://www.hkeaa.edu.hk/DocLibrary/HKDSE/Exam_Report/Examination_Statistics/dseexamstat22_5.pdf

Hue, M., & Kennedy, K. (2012). Creation of culturally responsive classrooms: Teachers' conceptualization of a new rationale for cultural responsiveness and management of diversity in Hong Kong secondary schools. *Intercultural Education, 32*(2), 119–132.

Hue, M., Leung, C., & Kennedy, K. (2015). Student perception of assessment practices: Toward 'no loser' classrooms for all students in the ethnic minority schools in Hong Kong. *Educational Assessment Evaluation and Accountability, 27*, 253–273.

Intercultural Communication Institute. (2006). Retrieved from http://www.intercultural.org

Irvine, J., & Gal, S. (2000). Language ideology and linguistic differentiation. In P. Kroskrity (Ed.), *Regimes of language: Ideologies, polities and identities* (pp. 35–84). School of American Research Press.

Kapai, P., & Singh, G. (2018). *HongKonger – 253 ethnic minority youth aspirations, challenges and identity.* The Zubin Mahtani Gidumal Foundation Limited.

Ki, W. W., Postiglione, G., et al. (2006). Unpublished petition letter to Legislative Council of Hong Kong.

Kroskrity, P. (2010). Language ideologies: Evolving perspectives. In J. Verschueren & J. Ostman (Eds.), *Handbook of pragmatics highlights: Society and language use* (pp. 192–211). John Benjamins.

Ladson-Billings, G. (1994). *The dreamkeepers*. Jossey-Bass Publishing.

Lau, K. C. (2015). *Learning Chinese in multilingual contexts: Cases of ethnic minority learners with high attainment in Chinese*. Unpublished PhD thesis, The University of Hong Kong.

Legislative Council Secretary. (2009). *Legislative Council document CB(3) CB(3) 158/09-10*. Retrieved from https://www.legco.gov.hk/yr09-10/chinese/counmtg/motion/m_papers/cm1118cb3-158-c.pdf

Li, D. (2017). *Multilingual Hong Kong: Languages, literacies and identities*. Springer.

Lo Bianco, J., & Aronin, L. (Eds.). (2020). *Dominant language constellations: A new perspective on multilingualism*. Springer.

Lo, Y. Y., & Lin, A. M. Y. (2015). Special issue: Designing multilingual and multimodal CLIL for EFL students. *International Journal of Bilingual Education and Bilingualism, 18*(3), 261–269.

Loh, E. K. Y., & Tam, L. C. W. (2017). The role of emotionality in teacher change: The case of Chinese language teachers in Hong Kong. *Teacher Development, 21*(3), 462–479.

Loh, E. K. Y., Chou, P. W. Y., Shum, M. S. K., & Ki, W. W. (Eds.). (2019). *The teaching and learning of Chinese language in a multilingual and multicultural context. [多語言、多文化環境下的中國語文教育:理論與實踐]*. Hong Kong University Press.

Marton, F., & Booth, S. (1997). *Learning and awareness*. Erlbaum Associates.

Marton, F., Tse, S. K., & Cheung, W. M. (Eds.). (2010). *On the learning of Chinese*. Sense Publication.

Norton, B. (2006). Identity: Second language. In K. Brown (Ed.), *Encyclopedia of language and linguistics* (2nd ed.). Elsevier.

Palmer, P. J. (1998). *The courage to teach: Exploring the inner landscape of a teacher's life*. Jossey-Bass Publishers.

Rose, D., & Martin, J. (2012). *Learning to write, reading to learn: Genre, knowledge and pedagogy in the Sydney School*. Equinoxe.

Sharma, A. (2012). *Low-income South Asian parents' concept of 'making it' in Hong Kong*. Unpublished Ph.D. thesis, The Univesity of Hong Kong.

Shum, M. S. K. (2019). The effect of using 'reading to learn pedagogy' to teach explanation genre to non-Chinese speaking students. In E. K. Y. Loh, P. W. Y. Chou, M. S. K. Shum, & W. W. Ki (Eds.), *Chinese language education in multilingual and multicultural environment*. Hong Kong University Press.

Shum, M., Gao, F., & Ki, W. (2016). School desegregation in Hong Kong: Non-Chinese linguistic minority students' challenges to learning Chinese in mainstream schools. *Asia-Pacific Journal of Education, 36*(4), 533–544.

Soto Pineda, C. (2016). *Empowering low-income ethnic minority students in Hong Kong through critical pedagogy: Limits and possibilities in theory and practice*. Unpublished Ph.D. thesis, The University of Hong Kong.

South China Morning Post. (2018). *UN committee tells Hong Kong to show proof that education policy is helping ethnic minority children integrate into society*. News report on Aug 13, 2018. Retrieved from https://www.scmp.com/news/hong-kong/education/article/2159545/un-committee-tells-hong-kong-show-proof-education-policy

Tse, S. K., Marton, F., Ki, W. W., & Loh, E. K. Y. (2007). An integrative perceptual approach for teaching Chinese characters. *Instructional Science, 35*, 375–406.

Tse, S. K., Ki, W. W., & Shum, M. S. K. (2012). *Learning and teaching of Chinese for non-Chinese language speaking students: Curriculum, materials, pedagogy and assessment [非華語學生的中文學與教: 課程、教材、教法與評估]*. The Hong Kong University Press.

Tse, S. K., Ki, W. W., & Shum, M. S. K. (2021). *Controversies in medium of instruction reform: The experience of Hong Kong*. Springer.

Tsung, T. H., Shum, M. S. K., Ki, W. W., & Zhang, K. (2012). *Studies of teaching Chinese as a second language to ethnic minority students in HK: Theories, challenges, and practices. [香港少數族裔學生學習中文的研究: 理念,挑戰與實踐]*. The Hong Kong University Press.

Westrick, J., & Yuen, C. (2007). The intercultural sensitivity of secondary teachers in Hong Kong: A comparative study with implications for professional development. *Intercultural Education, 18*(2), 129–145.

Wong, W. F., & Yip, H. L. (2014). *Unleavened bread: Exploration of Chinese as second language teaching and learning. [無酵餅:中文為第二語言教與學初探]*. Hong Kong Unison.

Part II
The Language Trajectory: Literacy Development—Character Learning and Reading Comprehension

Cognitive Processing Based Curriculum for the Facilitation of Chinese as a Second Language Young Learners' Chinese Character Learning

Elizabeth Ka Yee Loh, Tikky Sing Pui Chan, Renee Wei Yan Fung, and Stephanie Mei Lok Fung

Abstract Our three-year longitudinal study investigating the developmental orthographic awareness of Chinese characters among K1 to K3 CSL kindergarteners revealed that single character reading is a significant longitudinal predictor of their radical awareness development. It also laid a foundation for the learning of Chinese character meanings. Based on such the findings, a cognitive processing based curriculum aims at strengthening their orthographic awareness has been designed to facilitate their Chinese character learning has been developed. This chapter introduces the rationale of the curriculum design, learning objectives, teaching materials, as well as various pedagogies and learning activities and how they help to facilitate the development of CSL kindergarteners' orthographic awareness.

1 Introduction

Learning to read and write Chinese as a second language (CSL) has always been known to be extremely challenging due to the language's numerous characters and the complexity of its orthographic system, not to mention the lack of consistency in grapheme-phoneme congruence. In conventional classrooms, students are often encouraged to learn Chinese characters by rote learning (Loh et al., 2018; Xu & Padilla, 2013). This imposes a tremendous memory burden to novice CSL learners who struggle to achieve competence in Chinese literacy, as patterns formed by strokes are overwhelmingly intricate to learners, especially when the rules of how these characters are formed are not understandable. In recent decades, a body of

---

E. K. Y. Loh · R. W. Y. Fung · S. M. L. Fung
The University of Hong Kong, Pok Fu Lam, Hong Kong
e-mail: ekyloh@hku.hk; reneeyan@hku.hk; mlsfung@connect.hku.hk

T. S. P. Chan (✉)
The Education University of Hong Kong, Tai Po, Hong Kong
e-mail: spto@eduhk.hk

© The Author(s), under exclusive license to Springer Nature Switzerland AG 2024
J. Lo Bianco et al. (eds.), *Supporting the Learning of Chinese as a Second Language: Implications for Language Education Policy*, Language Policy 36,
https://doi.org/10.1007/978-3-031-66135-8_3

literature has looked into the promotion of orthographic knowledge to facilitate Chinese character acquisition in CSL students (Leong et al., 2011; Loh et al., 2018, 2021; Tsai et al., 2021; Wong, 2019; Xu et al., 2014) and investigated the role of orthographic knowledge in the development of reading skills in Chinese (Chan et al., 2021; Ho et al., 2003a, b; Liao et al., 2022; Tong et al., 2017; Wong, 2020). Overall, findings suggest that orthographic awareness plays a fundamental role in learning to read Chinese characters.

Questions of orthography and approaches to how it is understood and studied encompass a wide spectrum of factors. In general, orthographic awareness in Chinese language can be defined as the ability to grasp the orthographic principles and restrictions underlying the formation of Chinese characters (Wong, 2020). However, due to the nature and complexity of Chinese orthography, researchers have explored orthographic awareness from different perspectives, examining the contributions of a variety of subskills to Chinese character reading. For example, Ho et al. (2003a, b) conducted a study on Chinese reading and spelling skills from kindergarten to primary, with three native Chinese speakers in Hong Kong. The authors proposed a six-stage developmental model of Chinese orthographic knowledge, in which competence in orthographic processing is further divided into subsets of skills, including character configuration knowledge, structural knowledge, radical information knowledge, positional knowledge and functional knowledge for both phonetic and semantic radicals. As such, orthographic knowledge is holistically viewed as an integration of various subskills.

Conversely, some researchers sought to isolate the impact of functional information on character learning and to instead examine orthographic awareness from a mere perceptual standpoint (Loh et al., 2018, 2021). From this point of view, orthographic knowledge is regarded as the awareness of three types of visual and spatial information contained in single characters, including component knowledge (knowledge about the constituent components of characters), structural knowledge (knowledge of the configuration of the characters), and position regularity (knowledge the of positional constraints of components). Nonetheless, visual-spatial ability, despite its significant role in Chinese character learning, might not be sufficient in explaining how emergent L2 learners process Chinese characters, specifically how the meaning of a novel Chinese character is memorised, retained, and retrieved. It is supported in recent literature that semantic radicals have a unique contribution to L2 character recognition (e.g., Chan et al., 2021; Wong, 2020). It is, therefore, critical to consider the effects of both the structural and semantic information of Chinese characters in gaining a comprehensive understanding of orthography processing, shedding light on possible instructional designs that are effective in minimising L2 learners' memory load.

There has been ample evidence illustrating the importance of orthographic awareness to Chinese reading; however, its relationship with character-meaning identification and the effectual approach to fostering orthographic awareness in young CSL learners remain unclear. Given that relatively limited research has been carried out in this area, the present three-year longitudinal study aims to examine the effectiveness of a cognitive processing-based curriculum for promoting Chinese orthographic awareness in young CSL learners, and to look into the development of orthographic and character identification skills in these beginning learners of CSL.

2 Literature Review

2.1 Challenges of Learning Chinese Orthography Among CSL Learners in Hong Kong

Learning to read Chinese poses significant challenges to CSL learners due to the visual complexity of its orthographic units (Shen, 2005). Unlike alphabetic orthographies, the basic unit of written Chinese is characters which are made up of recursive stroke chunks, known as components, placed in different configurations within a square space. Characters can be categorised as either single or compound. A single character can stand as a free morpheme alone, or as constituent components of a compound character. For instance, the single character 口 ('mouth') serves as a compositional part of compound characters such as 吃 ('eat'), 如 ('if'), 哭 ('cry'), and 苦 ('bitter'). Compound characters are, therefore, made up of more than one constituent component. The spatial arrangements of these components generally fall into three basic categories, namely left-right (e.g., 好 'good'), top-down (e.g., 花 'flower') and wrapped configurations (e.g. 國 'country') (Loh et al., 2018). More than 80% of characters are constructed by a semantic component (which indicates the meaning of the character) and a phonetic component (which provides pronunciation cues). These constituent components exhibit positional regularities, where semantic components are typically at the left side or top of characters, whereas phonetic cues are found at the right or bottom (Feldman & Siok, 1997; Shu et al., 2003). Taking the character 吃 (/hek3/; 'eat') as an example, the component 口 on the left suggests the semantic category of the character, i.e. related to the mouth, and the component 乞 (/hat1/; 'begging') cues the sound of the character. Most of the time, semantic information of components is used for character recognition than phonetic cues due to abundant homophones, while the grapheme-and-phonology correspondence is comparatively less transparent and regular (Tong & Yip, 2015).

Given such unique structural characteristics as discussed above, teaching CSL learners basic components and compositional principles may be instrumental in their acquisition of Chinese characters. Yet, traditional rote learning instructions such as point-and-read and repeated copying remain prevalent in most mainstream classrooms in Hong Kong (Lau et al., 2020). Considering the vast quantity of Chinese characters, learning them one by one holistically by rote memorisation is cognitively demanding and ineffective for non-native learners. It is not uncommon for students of CSL in Hong Kong, who were taught with conventional approaches, to struggle with the Chinese script, reporting difficulties in differentiating and memorising visually similar characters, as well as decoding unfamiliar characters (Zhang et al., 2011). Moreover, unlike their native Chinese counterparts who have constant and repeated print exposure, CSL learners tend to have inadequate home and formal Chinese literacy experiences to support their orthographic learning through implicit observation (Loh et al., 2018). The linguistic challenges, together with inefficient instructional practices and support, accentuate the need to develop a Chinese curriculum that addresses the learning hurdles specific to CSL students.

2.2 Orthographic Awareness and Chinese Character Learning

Studies concerning early Chinese reading acquisition have shown that both L1 and L2 children learn Chinese characters through an analytical understanding of the orthographic conventions of the writing system, instead of mere rote visual memory (e.g. Anderson et al., 2013; Loh et al., 2018; Pak et al., 2005; Shen & Ke, 2007). Such awareness is reflected in multiple dimensions, such as the knowledge of one-to-one mapping between a syllable and its corresponding character, the ability to identify and separate components in a character, the sensitivity to the spatial configuration of a character, and the knowledge of functional and positional constraints of constituent components. Existing literature has explored the role of awareness in various orthographic aspects of Chinese character learning, among which radical awareness and structural knowledge were identified to be crucial in successful character recognition and meaning inference of novel characters (e.g. Loh et al., 2018; Lü et al., 2015; Shen & Ke, 2007; Tong et al., 2017). It is observed that adult beginning learners were able to apply orthographic knowledge contained in constituent components to infer meaning and pronunciation of unfamiliar characters shortly after learning the language (Jackson et al., 2003). L2 children demonstrated a similar developing trend where they were able to recognise and capitalise on the orthographic aspects of characters as they learn more characters throughout their school years (Chan et al., 2021; Loh et al., 2018). In a recent study, Chan and her colleagues (2021) further extended the body of research by investigating the connection between radical awareness and character semantic representation. Their results revealed that the effect of component knowledge on character meaning identification was mediated by radical knowledge. While orthographic awareness was not observed among children at K1, K2 students who had learnt some basic single characters in the previous school year were able to analyse the internal structure of characters and analogise new characters, indicating that radical awareness is built upon the knowledge of single component characters. On the other hand, structural knowledge, the ability to recognise different layouts for component placement within characters, is crucial for character recognition in terms of the discrimination between visually similar characters (Yeh & Li, 2002). Another study (Loh et al., 2018) further posited that structural knowledge has a more significant contribution than single component knowledge to the development of awareness in radicals' positional regularities.

The prominent role of orthographic awareness in Chinese character learning implies the desirability of an orthographic-focused Chinese instruction, specifically in enhancing knowledge on characters' structural features (i.e. the legal position and composition of components) and their linguistic properties (i.e. the semantic role of components). An orthographic-focused Chinese instruction can expedite the development of Chinese reading proficiency among CSL learners.

2.3 Effective Instructional Methods on Chinese Character Learning

There has been a growing interest among researchers in identifying pedagogical practices related to orthographic awareness that are effective in maximising character learning. Their findings confirmed the notion that explicit instruction with an orthographic focus is useful in cultivating orthographic sensitivity of CSL learners, and benefits their acquisition of Chinese characters (Tse et al., 2007; Wong, 2020). It has also been put forward that CSL students' orthography learning could be supported via the utilisation of cognitive aids for optimal perception and retention of target characters (Shen, 2013).

2.3.1 Integrative Perceptual Approach

The Integrative Perceptual Approach (IPA; Tse et al., 2007) is a systematic approach to Chinese literacy instruction, aimed at developing learners' orthographic awareness through explicit introduction of components and structures of characters within authentic and meaningful learning contexts. The IPA, underpinned by the phenomenographic theory of learning (Marton & Booth, 1997), places great emphasis on the guided discernment of critical orthographic features, progressing from perceiving characters in their whole forms to discerning parts (strokes, structures, and components) in relation to wholes (characters). Through multimodal texts, nursery rhymes, and games, young CSL learners are given ample opportunities to experience and analyse characters' internal structures by comparing them in clusters and semantic networks, and at the same time are encouraged to pay attention to the constituent components, pronunciation and meaning of characters as well.

Contrary to traditional teaching methods, IPA enhances character learning efficiency by building on children's learning interests and prior spoken vocabulary knowledge (Loh et al., 2015). As the meaning and pronunciation of these everyday words have already been previously acquired, children could easily grasp the correspondence between all three dimensions of characters, i.e. sound, meaning, and form through training in analytical processing of the orthography form.

Successful IPA interventions in both local preschools and primary schools have proven its facilitative effect on orthographic awareness and learning interest among young non-native students, evidencing its auxiliary role in the CSL curriculum (Lau et al., 2020; Lee et al., 2011; Loh et al., 2023; Tse et al., 2007). In addition, preschoolers who received IPA instruction demonstrated the ability to apply the learned component knowledge to infer meaning of unfamiliar characters. Strong evidence highlighted the role of character analytical skills as a powerful self-learning tool that enables learning beyond the classroom.

2.3.2 Orthographic Knowledge-Based Mnemonics

From a cognitive perspective, the challenges of character learning and memorisation among CSL learners can be overcome with the help of mnemonics. Mnemonics strategies direct learners' attention and organise what they need to learn by associating learning targets with their prior knowledge, through the use of visual and/or acoustic cues. According to the levels-of-processing theory (Craik & Lockhart, 1972), in which a deeper processing level enhances memory strength, mnemonics involves deep memory coding of challenging learning material. Since learners are encouraged to actively construct their own individual meaning, this in return maximises information retention and retrieval. Mnemonics also reinforces character learning through encoding orthographic information in both verbal and non-verbal stimuli, i.e., images, sound, tactile objects and body movements. It has been claimed that greater learning and retention outcomes could be expected when information is encoded in more than one modality (Dual coding theory; Clark & Paivio, 1991).

Numerous studies on learning Chinese characters with mnemonics have produced positive results, in which improved recall of novel Chinese characters was observed among CSL learners who were introduced to retrieval aids with a focus on semantic attributes of characters (e.g., Kuo & Hooper, 2004; Shen, 2004; Xu & Padilla, 2013). These findings are compatible with prior research on learners' perception, where L2 learners reported relative ease in learning component meanings in comparison to their pronunciation and writing (Shen, 2010). Taking advantage of the logographic nature of the Chinese script, mnemonic strategies for learning Chinese characters mainly involve establishing and cementing connection between character form and meaning, with the use of chunking, imagery, elaboration, and/or motor engagement as memory cues. Chunking as a Chinese learning strategy refers to the organisation of target characters in smaller, meaningful groups to increase memory capacity and achieve effective and efficient retrieval of character information. For example, in an intervention study conducted by Xu and Padilla (2013), word recognition scores of CSL learners who learned characters in radical-based groupings were substantially higher than those in random distributions. This suggests that target characters that are chunked into meaningful groups according to their shared radical boosted character learning and retention among beginning learners. Similar effects of such a character-centred approach were also observed in a study by Xu et al. (2014).

Researchers have also put forward instructional practices that incorporate visual inputs and elaborations to encode new characters. A popular encoding procedure is to present basic single characters, which are primarily pictograms and components of modern characters, alongside with their corresponding pictorial origin. Children can then draw on the perceptual similarity between the graphic representation and the character shape to retain character meaning (Tse et al., 2007). Chang et al. (2019) proposed an imagery-based mnemonic that utilises illustrations specifically designed to resemble target character forms and their meanings, and concluded that mnemonics that strengthen form-meaning representations lead to greater recognition of complex characters and character reproduction, regardless of their complexity. Shen (2004) compared three instructional approaches that engage learners in shallow (i.e. rote memorisation) or deeper processing levels (i.e. creating their own stories to memorise characters or learning character etymology and radical analysis). Results showed that both self-generated and teacher-provided mnemonics groups significantly outperformed the rote memorisation group in character meaning retention. A study in the computer-based learning context generated similar results as well (Kuo & Hooper, 2004).

An alternative learning strategy for Chinese characters is motor engagement, where learners actively use body movements or gestures to encode and consolidate visual and semantic information of Chinese characters. Xu and Ke (2020) reported that students who mimic the shape of target Chinese characters with their bodies demonstrated better understanding of character meaning than those not gesturing. It has been suggested that body movements or gestures, a powerful source of non-verbal modality, contribute to character meaning retention by creating visual-motor mental representations of characters. Mental representations encoded in joint modalities lead to deeper processing and faster recognition of the learning materials.

In sum, it is evident that young CSL children can benefit from explicit instructions regarding the internal structure of characters, and that IPA interventions are effective in bringing about CSL children's orthographic awareness and Chinese character learning. Besides, mnemonics can be introduced in CSL classrooms to reduce memory load and strengthen orthographic representations among beginning learners.

2.4 The Present Study

Orthographic awareness plays a crucial role in the development of the ability to read and write Chinese. This is specifically true for emergent learners who struggle to learn CSL. Thus, the explicit teaching of orthographic knowledge is needed. While a few studies have explored the developmental trends of Chinese in young CSL learners, or reported on intervention programmes for assisting ethnic minority children in Hong Kong to learn Chinese (Chan et al., 2021; Tse et al., 2021), few have investigated the effectiveness of interventions using a cognitive processing-based curriculum incorporating IPA and mnemonics to help emergent learners obtain skills for Chinese character reading at kindergarten level. Given the vast challenges faced by CSL young learners in building up literacy, the present study aims to investigate the effectiveness of a cognitive processing-based curriculum using IPA and mnemonic techniques in facilitating CSL preschoolers' Chinese learning. Specifically, we want to look at how the curriculum can help young children promote their orthographic knowledge to facilitate character identification. Two research questions are addressed in this study.

1. Does the cognitive processing-based curriculum help promote orthographic awareness in CSL students?
2. How do subtypes of orthographic awareness contribute to character meaning identification?

3 Methodology

3.1 Participants

Participants were 168 children (84 girls and 84 boys) from six local kindergartens in Hong Kong, including 67 K2 ($M_{age} = 50.16$ months; $SD = 0.52$), and 101 K3 ($M_{age} = 60.60$ months; $SD = 0.26$) students. Out of the six kindergartens, four used Cantonese as the medium of instruction while two utilised both English and Chinese due to their high concentration of ethnic minority students. All participating kindergarteners were non-native Chinese speakers of different ethnic backgrounds, including 43.5% Nepalese, 25% Pakistani, 18.5% Filipino, 13% others (e.g. Indian, Indonesian, and British).

3.2 Intervention Programme

The intervention programme for K2 and K3 students consisted of 70 thirty-minute sessions over the span of approximately 37 weeks. These sessions were divided equally under seven learning themes, all of which were ones contained in the local school-based curricula and highly relevant to the children's everyday lives. Since components are the basic constituent units of Chinese characters that carry meaning, 13 components (i.e., 口 'mouth', 手 'hand', 女 'female', 水 'water', 艸(艹) 'grass', 火 'fire', 足 'foot', 人 'man', 木 'tree', 糸 'silk', 土 'earth', 心 'heart', 言 'speech') were first selected based on their high frequency and low visual complexity. For each learning theme, eight bi-syllabic words with characters containing these components were then chosen with consideration of their relevance to the learning materials. The character configurations of the selected vocabulary items were left-right (e.g., 妹妹 'sister', 媽媽 'mother'), top-down (e.g., 花朵 'flower') and wrapped (e.g., 圖in圖書 'picture book'). Throughout each of the learning themes, the teachers, who had received training in using IPA and mnemonics techniques, would first present selected vocabulary items—usually bi-syllabic words containing characters that share the same component—through the use of multimodal texts such as storybooks and nursery rhymes. After that, the teacher would draw the students' attention to the orthographic features of the characters using IPA and mnemonic approaches.

For example, in one of the typical learning sessions, the teacher first introduced a nursery rhyme (specifically composed for learning characters containing the target component) for the CSL students to familiarise themselves with the pronunciation and meaning of words in a comprehensible context. The teacher then presented the printed form of the nursery rhyme to help the students map the sound and meaning with their corresponding print. After that, the teacher asked the students to search for characters containing the target component in the text, leading them to discern the similarities and differences among the characters. By doing so, the teacher guided the students to actively engage in processing orthographic information contained in the characters, strengthening the association on the component, radical, and character level. The teacher also invited the students to identify characters containing the same component in their surroundings, building up connections with their daily lives.

To help the children memorise the written forms of the characters, the teacher asked the children to use mnemonic strategies to memorise the character. For example, when teaching the component 女 /neoi5/ 'female', the teacher told the students that the original character comes from shape of a woman crossing her legs. Then, he or she illustrated how the character 妹 /mui6/ 'younger sister' looked like a girl wearing a dress by drawing the outline of a dress on the character. At the same time, the teacher used gestures to reinforce the shape of the character or component to help the students memorise the form. The teacher presented another character with the same component, for example, 姐 /ze2/ 'elder sister', and asked the children to brainstorm what the character 姐 /ze2/ might resemble. Afterwards, he or she invited students to improvise a picture and/or a gesture to represent the character.

3.3 Measures

A pre-test and post-test were administered at the participating schools to assess ethnic minority children's orthographic awareness at the beginning and end of the academic year. Given the multifaceted nature of orthographic awareness, the instrument used in this study comprised of four orthographic-related measures, namely a character configuration task, radical position task, radical awareness task, and character-meaning matching task. The entire assessment took around 20 minutes.

3.3.1 Character Configuration Task

The character configuration task examined students' sensitivity to the visual and spatial arrangement of characters, i.e. the orthographic awareness that each character is positioned within an imaginary square frame. For each item, students were presented with four different configurations of the same character. The target configuration was centrally positioned, with three distractors that were (1) elongated and located on the left or right half of the square frame, (2) compacted and situated on the top or bottom half of the frame, and (3) reduced in size and fitted into one quarter of the frame. They were then asked to select the configuration that conforms to proper spatial placement. The task consisted of a total of 10 items, and one point was given for each correct response. The Cronbach's alpha reliability coefficient for this task was .92, which shows a high internal consistency of the items in the scale.

3.3.2 Radical Position Task

Adapted from Ho et al. (2003a, b), this task measured students' knowledge of the legal position of components. Ten compound characters (7 left-right and 3 top-down structures) from upper grade level were selected as targets to ensure all items were novel to the students. For each item, the target was presented alongside three other options with identical components that violate the canonical position. Students were asked to choose the one that best resembled a Chinese character. One point was awarded for each correct answer. The maximum score for this task was 10. The Cronbach's alpha reliability coefficient was .45, which shows an acceptable internal consistency of the items in the scale.

3.3.3 Radical Awareness Task

With reference to similar radical analysis tests for L2 beginning learners (e.g., Chen, 2019; Wong, 2020), the radical awareness task was designed to test students' knowledge of the linguistic functions of constituent components. Fifteen characters with high-frequency radicals were chosen from kindergarten textbooks as targets. In this task, students were asked to identify the character that corresponds to the picture. The three alternatives provided included one with the same semantic component as the target, one that shared the same phonetic radical, and lastly an unrelated character. For instance, 跑 ('run'; semantic radical distractor), 洛 ('River Luo'; phonetic radical distractor;), 利 ('advantage'; irrelevant character) were presented alongside the target character 路 ('road'). The maximum score for this task was 15 and one point would be given for a correct response. The Cronbach's alpha reliability coefficient was .67, which shows an acceptable internal consistency of the items in the scale.

3.3.4 Character-Meaning Mapping Task

The ultimate goal of enhancing students' orthographic awareness was to facilitate children's ability to map form and meaning. Thus, a character-meaning mapping task was used to measure how well students can associate the meaning of the character with its orthographic information. This task required students to choose one out of the four pictures that represent the meaning of the character. Fifteen characters were obtained from teaching materials for kindergarteners, by two experienced teachers and researchers. Previous studies have successfully carried out similar tests for assessing form-meaning correspondence among young L1 and L2 children (Chan et al., 2020; Ho et al., 2003a, b). One score was given to each correct answer and the maximum score for this task was 15. The Cronbach's alpha reliability coefficient was .63 which shows an acceptable internal consistency of the items in the scale.

3.4 Data Analyses

The mean scores of the tasks and the percentage changes between the pre-test and post-test scores were computed. Cohen's d effect size (Cohen, 1992) was also calculated to examine the effectiveness of the IPA intervention in enhancing orthographic knowledge associated with Chinese reading at a character level. A hierarchical regression analysis was further performed to explore the unique contribution of various orthographic knowledge (i.e., character configuration, radical position, and radical awareness) to character meaning identification.

4 Results

4.1 Descriptive Statistics

To address the first research question, i.e. the effectiveness of the current intervention in promoting orthographic awareness, the mean scores, standard deviations and percentage changes of all measures have been calculated and are presented in Table 1. Significant improvement in all tasks was observed among CSL students who received IPA trainings, indicating their increased orthographic awareness in different aspects. The average percentage increase in post-tests ranged from 76.92% to 116.23% for K2 and 10.60% to 47.57% for K3 students. The percentage increase in the K2 group were observed in the character configuration task and radical awareness task, with 116.23% and 102.22% respectively. Meanwhile, in the K3 group, most improvement was observed in the radical awareness task and character-meaning mapping task.

To further test the efficacy of the intervention, the Cohen's d effect sizes of students' performances across tasks were calculated. The effect size ranged from 0.41 to 2.05. The IPA intervention was remarkably effective in enhancing K2 students' orthographic awareness, indicated by the large impact ($d > 0.80$) on all task scores. Corroborating with the percentage increase, the highest effect size was found in the character configuration task ($d = 2.05$), suggesting that the intervention is highly effective in promoting students' sensitivity towards the visual and spatial

Table 1 Mean scores, percentage changes, and effect sizes of all measures by grades

Measures	K2 Pre-test Mean	SD	n	K2 Post-test Mean	SD	n	Percentage change	d	K3 Pre-test Mean	SD	n	K3 Post-test Mean	SD	n	Percentage change	d
CCT	4.19	2.67	67	9.06	2.04	66	116.23%	2.05	8.49	2.52	100	9.39	1.86	97	10.60%	0.41
RPT	2.42	1.35	67	4.36	2.11	66	80.17%	1.10	3.91	1.91	100	5.03	2.14	97	28.64%	0.55
RAT	3.61	1.64	67	7.29	3.35	66	102.22%	1.39	5.55	2.60	101	8.19	3.27	97	47.57%	0.89
CMMT	3.90	1.53	67	6.89	2.87	66	76.92%	1.30	5.78	2.63	101	8.29	3.43	97	43.43%	0.82

Note. CCT Character Configuration Task, *RPT* Radical Position Task, *RAT* Radical Awareness Task, *CMMT* Character- Meaning Matching Task

aspects of Chinese characters. Specifically, students have become more aware of the dimensions and rules underlying the arrangements of Chinese characters in an imaginary square. Large effects were also observed in the radical position task, radical awareness task and character meaning task, with effect sizes of 1.10, 1.39 and 1.30 respectively. While the effects of the intervention varied among tasks in K3, the effect size value on radical awareness ($d = 0.89$) and character-meaning matching ($d = 0.82$) remained large among K3 students, while the effects on radical position ($d = 0.55$) and character configuration ($d = 0.41$) knowledge were moderate and small respectively.

4.2 Correlation Analysis

The second research question we wanted to examine was how orthographic awareness contributes to character meaning identification. To address this question, correlations among the four tasks were analysed and are indicated in Table 2. As shown in the table, the character-meaning matching task was significantly and positively correlated with all measures in both K2 and K3, with correlation strength ranging from weak to strong ($r = .29$ to .79). Specifically, the association between character-meaning matching and radical awareness was the strongest with the correlation coefficients at .79 in K2 and .68 in K3. All three measures of orthographic awareness had significant associations with each other, indicating moderate associations ($r = .33$ to .41) in both grades.

4.3 Regression Analysis

A stepwise hierarchical regression analysis was further performed to test the associations of various types of orthographic knowledge with character-meaning identification set as the dependent variable. Character configuration was entered in step 2 after statistically controlling students' grade level in step 1. Radical position was added to the equation in step 3 and radical awareness in step 4. As discussed in previous developmental studies on children's orthographic awareness (e.g. Ho et al., 2003a, b), radical awareness was considered to be an advanced orthographic skill

Table 2 Correlations among All Measures in Grade K2 (upper right) and K3 (lower left)

Measures	1	2	3	4
1 Character configuration task	–	.41**	.39**	.29*
2 Radical position task	.36**	–	.44*	.32**
3 Radical awareness task	.33**	.49**	–	.79***
4 Character-meaning matching task	.29**	.30**	.68**	–

*$p < .05$. **$p < .01$. ***$p < .001$

Table 3 Hierarchical regression analysis predicting character meaning identification

Variables	R^2	R^2 change	F change	β	t
Step 1	.04	.04	7.38**		
Grade				.21	2.72**
Step 2	.12	.08	14.51***		
Grade				.19	2.50*
Character configuration				.28	3.81***
Step 3	.17	.04	8.19**		
Grade				.16	2.16*
Character configuration				.20	2.52*
Radical position				.23	2.86**
Step 4	.54	.37	126.06***		
Grade				.12	2.11*
Character configuration				.04	.73
Radical position				−.02	−.37
Radical awareness				.70	11.23***

*$p < .05$. **$p < .01$. ***$p < .001$

which usually emerged after the acquisition of character configuration knowledge and radical position knowledge.

As shown in Table 3, the variables together accounted for 54% of the variance in character meaning identification. In the first model, grade level (as the control variable) contributed 4% of the variance in character-meaning identification, $F_{change} = 7.38, p < .01$. Character configuration was then included in the second model and explained an additional 8% of the variance in character-meaning identification, $F_{change} = 14.51, p < .001$. In the third model, in addition to character configuration, radical position was added. While both significantly predicted character-meaning identification, these two variables that bring structural knowledge of characters together contributed 17% of the prediction, $F_{change} = 8.19, p < .01$. In the final model, all variables measuring different aspects and stages of orthographic awareness were included. Results revealed that character configuration and radical position were no longer significant predictors after radical awareness was entered into the equation. Instead, radical awareness strongly predicted character-meaning identification, contributing a unique 37% to the variance ($F_{change} = 126.06; p < .001$). This suggests that radical awareness may play a much stronger role in character-meaning identification.

5 Discussion

The present study investigated the effectiveness of our cognitive processing-based intervention programme for promoting orthographic awareness in young CSL learners studying in kindergartens in Hong Kong. While several studies have investigated pedagogical approaches for the teaching and learning of CSL to beginning learners in Hong Kong and worldwide, few have evaluated the effectiveness of incorporating the IPA and mnemonics to facilitate orthographic awareness in young learners of Chinese in Hong Kong. Thus, the present study aimed to bridge the research gap by assessing the effectiveness of the current cognitive-based approach, combining the use of IPA and mnemonics—two proven approaches to support literacy development in CSL students—to optimise orthographic awareness in young CSL learners. In particular, their effectiveness in enhancing several aspects regarding the structural and functional domains of orthographic awareness have been addressed, namely, character configuration, radical position awareness and radical awareness, which were said to play a fundamental role in the development of Chinese literacy.

5.1 Effectiveness of IPA and Mnemonic Approaches to Enhancing Orthographic Awareness/Structural Knowledge

In general, the participants showed improvement in all tasks, reflecting their gain in sensitivity towards the orthography of Chinese characters.

From our results, L2 students seemed to have benefited from learning activities adopting IPA and mnemonic approaches in character learning. During these cognitive-based activities, not only did the students learn to discern the features in characters sharing a common component or radical through songs and texts, but also participated in a variety of component games, from placing missing components in grids to rearranging components to form characters, during which students paid attention to the visual and spatial information as well as structural and positional constraints of the components, gaining structural knowledge of Chinese characters. Concurring with previous research on the effectiveness of IPA in promoting L2 young learners' word reading skills and character component skills (Lee et al., 2011), learners in the current study manifested increased awareness of Chinese character components and strengthened character recognition ability. As suggested by Xu et al. (2014), novice learners may lack the strategy to interpret componential information and thus encipher characters as a whole unit or arbitrary spatial patterns, hence finding it difficult to acquire Chinese orthography knowledge. Systematically presenting characters that possess a common radical or component might therefore help to consolidate the acquisition of component knowledge, because learners gain the opportunity to decompose characters into smaller units (chunks and components) and to consistently focus on the visual patterns, positional regularities, and functional (i.e. semantic) information of a given radical or component. Such activities allowing students to actively engage in processing orthographical information contained in the characters could help to reinforce componential and structural knowledge.

Our findings also revealed that the intervention had an overall larger effect on students in the K2 group than those in K3. Results indicated that large effects were observed in the radical awareness task and character-meaning matching task for the K3 group, whereas effects for the character configuration task and radical position task were relatively small and medium respectively. The inconsistency of effects can be explained by three main reasons. First, the starting points (as reflected in the pre-test scores) of the K2 students had been relatively low compared to K3 students, particularly in the character configuration task, where the mean scores of the K3 students were double that of K2 students and were very close to full marks at the pre-test. This may imply that K3 students had already acquired a certain degree of structural knowledge. Because of this, the percentage change of the scores in the pre-test and post-test of the task was only small, and the impact of the intervention on the K3 students in this task may be less apparent. It is also worth noting that while the K2 group made remarkable improvement with a large effect size in the radical position task, the effect size of the K3 group was only medium. This could be accounted for by the fact that positional regularity knowledge is considered to be sophisticated and more challenging compared to other types of orthographic knowledge (Loh et al., 2021), and that awareness of positional regularities emerges early but gradually strengthens in later years (Ho et al., 2003a, b; Tong et al., 2017). Before the skill is fully grasped, one might need to gain enough exposure to characters with the same configuration and internalise the visual, spatial and perhaps functional information of the components. As such, our results might indicate that our K3 learners need extraneous support to gain a more comprehensive understanding of positional constraints of different components.

5.2 Clustering of Characters Sharing the Same Component to Strengthen Association Between Meaning and Form

Aside from structural knowledge, the current intervention was found to be effectual in promoting radical awareness as well as character meaning in both the K2 group and K3 group, with Cohen's *d* effect sizes being large. A plausible explanation is that during the intervention, characters taught using the IPA were recurrently presented in clusters sharing the same semantic component. As discussed earlier, students participating in the learning activities were engaged in processing the orthographic information of characters, reinforcing structural and positional regularities. This supports results from previous literature regarding IPA's effectiveness in promoting L2 young learners' word reading skills and character component skills (Lee et al., 2011), where learners manifested increased awareness to Chinese character components and strengthened character recognition ability. Concurrently, repeated occurrence of characters consisting of the same semantic-bearing component may yield a grouping effect (Xu et al., 2014), strengthening the association between meaning and form, which in turn, contributes to the better organisation of characters in the memory based on their functional information.

The enhanced radical awareness and character-meaning identification in our students could be further attributed to the use of mnemonic aids, such as pictures and body movements. During the learning activities in the Chinese enrichment classes, images and gestures were used to strengthen the connection between meaning and form. As Tsai et al. (2021) suggested, the use of pictures to elaborate on how the form of a character corresponds to the meaning established a meaningful context and provided hints for memory retrieval. Alongside with body movements or gestures for memorising the characters, which are said to increase learners' attention and memory recall (Xu & Ke, 2020), these heightened the learning effect. The utilisation of body movements serves as an effective and complementary learning strategy for young children. Not only do movements make it easier to remember characters by tapping into multiple modalities, it actively engages young learners in game-like learning experiences, helping to sustain learning motivation.

5.3 Development of Orthographic Knowledge in Young CSL Learners

Findings of the current research align with previous studies and models of orthographic development in Chinese, namely that young children are capable of developing a certain degree of character configuration knowledge at an early stage (Ho et al., 2003a, b; Li et al., 2012), that they learn to utilise structural knowledge and are capable of detecting the ill-formedness of Chinese characters to a certain extent (Shu & Anderson, 1999; Tong et al., 2017). In addition, our findings extended to the body of research which was predominately carried out on L1 children, suggesting that structural knowledge could emerge as early as K2 in L2 children with sufficient and explicit instruction. Results from the present study strongly imply that the initial stage of L2 Chinese orthographic development follows a pattern of orthographic processing similar to that of L1, with character configuration knowledge emerging before other types of orthographic skills. However, as suggested in previous literature (Ho et al., 2003a, b), when the children progress to higher grades, they begin to rely more on other types of radical knowledge in character recognition. This is consistent with the study by Chan et al. (2020) on the development of orthographic awareness in young L2 children, in that character-meaning identification is mediated by radical awareness and that the role of sensitivity to semantic radical and character identification becomes more significant as the children's orthographic awareness becomes more developed.

5.4 Limitations and Implications

It should be noted that there are limitations to this study. First of all, due to the scope of the current study and the nature of the intervention, other factors which might influence students' character identification skills, such as phonetic information awareness, has not been investigated. There has been inconsistency regarding whether phonological cue of a character is acquired before semantic information in the course of orthographic knowledge development. For example, the model on the progression of orthographic knowledge by Ho et al. (2003a, b) suggested that children rely more on semantic radicals than phonetic radicals at the beginning stages of Chinese characters learning. However, findings in a study by Tong et al. (2017) revealed that phonetic hints rather than semantic ones were more depended upon when young learners of Chinese learned to read. Hence, it might be worthwhile to further investigate the development of phonetic knowledge and its role in orthographical awareness and word identification.

Factors influencing the development of the subskill of positional regularity knowledge and pedagogical strategies for promoting such competence should be further examined. While the exact role of positional regularity knowledge to Chinese character learning remains unclear, our findings suggested that beginning learners of Chinese might need more support in acquiring knowledge in positional restrictions of components. As acknowledged in previous research, positional regularity is believed to be a more advanced skill among various types of orthographic knowledge (Loh et al., 2021), and the progression of young CSL learners' knowledge in this aspect might take longer time than other areas of orthographic awareness (Ho et al., 2003a, b; Tong et al., 2017). Therefore, it may be interesting for future studies to substantiate research on the relationship between positional regularity knowledge, other types of orthographic knowledge and character reading. In addition, future intervention programmes for CSL learners could focus more on instructional support, such as the provision of more explicit instructions, increased exposure and analytical component games, for enhancing knowledge on positional rules so as to facilitate learners' development of a complete set of orthographic skills.

Consistent with previous studies (e.g., Chan et al., 2021), the findings of the study suggested a developmental pattern of orthographic processing as well as highlighted the significance of semantic radical awareness in the acquisition of Chinese characters. The result also provided evidence in support of a systematic orthographic-focused curriculum at a kindergarten level, in which semantic radical awareness can be cultivated and enhanced through effective instructional approaches. To aid literacy development in Chinese character reading among young CSL learners, educators may incorporate more character analytical games and mnemonic strategies in CSL classrooms.

6 Conclusion

The present study is among the very first to demonstrate that a cognitive processing-based curriculum incorporating IPA and mnemonic techniques for character learning is effective in enhancing young CSL learners' orthographic awareness pertinent to Chinese character learning. More specifically, our results suggest that the development of various orthographic skills in emergent learners of CSL follows patterns of orthographic processing similar to those in L1 students, contributing further evidence for the significance of radical awareness to Chinese character reading. Given the multidimensional nature of orthographic awareness in Chinese, it is hoped that the present research can provide directions for future research and intervention for CSL literacy development.

References

Anderson, R. C., Ku, Y. M., Li, W., Chen, X., Wu, X., & Shu, H. (2013). Learning to see the patterns in Chinese characters. *Scientific Studies of Reading, 17*(1), 41–56. https://doi.org/10.1080/10888438.2012.689789

Chan, S. W., Cheung, W. M., Huang, Y., Lam, W. I., & Lin, C. H. (2020). Development and validation of a Chinese character acquisition assessment for second-language kindergarteners. *Language Testing, 37*(2), 215–234. https://doi.org/10.1177/0265532219876527

Chan, T. S. P., Loh, E. K. Y., & Hung, C. O. Y. (2021). A longitudinal study of Chinese as a second language kindergarteners' orthographic awareness and its association with their lexical learning performance. *Current Psychology, 42*, 4543–4554. https://doi.org/10.1007/s12144-021-01797-2

Chang, L.-Y. W., Chen, J.-Y., Perfetti, C. A., & Chen, H.-C. (2019). The effect of key-image mnemonics to support character learning of Chinese-as-foreign-language learners. *Journal of Chinese language teaching, 16*(2), 31–74.

Chen, T. (2019). Joint contributions of multilevel linguistic knowledge to character meaning retention in L2 Chinese. *Journal of Psycholinguistic Research, 48*(1), 129–143. https://doi.org/10.1007/s10936-018-9594-3

Clark, J. M., & Paivio, A. (1991). Dual coding theory and education. *Educational Psychology Review, 3*(3), 149–210. https://doi.org/10.1007/BF01320076

Cohen, J. (1992). A power primer. *Psychological Bulletin, 112*(1), 155–159. https://doi.org/10.1037/0033-2909.112.1.155

Craik, F. I., & Lockhart, R. S. (1972). Levels of processing: A framework for memory research. *Journal of Verbal Learning and Verbal Behavior, 11*(6), 671–684.

Feldman, L. B., & Siok, W. W. (1997). The role of component function in visual recognition of Chinese characters. *Journal of Experimental Psychology: Learning, Memory, and Cognition, 23*(3), 776–781. https://doi.org/10.1037/0278-7393.23.3.776

Ho, C. S. H., Ng, T. T., & Ng, W. K. (2003a). A "radical" approach to reading development in Chinese: The role of semantic radicals and phonetic radicals. *Journal of Literacy Research, 35*(3), 849–878. https://doi.org/10.1207/s15548430jlr3503_3

Ho, C. S. H., Yau, P. W. Y., & Au, A. (2003b). Development of orthographic knowledge and its relationship with reading and spelling among Chinese kindergarten and primary school children. In C. McBride-Chang & H. C. Chen (Eds.), *Reading development in Chinese children* (pp. 51–71). Praeger.

Jackson, N., Everson, M., & Ke, C. (2003). Beginning readers' awareness of the orthographic structure of semantic–phonetic compounds: Lessons from a study of learners of Chinese as a foreign language. In C. McBride-Chang & H. C. Chen (Eds.), *Reading development in Chinese children* (pp. 142–153). Praeger.

Kuo, M.-L. A., & Hooper, S. (2004). The effects of visual and verbal coding mnemonics on learning Chinese characters in computer-based instruction. *Educational Technology Research and Development, 52*(3), 23–38. https://doi.org/10.1007/BF02504673

Lau, C., Wang, Y., Chan, S. W., Chen, E. E., McBride, C., Tse, S. K., Richards, B., & Rao, N. (2020). Promoting Chinese literacy in South Asian preschoolers and their mothers in Hong Kong: An intervention study. *Early Education and Development, 31*(4), 561–581. https://doi.org/10.1080/10409289.2019.1690341

Lee, M. T., Tse, S. K., & Loh, E. K. Y. (2011). The impact of the integrative perceptual approach on the teaching of Chinese characters in a Hong Kong kindergarten. *Early Child Development and Care, 181*(5), 665–679. https://doi.org/10.1080/03004431003768006

Leong, C. K., Tse, S. K., Loh, E. K. Y., & Ki, W. W. (2011). Orthographic knowledge is important in comprehending elementary Chinese text by users of alphasyllabaries. *Reading Psychology, 32*(3), 237–271. https://doi.org/10.1080/02702711.2010.495605

Li, H., Shu, H., McBride-Chang, C., Liu, H., & Peng, H. (2012). Chinese children's character recognition: Visuo-orthographic, phonological processing and morphological skills. *Journal of Research in Reading, 35*(3), 287–307. https://doi.org/10.1111/j.1467-9817.2010.01460.x

Liao, X., Loh, E. K. Y., & Cai, M. (2022). Lexical orthographic knowledge mediates the relationship between character reading and reading comprehension among learners with Chinese as a second language (CSL). *Frontiers in Psychology, 13*, Article 779905. https://doi.org/10.3389/fpsyg.2022.779905

Loh, E. K. Y., Mak, M. T. F., & Tam, L. C. W. (2015). The road to successful Chinese language learning: Effective strategies for teaching and learning Chinese characters. In I. Hill & M. S. K. Shum (Eds.), *Infusing IB philosophy and pedagogy in Chinese language teaching* (pp. 174–194). John Catt Educational.

Loh, E. K. Y., Liao, X., & Leung, S. O. (2018). Acquisition of orthographic knowledge: Developmental difference among learners with Chinese as a second language (CSL). *System, 74*, 206–216. https://doi.org/10.1016/j.system.2018.03.018

Loh, E. K. Y., Liao, X., Leung, S. O., & Tam, L. C. W. (2021). How do Chinese as a second language learners acquire orthographic knowledge: Component, structure and position regularity. *Language Awareness, 30*(3), 297–316. https://doi.org/10.1080/09658416.2021.1972115

Loh, E. K. Y., Chan, T. S. P., & Fung, W. Y. R. (2023). Dynamic enrichment learning mode: A new way to facilitate the learning of Chinese as a second language in the mainstream curriculum. In Y.-T. Sung, C.-M Si, & J.-F. Hong (Eds.), *Teaching Chinese language in the international school context*. Springer.

Lü, C., Koda, K., Zhang, D., & Zhang, Y. (2015). Effects of semantic radical properties on character meaning extraction and inference among learners of Chinese as a foreign language. *Writing Systems Research, 7*(2), 169–185. https://doi.org/10.1080/17586801.2014.955076

Marton, F., & Booth, S. (1997). *Learning and awareness*. Lawrence Erlbaum.

Pak, A. K. H., Cheng-lai, A., Tso, I. F., Shu, H., Li, W., & Anderson, R. C. (2005). Visual chunking skills of Hong Kong children. *Reading and Writing, 18*, 437–454. https://doi.org/10.1007/s11145-005-6575-3

Shen, H. H. (2004). Level of cognitive processing: Effects on character learning among non-native learners of Chinese as a foreign language. *Language and Education, 18*(2), 167–182. https://doi.org/10.1080/09500780408666873

Shen, H. H. (2005). An investigation of Chinese-character learning strategies among non-native speakers of Chinese. *System, 33*(1), 49–68. https://doi.org/10.1016/j.system.2004.11.001

Shen, H. H. (2010). Imagery and verbal coding approaches in Chinese vocabulary instruction. *Language Teaching Research, 14*(4), 485–499. https://doi.org/10.1177/1362168810375370

Shen, H. H. (2013). Chinese L2 literacy development: Cognitive characteristics, learning strategies, and pedagogical interventions. *Language and Linguistics Compass, 7*(7), 371–387. https://doi.org/10.1111/lnc3.12034

Shen, H. H., & Ke, C. (2007). Radical awareness and word acquisition among nonnative learners of Chinese. *The Modern Language Journal, 91*(1), 97–111. https://doi.org/10.1111/j.1540-4781.2007.00511.x

Shu, H., & Anderson, R. C. (1999). Learning to read Chinese: The development of metalingusitic awareness. In J. Wang, A. W. Inhoff, & H.-C. Chen (Eds.), *Reading Chinese script: A cognitive analysis* (pp. 1–18). Lawrence Erbaum Associates Publishers.

Shu, H., Chen, X., Anderson, R. C., Wu, N., & Xuan, Y. (2003). Properties of school Chinese: Implications for learning to read. *Child Development, 74*, 27–47. https://doi.org/10.1111/1467-8624.00519

Tong, X., & Yip, J. H. Y. (2015). Cracking the Chinese character: Radical sensitivity in learners of Chinese as a foreign language and its relationship to Chinese word reading. *Reading and Writing, 28*(2), 159–181. https://doi.org/10.1007/s11145-014-9519-y

Tong, X., Tong, X., & McBride, C. (2017). Radical sensitivity is the key to understanding Chinese character acquisition in children. *Reading and Writing, 30*(6), 1251–1265. https://doi.org/10.1007/s11145-017-9722-8

Tsai, M. H., Chang, L. Y., Chen, H. C., & Lin, C. L. (2021). Effects of key-image mnemonics on Chinese instruction for first-grade students' achievement and interest toward Chinese learning. *International Journal of Educational Research, 109*, Article 101856. https://doi.org/10.1016/j.ijer.2021.101856

Tse, S. K., Marton, F., Ki, W. W., & Loh, E. K. Y. (2007). An integrative perceptual approach for teaching Chinese characters. *Instructional Science, 35*(5), 375–406. https://doi.org/10.1007/s11251-006-9011-4

Tse, S. K., Leung, C. Y., Tsui, P. F., Chan, K. Y., & Kwok, M. C. (2021). A longitudinal investigation into the Chinese language development of non-Chinese speaking preschoolers in Hong Kong. *Journal of Language Teaching and Research, 12*(1), 183–193. https://doi.org/10.17507/jltr.1201.20

Wong, Y. K. (2019). Role of decoding competence in the Chinese reading comprehension development of ethnic minority students in Hong Kong. *International Journal of Bilingual Education and Bilingualism, 22*(8), 1016–1029. https://doi.org/10.1080/13670050.2017.1329273

Wong, Y. K. (2020). The relationship between orthographic awareness and Chinese reading in Hong Kong's young CSL learners. *ECNU Review of Education, 3*(4), 678–693. https://doi.org/10.1177/2096531120930485

Xu, X., & Ke, F. (2020). Embodied interaction: Learning Chinese characters through body movements. *Language Learning & Technology, 24*(3), 136–159. http://hdl.handle.net/10125/44744

Xu, X., & Padilla, A. M. (2013). Using meaningful interpretation and chunking to enhance memory: The case of Chinese character learning. *Foreign Language Annals, 46*(3), 402–422. https://doi.org/10.1111/flan.12039

Xu, Y., Chang, L. Y., & Perfetti, C. A. (2014). The effect of radical-based grouping in character learning in Chinese as a foreign language. *The Modern Language Journal, 98*(3), 773–793. https://doi.org/10.1111/j.1540-4781.2014.12122.x

Yeh, S. L., & Li, J. L. (2002). Role of structure and component in judgments of visual similarity of Chinese characters. *Journal of Experimental Psychology: Human, Perception and Performance, 28*(4), 933–947. https://doi.org/10.1037/0096-1523.28.4.933

Zhang, Q., Tsung, L., Cruickshank, K., Ki, W. W., & Shum, M. (2011). South Asian students' educational experience and attainment: Learning Chinese as a second/additional language in Hong Kong. In L. Tsung & K. Cruickshank (Eds.), *Teaching and learning Chinese in global contexts: Multimodality and literacy in the new media age* (pp. 63–80). Continuum.

Comparing the Effects of Inhibitory Control on Chinese Reading Comprehension Between Learners of Chinese as a First and Second Language

Nissom Zheng Liang Sun ⓘ, Elizabeth Ka Yee Loh ⓘ, and Xian Liao ⓘ

Abstract Chinese reading comprehension is vital for both native speakers and Chinese as a Second Language (CSL) learners, including ethnic minority (EM) students from China's Autonomous Regions. These students, such as Uighur, Kazakh, Mongolian, and Tibetan, often learn Chinese after acquiring their own language and may attend prestigious universities in major cities. Good reading comprehension is essential for their academic success. Executive function (EF), comprising inhibitory control, cognitive flexibility, and working memory, plays a significant role in reading comprehension. Inhibitory control positively impacts primary school students' second language reading performance. However, its effects on senior secondary school native Chinese and CSL students remain unclear. In the current study involving 107 CSL students and 142 native Chinese students, participants were assessed using Chinese literacy, inhibitory control, and non-verbal intelligence instruments. Surprisingly, no correlation was found between reading and inhibitory control in native students, while a negative relation was observed in CSL students. These findings may offer new insights into inhibitory control's role in reading comprehension for both Chinese and CSL adolescent learners.

1 Background

Ethnic minority (EM) students of Mainland China, a special subgroup of second language learners of Chinese (CSL) with alphabetic language backgrounds living in autonomous regions of China, face difficulties in reading comprehension (Ban,

N. Z. L. Sun
Kyoto University, Kyoto, Japan
e-mail: sun.zhengliang.82s@st.kyoto-u.ac.jp

E. K. Y. Loh (✉)
The University of Hong Kong, Pok Fu Lam, Hong Kong
e-mail: ekyloh@hku.hk

X. Liao
The Education University of Hong Kong, Ting Kok, Hong Kong

© The Author(s), under exclusive license to Springer Nature Switzerland AG 2024
J. Lo Bianco et al. (eds.), *Supporting the Learning of Chinese as a Second Language: Implications for Language Education Policy*, Language Policy 36,
https://doi.org/10.1007/978-3-031-66135-8_4

2009). These students need to gain good Chinese proficiency to immerse themselves in mainstream society and for better ethnic integration. Therefore, since 2000, the Chinese education system has offered a program called Ethnic Minority Class (Shaoshu Minzu Neidi Gao Zhong Ban), for middle school-aged EM students to attend schools in First-tier cities[1] located throughout eastern China. This project aims to enhance EM students' educational level, including Chinese proficiency, to a near-native level through curriculum reform. However, many secondary EM students still lag behind their Chinese classmates in Chinese reading comprehension (Liang, 2019; Liu, 2004; Yang, 2014).

For CSL learners, it is essential to understand the Chinese language writing system, as its visual form-to-meaning system plays a more important role than in the alphabetic language system. As a logographic language, Chinese presents a complex orthography (Handel, 2019). Unlike the alphabetic language system in which each grapheme corresponds to one phoneme, each Chinese character, as the basic writing unit, corresponds to a syllabic morpheme (Perfetti & Harris, 2013). Given the difference between the units of writing systems, the decoding process of alphabetic language and that of logographic language are different. For a logographic language such as Chinese, the decoding process is much more complex than for alphabetic language systems such as English (Qiu, 1996; Rath, 2001; Troia, 2004). It is because the Chinese language system has more homophones, synonyms, and characters with more than one meaning or pronunciation. These features of the Chinese language system make orthographic knowledge and morphological awareness more essential than phonologic awareness in the decoding process (Chan et al., 2021; Leong et al., 2018; Loh et al., 2017).

Recently, there has been some controversy over the role of inhibitory control (one of the core aspects of executive function) in the second language learners' reading comprehension process (i.e. Keijzer, 2013; Linck & Weiss, 2015). As cross-language transfer is influenced by multiple cognitive and linguistic factors, inhibitory control has been found to help learners suppress the interference with their first language when they are reading in their second language (Chung et al., 2019). Due to the distance between first and second languages, second language learners would not only adopt a new approach during the reading process, but also inhibit the interference of their first language experience. What is more, since there are many Chinese characters sharing similar orthographic structures or representing different meanings according to the context, Chinese learners may rely on their inhibitory control to suppress their existing knowledge during the character decoding process. Considering the importance of Chinese language proficiency for the academic advancement of CSL students, it is essential to explore if inhibitory control is a factor that influences their reading performance.

---

[1] First-tier cities refer to those highly-developed cities in Mainland China, such as Shanghai, Guangzhou, Beijing and Shenzhen.

2 Literature Review

2.1 Chinese Language System

While Perfetti and Harris (2013) indicated the universal feature of reading comprehension, the unique constituents of the language systems, particularly the orthographic and phonological attributes, may have a potential effect on the reading process. Using Chinese reading as an example, due to the unique character of its writing system, many researchers claimed that the reading process is different from other alphabetic languages (Chao, 1968; Li & Thompson, 1981). This is because of the features of Chinese characters. As the basic unit of the Chinese writing system, the Chinese character represents a single morpheme. Chinese characters are formed through the logical combination of smaller meaningful parts called components. It is the components that illustrate the meaning and pronunciation, which makes decoding Chinese characters a complex process.

One of the major characteristics of Chinese characters is the essential role of components as the meaningful unit to form characters. The Chinese character is constructed of three layers, including the whole character, component, and stroke (Taft & Zhu, 1997). The stroke is the smallest unit that may or may not represent the meaning and pronunciation. At the component level, Chinese characters can be constructed by one component, which is named a single-unit character, and two or more components which are named as compound characters (Chen et al., 1996). As compound characters account for approximately 80% of Chinese characters (Zhou, 1980), the perception of components is essential for decoding Chinese characters.

Another unique characteristic of Chinese characters is the complex anatomy of how components are put into a square-like form. The organization of components within a character follows two foundational disciplines: (1) the structural constraint which refers to the visual-spatial layout of components within a character (Law & Leung, 2000); (2) the positional regularity which refers to the specific position of components within a compound (Tong & McBride-Chang, 2016). Components within the compound characters could be divided into two categories, according to the function of the components: morphological components, which represent the meaning of the characters, and phonetic components, which represent the pronunciation of the characters.

Because of these unique features of the Chinese writing system, decoding Chinese characters requires more skills and knowledge, which makes reading Chinese characters one of the main intimidators for learners of Chinese as a second language (Everson, 1998; Yin, 2003). The complexity of the Chinese orthographic system directly impacts their learning of reading comprehension (Packard et al., 2006; Tong et al., 2009). To investigate their Chinese reading difficulties, it is necessary to explore potentially related skills, including orthographic knowledge and morphological awareness, and how these skills relate to Chinese reading comprehension.

2.2 Chinese Comprehension Related Skills: Learning Difficulties of CSL Learners

2.2.1 Chinese Orthography

Chinese orthographic knowledge refers to a comprehensive understanding of the structure (character structure and component position) as well as functions (meaning and pronunciation) of Chinese characters (Ho et al., 2003). According to Packard et al. (2006), Chinese orthographic knowledge is a systematic property of the Chinese writing system. The acquisition of such a system strongly relates to the sound and lexical knowledge of the learners (Anderson et al., 2013). Although it has been argued that the clues of meaning or pronunciation provided by components are unreliable (Tse et al., 2007; Tong et al., 2014), function regularity of components is an essential aspect of Chinese orthographic knowledge that helps readers to decode the characters (Chen & Shu, 2001).

For CSL learners, Loh and her colleagues (2018) investigated the developmental trend of orthographic knowledge among Grade 5, 7, and 9 students. This study measures CSL students' orthographic knowledge from three aspects: structural knowledge, positional knowledge, and component awareness. Other than assessing students' character composition awareness (Ho et al., 2003), this study further required students to extract the components from characters and identify the structure of the character. The results show that CSL learners can build their orthographic knowledge, and that the developmental trend of their orthographic knowledge is similar to that of native Chinese children, as they first developed structural knowledge, followed by positional regularity awareness. Thus, it can be seen that orthographic knowledge has a developmental trend that constantly influences readers.

2.2.2 Chinese Morphology

Chinese morphological awareness refers to the understanding of the morphologic structure of words (Carlisle & Stone, 2005). Referring to the universal linguistic rules (Packard, 2000), morphological awareness contains two levels: morpheme and morphological structure. For the morpheme level, morphological awareness refers to the ability to identify and manipulate specific morphemes. For the structure level, it means the understanding of morphological structure within a Chinese word that contains two or more characters.

On the other hand, since the most commonly used Chinese word formation is compound characters (Packard, 2000), the newly formed word is semantically related to the original morpheme. The morpheme, as the smallest meaningful unit, contributes to the full meaning of the polysyllabic words. Moreover, the words sharing the same morpheme also have semantic relationships. Thus, the morphological structure of the character is believed to contribute to the acquisition of new words in reading (Wang et al., 2006).

Even though there are growing numbers of studies emphasizing the uniqueness of Chinese morphology as well as suggesting the role of morphological awareness, it is still unclear how to manipulate morphemes in terms of the executive perspective in Chinese. From a linguistic perspective, Zhou (1980) defined the Chinese morpheme as the smallest linguistic component but not a meaningful unit. On the other hand, Peng and Wang (1997) believed that the morpheme is the smallest meaningful unit within the Chinese word, according to the cognitive process. For second language learners, it is also essential to explore the formation of their Chinese morphological awareness, due to the huge difference between Chinese and the morphology of Indo-European languages or Turkic languages.

2.3 Reading Process and Cognitive Skills

There is increasing research that reported the role of executive function (EF) in the reading process. Among these research studies, most of them emphasized the contribution of cognitive skills, such as working memory, rather than inhibitory control. Recently, there is growing evidence showing the importance of inhibitory control to the learning of reading in both first and second languages.

Kieffer et al. (2013) noticed that only limited studies were conducted on whether inhibitory control and attention shifting contribute to reading comprehension. To measure the inhibitory control, the researchers used a self-developed task built on the traditional colour-word Stroop paradigm which asks the participants to name the words instead of colour as presented. Thus, the researchers selected 46 English native speakers and 74 English as second-language speakers as a comparison group to explore if the effect of inhibitory control is different due to their language background. It is found that inhibitory control has a direct effect on reading comprehension but no indirect relations through word reading to language comprehension. Besides, no group difference was found between English native speakers and ESL students. The findings revealed the potential of inhibitory control. As a top-down cognitive skill, it forms reading strategies to prevent irrelevant information from interfering with comprehension. However, this study has insufficient statistical power due to the small sample, and further study is needed.

Hung (2017) investigated the effect of EF with three core components, i.e. inhibitory control, working memory, and cognitive flexibility in Chinese reading comprehension, and the age-related difference was also considered. A total of 409 Chinese native students ranging from age 7 to 12 were recruited. Their reading skills, reading comprehension performance, and inhibitory control were assessed. The participants were separated into two groups, the younger group, and the older group, to find out whether the cognitive mechanism has different structural effects on reading comprehension according to the age of learners. The findings illustrated the significant predictability of EF on reading comprehension. More importantly, the reading comprehension performance of each age group was influenced by different factors for the EF. The results showed the difference in the relation between reading comprehension and EF across age. More specifically, inhibitory control has growing support for its role in reading comprehension, particularly for the late-middle childhood groups. Because of this, further studies on the contribution of inhibitory control on Chinese reading comprehension are essential. Nevertheless, previous studies only focused on the Chinese native learners rather than the second language students, which remains a research gap that the current study aims to address.

2.4 Theoretical Framework of the Current Study

For Chinese reading comprehension, the reader may construct a situation model based on their background knowledge and the integration of their linguistic knowledge that supports the mechanism of suppression to lay the foundation before mapping and shifting the meaning of the texts. (morphological awareness and orthographic knowledge), according to the Construction Integration Model (Kintsch, 1988). This theory provides the foundation for reading models of the current study that text comprehension could be explained by the combination of top-down and bottom-up processes. From the perspective of cognitive development, inhibitory control, as the core cognitive skill of executive function helps readers to prevent interference during decoding of the complex Chinese writing system and incorrect transfer from their first language, which may have a direct impact on reading comprehension. This hypothesized relation was built since inhibitory control may support the integration of text-based representation with the situational model during Chinese reading comprehension. For Chinese as a second language learners, inhibitory control may also support their suppression mechanism to prevent interference of their first language. To conclude, the current study builds the theoretical framework based on the potential relation among Chinese reading comprehension, linguistic knowledge and inhibitory control.

3 Research Question

Considering the characteristics of the Chinese writing system, inhibitory control could help the readers of Chinese in their decoding process for reading comprehension. It is worth investigating if there are any differences between the Chinese reading comprehension process of first and second language learners, with a special focus on the role of inhibitory control and its association with reading comprehension. Thus, the present study aims to address two research questions:

1. What are the multivariate relationships among inhibitory control, Chinese orthographic knowledge and morphological awareness, and how do they contribute to Chinese reading comprehension?

2. Is there any difference between Chinese and CSL students in relation to inhibitory control, Chinese orthographic knowledge and morphological awareness contributing to Chinese reading comprehension?

4 Methodology

4.1 Research Participants

107 Form 5 CSL students (49 girls and 58 boys), aged 16–18 years old, were recruited from a secondary school that admitted EM students. The present study applied the convenience sampling method as only a few schools would allow recruitment of CSL learners. One City-level Model secondary school with rich experience in operating EM classes was invited to join. On the other hand, 142 Form 5 native Chinese students (65 girls and 77 boys) were recruited as a comparison group.

Contrasting the educational environments of EM students in Hong Kong, where Integrated Education is implemented, with those in Mainland China, it's evident that EM students in Mainland China are often educated separately from native Chinese students, typically in a specialized instructional approach. This divergence underscores significant differences in the educational strategies and integration policies employed between the two regions, offering valuable insights on second language education policies for EM students.

4.2 Research Instruments

4.2.1 Chinese Reading Comprehension

The participants in the present study are asked to complete a test that was selected from the Territory-wide System Assessment (TSA) Chinese reading comprehension test for Form 3 students, and the Hong Kong Diploma of Secondary Education Examination (HKDSE) Chinese reading comprehension test for cross-region comparison.

There were two articles in the test, and students were asked to answer all the questions according to the contexts. The first article was selected from TSA, containing a total of 7 items for two types of questions: multiple-choice (5 items) and short answer (2 items). The second article was selected from HKDSE, containing a total of 5 items for three types of questions: true or false (3 items), multiple choice (1 item) and open-ended questions (1 item). Two marks were scored for each multiple-choice, true or false question and short answer. Six marks were scored for open-ended questions. All marks were made according to the model answers provided by the Hong Kong Examinations and Assessment Authority

(HKEAA). There were 14 scores for each article and 28 scores for the whole test. It took about 30 minutes for students to complete the whole test.

4.2.2 Orthographic Knowledge

Orthographic knowledge was measured by three subtests of a lexical decision task, orthographic choice in context task and phonemic awareness task.

Lexical Decision Task

The lexical decision task (Wang et al., 2003) aims to test students' orthographic awareness of the internal structure in Chinese characters. Participants need to determine whether the presented pattern is a real character or not, by using their orthographic knowledge of manipulations of structural complexity (left-right or top-bottom) and component compositional relationship (i.e. single or compound character). Both real and pseudo characters are designed with different stimuli. For the pseudo compound characters, each of the characters represents one of the three combinations: (i) illegal component and legal position, (ii) legal component, and illegal position, and (iii) illegal component and illegal position. For the real compound characters, each character represents one of the four combinations: (i) structural complexities of left-right, (ii) structural complexities of top-bottom, (iii) high frequency, and (iv) low frequency. There were 20 items for each type, rendering a total of 160 items. On average it took students 5 minutes to complete the whole test. One point was given for each correct response.

Orthographic Choice in Context Task

The orthographic choice in context task was modified from the study of Leong et al. (2018), to measure students' orthographic knowledge of words in context. Each question asked participants to select the correct answer from four two-character words provided to complete the meaning of the sentence. Based on the similarity of orthography or phonology, there were three kinds of two-word character distractors: (a) regular consistent, (b) regular inconsistent, (c) exception real, or pseudowords. There were 20 items, and on average it took students 5 min to complete the whole test. One mark was scored for each correct response, yielding a maximum of 20 points for the entire task.

Phonetic Awareness Task

The phonetic awareness task was modified from the study of Shu and her colleagues (2000), to measure students' orthographic knowledge of phonetics within the characters. Each question asked participants to select the correct answer from two two-character words with different phonetics components but the same pronunciation. There were 20 items in the whole test, that on average took students 5 min to complete. One mark was scored for each correct response, yielding a maximum of 20 points for the entire task.

4.2.3 Morphological Knowledge

Morphological knowledge assessment included two subtests; the morpheme recognition task and the morpheme discrimination test, which were modified from the study of Ku and Anderson (2003).

Morpheme Recognition Task

The morpheme recognition task assessed students' knowledge of morphological relationships between the two characters which formed one word. Participants were asked to judge whether the second word's meaning was derived from the first one. There were 20 items and on average it took students 5 min to complete the whole test. One mark was given for each correct response, yielding a maximum of 20 points for the entire task.

Morpheme Discrimination Test

The morpheme discrimination test was used to measure the understanding of students morpheme with different meanings in different two-character words. Each test item consisted of three two-character words that shared the same morpheme, and one morpheme of the word carries a different meaning. Participants were asked to identify the odd word with the morpheme that was inconsistent with the meaning of others. Considering the content of the current Chinese curriculum for CSL students, some modification of the word selection was taken as suggested by experienced secondary school teachers of the two sampled schools. On average, it took students 5 min to complete the whole test. One mark was scored for each correct response, yielding a maximum of 20 points for the entire test.

4.2.4 Inhibitory Control

In this study, inhibitory control, as one important aspect of EF, was measured by the subtest of Delis-Kaplan Executive Function System (D-KEFS) named the Colour-Word Interference Test (Delis et al., 2001).

The Colour-Word Interference test is a computerized task measuring the response inhibition of participants. Participants were asked to name the colour of the characters presented on the computer screen. There were three conditions: (1) in the baseline condition, a colour patch of either blue, red, green, or black; (2) in the congruent condition, the colour word is presented in congruent colour, for example, character 藍 (meaning 'blue') in blue; (3) in the incongruent condition, the colour word is presented in incongruent colour, for example, character 藍 (meaning 'blue') in red. The inhibition score was analysed from the difference in accuracy and response time (RT) in congruent and incongruent conditions. The task length was estimated to be 10 min. There were 18 items for each condition, rendering a total of 54 items. 1 point for each correct item yielded a maximum of 54 points for the entire task.

4.2.5 Nonverbal Intelligence

To exclude the students with special educational needs, Raven's Standard Progressive Matrices and Peabody Picture Vocabulary Test were applied in the current research.

This study applied the standardized test of Raven's Standard Progressive Matrices (Raven, 1958), which included five sets with 12 items each. In each set of tests, students were asked to pick one correct image from 6–8 alternatives according to the missing part of the target visual matrix. On average, students took 10 min to finish the whole test. One point will be given for each correct response.

4.2.6 Vocabulary

Standardized assessment of the receptive vocabulary of the Peabody Picture Vocabulary Test (Dunn & Dunn, 2007) in the Chinese version (Lu & Liu, 1998) was applied. In the test, students were asked to select one of four pictures that best describes the word meaning according to the word. It on average took 20 min for students to complete the whole test, unless the student failed to read 15 words consecutively, which would lead to an instant stop of the test. One point was given for each correct response.

5 Results

5.1 *Descriptive Statistics*

CSL students (n = 107) and Chinese native students (n = 142) were included in the design for comparison. All measures were first screened for missing values and outliers. The means and standard deviations of all measures were computed.

Table 1 presents the descriptive statistics that were conducted to test means and standard deviations, as well as correlations among all variables being measured in the present study.

5.2 *Correlations of All Variables Among CSL and Chinese Students*

To test the relations among all variables, correlation analyses for Chinese and CSL students were conducted. Correlations among all variables and reading comprehension of CSL students are presented in Table 2. Among the CSL student group, inhibitory control was shown to be moderately negatively correlated with reading comprehension, $r = -0.18, p < .01$.

Table 1 Descriptive statistics of all measures for CSL and Chinese students

Measures	Full score	CSL students (n = 107) Mean	SD	Chinese students (n = 142) Mean	SD
1. Reading comprehension	28	17.96	16.71	21.80	4.01
TSA	14	9.66	3.33	11.96	2.28
HKDSE	14	8.30	3.64	9.84	3.45
2. Inhibitory control	54	47.56	13.82	50.04	7.85
3. Orthographic phonetic choice	20	19.64	3.45	19.27	1.41
4. Orthographic choice task	20	19.45	14.01	19.90	0.29
5. Lexicon decision	20	19.15	14.53	19.52	4.84
6. Morpheme discrimination	20	18.62	6.21	19.14	1.12
7. Morpheme recognition	20	14.08	10.26	17.39	1.42
8. Lexicon knowledge	120	112.46	6.29	114.62	3.60
9. Raven test	24	22.50	6.48	23.24	1.09

Table 2 Correlations among all measures of CSL students (n = 107)

Measures	1	2	3	4	5	6	7	8	9
1. Reading comprehension	–								
2. Inhibitory control	.18*	–							
3. Orthographic phonetic choice	.13	.30**	–						
4. Orthographic choice task	.06	.07	−.03	–					
5. Lexicon decision	.21*	.17*	−.02	.01	–				
6. Morpheme discrimination	.10	.23*	.30**	−.07	.31**	–			
7. Morpheme recognition	.11	.20*	.033	.01	.28**	.10	–		
8. Lexicon knowledge	.08	.01	.18*	−.01	.19*	.30**	.17	–	
9. Raven test	−.08	.13	.14	−.02	.26**	.22	.17*	.23*	–

Note. *$p < .05$ **$p < .01$ ***$p < .001$

For Chinese native students, the correlation among the variables and reading comprehension was computed and presented in Table 3. The reading comprehension was shown to be moderately correlated with morpheme recognition (r = −0.22, $p < .05$). Still, there were no significant relationships between reading comprehension with other linguistic tasks. Moreover, no significant correlation was found between reading comprehension and inhibitory control.

5.3 Hierarchical Regression Analysis

The data of CSL students were examined using regression analysis, and the results are shown in Table 4. The inhibitory control and reading sub-skills were entered as

Table 3 Correlations among all measures of Chinese students (n = 142)

Measures	1	2	3	4	5	6	7	8	9
1. Reading comprehension	–								
2. Inhibitory control	.10	–							
3. Orthographic phonetic choice	.07	.08	–						
4. Orthographic choice task	.10	.03	.01	–					
5. Lexicon decision	.11	.03	.13	−.10	–				
6. Morpheme discrimination	.12	.15	.08	−.03	.16	–			
7. Morpheme recognition	−.22*	−.001	.02	−.08	−.01	.02	–		
8. Lexicon knowledge	−.09	−.03	.17	.13	−.11	.06	.02	–	
9. Raven test	−.04	.22*	−.11	.16	.00	.22*	.08	.12	–

Note. $*p < .05$ $**p < .01$ $***p < .001$

Table 4 Hierarchical regressions predicting reading from all measures of CSL students

	Final β	t
1. Inhibitory control	−.16	−2.40**
2. Orthographic phonetic choice	.92	1.32
3. Orthographic choice task	−.21	−1.03
4. Lexicon decision	.03	1.06
5. Morpheme discrimination	.34	1.31
6. Morpheme recognition	.10	.44
7. Lexicon knowledge	−.02	−.26
8. Raven test	−.1.74	−.61

Note. $*p < .05$ $**p < .01$ $***p < .001$

independent variables for multiple regression. The whole regression model is positive (F = 4.186, P < .05, R = 0.42). Among the reading comprehension of CSL students, inhibitory control significantly negatively influences the reading comprehension outcomes. None of the linguistic tasks significantly predicted the reading comprehension outcome. Given the results of the correlation of group comparison, where no relations were found between inhibitory control and reading comprehension in Chinese students, the hierarchical regression of Chinese students was not conducted.

5.4 Factor Analysis

5.4.1 EFA for the Relations Between Fundamental Linguistic Skills and Inhibitory Control

Exploratory factor analysis (EFA) was conducted to test the measurement model for the latent variables of interest. The result of the model fit for CSL students is presented in Table 5. As the model fit data illustrated, the one-factor model had shown good model fit with the data, which corresponded to the standard of selecting

Table 5 Estimated component loadings of EFA among CSL students

	Component	
	1	2
1. Morpheme discrimination	.76	
2. Orthographic phonetic choice	.68	
3. Lexicon knowledge	.64	
4. Orthographic choice task		
5. Morpheme recognition		.75
6. Lexicon decision		.71

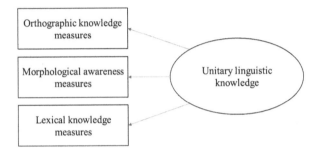

Fig. 1 Model fit analysis of single-factor of Chinese linguistic knowledge for CSL students

the simplest and most theoretically appropriate model (Preacher et al., 2013). Thus, the one-factor model of general linguistic skills with orthographic phonetic choice, morpheme discrimination and lexicon knowledge was selected in the present study.

5.4.2 CFA for the Relations Between Fundamental Linguistic Skills and Inhibitory Control

Confirmatory factor analysis (CFA) was conducted to determine the models of linguistic skills for CSL students. Based on the result of EFA, the single-factor model was suggested for CSL students as shown in Fig. 1. The indices for model fit included comparative fit index (CFI) and root mean square error of approximation (RMSEA). The results are presented in Tables 5 and 6 as an identified model. Regarding the EFA results, the model includes three measures, orthographic phonetic choice, morpheme discrimination and lexicon knowledge, as components within the model of general linguistic knowledge.

5.5 *Structural Equation Modelling*

The multivariate relations between inhibitory control, linguistic skills, and reading comprehension were examined with the SEM approach for CSL students. All of these relations were examined applying AMOS. The maximum likelihood estimator was used, and the bootstrap resampling method was performed with 5000 iterations

Table 6 Model fit indices for the confirmatory factor analysis of reading-related linguistic skills for CSL students (N = 107)

Model	X²	df	X² /df	CFI	RMSEA
1. Full three factors	Models not identified				
2. Two factors model	Models not identified				
3. One factor model	5.67	2	2.83	1.00	.00

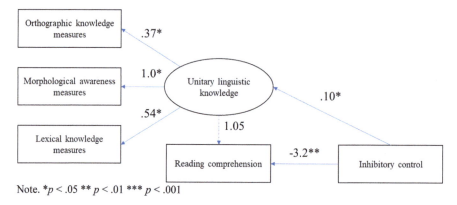

Note. *p < .05 ** p < .01 *** p < .001

Fig. 2 Path diagram of the relation between reading comprehension, inhibitory and linguistic skills among CSL students

(Muthén & Asparouhov, 2012). The bootstrapping confidence interval was set at 95%.

The diagram with standardized path coefficients is presented in Fig. 2. The overall model provided a moderate model fit as CFI = .98, X2 = 6.04, X2 /df = 1.51, RMSEA = .05. The overall model approximately accounted for the variance in reading comprehension. The solid line represents significant relationships and the dashed line represents insignificant relationships. The curved arrow represents the correlation between residual variances.

6 Discussion

6.1 Relationship Between Chinese Linguistic Skills and Inhibitory Control for CSL Learners

Although inhibitory control has no direct contribution to the specific linguistic skills of EM students, the results showed that inhibitory control has a predicting effect on unitary linguistic skills. It was expected that inhibitory control still maintains its role in low-level reading skills for CSL learners. The results were consistent with the previous studies, that inhibitory control supports reading development of second language learners (Linck et al., 2009). In the present study, the linguistic skills of CSL students in secondary school were supported by inhibitory control. As they were immersed in the environment of the targeted second language, inhibitory control would be activated in language control to reduce their first language involvement (Heidlmayr et al., 2014).

6.2 Relationship Between Chinese Linguistic Skills and Inhibitory Control for Chinese Learners

In the present study, Chinese students have already entered a more advanced stage of their first language learning, and Chinese linguistic skills have no relation with their inhibitory control. This result is aligned with the previous studies that inhibitory control holds a less important role for high-level first language users who have full control of their first language (Linck & Cunnings, 2015). Recently, it has been found that inhibitory control mechanisms enable learners in the early learning period to distinguish irrelevant information as well as resist interference, which facilitates their low-level linguistic skills for complex reading processes (Gandolfi & Viterbori, 2020). However, for adolescent students, their linguistic skills have already developed through years of learning, which could be reflected by the ceiling effect appearing in the present study. In other words, adolescent students could apply those fundamental skills without the support of inhibitory control mechanisms. Thus, inhibitory control, as a top-down cognitive skill, may not contribute to these linguistic skills but is directly involved in reading comprehension.

6.3 Relation Between Inhibitory Control and Reading Comprehension for Chinese Students

For Chinese senior secondary students, inhibitory control has no significant effect on reading comprehension. This result may be due to the reason that native speakers seldom rely on such cognitive ability in first language reading comprehension (MacWhinney, 2005). As native speakers, the effect of inhibitory control was less important for first language processing, as they have the strong skills and rich experience to control their first language. Recently, it was also found that secondary school Chinese students' inhibitory control has no independent or unique role in predicting their native reading comprehension performance, even when they have already developed all three EF skills (Hung, 2021).

Another explanation of the null inhibition results is that the Chinese learners in the present study are senior secondary school students, a group of research participants that previous studies seldom targeted. For example, Gandolfi and Viterbori (2020) found that the effect of inhibitory control plays an important role in language acquisition for preschool children. It is suggested that inhibitory control skills support early language development in young children. In contrast, since middle school students are well-trained in reading, it could reduce the potential contribution of inhibitory control in the reading process which was observed in previous research (Kieffer et al., 2013).

6.4 Relation Between Inhibitory Control and Reading Comprehension for CSL Students

Results of the present study found that inhibitory control negatively predicted the reading performance of CSL students. This finding is novel which is hard to reconcile with the growing body of literature determining inhibitory control's importance in reading comprehension of second language processing (i.e. Pivneva et al., 2012; Keijzer, 2013).

One potential explanation of the negative results of inhibitory control is that second language learners in the present study have a special learning experience and language background. CSL students learn the Chinese language as a compulsory course since primary school. They then use the language as a tool to learn other subjects in Chinese from the middle school stage. In EM class, students are required to speak Mandarin, while minority languages (e.g. Uyghur or Kazakh etc.) is prohibited during the lessons except for chatting, and no minority language lesson is offered by their school, which highly limits the development of their first language abilities. Such imbalanced development of EM students' languages would influence their skills to regulate the first language experience to benefit second language learning. Although many studies indicate the positive transfer from L1 to L2 (i.e. Su, 2001; Yang et al., 2017), the interference of EM students' L1 to Chinese reading might be limited, due to their low L1 proficiency (Liang, 2019). Since inhibitory control helps EM students to inhibit their first language during the Chinese reading comprehension process, the lack of first language learning could make the overlapped morphological structure across two language systems become more serious, rather than less, and difficult to access (Clercq & Housen, 2016).

7 Implication

7.1 The Practical Implication for Chinese Language Learning

As the results revealed, there was a strong negative association between inhibitory control and reading comprehension for CSL learners rather than Chinese students. This implies that CSL students who have better inhibitory control would perform worse in Chinese reading comprehension. As mentioned above, this may be related to the immersive Chinese learning environment yet lack of opportunity and support for their L1 learning. According to research in cross-language interference, the increase of L1 proficiency could help learners to utilize their L2 language. When students were heavily reduced in their first language learning yet overemphasized on their second language learning, such imbalanced language development may limit the readers using their first language experience to benefit their second language learning, even though the L1 proficiency of CSL students in the current study was relatively low. Thus, the result of the study may imply that teachers of second language learners should also pay more attention to the development of students' first language learning. In the pedagogical translanguaging perspective, applying resources from their original linguistic repertoire in learning the second language could reinforce students' process of linking old information to new information (Cenoz & Gorter, 2022). Thus, CSL students should have more opportunities to use their first language to support their learning. For example, second language teachers may design the curriculum based on the first language experience of students to build the bridge for positive interaction between two language systems.

7.2 Implications for a Theoretical Model of Reading Comprehension

The present study extends the existing understanding of the role of inhibitory control in Chinese language learning from young native learners to adolescent learners learning it as a second language. The results showed that inhibitory control explained the difference in linguistic skills and reading comprehension. Furthermore, the negative association between reading comprehension and inhibitory control suggested a more complex role during the CSL reading process, due to the unique decoding which was proposed by the previous theory of Perfetti and Stafura (2013), that cognitive skills support the reading comprehension process. Indeed, more emphasis should be placed on how cognitive skills, not just inhibitory control, would influence the learning outcomes for CSL learners with different language backgrounds. On the other hand, the results of the present study also suggest the importance of cognitive skills in the imbalanced development of L1 and L2. As the cross-language independence and interference would appear when second language learners happen to have imbalanced development of L1 and L2, second language learners may heavily rely on inhibitory control to overcome the interference from the language with higher proficiency. In the current study, since CSL learners have developed a high proficiency in Chinese compared with their first language (due to little enforcement of first-language learning), the role of inhibitory control could be influenced by such an imbalanced development of L1 and L2. This could then lead to the negative effect of inhibitory control for CSL learners in the current study.

8 Limitations

There were several limitations to the present study. First, the participants in the present study were EM students studying in first-tier cities with upper-intermediate levels of Chinese language proficiency. They have outperformed their peers who were studying in schools in the autonomous regions and earned the opportunity to study in First-tier cities with richer educational resources. Thus, the results of the present study could apply to this specific group of CSL learners only. Further studies are needed to explore the role of inhibitory control in Chinese reading with different age groups of CSL learners, such as bilingual students in international schools, where a different curriculum and textbooks are used.

Second, the reading comprehension measures that were selected from TSA and HKDSE are not specifically designed for the Chinese as second language learners in Mainland China. It is suggested to use more comprehensive measures to assess the Chinese reading ability of CSL students in Mainland China.

9 Conclusion

In sum, this study has the notable finding that inhibitory control could have a negative effect on reading comprehension for CSL learners. Comparing the differentiation in the relations among inhibitory control, Chinese linguistic skills, and reading comprehension between Chinese students and CSL students, it is essential to point out that even though CSL learners have a rich experience of learning Chinese in an immersive environment, their difficulties in learning Chinese should still be emphasized and considered, as these difficulties are different from the difficulties Chinese native students have. More importantly, the present study further highlighted the role of inhibitory control for middle school-aged students with different backgrounds: for senior secondary native Chinese students, inhibitory control has no role during their reading comprehension process; but for CSL students, inhibitory control has a negative effect on their CSL reading comprehension process.

References

Anderson, S., White-Schwoch, T., Parbery-Clark, A., & Kraus, N. (2013). A dynamic auditory-cognitive system supports speech-in-noise perception in older adults. *Hearing Research, 300*, 18–32.

Ban, Z. (2009). Xinjiang Shaoshuminzu Xuesheng Hanyu Yuedu Nengli de Peiyang [The cultivation of Xinjiang minority's reading ability]. *Journal of Hotan Teachers College, 28*(6), 118–119.

Carlisle, J. F., & Stone, C. A. (2005). Exploring the role of morphemes in word reading. *Reading Research Quarterly, 40*(4), 428–449.

Cenoz, J., & Gorter, D. (2022). *Pedagogical Translanguaging (Elements in language teaching)*. Cambridge University Press.

Chan, T. S. P., Loh, E. K. Y., & Hung, C. O. Y. (2021). A longitudinal study of Chinese as a second language kindergarteners' orthographic awareness and its association with their lexical learning performance. *Current Psychology: A Journal for Diverse Perspectives on Diverse Psychological Issues*. Advance online publication. https://doi.org/10.1007/s12144-021-01797-2

Chao, Y.-R. (1968). *A grammar of spoken Chinese*. University of California Press.

Chen, H., & Shu, H. (2001). Lexical activation during recognition of Chinese characters: Evidence against early phonological activation. *Psychonomic Bulletin & Review, 8*, 511–518.

Chen, Y.-P., Allport, D. A., & Marshall, J. C. (1996). What are the functional orthographic units in Chinese word recognition: The stroke or the stroke pattern? *The Quarterly Journal of Experimental Psychology A: Human Experimental Psychology, 49A*(4), 1024–1043. https://doi.org/10.1080/027249896392423

Chung, S. C., Chen, X., & Geva, E. (2019). Deconstructing and reconstructing cross-language transfer in bilingual reading development: An interactive framework. *Journal of Neurolinguistics, 50*, 149–161.

Clercq, B. D., & Housen, A. (2016). The development of morphological complexity: A cross-linguistic study of L2 French and English. *Second Language Research, 35*(1), 71–97.

Delis, D. C., Kaplan, E., & Kramer, J. H. (2001). *The Delis Kaplan executive function system: Examiner's manual*. The Psychological Corporation.

Dunn, L. M., & Dunn, D. M. (2007). *PPVT-III, Peabody picture vocabulary test*. Pearson.

Everson, M. E. (1998). Word recognition among learners of Chinese as a foreign language: Investigating the relationship between naming and knowing. *The Modern Language Journal, 82*(2), 194–204.

Gandolfi, E., & Viterbori, P. (2020). Inhibitory control skills and language acquisition in toddlers and preschool children. *Language Learning, 70*(3), 604–642.

Handel, Z. (2019). *Sinography: The borrowing and adaption of the Chinese script*. Brill.

Heidlmayr, K., Moutier, S., Hemforth, B., Courtin, C., Tanzmeister, R., & Isel, F. (2014). Successive bilingualism and executive functions: The effect of second language use on inhibitory control in a behavioural Stroop colour word task. *Bilingualism: Language and Cognition, 17*(3), 630–645.

Ho, C. S.-H., Yau, P. W. Y., & Au, A. (2003). Development of orthographic knowledge and its relationship with reading and spelling among Chinese kindergarten and primary school children. In I. C. McBride-Chang & H. C. Chen (Eds.), *Reading development in Chinese children* (pp. 51–71). Praeger.

Hung, C. O.-Y. (2017). *Age related changes in executive function and Chinese reading comprehension among primary school students in Hong Kong*. Unpublished Ph. D thesis, University of Hong Kong.

Hung, C. O.-Y. (2021). The role of executive function in reading comprehension among beginning readers. *British Journal of Educational Psychology, 91*(2), 600–616.

Keijzer, M. (2013). Working memory capacity, inhibitory control and the role of L2 proficiency in aging L1 Dutch speakers of near-native L2 English. *Brain and Language, 3*(3), 1261–1281.

Kieffer, M. J., Vukovic, R. K., & Berry, D. (2013). Roles of attention shifting and inhibitory control in fourth grade reading comprehension. *Reading Research Quarterly, 48*, 333–348.

Kintsch, W. (1988). The role of knowledge in discourse comprehension: A construction-integration model. *Psychological Review, 95*(2), 163–182.

Ku, Y. M., & Anderson, R. C. (2003). Development of morphological awareness in Chinese and English. *Reading and Writing, 16*(5), 399–422. https://doi.org/10.1023/A:1024227231216

Law, S. P., & Leung, M. T. (2000). Structural representations of characters in Chinese writing: Evidence from a case of acquired dysgraphia. *Psychologia, 43*, 67–83.

Leong, C. K., Tse, S., Ki, W., & Loh, E. K. Y. (2018). Orthographic knowledge promotes young Chinese Children's character writing performance. *International Journal of Disability, Development and Education, 44*(1), 1–23.

Li, C. N., & Thompson, S. A. (1981). *Mandarin Chinese: A functional reference grammar*. University of California Press.

Liang, D. (2019) *Neidi Gaozhong Xinjiangban Yuwen Yufa Jiaoxue Yanjiu* [Research on Chinese and grammar teaching in Xinjiang classes in the mainland]. Unpublished Master dissertation of Guangzhou University.

Linck, J. A., & Cunnings, I. (2015). The utility and application of mixed-effects models in second language research. *Language Learning, 65*, 185–207. https://doi.org/10.1111/lang.12117

Linck, J. A., & Weiss, D. J. (2015). Can working memory and inhibitory control predict second language learning in the classroom? *SAGE Open, 5*(4), 1–11.

Linck, J. A., Kroll, J. F., & Sunderman, G. (2009). Losing access to the native language while immersed in a second language evidence for the role of inhibition in second-language learning. *Psychological Science, 20*(12), 1507–1515.

Liu, Z. (2004). Tigao Shaoshu Minzu Xuesheng de Hanyu Yuedu Nengli zhi Wojian [Opinions on improving the Chinese reading ability of my students]. *Language and Translation, 3*, 76–77.

Loh, E. K. Y., Lau, C. P. T., & Leong, S. O. (2017). How ethnic minority students perceive patterns in Chinese characters: Knowledge of character components and structures. In D. Zhang & C.-H. Lin (Eds.), *Chinese as a second language assessment* (pp. 91–113). Springer.

Loh, E. K. Y., Liao, X., & Leung, S. O. (2018). Acquisition of orthographic knowledge: Developmental difference among learners with Chinese as a second language (CSL). *System, 74*, 206–216.

Lu, L., & Liu, H. X. (1998). *Xiuding Bibaode Tuhua Cihui Ceshi* [Peabody picture vocabulary test-revised]. Psychological Press.

MacWhinney, B. (2005). A unified model of language acquisition. In J. Kroll & A. M. B. de Groot (Eds.), *Handbook of bilingualism: Psycholinguistic approaches* (pp. 49–67). Oxford University Press.

Muthén, B., & Asparouhov, T. (2012). Bayesian structural equation modeling: A more flexible representation of substantive theory. *Psychological Methods, 17*(3), 313–335. https://doi.org/10.1037/a0026802

Packard, J. L. (2000). *The morphology of Chinese: A linguistic and cognitive approach*. Cambridge University Press.

Packard, J. L., Chen, X., Li, W., Wu, X., Gaffney, J. S., Li, H., & Anderson, R. C. (2006). Explicit instruction in orthographic structure and word morphology helps Chinese children learn to write characters. *Reading and Writing, 19*, 457–487.

Peng, D. L., & Wang, C. M. (1997). Basic processing units of Chinese character recognition: Evidence from stoke number effect and radical number effects. *Acta Psychologica Sinica, 29*, 8–16.

Perfetti, C. A., & Harris, L. N. (2013). Universal reading processes are modulated by language and writing system. *Language Learning and Development, 9*, 296–316.

Perfetti, C., & Stafura, J. (2013). Word knowledge in a theory of reading comprehension. *Scientific Studies of Reading, 18*(1), 22–37. https://doi.org/10.1080/10888438.2013.827687

Pivneva, I., Palmer, C., & Titone, D. (2012). Inhibitory control and l2 proficiency modulate bilingual language production: Evidence from spontaneous monologue and dialogue speech. *Frontiers in Psychology, 3*, 57.

Preacher, K. J., Zhang, G., Kim, C., & Mels, G. (2013). Choosing the optimal number of factors in exploratory factor analysis: A model selection perspective. *Multivariate Behavioral Research, 48*(1), 28–56.

Qiu, X. (1996). *Wenzixue Gaiyao* [Chinese writing]. Commercial Press.

Rath, J. (2001). Teachers' beliefs and teaching beliefs. *Early Childhood Research and Practice, 3*(1).

Raven, J. C. (1958). *Standard progressive matrices*. Psychological Corporation.

Shu, H., Anderson, R. C., & Wu, N. (2000). Phonetic awareness: Knowledge of orthography–phonology relationships in the character acquisition of Chinese children. *Journal of Educational Psychology, 92*(1), 56–62. https://doi.org/10.1037/0022-0663.92.1.56

Su, I. (2001). Transfer of sentence processing strategies: A comparison of L2 learners of Chinese and English. *Applied PsychoLinguistics, 22*(1), 83–112.

Taft, M., & Zhu, X. (1997). Using masked priming to examine lexical storage of Chinese compound words. In H.-C. Chen (Ed.), *Cognitive processing of Chinese and related languages* (pp. 233–241). Chinese University Press.

Tong, X., & McBride-Chang, C. (2016). Reading comprehension mediates the relationship between syntactic awareness and writing composition in children: A longitudinal study. *Journal of Psycholinguistic Research, 45*(6), 1265–1285.

Tong, X., McBride-Chang, C., Shu, H., & Wong, A. M. (2009). Morphological awareness, orthographic knowledge, and spelling errors: Keys to understanding early Chinese literacy acquisition. *Scientific Studies of Reading, 13*(5), 426–452.

Tong, X., Tong, X., Shu, H., Chan, S., & McBride-Chang, C. (2014). Discourse-level reading comprehension in Chinese children: What is the role of syntactic awareness?. *Journal of Research in Reading, 37*, S48–S70. https://doi.org/10.1111/1467-9817.12016

Troia, G. A. (2004). Building word recognition skills through empirically validated instructional practices. In E. R. Silliman & L. C. Wilkinson (Eds.), *Language and literacy learning in schools* (pp. 98–129). Guilford Publications.

Tse, S. K., Marton, F., Ki, W. W., & Loh, E. K. Y. (2007). An integrative, perceptual approach for teaching Chinese characters. *Instructional Science, 35*, 375–406.

Wang, M., Perfetti, C. A., & Liu, Y. (2003). Alphabetic readers quickly acquire orthographic structure in learning to read Chinese. *Scientific Studies of Reading, 7*(2), 183–208. https://doi.org/10.1207/S1532799XSSR0702_4

Wang, M., Cheng, C., & Chen, S.-W. (2006). Contribution of morphological awareness to Chinese-English biliteracy acquisition. *Journal of Educational Psychology, 98*(3), 542–553. https://doi.org/10.1037/0022-0663.98.3.542

Yang, C. (2014). Xibu Qianfada Diqu Shaoshu Minzu Zhongxuesheng Yuedu Xianzhuang Fenxi [An analysis of the reading status of ethnic minority middle school students in the underdeveloped western regions]. *Library Work and Study, 2*, 95–100.

Yang, M., Cooc, N., & Sheng, L. (2017). An investigation of cross-linguistic transfer, between Chinese and English: A meta-analysis. *Asian-Pacific Journal of Second and Foreign Language Education, 2*(15), 1–21.

Yin, J. H. (2003). Survey of American university students' memory strategy use of Chinese characters. *Journal of the Chinese Language Teachers Association, 38*, 69–90.

Zhou, Y. G. (1980). *Hanzi Shengpang Duyin Biancha* [Pronunciation of phonetics within compound characters]. Jilin People's Publishing House.

Space of Learning: The Application of Phenomenography and Drama in Chinese as a Second Language Learning

Elizabeth Ka Yee Loh, Joe Winston, and Wing-Wah Ki

Abstract Many ethnic minority students of Hong Kong are struggling in learning Chinese as a second language (CSL). In the past decade, a 'drama in education' (DiE) pedagogy has been used by some teachers to facilitate CSL teaching and learning. They found it effective in enhancing students' learning motivation and language proficiency, the learning outcomes produced being much beyond those of students in conventional CSL classrooms.

Based on a case study of a teacher in the first-time using DiE, we try to investigate why DiE pedagogy can be effective from the Phenomenography and its Variation Theory of Learning perspectives. The teacher's application of DiE is examined and research data is analysed. Results indicated that DiE pedagogy can bring in the combination of variation and invariance and the core features of Phenomenography for effective learning easily, and that DiE lessons are highly open yet well-structured. The use of Drama Conventions (i.e. short classroom drama activities) directed students to discern the sameness and differences in text meanings and language forms which sharpened their sense making and brought about new discernments on the nature and meanings of what they learnt. Learning space was provided for playful imagination and personal meaning making. While the DiE classroom seems to be more intellectually demanding, it provided more uplifting and engaging experiences for the learners who became more willing to overcome their learning difficulties. Recommendations in using DiE pedagogy in daily CSL classes are provided so that teachers can go from shallow to deeper water in adopting the pedagogy.

E. K. Y. Loh (✉) · W.-W. Ki
The University of Hong Kong, Pok Fu Lam, Hong Kong
e-mail: ekyloh@hku.hk; hraskww@hku.hk

J. Winston
University of Warwick, Coventry, UK
e-mail: j.a.winston@warwiak.ac.uk

© The Author(s), under exclusive license to Springer Nature Switzerland AG 2024
J. Lo Bianco et al. (eds.), *Supporting the Learning of Chinese as a Second Language: Implications for Language Education Policy*, Language Policy 36,
https://doi.org/10.1007/978-3-031-66135-8_5

1 Introduction

Due to globalization, more and more students are learning a second language. Some of them learn their target language in a foreign country with their native speaking counterparts as immigrants. They need to master the language so as to catch up academically and use it urgently as a tool for their local living and better integration into the society.

In Hong Kong, there has long been a visible ethnic minority (EM) population who are learning Chinese as a second language (CSL) in mainstream schools, with the majority originating from Southeast Asian countries such as Pakistan, India, Nepal, the Philippines since the British colonial period. Their population has grown faster since Hong Kong's return to Chinese sovereignty in 1997. They consider Hong Kong as their home, so they send their children to local schools for education. In the 2020–2021 academic year, EM kindergarteners amounted to 6.8%, while school-aged EM students aggregated nearly 4% of the whole student population (Hong Kong Audit Commission, 2021). However, only 1.3% of them have attended tertiary education, as compared to 12.5% for their Chinese counterparts. The drop-out rate of adolescents aged 13–19 was 13.1%, compared with 6.4% for Chinese (Hong Kong Census and Statistics Department, 2012), and only 47.4% of EM children can read and write Chinese (Hong Kong SAR Government, 2016). Their poor Chinese proficiency is a major hurdle for academic and career prospects, particularly after the return of sovereignty. Based on the Hong Kong SAR Government's report (2016) their unemployment rate was 19.8% (Hong Kong mean was 16.6%) and 33.6% of EM households with children fell under the poverty line (Hong Kong mean was 17.2%). Therefore, improving the effectiveness of CSL teaching and learning is crucial for the successful integration of EM groups into Hong Kong.

2 Improving Chinese as a Second Language Education

School is the only place for EM children to learn and practise Chinese language as their ethnic groups seldom interact with the Chinese. They also prefer using their mother tongues as family language because their family members may not know Chinese or they want to retain their heritage languages and culture.

Conventionally, learning a second language mainly relies on inputs from teachers and textbooks. A study by Tsung et al. (2013) revealed a lack of curricu, teaching materials or strategies specifically designed for CSL students. As the CSL proficiency among EM students is very diverse, teachers found it impossible to address individual needs. Furthermore, their students often forgot what they had learnt, needed to start over and learn from basic CSL teaching again and again which made the learning progress slow and boring (Loh & Tam, 2016).

At the same time, EM students are not motivated to learn as the textbook content cannot arouse their interest. The significant differences between their mother tongues (as phonological language), and Chinese (as orthophonological language) also make the recognition and memorisation of Chinese characters difficult (Chan et al., 2023; Liao et al., 2022; Loh et al., 2017, 2018, 2021; Wong, 2017, 2019). The traditional way to learn Chinese is through drilling the character-syllable-meaning connection until it is fluent which makes the learning process painful, laborious and ineffective (Tse et al., 2007). Tse and Loh (2008, 2009) found that EM students' Chinese proficiency lags three years behind their native Chinese counterparts. It is highly frustrating that after years of learning Chinese in school, their proficiency is still not coming close to their Chinese counterparts and insufficiently competent for actual use in real situations. Many of them have low learning motivation; some even give up learning Chinese. The situation has worsened due to the 3-year pandemic as face-to-face teaching was suspended intermittently, and the teaching time was reduced because of the city lockdown.

We found that 'Drama in Education pedagogy' (hereafter DiE) pedagogy could be a way out—it helps teachers cater to learners' learning diversity easily, arouse students' learning motivation and help them engage in the class that they do not aware they are learning Chinese, become willing to spend time to practise and memorise the learning contents and pay effort to overcome the learning difficulties. With the support of learning theories, we believed DiE can make the teaching and learning of CSL an enjoyable experience and speed up EM students' language development.

3 Drama in Education and Its Application in Second Language Education

Children acquire life skills through observing and imitating adults' discourse and behaviours. The ancient Greek philosopher Aristotle first proposed that drama is an imitation of life in *Poetics* (see Lucas, 1968). If we also agree that the imitation of life is an effective way of learning, using drama as a pedagogy could be a good choice and many pioneering educators introduced drama pedagogy into schools in Europe and the United States. Although they have different views on the way to apply drama in daily teaching, they all proved that it can make teaching more student-centred and enhance the learning and teaching effectiveness. For example, Finlay-Johnson (1912) believed that allowing students to participate in drama performances can help them absorb and digest knowledge, and students can display their learning outcomes through drama (see Bolton & Heathcote, 1999, p. 12). Cook (1919) indicated that the dramatic 'magic if' scenario created in the classroom can direct students to deeply comprehend the situations described in texts, and that the 'acting out' process gives them room to interpret the meaning of what they are learning (1917, see Bolton & Heathcote, 1999, p. 28). Heathcote (1976, see Wagner, 1999) further elaborated that, through improvisation, drama activities provide students with an experiential process of make believe which helps facilitate their learning. Bolton and Heathcote further (1999) pointed out that teachers should not just focus on 'acting out' in classroom but assed that self-reflection after the learning activities is more important and crucial. Teachers should give students clear learning objectives with rules and guidelines, yet allow them to explore freely within this framework, and guide them to reflect on their learning experiences during or after the drama activities.

DiE is not specifically aimed at language teaching, but language is an essential component of drama—the audience can deliberate on characters' personalities, their situation and positions, feel their tensions or criticise the characters and their behaviour through narrations, monologues and dialogues etc. So, it seems natural and appropriate to apply DiE to language education. In fact, European and American researchers and teachers have achieved notable results in applying DiE to the teaching of English as a mother tongue or a second language (such as Bolton, 1984; Heathcote, 1980; Neelands, 1992; O'Neill, 1983; Winston, 2012).

Based on the literature, 'drama' is used as a tool to facilitate teaching and learning, or as a 'platform' to demonstrate students' learning outcomes (such as Bolton, 1984; Heathcote, 1980; Neelands, 1992; O'Neill, 1983; Winston, 2012); yet self-reflection during and after drama activities is crucial for the consolidation of students' learning (Bolton, 1999). In this chapter, we want to investigate the effectiveness of using 'drama in CSL education' (instead of 'drama' education; Loh et al., 2019). The drama activities (also named as 'drama conventions') are short and simple, like students acting out certain scenes that teacher or students have selected from the textbooks in the make-believe situations, instead of full production of 'theatre drama'. The commonly used drama conventions include still image, thought tracking, reader's theatre, monologue, conscience alley, improvisation, the magic if, hot seating, panel discussion, in-role reading, in-role writing and teacher-in-role. This chapter examines the application of conscience alley, in-role writing and teacher-in-role.

4 The Application and Challenges of Drama in Chinese as a Second Language Education in Hong Kong

Some Hong Kong educators have used DiE to help primary and secondary school students learning Chinese language and literature (such as Ho, 2011; Liu, 2010; Loh, 2017, etc.). The results are encouraging and students with diverse language proficiency have benefited, for instance with their language ability enhanced, their motivation improved, better engagement in learning and increased willingness to make an effort to overcome their learning difficulties. However, the application of DiE to the teaching and learning of CSL is still in the beginning stage (Loh, 2015; Loh et al., 2019) and its promotion is not easy.

Many CSL teachers are inexperienced and do not have related professional training as this is not a prerequisite according to the Hong Kong Education Bureau.

So, they mainly rely on their own learning experiences, typified by drilling, memorising, practising and dictating the learning content which can work against the learning preferences of CSL students and damage their learning motivation. They also spend a lot of time explaining simple concepts, demonstrating how things work in great detail, and asking students to reproduce what they have shown as they worry that their CSL students' poor CSL proficiency is insufficient for them to learn independently. However, they are relatively conservative about adopting new pedagogies (Loh & Tam, 2017). They wonder how much the new pedagogy is more effective than their current practice, worry that their workload will be increased and mistrust the implementation procedure as they tend to prioritise high control and classroom discipline. They are hesitant to use DiE as they think the conventional CSL teaching is already challenging enough; adding that drama activities would make teaching even more complicated and difficult to handle. While some teachers are brave enough to deter a little away from the norm, they feel reluctant because of a lack of drama training. In a nutshell, they do not intend to try it and it is challenging to have their paradigm shifted (Loh & Tam, 2016; also see chapter "Success or Failure: The Important Role of Emotionality for CSL Teachers' Professional Development" of this book).

The motivation for our study was to examine the effectiveness of DiE in enhancing CSL teaching and learning in Hong Kong from a more in-depth perspective. In the following sections, based on the case of a teacher in his first two years of attempting DiE, we investigate the possible ways to practise DiE in daily CSL classrooms that the teacher can find manageable and effective, and examine and discuss the basic lesson 'syntax' (or 'lessons genre'). The purpose is to provide teachers with practical strategies to practice DiE and to face the possible challenges.

5 Phenomenography and the Variation Theory of Learning in Phenomenography

Following is a brief introduction to the phenomenographic theory of learning, highlighting certain features which are particularly relevant to the present study.

5.1 Phenomenography

The main idea of phenomenography is that people understand the nature of things from experiencing the changes of the phenomena. It involves different combinations of the four changing modes by discerning the difference and sameness of things. They are: (1) contrast; (2) generalisation; (3) separation; and (4) fusion. Related empirical studies indicate that these four changing modes play an important role in students' Chinese learning (Ki et al., 2005; Tse et al., 2010).

Contrast means the characteristics of things are perceived through comparison. The same things may have different characteristics, such as 'up and down' which are relative concepts and must be discovered through comparison (Ki et al., 2005).

Generalisation refers to our way of seeing things. For example, we may observe the strength of sound, the strength of light, and the strength of running water. Through the analogy of strength and weakness, it becomes a general principal to observe things (Ki et al., 2005).

Separation means students can distinguish different aspects, see more possibilities of things, and thus experience a larger space for thinking. In our daily living, many things become stereotyped; students just memorise the principles and there is no need to investigate the phenomenon behind. Therefore, it is very important for teachers to open up the space for learning and break these habitual concepts, letting students think about different interpretations of the same phenomenon (Ki et al., 2005).

Fusion is the opposite of *separation*. In the learning process, sometimes it is essential for students to know how to organically combine different things as a whole. For example, when examining the pronunciation of a Chinese character 樂, one may say 'lok6' as it forms the vocabulary '快樂' (lit. joy, faai3 lok6), but someone may say 'ngok6' as it can form another vocabulary '音樂' (lit. music, jam1 ngok6). Therefore, the students should organically integrate '樂' with other words to make a more concrete meaning and for the right pronunciation. But this principle for learning is difficult for many CSL students. Teachers should guide students to observe these two words simultaneously, identify the invariance (i.e. 樂) and the variant (i.e. 快 and 音) in order to pay attention to both at the same time, and perceptually integrate the two into an overall understanding of the phenomenon (Ki et al., 2005; Tse et al., 2010).

5.2 Variation Theory of Learning and How it Works in Teaching and Learning

The development of *Variation Theory* originates from *Phenomenography*. It aims to explain how people perceive the same phenomenon (invariant) with different perspectives (variance), and suggests that students must go through the following three processes to produce the perception of phenomena: (1) discernment; (2) variation; and (3) simultaneity.

Discernment means students need to experience the *critical features* (i.e. important aspects) of the learning object(s) from the surrounding things and stands out from the environment.

Variation implies that students should experience the three aspects of *changes, similarities and differences* of a phenomenon simultaneously to *discern* the *critical features* of this *learning object* perceptually.

Simultaneity highlights the prerequisite for students to experience the *transformation* of the *similarities and differences* of the learning object(s) at the same time by attending to and linking up more than one of these perspectives and identify their characteristics. These three processes are closely intertwined and indivisible (Ki et al., 2005).

Variation Theory is applied to examine the *variant* being generated in the teaching process and how it helps students master the *learning object* (e.g., a concept) effectively in lesson studies. Results show that students must know how to *perceive* and *discern* the *critical features*, particularly the *variant* and *invariance* perspectives from the phenomena which cannot be replaced by teachers' teaching (Ki et al., 2005). When applying Variation Theory to design teaching, teachers should bear in mind that some aspects should remain unchanged while other aspects change in one step (Ki et al., 2005).

In this study, we apply Phonomyography and Variation Theory to analyse a drama lesson to help explain why drama conventions can make CSL teaching and learning effective. We hope that this study can contribute some new light to the theory in this respect.

6 Case Study

6.1 Background of the Participants

The research school was established under the Hong Kong Government Direct Subsidy Scheme (DSS) which allows schools autonomy in student admission. Based on the information provided by the school, the student body consists of 70% non-native Chinese speaking students, with their nationalities ranging from the United Kingdom (UK), the United States of America (USA), Australia, Japan, Korea, mainland China, countries of Southeast Asia and others with more than 40 countries in total. Students can choose to sit for the local mainstream curriculum, but many of them are learning Chinese as a second language (CSL) in other international curricula.

The participants are 19 secondary three students (11 females, aged between 13 and 15) and their CSL teacher. They have been studying CSL (in traditional Chinese characters and Cantonese as the medium of instruction [MOI]) since primary school for five to eight years. They use English for daily communication. Although some of them are fluent in Cantonese and can read and write traditional Chinese characters, the school uses Putonghua and simplified Chinese characters as the MOI. Most of the students did not learn both the spoken and written forms before joining this school. Because of this, those who are fluent Cantonese speakers felt extremely frustrated and their learning motivation was low. The students are studying an international CSL curriculum. This teaching unit focuses on 'work and society', one of the themes of the syllabus.

Mr. Z is the class teacher and has over ten-year experience in teaching CSL. He had received no drama training prior to this study, and had great hesitation to apply DiE in his class as he thought the current teaching practice was good enough. He was invited by the authors to attend a DiE workshop for CSL teachers. He enjoyed participating in drama activities and agreed to bring drama conventions into his teaching.

Teacher Z, the authors and the research team designed two DiE lessons together (due to the word limit, this chapter reports the first lesson only). Teaching process was observed and video-recorded; Mr. Z and six student representatives (including both genders with high, medium and low CSL performance in the class) were interviewed afterwards to share their teaching and learning experiences for in-depth analysis. Six months after this lesson study, Teacher Z was interviewed again to share his later experiences with DiE, particularly his professional development. By that time, he was teaching another CSL class a selected Chinese novel and was confident enough to design his own DiE lessons.

6.2 The DiE Lesson

This lesson is a subtopic of 'work and society' teaching unit, titled 'volunteerism and career'. The teaching text, written by the school's teaching team, is about a working holiday. It describes the experience of a Taiwanese boy called Oliver, who wants to work abroad as a 'friendly organiser' in a resort after graduating from high school. The *learning objectives* are "vocabularies" related to the nature of the job, descriptions of different time slots in different venues organising various leisure activities for the resort visitors, personal feelings; and sentence patterns. Students are expected to use the knowledge they have learnt to express their personal views of the learning theme.

Teacher Z said students like this topic because working holiday sounds romantic yet risky and uncertain, but they did not like reading the text. He would ask students whether they wanted to go for the working holiday, then write a passage to share their thinking. He observed that students could not use the learnt vocabularies and sentence patterns in their writing and that the content was boring without personal views. With the support of the authors and the research team, Teacher Z added drama conventions to the teaching process. The drama lesson was carried out after finishing teaching the text and in the form of class groupwork with students assuming the responsibility of a friendly organiser to design their hospitality schedules for resort customers. So, they understood the job as a friendly organiser.

The lesson with drama activities lasted for 65 min (equivalent to one normal lesson of the research school). The selected drama conventions are *conscience alley*, *student in-role-writing* and *teacher-in-role*. The scenario is Oliver (teacher-in-role), considering whether he should go for the working holiday. Students are assigned into two groups. I*n-role* as Oliver's 'parents' or 'girlfriend' (both are not mentioned

Space of Learning: The Application of Phenomenography and Drama in Chinese...

in the text), they can support or be against Oliver taking the job, which creates tensions between the characters, making the situation more dramatic.

They need to use the provided sentence pattern to express their opinion as homework. During the drama lesson, Teacher Z gives them 5 min to practice reading it aloud:

> 'Oliver, I am your (parents / girlfriend). I (support / oppose) you to be a 'friendly organiser' in the resort because (students' advice). If you (accept / reject) the offer, I will (the possible consequences).'

'Oliver's parents' or 'girlfriend' take turn in the activity conscience alley. The teaching flow is as follows: (1) students line up facing each other, those supporting Oliver's initiative standing on the left-hand side, those against on the right-hand side, speaking their opinions when Oliver passes one by one; (2) *teacher-in-role*, pretends he is Oliver, walks through the "alley", listens to the advice of each member of the two groups, thus leading the *conscience alley* activity; (3) students read aloud their thoughts written on their worksheets to the teacher and the whole class one by one; students express their opinions to convince him (4) when Oliver reaches the end of the alley, he makes the decision; (5) after the *conscience alley* activity, teacher instructs students to post their worksheets on classroom windows, walk around to read others' work, and write down the advice they like in their notebooks; (6) students do 'in-role-writing' again as homework, in-role as Oliver's friend, writing a letter explaining the advantages and disadvantages of a working holiday job and giving him their advice.

To give readers a feel of the lesson's atmosphere and how the content is brought up in the drama activity, we extracted teacher and students' dialogues as the following:

(Teacher Z, the teacher gave students a worksheet in the last lesson with the target sentence pattern. The students have already been divided into two groups: 'Oliver's parents' group and 'girlfriend' group. They need to fill in to indicate which role they play and their advice on the worksheet.)

T   How many roles are there? What is the first one? Which are you playing? What is written on your worksheet? What is he going to do now?
S   Be a friendly organiser in the resort.
T   And you have to choose, there are two different words here: support. What is objection?
S   Object.
T   Okay, what is your advice? Now I will give you five minutes, tell your classmate who sits next to you, whether you support or object to Oliver's working holiday initiative and your reasons.

(Students help each other correct the pronunciations and revise the wordings; Teacher Z encourages everyone to have their own 'presentation style' with imagination and creativity.)

T   Ok. Time's up... First of all, I want to listen to my parents' opinions. For those who supports me to do the working holiday as a friendly organiser in the resort, please stand to my left-hand side and those who object stand to my right-hand side. 'Girlfriends', please wait and listen to my parents' opinions.

(Students in the parent group stand and line up in two lines, facing each other.)

T   Look at me, I am Oliver (*teacher-in-role*). You are my moms and dads. Do you support or are you against me? I will walk through the middle, come in front of you, and you have to read aloud your advice, okay?

(Teacher Z walks to the students standing in front of the two lines, inviting the student who is against to talk first.)

T   I want to be a friendly organiser in the resort... you are...
T   You can read it... it's okay. (Turns to the whole class) Listen, okay?
S1 Oliver, I am your mother. I oppose you to be a friendly organiser in the resort because I love you and miss you. If you go to the resort, I will be very angry.
T   Angry, okay, angry. Angry means feeling anger... (Teacher Z then turns to the supporter side.)
T   I am Oliver. I want to be a friendly organiser in the resort, you are...

This DiE activity is new to both teacher and students. They show a little nervousness at the beginning when taking on a role different from who they really are. Fortunately, the first few students started well, and soon everyone understands what this activity is like. All students try their best to read aloud their opinions. The spirit is high and the classroom atmosphere is relaxed yet engaging and warm. Everyone is curious to listen to what others are saying because everyone's words are different, some humorous which causes some laughter. After the parent group finish their sharing, Teacher Z invites the girlfriend group to play. The rhythm of the activity is quick, and two rounds of *conscience alley* take 15 min only.

Students also want to see how Teacher Z (*in-role* as Oliver) responds. He mainly responds with facial expressions and repeats students' speech with intonations showing acceptance or surprise. The purpose of repeating is to ensure the whole class can hear. At the same time, the research team writes down keywords of students' opinions on the whiteboard for immediate visual input and summarise key points after the activity.

We extracted a few points shared by the students:

S2   (a girl insists to play the role of father): I am your father (laugh), I support you to be a friendly organiser in the resort because I... agree with you (laugh)... you should try... different jobs... and travel. If you go, I will wait for you to come back.

S4   I am your father. I support you to be a friendly organiser in the resort because I love you (classmates' uproar), and you can learn English which will be very useful for your future.

S9   I am your father. I support you to be a friendly organiser in the resort because you would have a good work experience. If you got chosen ...I will be very happy.

S3   I am your girlfriend (laughs), I am against you going to the resort to be a friendly organiser because I... I like...you. If you go on a working holiday, I will commit suicide.

S6   I am your girlfriend. I am against you going to the resort to be a friendly organiser because your salary is very little. If you can earn more, I will support you and love you.

S10 I am your girlfriend. I object.... you go to the resort to be a friendly organiser, because I will miss you and I will be lonely. If you go, I will date another guy.

S5   I am your girlfriend. I support you to be a friendly organiser in the resort because you can try different jobs. If you have a new girlfriend, I will beat you.

S8   I am your girlfriend. I support you to be a friendly organiser in the resort because you can travel across the world. If you want to do this, I will wait for you.

S11 (A boy playing the role of Oliver's girlfriend): I am your girlfriend. I support.... You go to the resort to be a friendly organiser because I love you so much. I can wait for you... to come back. If you come back, I (laughs) I will love you more than before.

Teacher Z seems to appreciate the students' learning performance very much. He first expresses his gratitude to everyone, then proceeds to consolidate their opinions. He highlights a few Chinese words and phrases written on the whiteboard and asks the whole class to review the meanings and read them aloud. The words and phrases include: waiting (等待), useful (有用), work experience (工作經驗), angry (生氣), cannot make money (賺不到錢), lonely (寂寞).

Then the students *in-role-writing* is a letter to Oliver as a friend, sharing their advice by analysing the advantages and disadvantages of the proposed working holiday plan. To stimulate students' inspiration, Teacher Z asks students to post their worksheets used in *conscious alley* activity on the classroom windows: supporting views on one side and opposing views on the other. They walk around freely to read and copy opinions they like, and then use them in their own compositions. Teacher Z demonstrates the format of a letter to the students and the students start writing. Before the lesson ends, Teacher Z reiterates the points to be included in the composition, assigns the homework and dismisses the class.

To examine the impact of DiE on CSL teaching and learning, qualitative research data including lesson designs, teaching objectives, implementation of drama conventions, teacher and student interviews are collected. In-depth analysis is carried out based on the Phenomenography (Marton & Booth, 1997) and Variation Theory (Ki et al., 2005; Marton & Booth, 1997; Tse et al., 2010) to identify the variation and invariance of the learning objectives being unfolded in this lesson; and to identify what important aspects in the dramatic situation and critical features of language knowledge one may use to negotiate meanings in such a context that the students discerned.

6.3 Case Analysis

6.3.1 Variation and Invariance Are Combined in a Shared Space of Learning

Three invariance (IV) and four variations (V) in meanings and language forms are identified in this lesson: (V1) *Student-in-role* as father / mother / girlfriend; (V2) agree / disagree; (V3) the reasons; (V4) possible reactions / consequences of Oliver's working holiday plan (IV1) and presenting ideas with the provided sentence pattern (IV2) and the same acting format (IV3).

Students' learning outputs clearly demonstrated these four *variations* presented in the two *invariants* (i.e. IV2 and 3) *simultaneously* within the provided learning context (i.e. IV1). This directs their attention to compare and discern the *contrasts* in a rich multi-dimensional space of thinking and imagination. They are aware that even if they have the same relationship with Oliver (e.g., being his girlfriend), they still have different stances (i.e., agree or disagree with his plan). Furthermore, even if they hold a similar stance, they can have different reasons and react differently. As the meanings generated by the students and the words (i.e., language form) they used varied (related but not totally the same), this space of learning strengthened the connection between the invariance and variants of the learning objects.

6.3.2 Variation and Invariance Are Used to Organize a Creative Yet Well-Structured Lesson

Data also indicates that the drama conventions make this DiE lesson lively and fun. The teaching process is well-structured yet opens up a space of learning for students. On the one hand, the lesson provides playful free space for students' diverse inputs of imagination and personal meanings; on the other hand, the lesson demonstrates a robust activity structure that brings the contrasting meanings contributed by students together to stimulate sharp and focused *discernment*.

The space of learning is clearly set to guarantee that the DiE component will not hijack or lead the lesson astray. The teacher also brings the students through several clearly demarcated task episodes with variation and invariance between the tasks as evolving but connected parts of a meaningful whole. About the invariant goal (i.e., advising Oliver about the working holiday plan), the students cycle through the goal several times in different ways: drafting their ideas individually, with group assistance in practicing and revising the draft, reading aloud and acting out the ideas in conscience alley, displaying, reviewing and learning from others' opinions, and then individual writing composition.

6.3.3 Variation in Participants' Positions Between their Real Roles and the Imaginative Role in Play Brings New Experience and Insights into CSL Learning

Some variations in social dimension of the teaching and learning context are particularly vivid in this lesson which facilitate CSL students' effective learning. First, there is a repositioning in status of the teacher and students when the class prepares for the drama activity content. Second, when the teacher and students take up their fictitious roles in the drama activity, the nature of the transaction and the learning feedback becomes very different. These new interactive experiences stimulate both the students and the teacher to see CSL learning in a new light.

First of all, when preparing language content for the drama activity, the students are language users, using Chinese to express their thoughts, instead of learners in the usual classroom, memorising what their teacher teaches them. The teacher becomes a language assistant, providing support according to what his students want to express. This re-positioning adds new life into the teaching and learning process. Students enjoy playing their fictitious roles, which give them choice about what they want to say and learn. Some experience personal twists in meaning making, some use the opportunity to express personal views about the cultural constraints that they seldom express in real situations (like S2). Hence they find it interesting to choose what to say and see the spontaneous responses from Oliver (acted by the teacher) and the audience (fellow classmates). The teacher also enjoys providing help requested by the students and guessing the underlying meanings in students' interesting acts. The natural variation among students' expressions becomes a rich collective learning resource for their final composition, mainly coming from the learners instead of the teacher.

When the teacher and students take up their fictitious roles in the drama activity, the transaction among them is different. Students are not saying things as students but as significant others of the teacher in role as Oliver, in front of the class as audience, the teacher no longer responding as a teacher but as Oliver to what the students (i.e., Oliver's parents or girlfriend) said, instead of explicitly commenting on their learning performance. Though the response from the teacher is brief, like making a facial expression or airing a word, the students know whether the teacher understands and how he feels about it - this is a new kind of learning feedback. The students can think on the spot, review the communications and try to improve. This is like language in action (also referred to as 'languaging') that makes what the students are experiencing more challenging but also thrilling.

6.3.4 Challenges Experienced by the Teacher in Managing his Different Positions

While teacher in-role can add motivation and learning value to the lesson, some challenges are experienced by the teacher. First, he feels slightly nervous because this is his first time to act out in the class. He does not know how the students will respond to his acting and whether class discipline will be under control. But he chooses to trust his students. Second, he needs to take both the real role of a teacher and *in-role* as Oliver alternately during the drama activity. This incident happens several times, especially at the beginning of the drama activity:

(The teacher walks to the first student on the opposition side.)

T   I am Oliver. I want to be a friendly organiser at the resort...you are...
T   You can say it, say it, it's okay. (Turns to the whole class) Listen, okay?
S1 Oliver, I am your mother. I oppose you to be a friendly organiser of the resort, because I love you and miss you. If you go to the resort, I will be very angry.
T   Angry, okay, angry. Angry means feeling or showing anger.

(Then the teacher turned to the first student on the supporter side.)

In this selected episode, Teacher Z plays the role of a teacher encouraging his student to speak up ('You can say it, say it, it's okay.') and managing classroom discipline ('Listen, okay?'). He also takes up the instructor role to assist the class in understanding what the student has said ('Angry means feeling or showing anger.'). He is also *in-role* as Oliver, walking down the alley and listening to students' opinions simultaneously. But he has the *out of role* pressure to correct students' language mistakes which is understandable. However, this can create confusion in the drama activity.

7 Applying Phenomenography and Variation Theory to Analyse DiE Pedagogy

7.1 Variant and Invariance

The phenomenographic theory of learning is intended to explain how learning is brought about in different disciplines (Marton & Booth, 1997). It emphasises we should anchor on to a particular thing to be learnt (i.e., the 'object of learning') and consider the learners' backgrounds because the way of learning will change according to the nature of the learning object and its relation to the learners. It gives us new understanding about the nature of the object of learning and what is critical for learning it. We hope that examining DiE pedagogy through this phenomenographic lens can help us see how such an underlying mechanism is activated in CSL class, hence providing explanations about its striking learning effect and generating some 'pedagogical content knowledge'.

Our findings indicate that *variation* brought about in the DiE lesson is rich and diverse, including:

(a) students' identity, being a learner vs a language user;
(b) teacher's identity, being a language instructor and assistant;
(c) language used among the *students-in-role* towards the assigned situation;
(d) students' thoughts among the *students-in-role* towards the assigned situation;
(e) cultural experiences reflected in the students' thinking;
(f) teacher's *in-role* and *out-of-role* behaviours.

Each of these leads to new ways of designing CSL lessons and specific language items to be learnt.

Besides, the role of *invariance* is also made obvious which:

(a) provides the continuity between successive episodes in the lesson;
(b) *separates* the focus of variation and comparison within each episode;
(c) combines variation and invariance simultaneously, so that learners experience, discern and separate the important aspects of the object of learning organically, yet remain connected to each other as an integrative whole.

Being an experienced CSL teacher, Teacher Z demonstrates competence in adapting and using variation and invariance to organise his DiE lesson with a drama activity, which is tightly connected to his teaching objectives. More importantly, he witnesses the positive impact on his CSL students, even though switching between in-role and out-of-role in the teacher-in-role drama activity remains challenging for him.

7.2 Space of Learning

In this DiE lesson, it is obvious that a space of learning is created. Teacher Z illustrates how to provide his students with language scaffolds for the drama activity (i.e., the sentence pattern), yet they have the freedom to choose the role, their standpoints, the reasons and the possible consequences for the given context. Both Teacher Z and his students are aware that such a space of learning is not offered in conventional CSL classes; that DiE stimulates them to think more and to express their thoughts confidently.

S2 Before using drama... we spend most of the time doing reading and writing tasks or practising exam papers. When practising speaking, teacher asks questions and students take turn to answer... Besides, you should get the right answers.

S1 ... I feel like the drama is better than [other teaching method] before. Because it builds up confidence for everything. You are not afraid to speak, and you won't be afraid to say your —opinions... it helps us to think more, because we have to think of... more different perspectives that we could write it in or say it. Because we have not done that before, so we use our mind to ... simulate things.

S3 It was really fun to see a personal opinion.

S1 I...I like the working holiday. You can tell whatever you want. Like, whatever you are interested in, you could put that in. You could put your own viewpoints and see what happen to people reacting on this viewpoint... you are projecting your idea... with freedom.

S2 We can come up with our alternative ending..., then we will be more interested in it, because it is our own creativity and our work. So, we probably would put more attention to it.

The learning outputs are rich as the students use diverse language to share different thoughts, yet all are related to the learning objectives. The boundary of this created space of learning is clear, but sufficiently broad for students to express their true feelings and explore the language usage from the material, inter-personal and text-construction dimensions.

7.2.1 Material Dimension

As mentioned in the earlier section of this manuscript, students' CSL learning mainly relies on the inputs of their teacher and the textbooks. Nevertheless, their reading motivation is low due to the unattractive content and their poor reading ability (see Loh et al., 2019, 2020, 2021). In our case study, we observed students enjoy reading the text not only because the topic is fun, but because they also want to participate in the drama activity. This desire directs them repeatedly to read the text and memorise all the details about the characters they are going to play. Their reading motivation increased when they are *in-role-reading* and not even aware they are reading Chinese texts. They are willing to make additional efforts to overcome their reading difficulties. Furthermore, the space of learning allows them to present their personal views about the characters and the plots which brings up diverse perspectives, thus making learning interesting.

S2	It is more interesting (to read the text from a drama perspective) ... I like more interesting characters and I want to listen to more stories like this. Because you just can't believe the stories are true... it is just like fantasy. Because I like such things, so it makes me more interested in Chinese.
Teacher Z	My students are very active, but they are not doing what you ask them to do. With drama, they need to think within the frame (i.e. a given situation), project themselves into the situation, think what to do, then use their limited Chinese (to convey meanings). In the past, they just say whatever comes to their minds. Now they think about what to say based on what they have read... With drama activities, you can see what they have acquired and their thinking from their outputs.

Furthermore, students do not just have superficial understandings of the text. They dig deep into all the details to figure out the inner world and feelings of the characters. For example:

S1	I understood the paragraphs much better because we actually... went in-depth through every part, without really using a lot of time. So, it is effective... I enjoy a lot because it is very different... we have to be someone we probably never understand... So, it was different... we could... try a new emotion. We could learn the character's sadness and anger and all about that. So, I like that best.
S4	You are not actually that person, but you try to say for that person.

The space of learning generated by DiE not only allows students to 'try some new emotions' but expands their imagination, making learning much deeper, more sustainable and in a wholistic way.

S2	We won't forget them easily... we could keep them in mind for a while that help us remember them for a long time... can be more team efforts. You can find more words by yourself, (like you could normally) and you could make more interested in finding out more things.

7.2.2 Inter-Personal Dimension

To learn a language, students need to practise it. But second language learners always worry about their poor pronunciation or about making mistakes which will embarrass them in front of the class and so deters them from trying. DiE creates a safe zone in which students pretend they are someone else; they are willing to use Chinese to express their thoughts without pressure. Some students even project their own personal experiences into the role and enjoy that very much.

S2 Because a lot of us… we don't really like talking about ourselves because we always worried about getting wrong… don't really like embarrassing ourselves. To be someone else, even we don't really like (that person)… we won't be that person again after that lesson. So, we don't have to care about their reputation or anything. So, it is okay to make mistakes.

S1 You will feel like… maybe that is not the best idea, but you could always consider it. You could try to change their minds. If you get criticized, you would not feel that depressing as it's not you.

Interaction is important in drama. When interpreting the text and the characters, students may have different understandings. This gives them opportunities to understand each other's thoughts and support each other's learning in a collaborative way.

S2 I find it very funny, it is different from all the other lessons when we just pick up from books. It was a lot easier because we were working with people we know.

7.2.3 Text-Construction Dimension

Teacher Z asks his students to write a letter to Oliver as a friend, but writing is another challenging task for them. So Teacher Z asks students to post their conscience alley worksheets on the classroom windows, then walk around to read what their classmates have written, writing down the points they find useful for their composition. This not only stimulates more interesting ideas for their writing, but also expands their language exposure, which is helpful for enhancing their writing ability and confidence.

S1 If you write about yourself all the time, you just write the same thing over and over again. But if that is a different character, you can write new and different things, or different feelings.

S2 Eh.. I learnt the word which I didn't know how to write it before. And I write a lot of different new words… it was a teamwork again. So, I found… like my friends who knew some words I didn't know, and I used some words they didn't know, so we help each other. I think we all brought in our characters.

Although DiE brings many benefits, there are precautions that teachers should be aware of when using it. The following are Teacher Z's sharing about the challenges he encounters and we propose some possible solutions.

7.3 *Challenges of Using DiE Pedagogy*

Our findings reveal some challenging or uncomfortable moments experienced by the teacher. First of all, students' responses can be quite out of teacher's expectation so that he does not know how to respond. This intimidated him and made him hesitant to use DiE.

Teacher K   In drama, students' outputs are more diverse than we have expected, but we must respond to them. For example, there was one incident where I feel regret. We played a discussion, in which I told my true story that I took medicine for body slimming. The students were very engaged. They asked me many details about the medication and effects. Then they wrote what they would say to me as advice. After that they read out what they wrote. But when one student said, 'What you need is not to slimming yourself. What you need is to know how to love yourself.' Oh, I felt the emotion was so strong that I did not know how to respond. There was silence. I just said, 'I really don't know how to cope with this. Can we move on to another classmate?' I think I might have demotivated the student because I did not respond.

The reason why Teacher Z does not know how to respond to his student's 'advice' is because he revealed his true feelings during the drama activity. It is difficult to have this kind of intimate teacher-student communication in ordinary classrooms. In this case, the teacher can thank the student for their care and concern, tell the student that he feels touched. In fact, using drama activities in CSL classes not only strengthens the students' language proficiency, but also deepens the teacher-student relationship. One year after this case study was finished, we interviewed Teacher Z again. He said his teaching style changed dramatically after the case study, and he is still using DiE in his CSL classes. The pedagogy helps him develop very close relationships with his students; they liked him and his teaching so much!

Nevertheless, Teacher Z shared other challenges that he encountered when students were in as an employer and teacher was in role as the applicant attending a job interview:

Teacher Z   I felt powerless when I played the role as an applicant. The students took the opportunity said something mean to me which was inappropriate as a student and as an interviewer. However, as I was an applicant, I couldn't say anything when the drama activity was going on. I think I would play the role as one of the interviewers (i.e., employer) if I had the chance to do the activity again.

We want to point out that if inexperienced teachers want to apply *teacher-in-role* in their classes, they had better assign a powerful role for themselves, such as 'Oliver's parents' in this case study. The teachers will feel more comfortable and can control the class discipline by using the role as 'Oliver's parent', if needed. This is more like an ordinary classroom situation, where teachers have the power to monitor students' discipline.

8 Discussion and Conclusion

This chapter has reported a case study using DiE in a CSL class. The objective was to examine whether it is effective in enhancing CSL students' language learning, making it more sustainable and strengthen their learning motivation. The DiE lesson was examined, including the teaching objectives, lesson designs, implementation of drama conventions and teacher and students' responses. Inspired by Variation Theory and Phenomenography (Marton & Booth, 1997; Ki et al., 2005), we examined how the learning experience unfolded in the DiE lesson, what kinds of variation and invariance were brought about to stimulate students' discernment of important aspects in the dramatic situation and the language being used in order to negotiate meanings. We made use of qualitative data (i.e., teacher and student interviews) to illustrate the learning outcomes.

Results indicate that DiE lessons can be designed to be both highly open and structured. On the one hand, the lessons provide playful free spaces for students' diverse inputs of imagination and personal meanings; on the other hand, the lesson demonstrates robust activity structures in which students contribute contrasting meanings to stimulate sharply focused discernment of the objects of learning (i.e., content and language form).

8.1 CSL Teaching and Learning Effectiveness Can Be Boosted with the Use of DiE Pedagogy

Phenomenography points out that effective learning is about new discernment, the way of seeing things by combining variation and invariance on critical aspects of the object of learning. Teacher Z's lesson clearly indicates that combination of variation and invariance on three aspects simultaneously: students' understanding or imagination about the situation (i.e., teaching materials) and their personal reaction which elicited a variety of responses; Chinese words and grammar; and other multimodal expressions used by the students. Therefore, the variation and invariance on these three aspects connect and provide meanings for one another.

8.2 Essential Trajectory for Teachers Using DiE Pedagogy

We cannot generalize a developmental trajectory from the findings of a case study, but we see that certain abilities are important in adopting DiE. Using Teacher Z as an example, he displays good sense when using variation and invariance to help students discern meanings and language structure in the teaching text. He is not just having fun, but intensively helping students achieve specific learning objectives required in the examination syllabus, and hence his DiE pedagogy is purposeful.

He has a good ability in dreaming up certain fictitious situations at specific points of time and space, for students to bring out their diverse views and imaginations to compare and contrast (through *student-in-role*), to stimulate thinking and discernment relevant to their learning, important for DiE lessons. The dramatic situations he creates bring together variation and invariance (e.g., contrasting different understanding, imagination, and reaction of students in the same situation), the two important components for effective learning. Teacher Z points out that identifying students' cultural experiences helps him design better dramatic situations to stimulate their imagination.

Nevertheless, Teacher Z explicitly mentions that *teacher-in-role* is a challenge for him. He must have enough self-confidence, trust his students, allows himself and his students to enter a playful mode, not be paranoid about his imperfect acting or worry that students may do something nasty to undermine his authority in the drama activities. In fact, it can be difficult to differentiate whether the student is targeting unflattering comments at the person or the character. Therefore, teachers new to using drama are advised to assign a powerful role for their *teacher-in-role* activities.

Teacher Z repeatedly mentions that it is challenging to manage multiple roles in a DiE lesson, i.e., -+- switching between *in-role* and *out-of-role*. He needs to be *out-of-role* and perform his real teacher-role to direct the activity or regulate classroom order, give just-in-time instructional support to students having difficulties during the drama activity, or to ensure that students are paying attention to certain points that come out in the play which are important for learning. He feels this has brought confusion and disruption to the activity. We suggested that teachers can provide guidance to students even during *teacher-in-role*. Using Teacher Z's case as an example, he can use his role as 'Oliver' to encourage 'his parents' to speak out their true feelings, confirm or clarify their ideas by reiterating or rephrasing their words. With more experience in using DiE pedagogy, teachers will see that DiE classes can also be readily controlled from within the drama, particularly when the teacher plays an authority figure.

Based on the findings of this case study, we hope the pedagogical knowledge for effective and accessible DiE can be generated. For this, one more essential teacher quality is required: a disposition for opening themselves (and their classroom) up to trying out new pedagogical approaches collaboratively.

8.3 Generic Structure (Genre) That Can Help Teacher Planning CSL DiE Lessons

Although drama conventions are useful tools for CSL teaching and learning, they constitute only one part of an effective lesson and have to relate to the rest of the teaching unit. In this case study, the DiE lesson comes after the teaching of the text as an extended learning activity to deepen students' understanding and prepare for the final writing task. The teaching objectives, the original teaching content and the teaching process are largely unchanged, and the drama convention (i.e., conscience alley in this case study) is only one kind of learning activity. Students learn the required language knowledge and skills first and apply them during the drama activity. In fact, they are eager to participate in the drama activity, willing to ask more questions so as to overcome their learning difficulties, and this advanced their learning performance.

Teacher Z warms up the class by re-iterating what they have learnt from the text about Oliver's story and his working holiday initiative. He then teaches students the language components they will use in the drama convention (i.e., writing one sentence on a single stance for Oliver), brings the class atmosphere to a climax, and after the drama activity allows students to read each other's work and use that resource to write a composition (i.e., write a letter to Oliver demonstrating more comprehensive thinking about the pros and cons of his plan). The learning progression is logical and this remains important.

9 Conclusion

Make-believe play is a psychological human need as it provides space for one's imagination beyond the real world's limits, offering pleasure and excitement. Through thoughtful teaching design, DiE can be a powerful tool for CSL teaching and learning for, through play, it can touch the mind, heart and body of the learners. It can also facilitate deeper impressions and discernments of what is being learnt, which cannot be provided in an ordinary CSL classroom.

In this chapter, we have analysed the design and implementation of DiE pedagogy for CSL teaching. Findings indicate that the make-believe play freed students temporarily from the constraints of the normal world of the classroom, stimulating them to think more deeply and to speak their true feelings, instead of solely imitating what the teacher wanted them to say. The drama activity helped them reflect on their personal experiences, then speak out their responses. It touched upon their inner thoughts and emotions. Language-wise, the learners began to link the language-they-produced to the meaning-they-wanted-to-make, thus beginning to own the language and use it for meaning making.

This case study has aimed to clarify three myths about DiE: (1) drama education is not helpful to CSL teaching and learning; (2) it is time consuming, laborious, difficult to control and maintain discipline, and demands a lot of time being spent on rehearsals with students; (3) it is difficult for non-trained practitioners to handle. Furthermore, they feel their traditional ways of teaching are good even if their students hate learning CSL and show little sign of improvement even after years of studying the language.

In fact, Teacher Z's feedback indicates that a DiE lesson can be simple and easy to handle when the connection between teaching objectives, curriculum and drama conventions is clear and logical. A teaching design with drama components can naturally bring about variations and invariance in a condensed way for students to discern language forms and meaning connected to the learning text, and generalise the language and meaning discernment to other CSL contexts (Ki et al., 2005; Marton & Booth, 1997). Teacher Z's previous CSL pedagogical knowledge was readily used to interact with his experimental use of DiE pedagogy. His usage presents the example of providing learning scaffolds (such as basic language templates) before a DiE lesson in order to promote students' learning performance in the drama activity, similar to what teachers might do in conventional CSL classes.

Nevertheless, as the teacher was a novice in DiE, he was not initially aware that some aspects of this pedagogy might present him with difficulties, such as how to maintain his teacher image and authority in DiE lessons. Initially, these difficulties brought some uncomfortable moments for him as a teacher. With input from the researchers, however, Teacher Z gradually picked up useful practical strategies to improve his DiE pedagogy after the case study. For example, he now uses drama conventions like *still images* and *thought tracking* which allow students with diverse CSL proficiency to work together and use multimodality (e.g., imaginative photo-text narratives) to express their thoughts (Loh, 2015; Loh et al., 2019). He also considers the social experiences his students may have when designing the dramatic situations for DiE lessons so that their imaginations and emotions can be aroused readily. If *teacher-in-role* is used, he will design a high status authority role for himself, such as supervisor, interviewer, superintendent or school principal in order to regulate drama activities. He also thinks of ways to advance drama activities by pausing or bringing them to an end if unexpected things happen during the process that he feels unable to deal with. With all these arrangements, he feels safe and comfortable and enjoys himself when using DiE for CSL teaching. He has also observed noticeably improved attitude and behavioural changes in his students.

To make DiE pedagogy more accessible to teachers, it is valuable to examine its practices through collaboration with front-line CSL teachers, language and learning experts and DiE experts. The examination and theorisation of DiE practices can spotlight critical features of this pedagogy and make it more understandable, doable and meaningful. We believe DiE pedagogy can contribute to the development of a more powerful conception of CSL learning and teaching. Hopefully, both teachers and students will be able to enjoy participating in drama activities, leading to their own perceptual change and an ability to use DiE as one of their favourite pedagogies.

Acknowledgement We would like to thank the Language Fund of the Standing Committee on Language Education and Research (Reference number: 2015-0027) for the project sponsorship. We also want to thank the schools and teachers who participated in this project. Special thanks to Dr. Woo Po Sau Justine for her dedicated support to advance our teaching designs as a consultant; Dr. Shum Shui Kee Mark, Mr. Tang Kai Lun Francis, Dr. Loretta Tam, Miss Sophia Liu, Mr. Nixon Leung for their contributions and continued support to our work.

References

Bolton, G. M. (1984). *Drama as education: An argument for placing drama at the centre of the curriculum*. Longman.

Bolton, G. M. (1999). *Acting in classroom drama: A critical analysis*. Calendar Islands.

Bolton, G. M., & Heathcote, D. (1999). *So you want to use role play?: A new approach in how to plan*. Trentham Books.

Chan, S. P., Loh, E. K. Y., & Hung, C. O. Y. (2023). A longitudinal study of Chinese as a second language kindergarteners' orthographic awareness and its association with their lexical learning performance. *Current Psychology, 42*, 4543–4554. https://doi.org/10.1007/s12144-021-01797-2

Cook, H. C. (1919). *The play way: An essay in educational method*. Heinemann.

Finlay-Johnson, H. (1912). *The dramatic method of teaching*. Ginn and Company.

Heathcote, D. (1980). From the particular to the universal. In K. Robinson (Ed.), *Exploring theatre and education* (pp. 7–50). Heinemann.

Ho, S. Y. (2011). *Classroom as a stage for life: Teaching literature through drama (in Chinese)*. Hong Kong University Press.

Hong Kong Audit Commission. (2021). *Education support measures for non-Chinese speaking students*. Hong Kong SAR Government.

Hong Kong Census and Statistics Department. (2012). *The Hong Kong census 2011*. Hong Kong SAR Government.

Hong Kong SAR Government. (2016). *Hong Kong ethnic minority poverty situation report 2015*. Financial Secretary, and Census and Statistics Department, Hong Kong SAR Government.

Ki, W. W., Tse, S. K., & Shum, M. S. K. (2005). *Variation theory and the space of learning*. Hong Kong University Press.

Liao, X., Loh, E. K. Y., & Cai, M. (2022). Lexical orthographic knowledge mediates the relationship between character reading and reading comprehension among learners with Chinese as a second language (CSL). *Frontiers in Psychology*. https://doi.org/10.3389/fpsyg.2022.779905

Liu, P. L. (2010). Adding dramatic elements: The application of role-playing to primary school Chinese language class (in Chinese). *Hong Kong Teachers' Centre Journal, 9*, 79–88.

Loh, E. K. Y. (2015). Using drama in education to enhance Chinese language proficiency of non-Chinese speaking secondary school students. *IB Journal of Teaching Practice, 2*(2), 1–7.

Loh, E. K. Y. (2017). Reading comprehension in primary 4 students through drama in education and reading theories. In C.-W. Liu (Ed.), *Understanding and dialogue: Education of literature and language in the globalization context* (pp. 249–259). Zhejiang University Press.

Loh, E. K. Y., & Tam, L. C. W. (2016). Struggling to thrive: The impact of Chinese language assessments on social mobility of Hong Kong ethnic minority youth. *Asia-Pacific Education Researcher, 25*(5–6), 763–770.

Loh, E. K. Y., & Tam, L. C. W. (2017). The role of emotionality in teacher change: The case of Chinese language teachers in Hong Kong. *Teacher Development, 21*(3), 463–479. https://doi.org/10.1080/13664530.2016.1266381

Loh, E. K. Y., Tam, L. C. W., Lau, C. P. C., & Leung, S. O. (2017). How ethnic minority students perceive patterns in Chinese characters: Knowledge of character components and structures. In D. Zhang & C. H. Lin (Eds.), *Chinese as a second language assessment* (pp. 91–114). Springer.

Loh, E. K. Y., Liao, X., & Leung, S. O. (2018). Acquisition of orthographic knowledge: Developmental difference among learners with Chinese as a second language (CSL). *System, 74*, 206–216. https://doi.org/10.1016/j.system.2018.03.018

Loh, E. K. Y., Woo, J. P. S., Ki, W. W., & Tang, F. K. L. (2019). Drama in education pedagogy assists students in learning Chinese as a second language: Theories and research. In E. K. Y. Loh, P. W. Y. Chou, M. S. K. Shum, & W. W. Ki (Eds.), *Chinese language education in the multilingual and multicultural contexts: Theories and practice* (in Chinese) (pp. 87–102). Hong Kong University Press.

Loh, E. K. Y., Sun, K. W., Ki, W. W., & Lau, K. C. (2020). Collaborative knowledge building and sharing: Mobile app assists ethnic minority learning Chinese writing. In M. L. Tam (Ed.), *Theories, practice and teaching of Chinese functional writing* (pp. 261–286). Wanjuan House Publisher.

Loh, E. K. Y., Liao, X., Leung, S. O., & Tam, L. C. W. (2021). How do Chinese as a second language (CSL) learners acquire orthographic knowledge: Components, structure and position regularity. *Language Awareness, 30*(3), 297–316. https://doi.org/10.1080/09658416.2021.1972115

Lucas, D. W. (1968). *Aristotle: Poetics, introduction, commentary and appendixes*. Verlag C.H. Beck.

Marton, F., & Booth, S. (1997). *Learning and awareness*. Lawrence Erlbaum Associates Publishers.

Neelands, J. (1992). *Learning through imagined experience: The role of drama in the national curriculum*. Hodder & Stoughton.

O'Neill, C. (1983). Imagined worlds in theatre and drama. *Educating Through Drama, 24*(3), 158–165.

Tse, S. K., & Loh, E. K. Y. (2008). *Hong Kong territory-wide system assessment (TSA) 2007: Analysing the Chinese language performance of P3, P6 & IF ethnic minority students* (in Chinese). Unpublished research report, CACLER, Faculty of Education, The University of Hong Kong.

Tse, S. K., & Loh, E. K. Y. (2009). *Hong Kong territory-wide system assessment (TSA) 2008: Analysing the Chinese language performance of P3, P6 & F3 ethnic minority students* (in Chinese). Unpublished research report, CACLER, Faculty of Education, The University of Hong Kong.

Tse, S. K., Marton, F., Ki, W. W., & Loh, E. K. Y. (2007). An integrative perceptual approach for teaching Chinese characters. *Instructional Science, 35*(5), 375–406. https://doi.org/10.1007/s11251-006-9011-4

Tse, S. K., Marton, F., Ki, W. W., & Loh, E. K. Y. (2010). Learning characters. In S. F. Marton, S. K. Tse, & W. M. Cheung (Eds.), *On the learning of Chinese* (pp. 75–102). Sense Publishers.

Tsung, T. H., Shum, M. S. K., Ki, W. W., & Zhang, K. (2013). *Studies of teaching Chinese as a second language to ethnic minority students in Hong Kong: Theories, challenges, and practices* (in Chinese). Hong Kong University Press.

Wagner, B. J. (1999). *Dorothy Heathcote: Drama as a learning medium*. Heinemann.

Winston, J. (2012). *Second language learning through drama: Practical techniques and applications*. Routledge.

Wong, Y. K. (2017). Role of decoding competence in the Chinese reading comprehension development of ethnic minority students in Hong Kong. *International Journal of Bilingual Education and Bilingualism, 22*(8), 1016–1029.

Wong, Y. K. (2019). The role of radical awareness in Chinese-as-a-second-language learners' Chinese character reading development. *Language Awareness, 26*(3), 211–225.

Song-Stuck-In-My-Head: Acquisition on Adjectival Predicates for Secondary School Students in Hong Kong Learning Chinese as a Second Language Through Mandarin Songs

Ziv Wang Ngai Kan

Abstract The necessity of learning Chinese as a second language (CSL) in Hong Kong is increasing as there is an ever-growing population of ethnic minorities. Despite this, there is still no centralised second language Chinese curriculum for these students.

As one of the recognised examinations for CSL students in Hong Kong, the IGCSE (0547) examiner reports point out that overuse of 是(is) is one of the most frequently made grammatical mistakes by candidates. Based on Krashen's (*Principles and practice in second language acquisition*. Pergamon) five hypotheses, the Song-Stuck-In-My-Head Phenomenon (Murphey, T., *Popular Music* 8:185–193, 1989), as well as VanPatten's (*Input processing and grammar instruction in second language acquisition*. Greenwood Publishing Group) input processing theory, a theoretical framework is generated as the foundation of this study to test whether students who learn CSL can acquire the target grammar point (i.e., the adjectival predicate) by listening to Mandarin songs with structured input activities conducted in classes. A quasi-experimental design was used in this research, with 69 Hong Kong secondary school students participating. After a four-week intervention, students who listened to Mandarin pop songs with structured input activities showed improvement in the usage of the target grammar point. This experimental group outperformed the control group and the other experimental group who listened to Mandarin pop songs without input processing activities. The intervention details and the results will be reported in this chapter.

1 Introduction

The population of ethnic minorities (EM) in Hong Kong has risen from 451,183 in 2011 (Census and Statistics Department, 2011) to 584,000 in 2016 (Census and Statistics Department, 2016). These EM groups include Pakistani, Filipinos,

Z. W. N. Kan (✉)
Fairview International School, Kuala Lumpur, Malaysia

Nepalese, Indians, Whites, Thais, Vietnamese, Japanese and Indonesians. This trend is drawing more and more attention from both the public and academic sectors as policies ought to be adjusted to suit the needs of this growing population.

In Hong Kong, mastering Chinese is not only a prerequisite for tertiary education but also job applications. This is especially the case when applying for civil servant positions in Hong Kong. Therefore, it is suggested that supporting EM in learning Chinese would not only allow them an increased opportunity in pursuing tertiary education. But in the long term, it enables them to integrate seamlessly into society through academic and career opportunities (Loh et al., 2018).

The Cambridge International Examinations International General Certificate of Secondary Education Chinese (Mandarin) Foreign Language (0547) (CIE IGCSE Chinese (Mandarin)- Foreign Language) is one of the few international examinations which enable students who learn Chinese as a second language (CSL students) to fulfil the application requirements of applying to universities in Hong Kong. This exam naturally draws the attention of Hong Kong CSL teachers as they start exploring curriculum development to ensure that their students are equipped to meet the requirements for applying to tertiary education.

1.1 Overuse of 是

The focus of this study starts from the examiner's reports of the CIE IGCSE Chinese (Mandarin)- Foreign Language paper. In the years 2013 and 2014 consecutively, one mistake frequently made by candidates mentioned in the reports was the overuse of 是(is). One of the reasons CSL students make this grammatical mistake is they have not learnt the required adjectival predicate in Chinese. In English sentences, verbs are needed regardless of the category of their predicate (example: I am beautiful). However, when adjective becomes predicate in Chinese sentences, verbs are not required (Example: 我很漂亮。 I am beautiful). CSL students who speak English as their first language may have difficulty transferring information from English to Chinese. This study aimed at investigating a pedagogy helping students acquire adjectival predicate in Chinese to avoid the overuse of 是.

2 Background of the study

Hong Kong does not have a centralised grammar curriculum for teaching CSL students. As such, teachers have to explore different pedagogies. Teachers tend to use traditional grammar instruction in the classroom. However, Krashen (1982) insists it is more beneficial for students to master a language through acquisition (subconsciously learning) than through learning (consciously learning).

Based on Krashen's (1982) Second Language Acquisition Hypothesis, it is believed that language output is more fluent if students master a language through acquisition instead of learning. But acquisition would only occur when learners have sufficient comprehensible input, especially when their affective filter is low.

Music is brought into the discussion because it can regulate human emotions (Williamson, 2014). Moreover, Murphey (1989) suggests that Song-Stuck-In-My Head Phenomenon (SSIMH Phenomenon, which refers to songs being involuntarily repeated in our head) could contribute to second language acquisition as it can enhance language exposure inside learners' heads.

Researchers continue to explore the role of music in a second language classroom. They are investigating whether music can enhance the capabilities of second language students. For example, their pronunciation (Terrell, 2012), their motivation (Pyper, 2005), the increase in the frequency of using the target language (Euyoque-Garcia, 2002), raise the awareness of cultural understanding (Redmond, 2013) as well as acquiring grammar point (Ayotte, 2004) when music is used.

It is worth investigating if music positively impacts learners when used in conjunction with CSL students acquiring adjectival predicates in Chinese.

2.1 Research Question

In accordance with these considerations of the absence of a centralised grammar curriculum and the sense that the researcher derives from the academic literature on language output it is worth investigating if music positively impacts learners when used in conjunction with CSL students acquiring adjectival predicates in Chinese. As a result the driving research question that is reported in this chapter concerns whether CSL students reduce the overuse of 是 after listening to Mandarin songs with structured input activities?

3 Literature Review

This section includes the usage of 是(is) in Chinese, some second language acquisition theories, grammar pedagogies for second language learners, some music features that could contribute to CSL classrooms, and an initial research framework for this proposed study.

3.1 The Cause of Overuse of '是'

A discussion is needed in order to understand the cause of students who learn Chinese as a second language to make the mistake of overuse of '是'.

3.2 The Usage of '是' in Chinese and the Use of 'is' in English

'是' can be translated as 'verb to be' in English. 呂叔湘 (1979) defines it as a verb. It confirms the predicate.

The term '是' can be translated as the 'verb to be' in English. 呂叔湘 (1979) categorises it as a verb. It affirms that the predicate follows and becomes negative when preceded by '不' (not).

However, the application of this word does not align with the usage of the 'verb to be' in English. Unlike English sentences, Shei (2014) states that it is not obligatory to include the 'verb to be' in a Chinese sentence. Verbs are not required in sentences where adjectives or adverbs function as predicates. In contrast, it is mandatory to include verbs in all English sentences. Students learning Chinese as a second language may insert '是' (is) into every sentence, even those with adjectival predicate sentences in Chinese, leading to the overuse of '是' (is).

3.2.1 The Occasions Where '是' Is Needed in Sentences

There are two types of sentences in which '是' (is) is required. One is where it functions as a verbal predicate, and the other is where the sentence structure '是…的' is present. When '是' (is) serves as a verbal predicate, it connects subjects while conveying a tone of affirmation. Both subjects and objects can be nouns, pronouns, verbs, adjectives, and phrases. In the '是…的' sentence structure, the aim is to emphasise when, where, or how an action is executed.

3.2.2 The Occasions Where '是' Is Not Needed in Sentences

According to Shei (2014) there are verb-less sentences in Chinese language. It happens when adjectives or adverbs serve solely as the predicates of sentences. In this study, it focused on adjectival predicate sentences as it is a verb-less sentence in Chinese and the usage is different from English which may cause learners making the mistake of overuse of '是'.

3.2.3 Adjectives and Adjectival Predicate Sentence in Chinese Language

王還 (1995) defines adjectives as words that 'display the status of people, objects, or behaviour, as well as the nature and status of actions'. 房玉清 (2008) further elaborates on the distinct characteristics of adjectives in Chinese. They include:

1. Most can be modified by the adverb '很' (very).
2. Most can function as predicates.
3. Some can act as attributes to modify nouns, while others can serve as adverbial modifiers or complements to modify verbs.
4. Generally, they cannot be followed by objects.
5. Some can be used in an overlapping manner to emphasise.

According to 房玉清 (2008), there are certain characteristics of adjectival predicate sentences in Chinese:

1. The adjectival predicate does not require the copula '是' (is) in the sentence.
2. '了', '起', '來' can be added to the sentences to indicate the change or development of the subjects.

In verb-less adjectival predicate sentences, '很' (very) is commonly used. The meaning of 'very' is diminished, but it must be included in the sentence. This could be a challenging grammar point for students learning Chinese as a second language to master, as there is no equivalent sentence structure in English where the verb 'to be' is not needed, but 'very' is added into the sentence without any actual meaning. If students cannot master this grammar point, it could lead to the overuse of '是'. This study aims to use Mandarin songs to help learners acquire this grammar point without explicitly teaching them the rule.

3.3 Second Language Acquisition Theory

Five Hypotheses suggested by Krashen (1981) are the backbones of this study. They include:

1. Acquisition-Learning Hypothesis. Krashen distinguishes the difference between acquisition (subconscious acceptance of language) and learning (learning the language rules consciously). Knowledge developed through acquisition is more likely to become long-term memories than knowledge developed through learning.
2. Input Hypothesis. Acquisition occurs only when learners are exposed to comprehensible language input but also slightly challenging for them. At the beginner stage, input is the priority instead of output until learners have acquired sufficient amount of language input.
3. Monitor Hypothesis. The language knowledge gained from learning will act as a monitor and correct learners' language output errors. Krashen (1981) emphasises the contribution of monitor should be limited as it will slow down the language output process and affect communication. Hence, acquisition should be the priority in mastering grammar rules.
4. Natural Order Hypothesis. This hypothesis suggests that every second language learner utilises a similar order in mastering the target language. Farley and McCollam (2005) conducted a study by using input processing activities teaching

a Spanish grammar point which was classified as 'not ready'(p. 52) for second language learners. The result suggests that pedagogies would help students to learn specific grammar points.
5. Affective Filter Hypothesis. It refers to some factors such as feeling, attitude, emotions, motivation, and needs may affect learners mastering the target language even if comprehensible input is provided. Music is brought to this study as Williamson (2014) suggests that music has the function of regulating people's emotions particularly in teenagers. It is hoped that music would lower students' affective filter and facilitate acquisition.

Based on the hypothesis of 'flow' (Csikszentmihalyi, 2013), Krashen (2011) develops a compelling input hypothesis. It is believed that people exposed to comprehensible yet compelling language input cause language acquisition to occur even though the learners might not be aware Krashen (2015) further suggests that reading material, music, visual and kinaesthetic stimuli can all create the flow status for learners. This study hypothesises that melody and lyrics can be a compelling input for learners to be immersed in the content of the lyrics, and they can acquire the target grammar point subconsciously.

3.4 Explicit and Implicit Grammar Teaching

This section will discuss different types of grammar teaching pedagogies and the one suitable for the present study.

There are two main categories in grammar teaching: explicit instruction and the meaning-focus approach. Skehan (1996) supports teaching students grammar rules and argues that an absence of grammar instruction may lead to fossilisation and lower the accuracy of language output. However, Long (1991) argues that explicit instruction cannot help students' communicative competence.

In the meaning-focus approach, it is believed that students would acquire the grammar rules when they are immersed in the language input. The teaching objectives would focus on the input content instead of explaining grammar rules. Examples of this approach are Natural Approach (Krashen & Terrell, 1983) and Teaching Proficiency Through Reading and Storytelling (TPRS) (Ray & Seely, 2004).

'Focus on form' is proposed to balance explicit instruction and the meaning-focused approach. It aims at raising learners' awareness of a target gramma point through processed input while the main focus is still on the meaning of the language input. Input Processing (VanPatten, 1996) is an example of this approach.

Lao and Krashen (2000) conducted research to use popular literature reading to help students who learn English as a second language to acquire the target language. The results were positive. The experimental group outperformed in both vocabulary growth and reading rate compared to the group who receive traditional teaching approach.

Table 1 Variables that determine the importance of grammar

Teaching approach Learner's factors	Meaning-focus approach	Focus on forms	Explicit instruction
Learner variable			
Age	Children	Adolescents	Adults
Proficiency level	Beginning	Intermediate	Advanced
Educational background	Preliterate, No formal education	Semiliterate, Some formal education	Literate, Well educated
Learning duration	Short	In between	Long
Mother tongue/non-mother tongue	Mother tongue	Translanging	Non-mother tongue
Instructional variable			
Skills	Listening, reading	Speaking	Writing
Register	Informal	Consultative	Formal
Need/use	Survival communication	Vocational	Professional

Celce-Murcia (1991, p. 4)

There are some factors to consider when choosing the most suitable grammar teaching approach for students. Celce-Murcia (1991, p. 4) proposes six variables that would affect the approach's effectiveness. They are learner variables (age, proficiency level, educational background, learning duration, mother tongue/ non-mother tongue) and instructional variables (skills, register, and need/use). When the three grammar teaching approaches are compared, it shows that meaning-focus or focus on form approaches are more suitable for young and beginner-level learners.

The comparison is shown in the Table 1 above.

Research (Rodrigo et al., 2004) was conducted to test whether comprehensible input could help intermediate level students to acquire second language. It was found that students who were in comprehensible input approach group outperformed in both the number of vocabulary acquired as well as the accuracy of grammar.

3.5 Input Processing and Structured Input Activities

VanPatten (1996) proposed input processing which aims to explain how learners acquire grammar in a second language. It has some relationships with the Comprehensible Input Hypothesis (Krashen, 1981).

VanPatten (1996) firstly distinguishes the difference between input and intake. He explains intake is a subset of input in which learners' working memory has been processed and is available for further processing. Based on this theory, a pedagogy of processing instruction (Wong, 2005) is proposed, which includes three steps:

Firstly, learners are given explicit information about the target grammar point they are going to learn, then they are told about the input processing strategy that may lead them to process the input correctly, and finally they are given structured input activities.

With explicit grammar instruction, this pedagogy is developed from a different perspective than Krashen's five hypotheses (1982), except for structured input activities, which may still raise students' awareness of the target grammar point without distracting them from the content. This is why structured input activities were used in this study alongside music to facilitate students in acquiring the target grammar point. Wong (2005) gives solid guidelines for designing structured input activities. They are: presenting one thing at a time, keeping meaning in focus, moving from sentence to connected discourse, using both oral and written inputs, and having learners do something with the input.

When designing teaching materials for the songs chosen for this study, these principles were considered.

3.6 Din

Din is first introduced by Barber (1980), which refers to an involuntary rehearsal of a new language inside the head of those learning a second language. Krashen (1983) further explains this phenomenon because of the Language Acquisition Device (LAD) operations. A few conditions need to be fulfilled for this phenomenon to occur. They include: the input is comprehensible, it contains significant patterns, and learners are immersed in the target language environment for at least one to two hours.

It is believed that Din can be helpful in language acquisition as learners would experience increased exposure to the target language. Music is brought to the discussion in this study as its repetitive structure and SSIMH phenomenon have a similar effect as Din and might help language acquisition.

3.7 Music

Music is brought into this study because some of its features are believed to be helpful in facilitating language acquisition.

Firstly, Margulis (2014) believes that "music is a fundamentally human capacity". Hence, music should be easily accepted by students from different cultures. Secondly, Williamson (2014) finds that music could regulate human emotion, especially in adolescents. It is hypothesised that music could lower learners' affective filter and acquire the target grammar point more quickly. Moreover, repetitive music structures are its "designed feature" (Fitch, 2006). Margulis (2014) suggests this feature could create a "flow state," which is one factor in facilitating acquisition. Williamson (2014) believes that this structure is one of the reasons triggering the SSIMH phenomenon.

Furthermore, a repetitive structure in melody necessitates repetition in the lyrics. It boosts the input of a language structure as well as the exposure of learners to the target language.

3.8 Music and Language Education

Music is not a stranger in second language education. Murphey (1989) tries to bring pop music into language lessons and suggests different teaching strategies for helping second language learners acquire English pronunciation, vocabulary, and culture through English pop songs. Murphey (2013) also tries to analyse the lyrics of songs from Music & Media's 100 Chart and concludes some characteristics of pop songs which include they are usually musically short, being repetitive, the word-per-minute of the songs were half of the rate of normal speech, the majority of the songs in the corpus had no specific names, time, place or gender in lyrics, and they were generally conversational.

These principles were taken into consideration when choosing songs for this study in order to maximise the probability of triggering SSIMH Phenomenon and facilitating acquisition of the target grammar point occurred.

4 An Initial Framework for the Present Study

After reviewing different aspects related to this study, a proposed theoretical framework is generated as follows:

There are three aspects involved in this study: grammar, pedagogy in second language grammar and music.

Since this study aims to help students who learn Chinese as a second language acquire the adjectival predicate in Chinese, the target grammar point is placed under second language grammar, which is under the pedagogical grammar category.

The pedagogy used in this study was combined with implicit learning and instructed input activity, one of the input processing activities. It is under focus on form category. It is hoped that the song lyrics would serve as comprehensible input and acquisition would occur, and structured input activities could help in raising learners' awareness of the target grammar point while the primary focus is still on the meaning of the lyrics.

Lastly, music would have serval functions in the present study. The first one would be that music itself could regulate emotions, lower the affective filter, and increase the exposure of the lyrics as language input. Also, the room for interpretation of lyrics could have a higher chance to engage the learners to make it a compelling input to acquire the target grammar point in the process. SSIMH Phenomenon could also play a role in this study as it would create a similar situation like Din and facilitate the occurrence of acquisition (Fig. 1).

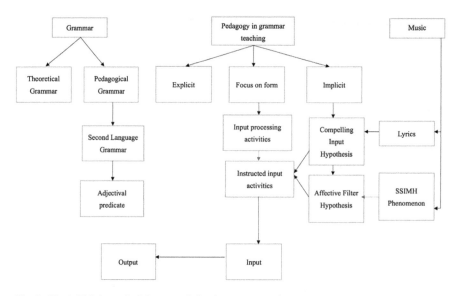

Fig. 1 The initial theoretical framework for the present study

5 Research Design

A study was conducted in a secondary school in Hong Kong to answer the research question proposed in the last section. Quantitative methods were used in this study.

5.1 Quasi-Experimental Study

This quasi-experimental study investigated the causal relationships through intervention in the students' learning outcomes. A four-week intervention was conducted in the target school to examine the effectiveness of acquisition of the adjectival predicate for CSL students with the help of different musical inputs.

Participants recruited from the target school were allocated into four groups. Two served as controlled groups, while the other two served as experimental groups which received different treatments. One group listened to the Mandarin songs chosen. In contrast, another experimental group listened to the same songs with structured input activities designed based on the lyrics of the songs with the adjectival predicate. The controlled groups continued with their regular lessons during the intervention.

5.2 Participants

Four groups of students studying in Forms two and three from the target school were recruited for this study. Their age ranged from around 12–15 years old (Mean = 13.8, S.D. = 8.7). Group 1 and Group 3 were control groups. It consisted of 21 (15 male and 6 female) students and 18 (7 male and 11 female) students. Group 2 and Group 4 are experimental groups. It consisted of 21 (8 male and 13 female) students and 19 (10 male and 9 female) students. The ethnicities in all groups included Indian, Pakistani, Nepalese, Malaysian, South Korean and Filipinos. They could read passages of approximately at least 300 words and write 150 words related to the topics covered in CIE IGCSE Chinese (Mandarin)- Foreign Language syllabus.

Table 2 below showed the basic background for the participants.

5.3 Research Instruments

Various instruments were used in the data collection.

5.3.1 Pre-test and Post-test

Two tests were administered for all four groups one week before and one week after the intervention. The test required students to identify the misuse of 是(is) in adjectival predicate sentences and replace those sentences with 很(very). Test scores and answers were not disclosed to students to prevent them from memorising the correct answers and affecting the post-test results.

Both tests contained two parts: correcting sentences and translation questions. There were five correcting sentences and five translation questions related to the adjectival predicate in each test that carried ten marks. Participants were required to complete the tests within 15 minutes. In the part of correcting sentences, there were three out of five questions in which adjectival predicate was needed but misused by 是(is) in the questions. Participants were required to spot those sentences and correct them with the adjectival predicate.

Table 2 Background of the participants in the study

	Control groups		Experimental groups	
Group number	Group 1	Group 3	Group 2	Group 4
Grade levels	Form 2	Form 3	Form 2	Form 3
Number of students	21	18	21	19
Gender of students	Male: 15 Female: 6	Male: 7 Female: 11	Male: 8 Female: 13	Male: 10 Female: 9
Types of intervention	Nil	Nil	Music Structured input activity	Music

5.3.2 Questionnaire

A questionnaire that contained four parts was given to participants to fill in. Each section aimed at investigating students' perceptions of the four songs chosen in the study. One week after each song was introduced to the participants, they were asked to fill in one questionnaire section. A Likert scale from 1(strongly dislike) to 5 (strongly like) was given to students to ask how much they liked and how catchy they thought the songs were. Another aspect of data collected from the questionnaire was asking students whether they had experienced SSIMH Phenomenon. Lyrics with pinyin were provided in the questionnaire for students to highlight the part of the songs that stuck in their heads.

5.3.3 Mandarin Songs

Based on the literature review, there are some principles need to taken to consideration when choosing the songs of the study. They include:

1. The songs have to contain high frequency of the target grammar point in lyrics particularly on adverbial 很 with the adjectival predicate,
2. The songs generally did not specify gender, time or places in order to make audience easier engage with the songs,
3. The frequency of appearance of the target grammar point in chorus part should be high as it has higher probability triggering SSIMH Phenomenon.

Four Mandarin songs were chosen for this study. They were '愛很大 (Love is big)', '外面的世界 (The world outside)', '戀 (Love)' and '最近比較煩 (A bit annoyed lately)'. They all have repetition of chorus for 2 to 3 times, the frequency of adverbial '很' with adjectival predicate across the songs or in the chrous were high. The lyrics in the songs did not specify gender, time or place except Song 4 '最近比較煩 (A bit annoyed lately)' which was sung by four female singers. '姊妹 (sisters)' was mentioned in the lyrics to express the close friendship between the singers.

The Table 3 below shows the basic information about the songs chosen in this study. All songs were sung in Mandarin.

5.3.4 Intervention Lessons

Teaching materials were devised based on the scenarios depicted in the song lyrics, incorporating input processing activities. The objective was to employ structured input activities to enhance students' awareness of the target grammar point, while maintaining their focus on the contextual aspects of the lyrics.

For Experimental Group 2 students, the materials comprised two sections. The initial segment entailed the lyrics of four songs, featuring Chinese characters and accompanying pinyin, with the exclusion of all adjectives. Students were tasked with

Table 3 Information of the songs used for intervention

	愛很大 (love is big)	外面的世界 (the world outside)	戀 (love)	最近比較煩 (a bit annoyed lately)
Gender of the singer(s)	Male	Female	Female and Male	Females
Repetition of chorus	3.5 (last part of the chorus repeated once more)	2	3	2
Number of adjectives	46	14	29	65
Frequency of adverbial "很" with adjectival predicate	30	14	19	4
Frequency of adverbial "很" with adjectival predicate in chorus	28	6	3	0

listening to the songs and completing the missing lyrics. The latter section encompassed various structured input activities, adhering to the principles advocated by VanPatten (1996), including the prioritization of the first noun principle and the steady introduction of one objective at a time. The lesson activities encompassed discussions on the perspectives of the singers, exploration of participants' emotive responses towards the songs, and voting for the preferred versions of the songs. Detailed teaching materials and lesson plans can be found in the appendix.

Alternatively, a distinct set of materials was tailored for Group 4 students, who solely received the musical component as an intervention. The initial part of the materials mirrored the contents of Group 2's materials, involving a fill-in-the-blanks exercise on a lyrics sheet with all adjectives removed. The activities presented in the subsequent section were akin to those in Group 2's materials; however, the structured input principles were not systematically followed in the presentation of the target grammar point. This arrangement aimed to explore the disparity resulting from the presence or absence of structured input activities during the listening of the same songs.

5.4 Research Procedure

There were three stages of data collection in this study: before the intervention, during the intervention and after the intervention.

Before the intervention, a pre-test was administered to all four groups of participants to assess students' abilities in mastering adjectival predicates in Chinese.

During the intervention, the control groups continued their usual lessons as scheduled. The participants would receive explicit grammar instructions.

Table 4 Research procedure for each group

	Group 1 (controlled group)	Group 2 (experimental group: music and structured input activities)	Group 3 (controlled group)	Group 4 (experimental group: music only)
Before intervention	Background survey and pre-test	Background survey and pre-test	Background survey and pre-test	Background survey and pre-test
Week 1	Normal lessons	Introducing song 1 with structured input activities	Normal lessons	Introducing song 1
Week 2	Normal lessons	Introducing song 2 with structured input activities	Normal lessons	Introducing song 2
Week 3	Normal lessons	Introducing song 3 with structured input activities	Normal lessons	Introducing song 3
Week 4	Normal lessons	Introducing song 4 with structured input activities	Normal lessons	Introducing song 4
After intervention	Post-test	Post-test	Post-test	Post-test

The two experimental groups received different interventions. For Group 2 students, one song was introduced to them every week. The lessons firstly started with playing the song once without providing lyrics to students. Then they were required to fill in the missing adjectives on lyrics sheets. The songs' meaning was explained to the students, and instructed input activities were conducted. The lesson structure for Group 4 intervention was similar, but the activities conducted were not instructed input activities. Students were provided with YouTube links to the songs to access the music in their leisure time. Songs were played once every day during the start of the lesson that week for both groups. Questionnaires were administered to both groups of participants one week after each song was introduced to understand the frequency with which songs were listened to, what they thought of the songs and whether the SSIMH Phenomenon occurred.

One week after the intervention, a post-test was administered to all four groups of participants to assess how much the students had mastered the target grammar point. Moreover, four students from Group 2 (two male and two female) and five students from Group 4 (two make and three female) aged 12–14 with different levels of CSL proficiency were invited to a semi-structured interview to investigate their perceptions on the songs and whether the SSIMH Phenomenon occurred during the intervention.

Above Table 4 shows the procedure of the research for each group.

6 Results and Discussion

After a four-week-intervention, data from the pre-test and post-test as well as the questionnaire were collected, and they will present as follow:

6.1 Results of the Pre-test and Post-test

Table 5 shows the results of the pre-test and post-test. The total mark for both tests was 10. Both experimental groups, i.e., Group 2 and Group 4, progressed from the mean score of 3.25 to 4.25 and 1.63 to 2.37, respectively. When the values of both tests are put through a paired sample t-test, the t-value is *2.48** and *2.16** ($p < 0.05$). It means the impact of music in helping learners in acquiring adjectival predicates was positive. In contrast, the effect was more significant when students introduced music alongside structured input activities.

For the control groups, in pre-test and post-test, Group 1 and Group 3 are 8 to 7.63 and 7.93 to 7.79, respectively. When they are put in a paired sample t-test, the t-values are *−0.79 (p = 0.44)* and *−0.29 (p = 0.78)*, which indicate that the participants did not acquire the target grammar point through traditional grammar teaching.

Both experimental groups improved by overusing the target grammar point after the intervention based on the results above. The improvement for Group 2 (with music and structured input activities) is 2.48*, which is slightly greater than that of 2.16* for Group 4 (music only). In contrast, both control groups had a mild decrease in scores after 5 weeks of learning (see Table 5)

The results show that music with structured input activities might contribute to helping CSL students to acquire adjectival predicates. Music alone had an impact, but it was not as effective as music with structured input activities.

6.2 Results of the Questionnaire

A few questions were asked to the participants.

The first question was how much they liked the songs used in intervention lessons. Both experimental groups ranked the songs in identical order from the

Table 5 Pre-/post-test result comparison

	n	Pre-test Mean	SD	Post-test Mean	SD	Paired sample t-test t-value	Sig
Control groups							
Group 1	16	8.00	2.10	7.63	2.85	−0.79	0.44
Group 3	14	7.93	3.05	7.79	2.69	−0.29	0.78
Experimental groups							
Group 2 (music & structured input activity)	19	3.25	2.07	4.25	2.75	2.48	0.02*
Group 4 (music only)	19	1.63	1.30	2.37	2.19	2.16	0.04*

*$p < 0.05$

ones they liked the most to their least favourite: Song 1, Song 4, Song 3 and Song 2. The details are shown as below (Table 6).

The second question was about how catchy the participants thought of the songs. The data shows that Song 1 was the 'catchiest' across both experimental groups. Song 4 comes second, followed by Song 3, then Song 2. The ranking of these songs is the same as that in the previous question (Table 7).

The last part of the questionnaire aimed at investigating whether the participants experienced the SSIMH Phenomenon from any of the songs introduced throughout the week. Thirteen participants from both groups reported that they had this experience towards Song 1, which made 26 students in total. The order was the same as how much they liked the songs and how catchy they thought they were (Table 8).

The questionnaire also provided participants with lyrics and pinyin to all songs they used in this study. Students were asked to highlight the parts of the songs that triggered the SSIMH Phenomenon. Since Song 1 was the participants' favourite song and also triggered the most participants, it is worth looking into which part of the song they remembered the most.

There were six students from Group 2, and ten students from Group 4 could specify which part of the song they had this reaction towards.

The chorus was the most popular part of the song that triggered the SSIMH Phenomenon. All 16 students pointed out that part of the song stuck in their heads, i.e. the three characters '爱很大 (Love is big)'. This phrase is repeated eight times every time the chorus plays, and it was the target grammar point for this study. Two students from Group 2 and three from Group 4 highlighted the entire chorus. There were two students from Group 2 and four students from Group 4 that highlighted the line that preceded the chorus.

Table 6 The level of students liking the songs

Groups	Song 1 Mean	SD	Song 2 Mean	SD	Song 3 Mean	SD	Song 4 Mean	SD
Group 2	3.45	1.14	2	1.03	2.48	1.12	3.05	1.24
Group 4	3	1.00	2.53	1.07	2.63	1.21	2.82	1.24

Table 7 The catchiness of the songs

Groups	Song 1 Mean	SD	Song 2 Mean	SD	Song 3 Mean	SD	Song 4 Mean	SD
Group 2	3.68	1.17	1.85	1.04	2.48	1.12	3.10	1.07
Group 4	3.58	1.21	2	1.17	2.42	1.17	2.82	1.07

Table 8 The frequency of participants experiencing SSIMH Phenomenon

Groups	Song 1	Song 2	Song 3	Song 4
Group 2	13	1	3	6
Group 4	13	4	3	5

6.3 Answer to the Research Question

After the intervention, the pre-test and post-test results indicated that music (Group 4) could impact students in acquiring adjectival predicates. At the same time, it was more significant for music to be coupled with structured input activities to help learners misuse 是 with the adjectival predicate became less frequent.

6.3.1 The Relationship Between Acquisition of the Target Grammar Points and the Connection with Music

The results support the hypothesis behind this study. In the proposed theoretical framework, it is hypothesised that lyrics could serve as comprehensible input. The results of the pre- /post-tests show that both experimental groups who received music in intervention outperformed the other two controlled groups. It suggests that music could be a factor to facilitate learners acquiring the target grammar point.

This study hypothesised that music not only lowers the learners' affective filter but provides them with sufficient comprehensible input through its repetitive structure. The pre- /post-test results show that participants from experimental groups progressed from 3.25 to 4.25 and 1.63 to 2.37, respectively, while both controlled groups did not progress. When music is the only common intervention received in both experimental groups, it suggests that music has a role in helping participants acquire adjectival predicates in Chinese.

6.3.2 The Relationship Between Acquisition of Target Grammar Point and SSIMH Phenomenon

Another factor that was hypothesised in helping learners in acquiring the target grammar point was the SSIMH Phenomenon. In the theoretical framework, the role of the SSIMH Phenomenon could have a similar function as Din and, therefore, would facilitate acquisition occur.

According to the questionnaire results, Song 1 caused the largest number of students to experience the SSIMH Phenomenon. Students were able to highlight the chorus part of Song 1. Participants could easily associate with this part after they were told the objective of this study after the intervention. Hence, language acquisition could have occurred subconsciously.

6.3.3 The Impact of Structured Input Activities Enhancing Acquisition on the Target Grammar Point

The pre-test and post-test results show that both experimental groups outperformed after the intervention compared with the controlled groups. In group 2, which received music and structured input activities, the pre-and post-test mean scores increased from 3.25 to 4.25 out of 10, with a significant t-value of 2.48* (p = 0.02). This group progressed the most among all groups.

The theoretical framework suggested that acquisition would only occur when music and structured input activities are provided to students where the lyrics could serve as the comprehensible input. Structured input activities could raise students' awareness of the target grammar point while the focus is still on the content of the language input. Group 2 participants who received music and structured input activities in the intervention progressed more than Group 4, who just received music in their intervention during the post-test. It could be concluded that structured input activities could raise students' awareness of the target grammar point while their focus was still on the content of the lyrics.

7 Conclusion

7.1 Use of Songs in CSL Classroom

Different studies (Ayotte, 2004; Euyoque-Garcia, 2002; Pyper, 2005; Terrell, 2012; Redmond, 2013) were conducted to investigate whether songs could help in different aspects of second language acquisition. The studies focused on CSL are limited as most of the studies mentioned above focused on learning European languages as the target languages.

This study tried to use Mandarin songs and focused on helping CSL students to acquire adjectival predicate. The result of the study suggests that the hypothesis in this study could help students in avoiding the overuse of 是 (is), especially when songs were used alongside with structured input activities.

7.2 Sustainability

One year after the interview was conducted, the researcher had a chance to have an informal conversation with two participants. One of the participants could still sing the first line of the chorus from Song 1 ("愛很大, 有你有我有他") with the correct melody and lyrics. They said they liked the song but had not listened to it after the intervention.

The encounter with the participants above can be concluded with two points. Firstly, the song is deeply rooted in the participants' minds. After one year of not listening to the song, she could still recall one line of the song. Secondly, the chorus seems to be the most memorable part of the song. This echoes the results of Tsai et al.'s (2014) study.

8 Limitation

8.1 Generalisation of the Study

Due to various reasons, the findings of this study might be limited and cannot be generalised to other contexts. Convenient sampling was used in this study due to the school class setting. Moreover, there was only one grammar point being investigated in this study. There is no evidence supporting the same effect for the CSL students on other grammar points.

8.2 Recommendations for Future Study

This study suggests that music with structured input activities might facilitate students who learn Chinese as a second language to acquire adjectival predicates. However, other grammar rules were not covered in this study. Hence it is still under investigation how second language learners would respond when songs are used to acquire other grammar points.

Appendix I: Lyrics of the Songs Chosen for Intervention for the Main Study

Song 1 愛很大 sung by Waterman
Music: 廷廷
Lyrics: 龔大中

徹底崩壞的 重生了
曾經傷害的 癒合了
不願離開的 回來了
害怕孤單的 幸福了
看愛的夜空有流星的河
聽愛的心中奇蹟在唱歌
我們每一個 都是被祝福的
因為我們的**愛很大**

愛很大 有你有我有他
愛很大 我們一起大聲唱
愛很大 發射溫暖的陽光
愛很大 黑夜過後就是天亮

愛很大 不再分你我他
愛很大 我們什麼都不怕
愛很大 張開夢想的翅膀
愛很大 沒有到不了的地方

冰冷凍結的 融化了
哭泣流淚的 微笑了
支離破碎的 完整了
枯萎凋謝的 開花了
看愛的天空有和平的鴿
聽愛的心中交響著快樂
我們每一個 都是被祝福的
因為我們的**愛很大**

愛很大 有你有我有他
愛很大 我們一起大聲唱
愛很大 發射溫暖的陽光
愛很大 黑夜過後就是天亮

愛很大 不再分你我他
愛很大 我們什麼都不怕
愛很大 張開夢想的翅膀
愛很大 沒有到不了

愛很大 有你有我有他
愛很大 我們一起大聲唱
愛很大 發射溫暖的陽光
愛很大 黑夜過後就是天亮

愛很大 不再分你我他
愛很大 我們什麼都不怕
愛很大 張開夢想的翅膀
愛很大 沒有到不了
愛很大 愛很大 愛很大 愛很大 很大很大很大……

Song 2 外面的世界 sung by Karen Mok
Music: 齊秦
Lyrics: 齊秦

在很久很久以前
　你擁有我　我擁有你
　在很久很久以前
　你離開我去遠空翱翔＊

外面的世界很精彩
外面的世界很無奈
當你覺得外面的世界很精彩
我會在這裡衷心的祝福你

＃每當夕陽西沉的時候
　我總是在這裡盼望你
　天空中雖然飄著雨
　我依然等待你的歸期＃

REPEAT＊

外面的世界很精彩
外面的世界很無奈
當你覺得外面的世界很無奈
我還在這裡耐心的等著你

REPEAT＃

我依然等待你的歸期

Song 3 戀 sung by 光良/李心潔
Music: 光良
Lyrics: 李心潔

不願承認	不願面對	**我真的愛你很深很深**
一個笑容	一句話語	**都讓我心跳　很快很快**
每個思索	每個慾望	**全被你佔據很滿很滿**
無法平靜	不想透露	**因為愛你快樂　很久很久**

情願	醉死在夢裡	當一切都變得無力
情願	為你而美麗	當你呼喚我的名字
情願	默默的隱藏	當它只是一個錯誤
情願	很久的以後	當一切都被時間沖淡　我只會更愛你

Song 4 最近比較煩 by 鄭希怡 蔡卓妍 鍾欣潼 容祖兒
Music: 李宗盛 周華健 黃品冠
Lyrics: 谷德昭 林子萱

最近比較煩　比較煩　比較煩
從一開始就不怎麼喜歡上班
卻每天工作到很晚
喜歡電視劇也沒法收看

最近比較煩　比較煩　比較煩
總覺得愛情不是想像的簡單
現在只想要個肩膀
擋著大風雨撐起把雨傘

最近比較煩　比較煩　比較煩
結婚的禮物沒一份特別喜歡
我的媽媽不厭其煩每天追趕
[Yumi 什麼時候生一個 baby]
真心 她很趕

最近比較煩　比較煩　比較煩
我長得不賴怎麼沒有人喜歡
沒一個真心的胸膛
也許是我注定要流浪

最近比較煩　比較煩　比較煩
我覺得我的世界要做夢不難
把夢想實現　很困難
努力加運氣　這個超難

最近比較煩　比你煩　也比你煩
我很久沒有站在舞台上方
現在的模樣　有點不習慣
卻喜歡唱歌有你們作好伙伴

人生太多比較所以麻煩
現在每天只想回家吃飯
我的狗狗教我快樂不難
臉要掛上微微笑的模樣
沒有什麼　天大遺憾
看著前方　隨風起帆
世界不會給你太多麻煩

某個師傅說我成功很難
害我事倍功半十年時光
相愛不難　相處卻不簡單
喜歡煮飯　努力學習平凡
麻煩　麻煩　麻煩　麻煩
麻煩　我很麻煩　麻煩　麻煩　麻煩

最近比較煩
比較煩
我比較煩
我其實沒有想像的那麼堅強
不要在意勢利的眼光
專注在自己要走的方向

最近比較煩
比較煩
比較煩
人生　這一段總有你們陪伴
姊妹的關心充滿溫暖
將來有寶寶一起煮飯...

不煩　我不煩　只一點煩　你比我煩
我不煩　我不煩　只一點煩　那不算煩
我不煩　我不煩　只一點煩　你和我一樣
我不煩　我不煩　只一點煩　那不算煩　不煩

Appendix II: Teaching Materials and Lesson Plans for Intervention Lessons

Waterman 爱很大
https://www.youtube.com/watch?v=W3LJACdGQ6c

kuàilè wēnnuǎn xìngfú gūdān dà bīnglěng pà
快乐 温暖 幸福 孤单 大 冰冷 怕

chèdǐ bēng pī de chóngshēng le
彻底 崩 坏 的 重 生 了
céngjīng shānghài de yùhé le
曾经 伤害 的 愈合 了
bù yuàn líkāi de huílái le
不 愿 离开 的 回来 了
hàipà ___ de ___ le
害怕 的 了
kàn ài de yèkōng yǒu liúxīng de hé
看 爱 的 夜空 有 流星 的 河
tīng ài de xīnzhōng qí jì zài chànggē
听 爱 的 心中 奇迹 在 唱歌
wǒmen měi yī gè dōu shì bèi zhùfú de
我们 每 一 个 都是 被 祝福 的
yīnwèi wǒmen de ài hěn ___
因为 我们 的 爱 很
ài hěn ___ yǒu nǐ yǒu wǒ yǒu tā
爱 很 有 你 有 我 有 他
ài hěn ___ wǒmen yīqǐ dà shēng chàng
爱 很 我们 一起 大 声 唱
ài hěn ___ fāshè de yángguāng
爱 很 发射 的 阳 光
ài hěn ___ hēiyè guòhòu jiùshì tiānliàng
爱 很 黑夜 过后 就是 天 亮
ài hěn ___ bù zài fēn nǐ wǒ tā
爱 很 不再 分 你 我 他
ài hěn ___ wǒmen shénme dōu bù
爱 很 我们 什么 都 不
ài hěn ___ zhāngkāi mèngxiǎng de chìbǎng
爱 很 张 开 梦 想 的 翅膀
ài hěn ___ méiyǒu dào bùliǎo de dìfāng
爱 很 没有 到 不了 的 地方
dòngjié de rónghuà le
___ 冻结 的 融化 了
kūqì liúlèi de wēixiào le
哭泣 流泪 的 微笑 了
zhīlí pòsuì de wánzhěng le
支离 破碎 的 完 整 了
kūwěi diāoxiè de kāihuā le
枯萎 凋谢 的 开花 了
kàn ài de tiānkōng yǒu hépíng de gē
看 爱 的 天空 有 和平 的 鸽
tīng ài de xīnzhōng jiāo xiǎng nà zhào
听 爱 的 心中 交 响 那
wǒmen měi yī gè dōu shì bèi zhùfú de
我们 每 一 个 都是 被 祝福 的
yīnwèi wǒmen de ài hěn ___
因为 我们 的 爱 很

听完这首歌你有什么感觉？

我觉得	很	感觉	同意 / 不同意
		开心	
		伤心	
		无聊	
		其他：	

歌词中提到"哭泣流泪的微笑了"，你觉得这是一个怎样的微笑？

我觉得这个微笑	很	1._____
		2._____
		3._____

听完这首歌，你觉得歌手应该是怎样的一个人，画下来并形容一下。

请填上他的特征：

他的眼睛		
他的鼻子	很	
他的耳朵		
他的口		
他		

听完这首歌你有什么感觉?

我觉得	很	感觉	同意 / 不同意
		开心	
		伤心	
		无聊	
		其他:_____	

歌词中提到"哭泣流泪的微笑了",你觉得这是一个怎样的微笑?

我觉得这个微笑	很	1._____ 2._____ 3._____

听完这首歌,你觉得歌手应该是怎样的一个人,画下来并形容一下。

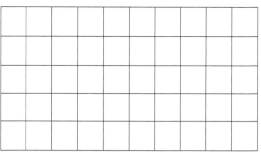

请填上他的特征:

他的眼睛		
他的鼻子	很	
他的耳朵		
他的口		
他		

你觉的这首歌想说什么?

你喜欢这首歌吗?你会给它多少分?请圈出来。5分最高1分最低

1	2	3	4	5

Lesson Plan

Class: Group 2
Time: 65 minutes
Lesson objectives:

1. To learn adjectives from the songs
2. To learn adverbial 很 with adjectival predicate

Time	Activities	Material needed	Theory
5'	Introducing the song to students Asking students their opinion on the song verbally	recording	Starting with music Murphey, 2013
10'	Lyrics sheet with pinyin are provided to students while adjectives are taken out. Students need to fill in the blanks	Recording Lyrics sheet	Text completion and construction Murphey, 2013
10'	Students need to complete task 1 on worksheet. Giving opinion on what do they think of the scenario of the song	Recording Lyrics sheet	Processing input activity (Vanpatten)
15'	Students are asked to imagine the appearance of the singer by just listening to the song They are required to draw and write a short description	Recording Lyrics sheet	Processing input activity (Vanpatten)
5'	Introducing the background of the chorus	Recording Lyrics sheet	
15'	4–5 students in a group Discussion on whether the song is about. After discussion they are required to write down their thoughts in 50 words	Recording Lyrics sheet	Pop song: discussion Murphey, 2013
5'	Plenary Revision on the adjectives covered in this lesson	Recording Lyrics sheet	

Song will be played when students are completing the tasks given

莫文蔚 外面的世界
https://www.youtube.com/watch?v=W3LJACdGQ6c

wú nài　jīngcǎi　jiǔ
无奈　精彩　久

```
          zài hěn           hěn        yǐ qián   nǐ yōngyǒu wǒ   wǒ yōngyǒu nǐ
       ★ 在 很 _____ 很 _____ 以前 你 拥有 我　我 拥有 你
          zài hěn           hěn        yǐ qián   nǐ líkāi wǒ qù yuǎn kōng áoxiáng
         在 很 _____ 很 _____ 以前 你 离开 我 去 远 空 翱 翔 ★

          wàimian de shìjiè hěn              wàimian de shìjiè hěn
         外面 的 世界 很 _____  外面 的 世界 很 _____
          dāng nǐ jué de wàimian de shìjiè hěn
         当 你 觉得 外面 的 世界 很 _____
          wǒ huì zài zhèlǐ zhōngxīn de zhùfú nǐ
         我 会 在 这里 衷心 的 祝福 你

          měidāng xīyáng xī chén de shíhou wǒ zǒngshì zài zhèlǐ pànwàng nǐ
       # 每 当 夕 阳 西 沉 的 时候 我 总 是 在 这里 盼 望 你
          tiānkōng zhōng suīrán piāo zháo yǔ wǒ yīrán děngdài nǐ de guīqī
         天 空 中 虽然 飘 着 雨 我 依然 等 待 你 的 归期 #
         REPEAT ★

          wàimian de shìjiè hěn              wàimian de shìjiè hěn
         外面 的 世界 很 _____  外面 的 世界 很 _____
          dāng nǐ jué de wàimian de shìjiè hěn
         当 你 觉得 外面 的 世界 很 _____
          wǒ hái zài zhèlǐ nàixīn de děng zháo nǐ
         我 还 在 这里 耐心 的 等 着 你
         REPEAT #

          wǒ yīrán děngdài nǐ de guīqī
         我 依然 等 待 你 的 归期
```

你觉得歌手有什么感觉？

她	很	感觉	同意 / 不同意
		开心	
		伤心	
		无奈	
		其他：_____	

歌词中提到"外面的世界很精彩"，你觉得那个世界应该有什么？

那个世界有		所以	很	精彩。

你觉得那首歌应该是谁唱给谁听的呢？为什么？

你喜欢这首歌吗？你会给它多少分？请圈出来。5分最高1分最低

| 1 | 2 | 3 | 4 | 5 |

Lesson Plan
Class: Group 2
Time: 65 minutes
Lesson objectives:

1. To learn adjectives from the songs
2. To learn adverbial 很 with adjectival predicate

Time	Activities	Material needed	Theory
5'	Introducing the song to students Asking students their opinion on the song verbally	recording	Starting with music Murphey, 2013
10'	Lyrics sheet with pinyin are provided to students while adjectives are taken out. Students need to fill in the blanks	Recording Lyrics sheet	Text completion and construction Murphey, 2013
10'	Students need to complete task 1 on worksheet. Giving opinion on what do they think of the scenario of the song	Recording Lyrics sheet	Processing input activity (Vanpatten)
15'	Students are asked to do group discussion what do they have in the world outside to make it so 精彩	Recording Lyrics sheet	Processing input activity (Vanpatten)
15'	Group discussion on what relationship would be between the singer and the one she sings to	Recording Lyrics sheet	
10'	Presentation on what relationship would be between the singer and the one she sings to	Recording Lyrics sheet	
5'	Plenary Revision on the adjectives covered in this lesson	Recording Lyrics sheet	

Song will be played when students are completing the tasks given

李心洁 / 光良 恋
https://www.youtube.com/watch?v=pG1sH8V4_Ng
https://www.youtube.com/watch?v=Hy8_wQE0z9E

jiǔ kuài mǎn shēn měi lì wú lì
久　快　满　深　美丽　无力

bù yuàn chéngrèn bù yuàn miànduì wǒ zhēn de ài nǐ hěn　　　　hěn
不 愿 承认 不 愿 面对 我 真 的 爱 你 很 _____ 很
yī gè xiàoróng yī jù huà yǔ dōu ràng wǒ xīntiào hěn　　　　hěn
一个 笑 容 一句 话 语 都 让 我 心 跳 很 _____ 很
měi gè sīsuǒ měi gè yùwàng quán bèi nǐ zhànjù hěn　　　　hěn
每个 思索 每个 欲望　全 被 你 占 据 很 _____ 很
wúfǎ píngjìng bù xiǎng tòulù yīnwèi ài nǐ kuàilè hěn　　　　hěn
无法 平 静 不 想　透露 因为 爱 你 快乐 很 _____ 很
qíngyuàn zuì sǐ zài mèng lǐ dāng yīqiè dōu biàn dé
情 愿 醉 死 在 梦 里 当 一切 都　变 得 _____
qíngyuàn wéi nǐ ér _____　dāng nǐ hūhuàn wǒ de míngzi
情 愿 为 你 而 _____　当 你 呼唤 我 的 名字
qíngyuàn mòmò de yǐncáng dāng tā zhǐ shì yī gè cuòwù
情 愿 默默 的 隐 藏　当 它 只 是 一 个 错误
qíngyuàn hěn jiǔ de yǐhòu dāng yīqiè dōu bèi shíjiān chōngdàn
情 愿 很 久 的 以后　当 一切 都 被 时间　冲 淡
wǒ zhǐ huì gèng ài nǐ
(我 只 会 更 爱 你)

听完这首歌你觉得歌手的心情怎么样？

她	很	感觉	同意 / 不同意
		开心	
		甜蜜	
		不知所措	
		其他: _____	

歌词说「一句话语 都让我心跳很快很快」，你觉得他应该跟她说了什么？

你觉得唱歌的人会是第一次喜欢别人吗？为什么？请跟同学讨论一下。

	原因	歌词
第____次喜欢别人		

其实这首歌也有男生唱过。
你觉得谁适合这首歌？为什么？
我喜欢 男生 / 女生 唱这首歌，因为

他 / 她	很	_____。

你喜欢这首歌吗？你会给它多少分？请圈出来。5分最高1分最低

1	2	3	4	5

Lesson Plan

Class: Group 2
Time: 65 minutes
Lesson objectives:

1. To learn adjectives from the songs
2. To learn adverbial 很 with adjectival predicate

Time	Activities	Material needed	Theory
5'	Introducing the song to students Asking students their opinion on the song verbally	recording	Starting with music Murphey, 2013
10'	Lyrics sheet with pinyin are provided to students while adjectives are taken out. Students need to fill in the blanks	Recording Lyrics sheet	Text completion and construction Murphey, 2013
10'	Students need to complete task 1 on worksheet. Giving opinion on what do they think of the scenario of the song	Recording Lyrics sheet	Processing input activity (Vanpatten)
15'	Discussion 4–5 students in a group Whether students think it should be the first love for the singer. Students should find evidence from the lyrics.	Recording Lyrics sheet	Pop song: discussion Murphey, 2013
5'	Introducing the song sung but a male singer	Recording Lyrics sheet	Background music Murphey, 2013
15'	4–5 students in a group Discussion on whether a male or female singer is more suitable for the song	Recording Lyrics sheet	Pop song: discussion Murphey, 2013
5'	Plenary Revision on the adjectives covered in this lesson	Recording Lyrics sheet	

Two songs will be played when students completing the tasks given

鄭希怡 容祖兒 蔡卓妍 鍾欣潼 最近比較煩
http://www.youtube.com/watch?v=OrDxlcfdv0o

Sa:
最近比較煩 比較煩 比較煩
從一開始就不怎麼喜歡上班
卻每天工作到很晚
喜歡電視劇也沒法收看

Joey:
最近比較煩 比較煩 比較煩
總覺得愛情不是預像的簡單
現在只預留個遺憾
接著大風雨撐起把雨傘

Yumiko:
最近比較煩 比較煩 比較煩
結婚的禮物(沒一份特)很難
我叫媽媽不要其煩每天追錢
[Yumi 什麼時候生一個 baby]
其心 始怪跟

Gillian:
最近比較煩 比較煩 比較煩
我身得不確怎麼沒有人喜歡
沒一個心的胸圍
也許是我注定要流浪

Joey:
最近比較煩 比較煩 比較煩
我覺得我的世界要夢不嘛
把夢想實現很困難
努力加運氣 這個題難

Yumiko:
最近比較煩 布煩 也比煩
我很久沒有站在舞台上方
現在仍繼續 有點不習慣
如喜歡場有有你的好伙伴

Joey: 人生太多比戰所以麻煩
Yumiko: 現在每天只預回來吃飯
Sa/Gillian: 我的的狗表我快樂不嘛
據著掛上跑跑笑的模樣
All: 沒有什麼天大遺禍
看著前力 搔風起吶
世界不會給你太多麻煩

Yumiko: 某個師傅敗我成功很難
害我事倍功半十年時光
Sa: 相累不嘛 相逢卻不簡單
Joey: 看歌嘉疲 努力摩眉甲凡
All: 麻煩 我很很煩 麻煩 麻煩
麻煩 我很很煩 麻煩 麻煩

Yumiko: 最近比較煩
Sa: 比較煩
Gillian: 我比較煩
我其真沒有預像的原度驅強
Joey: 不是在意勝利內強光
Yumiko/Sa: 尋找在自己要走的方向

Gillian: 最近比較煩
Sa: 比較煩
Joey: 比較煩
人生 造一規踏有你門陪伴
Sa/Gillian: 姊妹內關心充滿過暖
Yumiko: 將來有寶貝一起煩惱...

All:
不煩 我不煩 只一點點 你比我煩
我不煩 我不煩 只一點點 那不算煩
我不煩 我不煩 只一點點 你和我一樣
我不煩 我不煩 只一點點 原不煩煩 不煩

听完這首歌你有什么感覺？

我覺得	很	感覺	同意 / 不同意
		开心	
		伤心	
		无聊	
		其他	
		_____	

歌詞中提到"哭泣流淚的微笑了？"，你覺得這是一個怎樣的微笑？

我覺得這個微笑	很	

听這首歌，你覺得歌手應該是怎樣的一个人，畫下來并形容一下。

請填上他的特征：

他的額頭		
他的鼻子		
他的耳朵	很	
他的口		
他		

你覺的這首歌想说什么？

你喜歡這首歌嗎？你會給它多少分？請圈出來，5分最高 1分最低

1	2	3	4	5

Lesson Plan
Class: Group 2
Time: 65 minutes
Lesson objectives:

1. To learn adjectives from the songs
2. To learn adverbial 很 with adjectival predicate

Time	Activities	Material needed	Theory
5'	Introducing the song to students Asking students their opinion on the song verbally	recording	Starting with music Murphey, 2013
10'	Lyrics sheet with pinyin are provided to students while adjectives are taken out. Students need to fill in the blanks	Recording Lyrics sheet	Text completion and construction Murphey, 2013
10'	Students need to complete task 1 on worksheet. Giving opinion on what do they think of the scenario of the song	Recording Lyrics sheet	Processing input activity (Vanpatten)
15'	Students are asked to imagine the appearance of the singer by just listening to the song They are required to draw and write a short description	Recording Lyrics sheet	Processing input activity (Vanpatten)
5'	Introducing the background of the chorus	Recording Lyrics sheet	
15'	4–5 students in a group Discussion on whether the song is about. After discussion they are required to write down their thoughts in 50 words	Recording Lyrics sheet	Pop song: discussion Murphey, 2013
5'	Plenary Revision on the adjectives covered in this lesson	Recording Lyrics sheet	

Song will be played when students are completing the tasks given

References

Ayotte, S. (2004). *The acquisition of verb forms through song.* Unpublished doctoral dissertation of Michigan State University.

Barber, E. (1980). Language acquisition and applied linguistics. *ADFL Bulletin, 12,* 2632–2632.

Celce-Murcia, M. (1991). Grammar pedagogy in second and foreign language teaching. *TESOL Quarterly, 25*(3), 459. https://doi.org/10.2307/3586980

Census and Statistics Department. (2011). *2011 population census summary results.* Retrieved from https://www.census2011.gov.hk/pdf/EM.pdf

Census and Statistics Department. (2016). *2016 population by-census summary results.* Retrieved from https://www.bycensus2016.gov.hk/data/snapshotPDF/Snapshot10.pdf

Csikszentmihalyi, M. (2013). *Flow: The psychology of happiness*. Random House.
Euyoque-Garcia. (2002). *The impact of music upon oral language proficiency in a group of second-language kindergartners*. Unpublished master's thesis of California State University.
Farley, A., & McCollam, K. (2005). Learner readiness and L2 production in Spanish: Processability theory on trial. *Estudios de lingüística aplicada, 40*, 47–69.
Fitch, W. T. (2006). The biology and evolution of music: A comparative perspective. *Cognition, 100*(1), 173–215. https://doi.org/10.1016/j.cognition.2005.11.009
Krashen, S. D. (1981). *Second language acquisition and second language learning*. Oxford University Press.
Krashen, S. D. (1982). *Principles and practice in second language acquisition*. Pergamon.
Krashen, S. D. (1983). The din in the head, input, and the language acquisition device. *Foreign Language Annals, 16*(1), 41–44. https://doi.org/10.1111/j.1944-9720.1983.tb01422
Krashen, S. D. (2011). *The compelling (not just interesting) input hypothesis*. Conference paper presented at The English Connection (KOTESOL), Korea. Retrieved from https://koreatesol.org/sites/default/files/pdf_publications/TECv15n3-11Autumn.pdf
Krashen, S. D. (2015). The Ecstacy Hypothesis. *Peerspectives, 14*, 7–9. Retrieved from http://www.sdkrashen.com/content/articles/2015._the_ecstacy_hypothesis.pdf
Krashen, S. D., & Terrell, T. D. (1983). *The natural approach: Language acquisition in the classroom*. Prentice Hall Europe.
Lao, C. Y., & Krashen, S. (2000). The impact of popular literature study on literacy development in EFL: More evidence for the power of reading. *System, 28*(2), 261–270. https://doi.org/10.1016/s0346-251x(00)00011-7
Loh, E. K. Y., Tam, L. C. W., & Lau, K. C. (2018). Moving between language frontiers: The challenge of medium of instruction policy for Chinese as a second language in Hong Kong. *Language Policy, 18*(1), 131–153. https://doi.org/10.1007/s10993-018-9465-7
Long, M. (1991). Focus on form: A design feature in language teaching methodology. In K. De Bot, R. Ginsberg, & C. Kramsch (Eds.), *Foreign language research in cross-cultural perspectives* (pp. 39–52). John Benjamins. https://doi.org/10.1075/sibil.2.07lon
Margulis, E. H. (2014). *On repeat: How music plays the mind*. Oxford University Press.
Murphey, T. (1989). The when, where, and who of pop lyrics: The listener's prerogative. *Popular Music, 8*(2), 185–193. https://doi.org/10.1017/s0261143000003378
Murphey, T. (2013). *Music and song – Resource books for teachers*. Oxford University Press.
Pyper, M. J. (2005). *Music and motivation in the second language college classroom*. Unpublished doctoral dissertation of Michigan State University.
Ray, B., & Seely, C. (2004). *Fluency through TPR Story-telling* (4th ed.). Command Performance Language Institute.
Redmond, M. L. (2013). *Action research in the world language classroom*. IAP.
Rodrigo, V., Krashen, S., & Gribbons, B. (2004). The effectiveness of two comprehensible-input approaches to foreign language instruction at the intermediate level. *System, 32*(1), 53–60. https://doi.org/10.1016/j.system.2003.08.003
Shei, C. (2014). *Understanding the Chinese language: A comprehensive linguistic introduction*. Routledge.
Skehan, P. (1996). A framework for the implementation of task-based instruction. *Applied Linguistics, 17*(1), 38–62. https://doi.org/10.1093/applin/17.1.38
Terrell, S. (2012). *Elements of music and speech: A methodology to incorporate the elements of music into teaching pronunciation to speakers of English as a Second Language*. Unpublished doctoral dissertation of The University of Texas.
Tsai, C., Chen, R., & Tsai, T. (2014). The arousing and cathartic effects of popular heartbreak songs as revealed in the physiological responses of listeners. *Musicae Scientiae, 18*(4), 410–422. https://doi.org/10.1177/1029864914542671
VanPatten, B. (1996). *Input processing and grammar instruction in second language acquisition*. Greenwood Publishing Group.

Williamson, V. (2014). *You are the music: How music reveals what it means to be human.* Icon Books.
Wong, W. (2005). *Input enhancement: From theory and research to the classroom.* McGraw-Hill Humanities, Social Sciences & World Languages.
吕叔湘. (1979). 漢語語法分析問題. 北京: 商務印書館.
王還. (1995). 对外汉语教学语法大纲. 北京: 北京語言學院出版社.

Part III
The Language Trajectory: Reading and Writing Development

Learning Chinese as a Second Language in Hong Kong: The Needs of the Learners in Writing

Mark Shiu-kee Shum and Dan Shi

Abstract Chinese language has been considered to be of importance for South Asians with low socio-economic status to obtain upward mobility (Shum MSK, Gao F, Tsung L, Ki WW. J Multiling Multicult Dev 32(3):285–297, 2011). However, South Asian ethnic minority students as a disadvantaged group of second language learners, lack efficient pedagogical support in Chinese language learning in Hong Kong. This study aims to understand the writing difficulties and learning needs of these students in order to prepare them for targeted pedagogic intervention for better Chinese language acquisition. Based on the students' pre-tests and interview data, genre-based "Reading to Learn, Learning to Write" (R2L) assessment criteria were used to evaluate and identify the deficiencies in the students' writings. The findings lay a solid foundation for teaching that would be specific to the needs of language learning of South Asian ethnic minority students in Hong Kong.

1 Introduction

In Hong Kong, Chinese language became a compulsory subject for all students after Hong Kong reunified with China in 1997. Besides the local residents in Hong Kong, there exists over 8% of South Asian ethnic minorities among its whole population, who are mainly Indonesians, Filipinos, Indians, Pakistanis, Nepalese, Thai and others. They immigrated to Hong Kong with different historical, socio-economical, and family reasons, sharing different labour force from various walks of life for living. For local South Asian students who learn Chinese as a second language, insufficient language learning skills and inappropriate teaching pedagogy led to their

M. S.-k. Shum (✉)
The University of Hong Kong, Pok Fu Lam, Hong Kong
e-mail: mskshum@hku.hk

D. Shi
University of Nottingham Ningbo China, Ningbo, China
e-mail: Dan.Shi@nottingham.edu.cn

low proficiency in Chinese (Troia, 2006; Tsung et al., 2010; Zhang et al., 2011). It is thus essential for schools to teach knowledge of Chinese written language, as well as to teach it explicitly (Berninger & Winn, 2006). Through explicit teaching and learning at the end of their schooling, South Asian students will attain a higher proficiency in the various literacy tasks (genres) demanded by schools and by society. It is of great importance to teach the knowledge of Chinese written language explicitly. However, it is even more fundamental to identify the specific aspects of knowledge with regard to Chinese written language that local South Asian students are lacking in prior to in-class teaching. Once the symptoms have been determined, the pedagogic intervention is more straight to the point in catering for the learning needs of the South Asian students in Chinese language education.

Accordingly, the current study is aimed at understanding the writing difficulties and learning needs of the South Asian ethnic minority students in Hong Kong in order to prepare them for targeted pedagogic interventions for better Chinese language acquisition, especially in Chinese language writing. It has applied Halliday's (1985) Sydney School genre-based approach to the field of second language learning for ethnic minorities in Hong Kong, with the use of "Reading to Learn, Learning to Write" (R2L) assessment criteria in Context, Discourse, Grammar, and Graphic Features for writing evaluation across genres. The work attempts to enhance teaching and learning Chinese as a Second Language (CSL) by making use of a genre-based approach, with the South Asian ethnic minority students in Hong Kong as our research participants. The genres focused on in the current study are narration and explanation. According to the students' writing of these two genres, the situation related to their Chinese language writing has been identified in order to provide pedagogic support to facilitate their learning.

2 Literature Review

From a textual perspective, writing is an integral aspect of literacy, in collaboration with reading (Hyland, 2007). The ability to read and write holds the key to participation in social practices, with involvement of human activities. In addition to its communicative role in socio-cultural events, writing is also perceived as "a cognitive act" representing the writer's imagination, knowledge and experiences (McCutchen, 2006). Recent research shows the influence of cognitive factors on students' writing performance (Guan et al., 2014; Shum et al., 2014). One important factor is working memory, which has been found to have a direct bearing on Chinese text comprehension and writing (Guan et al., 2014; Shum et al., 2014). Furthermore, as noted by Hyland (2007), writing has been understood as "personal empowerment" that enables students to gain access to socio-cultural resources and engagement (Hyland, 2007).

The pedagogy of writing has been developed over years of educational practice ranging from the traditional learning of language structure organization in writing to the recent development of the genre-based approach to writing (Hyland, 2012). The genre-based approach attaches great importance to text types and meanings in writing that are integral to different social contexts and purposes (Hyland, 2003). As demonstrated by Donovan and Smolkin (2006), exposure to a diversity of genres in writing is conducive to the teaching and learning of writing to/by second language learners in their primary and secondary schooling (Hyon, 1996). The current research proposes to find ways of enhancing the writing achievement of ethnic minority students in Hong Kong by identifying their Chinese language writing difficulties and learning need within secondary school settings. Since 2000, various studies have been done in identifying the subject-specific genres in Chinese found in the Hong Kong public examinations in the school subjects; Physics, Chemistry, Biology, History, Geography, Economics and Liberal Studies (Shum et al., 2003a, b, 2004, 2006, 2012a, b; Shum, 2004, 2006). Subject-specific genre pilot teaching in collaboration with the Education Bureau was also conducted in order to promote the learning of various school subjects in Chinese (Shum & Ki, 2008). The finding revealed a significant improvement by students in learning school subjects through Chinese. These above-noted research studies of learning through Chinese have laid the basis for the proposed study of learning Chinese as a second language, which is geared towards enriching the existing body of knowledge of genre-based literacy for second language Chinese learners in Hong Kong.

3 Methodology

With the support of funding from the Hong Kong Education Bureau, there has been a provision of Student Support Programmes (SSP) on Chinese language learning for South Asian ethnic minority students since 2007. A strong relationship has thus been built between the schools that recruit non-Chinese speaking students and the research team. Among those schools, two local direct subsidy schools, in which a large proportion of enrolled students are South Asian ethnic minorities, have shown their interest and willingness in participating in this proposed research. Supported by these two secondary schools, the present research can be undertaken more widely to facilitate the South Asian ethnic minority students in Hong Kong in learning Chinese and enhancing their capability of Chinese written composition.

A taxonomy of genres from the literacy tasks in schools and in society has been developed (Shum, 2015). The functions and forms of some basic genres in school curriculum in Hong Kong are shown in Table 1 (Shum, 2015). It is essential for students to master these genres in order to achieve academic success. This research focuses on the two most common genres: narration and explanation. With a view to understanding the obstacles faced by non-Chinese speaking students in Chinese language writing, a pre-test of task writing before pedagogic intervention was undertaken to measure the students' performance in their genre-based Chinese written composition of narration and explanation. The participants were secondary Form 2 students who should have some sense of the two genres. All the writings were evaluated and analyzed by "Reading to Learn" assessment criteria.

Table 1 Functions and Forms of Basic Genres in Hong Kong School Curriculum

Genre	Function	Schematic structure
Narration	*Resolving a complication in a story*	Orientation^Complication^Resolution^Evaluation
Description	*Describing a person or a phenomenon*	Overview of description^Description 1-n ^ Conclusion
Explanation	*Explaining a sequence or multiple causes or multiple effects*	Phenomenon^Explanation Sequence 1-n
Exposition	*Arguing for a point of view*	Position^ Argument 1-n^ Reposition
Review	*Evaluating a book or a literary text*	Orientation^Text description^ Comment

The "Reading to Learn" assessment criteria are based on four textual components, i.e. Context, Discourse, Grammar, and Graphic Features. Context mainly covers the scoring items of writing purpose, staging, phases, field, tenor and mode, while Discourse focuses on the lexico-grammatical aspects of lexis, appraisal, conjunction, reference and grammar used in the writings. The last dimension, Graphic Features, emphasizes the students' fundamental skills of spelling, punctuation and text presentation. The scoring system and assessment criteria of each dimension range from 0 to 3, with 14 items in total constituting the highest score of 42. All the students' writings were sent to two independent markers who had been trained to mark via the "Reading to Learn" assessment criteria and were also experienced in the marking of GCSE Chinese examination writings. The writing samples composed by the student representatives of low, medium and high levels of achievement nominated by the teachers of these two targeted local secondary schools are analyzed and discussed. Focus group interviews were conducted to solicit information from the students themselves from the insiders' point of view in perceiving their own difficulties and learning needs in Chinese language writing.

4 Results and Discussion

Figure 1 shows the assessment results of the students' writing performance in the composition of narration and explanation. All the students with different levels of achievement were invited to participate in the writing tasks of genre writing without any intervention. The purpose of the genre-based literacy tasks designed for the students is to help diagnose the weakness and problems existing in their writings that hinder their literacy development at the secondary institutional level. The "Reading to learn" writing assessment is composed of 14 items covering four main dimensions: Context, Discourse, Grammar, and Graphic Features. Each dimension has different foci and emphases in mediating the ingredients that constitute a good piece of writing. As shown in Fig. 1, it was found that the students with all levels of achievement (low, medium, high) performed better in narrative writing than in explanatory writing, especially in the dimensions of Context and Discourse.

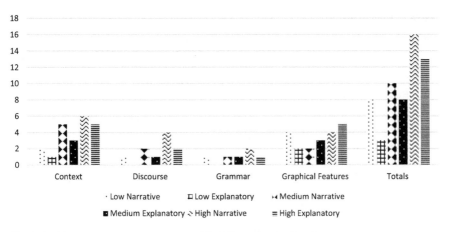

Fig. 1 Writing assessment across genres with different levels of students

In the dimension of Context, most of the students could fulfil the purpose of writing with different genres. The narration is composed to engage the readers in story telling for recreation, while the explanation intends to provide information for readers with the function of informing. As to Staging and Phases, the students were found to be more familiar with the stages of narrative writing than with those of explanation. Phase can be referred to as the steps that a text follows within each stage, which can hardly be detected either in their narrative or their explanatory writings. The three core elements of Field, Tenor, and Mode in Context were scored approximately around 1 and 0. Most of the students in all three ranges of achievement were able to show a weak evidence of Field and Mode in constructing the main content of the text with a fundamental level of written language. However, no evidence of Tenor was found, especially for low and medium levels of students, who failed to build relationships with the readers in engaging them in the plot and informing them of factual messages. With respect to the discourse, attention was diverted to the lexico-grammatical level rather than the contextual level. The use of lexis, as a key element in Field construction, indicates the basic lexical resources that the students have got mastery of at their current stage of schooling. However, little evidence was found in the use of Appraisal, Conjunction or Reference in the students' writings. Few evaluating words were found as Appraisal for personal feeling expression, behavioural action judgement and environment appreciation, with few conjunctions in sentence connection and unclear use of pronouns in references. Detailed analysis was undertaken in the following sample case studies in which the written samples were nominated by the teachers to represent different levels of performance.

Table 2 shows the writing performance of one of the student representatives as a high achiever in the genre-based composition tasks of narration and explanation. In the pre-test before teaching, each student was required to write a narration about a school picnic and an explanation regarding their favourite sports. As shown in the sample writings of the high achiever, it was found that the student had difficulty in

Table 2 High Achiever

Narration	Explanation
星期一，學校有一個旅行。我、朋友、老師和同學一起去旅行。我們一起去沙田旅行。*(Orientation)* 我們做了很多活動。我們玩了籃球、足球和很多活動。我和小文一起玩籃球玩得很開心。*(Record of events)* 小文 有參加了學校籃球比賽。可是小文沒法子拿到冠軍。她很不開心。*(Complication)* 老師、同學和朋友鼓勵她，讓我相信自己的能力。*(Resolution)* 我學到我們要相信自己的能力。*(Evaluation)* Monday, school had a "picnic". My friends, teachers, classmates and I went to picnic together. We went to Shatin for picnic together. *(Orientation)* We did many activities. We played basketball, football and many activities. Siu Man and I played basketball together happily. *(Record of events)* Siu Man had participated the school basketball competition. However, Siu Man could not get the champion. She was very unhappy. *(Complication)* Teachers, classmates and friends encouraged her, let me believed my ability. *(Resolution)* I had learnt we have to believe our own ability. *(Evaluation)*	我最喜歡的運動項目是打羽毛球。他是一個打球的運動。 *(Phenomenon)* 我也最喜歡同我的最好的朋友一起打羽毛球。她們也喜歡打球。 *(Explanation 1)* 我和我的最好的朋友一起在星期六和日打球。我們打得很開心! *(Explanation 2)* My favourite sport is playing badminton. It is a ball game. *(Phenomenon)* I also like playing badminton with my best friend together. They like playing ball too. *(Explanation 1)* My best friend and I play badminton together on Saturday and Sunday. We play very happily! *(Explanation 2)*

telling the difference between recount and narration. Students tend to confuse narration with recount. Although recount and narration share the same function of engaging, they are distinct from each other in genre construction. The purpose of a narrative story is to engage the readers by solving a problem or resolving a complication among the major characters designed in the plot, while a recount aims to record a series of events without any involvement of complications.

As shown in Table 2, the high achiever is able to partially fulfil the writing purpose based on the understanding of the narrative writing task of a memorable experience on a school picnic trip, where a complication event arises with the lesson learnt from the happenings afterwards. The writing begins with an orientation which introduces the day, people involved and the place of school picnic. It is then followed by a record of events of different activities organized, and a complication indicating a discouraging event that Siu Man did not obtain the champion in the basketball competition. The writing is finally concluded by a resolution which describes how teachers and classmates encourage Siu Man with an evaluation which summarizes the lesson he has learnt. However, the writing is mixed up the stages of narrative and recount with a record of events and different activities joined during the school picnic, followed by a rushed ending of an evaluation with personal feeling expression as a typical usage of appraisal. Due to the different language systems, the student also found difficulty in writing Chinese characters and felt confused in the word choices with similar forms.

In terms of explanatory writing, the student was able to construct the writing with distinctive stages for explanations which include phenomenon and a series of explanations. The writing is started by indicating her favourite sport, i.e. playing badminton. It is followed by explaining the type of sport it belongs to, the people who play with her and the frequency of doing the sport in a week. It is then concluded by expressing the feeling of playing badminton. From the writing, it was reflected that the student was able to identify some key stages and requirements of writing an explanatory writing. In terms of language use, the student was able to use various process and appraisal in the pre-test. For the process, the student could use relational process, mental process and material process in the writing (e.g. "是" (is) to clarify the favorite sport, "喜歡" (like) to indicate her feeling, and "打" (hit, play) to indicate the action for the sport). As to the appraisal, she used the appreciation appraisal "最喜歡的" (most favourite) to describe the value of playing badminton and used the affect appraisal "很開心" (very happily) to express the feeling of playing it with her friend. However, little attention was paid to the use of cohesion especially in the explanatory writing to connect the ideas, and at the meantime, the student was not able to apply as much lexicogrammar as those used in narrative writing in expressing their ideas. Although the sample writing has correct syntactic structure, a diversified use of sentence is suggested with space for improvement to avoid a monotonous use of simple SVO structure as majority.

As a representative of high achievers, the student had a relatively better command of lexico-grammatical resources in comparison with the medium and low achiever, and a clear track of the person or thing throughout the text by using appropriate personal and demonstrative pronouns, though with a lack of conjunctions to help establish logical relationships between sentences in the explanatory writing. Their insufficient genre knowledge results in their confusion in genre writing with narration and recount. The inappropriate development of stages and phases further leads to a weak construction of plot, settings and characters in stories and encourage a more flourishing development in the field of information in factual texts. Without an attractive storyline or convincing explanation, it would be difficult for readers to be emotionally engaged and objectively informed in texts.

Table 3 shows the writing performance of one of the medium achievers in fulfilling the literacy task of narrative and explanation writing in L2 Chinese language classroom. Like the representative high achiever in Table 2, the medium achiever was also able to understand the task requirement and appropriately realize the writing purpose in genre-based composition. However, it is found that the student wrote the narration with incomplete schematic structure. The text starts

Table 3 Medium Achiever

Narration	Explanation
今年學校的旅行，我們去了countryside。我們、同學和老師一起去旅行。我和我的同學一起打藍球、打排球、打本球和吃。 *(Orientation)* 旅行時有一有趣的事情發生, 我的朋友lost 他的書。*(Complication)* 我學到Take care of your belongings. *(Evaluation)* Our school picnic of this year, we went to countryside. We, classmates, and teachers went picnic together. My classmates and I played basketball, played volleyball, played baseball and ate. *(Orientation)* There was an interesting thing happened during picnic, my friend 'lost' his book. *(Complication)* I have learnt 'Take care of your belongings'. *(Evaluation)*	我最喜歡的運動時木球, 因為玩木球是我很開心。 *(Phenomenon)* 木球是一chong yong木和球的運動。 *(Explanation 1)* 我和我的哥哥一起玩木球, 我的哥哥kao我玩木球。我和我的哥哥mui天一起玩木球, 玩木球很好玩。 *(Explanation 2)* My favourite sport "time" cricket, because playing cricket is I am very happy. *(Phenomenon)* Cricket is a 'chong' 'yong' wood and ball sport. *(Explanation 1)* My elder brother and I play cricket together, my elder brother 'kao' me play cricket. My elder brother and I play cricket 'mui' day, playing cricket is very funny. *(Explanation 2)*

with an orientation clearly indicating where they went for a school picnic and what they did during that picnic, followed by the complication of a special event that his friend lost the book, yet a resolution describing how they address the issue is missing. Although the student intended to write evaluation, it was not clarified in detail lacking in comprehensiveness in the construction of the narration. It can be seen from the writing that the student was able to describe the place, the people involved and the activities done in the school picnic by using the material processes "去" (went), "打" (played) and "吃" (ate) to carry out the activities they had done during the day. However, the student used limited functional language by only referring to the appreciation appraisal "有趣的" to describe the happening and no cohesion was deployed to show the sentence relationship. The student's composition of the explanatory writing also concords with the stages of phenomenon identification about their favourite sports at the very beginning and the explanation of the identified sport in detail immediately afterwards. However, the student only briefly touched upon the staging distribution of this genre specific text, without further development in phases. Based on the understanding of the task requirement, the student has a fundamental awareness of plot construction in stories as well as field elaboration in explanation. But due to a lack of elaboration in complication, the writer also fails to build tensions to attract the reader's attention in the narrative writing.

As seen from the text, it can be noticed that the writer misleadingly used many English wordings to replace Chinese character writings in both narrative and explanatory writing because of a relatively lower level of Chinese language proficiency, especially in the lexico-grammatical scale of language acquisition. Most of the words written in English are the core words that are indispensable for field construction, which hinder the text comprehension of Chinese language readers (e.g. Cricket is a 'chong' 'yong' wood and ball sport), where the student used phonics with similar pronunciation to replace the Chinese word "種" (kind) by 'chong' and "用" (made up of) by 'yong'. The text is also deficient in the application of the lexical resources of appraisal to express emotional feelings towards a series of happenings during the trip in a school picnic as well as to appreciate the writer's favourite sport to engage the readers. With little involvement of conjunctions, the logical relationship between the sentences throughout the whole text has been weakened to some extent and co-structured with a relatively loose bunch of sentences, leading to a weak performance on the graphic features.

Table 4 shows the student's performance of narrative and explanatory writing as sample texts of the low achievers. Due to the student's weak Chinese language proficiency, the student's writing performance tends to be restricted by their limited lexico-grammatical resources. In comparison with the writing samples composed by the high and medium achievers, the student at the relatively low level of achievement was not able to write a complete text of narration and explanation. The first text of narration is a typical recount, only describing a flow of events happening in the school picnic mechanically recording the events (dancing and singing Chinese songs) the student experienced one after another during the school trip. It fails to show any complication or conflict involved which indicates a problematic happening and the resolution showing relevant solutions as well as the evaluation expressing the feelings towards the happenings. It becomes even worse in explanation writing with only one incomplete sentence composed with no identification of phenomenon and elaboration for detailed explanation. The field thus fails to be well constructed, with no climate of expectation for reader engagement.

When it comes to the dimension of discourse, no traces were detected for any use of appraisal, conjunction and reference. There are no expressions of personal feelings, no judgement of moral behaviours in narration and no appreciation of the phenomenon under explanation. Each sentence exists separately, with no conjunctions logically relating them into a whole. The student has little sense of reference to keep track of the person and thing with personal and demonstrative pronouns. This pre-test reflects the student's weak foundation of Chinese literacy by knowing only a few simple Chinese characters and using most English wordings for meaning

Table 4 Low Achiever

Narration	Explanation
on Sunday, 我去學校旅行。我和老師, 朋友去旅行。(*Orientation*) 我們做Dancing和Sing中文 Songs All Night。After Sunday (*Record of Events*) on Sunday, I went to school picnic. My teachers, friends and I went travelling. (*Orientation*) We did Dancing and sing Chinese Songs All Night. After Sunday (*Record of Events*)	我最喜歡的運動項目是 (*Phenomenon*) My favorite sport is (*Phenomenon*)

expression (e.g. using the English words "dancing, "sing", "song", "All night" and "After Sunday" to replace the Chinese words "跳舞", "唱", "歌", "整晚" and "星期天後" respectively). These two incomplete texts are both presented in one paragraph. Paragraphs are not used in the writings. Thus, deficiency in all these dimensions indicates students' low performance in genre writing. The results further enrich our understanding of the under-developed educational experiences of South Asian ethnic minority students in Hong Kong, especially in writing, from a linguistic perspective (Shum et al., 2012a, b).

5 Challenges Faced by Different Levels of Students in Chinese Writing

With a view to having a more thorough understanding of the students' challenges in Chinese language writing, text analysis was triangulated with semi-structured focus group interviews with the students. Each level of students, low, high, and medium achievers, was composed of two student representatives, with a total of six engaged in the interviews. The purpose was to supplement the pre-test data to explore the students' writing difficulties and learning needs from their own perceptions. Based on the interview data, the findings indicate that the students with different levels of achievement have a different focus on their perceived difficulties and learning needs in Chinese language writing.

5.1 Lack of Knowledge About Text Structure (High Achiever)

H1: Remembering the structure of the writing, like depends on letter. You have to remember the sequence of a letter...But then...but if you don't memorize the different structures of the writing skills, it's hard to for you to follow the process. Like if you're supposed to write the letter, but you don't remember the process, then you lose marks.

H2: If you forget the structure, you're gonna lose marks and it will affect your writing skills.

H3: I want to express my feelings or I want to write the words but I don't know how to write, so it's difficult for me to, you know, finish my writing very clearly. And I'm not sure... I can't be hundred percent sure if the teacher can understand, so that affects my marks.

As to the high achievers, most of the students indicated that their lack of knowledge about the schematic structure of genre-based text hindered their writing performance when they were asked about their difficulties faced in Chinese language writing. It was their deficiency of understanding of text structure that led to their poor performance in writing and even negatively influenced their writing skills and their cognitive thinking. Learning how to write properly depends pretty much on the students' genre knowledge of how the text is structured. The prerequisite for writing is to be aware of the text structure as to what is conventionally included in the context of culture for narrative and explanatory composition in order to realize their social functions of engaging and informing. Without genre knowledge, even if the high achieving students have all been equipped with ideas and lexico-grammatical resources ready for written composition, they can still not be able to write clearly and effectively due to an insufficient involvement of appropriate staging and phasing for text development. Students' contextual knowledge of genre constrains their writing creativity as well as their development of language skills in the dimension of Discourse.

5.2 Lack of Lexical Source and Variation (High/Low Achiever)

H1: *For English exactly, really, because we are very fluent in speaking. So we know what we're writing. So instead of saying 'I feel really happy', we can say 'I felt great' or 'I felt... I have really good time' Ah, Yea...but for Chinese sometimes we don't know how to describe other than using the same word over and over.*

L1: *Well, I guess I can express myself in Chinese using my basic knowledge of Chinese sense like what I've learnt in Primary because I do know like my name is that, I am that age and I am that, so I can like express my knowledge, I express myself, like writing Chinese, but I even like write more interesting stuffs because I can't just write I like that stuff, I like this stuff. So I need to write...err... learn more stuff like to know what I'm writing.*

L2: *English is much easier than Chinese. But sometimes for Chinese, the words are really hard for me. I can't find them easy, it's gonna difficult.*

Lack of lexical source and variation is another difficulty that the students with high and low levels of language proficiency usually come across in their writing practice of literacy tasks. It is mostly reflected in the use of Appraisal in the writings to express the authors' emotions and to appreciate the surroundings in narration and explanation. In English writing, they are equipped with sufficient lexico-grammatical choices to realize meaning diversity in their writing. Instead of using "happy" to express the feeling of pleasure, they are also capable of using "feeling great", "having a good time", "cheerful", even "delighted", etc. to show their enjoyment of the event they are engaged in. However, in Chinese writing, although the students of high achievers have acquired the fundamental lexis to express happiness in Chinese as "開心", they have not yet been explicitly taught how to describe feelings and thinking with some other words with similar meanings. This limitation of lexical resources is the main reason why the students have to use a word over and over again, resulting in word repetition rather than lexical variation in their Chinese writings. For lower-level students, they are confident in the basic written Chinese knowledge of their name, age and hobby to express and introduce themselves in writing, yet they are highly motivated and interested in using Chinese to write more interesting things covering a wider range of knowledge through learning how to write. Their limited lexical resources constrain their ways of expression of ideas and thoughts in writing even though they have strong motivation in learning.

5.3 *Difficulty in Memorizing Vocabulary and Writing (Medium/Low Achiever)*

M1: Sometimes we don't know how to write the vocabularies, we often forget... I often forget how to write some vocabularies which I should remember.

M2: It is easy to understand the question but sometimes it is hard to write the like... answer the questions in Chinese, because I don't know how to write some of the words. It's hard.

L1: Actually my favourite subject is Chinese. I really want to learn Chinese. But sometimes I forgot the words, so I feel it's hard for me to learn Chinese. Yea, actually I really want to learn Chinese. But, but I can't really remember all the words.

L2: I like writing Chinese writing. It came interesting to me but I find some word quite difficult because whenever I write a stroke, it's always like one stroke here but sometimes it counts wrong because it's straight, we usually see it on a paper it's like this, but basically it's like this.

L3: Sometimes if I, like, I can speak Chinese but then when it comes to writing, I can understand the question but then when I answer, I cannot write some of the Chinese words.

As for the medium and low achievers, the most challenging part in the midst of Chinese language writing is their difficulty in Chinese word memorizing and writing. Most of the students found it extremely difficult to write in Chinese. It is even more demanding for non-Chinese speaking students to memorize the Chinese words, not only with respect to their meaning, but also to the formatting of the stroke-based characters. As Chinese and English originated from different language systems, they have developed two totally different writing systems. Differently from English, Chinese characters are composed by non-alphabetic stroke-oriented constituents. To non-Chinese speaking students, the writing of Chinese characters is like drawing, which seem quite interesting to them but at the same time causes many practical problems to their memory as well as for word memorizing and writing.

During the process of Chinese writing, the students could well understand the literacy writing tasks that they were required to complete. However, having been kept informed of the topics that needed to be written up, most of the students at the low and medium level were not able to construct their thinking and feelings into writings with Chinese characters with meaning potential. However, meanings can be relatively easier to make by speaking as shared from the perspective of the students' own experience. When it comes to writing about the same question, students may fail to write their utterances into Chinese characters due to their forgetting of the stroke construction of the words that have come up in their minds. Thus, in regard to students' meaning making, writing is more challenging than speaking. Writing prevents the students' ideas from being realized. Hence, there is a great need for intensive strategies to help students to learn to recognize and write Chinese characters and wordings in order to facilitate their Chinese language writing for literacy improvement.

6 Conclusion

This study is of great significance in language teaching, learning and assessment. In order to facilitate the teaching process, identifying the symptoms faced by the students is a prerequisite to a thorough understanding of their learning process. Hence, with a view to helping students improve their writing skills, revealing their difficulties and learning needs in their L2 Chinese writing is the first step and a key to gaining access to the ways that improve the students' writing capacity. Based on the text analysis by means of Reading to Learn (R2L) assessment criteria, the students' writing difficulties at word level, sentence level and whole text level have been revealed by examining students with different levels of learning ability.

At the whole text level, the students at all levels of achievement were found to have difficulty in constructing correctly the schematic structure and the staging of narration and explanation. Their writing performance in these two genres indicates that explanatory composition is harder than narration writing. Without the support of accurate stages and detailed elaboration in phases, the writing purpose can only be partially fulfilled, leading to an underdevelopment of field, tenor, and mode for content delivery and reader engagement. At the sentence and word levels, the students were confronted with a deficiency of lexico-grammatical knowledge for syntactical and lexical variation to build the field. Some students with weaker language proficiency experienced special difficulty in Chinese character writing, even using English for meaning-making in Chinese language writing. In the process of discourse construction, students had little awareness of using appraisal to express personal feelings or subjective reflection towards the happenings in narrative writing, and did not use it to appreciate the target surroundings in explanatory composition. All writings were loosely constructed, without strong connections by conjunctions. Repetition of noun subjects instead of using pronouns was usually detected in the writings of the relatively lower achievers.

The students themselves were also aware of their own deficiency in Chinese language writing, which corresponds to and is well reflected in their writing performance. As to the high achievers, lack of genre knowledge about text structure and lexical variation are the main challenges faced by non-Chinese speaking students in the course of L2 Chinese writing. Differently from the high achievers, students at the low and medium levels found Chinese word memorizing and writing extremely difficult, thus hindering their thinking in writing when engaged in the literacy tasks. Hence, students at different levels of achievement have different kinds of difficulty in the language learning process. Once the symptoms of the students' learning problems have been identified, there is a great need for pedagogic instruction that is straight to the point, thus catering for the students' learning needs with different pedagogic devices.

References

Berninger, V. W., & Winn, W. D. (2006). Implications of advancements in brain research and technology for writing development, writing instruction, and education evolution. In C. A. MacArthur, S. Graham, & J. Fitzgerald (Eds.), *Handbook of writing research*. The Guilford Press.

Donovan, C. A., & Smolkin, L. B. (2006). Children's understanding of genre and writing development. In C. A. MacArthur, S. Graham, & J. Fitzgerald (Eds.), *Handbook of writing research*. The Guilford Press.

Guan, Q. C., Ye, F. F., Wagner, R. K., Meng, W. J., & Leong, C. K. (2014). Text comprehension mediates morphological awareness, syntactic processing, and working memory in predicting Chinese written composition performance. *Journal of Education Psychology, 106*(3), 779–798.

Halliday, M. A. K. (1985). *An introduction to functional grammar*. Edward Arnold.

Hyland, K. (2003). Genre-based pedagogies: A social response to process. *Journal of Second Language Writing, 12*, 17–29.

Hyland, K. (2007). *Teaching and researching writing*. Foreign Language Teaching and Research Press.

Hyland, K. (2012). *Second language writing*. Cambridge University Press.

Hyon, S. (1996). Genre in three traditions: Implications for ESL. *TESOL Quarterly, 30*(4), 693–722.

McCutchen, D. (2006). Cognitive factors in the development of children's writing. In C. A. MacArthur, S. Graham, & J. Fitzgerald (Eds.), *Handbook of writing research*. The Guilford Press.

Shum, M. S. K. (2004). Learning subject specific genres of chemistry through variations. In W. W. Ki, S. K. Tse, & M. S. K. Shum (Eds.), *Variation theory and the space of learning* (pp. 81–101). Hong Kong University Press.

Shum, M. S. K. (2006). Exploring an approach for teaching subject specific genres in Chinese: The case of post-colonial Hong Kong. *Australian Review of Applied Linguistics, 29*, 6.1–6.22.

Shum, M. S. K. (2015). *Subject specific genres of Liberal Studies and the skills of expression*. Hong Kong Educational Publishing Company.

Shum, M. S. K., & Ki, W. W. (2008). *Improving language and learning across the curriculum through subject specific genre teaching*. Education Bureau & the University of Hong Kong.

Shum, M. S. K., Tse, S. K., Ki, W. W., Kwong, W. L., Chan, W. F., & Lo, W. C. (2003a). *Subject specific genres of school chemistry: A resource book*. Support Centre for Teachers Using Chinese as the Medium of Instruction. The University of Hong Kong.

Shum, M. S. K., Tse, S. K., Ki, W. W., Yu, S. K., Chan, M. T., Lai, Y. W., et al. (2003b). *Subject specific genres of school economics: A resource book*. Support Centre for Teachers Using Chinese as the Medium of Instruction. The University of Hong Kong.

Shum, M. S. K., Tse, S. K., Ki, W. W., Chan, C. Y., Yuen, K. C., Yu, N. S. S., et al. (2004). *Subject specific genres of school biology: A resource book*. Support Centre for Teachers Using Chinese as the Medium of Instruction. The University of Hong Kong.

Shum, M. S. K., Tse, S. K., Ki, W. W., Chan, C. W., Kwan, W. B., & To, W. S. (2006). *Subject specific genres of school geography: A resource book*. Support Centre for Teachers Using Chinese as the Medium of Instruction. The University of Hong Kong.

Shum, M. S. K., Gao, F., Tsung, L., & Ki, W. W. (2011). South Asian students' Chinese language learning in Hong Kong: Motivations and strategies. *Journal of Multilingual & Multicultural Development, 32*(3), 285–297.

Shum, M. S. K., Gao, F., & Tsung, L. (2012a). Unlocking the racialized and gendered educational experiences of South Asian females in Hong Kong: The case study of Pakistani girls. *Asian Ethnicity, 13*(3), 251–262.

Shum, M. S. K., Ki, W. W., & Lam, J. W. I. (2012b). *Assessment for learning: Enhancing students' writing ability in Liberal Studies by subject specific genre teaching*. Centre for Advancement of Chinese Language Education and Research. The University of Hong Kong.

Shum, M. S. K., Ki, W. W., & Leong, C. K. (2014). Cognitive and linguistic factors affecting alphasyllabary language users comprehending Chinese text. *Reading in a Foreign Language, 26*(1), 153–175.

Troia, G. A. (2006). Writing instruction for students with learning disabilities. In C. A. MacArthur, S. Graham, & J. Fitzgerald (Eds.), *Handbook of writing research*. The Guilford Press.

Tsung, L., Zhang, Q. Y., & Cruickshank, K. (2010). Access to majority language and educational outcomes: South Asian background students in postcolonial Hong Kong. *Diaspora, Indigenous, and Minority Education: Studies of Migration Integration, Equity, and Cultural Survival, 4*(1), 17–32.

Zhang, Q. Y., Tsung, L., Cruickshank, K., Ki, W. W., & Shum, M. S. K. (2011). South Asian students' educational experience and attainment: Learning Chinese as a second/additional language in Hong Kong. In L. Tsung & K. Cruickshank (Eds.), *Teaching and learning Chinese as global contexts*. Continuum.

Using 'Reading to Learn, Learning to Write' (R2L) Pedagogy to Teach Explanation Genre to Non-Chinese Speaking Students in Hong Kong

Mark Shiu-kee Shum , Jojo Wan Shan Yung , and Dan Shi

Abstract The previous chapter has explored the writing needs of non-Chinese speaking (NCS) students learning Chinese as a second language (CSL). Based on text analysis, the students' writing difficulties at word level, sentence level and whole text level have been identified by examining students with different levels of learning ability. In order to provide pedagogical support to cope with the students' learning needs, this chapter introduces the "Reading to Learn, Learning to Write" (R2L) Pedagogy, explains its theoretical underpinning, and illustrates how this pedagogy can be applied in daily CSL classroom teaching. In the form of a case study which involves classroom observation, interviews and text analysis, the chapter aims to describe how R2L Pedagogy which can provide students with all-round support was applied in a Chinese second language writing class dealing with the explanation genre, and to evaluate the effectiveness of the R2L Pedagogy on enhancing the writing ability of NCS students. Through integration of reading and writing, the R2L pedagogy provided students with abundant support in language input and output. The research results indicated that NCS students showed great improvements in writing after R2L teaching.

1 Introduction

Hong Kong is an international community, with about 8.4% of its people being non-Chinese ethnicities (Census and Statistics Department, 2021). The Hong Kong Census and Statistics Department (2021) has made a statistical report on these ethnic

M. S.-k. Shum (✉)
The University of Hong Kong, Pok Fu Lam, Hong Kong
e-mail: mskshum@hku.hk

J. W. S. Yung
Hong Kong Metropolitan University, Homantin, Hong Kong
e-mail: jwsyung@hkmu.edu.hk

D. Shi
University of Nottingham Ningbo China, Ningbo, China
e-mail: Dan.Shi@nottingham.edu.cn

minorities with a detailed analysis of its demographic characteristics. After excluding foreign domestic helpers who are not permanently settled in Hong Kong, there were 301,344 ethnic minorities in 2021, making up 4.1% of the whole Hong Kong population (Census and Statistics Department, 2021). They are mostly composed of Indians, Nepalese, Pakistanis, Filipinos, Indonesians, Thais, and others. Most of them arrived in the British colonial period working as policemen, members of military forces, safety guards, construction workers etc. Their children, before Hong Kong reunited with China in 1997, chose to learn French or their home languages like Urdu, Hindi, Nepalese etc. besides English. After the handover in 1997, Chinese language, with its heightened status in Hong Kong, holds a key for non-Chinese speaking students with low socio-economic status to obtain upward mobility (Shum et al., 2011).

However, after the handover, the main medium of instruction in schools in Hong Kong is Chinese (Cantonese as the spoken form and traditional Chinese characters for the written form). In fact, the Chinese competency levels among the non-Chinese speaking students are considered inadequate for them to be taught by Chinese medium of instruction (CMI). For instance, Ku et al. (2005) found that 88.5% and 91% of non-Chinese speaking students in their research reported deficiencies in Chinese reading and writing skills respectively. Tsung et al. (2008) revealed that the non-Chinese speaking secondary school students generally had a limited Chinese vocabulary, especially the vocabulary of abstract concepts. The students were weak at discerning relations and the focuses of a speech or text. Their lowest competency was in writing, with 49% of students reported as 'poor'. A study done by the Centre for Civil Society and Governance (2012) also found that the major obstacles existing for non-Chinese speaking students learning Chinese lie mainly in learning to read and write. Yet proficiency in Chinese has become vital for non-Chinese speaking students to further study and work in Hong Kong, with Chinese language requirements for university entrance or entering into CMI schools in Hong Kong as well as for job applications to local conditions of public civil service (Loper, 2004). Therefore, the cultivation of students' reading and writing capability in Chinese is a pressing issue so as to help non-Chinese speaking students in Hong Kong to acquire Chinese language and to reinforce their Chinese language proficiency.

In response to the above issue, in this chapter, 'Reading to Learn, Learning to Write Pedagogy' (R2L). which is based on Systemic Functional Linguistic theory and the Genre-based Approach, was applied to teach Chinese as a second language to non-Chinese speaking students in Hong Kong. This pedagogy, which originated from Australia, was successfully undertaken in countries like Sweden, Finland, Denmark, Spain, Portugal and Indonesia in teaching English as a second language. Yet, the effectiveness of its application in teaching Chinese as a second language has yet to be further studied and its adaptation to Chinese contexts remains challenging. Thus this chapter aims to evaluate the effectiveness of the R2L Pedagogy in enhancing Chinese written composition performance by non-Chinese speaking students in Hong Kong. It intends to attach more empirical evidence of the gap between the curriculum expectation and actual proficiency to allow the policy officials and educators to better plan provision to support NCS.

2 Literature Review

2.1 Halliday's Systemic Functional Linguistics and Genre-Based Approach

In light of this need to understand the precise proficiency capability needs of learners, the Hallidayan system Systemic Functional Linguistics (SFL) was selected for the study. SFL proposes a functional model of language which emphasises the social functions of language. It includes the ideational meta-function to experience the inner and outer world, the interpersonal meta-function to connect each of these, and the textual meta-function to transform the above two functions into spoken or written texts (Halliday, 1994). The tripartite structure accounts for how language is intrinsically fashioned to make meaning. For language acquisition, Halliday pointed out that to learn a language is to learn how to mean (Halliday, 1975). In the past few decades, SFL theory has led to the study of language use in the social context, or genre as staged goal-oriented sociolinguistic process (Martin & Rose, 2008; Martin, 2009).

Inspired by Halliday's concept that 'Language is as it is because of the functions in which it has been involved' (Halliday, 1975; Halliday & Mathiessen, 2004), SFL theory has been applied in the development of the language teaching methodology known as Genre-based Pedagogy (Martin & Rothery, 1990; Rothery, 1994; Martin, 1999). In this approach, the aim of language teaching is to facilitate the students in completing literacy tasks in school and in society, and these literacy tasks can be identified and organised as taxonomy of genres (Rose & Martin, 2012: 128, 130). This pedagogy first identifies the kind of texts (genres) that students will have to write in their academic learning, and then provides a stage-oriented process to guide students to experience different levels of language and to scaffold their reading and writing competency through extensive classroom reading and writing activities surrounding selected texts. The teaching and learning cycle of Genre-based Pedagogy features three main phases of activity, namely Deconstruction, Joint Construction and Independent Construction (see Fig. 1). The Deconstruction phase foregrounds modelling of texts, establishing one genre as the goal and supporting students with detailed discussion of selected texts; the Joint Construction phase involves scribing another example of the genre based on suggestions from students; and the Independent Construction phase hands over responsibility to students for writing a further text in the genre on their own (Rothery, 1994).

2.2 Reading to Learn, Learning to Write Pedagogy

'Reading to Learn, Learning to Write Pedagogy (R2L)' proposed by Rose and Martin (Rose, 2008, 2012; Rose & Martin, 2012) is a further extension of Genre-based Pedagogy, to integrate the teaching of reading and writing across the

Fig. 1 Genre-based pedagogy: Teaching and learning cycle. (Rothery, 1994)

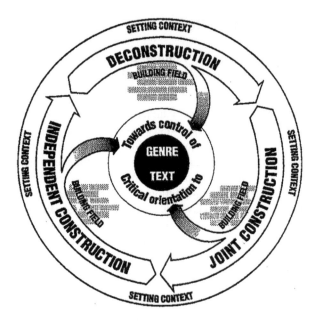

Fig. 2 3 Levels of strategies in reading to learn pedagogy. (Rose & Martin, 2012)

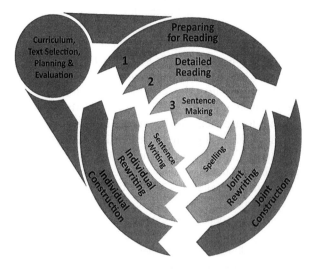

curriculum at all levels of school and beyond. It was first designed to provide pedagogical support for a disadvantaged group, helping aboriginal students in Australia with English language learning, which has been found effective in pedagogic practices (Rose, 2012). Then the pedagogy was widely adapted to second language English teaching in South Africa, Indonesia, Sweden, Finland, Denmark, Scotland, Portugal, Spain etc. with significant success (Acevedo, 2010; Rose, 2012). There are three levels of support in the teaching process (see Fig. 2). The first level includes Preparing for Reading, Joint Construction and Individual Construction, which prepares students for text comprehension and uses these reading texts as models for teacher-guided writing and student-independent writing. The second level includes Detailed Reading, Joint and Individual Rewriting, which equips students with an intensive comprehension of the reading texts and helps them with the application of the schematic structure and lexicogrammatical features learnt to their own writings. The third level includes Spelling, Sentence Making (sentence resequencing) and Sentence Writing (independent sentence structuring), which focuses on developing students' fundamental language skills at the word and sentence level, designed especially for low achievers.

The application of the three different scaffolding levels can be adjusted corresponding to students' different achievement levels. For high achievers, only the first and the second levels are employed, starting from Preparing for Reading, Detailed Reading, followed by Joint Rewriting and Joint Construction, before Individual Construction. For students with medium level of achievement, Individual Rewriting after Joint Rewriting will be practised before Joint Construction. For low achievers, more pedagogical support will be provided by scaffolding from the third level of Spelling, Sentence Making and Sentence Writing. Compared with Genre-based Pedagogy, R2L Pedagogy aims to offer more scaffolding to the students with low writing achievement. In summary, R2L Pedagogy is a very flexible teaching strategy, and teachers can design their teaching and learning cycle according to the learning needs of the students.

3 Aim of the Study and Research Questions

The current study is designed to understand whether the R2L Pedagogy helps to improve students' genre writing achievement, if so, how this can be applied in classroom practices. Since the previous chapter identified that non-Chinese speaking students were found to have more difficulty in writing explanation composition than narration writing, this study would choose explanation genre as the focus of teaching and learning.

The research questions of this study are as follows:

1. Do students improve their writing performance of explanation genre after their teacher's classroom teaching with R2L pedagogy?
2. What are the differences between their pre-test and post-test Chinese compositions of students at different levels of language skills (high, medium, low)?

4 Research Design

This study is a qualitative case study, which mainly uses a variety of research tools to collect data, such as teacher and student interviews, class observation, and comparison of pre-test and post-test. On the one hand, it can enrich the sources of research data, and on the other hand, it can make multiple cross-examinations (Merriam, 1998; Yin, 2003), so as to increase the reliability and validity of the research data.

4.1 Information Background of the Participating Teacher and NCS Students

A total of eighteen NCS students were selected as the participants in this study. All of them were secondary three students from local secondary schools in Hong Kong. They mainly came from South Asian countries such as Pakistan, the Philippines, India and Nepal. They all participated in a Chinese language learning support programme which was organized by a tertiary institution in Hong Kong and attended classes for three hours each Saturday. These students had lived in Hong Kong and studied Chinese for at least six years. They had basic listening and speaking skills in Chinese, but their reading and writing skills were relatively weak. According to the teacher's pre-assessment of the students' explanation writings, the level of Chinese language proficiency of these students was medium.

The teacher participant involved in the study was a well-qualified Chinese teacher with seven years' experience in teaching NCS students. She had studied her master's degree courses related to Systemic Functional Linguistics at university and studied the theory of the Genre teaching approach and the R2L teaching method, so she had a deep understanding of that theory.

4.2 Methodology

4.2.1 Semi-structured Interview

In this study, semi-structured interview was used to collect research data. The advantage of interviews is that the researchers can "get into" the interviewees' hearts, understand their psychological activities and inner thoughts, and honestly speak out their own thoughts and motivations (Lincoln & Guba, 1985) and personal experience (Connelly & Clandinin, 1994). The purpose of the interview in this study is to understand their opinions on the evaluation of the effectiveness of Chinese teacher and NCS students on the application of R2L teaching method and comparison of the differences between the students' writing performances in the pre-test and post-test.

4.2.2 Class Observation

In each class, the researchers went to the classroom in person to watch the class and make video recordings. The purpose of class observation was to examine how the

Chinese teacher applied the R2L teaching method to explanation genre teaching of NCS students and observe the students' reaction and performance in class, so as to evaluate the effectiveness of the Chinese teacher's application of the R2L teaching method.

4.2.3 Comparison of Pre-test and Post-test Explanation Writing

In this study, the writing assessment criteria of R2L Pedagogy were used to mark all the students' writing texts. The writing assessment criteria, as introduced in the previous chapter, are divided into four parts: Context, Discourse, Grammar and Graphic Features. Each part has its own detailed description, and the total score of the writing assessment criteria is 42 points (Rose, 2012; Rose & Martin, 2012).

4.3 Scoring Criteria

In order to evaluate the effectiveness of the R2L teaching method, the researchers collected all the participating students' pre-test writing papers and post-test writing papers, invited two experienced teachers to use the writing assessment criteria of R2L to score, and took their average scores as the final scores of the students' writing. The invitation of two independent experienced teachers as examiners refers to the Consensual Theory of Amabile (1996). Amabile pointed out that if something needs to be evaluated, it can be comprehensively evaluated by people who have a considerable knowledge of that thing. If two or more professionals have relatively consistent opinions on this thing, the relevant evaluation results will be quite reliable (Amabile, 1996). In this study, both experienced Chinese teachers had over eight years of experience in teaching Chinese to NCS students, with a focus on training NCS students for GCSE Chinese examinations. Thus, both teachers had a clear understanding of the writing grading of NCS students, thus ensuring that their grading was highly reliable.

4.4 Functional Structure of the Explanation Genre

In this study, the researchers mainly tested the explanation text. The functional structure of explanation text is mainly referred to the research of Shum (see Shum, 2010: 124–125). The function of explanation text is to explain things or phenomena according to space-time or causal relationship. It is mostly used to explain the evolution or formation process of natural or social phenomena. The explanation genre has its own Schematic Structure to realize the communication function of its texts:

Phenomenon^Explanation Sequence 1 – n^Conclusion

5 Research Findings and Discussion

5.1 Interview with the Chinese Teacher and NCS Students Before Teaching

Before the teaching, the researchers arranged for the students to take a pre-test of explanation writing and interviewed them. Students generally reported that they did not know how to arrange the content of the explanation passages; they encountered many difficulties in the structure of the passages. For example, one student said: "I do not know how to write, I do not know what the structure of the explanation passage is."

In addition, some students also failed to master some words and sentence patterns to explain and elaborate the topic. For example, one student pointed out: "I don't know which words are objective to introduce things. I only know a few words and I have no idea about what connective words to use." Therefore, all the students hoped that the Chinese teacher could teach them how to write an explanation passage that met the requirements of the explanation genre, and increase the words and connectives related to the text category.

By contrast, the Chinese language teacher thought that none of the students' writing texts was in conformity with the requirements of the explanation commentary. She said: "Their written texts, in general, are not very good. There is no explanation of the characteristics and the schematic structure is not correct. Some high achievers can write a little bit of content; but most of them can just write a few words, some low achievers even write a lot of English words and sentences instead of Chinese expressions. They can't objectively explain phenomenon and introduce items." The Chinese teacher considered that her students' pre-test writings were quite poor, there was a lot of confusion in their writings, they lacked vocabulary and had many sentence errors. Thus, she hoped that through some relevant model text teaching, she could help those students to master the discourse structure of explanation genre, increasing their application of related words and skills, so as to improve their explanation content coherence and make smooth sentences.

5.2 Teaching Objectives

After assessing the NCS students' pre-test results, the Chinese teacher set her teaching objectives as follows:

(i) Students can report the context of the explanation writing.
(ii) Students can identify the functional words in the explanation text.
(iii) Students can use explanation functional sentence patterns to write complete sentences.
(iv) Students can construct a well-structured composition in the explanation genre.

Fig. 3 R2L teaching procedure which Chinese teacher had selected

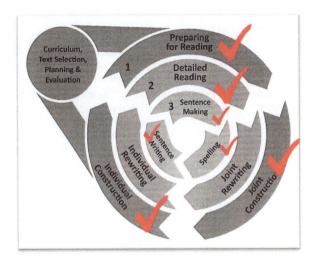

According to the above teaching objectives, the R2L teaching steps the teacher used involved four iterations:

1. The first teaching: (i) Preparing for reading; (ii) Detailed reading; (iii) Spelling
2. The second teaching: (i) Preparing for reading; (ii) Detailed reading; (iii) Sentence making
3. The third teaching: (i) Preparing for reading; (ii) Detailed reading; (iii) Intensive strategies
4. The fourth teaching: (i) Detailed reading; (ii) Joint construction; (iii) Individual construction (Fig. 3)

5.3 Teaching Process

Teaching section	Teaching process	Steps of R2L used
The first teaching	1. Preparing for reading: the students were divided into groups. Then discussed a situation about a salesman selling the latest electronic products to customers. After the discussion, wrote down the characteristics of the marketing situation in groups, and then reported the content of the marketing situation together, and shared their own group agreement to take measures.	1. Preparing for reading
	2. Listening to the recording: The teacher played the recording about the introduction of the situation, and the students listened to the recording and answered the questions.	2. Detailed reading

(continued)

Teaching section	Teaching process	Steps of R2L used
	3. Detailed reading: The teacher explained to the students the content and the meaning of the words of an expository article *TV program* by asking questions.	3. Spelling
The second teaching	1. Preparing for reading: The teacher divided the class into groups, each of which was responsible for a situation in which an electronic product was introduced and discussed and wrote the first draft together. Each group will role-play each scenario in front of the podium and be graded by the teacher and other students.	1. Preparing for reading
	2. Detailed reading: The teacher reviewed the key words and structure of the sample text *TV program* for the students by asking questions.	2. Detailed reading
	3. Sentence making: The teacher messed up the order of the key sentences in the text and then instructed the students to reorganize the sentences.	3. Sentence making
The third teaching	1. Preparing for reading: The teacher first divided the class into groups and then showed a few videos about the object scenarios, reminding each group to be responsible for presenting the questions about the object scenarios and pointing out the differences in the text written for each scenario. Different groups of students were willing to come to the podium to share their group's views on the introduction videos.	1. Preparing for reading
	2. Detailed Reading: Teachers and students worked together to deconstruct the content and words of the sample text *Facebook*.	2. Detailed reading
	3. Intensive strategies: The teacher prompted the students to compare the similarities and differences in wording and text structure between the texts *Introducing Digital Cameras* and *Introducing Electronic Blackboard*.	3. Intensive strategies
The fourth teaching	1. Detailed Reading: Teachers and students worked together to deconstruct the content and words of the sample text *Introducing High-definition TV set*.	1. Detailed reading
	2. Joint Construction: The whole class worked together to create an essay based on a common favourite object theme.	2. Joint construction

According to the above teaching process, we can see the specific application of Chinese teachers' R2L teaching method in teaching the explanation genre. At first, the Chinese teacher tried to use the "Preparing for reading" and "Detailed reading" steps. In the aspect of "Preparing for reading", the Chinese teacher set up a daily life situation of a salesman introducing the electronic products to customers before explaining the model text, and let the students discuss the content and arguments of the situation in groups, so that they could initially understand the application characteristics of explanation genre in class to arouse their interest in learning Chinese. In the aspect of "Detailed reading", the Chinese teacher attached importance to explaining the general idea and meaning of the text by asking questions and inviting the students of different abilities to answer questions. Besides giving students affirmation and appreciation, the Chinese teacher also gave the students further explanation to the questions that they asked.

In the following three iterations of teaching, the Chinese teachers mainly implemented the steps of R2L teaching method, such as "Detailed reading", "Joint construction", "Spelling" and "Sentence making". In the aspect of "Detailed reading", the Chinese teacher attached importance to explaining to the students the main content of the texts, and the meaning and use of the keywords of the texts, by asking questions.

In order to enhance students' understanding of the structure of explanation texts, the teacher attached great importance to the in-depth explanation and application of the structure of the explanation texts in the aspect of "Joint construction". She specially arranged all the students to write a new explanation text in the form of giving guidelines and tips, letting the students create a complete explanation article with the complete schematic structure to consolidate their knowledge of the explanation texts' schematic structure and their application ability with explanation genre words, such as some words about phenomena, and introduced items, such as "in recent years近年來", "more越來越多", "every每一個", etc. In the application of sentence patterns, the Chinese teacher also paid attention to the explanation texts of some specific sentence patterns, such as "for example例如……" and "take... as an example以……為例", so as to strengthen the richness and diversity of examples. The other sentence patterns like "both... 既……又……" and "Not only... but also... 不但……而且……", could help students to write their sentences of the explanation genre more clearly and accurately.

As observed in the class, the Chinese teacher was flexible in the use of the R2L teaching method and could appropriately adjust and mobilize the use of some teaching steps according to students' immediate response and their Chinese language proficiency level. The whole class atmosphere was lively, all students were engaged in various collective creation activities and group discussion activities. The interaction between teacher and students was quite strong.

5.4 The Effectiveness of Explanation Genre Teaching

5.4.1 Comparison of Test Scores of Explanation Texts

Table 1 below shows the comparison of test scores of the pre-test and post-test of explanation writing of the secondary three NCS students in this study:

Table 1 Comparison of the test scores of the whole class in explanation writing

	Context (Total marks:18)	Discourse (Total marks:12)	Grammar (Total marks:3)	Graphic feature (Total marks:9)	Total marks (Total marks:42)
Pre-test	5.7	5.2	1.3	4.1	16.3
Post-test	12.1	8.4	2.2	5.8	28.5
Progress rate	112%	62%	69%	41%	75%

As shown in Table 1, the average score of the whole class was 16.3 in the pre-test and 28.5 in the post-test, with an improvement rate as high as 75%, reflecting a great increase in the overall level of explanation writing of the students. In terms of the scores of each sub-item, the improvement rate of the students in Context, Grammar, Discourse and Graphic feature has been significantly improved, especially in the improvement rate of Context, up by 112%, and Grammar, up by 69%; the improvement rates of Discourse and Graphic features were up by 62% and 41% respectively. This reflected the students' significant progress in mastering the schematic structure, the application of functional words, the writing of sentences, and the use of punctuation, after being taught by the Chinese teacher using the R2L teaching method. In order to better understand the change of students' writing text, the researcher compared the writing texts of pre-test and post-test of three students with different Chinese language abilities and analyzed the change of their writing performances.

5.4.2 Texts Analysis for High Achiever

Pre-test writing: Introducing Computer	Post-test writing: Introducing Smart Phone
電腦的外形有很多種。我用的電腦是四方形。電腦有很多不同和很有用(*Appraisal*)的功能，例如(*Conjunction*):我們可以用電腦玩很多不同類型的 games、聽歌、看 movies、看不同的書、在網上自典 check 字和可以學不同語言的字還可以在網上做公課，很方便(*Appraisal*)。我經常都會用電腦，因為(*Conjunction*)我可以聽很新和不同的歌、我都會在電腦上做公課，因為(*Conjunction*)在電腦上做公課，我覺得很方便(*Appraisal*)和一旦(*Conjunction*)有字不知道可以看網上的自典。我沒有東西做的時候(*Conjunction*)，我都會用電腦用來過時間。(*Explanation*) Computers come in many shapes. The computer I use is boxy. Computer has many different and very **useful** (*Appraisal*) functions, **for example** (*Conjunction*): we can use the computer to play a lot of different types of games, listen to music, watch movies, read different books, self-check word on the Internet and can learn different language words, and do homework on the Internet, very **convenient** (*Appraisal*). I often use the computer, **because** (*Conjunction*) I can listen to very new and different songs, I will do homework on the computer, **because** (*Conjunction*) do homework on the computer, I think it is very **convenient** (*Appraisal*) and **once** (*Conjunction*) there is any word that I	我今日要介紹智能手機。智能手機現在很流行(*Appraisal*)，人人都有只少一部智能手機。(*Phenomenon Identification*)智能手機有很多不同的外形，例如(*Conjunction*):有大和小。大多數的手機都是四方形。還有很多不同的顏色。智能手機有很多類型，例如(*Conjunction*):有些手機在水裡都可以用，不同的公司會出不同的智能手機。智能手機的功能有很多，例如(*Conjunction*):可以用來用別人說東西、可以玩遊獻、聽音樂、做公課、上網和當(*Conjunction*)你沒有事做，可以用手機打發時間。(*Explanation*)所以(*Conjunction*)，現在人人都有智能手機，智能手機還十分方便(*Appraisal*)。(*Conclusion*) Today I'm going to talk about smart phones. Smart phone is very **popular** (*Appraisal*) now, everyone has at least one smart phone. (*Phenomenon Identification*) Smart phones come in many different shapes, **for example** (*Conjunction*), big and small. Most cell phones are boxy. And lots of different colors. There are many types of smart phones, **for example** (*Conjunction*), some mobile phones can be used in water, different companies will produce different smart phones. Smart phone has many functions, **for example** (*Conjunction*): can be used to talk to others, can play games,

(continued)

Pre-test writing: Introducing Computer	Post-test writing: Introducing Smart Phone
don't know, I can check it via the online dictionary. **When** *(Conjunction)* I don't have anything to do, I will use my computer to pass the time. *(Explanation)*	listen to music, do homework, surf the Internet and **when** *(Conjunction)* you have nothing to do, can use the mobile phone to kill time. *(Explanation)* **So** *(Conjunction)*, now everyone has a smart phone, smart phone is very **convenient** *(Appraisal)*. *(Conclusion)*

Comparison of the pre-test and post-test of the high achiever is as follow:

R2L assessment criteria	Pre-test	Post-test
Context	The writer could introduce the different characteristics of the computer point by point and present the basic explanatory structure.	The article was divided into two paragraphs, which could clearly introduce the characteristics of smart phones point by point, and more in line with the text structure of the "Phenomenon ^ Explanation Sequence 1-n ^ Conclusion" in the explanation.
	The internal stage of the explanation passage was not clearly demonstrated in the paragraph, and it lacked topic sentences and explanatory sections.	The content of the middle paragraph of the article could conform to the internal stage of the "topic sentence—explanation (examples)" of the explanation paragraph.
	The readers could get to know the basic characteristics of computers through the writer's introduction.	The article was more informative and could attract readers' interest in reading.
Discourse	The writer could initially use evaluation words to introduce the characteristics of computers, such as "useful", "convenient", but the words are monotonous.	The writer could use different evaluation words to introduce the characteristics of smart phones, such as "popular", "convenient"; and the words were more accurate.
	The writer could use different conjunctions to connect the meanings between different sentences, such as "because", "once", "for example".	The writer could use different conjunctions to connect the meanings between different sentences, such as "so", "when", "for example".
	The writer failed to use any reference words and pronouns.	The writer could accurately use different reference words and pronouns, such as "everyone", "some", etc.
Graphic feature	The writer's use of punctuation was reasonably accurate. The writer failed to segment.	The writer could use different punctuation marks correctly. Paragraphs were separated clearly, and each paragraph had a clear topic.

According to the above comparison of the written text of pre-test and post-test for the High Achiever student, it can be seen that the student basically understood that the purpose of writing explanation text was to provide information and inform readers, which is consistent with the research findings of the previous chapter

(Shum & Shi). In the pre-test text, the student could briefly introduce the appearance, type and function of the computer as well as his own use of the computer, but he added a lot of content involving personal subjective practices in the pre-test text, such as lots of "I" information mentioned in the text: "我經常" ("I often"), "我可以" ("I can"), "我都會" ("I will"), "我覺得" ("I think"), "我沒有" ("I don't"), "我都會" ("I will"), etc., which is not consistent with the writing characteristics of explanation genre that explanation writing should introduce things objectively rather than talk about subjective wishes. All these reflect students' lack of contextual knowledge in explanation writing.

In addition, as mentioned in the previous chapter by Shum and Shi, the high-level student lacked the knowledge of text structure for writing Chinese texts, which was also reflected in the pre-test text of this student. Because the student lacked the knowledge of the schematic structure of explanation genre, he only listed the information about the computer that he knew, without careful thinking and carving of the structure, format and organization of the article. Therefore, the section of the pre-test text was only one paragraph, the schematic structure was not clear, and did not know how to segment. However, in the post-test text, the content was all an objective introduction to the situation of smart phones, including the shape, colour, type and function etc. The student knew how to divide the article into two paragraphs, and the whole content conformed to the schematic structure of the explanation, including explaining the phenomenon and talking about the popularity of smart phones. Then it focused on the various features of smart phones. Finally, the popularity of smart phones and their convenience were summarized.

It can be seen that the student's post-test text was clearer and more well-organized in terms of schematic structure, and the vocabularies were more accurate. More connective words were used, and the sentence structure was more complex than the pre-test text.

5.4.3 Texts Analysis for Medium Achiever

Pre-test writing: Introducing Computer	Post-test writing: Introducing Smart Phone
我的電腦是黑和白色,哪電腦不太大不太少。香港有不同電腦,*(Phenomenon Identification)*有 super computer 有 mini-computer, 不過*(Conjunction)*上學校你會看者 micro computer, 老師會用 mini-computer 給枝同學看東西。我們可以用電腦看東西和可以聽音樂, 電腦有很多功能。我喜歡*(Appraisal)*用電腦, 因為*(Conjunction)*我喜歡*(Appraisal)*聽音樂。*(Explanation)* My computer is black and white. It's not too big or too small. There are different computers in Hong Kong, *(Phenomenon Identification)* there are super computers, there are mini-computers, **but** *(Conjunction)* in school you	年來、香港有很多人用智能手機, 所以*(Conjunction)*在香港智能手機很流行*(Appraisal)*。*(Phenomenon Identification)* 智能手機手機有不同碼和不同顏色, 列如*(Conjunction)*:黑色、白色、紅色, 智能手機有高清手機也*(Conjunction)*有三星手機。*(Explanation)* 智能手機有很多功能, 有照相、可以聽音樂和網站 Facebook。*(Explanation)*今年你只要pay 一千三十五元買這智能手機, 我們會給你(special)折。快點買吧!*(Conclusion)* In recent years, many people use smart phones in Hong Kong, **so** *(Conjunction)* smart phones are very **popular** *(Appraisal)* in Hong Kong.

(continued)

Pre-test writing: Introducing Computer	Post-test writing: Introducing Smart Phone
can see micro computers, teachers use mini-computers to show things to their classmates. We can use the computer to watch TV and listen to music. The computer has many functions. I **like** *(Appraisal)* using computer **because** *(Conjunction)* I **like** *(Appraisal)* listening to music. *(Explanation)*	*(Phenomenon Identification)* Smart phones come in different sizes and colors, **such as** *(Conjunction)* black, white and red. Smart phones come in HD, **as well as** *(Conjunction)* Samsung phones. *(Explanation)* Smart phone has many functions, taking pictures, listening to music and browsing the website Facebook. *(Explanation)* This year you only need to pay 1035 dollars for this smart phone. We will give you a special discount. Hurry up and buy! *(Conclusion)*

Comparison of the pre-test and post-test of the medium achiever is as follow:

R2L assessment criteria	Pre-test	Post-test
Context	The writer could briefly introduce the different characteristics of the computer but failed to present the basic explanation structure.	The article was divided into three paragraphs, which could introduce the characteristics of smart phones point by point, and more in line with the text structure of the "Phenomenon ^ Explanation Sequence 1-n ^ Conclusion" in the explanation.
	Paragraphs failed to clearly demonstrate the internal stage of the explanation text, and paragraphs lacked topic sentences and explanatory sections.	The content of the middle paragraph of the article could conform to the internal stage of the "topic sentence—explanation (examples)" of the explanation paragraph.
	Readers failed to understand the basic features of computers through the writer's introduction.	The article was more informative and could attract readers' interest in reading.
Discourse	The writer could initially use an evaluation word to introduce the characteristics of the computer, such as "like", but the word was monotonous.	The writer could use different evaluation words to introduce the characteristics of smart phones, such as "popular", the word was relatively accurate.
	The writer could use conjunctions to connect meanings between different sentences, such as "but" and "because".	The writer could use different conjunctions to connect the meanings between different sentences, such as "so", "and", "for example", etc.
	The writer failed to use any reference words and pronouns.	The writer could accurately use different reference words and pronouns, such as "many people", "we", etc.
Graphic feature	The writer's use of punctuation was inaccurate. The writer failed to segment.	The writer could use different punctuation marks correctly. Paragraphs were separated clearly, and each paragraph had a reasonably clear theme.

As can be seen from the comparison of pre-test and post-test texts of Medium Achiever student, his pre-test text lacked understanding of the schematic structure and contextual knowledge of explanation genre. Moreover, as mentioned in the previous chapter by Shum and Shi, Medium Achiever student's vocabulary was very insufficient, and students could not use a lot of Chinese vocabularies to express their introduction to computers, but could only use some English words to do so And this makes the content and vocabulary of the article pale. In addition, the student lacked sufficient choice of vocabulary and grammar to achieve the diversity of writing meaning, which led to a lack of changes in the vocabulary of the article. For example, the author keeps repeatedly using the words "用電腦" ("use the computer"), "我喜歡"("I like") and so on, and failed to correctly use other words to express his ideas. As a result, limited vocabulary resources limited the way this student could express his ideas and thoughts in his writing.

In addition, the previous chapter also mentioned that Medium Achiever student faced great difficulties in memorizing and writing Chinese words, which was also reflected in this student's article. Because he couldn't remember a lot of Chinese words in the article, this led to his many misspelled words, such as "哪", "者", "衪", "酉" etc.: those were obviously wrong characters. It reflected that the student's vocabulary resources were very limited and that he had great difficulty in memorizing and writing Chinese words.

As for the post-test text, the student's vocabulary had increased and the variation of vocabulary had also made great progress. Although there were still many mistakes in writing Chinese vocabularies and there were some English words appeared in the student's text, which reflected that his Chinese word level needed to be improved. The student could obviously write more words and know how to use more different words to introduce the characteristics of smart phones. Moreover, the schematic structure of the students' post-test text had made great progress compared with the pre-test text. The students' segmentation was more accurate, and the content of each paragraph could also correspond to the requirements of the schematic structure of explanation genre.

5.4.4 Texts Analysis for Low Achiever

Pre-test writing: Introducing Computer	Post-test writing: Introducing Smart Phone
我很喜歡*(Appraisal)*電腦, 因為*(Conjunction)*我們可以用電腦to play game、chat and search for information。我經常使用電腦, 因為*(Conjunction)*電腦的game很好玩*(Appraisal)*。我的朋友都很喜歡*(Appraisal)*用電腦。我們可以用電腦上網學英文和中文。*(Explanation)* I **like** *(Appraisal)* computers very much, **because** *(Conjunction)* we can use them to play games, chat and search for information. I often use the computer, **because** *(Conjunction)* the	近年來, 智能手機是很**important** *(Appraisal)*。*(Phenomenon Identification)*我們可以用智能手機看電影、玩遊戲和聽音樂。智能手機現在流行*(Appraisal)*。智能手機是很小的, 我們的手和智能手機的大小差不多。智能手機有很多不同的顏色, 例如*(Conjunction)*, 黃、黑、白等等*(Conjunction)*。*(Explanation)* 在香港, 有很多人有智能手機, 因為*(Conjunction)*, 智能手機很便宜。*(Conclusion)* In recent years, smart phones are very

(continued)

Pre-test writing: Introducing Computer	Post-test writing: Introducing Smart Phone
computer game is very **interesting** *(Appraisal)*. My friends **like** *(Appraisal)* using computers very much. We can use computers to surf the Internet to learn English and Chinese. *(Explanation)*	**important***(Appraisal)*.*(Phenomenon Identification)* We can use smart phones to watch movies, play games and listen to music. Smart phones are **popular** *(Appraisal)* now. Smart phones are small and our hands are about the same size as smart phones. Smart phones have many different colors, **for example** *(Conjunction)*, yellow, black, white **and so on** *(Conjunction)*. *(Explanation)* In Hong Kong, a lot of people have smart phones, **because** *(Conjunction)* smart phones are cheap. *(Conclusion)*

Comparison of the pre-test and post-test of the low achiever is as follow:

R2L assessment criteria	Pre-test	Post-test
Context	The writer could not introduce the different characteristics of the computer, he also failed to present the basic explanation structure.	The article was divided into two paragraphs, which could introduce the characteristics of smart phones point by point, and more in line with the text structure of the "Phenomenon ^ Explanation Sequence 1-n ^ Conclusion" in the explanation.
	Paragraphs failed to clearly demonstrate the internal stage of the explanation text, and paragraphs lacked topic sentences and explanatory sections.	The content of the middle paragraph of the article could conform to the internal stage of the "topic sentence—explanation (examples)" of the explanation paragraph.
	Readers failed to understand the basic features of computers through the writer's introduction.	The article was more informative and could attract readers' interest in reading.
Discourse	The writer could initially use an evaluation word to introduce the characteristics of the computer, such as "like", "interesting", but the words were inaccurate.	The writer could use different evaluation words to introduce the characteristics of smart phones, such as "popular", the word was relatively accurate.
	The writer could use a conjunction word to connect meanings between different sentences, such as "because".	The writer could use different conjunctions to connect the meanings between different sentences, such as "because", "for example", etc.
	The writer was able to use the reference word accurately, such as "we".	The writer could accurately use different reference words and pronouns, such as "we", "many people".
Graphic feature	The writer's use of punctuation was inaccurate. The writer failed to segment.	The writer could use different punctuation marks correctly. Paragraphs were separated clearly, and each paragraph had a clear theme.

It can be seen from the above two texts that the writing titles in both the pre-test and post-test were mainly about an electronic product, and the number of words in the post-test increased significantly compared with that in the pre-test. In the pre-test, the student could only write down the appearance, type and function of the computer and describe his habit of using the computer. The explanation text pays more attention to convey clear, complete, and accurate information in an objective form (Shum, 2010), rather than express their personal feelings about things. The student showed more personal love for computers in the pre-test, which reflected his lack of understanding of the characteristics of explanation writing.

In addition, the student's vocabulary was not enough to give a further introduction to the shape, type and function of the computer, and there were many English words in his pre-test writing. In the post-test writing, the student could introduce the appearance and functions of smart phones in detail and objectively, such as different colours and being able to watch movies. In addition to his accurate use of words, he also used different sentence patterns to arrange the content of paragraphs. For example, sentence patterns and words such as "in recent year近年來", "in Hong Kong在香港" and "many people很多人" could effectively bring out the content of a social phenomenon that needed to be explained at the beginning of the article. While "for example...例如……等等" was useful to give specific examples to introduce the appearance and functions of smart phones.

Thus, it can be seen that the students' post-test writings had made significant progress in terms of words, sentence patterns, paragraph content, and even the structure of the whole article, from their pre-test writings of explanation genre.

5.4.5 Relationship Between Students' Pre-test and Post-test Writing Performance and R2L Teaching

According to the above analysis of pre-test and post-test writing performance of students with different Chinese proficiency, it can be seen that the Chinese language teacher can effectively improve students' explanation writing ability after using R2L Pedagogy. From the text analysis, the post-test texts of the three students had made significant progress comparing with the pre-test texts.

In terms of context, the post-test texts of the three students could show a relatively complete explanation text schematic structure, which accords with the structure of "Phenomenon ^ Explanation Sequence 1-n ^ Conclusion". In order to help students solve the problems such as loose and chaotic internal stage and unclear segmentation in the pre-test writing, the Chinese language teacher specially added detailed explanation of schematic structure in the Detailed Reading process and conducted various group activities related to the paragraph structure in the "intensive strategy" process so as to strengthen students' understanding of the internal stage of each paragraph of the explanation text.

Moreover, the Chinese teacher arranged some group writing activities for students such as Joint-Construction and Joint-Rewriting of explanation, which could effectively help students to consolidate their knowledge of the structure of explanatory texts, and strengthen their logical thinking and expression ability of writing expressions, as well as their ability to make clear and reasonable paragraphing.

In addition, students needed to extract all the joint writing passages in their own notebook, which also helped them to consolidate the knowledge learned in class. The activities of Joint-Rewriting and Joint-Construction of an explanation text could effectively help the students' post-test text to present clear segments, and the internal stage of each paragraph was consistent with the structure of "topic sentence— explanation (examples)".

In terms of discourse, the three students' post-test texts significantly improved their vocabulary usage. Basically, they could use different words to introduce the features of smart phones, and their sentence patterns were diversified, with fewer grammatical and syntactic errors, and the meaning of the sentences was clear and logical. In view of students' less or inappropriate use of conjunctions and reference words and pronouns in their pre-test writing, the Chinese teachers put special emphasis on students' application skills in word-making in the teaching process.

In the process of Detailed Reading of the text, the teacher not only focused on the content of the text, but also taught the sentence structure and the application skills of the conjunctions in the text, and required the students to practise writing sentences, so as to increase their knowledge of the connective sentence structure and their practical application skills in sentence writing.

At the same time, emphasis was placed on explaining the functions and different uses of the reference words and pronouns to students, and especially using different reference words and pronouns to write in the process of jointly constructing a new passage, which would help strengthen students' understanding and application skills of the reference words and pronouns of explanation.

In terms of the graphic feature of the writing performance, the teacher also attached importance to explaining the characteristics of paragraph segmentation and the application skills of various punctuation marks to students. In different group writing and sentence making activities, they also practised how to segment and use different punctuation marks to improve their segmentation skills and correct use of different punctuation marks.

5.4.6 Interview with the Chinese Language Teacher and the NCS Students

The researchers conducted an interview with the Chinese language teacher and the NCS students after teaching. The Chinese teacher pointed out that the students' participation in class rose a lot because the students preferred a higher interactive teaching mode. This is conformed with what Halliday says, "Language is a form of interaction, and it must be learnt through interaction." (Halliday, 1975). Through group learning and working together to complete different class activities, the students could improve their learning motivation, at the same time to strengthen their oral skills in Chinese. Some students said they enjoyed the explanation teaching: "the Chinese teachers' class was very interesting, there was a lot of group work, explanation writing was not too difficult". There were also students thinking that "group activities can let us understand the difference between myself and the other classmates; we learned a lot from other classmates who had already known the language knowledge."

It can be seen that the NCS students had positive comments on the teaching research, not only on their intention and motivation in class, but also on the knowledge of explanation reading and writing, which reflected the students' affirmation of the effectiveness of this teaching research.

From the above analysis, it can be seen that the Chinese teacher attached great importance to explaining the general idea of the words and paragraphs in detail when applying R2L Pedagogy. R2L Pedagogy attached importance to the steps of "Detailed reading" and "Spelling", which was a teaching strategy to deconstruct the content and meaning of words and texts. It emphasized the integration of reading and writing, so that reading drives writing, reading and writing abilities could both be improved. In the teaching process, the teacher invited students of different levels to give responses by asking questions of different degrees of difficulties, so as to build confidence of all the students and improve their understanding of the content of the explanation texts. The steps of "Spelling" included writing words, filling in blanks, marking keywords with colour pens or highlighters, etc., so as to deepen students' impression of the meaning and writing of words they had learned. In addition, when using R2L teaching steps, the teacher made appropriate adjustments according to teaching needs and students' language proficiency level. For example, the Chinese teacher attached importance to the "Preparation for reading" step of R2L teaching method, setting up a daily life situation to arouse students' interest in learning explanation genre. Thus, the teacher showed flexibility in applying the R2L Pedagogy according to the students' needs. The findings will help theory-building in the field of Chinese as a second language pedagogies, curriculum development and teacher education in Hong Kong and beyond.

6 Conclusion

This study has explored the application and effectiveness of R2L Pedagogy in teaching explanation genre for a class of NCS students through a case study, which is suggested to be read in conjunction with the previous chapter to allow greater depth of understanding of the challenges and possibilities for CSL/NCS students. The researchers summed up the research findings with the research tools which included teacher and students interviews, class observations and text analysis, that the Chinese teacher taught in application of R2L Pedagogy, attaching importance to the teaching steps "Detailed reading", "Spelling", "Joint construction" and so on, and guided the student to understand the text contents and word meanings, and in the process of group discussion and collaborative writing to acquire useful knowledge of reading and writing. From the interview opinions of the Chinese language teacher and students after teaching and the comparison of students' pre-test and post-test writing performance, it can be seen that R2L Pedagogy could improve NCS students' writing performance at the whole text level, the sentence level, and the vocabulary level. This reflected that the R2L Pedagogy could effectively improve the ability of NCS students to write Chinese explanation texts and motivate them to participate actively in classroom activities. The research results provide evidence that the teaching strategy is effective in teaching Chinese to the non-Chinese speaking students in Hong Kong, and the disparity between low and high achievers has been narrowed, which can supplement the findings from Australian and European research groups in English literacy studies. It is hoped that the findings will help theory-building in the field of Chinese as a second language pedagogies, curriculum development and teacher education in Hong Kong and beyond.

References

Acevedo, C. (2010). *A report on school-based action research: Will the implementation of teaching to learn in Stockholm schools accelerate literacy learning for disadvantaged students and close the achievement gap?* Multilingual Research Institute, Stockholm Education Administration.
Amabile, T. M. (1996). *Creativity in context: Update to "The social psychology of creativity".* Westview Press.
Census and Statistics Department. (2021). *Thematic report: Ethnic Minorities.* Hong Kong Websites of the Census and Statistics Department.
Connelly, F. M., & Clandinin, D. J. (1994). Telling teaching stories. *Teacher Education Quarterly, 21*(1), 145–158.
Halliday, M. A. K. (1975). Learning how to mean: Explorations in the development of language. .
Halliday, M. A. K. (1994). *An introduction to functional grammar* (2nd ed.).
Halliday, M. A. K., & Mathiessen, C. M. I. M. (2004). *An introduction to functional grammar* (3rd ed.). University Press.
Ku, H. B., Chan, K. W., & Sandhu, K. K. (2005). *Education of South Asian ethnic minority groups in Hong Kong.* Centre for Social Policy Studies, Department of Applied Social Science, The Hong Kong Polutechnic University and SKH Lady MacLehose Centre.
Lincoln, Y. S., & Guba, E. G. (1985). *Naturalistic inquiry.* Sage.
Loper, K. (2004). *Race and equality: A study of ethnic minorities in Hong Kong's education system.* Centre for Comparative and Public Law, Faculty of Law, the University of Hong Kong.
Martin, J. R. (1999). Mentoring semogenesis: Genre-based literacy pedagogy. In F. Christie (Ed.), *Pedagogy and the shaping of consciousness: Linguistic and social processes.* Continuum.
Martin, J. R. (2009). Genre and language learning: A social semiotic perspective. December 2009. *Linguistics and Education, 20*(1), 10–21.
Martin, J. R., & Rose, D. (2008). *Genre relations: Mapping culture.* Equinox.
Martin, J. R., & Rothery, J. (1990). *Literacy for a lifetime – Teachers. Notes.* Film Australia.
Merriam, S. B. (1998). *Qualitative research and case study applications in education: Revised and expanded from case study research in education* (2nd ed.). Jossey-Bass Publishers.
Rose, D. (2008). Writing as linguistic mastery: The development of genre-based literacy pedagogy. In R. Beard, D. Myhill, J. Riley, & M. Nystrand (Eds.), *The SAGE handbook of writing development.* Sage.
Rose, D. (2012). *Reading to learn: Accelerating learning and closing the gap* (Vol. 1–10). Teacher training books and DVDs. Reading to Learn Company.

Rose, D., & Martin, J. R. (2012). *Learning to write, reading to learn: Genre, knowledge and pedagogy in the Sydney school*. Equinox Publishing.

Rothery, J. (1994). *Exploring about language in English (Write it right resources for literacy and learning)*. Metropolitan East Disadvantaged Schools Program.

Shum, M. S. K. (2010). *The functions of language and the teaching of Chinese: Application of systemic functional linguistics to Chinese language teaching* (2nd ed.). Hong Kong University Press.

Shum, M. S. K., Gao, F., Tsung, L., & Ki, W. W. (2011). South Asian students' Chinese language learning in Hong Kong: Motivations and strategies. *Journal of Multilingual & Multicultural Development, 32*(3), 285–297.

Tsung, L. T. H., Shum, M. S. K., & Ki, W. W. (2008). *Teaching Chinese to South Asian students in Hong Kong: Policies and issues*. Paper presented at the conference on minority language education in China: Issues and perspectives, April 19. The University of Hong Kong.

Yin, R. K. (2003). *Case study research: Design and methods* (3rd ed.). Sage.

When Stanislavski Met Halliday: A Case Study

Justine Po-Sau Woo

Abstract The justification for incorporating Stanislavski's System and the associated research becomes evident when considering its effectiveness in enhancing writing skills for Chinese as Second Language students (CSL). Hence, as demonstrated in this chapter, the case study presented herein possesses a wider value for the field of CSL research, extending beyond its specific context. In the context of Hong Kong, the presence of a rising population of ethnic minority students has led to an increased need for acquiring Chinese as a second language after the language policy change in 1997. This chapter centres around a case study that examines the application of Stanislavski's System in addressing challenges encountered in Chinese narrative writing among students learning Chinese as a Second Language in a local secondary school in Hong Kong. The study's theoretical framework consists of three main pillars: (1) the second language acquisition theories, specifically the Input Hypothesis Model proposed by Krashen (The input hypothesis: issues and implications. Longman, 1985), and the Interactive Hypothesis put forth by Long (Long MH. Input and second language acquisition theory. In: Gass SM, Madden CG (eds) Input in second language acquisition. Newbury House, pp 377–393, 1985, The role of the linguistic environment in second language acquisition. In Ritchie WC, Bhatia TK (eds) Handbook of second language acquisition. Academic, pp 413-468, 1996); (2) Stanislavski's System (Creative work with actors: a discussion on directing. In: Cole T, Chinoy H (eds) (1976). Directors on directing. Macmillan, 1936, An actor's work. Routledge, 2008); and (3) the genre theories regarding narrative writing, which are based on Halliday's Systemic Functional Grammar (Introduction to functional grammar, 1st edn. Arnold, 1985). The research participants in this study consisted of a Chinese language teacher and her class of Form 2 ethnic minority students (N = 9). The collaboration between the practitioner-as-researcher and the schoolteacher involved the application of Stanislavski's System (Stanislavski K. Creative work with actors: a discussion on directing. In: Cole T, Chinoy H (eds) (1976). Directors on directing. Macmillan, 1936, Stanislavski K. An actor's work. Routledge, 2008)

J. P.-S. Woo (✉)
The University of Hong Kong, Pok Fu Lam, Hong Kong

within the context of a Chinese narrative writing class over a period of one year. The analysis of students' writings was conducted employing Halliday's Systemic Functional Grammar (Halliday MAK, Matthiessen CMIM. An introduction to functional grammar, 3rd edn. Routledge, 2004, Halliday MAK, Matthiessen CMIM. Halliday's introduction to functional grammar, 4th edn. Routledge, 2013). The study hired a pre-experimental research design to assess the efficacy of Stanislavski's System in improving the Chinese narrative writing skills of non-native Chinese speaking (NCS) students. The findings indicated enhancements in the overall writing performance. As a result of the discovery of more emotive lexicons, the students' capacity to convey their emotions through the written form of Chinese improved as well.

1 Introduction

The aim of this chapter is to propose the application of Stanislavski's System to enhance narrative writing in Chinese as a Second Language for secondary school students. The results of writing improvement are examined by the transitivity theory of Halliday's Functional Grammar. Firstly, this chapter will offer a brief overview of the research area and the research gap in the application of Stanislavski's System (Stanislavski, 1936, 2008) in second language writing. Secondly, Halliday's Functional Grammar (Halliday & Matthiessen, 2004, 2013) and the elements of transitivity in narrative writing will be briefly outlined; then a case study of practice in enhancing narrative writing in Chinese as a Second Language through Stanislavski's acting system will be offered, in which the connection of Stanislavski's System and Halliday's Functional Grammar will be demonstrated. Finally, the discussion and conclusion will highlight the effects and implications of Stanislavski's System and Halliday's Functional Grammar as a Learning and Teaching model, from the perspective of the second language acquisition theories, i.e., the Input Hypothesis Model of Krashen (1985) and the Interactive Hypothesis of Long (1985, 1996).

In Hong Kong, due to the increasing number of ethnic minority students, there is a growing need to learn Chinese as a second language after the change in language policy in 1997. The case study in this chapter focuses on how to ease the difficulties in Chinese writing, by adopting Stanislavski's System in learning Chinese narrative writing as a second language in one of the Hong Kong secondary schools. Stanislavski's System is suggested as a pedagogy for learning and teaching narrative writing, being a strategy of drama-in-education. Halliday's Systemic Functional Grammar is adopted as a framework to analyse the elements of narrative writing.

2 Drama and Writing

Drama is an effective way of learning (Heathcote, 1984; see also Bolton, 1984, 1999; Loh, 2015; Neelands, 1992; O'Neill, 1995). Increasingly, benefits can be found of using drama in the learning of writing in general, ranging from primary school to middle or secondary school level.

Eighty-four fourth graders and seventy eighth graders participated in Wagner's (1986) study of the impact of role acting on persuasive letter writing. The findings of the study indicate that eighth-grade students demonstrated superior writing skills compared to fourth-grade students. Additionally, it was observed that female students exhibited significantly stronger writing abilities than their male counterparts at the fourth-grade level, although this difference in gender was not observed at the eighth-grade level. The impact of drama on the writing proficiency of adolescents was investigated by Neelands et al. (1993) through the utilisation of diverse dramatic conventions. Through drama and writing activities, they discovered that not only did students' writing attitudes improve, but also their understanding and empathy for a wide variety of individuals.

A comparative analysis of the impact of pre-writing exercises incorporating drama and drawing was conducted by Moore and Caldwell (1993), as opposed to the conventional practice of discussion, on the development of narrative writing skills. This was accomplished through paired improvisations and individual role play, followed by the creation of storyboards depicting the major characters, settings, and scenes. At the second and third grade levels, the drama and drawing groups dramatically outperformed the discussion group in terms of writing quality. Moreover, McNaughton (1997) also discovered that drama was more effective than discussion in fostering the imaginative writing skills of four to seven years old primary school students. She employed a variety of drama strategies, including teacher-in-role, improvisation, mime, tableaux, interview, meetings, simulations, hot-seating, writing-in-role, etc. The techniques were described as drama conventions according to Neelands and Goode (2015).

The relationship between drama and writing within primary and secondary educational settings was investigated by Cremin et al. (2006). They discovered that dramatic play and process drama boosted students' creativity and imagination, allowing for a condition of "flow" when writing.

In those previous studies, drama strategies, i.e., "role-play", "drama conventions", "dramatic play" or "process drama" were employed. It seems the processes of those strategies involve *acting out* in the enactment of specific roles or engagement in particular situations. However, what types of acting style or acting elements are involved, and how are the learning or teaching activities among students and teachers articulated through the acting out processes? Thus, there is a research gap of applying Stanislavski's acting system as a mediation of learning narrative writing.

3 Stanislavski's System

Stanislavski was the stage name adopted by Konstantin Sergeyevich Alexeyev in 1884. He was born in Moscow, Russia in 1863 and died at the age of 75. He was an actor, director, producer, and founder of the Moscow Art Theatre (in 1898). During the nineteenth century, realism was an important theatrical movement. Stanislavski was one of the followers of realism throughout his career. His to theatre was quite an experimentation during that period. He documented his evaluation and reflection of his works, and then established the system of acting as a practitioner—the Stanislavski's System (Benedetti, 2000).

3.1 The System

Stanislavski's System was developed over a period of 40 years. Stanislavski's main focus was on an actor's work. He kept investigating the 'conscious means to the subconscious' and the 'creative statuses' of an actor as a whole person. Later, he was attracted by the scientific conception of the interaction of brain and body. He encouraged actors to act both physically and psychologically, to (better) sense the surrounding environment, to feel the emotion and the moment-to-moment, like experiencing real life (Stanislavski, 1936, 2008). To understand more about Stanislavski's System, the following are the basic elements of acting (Stanislavski, 1936, 2008):

3.2 Sense Memory

In Stanislavski's belief, actors should be able to bring their emotion and personality to the stage when playing their character. "Sense memory" refers to the recall of physical sensations of the surrounding environment, especially during emotional events, instead of the emotions themselves. Five major senses are used to perceive the world: sight, sound, taste, smell, and touch.

3.3 Emotion Memory

Stanislavski emphasised that actors should honestly feel the emotion. Actors need to put themselves in the mindset of the character's situation, so that they genuinely experience the feelings of the characters. If actors were not able to connect with the character's emotional state, Stanislavski encouraged actors to reach into their personal memories and draw upon similar life experiences.

3.4 Given Circumstances

The given circumstances are the information about the character and the play as a whole. For example, what is the background of the character? What is the situation in the scene and in relation to the other characters? This information is important for building a character and bringing the scenes alive.

3.5 Magic If

The **'magic if'** is a technique that enables actors to put themselves into the character's situation. The imagination of being in a role and in a certain situation stimulates the motivation that enables the actor to play the role and to empathise with the situation.

3.6 Inner Action

Inner actions are the psychological indicators of the desires and aspirations of characters. They are the objectives of the character that he/she is trying to achieve. An **objective** is the primary reason for any action. Actors should express the meaning of the objective in terms of a verb, such as "I want to ..." instead of a noun.

3.7 Physical Action

Stanislavski suggested that it is possible to construct a role through its physical dimensions. Characters show their appearances through body movement and gestures. Stanislavski believed physical action has an inherent psychological resonance. As long as actors are psycho-physically open and listening out for that resonance, the physical dimensions of the characters will never just be empty forms.

4 Halliday's Functional Grammar

Michael Alexander Kirkwood Halliday was born in Leeds, England in 1925. He was a renowned linguist who developed the internationally influential Systemic Functional Linguistics (SFL) model of language (a.k.a. Systemic Functional Grammar). He went to China and studied Chinese at Peking University in 1947. Later, he returned to the United Kingdom and completed a PhD in Chinese at Cambridge. In 1976, he established the Department of Linguistics at the University of Sydney (Christie, 2018). Halliday saw language as a social construction. His approach believes that the human capacity for language is by "nurturing" during life and experiences, instead of just by "nature" itself.

4.1 Systemic Functional Linguistics (SFL)

SFL views language as a meaning-making resource. It emphasises the whole text rather than isolated works. The "form" and "function" of language are equally

Table 1 Relations between language, registers, and meanings

Registers	Language	Meanings	Description
Field	Ideational metafunction	Experiential	Express the experience of the world through language (transitivity system).
Tenor	Interpersonal metafunction	Interpersonal	Express the nature of the relation between the author and the reader, and the attitude of the author towards the theme exposed (mood types, system of polarity and system of modality).
Mode	Textual metafunction	Textual	Determines the way in which a text—oral or written—is organised, its relation with previous texts and the surrounding context (thematic organisation).

Eggins (2004), Halliday (1978), Halliday and Matthiessen (2013)

important. In SFL, text is considered as "a process of making meaning in context" (Halliday & Matthiessen, 2013). Texts exist in the context of the situation, which exists within the larger context of culture. The writing practices of a culture are characterised by specific forms of texts used for different purposes, which involve specific language features. Therefore, different genres show different purposes and different text structures (Hyland, 2013).

In terms of using different functions for communication, genres indicate different language choices as defined by the register, i.e., field, tenor, and mode (Table 1).

Language reflects the field and ideas of the text through clauses formed by processes, participants, and circumstances. The Tenor of a text reflects the relationship between the author and the reader. The Mode reflects language choices depending on whether the text is oral, written, or multimodal. These variables characterise the language metafunctions: "experiential", "interpersonal", and "textual" (Halliday & Matthiessen, 2013, pp. 30–32).

4.2 Transitive Model

Transitivity traditionally refers to: who does what to whom? In a Transitivity system, verbs are classified into two groups: transitive and intransitive. In SFL, transitivity is a major component in the experiential function for "transmission of ideas", representing 'processes and 'experience'. It construes 'the world of experience' as a set of "process types". Each process type provides its own function (Halliday & Matthiessen, 2004, p. 170).

4.2.1 Process

Process is the product of human's perception of the world. It refers to a semantic verb, such as: doing, happening, feeling, sensing, saying, behaving, and existing. It expresses events like relational, physical, mental, or emotional state in the semantic system of the clause, in which process is classified into material, relational, mental, verbal, behavioural, and existential processes. They are socially and culturally constructed, with participants, any animate or inanimate noun phrase in circumstances expressed by adverbial and prepositional phrases. (Halliday & Matthiessen, 2004, 2013)

Material Process

The material process is externalised and embodies an action verb of doing or happening. A 'doer' is labelled as Actor and optionally Goal, affected by the process and circumstances that provide details of the verb (Halliday & Matthiessen, 2004, 2013).

Behavioural Process

The behavioural process stands between material and mental processes related to physiological and psychological behaviours. It shows emotive status, such as smiling, crying, and laughing. (Halliday & Matthiessen, 2004, 2013)

Mental Process

The mental process is classified into three categories of cognition, perception, and affection. It represents the content of consciousness. In the mental process, participants are labelled as Sensor and Phenomenon (Halliday & Matthiessen, 2004).

Verbal Process

The verbal process of direct or indirect report speech sits on the border between mental and relational processes. It relates to "any kind of symbolic exchange of meaning" or the ideas in human consciousness with their linguistic representation of 'Sayer' (Halliday & Matthiessen, 2004, pp. 179–195).

Relational Process

The relational process is classified into intensive, attributive, identifying, circumstantial, and possessive. Relational processes are concerned with the processes of description regarding the abstract relations. The irreversible attributive process assigns a quality or adjective to a participant, titled as Carrier, realised by a noun or a nominal phrase. (Halliday & Matthiessen, 2004).

Existential Process

The existential process refers to processes of existing with "a there and to be" with no representational function. An 'Existent' can be an entity, event, or action (Halliday & Matthiessen, 2004, pp. 256–259).

4.2.2 Circumstances

The transitive model is based on the configuration of Actor Process. It consists of three components:

1. A process unfolding through time;
2. The participants involved in the process;

3. Circumstances associated with the process (Halliday & Matthiessen, 2004, p. 175).

The circumstantial elements occur in all types of process, with the same significance wherever they occur. One of the perspectives of "circumstances" is referring to the location of an event in time or space, its manner or its cause; and the notions of 'when, where, how and why (WH-)' something happens are provided through a traditional explanation, by linking circumstances to the four WH- forms that are adverbs rather than nouns. For the circumstantial elements, please see the following (Halliday & Matthiessen, 2004, pp. 262–277):

Extent—indicates the extent of the unfolding of process in space-time:

- distance (spatial: how far?), duration (temporal: how long?), frequency (temporal: how many times?).

Location—indicates the location of the unfolding of process in space-time:

- the place (spatial: where? [there, here]), time (temporal: when? [Then, now]).

Manner—indicates the way in which the process is actualised:

- means—refers to the means whereby a process takes place (how? [thus]),
- quality—typically expressed by an adverbial group (how? [thus]),
- comparison—typically expressed by a prepositional phrase with like or unlike, or an adverbial group of similarity or difference (how? like what?),
- degree—typically expressed by an adverbial group with a general indication of degree (how much?).

Cause—explains the reason why the process is actualised:

- reason—represents the reason for which a process takes place—what causes it; sense of 'because' (why?),
- purpose—represents the purpose for which an action takes place, the intention behind it; sense of "in order that" (why? what for?),
- behalf—represents the entity, typically a person, on whose behalf or for whose sake the action is undertaken, who it is for (who for?).

Contingency—specifies an element on which the actualisation of the process depends. There are three sub-types:

- condition—outlines circumstances that have to be obtained for the process to be actualised, having the sense of 'if',
- concession—construed as frustrated cause with the sense of 'although',
- default—has the sense of negative condition, i.e., 'if not, unless'.

Accompaniment—a form of joint participation in the process and represents the meanings 'and', 'or', and 'not' as circumstantial:

- comitative—represents the process as a single instance of a process, although one in which two entities are involved, i.e., 'accompanied by' or 'not accompanied by' (who/ what with, who/ what else),

- additive—represents the process as two instances, i.e., 'in addition to' or 'as alternative to' (who/ what else, not who/ what) –

Role—construed by the meanings of '(to) be' and '(to) become'. The Role includes the subcategories of Guise ('be') and Product ('become'):

- guise—corresponds to the interrogative 'what as' and construes the meaning of 'be' (attribute or identity) in the form of a circumstance,
- product—corresponds to the interrogative 'what into?', with the meaning of 'become', similarly as attribute or identity.

Matter—relates to verbal processes; 'which is described, referred to, narrated, etc.' The interrogative is 'what about?'.

Angle—relates either to the Sayer of a 'verbal' clause, with the sense of 'as... says', or to the Sensor of a 'mental' clause, with the sense of 'as...thinks'.

- source—represents the source of information (who says? who thinks?),
- viewpoint—represents somebody's viewpoint (which standpoint?).

5 When Stanislavski Met Halliday

Even though Stanislavski's System and Halliday's Functional Grammar are two separate domains—Stanislavski's System is linked to acting and theatre, while Halliday's Functional Grammar is related to linguistics—the two theories are related to one another. Stanislavski's System and Halliday's Functional Grammar, on the other hand, both place an emphasis on the significance of context and the construction of meaning within their respective disciplines. Stanislavski's System places a greater emphasis on an actor's understanding of the given circumstances as well as the emotional and physical actions that are necessary to create a believable character, whereas Halliday's Functional Grammar places a greater emphasis on the importance of context and language choices in the process of creating meaning in a text. The meaning of a text or performance is, however, greatly impacted by the social and cultural context in which it was made and is understood. This is something that is acknowledged by both methods of analysis. As a result, the two theories may function well together in offering a more complete explanation of how meaning is formed and expressed in a variety of circumstances, provided that they are complementary to one another.

6 Research Questions

The potential for synergy between Stanislavski's System and Halliday's Functional Grammar is evident, as it may enhance our comprehension of the complex processes involved in meaning development and communication across various contexts. This phenomenon may be attributed to the shared focus of both theories on the transfer of meaning. To examine the effectiveness and execution of Stanislavski's System when combined with Halliday's Functional Grammar, there are two research questions:

On Learning
    How do the students improve their writing performances after using Stanislavski's System on learning narrative writing in Chinese as a second language?
On Teaching
    What is the teaching model of applying Stanislavski's System in teaching narrative writing in Chinese as a second language?

7 Methodology

The research presented here consists of a case study examination applying Stanislavski's System to enhance narrative writing in Chinese as a Second Language. The study was conducted in a regular classroom setting for a group of mixed mode F2 level students at a local secondary school in Hong Kong. The participants involved in this research included nine non-native Chinese-speaking (NCS) students, aged between 12 and 14, with diverse ethnic backgrounds such as Indian ($n = 3$), Filipino ($n = 2$), Nepali ($n = 2$), Pakistani ($n = 1$), and Venezuelan ($n = 1$). Additionally, a schoolteacher with 19 years of experience in teaching the Chinese language, including 2 years of teaching Chinese as a second language, collaborated in the study. The teacher-researcher involved in the study had 25 years of experience in facilitating Stanislavski's System in theatre directing, acting, and applied drama.

The study utilised a collaborative action research approach in which the teacher-researcher developed and implemented the new pedagogy. The Chinese language teacher from the school played an active role as a co-teacher. Through this collaboration, they were able to offer suggestions and make modifications after each cycle, as well as examine and evaluate the practise with critical reflection for continuous improvement of classroom practises. (Miller & Pine, 1990; Mills, 2003; Wilson, 2009; Mcniff & Whitehead, 2010; Koshy, 2010). Four spiral cycles were planned for the intervention, with each cycle consisting of four stages: planning, acting, reflecting, and re-planning (Kemmis & McTaggart, 1992).

Over the course of a semester, 18 lessons were designed and executed using Stanislavski's acting method as pre-writing activities. To assess the effectiveness of the intervention, pre-tests and post-tests of narrative writing written by students were collected before and after implementing the system in class. The text analysis was conducted using the transitivity model of Halliday's Functional Grammar, and the effect size of *Process* and *Circumstances* elements of narrative writing were measured.

Cohen's b effect size (Cohen, 1988) was used to measure the effectiveness of the intervention, with general guidelines indicating small (0.2), medium (0.5), and large (0.8) effects. By examining the impact of Stanislavski's System on the writing performance of students learning Chinese as a second language, this research aims to contribute valuable insights into innovative teaching methods and pedagogical strategies for enhancing language learning outcomes.

7.1 Data Collection

The study employed a comprehensive data collection process that consisted of a wide range of sources. The researcher's reflective log, which contained 32 entries, provided valuable insights into her thought process and experiences. Classroom videos were also collected, comprising nine clips capturing double lessons, resulting in a total of 18 individual lessons. Audio recordings were also one of the important components, with 32 mp3 files gathered alongside 74 written texts, providing a comprehensive perspective on the classroom observation. Lastly, the study included 11 students' interview audio recordings, which offered distinctive personal viewpoints on the learning process.

8 Findings and Discussion

Given the significance of assisting new Chinese language learners to write more effectively, what did the data from this case study reveal? The following analyses are the findings for answering the research questions: one on the perspective of learning—(1) the improvement of the students' writing performances as effects of the Stanislavski's System on writing performance in terms of SFL's transitivity theory; and the other one on teaching—(2) the teaching model of using Stanislavski's System.

Hence, the implication for learning and teaching narrative writing in Chinese as a second language by using the *Stanislavski's System* would be explained together with the transitivity theory of *Halliday's Functional Grammar*.

8.1 Improvement of the Students' Writing Performances After Using the Stanislavski's System on Narrative Writing in Chinese as a Second Language

The students' writing results (n = 9) are compared with their pre-test and post-test performances. The number of *Process* lexicons and *Circumstance* lexicons were measured, and the findings are shown through the effect size (Cohen's b).

The overall effect size is 1.56. It shows the students have a very good improvement after using the Stanislavski's System on learning narrative writing in Chinese as a second language.

Analysis of the data also shows that the students have a higher progress in writing *Process* lexicons with the effect size of 1.58 compared to *Circumstance* lexicons with effect size 1.10 (see Table 2).

For the improvement within the different *Process* lexicons, *behavioural Process* has the highest improvement with an effect size of 3.53. The second highest improvement is *Material Process* and the third is *Mental Process* with an effect size of 1.54 and 1.13 respectively (see Table 3).

For the improvement within the different *Circumstance* lexicons, the *Time* element has the highest improvement with an effect size of 1.70. The second is *Place* with an effect size of 1.45 (see Table 4).

Table 2 Overall writing performance of students (n = 9)

Transitivity	Pre	Post	%	M1	M2	SD1	SD2	Effect size
Process	28	106	278.57	3.11	11.78	2.80	8.20	1.58
Circumstance	33	61	84.58	3.67	6.78	1.58	4.06	1.10
Overall	61	167	173.77	6.78	18.56	4.09	10.97	1.56

Table 3 Students' writing performance of process Lexicon (n = 9)

Process	Pre	Post	%	M1	M2	SD1	SD2	Effect size
Material	15	40	166.67	1.67	4.44	1	2.60	1.54
Mental	6	36	500	0.67	4	1.32	4.56	1.13
Relational	4	10	150	0.44	1.11	1.01	1.90	0.46
behavioural	0	7	700	0	0.78	0	0.44	3.53
Verbal	2	10	400	0.22	1.11	0.67	1.54	0.81
Existential	1	3	200	0.11	0.33	0.33	0.71	0.43
Overall	28	106	278.57	3.11	11.78	2.80	8.20	1.58

Table 4 Students' writing performance of circumstance Lexicon (n = 9)

Circumstance	Pre	Post	%	M1	M2	SD1	SD2	Effect size
Time	10	24	140	1.11	2.67	0.33	1.50	1.70
Place	7	19	171.43	0.78	2.11	0.67	1.17	1.45
Cause	3	6	100	0.33	0.67	0.71	0.87	0.42
Manner	2	1	−50	0.22	0.11	0.44	0.33	−0.29
Extent	0	1	100	0	0.11	0	0.33	0.67
Matter	2	1	−50	0.22	0.11	0.44	0.33	−0.29
Contingency	0	2	200	0	0.22	0	0.67	0.67
Accompany	9	7	−22.22	1	0.78	0.71	1.20	−0.23
Angle	0	0	0	0	0	0	0	0
Role	0	0	0	0	0	0	0	0
Overall	33	61	84.85	3.67	6.78	1.58	4.06	1.10

8.2 The Teaching Model of Using Stanislavski's System in Teaching Chinese as a Second Language

Four cycles of teaching were practiced throughout the whole intervention (see Table 5).

The first cycle is for the preparation of adapting acting in class. Basic acting exercises of 'magic if', 'sense memory', 'physical action' and 'imagination' were introduced to prepare students step-by-step; from "who are you", to "private moment" and then "public place with somebody" for the later acting improvisation activities (see Table 6 for the details of cycle 1).

Table 5 Using Stanislavski's System on teaching Chinese narrative writing as second language

Narrative Writing (Topic)	Cycle 1 →	Cycle 2 →	Cycle 3 →	Cycle 4
	Preparation for acting	Making a story with Schematic Structure	Write an experience: School Life	Emotion Memory: Writing a Personal Story
Experiencing Stanislavski's System	Step 1 →	Step 2 →	Step 3 →	Step 4
	Observation Magic If: Make Believe	Observation Sense Memory Physical action: Body & Speech	Given Circumstances: Where, Why	Inner action: Psychological Drive & Feelings
	Concentration Imagination	Given Circumstances	Through-action: how, conflict, objective	
	Sense Memory Physical Action Communication	Inner action Communication		

Table 6 Cycle 1 preparation

Lesson	Content	Acting (Stanislavski)	Writing (SFL)
1,2	Who are you? **Read aloud**: a short script about 'I', a student. Teacher asked, **who** was 'speaking' in the script? Students described **who** he was and **how** he behaved through the text. Teacher asked the students to imagine, '**WHO are you**?' Students answer verbally and **write about "Who I am"** individually.	Observation Magic if Imagination Who	Describe "myself" **Who Relational Process**
3, 4	A private place Introduction: what is *a private place* What you **SEE**, what you **SMELL**, what you **HEAR** over there? **What if**, you were there by yourself?	Observation Magic if **Sense memory Physical Action** Given	Open up writers' **senses** Transitivity **Material Process**

(continued)

Table 6 (continued)

Lesson	Content	Acting (Stanislavski)	Writing (SFL)
	Exercise: 　1. Design your private place 　2. What you do (your action) in the *private place*? 　3. Draft your own idea on paper 　4. **Act it out** (individually) 　5. Feedback by the audience 　6. **Write it down**: WHO (I)+ WHERE (the place) + ACTION (doing)	Circumstances **Who + Where**	**Mental Process** Circumstances: **Actor + Place**
5, 6	A public place 　Introducing what public place would be 　Answers by students 　What you **SEE, SMELL** or **HEAR** over there? 　Exercise: 　　1. Work in pairs: **imagine** you are in a **public place.** What will you do over there? 　Act it out (in pairs) 　Guessing and feedback by audience 　Write it down: individually write a narrative piece with their own scenario *Additional bonus with believable performance (sense of truth) and clear **feedback in Chinese**	Observation Magic if **Sense Memory** Given Circumstances **Who +Where + What** **Physical action,** Body + speech **Communication**	Who **Senor + Actor** Circumstances **Space + Time** What **Mental Process** **Material Process** **Verbal Process**

In the second cycle, the acting techniques learned from the first cycle were used to build a story with narrative schematic structure (see Table 7 for the details of cycle 2).

In the third cycle, a set of given circumstances were emphasised, i.e. where and why. Students were encouraged to create a series of through-action to express their school life experience as a writing topic (see Table 8 for the details of cycle 3).

In the last cycle, in-depth feelings arose through an exercise of emotion memory, which inspired students to write their own personal stories (see Table 9 for the details of cycle 4).

8.3 The Implication for the Learning and Teaching Model of Stanislavski's System and Halliday's Functional Grammar

8.3.1 Acting to Learn

Acting seems an effective way to let students rehearse what they are going to write. According to the Input Hypothesis Model of Krashen (1985), language acquisition

Table 7 Cycle 2 Making a story with schematic structure

Lesson	Content	Acting (Stanislavski)	Writing (SFL)
7, 8	Schematic Structure (Staging): How and Ending Revision: who, where, what 　Introducing narrative staging 　**Schematic Structure**: 　Concept building: 　　1. **Orientation** vs when + who + where 　　2. **Process** vs who + what (action 1) 　　3. **Complications** vs why + how (action 2, 3…) 　　4. **Resolution** vs how (action 4,5…) 　　5. **Ending** (happy? Tragic? Opening?) 　Make your own story in group 　**Act it out** 　Feedback from others 　**Draft** it down with the **schematic table** (worksheet)	Observation Sense Memory **Given circumstances** When + Who + Where What + Why + How **Magic If** **Physical action** Body + Speech **Inner Action** Objective **Communication**	**6-W** **Circumstances** When+Who +Where What + Why + hoW **Process** Material Process Mental Process Verbal Process **Draft** (In Schematic Structure)
9, 10	Writing Revision of the content and **Chinese vocabulary** from their **own draft** of last lesson; Revision of the narrative **schematic structure vs action** list: 　1. **Orientation** vs background 　2. **Process** (complications-> resolution) /recount (step 1 -> step 2) vs action list 　3. **Ending** vs As a Result 　4. **Evaluation** vs Feelings/thoughts **Writing**: write their own story based on the draft	The acting experience becoming the inner images during writing.	**Vocabulary building** ↓ **Schematic Structure** ↓ **6-W Circumstances** When+Who +Where What + Why + hoW ↓ **Process** Material Process Mental Process Verbal Process ↓ **Writing**

happens through comprehensive input. That means the understanding of 'meaning' comes first and the 'form' follows. For Chinese as a second language learners, it may be difficult for them to speak out their ideas and feelings in Chinese. However, since Physical Action in Stanislavski's System helps students to express the meanings through their body movements and gestures, 'using body movement for expressing oneself (myself) and communicating to others (student 206)' seems easier. It is

Table 8 Cycle 3 Write about their experience—My school life

Lesson	Content	Acting (Stanislavski)	Writing (SFL)

11, 12	Action Topic: My school life (我的學校生活)
	Revision: Schematic Structure
	Task: How to express 'timeline' in Chinese—introducing vocabulary of describing "**when**":
	  1. **Recess** 小息時/ action 1 or 2
	  2. **Lunchtime**午飯時/ action 2 or 3
	  3. **During the lesson**上課時 / action 3 or 4
	  4. **After school** 放學後/ action 4 or 5
	  5. **Ending** →At the end 終於
	    Any story happening IN SCHOOL (**Where**)?
	    Create a story 'My School Life' in the group
	    Action: **What** happen? **Why** → **How**
	    Act it out
	    Feedback from others
	    Write a **draft**—on the worksheet
		Observation
		Sense Memory
		Given circumstances
		When + Who + Where
		What + Why + How
		Magic If
		Physical action
		Body + Speech
		Inner Action
		Objective
		Communication
			6-W
			Circumstances
			When+Who
			+Where
			What + Why + hoW
			Process
			Material Process
			Mental Process
			Verbal Process
			Draft
			(In Schematic Structure)

13, 14	Writing Revision of the content and **building Chinese vocabulary** from their own draft: Revision: the narrative **schematic structure** 1. **Orientation** vs **background** 2. **Process** (complications-> resolution) /recount (step 1 -> step 2) vs action list 3. **Ending** vs As a Result 4. **Evaluation** vs Feelings/thoughts **Writing**: write about the school life based on the draft	The acting experience becoming the inner images during writing.	**Vocabulary building** ↓ **Schematic Structure** ↓ **Circumstances** ↓ **Process** ↓ **Writing**

because 'actions help to memorise the vocabularies (student 203)'. Students can 'write what have spoken (student 209)' in acting. It shows that 'meaning' is created through acting and the 'form' comes after that. It also can be explained that as Stanislavski's System emphasises the 'creative status' of an actor as a whole person, students created their scenes to 'act physically and psychologically' to 'sense the surrounding environments', 'experiencing life' (Stanislavski, 1936, 2008). This 'experiencing life' process during acting seems like a rehearsal for narrative writing as it matches the saying of Halliday—language is 'a process of making meaning in context' (Halliday & Matthiessen, 2013).

Table 9 Cycle 4 Emotion memory: writing a personal story

Lesson	Content	Acting (Stanislavski)	Writing (SFL)

15, 16	Action Topic: An Unforgettable Memory
	Emotional recall. Stimulus: a farewell song
	   Listening to a song
	   Read the lyrics and find out **vocabularies** which **expressing emotions**
	   Teacher asked the narrative elements in the lyrics: **who, when, what** and asked the students to write **vocabularies about emotions** on the board
	   Students explained the **meanings**
	   Teacher asked about **students' experience inspired by the song**
	   Draft a story of an unforgettable experience
		Emotion memory
		Given circumstances
		When + Who + Where
		What + Why + How
		Magic If
		Inner Action
		Objective
			Inspiration from an emotion memory
			↓
			Circumstances
			↓
			Process
			Material, mental, verbal and behavioural process
			↓
			Draft
			(In Schematic Structure)

17, 18	Writing Revision: the narrative **schematic structure** vs **action**: 1. **Orientation** 2. **Process** (complications-> resolution) / recount (step 1 -> step 2) 3. **Ending** 4. **Evaluation** **Writing**: write an unforgettable memory		**Vocabulary building** ↓ **Schematic Structure** ↓ **Writing**

In Table 10, the process of acting in a group is demonstrated and a piece of individual writing serves as an output in the third teaching cycle. It illustrates the body action and verbal text created in the acting process and the written text as a result. In the acting out process, the experience is expressed through verbal language. It can be explained with the REGISTER, in which (1) ideational metafunction of the FIELD—*the school life*, shows the EXPERIENTIAL meaning through the choice of language use; (2) interpersonal metafunction of TENOR indicates the relation not only between the author and the readers, but also among characters *A, J & K*. It shows the INTERPERSONAL meaning in the experience; and (3) textual metafunction of MODE is transformed from oral (acting in group) to written (individual writing) text, according to the analysis of Halliday's Functional Grammar.

8.3.2 Acting Creates Emotion

Acting in a group provides opportunities for students to communicate and exchange ideas within their group and share them with others. According to the Interactive Hypothesis of Long (1985, 1996), during the interactive process of acting, it is a natural process of producing language within the context of what they create to perform in front of the audience. This is because, performing in front of the audience,

Table 10 Demonstration of the outcome of group acting and individual writing

Acting in Group (Physical Action)			Individual writing
Body action		Verbal speech	Written text
	A、J、K speak to the audience.	Together: 我哋係好朋友 (We are best friends)	[Orientation] K、A和J成立一個組合叫「BFF」, 意思是「Best Friends Forever」, 所以他是好朋友。 (One night in a park in Tokyo, K, A and J established a group called "BFF" which means 'Best Friends Forever'. Therefore, they were good friends.)
	K towards audience. A & J look at K.	K: The next day, at the road	[Process] 第二天, 他們在街上吃雪糕, (The next day, they were eating ice-cream on the street.)
	On the road, A & J are arguing and fight each other. J wants to stop them.	J: 唔好, 唔好打! (No. Don't fight!)	A碰到K, 他的雪糕掉了, K生氣地推A, 所以她的雪糕都掉, 接着, 他們一齊開始吵架, (A pushed K and made his ice-cream fall on the ground. K pushed A back angrily. A's ice-cream fell on the ground too. Both of them started arguing and fighting.)
	K drops his pen on the road.		K不小心弄跌他的筆在馬路上, (K's pen fell into the road)

(continued)

Table 10 (continued)

Acting in Group (Physical Action)			Individual writing
Body action		Verbal speech	Written text
	J walks out and helps to pick up the pen.		J在路上拾起它, (J went to pick it up.)
	Suddenly, a truck comes in and crashes into J. K & J are very frightened and scream out loud.	A, J, K:呀! (Ah!)	[**Complication**] 但她被貨車撞到, (She was hit by a truck.)
	K looks at the audience.	K: Next scene. Funeral	
	J lying on the floor. A & K look at J's body and cry. A wipes her tears and K cover his mouth.	A, K: 嗚…… (woo)	
	K stands up and talked to A.	K: 我唔想同你做朋友! (I don't want to be your friend anymore.)	
	A is surprised	A: 點解呀? (Why?)	

(continued)

Table 10 (continued)

Acting in Group (Physical Action)			Individual writing
Body action		Verbal speech	Written text
	A wipes off her tears.		
	K points to A, steps his right foot. (Scene change)	K: 我唔想呀…因為你做嘅! (I don't want to... because you have done such a thing!)	所以K和A不想做朋友。 (Therefore, K and A couldn't be friends anymore.)
	A appears in a university classroom		**[Resolution]** 十年之後, A在她的大學課 (After ten years, A attended a class in university)
	K enters and touches A's shoulder.		
	A turns back and looks at K.		見到K (A bumped into K.)
	K apologises to A and says…	K: Sorry	所以K說:「I'm so sorry…」, (K said, 'I am so sorry…')

(continued)

Table 10 (continued)

Acting in Group (Physical Action)			Individual writing
Body action		Verbal speech	Written text
	[Ending] A accepts and nobs her head.	A:I forgive you. K: 十年之後 我哋做番朋 友, 因為我好 掛住你! (Let's be friends again after 10 years. because I miss you so much!)	[Ending] 所以他們是朋友 了。 (Therefore, they became friends again.)

expression is generated not only in the form of verbal text but also in the form of prosody of tone and emotion. As emotion cannot be acted without a reason, it is a reaction of a specific action (Stanislavski, 1936, 2008). Therefore, when students act, their emotions are revealed subconsciously during the communication among student-actors.

Refer to the demonstration of acting in Table 10 again, where emotions are found as reactions:

1. A argued with K [Action] → A & K fought with each other [Reaction] →他們吵架 (They fight) [written]
2. J was hit by a truck (Action) → A & K were frightened (Reaction)
3. A & K attended J's funeral (Action) → A & K were crying (Reaction)
4. K said he didn't want to be friends with A because of J's death (Action) → A wipes off her tears (Reaction)
5. A met K again after ten years (Action) → K felt sorry for A (Reaction) → 十年之後, A見到K, K説:「I'm so sorry...」 (After 10 years, A bumped into K. K apologised) [written]

Language is produced through socialisation (Halliday, 1985; Halliday & Matthiessen, 2004, 2013). Acting in groups enhances students' ability to express themselves through improvisation. Thus, it is an activity of socialisation, which provides students with the opportunity to create more verbal text with emotions, which inspires students to express their feelings and use more emotive vocabularies in the written text.

8.3.3 Acting as Scaffolding of Narrative Writing

The Stanislavski's System seems to provide effective scaffolds for narrative writing for Chinese as a second language learners. Since in Halliday's Functional Grammar transitivity is a major component in the experiential function for representing 'processes and 'experience', it indicates the authors' cognitive awareness of construing 'the world of experience' (Halliday & Matthiessen, 2004). Through physical action, sense memory and emotion memory, the acting strategies arouse the actors' long-term memory in their life experience (Stanislavski, 2008). In addition, various acting exercises open up students' senses and awareness of their living environment and experience, as they progress through the different cycles. These acting activities work appropriately to provide scaffolds for narrative writing.

In cycle one (Preparation) of the teaching model, a series of Processes (Verb) input worked well through acting exercise:

- Who I am → Relational Process, e.g. 我是男孩子 (I *am* a boy).
- Sensory Memory → Mental Process, e.g. 我看見藍色裙子 (I *saw* a blue skirt).
- Physical Action (body) →Material Process, e.g. 我跑 (I *run*).
- Physical Action (speech) → Verbal Process, e.g. 「對不起!」K說。 ('I am sorry' K *said.*).

After building up the awareness of senses and actions in writing several process categories, Schematic Structure was introduced in cycle two (Making Story) and practiced in cycle three (Making a Story about School Life).

Schematic Structure:

- Orientation → when + who + where
- Process → who + what (action 1)
- Complications → why + how (action 2, 3…)
- Resolution → how (action 4,5…)
- Ending

In order to illustrate a scene realistically, as many details as possible about the scene are needed. *Given Circumstances* is an important element in the System for setting up a scene. Thus, *When, Who, Where, What, Why,* and *How* become the basic elements of *Given Circumstances* in acting. Simultaneously, those *WH-* forms become the circumstantial elements occurring in all types of process in narrative writing (see Fig. 1).

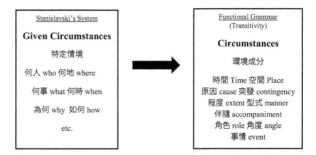

Fig. 1 Given circumstances in acting vs circumstances in SFL

In the last cycle (Emotion Memory), after students can manage the recounting of events and basic narrative skills, Emotion Memory may be introduced to enhance students' expression of their feelings in narrative writing.

- Emotion Memory → behavioural Process, e.g. 她哭了 (She *cried*).

9 Conclusion: Consideration and Limitation

While not all language educators may be convinced of the importance of drama in language teaching and learning, the current study suggests that Stanislavski's System offers an effective solution for teaching narrative writing in Chinese as a second language to junior secondary school students. By engaging in acting activities, students can collaborate with peers and explore writing topics based on their own life experiences. Acting as a whole-person activity reduces the burden of writing and allows students to focus on the ideas and meaning of expression. The analysis of Halliday's Functional Grammar reveals that students' writing performances show significant improvement (effect size 1.56) when they utilise more emotive (behavioural process) lexicons to express themselves in writing. This underscores the value of integrating drama practice and exercises into language education, aligning with both policy and pedagogical goals for enhanced second language learning.

Although this chapter's study has limitations, it provides valuable insights and establishes a strong foundation for future research. The metaphorical link between Stanislavski and Halliday and the limited scope and sample size of the study may restrict its generalizability. Additionally, the analysis may not provide a comprehensive and definitive analysis. However, these limitations present opportunities for further exploration, spark interest, and invite continued investigation into the integration of drama and language education.

References

Benedetti, J. (2000). *Stanislavski: An introduction*. Routledge.
Bolton, G. (1984). *Drama as education*. Longman.
Bolton, G. (1999). *Acting in classroom drama: A critical analysis*. Heinemann Drama.
Christie, F. (2018). Michael Halliday 1925–2018. *Australian Journal of Language and Literacy, 41*(3), 141–143.
Cohen, J. (1988). *Statistical power analysis for the behavioural sciences* (2nd ed.). Lawrence Erlbaum Associates.
Cremin, T., Goouch, K., Blakemore, L., Goff, E., & Macdonald, R. (2006). Connecting drama and writing: Seizing the moment to write. *Research in Drama Education: The Journal of Applied Theatre and Performance, 11*(3), 273–291.
Eggins, S. (2004). *An introduction to systemic functional linguistics*. Continuum.
Halliday, M. A. K. (1978). *Language as social semiotic*. Edward Arnold.

Halliday, M. A. K. (1985). *Introduction to functional grammar* (1st ed.). Arnold.
Halliday, M. A. K., & Matthiessen, C. M. I. M. (2004). *An introduction to functional grammar* (3rd ed.). Routledge.
Halliday, M. A. K., & Matthiessen, C. M. I. M. (2013). *Halliday's introduction to functional grammar* (4th ed.). Routledge.
Heathcote, D. (1984). Drama and learning. In L. Johnson & C. O'Neill (Eds.), *Dorothy Heathcote: Collected writings on education and drama* (pp. 90–102). Hutchinson.
Hyland, K. (2013). *Genre and second language writing*. The University of Michigan Press.
Kemmis, S., & McTaggart, R. (Eds.). (1992). *The action research planner* (3rd ed.). Deakin University Press.
Koshy, V. (2010). *Action research for improving educational practice. A step-by-step guide* (2nd ed.). Sage.
Krashen, S. (1985). *The input hypothesis: Issues and implications*. Longman.
Loh, E. K. Y. (2015). Using drama in education to enhance Chinese language proficiency of non-Chinese speaking secondary school students. *IB Journal of Teaching Practice, 2*(2), 1–7.
Long, M. H. (1985). Input and second language acquisition theory. In S. M. Gass & C. G. Madden (Eds.), *Input in second language acquisition* (pp. 377–393). Newbury House.
Long, M. H. (1996). The role of the linguistic environment in second language acquisition. In W. C. Ritchie & T. K. Bhatia (Eds.), *Handbook of second language acquisition* (pp. 413–468). Academic.
McNaughton, M. J. (1997). Drama and children's writing: A study of the influence of drama on the imaginative writing of primary school children. *Research in Drama Education, 2*(1), 55–76.
Mcniff, J., & Whitehead, J. (2010). *You and your action research project*. Routledge.
Miller, D. M., & Pine, G. J. (1990). Advancing professional inquiry for educational improvement through action research. *Journal of Staff Development, 2*(3), 56–61.
Mills, G. E. (2003). *Action research: A guide for the teacher researcher*. Merrill/Prentice Hall.
Moore, B., & Caldwell, H. (1993). Drama and drawing for narrative writing in primary grades. *Journal of Educational Research, 87*(2), 100–110.
Neelands, J. (1992). *Learning through imagined experience: The role of drama in the national curriculum*. Hodder & Stoughton.
Neelands, J., & Goode, T. (2015). *Structuring drama work* (3rd ed.). Cambridge University Press.
Neelands, J., Booth, D., & Ziegler, S. (1993). *Writing in imagined contexts: Research into drama-influenced writing*. University of Toronto Press.
O'Neill, C. (1995). *Drama Worlds: A framework for process drama*. Pearson Education Canada.
Stanislavski, K. (1936). Creative work with actors: A discussion on directing. In T. Cole & H. Chinoy (Eds.), *(1976). Directors on directing*. Macmillan.
Stanislavski, K. (2008). *An actor's work*. Routledge.
Wagner, B. J. (1986). *The effects of role playing on written persuasion: An age and channel comparison of 4th and 8th graders*. Unpublished doctoral dissertation of University of Illinois at Chicago.
Wilson, E. (Ed.). (2009). *School-based research: A guide for education students*. Sage.

A Multiple-Case Study of 1.5 Chinese Students' Writing Strategies

Feifei Feng

Abstract Writing has always been recognized as the most difficult and challenging part of language learning. Research on writing strategies has increased a lot recently, while less was found in Chinese field. Meanwhile, the number of 1.5 Chinese students shows a rapid growth trend, and this group's writing strategy research needs more attention. To fill the research gap of 1.5 Chinese, this study focuses writing strategies in different writing stages of 1.5 Chinese students with different writing abilities. This study adopts target sampling, and 4 IBDP Chinese B students from an international school of Hong Kong join in, with 2 of them are more skilled Chinese writer and the other 2 less skilled. In this study, interviews, think aloud protocols and stimulated recall are conducted with the students, meanwhile observation form and process log are done by the researcher. With the varieties of qualitative data, the study aims to meet triangulation principle and enhance the study's trustworthiness as well. The study identified 32 types writing strategies in total. The group of more skilled students used writing strategies more frequently and effectively in various writing stages than the group of less skilled students. Meanwhile, the writing strategies used by more skilled students are more interactive, thus their writing was more effective. However, the use of writing strategies of less skilled students often lacked of correlation and even contradictory with each other, thus it affected their writing performance. Basing on the research findings, this study makes both theoretical and pedagogical contributions to 1.5 Chinese writing strategy research and teaching. Further research on this field is expected and directions are also proposed.

1 Introduction

1.1 Chinese Language Learning in a Global Context

In the twenty-first century, language skill now has an important place in education. Bilingual or trilingual learners have a greater competitive advantage and gain more

F. Feng (✉)
Singapore International School (Hong Kong), Wong Chuk Hang, Hong Kong

opportunities, compared to their monolingual counterparts (Chibaka, 2018). With the rapid development of the Chinese economy, Chinese has become a very popular language around the world. Over the last three decades, the number of learners of Chinese as a second/foreign language has dramatically increased. According to the official news released by Hanban, the total number of learners of Chinese as a non-native language had reached 100 million by March 2014; and in 2013, a total of 5 million people participated in various Chinese language exams across 114 countries and regions (Zhao, 2017). Many popular programs worldwide provide Chinese as a Second Language subject courses, for example IB (International Baccalaureate), IGCSE (International General Certificate of Secondary Education), GCE A-level (The General Certificate of Education Advanced Level), and AP (Advanced Placement).

1.2 1.5 Chinese Language Learners

The term 'Generation 1.5' was raised by American scholars, used to describe students whose family language differs from the dominant language in education and society. This leads to limited literacy in their first language as well as their region's dominant language, especially for academic purposes. Among Chinese language learners, there is a group of students whose Chinese language proficiency is in between first and second language, however, this group is not clearly defined in academia. In Hong Kong, students learn Chinese through a very special method of language acquisition. Chinese is a second language, but it is also not totally new to them (Wong & Yeung, 2003). In Singapore, Chinese language acquisition is taught as a mother tongue subject, Chinese is a still a 1.5 language for many students (Wang, 2006; Ye et al., 2014). 1.5 Chinese learners may have a Chinese cultural background, while their dominant language is English or another language. Here are some main characteristics of 1.5 Chinese learners:

- They typically speak two or more languages fluently.
- They learn Chinese mainly through interactions, and their skills of listening and speaking are near-native.
- They perform relatively weakly in Chinese reading and writing.
- They usually have a cross-cultural identity, while being confused about their own identity and culture.

In recent decades, there has been a rapid growth of 1.5 Chinese language learners. This is also reflected in many exams' subject reports, where students who take Chinese as a Second Language performed very well. However, according to Cummins' (1981, 2021) Common Underlying Proficiency Hypothesis (Fig. 1), the 1.5 Chinese language learners can perform well in interpersonal communication skills (BICS), but not in cognitive academic language proficiency (CALP), especially with reading and writing.

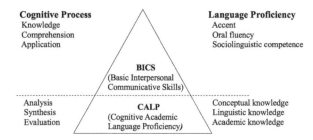

Fig. 1 The difference between BICS and CALP (Cummins, 1981, 2021)

Writing has always been recognized as the most difficult and challenging part of language learning. As for Chinese language learning, the development of interpersonal communication skills and academic reading and writing skills may always be inconsistent, usually with a huge gap between Chinese spoken and written abilities (Zhao, 2008). Thus, this study focuses on 1.5 Chinese learners, and because of the complexity of the Chinese language, it aims to do an in-depth analysis on their Chinese learning.

1.3 Research Gap in Chinese Writing Strategies

For many decades, research and practice in language teaching has identified the four skills — listening, speaking, reading and writing — as being of paramount importance. Among them, writing always shows its importance and difficulties at the same time. Writing is a very complicated process, as the writer needs to have the ability to express thoughts, feelings, transform information, organize grammatical structures and so on. The product-based approach is dominant in previous writing research, which treats writing as a linear process. Following the development of cognitive linguistics and its impact, after the 1980s, the research as well as the teaching and learning practice of writing shifted to a process-based approach (Bereiter & Scardamalia, 1987; Flower & Hayes, 1981; Hayes, 1996). According to cognitive psychology researchers, writing is essentially a "non-linear, exploratory and generative process whereby writers discover and reformulate their ideas as they attempt to approximate meaning" (Zamel, 1983, p. 165). During the recursive writing process, writers use various of strategies to achieve a complete product; for instance, translation, planning, reviewing, information organization, evaluation, modification, L1 transfer and so on.

The cognitive perspective on writing strategy research has been dominant for many decades, however, research findings were scattered and even the popular strategy taxonomy (Oxford, 1990, 1996; O'Malley & Chamot, 1990) was criticized for its lack of a theoretical framework. Since the 1990s, several researchers began to investigate strategies by adopting a sociocultural approach, with the number being small but very inspiring. When reflecting on second language acquisition research, Larsen-Freeman (2007, p. 784) comments: "Our field is beset by dialectics: learning versus use, psychological versus social, acquisition versus participation, and yet, it is focusing on the dynamic coupling of each pair that is likely to be the most productive."

Research on writing strategies has increased a lot recently, though less was found in the Chinese field. Meanwhile, as previously mentioned, the number of 1.5 Chinese students is rapidly increasing, and this group's writing strategy research needs more attention. Thus, to fill the research gap, this research studies the 1.5 Chinese learners' writing strategies; attempts to investigate IB Diploma Program (DP) language acquisition subject—Chinese B students' writing strategies from both cognitive and sociocultural perspectives; and tries to find out the relationship between language ability, different contexts, strategy use and learning outcomes. The research questions ask:

1. What writing strategies are used by the more skilled and less skilled IBDP 1.5 Chinese student writers during different writing stages?
2. What writing strategies are used by the more skilled and less skilled IBDP 1.5 Chinese student writers in different teaching contexts?

2 Literature Review

Writing is a skill that it is hard to be acquired naturally or directly through reading. It is very difficult for most language learners. However, it will be easier to achieve the writing goals if one has the right tools. Writing strategies are the tools writers need to use during the writing process, meanwhile they depend on personal effort or agency to be effective (Paris et al., 1985). This chapter will critically review three major approaches to language learning strategy (LLS) research as well as some previous research findings.

Language learning strategies define the approach that learners adopt in learning a second language (L2), and there are three major approaches to LLS research: O'Malley and Chamot's (1990) cognitive model, Oxford's (1990) six-factor taxonomy, and Cohen's (1998) LLS and language use strategies. LLS can be defined as "thoughts and actions, consciously selected by learners, to assist them in carrying out a multiplicity of tasks from the very onset of learning to the most advanced levels of target-language performance" (Cohen, 2011, p. 7). Then what is the definition of writing strategies? According to the classification of learning strategy by skill area, strategies are viewed in terms of their roles in listening, reading, speaking, and writing (Cohen, 2014). Oxford (1990) proposed the Strategy Inventory for Language Learning (SILL), which was recognized as one of "the most comprehensive learner strategy survey methods" (Ellis, 1994, p. 539) and is widely applied in second language writing strategy research. The strategy system consists of direct and indirect strategies, with specific different subcategories. The direct strategy category includes memory strategies, cognitive strategies and compensation strategies; while the indirect strategy category includes metacognitive strategies, affective strategies and social strategies. However, there is no consistent answer to the definition of a learning strategy. In addition, such taxonomy for classifying learner strategies merely quantifies them and ignores the qualities of strategies.

Much of previous research on writing strategy focused on the cognitive process of writing (Cumming, 1989), and recently some studies have focused on sociocognitive aspects of writing, through a sociocultural perspective (Lei, 2008, 2009; Prior, 2006; Zhao, 2011). A lot of research demonstrates a correlation between writing strategy use and writing proficiency. There is also some research focused on peer/teacher feedback on writing, computer use etc. The majority of research about writing in L2 investigated ESL writing, but writing strategy research in Chinese as a second/foreign language only started in the late 1980s with a very small amount.

According to a critical review of research on strategies of learning Chinese as both a second and foreign language by Jiang and Cohen (2012), there were only three relevant studies from 1980–1989; and it developed into fifteen publications in 1990–1999 and increased greatly to sixty-nine in the twenty-first century. Meanwhile, Chinese reading strategy and Chinese character learning strategy are the two prime focuses. Among all these studies, quantitative methods prevailed and questionnaire surveys were overwhelmingly used. Qualitative research on L2 writing strategy was also employed by researchers, such as verbal reports, case studies and experiment approaches, providing very in-depth, multi-faceted and vivid research data.

The LLS research field itself has witnessed the transition from a psychological to sociocultural perspective. Therefore, writing strategy research from a sociocultural perspective is in line with this trend and of great significance. Furthermore, it is still unclear about the relationship between individual learner differences, writing strategies and learning outcomes. Writing is very important, but second language and 1.5 language writing strategy research is still under development. Thus, more research on L2 and L1.5 Chinese writing strategy is needed.

3 Methodology

This research adopts a case study approach. In a case study, in-depth and multifaceted investigation can be done of a single social phenomenon, and vivid research data will be provided in a real-life environment.

3.1 Participants and Sampling

The researcher is a Chinese teacher of the IBDP Chinese B Higher Level course. Not only is it convenient to engage this group of students in this research, it is also meaningful to study students' writing strategies, for further improvement in language teaching practice.

There are four students taking the IBDP Chinese B Higher Level subject, including two boys and two girls, aged from 16–17 years old. They speak English with each other at school, and they also speak fluent Cantonese with their family members at home. In their daily life, English is their dominant language, given that the language of education of most subjects, communications and popular culture is English. Though they study in an international school, which promotes bilingual education, their Chinese language class time is very limited (around 4–5 hours per week). These students are very typical 1.5 Chinese learners; their Chinese language proficiency is between first and second language, and their listening and speaking abilities are stronger than their reading and writing abilities.

3.2 Research Methods

3.2.1 Interviews

Student participants had been invited to attend interviews four times for research data collection. The first is about their learning experience of Chinese as a second language, and the other three are based on DP Chinese B Higher Level written assignments in different learning stages: (a) at the beginning of the DP1 academic year, (b) in the middle of the DP1 academic year, and (c) at the end of the DP1 academic year. Each interview last ten to fifteen minutes and was audio-recorded. The audio files were encrypted and saved onto CD-ROMs. Students have the right to review the recording and erase part of or the entire recording.

The semi-structured interview method was adopted in this qualitative research, because it has two-way communication between the interviewer and interviewee, while the process remains under control of the interviewer. By the method of unstructured interview, it is easy to enter the inner world of participants who are experiencing writing with Chinese as a second language. Thus rich, complete, and in-depth information can be collected during the structured but also flexible interview process.

3.2.2 Think Aloud and Stimulated Recall

Aside from interviews, the think aloud and stimulated recall methods were employed in the study as well. Student participants were asked to finish a written assignment with the teacher, and say their thinking out loud during the writing process. Each think aloud activity last thirty to sixty minutes and were audio-recorded. Think aloud was conducted in a comfortable classroom environment that students are familiar with, and warm up exercises were done before formal recording.

After the students complete their writing, the researcher conducted stimulated recall, about 10–20 minutes on the same day. Basing on the think aloud process, researcher's observation logs and students' writing work, the researcher asked students to recall their writing process and discuss the use of writing strategies.

The entire sessions of think aloud and stimulated recall were recorded. The researcher transcribed the audio files of the think aloud and stimulated recall for further data analysis.

3.2.3 Text Analysis

The students' written assignments were collected and analysed. The text analysis is to prove and verify the writing strategies data collected from interviews, think aloud and stimulated recall activities. The rubrics of IBDP Chinese B writing was used to assess the students' writings. The researcher serves as IBDP Chinese B examiner and has good knowledge of assessment, another IB examiner was also invited to mark the students' writing, to ensure the accuracy of marking.

3.2.4 Data Analysis

For the data collected in this study, the researcher used the following three tools for analysis: checklist, coding and effectiveness assessment. The checklist combined Grabe and Kaplan (1996) writing strategy list and the writing strategies detected in this research's pilot study. With the checklist, the research coded the transcripts of think aloud and stimulated recall, and then double verified with researcher's observation logs and students' writings. The researcher also rated the effectiveness of strategy according to the following rubrics (Table 1).

4 Findings

In this study, the researcher identified 32 types of writing strategies in total, including 17 types of cognitive strategies and 15 types of meta-cognitive strategies. Cognitive writing strategy refers to the writer's procedural organization in the writing process, and the writer's underlying language knowledge and topic knowledge. Metacognitive writing strategy refers to the writer's planning, monitoring and

Table 1 Writing strategy effectiveness rubrics

Marks	Level descriptor
3	Strategy is used appropriately, and helps improve the writing.
2	Strategy is used appropriately, but its applicability may not be suitable.
1	Strategy is used not appropriately.

adjustment of the writing process. On the basis of a comprehensive writing plan, the author evaluated the constraints of rhetoric and content, as well as the relationship between composition and their writing goal.

Table 2 lists all the writing strategies identified at different writing stages, and divides the writing strategies into two main categories: cognitive and metacognitive. They are also classified into three different subcategories: linguistic level, textual level and pragmatic level. The linguistic level writing strategy refers to the writer's attempt to interpret the question accurately and polish their language appropriately. The textual writing strategy refers to materials selection and organization, so as to achieve their writing goals. The writing strategy at the pragmatic level is that the writer evaluates the context, audience and other criteria to determine the exact writing purpose for the composition.

To answer research question 1, what writing strategies are used by the more skilled and less skilled IBDP 1.5 Chinese student writers during different writing stages? In this study, the types of writing strategies used by more skilled and less skilled 1.5 Chinese students were identified and counted. The researcher also counted how many times did students use strategies in different stages and record it as the frequency. Meanwhile, the researcher also assessed the effectiveness of each writing strategy used. If the writing strategy was used without effect, 1 point was given; if writing strategy was used unskilfully with some help, 2 points was given; if writing strategy was well used to aid writing performance, 3 points was given. Table 3 shows the details. From the data we can found: in all writing stages, including planning, transforming and revising, there is a significant difference between the two groups. The more skilled group has clear advantages in terms of writing strategy types, frequency and especially in effectiveness. Therefore, they perform better in Chinese writing than the less skilled group.

In the process of planning, the effectiveness of cognitive strategy can positively lead to metacognitive strategy, thereby improving the quality of Chinese writing. During the planning stage, the more skilled student writers interpreted the question accurately, made an outline directly related to the topic and established a clear writing purpose. As a result, it met the IB writing requirements and earned a high grade. Meanwhile the less skilled student writers misinterpreted the question, lacked a clear linkage to the topic, and rarely used pragmatic level strategies, all of which had negative impact on their writing.

In the process of transforming, the frequency of metacognitive writing strategy can positively impact the writing quality. During the transforming stage, the more skilled student writers frequently used metacognitive writing strategies, particularly the textual level and pragmatic level strategies. Meanwhile the less skilled student writers mainly relied on the cognitive strategies of the linguistic level, and seldom adopted metacognitive strategies. This implies that less skilled student writers encountered many difficulties with vocabulary; thus, they were unable to present their planning well in the target language.

In the process of revising, students check the quality of their own work, evaluating and modifying it to meet the writing objectives. The more skilled student writers were good at using the metacognitive writing strategies from linguistic,

A Multiple-Case Study of 1.5 Chinese Students' Writing Strategies 233

Table 2 Writing strategies used by 1.5 Chinese students

		Planning	Transformation	Revising	Throughout the writing process
A: Cognitive strategies	Linguistic	A1 interpret questions A2 mark key points A3 list vocabulary	A10 write to confirm the character form A11 replace with simple words	/	/
	Textual	A4 plan key points A5 filter materials A6 outline A7 draft A8 Chinese target language thinking A9 English / Cantonese thinking	A12 introduce thematic focus A13 apply materials to writing A14 English / Cantonese translation	A15 reread full text A16 self-questioning A17 avoid review	
B: Metacognitive strategies	Linguistic	/	/	B7 check language expression B8 modify	/
	Textual	/	B2 linkage B3 add to writing plan B4 arrange structure	B9 review by paragraphs B10 review structure	B12 interdisciplinary knowledge imitation and transfer
	Pragmatic	B1 rhetoric / genre consideration	B5 evaluate language effect B6 evaluate content effectiveness	B11 self-evaluation	B13 consider writing purpose and effectiveness B14 time management

Table 3 Writing strategies used by 2 groups in panning, transforming and revising stages

		More skilled 1.5 Chinese writers	Less skilled 1.5 Chinese writers
Planning	Types	11	10
	Frequency	50	29
	Effectiveness	151	55
Transforming	Types	11	10
	Frequency	61	65
	Effectiveness	183	128
Revising	Types	8	5
	Frequency	48	27
	Effectiveness	144	45

textual and pragmatic levels. Meanwhile the less skilled student writers could not successfully employ revising strategies, and even avoided reviewing to ignore writing errors, in order to end the writing process as quickly as possible.

To answer research question 2, what writing strategies are used by the more skilled and less skilled IBDP 1.5 Chinese student writers in different teaching contexts? In this study, there were two teaching interventions; one was traditional teaching context, which emphasized tool mediation and rule mediation; while the other one was the collaborative teaching method, which incorporated tool mediation, rule mediation and community mediation. Table 4 shows the details of writing strategy use in two instructional circumstances.

In the first teaching context, more skilled student writers performed better than less skilled student writers, because their writing strategies were significantly correlated to each other. Less skilled student writers were more aware of using writing strategies; therefore, the number of writing strategy types and their frequency were even higher than the more skilled group. Thus, the gap between the two groups has narrowed. In the planning stage, the teaching had little impact on the more skilled group. On the other hand, the teaching was clearly beneficial to the less skilled group. Their writing strategy type, frequency and effectiveness all increased, which aided their overall writing plan. In the transforming stage, the more skilled group focused on metacognitive strategy use. They did not have many language difficulties, so could effectively apply materials to writing, add to writing plans, and undertake self-evaluation during the writing process. As for the less skilled group, they made an improvement in language, though Chinese vocabulary remains a big challenge for them. Meanwhile, they began to consciously use metacognitive strategies to improve their writing. In the revising stage, the more skilled group could revise more effectively than the less skilled group; however, the less skilled group's revising strategy frequency and effectiveness has obviously improved. To sum up, the traditional teaching instruction context does not produce a clear effect in the more skilled group, but it has very positive effects on the less skilled group's planning and metacognitive writing strategy use.

Table 4 Writing strategies used by 2 groups in different teaching contexts

		Traditional teaching (tool mediation and rule mediation)		Collaborative teaching (tool mediation, rule mediation and community mediation)	
		More skilled 1.5 Chinese writers	Less skilled 1.5 Chinese writers	More skilled 1.5 Chinese writers	Less skilled 1.5 Chinese writers
Planning	Types	10	14	10	12
	Frequency	40	72	38	39
	Effectiveness	120	139	114	108
Transforming	Types	11	13	11	13
	Frequency	56	54	58	58
	Effectiveness	168	112	174	141
Revising	Types	7	7	6	6
	Frequency	52	31	39	46
	Effectiveness	146	41	117	95

In the second teaching context, both the more skilled group and less skilled group showed improvement in their writing marks. The gap between them had further narrowed. During planning, both groups used cognitive writing strategies more frequently than metacognitive writing strategies, and they admitted that the collaborative teaching had positive effects on their writing. The less skilled group could interpret questions accurately and transfer the class contents to the writing context naturally. During transforming and revising, both groups used metacognitive writing strategies more frequently than cognitive writing strategies. The less skilled group used strategies correlatively, and it enhanced the writing strategy's effectiveness and writing quality. To conclude, as demonstrated by the data and the participants' own observations, the collaborative teaching method had a positive effect on both the more skilled and less skilled student writers.

5 Conclusion

5.1 Responses to Research Questions

According to the research results analysis, this study identified 32 types of writing strategies in total, which can be summarized into two categories: cognitive writing strategies and metacognitive writing strategies. This study also found that writing strategies work in clusters but not independently, and that cognitive writing strategies interacting with metacognitive writing strategies can effectively improve the writing qualities of 1.5 Chinese learners. As for the two groups of students with different language abilities, more skilled students use writing strategies more frequently and effectively in various writing stages than the group of less skilled students. Meanwhile, the writing strategies used by more skilled students are more interactive; thus, their writing was more effective. However, the use of writing strategies of less skilled students often lack correlation and even contradictory with each other; therefore, affecting their writing performance.

Based on the research findings, this study makes both theoretical and pedagogical contributions to 1.5 Chinese writing strategy research and teaching. Further research in this field is expected and future directions are also proposed.

5.2 *Implications for Further Research*

Socio-cultural theories have developed and gained recognition in the language acquisition research field over the years. With the awareness that language is interactive, it is clear that we should analyze Chinese writing from the perspective of teaching implementation and environmental influence, rather than solely from the learner's individual cognitive process.

We now know many types of writing strategies which can help language learners; however, different scholars have different categorizing criteria and a lack of consensus. Meanwhile, is there any hierarchy among the writing strategies and how they work together with each other? These questions still need to be clarified in future research. Moreover, in view of the complexity and particularity of 1.5 language learners, as well as their increasing numbers, more research is needed in this field.

5.3 *Implications for Pedagogy*

First, writing is always the biggest challenge for language learners, including 1.5 Chinese students. According to the revised Bloom's taxonomy (Anderson & Krathwohl, 2001), the structure of the knowledge dimension includes: Factual, Conceptual, Procedural and Metacognitive; and the structure of the cognitive process dimension includes: Remember, Understand, Apply, Analyse, Evaluate and Create. Adopting a collaborative teaching approach, students can understand the knowledge and skills well, and at the same time, train higher-order thinking skills. Compared to traditional teaching methods, the collaborative teaching and learning approach can effectively guide students to not just focus on the contents and language expressions of their own writing, but to also pay attention to: in what ways the concepts are embedded, to what extent the writing purpose is accomplished, and what the target audience's responses are. These strategies can help 1.5 Chinese learners develop strong audience awareness and diagnose their own writing's effectiveness under the marking criteria. It can also be transferred to other disciplinary contexts, and help with students' learning in other subjects. Thus, language teachers are encouraged to adopt the collaborative teaching approach in their lessons and students can benefit from it.

Second, a successful teaching should consist of three indispensable elements: curriculum design, management techniques and instructional strategies. In teaching practices, we found many teachers lack knowledge about writing strategies. Teachers usually teach students some specific writing ways, but students do not know how to choose and apply them, nor are they able to transfer them to other subjects' learning contexts. In recent years, the Writer's Workshop has been quite popular in the USA and was introduced to many countries. Writer's Workshop emphasizes the importance of writing strategies, with teachers conducting mini-lessons to teach writing strategy and guiding students to enhance their writing skills. Therefore, it is necessary for curriculum designers to incorporate writing strategies into curriculum mapping and scheme of work. Teachers can then teach students the knowledge of writing strategies and know how to use them effectively.

To sum up, this study investigated the 1.5 Chinese learners' writing strategies in different teaching contexts. As the number of 1.5 learners has been increasing in recent decades, more research is called to fill in the gap and the 1.5 learners will benefit from optimized curriculum design. Questions remain regarding relationship between writing strategies and writing abilities, how writing strategies reflect learners' cognitive physiological development, and to what extent the writing strategies produce effects in differentiated language learning conditions. All these questions need to be explored by further research.

References

Anderson, L. W., & Krathwohl, D. (Eds.). (2001). *A taxonomy for learning, teaching, and assessing: A revision of Bloom's taxonomy of educational objectives*. Longman.
Bereiter, C., & Scardamalia, M. (1987). *The psychology of written composition*. L. Erlbaum Associates.
Chibaka, E. F. (2018). Advantages of bilingualism and multilingualism: Multidimensional research findings. *Multilingualism and Bilingualism*, 15. Retrieved from: https://www.intechopen.com/chapters/59744
Cohen, A. D. (1998). *Strategies in learning and using a second language*. Longman.
Cohen, A. D. (2011). *Strategies in learning and using a second language* (2nd ed.). Routledge.
Cohen, A. D. (2014). *Strategies in learning and using a second language*. Routledge.
Cumming, A. (1989). Writing expertise and second-language proficiency. *Language Learning, 39*(1), 81–135.
Cummins, J. (1981). Empirical and theoretical understanding of bilingual education. *Journal of Education, 163*, 16–29.
Cummins, J. (2021). *Rethinking the education of multilingual learners: A critical analysis of theoretical concepts* (Vol. 19). Multilingual Matters.
Ellis, R. (1994). *The study of second language acquisition*. Oxford University Press.
Flower, L., & Hayes, J. R. (1981). A cognitive process theory of writing. *College Composition and Communication, 32*(4), 365–387. Retrieved from http://eproxy.lib.hku.hk/login?url=http://search.ebscohost.com/login.aspx?direct=true&db=eric&AN=EJ256235&site=ehost-live&scope=site
Grabe, W., & Kaplan, R. B. (1996). *Theory and practice of writing: An applied linguistic perspective*. Longman.

Hayes, J. (1996). A new framework for understanding cognition and affect in writing. In *The science of writing: Theories, methods, individual differences, and applications* (pp. 1–27). Lawrence Erlbaum Associates, Inc..

Jiang, X., & Cohen, A. D. (2012). A critical review of research on strategies in learning Chinese as both a second and foreign language. *Studies in Second Language Learning and Teaching, 2*(1), 9–43.

Larsen-Freeman, D. (2007). Reflecting on the cognitive–social debate in second language acquisition. *The Modern Language Journal, 91*, 773–787.

Lei, X. (2008). Exploring a sociocultural approach to writing strategy research: Mediated actions in writing activities. *Journal of Second Language Writing, 17*(4), 217–236. Retrieved from http://www.sciencedirect.com/science/article/pii/S1060374308000131

Lei, X. (2009). *Understanding writing strategy use from a sociocultural perspective: A multiple-case study of Chinese EFL learners of different writing abilities*. Unpublished PhD dissertation of The University of Hong Kong.

O'Malley, J. M., & Chamot, A. U. (1990). *Learning strategies in second language acquisition*. Cambridge University Press.

Oxford, R. L. (1990). *Language learning strategies: What every teacher should know*. Heinle & Heinle Publisher.

Oxford, R. L. (1996). *Language learning strategies around the world: Cross-cultural perspectives*. National Foreign Language Resource Center.

Paris, S. G., Newman, R. S., & Jacobs, J. E. (1985). Social contexts and functions of children's remembering. In *Cognitive learning and memory in children* (pp. 81–115). Springer.

Prior, P. (2006). *A sociocultural theory of writing. Handbook of writing research* (pp. 54–66). The Guilford Press.

Wang, H. (2006). Xinjiapo huawen jiaoyu jiaodian zhiyi: Hanzi—Jiyu zhongxiaoxue jiaocai yuliaoku de jiliang fenxi [One of the focuses of Chinese language education in Singapore: Chinese characters: A quantitative analysis based on a corpus of teaching materials for primary and secondary schools]. *Journal of Chinese Language Studies, 2*, 242–255.

Wong, Y. Y., & Yeung, S. Y. (2003). *Hanying yanyu yu wenhua [Chinese-English proverbs and culture]*. Shanghai Foreign Language Education Press.

Ye, Y. T., Li, X. L., & Jian M. R. (2014). *1yu, 2yu, 1.5yu? Huayu jiaoxue mianmianguan—cong Taiwan, Meiguo, Xinjiapo tantao huayu jiaoxue zhi qujing [L1, L2, L1.5? Aspects of Chinese language teaching--Discussing the approaches of Chinese language teaching in Taiwan, the United States and Singapore]*. Paper presented in the International Conference of International Cooperation and Education Aid. National Chi Nan University.

Zamel, V. (1983). The composing processes of advanced ESL students: Six case studies. *TESOL Quarterly, 17*(2), 165–188.

Zhao, J. M. (2008). Hanyu zuowei dier yuyan jiaoxue: Linian yu moshi [Teaching Chinese as a second language: Concepts and models]. *Chinese Teaching in the World, 1*, 93–107.

Zhao, J. F. (2011). *Investigation into the writing strategies of Chinese EFL college students from the perspective of sociocultural theory: A case study*. Jilin University.

Zhao, X. X. (2017). *Hanyu jiasu chengwei "Guojixing yuyan" [Chinese accelerates to become an "international language"]*. Retrieved from http://world.people.com.cn/n1/2017/0923/c1002-29553960.html

Enhancing the Liberal Studies Writing Skills of Non-Chinese Speaking Students Through Genre-Based Teaching

Mark Shiu-kee Shum ⓘ, Elizabeth Ka Yee Loh ⓘ, and Hiu Ching Chan

Abstract In Hong Kong, Liberal Studies (LS) was one of the four compulsory subjects in the Senior Secondary curriculum from 2009, and students had to study it for tertiary advancement. Yet it is extremely challenging for non-Chinese speaking (NCS) students to use Chinese as the medium of instruction for Liberal Studies, especially when writing their answers in Chinese in public examination. In response to their learning needs, a research team at the University of Hong Kong (HKU) launched a pilot study about using genre-based teaching to enhance the writing skills of NCS students. Based on Functional Linguistics (Halliday, M. A. K. *An introduction to functional grammar* (2nd ed.). Edward Arnold, 1994) and Genre theory (Martin, J. R. Mentoring semogenesis: 'Genre-based' literacy pedagogy. In F. Christie (Ed.), *Pedagogy and the shaping of consciousness: Linguistic and social processes* (pp. 123–155). Continuum, 1999), Mark Shum at HKU had previously identified the genres in major subjects in the secondary curriculum that students are expected to master (Shum, M. S. K., *Australian Review of Applied Linguistics* 29:1–22, 2006), including LS. Based on the research findings of the genres of Liberal Studies (Shum, M. S. K., *Subject specific genres of liberal studies and the skills of expression*. Hong Kong Educational Publishing Company, 2015), the research team conducted genre teaching in a class of non-Chinese speaking students to enhance their writing skills with the factorial explanation genre, which is one of the important genres of LS. This paper reports the strategies of the genre-based pedagogy and the outcomes of the genre-based teaching by class observation, interviews and text analyses of students' scripts of pretest and posttest. The results indicated that after genre teaching, the written performance of NCS students was improved in terms of genre identification, sentence patterns and overall construction of the texts. The interviews reflected that the students welcomed this kind of learning

---

Starting from academic year 2021/22 school year, Liberal Studies has been replaced by a new subject, namely Citizenship and Social Development (Education Bureau, 2021).

M. S.-k. Shum (✉) · E. K. Y. Loh · H. C. Chan
The University of Hong Kong, Pok Fu Lam, Hong Kong
e-mail: mskshum@hku.hk

© The Author(s), under exclusive license to Springer Nature Switzerland AG 2024
J. Lo Bianco et al. (eds.), *Supporting the Learning of Chinese as a Second Language: Implications for Language Education Policy*, Language Policy 36,
https://doi.org/10.1007/978-3-031-66135-8_11

and teaching model and they felt more confidence in writing LS essays in Chinese. The findings will have important implications for enhancing Non-Chinese Speaking students' mastery of Chinese language of other subjects and offer a new model of content and language integrating learning and teaching for Hong Kong and beyond.

1 Introduction

1.1 Liberal Studies as a Compulsory Subject

In Hong Kong, there were major education reforms after the 1997 handover. Regarding the secondary curriculum, in the British colonial period there were five years for secondary education (Form 1—Form 5) and two years for matriculation education (Form 6—Form 7). In 2006, Hong Kong moved to the present new '3 + 3' school structure, namely three years for junior secondary and three years for senior secondary. In the new senior secondary (NSS) curriculum, Liberal Studies (LS), together with Chinese Language, English Language and Mathematics, became one of the four compulsory subjects of the university entrance requirement. It was introduced in September 2009 and was examined for the first time in April 2012. This subject consists of three major areas: "Self and Personal Development", "Society and Culture", and "Science, Technology and the Environment". LS employed an inquiry-based approach that aimed to develop reflective and independent thinking as well as a critical and multi-perspectival approach to contemporary issues, something much needed by students as a means of equipping them as lifelong learners in the knowledge-based era. It "plays a unique role in the NSS curriculum by helping students to connect concepts and knowledge across different disciplines, to look at things from more than one single perspectives, and to study issues covered by any single disciplines" (Education and Manpower Bureau (EMB), 2021: 36). As a school subject of this nature, LS focuses very much on generic skills and students who want to be successful in this subject must demonstrate a good mastery of both language and logical thinking skills.

The introduction of LS as a core subject in the NSS Curriculum realized a main aspect of the spirit of the Hong Kong education and curriculum reforms of the early 2000s which aimed to promote critical thinking skills and all-round development in students and it is also "a response to the needs of the Hong Kong community which asks for a cross-curricular learning opportunity for all senior secondary students" (Curriculum Development Council & Hong Kong Examinations and Assessment Authority (CDC & HKEAA, 2005: 1). The distinctive nature of LS sets it aside from the traditional content subjects (Physics, Chemistry, Biology, Geography, Economics, History) in schools. Instead of requiring students to learn a specific field of knowledge, LS, with its multi-perspective and multi-disciplinary nature, requires students to use their critical thinking skills to explain issues based on given facts, to make judgments based on evidence, and to deliver arguments using sound reasons.

These features of LS, when reflecting on language, have resulted in a set of patterns of discourse different from and more demanding than those of the traditional content subjects.

1.2 Difficulties NCS Students Encountered when Learning LS in Chinese

By its very nature, LS deals with living subjects and current issues. The absence of prescribed textbooks makes the flexible curriculum highly challenging. Thus students of the subject have to consult local newspapers and magazines frequently. In Hong Kong, most newspapers and magazines are in Chinese. As a matter of fact, most of the schools in Hong Kong choose to teach LS in Chinese.

This chapter deals with non-Chinese speaking secondary school students learning Liberal Studies in Chinese. The first languages of these students are languages other than Chinese. The difficulties they have encountered when studying the Chinese Language Subject are reported in chapter "Learning Chinese as a Second Language in Hong Kong: The Needs of the Learners in Writing". When it comes to studying Liberal Studies, which requires a good mastery of multi-perspective and multi-disciplinary knowledge, good language ability, and high order thinking skills, such students feel this to be very difficult indeed, especially when using Chinese writing to express subject-specific concepts.

2 Literature Review

2.1 The Relation Between Language and Learning

Language is the major meaning-making system available to human beings (Halliday, 1978). In all areas of school learning and teaching, language has a central role in the construction of meaning. What is of critical important to an understanding of the role of language in constructing school knowledge is the recognition that language functions to build the meanings characteristics of different school subjects. While the construction of all school subjects necessarily draws upon the same linguistic system, each can be drawn in different ways to build the meanings characteristic of the school subjects of concern (Christie, 1984). Research from a variety of other theoretical perspectives has shown that subject areas have their own characteristic language forms and hence entail distinctive literate practices (Street, 1984) has shown that subject areas have their own characteristic language forms and hence entail distinctive literate practices. From the early 1990s, some scholars further explored the ways in which different types of language are used to build specialized knowledge of very different kinds across the curriculum (Christie, 1984, 1985, 1996). The methodology adopted draws in part on Halliday's Systemic

Functional Linguistic theory (Halliday, 1994; Halliday & Mathiessen, 2004 and in part on Martin's work on genre theory (Martin, 1986, 1992). In Martin's definition, genres are characterized as staged, goal oriented social processes: social since texts are always interactive events; goal oriented in that a text unfolds towards its interactants' purposes; staged, because it usually takes more than one step to reach the goal (Martin, 1999).

2.2 Studies of Subject-Specific Literacy

Intensive studies of subject-specific literacy in various subject areas have been carried out within a framework of Systemic Linguistics. The impetus for much of this work was the research of Martin (1986) and his colleagues at the University of Sydney. Christie investigated writing in primary school curriculum areas (Christie, 2005) and in collaboration (Christie et al. 1990, 1992) published curriculum materials focusing on literacy development across curriculum areas. Derewianka and Christie worked on investigating subject literacies and their challenges across the years of secondary education, with reports published with respect to subject History and English (Derewianka & Christie, 2005). The language of school science was substantially examined by Lemke (1990) focusing on 'Talking science', and by Halliday and Martin on 'Writing science'. The latter, which includes accounts of generic structure and lexicogrammatical and discourse semantic features of school science books, formed the basis for further research.

Veel (1997) described the idealized knowledge path in school science as constructed by the form of the school science texts. This involved a progression from genres concerned with "doing science" (procedure, procedural account) to those "organizing scientific information" (descriptive and taxonomic reports), then "explain events scientifically" (sequential, causal, theoretical, factorial, consequential explanations and explorations), and ultimately "challenging science" (exposition and discussion). For subject history, Veel and Coffin (1996) pointed out that as one shifted from chronicling history to explaining history and then to arguing history, there was a progressive increase in lexical density, grammatical metaphor, abstract participants and causal relations. They suggested that explicitly teaching about language—teaching genre, grammar, discourse—as an integral part of school history, can help students to develop a critical orientation through an understanding of the texts' construction.

2.3 Related Work Conducted in Hong Kong After the 1997 Handover

Since 1998, research in subject-specific literacy spread from the English speaking world to one Chinese-language community, i.e. Hong Kong, where the medium of instruction of most secondary schools changed from English to Chinese after the 1997 handover, and the need arose to explore, with teachers, the Chinese language features of various school subjects. From 2000 to 2006, with the help of the Research Grant Council (RGC) General Research Fund (GRF) and Quality Education Fund, Shum and his team conducted a series of research procedures to analyze secondary school public examination papers (Hong Kong Certificate of Education Examination, HKCEE), students' answer scripts, and the textbooks of Chemistry, Physics, Biology, Economics, Geography and History, to establish the subject-specific genres of the above disciplines. The findings from this series of studies were published in the form of genre analysis of six subjects (Shum et al., 2003a, b, 2004a, b, 2006a, b). To deepen the research from product to process, Shum and his team extended the scope of research from data related to public examination and textbooks to data related to classroom learning and teaching; from identification of the students' writing problems to the research on strategies and pedagogies that would contribute to empowering secondary school students with subject specific literacy (Shum, 2010).

As noted in the Introduction, as the essential component of the education reform, from 2009, Liberal Studies (LS) evolved to become one of the four compulsory subjects in the New Senior Secondary Curriculum in Hong Kong. To cope with the urgent need of teacher training, with the help of Research Grant Council (RGC) General Research Fund (GRF), in 2009, Shum and his team explored the language features of the subject so as to enhance effective learning and teaching. As a result, the genres of LS were identified as follows (Fig. 1 and Table 1).

In the above, nine genres were identified with explanation, argumentation, recommendation and interpretation as the dominating genres which are consistent with the spirit of LS. With the identification of the genres of LS, the research team organized their research project to collaborate with LS teachers to develop genre pedagogy to assist students in the mainstream classrooms to overcome the writing difficulties the students had encountered. The finding revealed a significant improvement by students in learning LS through genre teaching (Shum et al., 2012). The above-noted research of LS genre teaching in the mainstream class has laid the basis for the present study of supporting non-Chinese students learning LS through Chinese, which is geared towards enriching the existing body of knowledge of genre-based literacy for second language Chinese learners in Hong Kong.

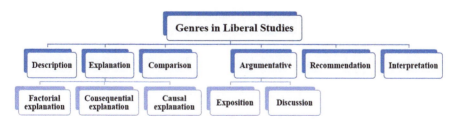

Fig. 1 Genre map of Liberal Studies (Shum, 2015)

Table 1 The functions and forms of LS genres in Hong Kong school curriculum (Shum, 2015)

Genre	Function	Schematic structure
Description	Describing a phenomenon	General statement^Description 1-n^ (Summary)
Factorial Explanation	Explaining factors constituting a phenomenon	Phenomenon^Factor 1-n^ (Reaffirmation of factors)
Consequential Explanation	Explaining the effects caused by a phenomenon	Phenomenon^Effect 1-n^ (Reaffirmation of effects)
Causal Explanation	Explaining a sequence causing a phenomenon	Phenomenon^Explanation sequence 1-n^(Summary)
Comparison	Comparing 2 or more from certain aspects	Comparison aspects^Elaboration 1-n^ (Summary)
Exposition	Arguing for a point of view	Position^Argument 1-n^Reiteration
Discussion	Discussing an issue from multiple perspectives	Position^Argument 1-n^Reiteration
Recommendation	Providing recommendation in a given situation	Overview^Suggestion1-n^ (Reaffirmation of Suggestions)
Interpretation	Interpreting the message of a(n) text/image	Message^Data Description 1-n^ Message Reaffirmation

2.4 Genre-Based Literacy Methodology

The description of written genres developed in tandem with a long term literacy intervention, designed to provide access for all students to the linguistic resources required for educational success (Rose, 2010). On the principle of 'guidance through interaction in the context of shared experience', Rothery (1994) and her colleagues designed a teaching-learning cycle for classroom language learning contexts. This Genre-based pedagogy consisted of three main stages: (i) Deconstruction (guiding students to recognize the cultural context, staging and key linguistic features in model texts, (ii) Joint Construction (guiding the whole class to construct another text in the same genre), and (iii) Independent Construction (in which students write their own texts in the same genre)—see Fig. 2.

The current chapter extends the study of LS genre teaching from mainstream class to non-Chinese speaking students who learn Liberal Studies in second language Chinese, a language other than their mother tongues. The research team aimed at using genre-based pedagogy and its latest development model 'Reading to Learn, Learning to Write'(R2L) pedagogy to support non-Chinese speaking students' to improve their writing skills of LS.

Space will not permit a detailed review of the Genre-based Approach and the R2L Pedagogy in this chapter. Please refer to chapter "Using 'Reading to Learn, Learning to Write' (R2L) Pedagogy to Teach Explanation Genre to Non-Chinese Speaking Students in Hong Kong" for detailed descriptions of the theories.

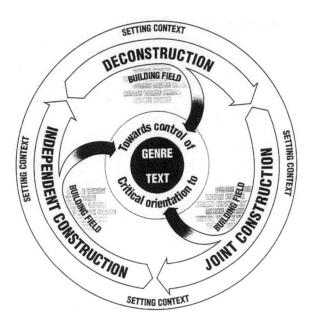

Fig. 2 Genre-based pedagogy: teaching and learning cycle (Rothery, 1994)

3 Aim of the Study and Research Questions

The current study is designed to gain understanding of how genre-based pedagogy helps to enhance non-Chinese speaking students' Liberal Studies writing skills, and, if it does so, how it can be applied in classroom practices. According to the teachers, factorial explanation is one of the important genres in Liberal Studies. This study would choose this genre as the focus of teaching and learning.

The research questions of this study are as follows:

1. Do students improve their writing performance of the factorial explanation genre in Liberal Studies after their teacher's classroom teaching with genre-based pedagogy?
2. What are the differences between their pre-test and post-test of factorial explanation writing of students at different levels of language skills (high, medium, low)?

4 Methodology

4.1 Research Context and Participants

The study was conducted in a government subsidized secondary school with a large population of non-Chinese speaking students. The first languages of those students are languages other than Chinese, while all subjects (apart from English language) in the school are delivered in Chinese. For this reason, the non-Chinese speaking students feel it difficult to master those subjects. When it comes to Liberal Studies, which requires a demanding Chinese proficiency and high order thinking skills, they feel it to be even more difficult to learn, especially writing.

To explore the effect of genre teaching on enhancing the Liberal Studies writing skills of non-Chinese speaking students, a total of six non-Chinese secondary five students who joined after-school Liberal Studies tutorial classes and their teacher were invited to participate in this pilot study. The students who were nominated by the school represented different levels of academic achievements, namely high, medium and low. A quasi-experimental pre-post-design was adopted to explore the effect of genre-based pedagogy as an intervention.

Before conducting the experiment, the researchers met with the teacher to discuss genre-based pedagogy in relation to teaching writing as developed by the Sydney School to ensure mutual understanding of the pedagogy used in the intervention. The researchers also analyzed the common genres used in Liberal Studies to facilitate the teacher's selection of genre used in this pilot study. The factorial explanation, as one of the most common genres that students need to acquire, was chosen as the teaching genre in the intervention. Thus, the teaching goal of the intervention was to enhance students' writing skills on the genre of factorial explanation (Fig. 3).

To achieve the teaching goal, ten hours of pilot teaching in four lessons were conducted with the application of the genre-based pedagogy. To understand students' difficulties in response to the genre of factorial explanation, the teacher participant first carried out a pre-test in the first lesson to measure students' genre writing performance on factorial explanation. To match students' learning progress and respond to the learning need in preparing for the Hong Kong Diploma of Secondary Education (HKDSE) Examination, the pre-test used was modified from the 2013 Liberal Studies HKDSE examination question paper. It is noted that in Hong Kong, at the end of the sixth year of secondary school, students sit in the HKDSE examination. The Liberal Studies HKDSE examination is set in Chinese and in English. The HKDSE examination determines entry to subsequent schooling that opens up the possibility of university entrance, the questions set for both languages are identical in content for the purpose of fairness. The genres assessed in both Chinese and English paper are also the same. Hence, the genres of the Liberal Studies subject that students in both English medium schools and Chinese medium schools need to master are basically the same, in terms of schematic structures and linguistics features. Since the secondary school attended by the NCS students participating in this study had chosen the Chinese paper, the students needed to answer the questions in Chinese. The question selected for the pre-test is related to the topic of *obesity* (*Based on the information provided and your own experience, what are the three causes of obesity?*). The topic of *obesity* was selected as students had been equipped with the subject content in the Liberal Studies classes.

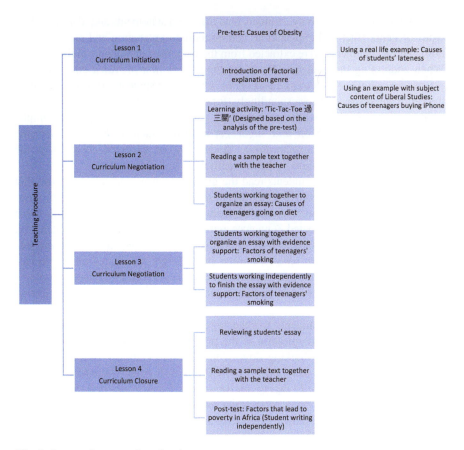

Fig. 3 Intervention: genre-based pedagogy treatment

After the pre-test, the teacher initiated the curriculum by using a real-life example (*What are the causes of students' lateness?*) and then an example which added the subject content of Liberal Studies (*What are the causes of teenagers buying iPhone?*). The examples were used to introduce the genre of factorial explanation.

Before the delivery of the second lesson, the researchers used R2L Writing Assessment Criteria (please refer to chapters "Learning Chinese as a Second Language in Hong Kong: The Needs of the Learners in Writing" and "Using 'Reading to Learn, Learning to Write' (R2L) Pedagogy to Teach Explanation Genre to Non-Chinese Speaking Students in Hong Kong") to assess the performance of students in the pre-test and identify the difficulties that students faced when constructing an essay of the factorial explanation genre. Based on the analysis, the teacher designed the second lesson (namely 'Tic-Tac-Toe 過三關') which aims to tackle students' difficulties in three steps.

In the first learning activity, students read the given statements and identified their types of genre (factorial explanation, consequential explanation and recommendation). Those statements were extracted from the responses of students in the pre-test. When addressing the question (*Based on the information provided and your own experience, what are the three causes of obesity?*), some students correctly identified the genre and responded correspondingly (for example, *eating too much oil, salt and sugar leads to obesity.*), while some students got the genres mixed up (for example, people *eating too much oil and sugar get diseases, such as heart disease and diabetes—consequential explanation*). Students were expected to identify the genre of factorial explanation in the first activity.

In the second activity, students read the given sentences and selected those that could be used in constructing a paragraph to respond to the question in the pre-test. Again, those sentences were extracted from the work of students. While some students correctly constructed sentences with the nature of factorial explanation (for example, *Taking hamburger as an example. It is higher in oil that exceeds daily intake. That leads to obesity.*), some students got the genres mixed up (for example, *Parents can encourage children doing more exercises—recommendation*). Students are expected to construct a paragraph of factorial explanation in the second activity.

In the third activity, students worked together to organize the structure of the essay in responding to the question in the pre-test. A flowchart was provided for students to construct the thinking flow of the factors of obesity step-by-step (for example, *eating too much fast food→ fast food is mainly fried → fast food is high in oil → this may exceed daily energy intake → this leads to obesity*). Students are expected to construct an essay of factorial explanation with a paragraph structure including a topic sentence showing the factor and an extension to elaborate the factor in the third activity.

4.2 Deconstruction or Modelling

After the three learning activities, students read a sample text together with the teacher to learn the function and the schematic structure of an essay of the factorial explanation genre. The sample text in Chinese was designed in a way that gathers students' exemplary work (to increase their learning motivation) and reflects the function of the genre. Below are the original Chinese sample text and its English translation version.

Topic: *Based on the information provided and your own experience, what are the three causes of obesity?*

Introduction (Identification of the phenomenon)	導致肥胖有三因素，包括飲食習慣、消閒習慣及工作模式的轉變，現解說如下。 [Translated work] There are three factors leading to obesity. They are eating habit, changes of leisure activities and changes of working mode. The explanations are as below.	
Factor 1	*首先*，在飲食習慣方面，現代人喜歡進食西方的快餐食物，導致肥胖。這些快餐食物多是煎炸食物，含大量油份，人們長期攝食，會超出人體每天所需的份量，讓膽固醇含量超標，導致身體脂肪累積。以麥當勞的炸雞和薯條為例，都是油炸的食物，膽固醇含量超高。因此，都市人長期進食，就會導致肥胖。	Topic sentence Extension of the topic sentence Example Summary Topic sentence
	[Translated work] *First*, in the aspect of eating habit, modern people have a tendency to consume western-style fast food, resulting in obesity. Fast food is mainly fried food. It is high in trans fats. Eating too much trans fat may exceed daily energy intakes needed. That leads to weight gain. Take McDonald's chicken nuggets and French fries as examples. They are all fried food with high trans fats. Hence, if people keep eating those foods, obesity is the result.	Extension of the topic sentence Example Summary
Factor 2	*其次*，在消閒習慣方面，現代人所選擇的休閒活動有所改變，減少了運動量，導致肥胖。因科技的電訊發展，人們可以在家中看電視和電腦遊戲，由於在家中已經得到消閒娛樂，所以他們減　少了做運動。當人們長坐，而沒有做運動，就會累積脂肪。由於脂肪並沒有得到消耗，長此下去　就會變得愈來愈胖。以電腦遊戲為例，電腦提供各種運動遊戲，但手只需要利用滑鼠或遊戲手掣，就能使虛擬人物進行活動，但對自身的運動量要求不大，根本不能大量消耗脂肪。因此，這種消閒模式的轉變，導致了肥胖。	Topic sentence Extension of the topic sentence Example Summary Topic sentence

(continued)

	[Translated work] *Second,* in the aspect of leisure habits, people nowadays participate in leisure activities with less body movement that leads to obesity. Because of the development of the technology, people can stay at home to enjoy various types of leisure activities, for example, watching TV and playing video games. They gain weight much more easily when joining those leisure activities with less need of body movement. Take playing video games as an example. Nowadays, there are so many video sport games for selection, but what people just need is to control the mouse or console for the movement of the character, instead of our own body movement in consuming energy. Fats are easily accumulated. Hence, the changes of leisure activities lead to obesity.	Extension of the topic sentence Example Summary
Factor 3	另外，在工作模式方面，部分人長時間逗留在辦公室工作，並多於快餐用膳，導致肥胖。以往的人多以勞動維生，如農業、工業工作，但隨著時代及產業的轉變，部分人從事第三產業的工作，例如商業。他們大多留在辦公室工作，活動量較以往低，加上現化人工作時間長及近湊，不少人選擇以快餐進行午膳，食物較多油份。由於活動量，脂肪攝取量就比消耗量高，導致脂肪累積，導致肥胖。	Topic sentence Extension of the topic sentence Example Summary Topic sentence
	[Translated work] *Also,* in the aspect of working mode, some people spend long hours confined to office work and rely heavily on fast food for meals, leading to obesity. In the past, people worked in agriculture and industry that required more labor work. Nowadays, more people work in the tertiary service sector instead. They sit in the office for most of the time. This requires less use of energy. Moreover, people have longer working hours and more workload. They prefer fast food than regular meals. Those food are with more oils. Due to lower amount of activity, energy intake is greater than expenditure. The accumulation of fats leads to obesity.	Extension of the topic sentence Example Summary
Conclusion	總括而言，以上為導致指出及解釋導致肥胖的三個因素。 [Translated work] To conclude, the above are the factors leading to obesity.	

4.3 Co-construction

At the end of the second lesson, students worked together to organize the structure of the essay in responding to a new question (*What are the two causes of teenagers going on diet?*). A magazine was given to each group. Students read the advertisements related to dieting for hints. A thinking flowchart again was provided for students to co-construct the thinking flow of the factors step-by-step (for example, *social media depicts slim as a sign of beauty→ social media distorts the belief and value of teenagers towards beauty → teenagers want to gain public recognition → they follow what the social media depicts about beauty → they go on diet to get slim*). Students are expected to equip the ability to organize a structure of an essay of factorial explanation genre before writing an essay.

In the third lesson, students consolidated the skills learned in the second lesson. Students were given a new question again (*what are the three factors of teenagers' smoking?*) to co-construct the whole structure of the essay of factorial explanation genre with the use of a flowchart (for example, *peers smoke→ teenagers are influenced by peers → teenagers smoke to gain acceptance and recognition from peers → teenagers do not want to be excluded and bullied → they smoke even they do not like smoking*). This time, students were given newspaper articles. They need to locate evidence related to teenagers' smoking in supporting the factors (for example, *according to the research conducted by the University of Hong Kong, secondary school students are 12 times more likely to smoke if their friends have smoking habit.*). Students are expected to organize the whole structure of the essay of factorial explanation genre with a paragraph structure, including a topic sentence showing the factor, an extension to elaborate the factor, an example as an evidence to support the factor and a short summary. Student then worked independently to finish the whole essay by developing two other factors in responding the question. Teacher then used R2L Writing Assessment Criteria to assess the essay performance of students.

In the final lesson, the essays wrote by students in the third lesson were first reviewed. Students got back their essays with marked individual feedbacks. The newspaper articles distributed in the third lesson were used again to discuss the appropriate and relevant selection of evidence to support the factors. The sample text developed that gathers students' exemplary work were used to explain the structure and the function of the essay of factorial explanation genre. On one hand, there was variation in the students' performance. By showing the good work from the others, students could learn from each other. On the other hand, the teacher attempted to include everyone's work in the sample text. This aims at increasing the writing motivation of each student. Below are the original Chinese sample text and its English translation version.

Topic: *What are the factors of teenagers' smoking?*

Introduction (Identification of the phenomenon)	導致青少年吸煙有兩個因素,包括朋輩影響及父母影響。現解說如下。 [Translated work] There are two factors leading to teenagers' smoking. They are peer influence and parent influence. The explanations are as belows.	
Factor 1	*首先*,在朋輩影響方面,部分朋輩在社交活動中吸煙,為了得到朋輩的認同,青少年也選擇跟隨吸煙。在朋輩壓力影響下,青少年希望得到朋友的認同及接納,而不是被排擠甚至欺凌,便選擇跟隨群體抽煙。香港大學一項中學生研究發現,若朋友吸煙,受訪學生現有吸煙的比率就會比其他人高出12倍,反映青少年希望透過抽煙得到身份認同。因此,為了能交到朋友,青少年選擇吸煙。 [Translated work] *First*, in the aspect of peer influence, when peers smoke, teenagers have a higher chance to follow in order to gain recognition. Teenagers want to gain acceptance and recognition, instead of exclusion and bullying. Under the pressure, they follow the group to smoke even they may be not interested in smoking. According to the research conducted by the University of Hong Kong, secondary school students are 12 times more likely to smoke if their friends have smoking habit. The result reflects teenagers need the identity recognition through smoking. Hence, to make friends, teenagers choose smoking.	Topic sentence Extension of the topic sentence Example Summary Topic sentence Extension of the topic sentence Example Summary
Factor 2	其次,在父母影響方面,部分父母有抽煙的習慣,導致他們的子女也跟隨抽煙。青少年由細到大與家人成長,受家人影響。若父母吸煙,青少年就會合理化吸煙的行為。當青少年遇到引誘或壓力吸煙,父母亦無力阻止。哥倫比亞大學醫學中心發現,如果父母抽煙,有百分之15的青年會選擇抽煙。因此,父母對青少年是否吸煙,有很大的因素。 [Translated work] *Second*, in the aspect of parent influence, as some parents have smoking habits, their children are more likely to follow. Teenagers grow with their parents and learn from parents. They easily follow the behaviors of parents, including the smoking behavior. When they group up, they may develop a smoking habit due to stress and lure. Their parents are not easy to stop them as they are also the smokers. According to the research conducted by Columbia University Medical Centre, teenagers have 15 percent higher chance in smoking when their parents are smokers. Hence, the smoking habit of parents is a big factor of teenagers' smoking.	Topic sentence Extension of the topic sentence Example Summary Topic sentence Extension of the topic sentence Example Summary
Conclusion	總括而言,以上為導致青少年吸煙的兩個因素。 [Translated work] To conclude, the above are the factors leading to teenagers' smoking.	

4.4 Independent Construction

When students equipped the writing skills of the factorial explanation genre, they did a post-test of writing an essay independently as a curriculum closure. The post-test was modified from the 2016 Liberal Studies HKDSE examination question paper with the topic of *poverty* (*Based on the information provided and your own experience, indicate and explain three factors that lead to poverty in Africa.*) The topic of *poverty* was taught in the Liberal Studies classes. A thinking flowchart was distributed for students to organize the whole structure of the essay. When they finished the thinking flowchart, they started writing the essay. Finally, the researchers used R2L Writing Assessment Criteria to compare the students' writing performance on the factorial explanation genre between the pre-test and post-test.

5 Results and Discussion

5.1 The Effectiveness of Genre-Based Teaching

5.1.1 Comparison of Test Scores of Factorial Explanation Texts

Table 2 below shows the comparison of test scores of the pre-test and post-test between high, medium, and low achievers in this study:

As shown in Table 1, three levels of achievers showed positive growth in their post-test scores. Among them, the growth of the medium achiever is 14 marks, while the growth of the low achiever is 11 marks. The growth of students' performance, especially the medium and low achievers is attributed to students' ability to identify the genre (the factorial explanation) and to develop a correct structure. To gain a better understanding of students' changes in performance in the pre-test and post-test, the texts of high, medium, and low achievers are analyzed.

Table 2 Comparison of the test scores of high, medium, and low achievers

	Pre-test (total marks: 42)	Post-test (total marks: 42)	Increase in marks
High achiever	18	28	10
Medium achiever	10	24	14
Low achiever	7	18	11

5.1.2 Texts Analysis for High Achiever (Conjunctions Are in Italics)

Pre-test writing: Explaining the factors that contribute to obesity	Post-test writing: Explaining the factors that contribute to poverty in Africa
[Student's original work] 從資料中，飲食、休閒、員工方面顯示了肥胖形成的因素 *(Phenomenon Identification)*	[Student's original work] 導致非洲仍處於貧困的因素，從疾病、缺乏農業科技及貪污方面的影響來現解說如下。*(Phenomenon Identification)*
首先，在飲食方面，人們進食太多多油、多鹽和多脂肪的食物，導致肥胖的問題，例如資料中的人物的飲食均衡不健康，以漢堡包和炸雞為例，用了太多的油炸，超出人體每天所需的份量，令膽固醇提升，導致出現疾病，*例如*心臟病、呼吸管道疾病等。*故此*，從圖中我們看見了進食太多不健康的食物會導致肥胖。*(Factor 1)*	*首先*，在疾病方面，*因*非洲的環境非常惡化，*仍此*產生疾病，例如有瘧疾，這個病是來源蚊滋生，*於是*市民容易感染，*而且*令死亡率高和會令失業率低，不會夠的人做工作，令經濟的發展差，*所以*非洲的人沒有足夠的錢照援。*因此*，有疾病的影響，非洲的人仍處於貧困。*(Factor 1)*
然後，在休閒方面，人們會用長時間電腦或看電視等，他們會集中在看電視和用電腦這些會令他們的骨肉不強壯，*因為*他們只坐，不會做運動，這些的行為也會導致肥胖。從資料的圖表，我們可以看到那位人物的狀況，他*不但*食不健康的食物，*而且*也不做運動，反而看電視和用電腦。這些的行為也能有肥胖的問題。*(Factor 2)*	*其次*，在科技方面，*因*非洲缺乏農業科技，沒有機器取代，*所以*用人手製造農業，*於是*不少的人都不會做農業，*因為*農業的科技的收入低，*而且*沒有足夠的員工做農業，令零售商沒有食物出售，*如果*有先進的機器，*例如*自動種子機器，*但*非洲沒有機器，*於是*用人手製造農業。*因此*，非洲缺乏農業科技，*所以*非洲仍處於貧困。*(Factor 2)*
最後，從零售業或快餐的餐廳的員工方面，員工在工作上每天都會吃餐廳裏的食物，這些的食物令他們容易快速地造成肥胖，*因為*快餐的食物含有太多的卡路里，令他們會每天積累太多脂肪。從麥當勞員工為例，他們吃的食物多數有油的成份，*而且*餐廳裏沒有太多健康食品，員工沒有選擇。*而且*這些的員工因付出了太多的時間在麥當勞，令他們上癮。*故此*，員工也容易出現肥胖的問題。*(Factor 3)*	*最後*，在貪污方面，一些貪心的官員會取走一些用到市民身上的錢，令市民沒有錢來生活，令他們的生活質素降低，他們*因*沒有足夠的錢，*所以*很難負擔醫療費和食飲方面，就*例如*發展工商沒有比(給)市民錢，就不少的市民不會做工作。*(Factor 3)*
	[Translated work] The factors that keep Africa in poverty can be explained from the perspectives of

(continued)

[Translated work] According to the data, diet, leisure time and staff situation show the factors of obesity. *(Phenomenon Identification)*	disease, lack of agricultural technology and corruption as below. *(Phenomenon Identification)*

[Translated work] According to the data, diet, leisure time and staff situation show the factors of obesity. *(Phenomenon Identification)*

First, in terms of diet, for people, eating a lot of oily, salty and fatty food will cause the problem of obesity. For example, the person in the data has unhealthy diet balance, taking hamburger and fried chicken as examples, it used too much frying oil, exceeding the daily need of the human body, causing the rise of cholesterol which gives rises to diseases, such as heart problem and inspiration tract diseases etc. So, from the picture, we can see taking too much unhealthy food will cause obesity. *(Factor 1)*

Then, in terms of leisure time, people will use long time working on computers or watching TV etc. Focusing on watching TV and working on computer will make their bone and flesh not strong. It is because they are only sitting and not doing exercise. These kinds of doing will also cause obesity. From the chart of the information, we can see the situation of that person. He not only eats unhealthy food, but also doesn't do exercise, instead he watches TV and uses computer. These also can cause the problem of obesity. *(Factor 2)*

Finally, from the perspective of staff who work in retailing business or fast food restaurants, every day when they work, the food they eat in the restaurants will easily and quickly make them fat. It is because the fast food contains a lot of calories, making them to accumulate too much fat every day. Taking an example of the McDonald's staff, they eat mostly oily food, and there are not many healthy food in the restaurants for them to choose. And these staff spend too much time in McDonald, making them addicted to the food. So the staff will easily face the problem of obesity. *(Factor 3)*

---

disease, lack of agricultural technology and corruption as below. *(Phenomenon Identification)*

First, in terms of diseases, because the environment of Africa deteriorated, it caused diseases such as malaria. The source of this disease is the breeding of mosquitos, thus the citizens are easily infected. And it caused high death rate and low unemployment rate. That makes not enough people to work, causing poor development of economy. So African people do not have enough financial support. Therefore, the influence of diseases keeps African people in poverty. *(Factor 1)*

Second, in terms of technology, as Africa is lack of agricultural technology, there are no machines to replace, so people just use bare hands to do agriculture. Then not many people do agriculture, as the salary of agriculture technology is low. And not enough workers work in agriculture, causing the retail merchants to have not enough food to sell. If there are advanced machines like automatic seed machines. But Africa has no machines, they have to use bare hands to produce agriculture. Therefore, Africa is lack of agriculture technology, so Africa remains poor. *(Factor 2)*

Finally, in terms of corruption, some greedy government officials took away the money that should be used for the citizens. That caused the people to have no money to live, causing their living quality to be lowered. Thus they have not enough money to spend on medical expenditure and food. For example, if you are to develop industry and commerce without providing money to the citizens, therefore most citizens will not do the jobs. *(Factor 3)*

In general, the high achiever showed a basic understanding of the structure of the factorial explanation genre from both pre-test and post-test. The student could clearly start a paragraph with a topic sentence indicating a key factor contributing to obesity or poverty. S/he could also elaborate on the key factors with examples. In the pre-test, the paragraphs about the first two factors (diet and leisure time) leading to obesity are clearly constructed. However, the focus and the example given for the third factor are not logical and appropriate. For example, the student elaborated that staff working in fast food shops eat fast food every day, but this may be not the real situation. Above all, the topic on the issue of obesity addressed to all the people and not just confined to people working in retailing business and fast food restaurant. In contrast, in the post-test, the three factors (diseases, technology, and corruption) leading to poverty in Africa are clearly constructed with elaboration and accurate examples. For instance, the student could indicate corruption as one of the key factors of poverty in a topic sentence. S/he then could elaborate with an example that 'some greedy government officials took away the money that should be used for the citizens and draw to a conclusion that 'caused the people to have no money to live'.

In addition, the high achiever showed a more accurate use of vocabulary and phrases in the post-test. In the pre-test, the student attempted to use a wide variety of vocabulary and phrases related to obesity but was wrongly used occasionally. For example, the student wrote 'spend too much time in McDonald, making them addicted to the food' instead of 'eat too much fast food, making them addicted to the food'; while in the post-test, the student has a more accurate use of vocabulary and phrases overall. Moreover, the writer could use 'no machines' and 'use bare hands to produce agriculture' to explain how the factor of lacking agricultural technology leads to poverty. Furthermore, the students got improvements in using conjunction, and s/he was able to use different conjunctions to connect sentences, for example, 'therefore', 'so' etc.

In summary, in the post-test, the high achiever could clearly explain the factors involved in the phenomenon of poverty in Africa and construct a clearer and more organized schematic structure of the factorial explanation genre.

5.1.3 Texts Analysis for Medium Achiever (Conjunctions Are in Italics)

Pre-test writing: Explaining the factors that contribute to obesity	Post-test writing: Explaining the factors that contribute to poverty in Africa
[Student's original work] 根據資料A，說出一個男人肥胖的原因，原因就有四個漢堡包，電視，炸雞和電腦。這個是他肥胖的原因。這個男子的身形是很大！和這個資料都有問題目是：那麼來個腰圍日又如何"？*(Phenomenon Identification)* *首先*，在吃漢堡包和炸雞的方面，要對他們的身體有壞處。他吃了很多漢堡包的話，這個就會他容易有不同病，*例如*：心臟病，糖尿病等等的東西，也*如果*吃完後，不做運動，他們就會容易肥。*(Factor 1)* *所以*如果他們不做運動和很多漢堡包的說，這個對的身體會有很多壞處，*因為*這個食物是不容易消化的食物，也人們會用很多油，糖等等東西在這個食物，*所以*對身體不好。*(Effect 1)—A stage that should belong to Consequential Explanation* *然後*，在看和玩電視和電腦，這個要對的生活不好和身體。這個電子的東西，對人們是很吸引，人們都會不想上班，回校。*所以*我覺得上面圖A的人們是沒有工做，*所以*他們每天都在家看電視或這玩電腦，*所以*這個兩個東西對他們的生活和身形會有不好地方，*因為*這個會都他們覺得懶，*所以*他們會不做運動或這上班。*(Effect 2) –A stage that should belong to Consequential Explanation* *最後*，在懶惰的方面，弄到他們不想做東西。*如果*他們是一個懶惰，他們就會不想回工，煮食，做運動，等等的小事都會不想，*因為*懶惰，每天都休息。這個懶	[Student's original work] 導致非洲仍處於貧困的三個因素是疾病，缺乏農業科技和貪污方面。*(Phenomenon Identification)* *首先*，在疾病方面，非洲會有很多病死，*所以*就會有很少人去工作，這個會令到國家的經濟會低。*因為*非洲有很多不同的病例如：瘧疾等等。每日會有很多人們死，也會有少人上班工作。*因此*會令都非洲仍處於貧困。*(Factor 1)* *然後*，在缺乏農業科技的方面，因為非洲的機器很少，*例如*：無耕耙(種)機器，無卡車等等的機器。*所以*就會用人手工作，*但是*非洲有缺乏人手，*所以*個收成也會很低，也不會賺都錢。*因此*，會令到非洲仍處於貧困。*(Factor 2)* *最後*，在貪污方面，官員取起用到市民身上的錢，本來這個錢會是用到人們的生活（衣，食，住，行），這個會都市民的生活素質低。這個錢本來途用的地方是醫療，科技，國家發民(展)等等的東西。*但是*他們不用了，令到非洲仍處於貧困。*(Factor 3)* 總括而言，以上為導致非洲仍處於貧困的三個因素。*(Reinforcement of Factors)* [Translated work] The three factors that keep Africa in poverty are disease, lack of agricultural technology and corruption. *(Phenomenon Identification)* First of all, in terms of diseases, there will be many people who die due to some diseases in Africa, so only few people can go to work, which will make the country's economy low. Because there are many different diseases in Africa such as malaria.

(continued)

惰對他們的身形會有很大的變化。**(Effect 3)** –A stage belonging to Consequential Explanation) 在這個三個方面，吃漢堡包和炸雞，看和玩電視和電腦和懶惰方面，對弄到他的身體會很大變化。*(Conclusion)* [Translated work] According to data A, to name the reasons why a man is obese, there are four, including hamburgers, television, fried chicken and computer. This is why he is fat. His figure is huge! This material also has a title: So what about a waistline day? *(Phenomenon Identification)* First, in terms of eating hamburgers and fried chicken, it is bad for their bodies. If he eats a lot of hamburgers, he will be prone to various diseases, such as heart disease and diabetes. and if they don't exercise after eating, they will easily become fat.*(Factor 1)* So if they don't exercise and eat a lot of hamburgers, this will do a lot of harm to the body, because this food is not easy to digest, and people will use a lot of things like oil, sugar in this food, so it will be not good to the body. *(Effect 1)—A stage that should belong to Consequential Explanation)* Then, watching and playing TV and computer, this is not good for life and health. This electronic thing, is very attractive to people, and people will not want to go to work or go to school. So I think the people in picture A above have no job, so they watch TV or play computer at home every day, so these two things will be bad for their life and body figure, because it will make them feel lazy, so they won't do sports or go to work. *(Effect 2) –A stage that should belong to Consequential Explanation)* Finally, in terms of laziness, it leads to their unwillingness to work. If they are lazy, they will not want to come work, cook, do sports, since they are lazy and want to rest every day. This laziness will result in a big change of their body figure. *(Effect 3) –A stage that should belong to Consequential Explanation)* In these three aspects, eating hamburgers and fried chicken, watching and playing TV and computer, and being lazy, will make a huge change to his body. *(Conclusion)*	Many people die every day, and only few people are able to go to work, so Africa remains poor. *(Factor 1)* Then, in terms of the lack of agricultural technology, because there are very few machines in Africa, for example tillage machines and trucks. So people will work with bare hands, but there is a shortage of labour force in Africa, so the harvest will be very small and it will not make any money. So Africa remains poor. *(Factor 2)* Finally, in terms of corruption, government officials took the money that was spent on citizens, which originally should be used for people's lives (clothing, food, housing, transportation), causing the citizens' quality of life to be low. The money is supposed to be used in medical and national development, but the government does not use it in the right place, so Africa remains poor. *(Factor 3)* To conclude, the above is the three factors that keep Africa in poverty. *(Reinforcement of Factors)*

In terms of the choice of genre, in the pre-test, the medium achiever identified the function of the topic wrongly, s/he used consequential explanation genre instead of the factorial explanation genre to develop the text. So the whole text was to explain the consequences of eating hamburger and fried chicken, watching TV and playing with computer, and being lazy. For instance, the student wrote 'in terms of eating hamburgers and fried chicken, it is bad for their bodies'. S/he explained the consequence of eating too much fast food, but not the factor leading to obesity. S/he then continued his elaboration with examples of various types of diseases. The content is not relevant to the writing requirement. In contrast, the text in the post-test displayed the fact that the student could master the structure in the factorial explanation genre. Each paragraph was started with a topic sentence that clearly indicates the factor leading to poverty with examples. S/he could logically explain why Africa remains poor. For example, s/he wrote 'only few people can go to work, which will make the country's economy weak'.

Another improvement can be shown in the use of vocabulary and phrases in the post-test. In the pre-test, the vocabulary or phrase level related to the factors of obesity is insufficient. Most of the vocabulary and phrases used are not related to the consequences of obesity, for example, 'bad for their bodies', 'not good for life and health', 'bad for their life and body figure' etc. The insufficient vocabulary or phrase level can also be reflected in the creation of vocabulary and phrases. For example, the student used 'not want to come work' to express 'not want to go back to work'. Some sentences even do not make meanings to the theme. For example, in the pre-test, the student directly copied from the data and wrote 'This is why he is fat. His figure is huge! This material also has a title: So what about a waistline day' without elaboration. Although the medium achiever wrote a lot in the pretest, most of the contents were not relevant to the writing requirements. In contrast, in the post-test, the student was able to use precise phrases and wordings related to the factorial explanation genre, for example, 'the three factors that keep Africa in poverty are…', 'the above is the three factors that keep Africa in poverty' etc. Besides, the post-test showed that the student got significant improvement in the use of appraisal and conjunction words.

In summary, the medium achiever could master the structure of the factorial explanation genre and explain logically the factors involved in the phenomenon of poverty in Africa.

5.1.4 Texts Analysis for Low Achiever (Conjunctions Are in Italics)

Pre-test writing: Explaining the factors that contribute to obesity	Post-test writing: Explaining the factors that contribute to poverty in Africa
[Student's original work] 資料顯了導致肥胖的三個因素,就是飲食方面,休息時間方面,和工作方面的。*(Phenomenon Identification)* *首先*,在人們飲食方面,人們可以咸(減)小吃漢堡包,炸雞等等,*因為*有多油,多鹽和多脂肪,以麥當勞為例,用上六匙油炸,令膽固醇第高,*而且*會有病 *(Suggestion 1)- A stage that should belong to Recommendation Genre*。 *然後*,休息時的方面,現在好多人道(用)電腦,看電(視),這個會導致肥胖, *(Factor 1) 因為*人們會化好多時間看電視,用電腦,他們不會去做運動,父母可以鼓勵他(們)的孩子去做運動,*例如*有氧運動,*而且*叫他不用電腦,看電視,*因為*可以導致則(傷)眼。*(Suggestion 2) - A stage that should belong to Recommendation Genre* *最後*,在工作方面,人們做工的時後多素都吃麥當勞,肯德基和漢堡包,*因為*他們有好小時間,*所以*去這個地方,*因為*這個就是附近他的工作。做工作也可以導致肥胖,*因為*有些工作要坐做,*例如* business,要好小後,*所以*工作導致肥胖。*(Factor 2)*	[Student's original work] 導致非洲仍處於貧困的三個因素,就疾病、缺乏農業科技和貪污,現解說如下。*(Phenomenon Identification)* *首先*,在醫料(療)方面,疾病會令非洲仍處於貧困。非洲有好多人會死亡,*因為*有病。例如家裏如果父親死亡,*因為*有疾病例如瘧疾,這個家沒有人做工,*而且*好少人會出去做工,*因為*他們不想有疾病,沒有人做工會令國家經濟差,*因此*疾病會令非洲仍處於貧困。*(Factor 1)* *然後*,在缺乏農業科技方面,非洲缺乏農業科技會令有非洲仍處於貧困。非洲機器少,好少人會做工,*而且*收入會低,*因為*人們不想用手做功,*但*到沒有機器例如卡車,*所以*國家會兼(賺)好少錢。*因此*缺乏農業科技會令非洲仍處於貧困。*(Factor 2)* *其次*,在貪污方面,貪污會令有非洲仍處於貧困。非洲的官員會取在用到市民上的衣,食,住,行,*例如*官員拿市民的錢,市民就起不到屋,他們會在不好的環境住。*而且*市民會改善不到生活,生活上用的素質會差,*因此*貪污會令非洲仍處於貧困。*(Factor 3)* 總括而言,以上為導到非洲人處於貧困的三個因素。*(Reaffirmation of Factors)*

(continued)

總括而言，以上為導致肥胖的恩素。 *(Reaffirmation of Factors)* [Translated work] The data shows three factors that lead to obesity, which is diet, resting time, and work. **(Phenomenon Identification)** First, in terms of people's diet, people can reduce eating snacks such as hamburgers, fried chicken, because they are oily, salty and fatty. Take McDonald's as an example, they usually fry with six spoons of oil, it increases its cholesterol level and will cause illness. **(Suggestion 1)- A stage that should belong to Recommendation Genre。** Then, in terms of resting time, nowadays many people use computers and watch TV, which will lead to obesity. **(Factor 1)** Because people will spend a lot of time watching TV and using computers, they won't do any sports, parents can encourage his (their) children to do sports, such as aerobic exercises, and tell him not to use the computer and watch TV, because it can cause eye problems. **(Suggestion 2) - A stage that should belong to Recommendation Genre** Finally, in terms of work, people eat McDonald's, KFC and Burger King for lunch when they are working, because they have very little time, so people tend to go to these restaurants, also because these restaurants are often near to their workplace. Working can also cause obesity, since some job require us to sit and work in office, such as business, so working can lead to obesity too. **(Factor 2)** To conclude, the above are the factors that leads to obesity. **(Reaffirmation of Factors)**	[Translated work] The three factors that keeps Africa in poverty are disease, lack of agricultural technology and corruption, which are explained below. *(Phenomenon Identification)* First, in terms of health care, diseases will keep the country in poverty. Many people in Africa will die, because of disease. For example, at home, if the father dies because of a disease such as malaria, no one in the family can work, and less people will be willing to go out to work because they don't want to be sick. Lacking work force will cause the country to have a weak economy, so diseases will keep Africa in poverty. *(Factor 1)* Then, in terms of lack of agricultural technology, the lack of agricultural technology in Africa will keep Africa in poverty. Africa has very few machines, only a small amount of people will go to work, and the income will be low, because people don't want to do work with their bare hands, but there are no machines such as trucks, so the country will make less money. Therefore, the lack of agricultural technology will keep Africa in poverty. *(Factor 2)* Second, in terms of corruption, corruption will keep Africa in poverty. Government officials will take away the resources used for citizens' clothing, food, housing, and transportation. For example if the government officials take the money from the citizens, the citizens will not be able to build houses, thus living in a bad environment. Moreover, citizens will not be able to improve their lives, and the quality of life will be poor. Therefore, corruption will keep Africa in poverty. *(Factor 3)* To conclude, the above are the factors that keeps African in poverty. *(Reaffirmation of Factors)*

In the pre-test, the student aimed to construct a text to explain three factors (diet, resting time, and work) of obesity in the introductory stage. However, in developing the explanation stages, s/he mixed with the recommendation genre by giving suggestions to readers about what people can do to have a healthy body and life, for example, 'people can reduce eating snacks such as hamburgers, fried chicken, because they are oily, salty and fatty', 'parents can encourage his [their]children to do exercises, such as aerobic exercises' etc. Thus, these contents are not relevant to the theme. Moreover, the student tried to develop stages to explain the cause of obesity, but the factors explained are not logical. For example, s/he wrote 'people eat

McDonald's, KFC and Burger King for lunch......because these restaurants are often near their workplace'. In contract, in the post-test, the low achiever demonstrated a better understanding of the requirement of the writing task, thus s/he constructed the text in a well-structured factorial explanation genre. S/he started with a topic sentence indicating the factors, namely health care, agricultural technology, and corruption. Each paragraph briefly explained how a factor contributed to poverty in Africa, though without in-depth elaboration. Yet the student was able to offer examples on all the key factors. For example, s/he wrote 'but there are no machines such as trucks, so the country will make less money'.

Compared with the high and medium achievers, the improvement of the low achiever in terms of the use of vocabulary and phrases was less obvious. In the pre-test, as the student mixed the factorial explanation genre with the recommendation genre, there are vocabulary and phrases related to the recommendation genre being used are not relevant to the theme of obesity. In the post-test, the student managed to use a few items of function words related to the factorial explanation genre, such as 'cause' and 'lead to'. Moreover, s/he got progress in the use of conjunction.

In summary, in the post-test, the low achiever had great progress at whole text level and got mastery of the factorial explanation genre, but there is room for improvement at the levels of sentence and vocabulary.

5.2 Relationship Between Students' Pre-test and Post-test Writing Performance and the Genre-Based Teaching

Judging from the texts of the pre-test, some students, like the low and medium achievers, had difficulties in identifying the correct genre (the factorial explanation) from the writing task. They mixed the factorial explanation genre with the consequential explanation and the recommendation genres. Hence, after the pre-test, the teacher analyzed the texts of the students and extracted both correct and incorrect sentences from the texts (**deconstruction**). The teacher then guided the students to recognize the characteristics of the sentences of the factorial explanation genre, for example, the vocabulary and phrases used ('cause', 'lead to', etc.). The activities were designed to facilitate students to distinguish between the genres of factorial explanation, consequential explanation, and recommendation. As a result, in the post-test, all achievers could identify the writing task and develop a well-structured factorial explanation genre.

When students were able to master the sentences with the factorial explanation elements, the teacher further supported students in developing paragraphs and then the whole structure. From the pre-test, it can be seen that the high achiever could construct a paragraph starting with a topic sentence that clearly indicates the factor of obesity. Although they could provide examples to elaborate on the factors, the elaboration was not in-depth. As for medium and low achievers, as they failed to recognize and develop the structure of the factorial explanation, and the paragraphs they developed are irrelevant to the theme of obesity. To address the problems, a series of activities were designed:

First, the flowchart activities were delivered so that students could work together and co-construct the thinking flow of the factors of obesity step-by-step (**co-construction**). For example, students built a thinking flow as follows: Eating too much fast food (Topic sentence) → fast food is mainly fried (Extension of the key factor) → fast food is high in oil (Extension of the key factor) → this may exceed daily energy intake (Extension of the key factor) → this leads to obesity (Consequence). The learning activity aimed at strengthening students developing topic sentences with elaboration.

Second, students together read a sample text that is integrated from their exemplary works in the pre-test (**modeling**). This process aimed at increasing students' comprehension of the structure of the factorial explanation, including a topic sentence, an extension of the topic sentence, an example(s), and a summary.

Third, repeated group work was provided so that students could work together to develop the whole structure of the factorial explanation genre (**co-construction**). The group work included writing about the factors of teenagers going on a diet and smoking. This aimed at increasing students' mastery of the development of the structure.

Fourth, the group activity of newspaper articles reading increased students' ability in adding an example(s) when elaborating on the key factor (**co-construction**). This activity was only delivered when the students mastered the development of the topic sentence and the extension of the topic sentence.

Finally, students worked individually to write a text in the factorial explanation genre (**independent construction**). This is to ensure that every student could get mastery of the ability to develop a well-structured essay according to the writing task.

With a series of activities aimed at developing students' ability in recognizing and developing the structure of the factorial explanation genre, it can be seen that the high achiever could clearly identify the factors leading to poverty, explain the factors point by point, develop each paragraph with a topic sentence related to the key factor, and with clear examples to elaborate. Similarly, the medium achiever could identify the factors leading to poverty, explain the factors point by point, and develop each paragraph with a topic sentence and examples, although there was still room for improving the elaboration part. Also, the low achiever could identify the factors, and briefly explain them, although without much in-depth elaboration.

5.3 Interview with the Liberal Studies Teacher

Throughout the study, the teacher participant worked closely with the researchers to conduct the pilot teaching with the use of the genre teaching approach and the application of R2L pedagogy. To understand more about the teacher's perception, she was interviewed after the intervention.

It was the first time the teacher had used the genre teaching approach to support the learning of non-Chinese speaking students with the writing skills of Liberal Studies. She was satisfied with such a great improvement in the students' writing skills in the genre of factorial explanation in the post-test. She shared the difference between her original teaching and the piloting teaching approaches:

> **Teacher:** *In the past, I focused more on delivering subject content of Liberal Studies. Liberal Studies have six modules, namely Personal Development & Interpersonal Relationships, Hong Kong Today, Modern China, Globalization, Public Health, Energy Technology & the Environment in total. For Chinese speaking students, they can easily access those subject content through social media and daily life discussion. But for non-Chinese speaking students, they cannot easily understand social media in Chinese. And they do not discuss the topics with the family members in daily life. Hence, they rely on teacher, that is me, to learn the subject content. I was always worried that students missed the subject content so that they may have no idea what to answer in the HKDSE Liberal Studies Examination. But there is a problem focusing too much on subject content. Students do not read the question carefully and identify the genre of the question type. They just write down what they know about the subject content. In this pilot teaching, I facilitate students to identify the factorial explanation genre, the schematic structure of the genre, and the process from constructing a sentence to a paragraph and to an essay of factorial explanation genre.*

From the sharing of the teacher about her teaching approaches, it can be discerned that subject content is important in Liberal Studies for students in constructing an essay with keywords and ideas related to the topics in six modules. However, this is far from enough for students in addressing the question accurately and correctly. The teacher used the genre teaching approach to facilitate students to identify the genre of the question and then the schematic structure of the genre. Students do not just write down keywords related to the subject content, but systematically and strategically they put those keywords into meaningful sentences and paragraphs in responding to the question of factorial explanation genre.

With teacher's effort and experience in designing the lessons, the genre-based pedagogy was effectively implemented. The teacher reflected upon the use of the pedagogy and its benefits in enhancing the writing skills of the students:

> **Teacher:** *Many of the written texts used throughout the four lessons were extracted from the exemplary work of students. In the first lesson, students did the pre-test. The responses from the pre-test were then used to develop the sample text. When students found their part of the responses were shown in the sample text, they were excited and more eager to read to learn.*
>
> *Another thing was the design of learning activities. The paragraphs written by students on the pre-test were deconstructed into sentences. The sentences were shown in the learning activities for students to read, and then to identify the relevant sentences that should be used in co-constructing paragraphs of factorial explanation genre in the second lesson. Students then responded to a new question of factorial explanation genre independently in the third lesson. Then, another sample text was developed to consolidate students' understanding of the schematic structure of the genre. Before doing the post-test, students read to learn the sample text in the final lesson. They had gained more confidence in writing an essay of factorial explanation genre in the post-test.*

Although only four lessons were delivered by the teacher in this pilot study, her reflection showed that the lessons designed were authentic, intensive and systematic as a means of getting students to learn the writing skills of the factorial explanation genre effectively. In terms of authenticity, students read their own and peer exemplary works, instead of sample works written by teachers only. From the researchers' observation, it was evident that students were more motivated to read and learn. In terms of intensity, students read to learn two sample texts in four lessons. Every time students finished writing an essay in the factorial explanation genre, they could read the sample text in the next lesson, which consolidated their understanding of the schematic structure of the factorial explanation genre. In terms of systematicity, the students learned to write an essay in the factorial explanation genre step-by-step, from identifying the genre by reading the related sentences, to co-constructing paragraphs in the factorial explanation genre, to writing an essay independently.

5.4 Interview with the NCS Students

The researchers also conducted an interview with the NCS students after teaching. Students gave comments on genre-based teaching and the improvement of their performance in the post-test.

In terms of genre-based teaching, students' comments are as follows:

Student 1: *At the beginning, we knew nothing. Then, we learned from simple to difficult, teacher taught us step-by-step and inspired us how to write an article.*

Student 2: *The group collaboration has huge support. Individually, I don't know if I write right it or wrong. But with discussion and collaboration, I know if my thoughts are the same as others.*

From the students' comments, it can be seen that the ***deconstruction*** process supports students' learning from simple to difficult by learning these three critical features(i) first, the vocabulary, phrases and sentences related to the themes and to the factorial explanation genre in the genre-recognition activity, (ii) secondly, the paragraphs with the structure of a topic sentence, an extension of the topic sentence, the example, and the summary in the flowchart and sample text reading activities, and (iii) finally, the whole schematic structure of the factorial explanation genre in co-construction and independent construction activities.

Also, in the process of ***co-construction***, students worked together to discuss and develop flowcharts and texts related to the factorial explanation genre. These activities support students to have a better understanding of the schematic structure of the factorial explanation genre. The benefits mentioned are revealed in the positive results shown in the post-test.

In terms of the improvement of student's performance in the post-test, students' comments are as follows:

Student 3: *I think I improved a lot in writing. I got fewer errors and more vocabulary. The teacher gave me a clear direction to write the text.*

Student 4: *I found big improvement in my writing. I know how to construct paragraphs with more content and write some factors. Now I know how to read the questions. When I recognize the question as a factorial explanation genre, I should write factors. When I recognize the question as a recommendation genre, I should write suggestions.*

From the comments by the students, it can be seen that they felt satisfied with their improvement in the post-test. The genre-based teaching supports students to reduce mistakes by learning how to recognize various genres, to write accurately by learning keywords related to the theme and the factorial explanation genre, and to have a direction to write by learning the schematic structure of the target genre.

Also, with the genre-based teaching, students mastered the skills of reading questions. When students recognized the keywords of the factorial explanation in the question, they knew that a schematic structure of the factorial explanation genre should be developed. The genre-based pedagogy supports students to recognize the genre and prevent mixing it with other genres (consequential explanation and recommendation genres), like what they did in the pre-test.

Although only a 10-hour genre-based teaching and learning cycle was delivered (including the time for pre-test), students could see the changes before and after the intervention. They were welcome to have more similar genre-based teaching in the future. They found this does not only benefit on Liberal Studies but also other subjects as well.

6 Conclusion

In this study, with the introduction of genre-based pedagogy in teaching NCS students Liberal Studies using Chinese as the medium of instruction, improvements in the writing skills of the students were significant at the word level, the sentence level and the whole text level. The data showed that there were great changes in the writings of the medium and the low achievers. At the same time, the improvements in that of the high achiever was also obvious, especially in the skills of setting up a topic sentence, providing elaboration, and offering examples.

Moreover, the beauty of the whole teaching and learning cycle is that the teacher inspired the students with the knowledge of genres and their functions. In this unit of teaching, the teacher's instruction to students was, namely factorial explanation, but also included consequential explanation and recommendation, and comparison among the three. This demonstrates a good use of Variation Theory of Marton (Marton & Booth, 1997) that the teacher organized classroom activities to enable students to make contrast among different functions of the genres, namely factorial explanation, consequential explanation and recommendation. Students then were inspired by the teacher that to write it right, they had to read the topic/question carefully to identify its function and then use appropriate form (genre) to realise the meaning. Hence to be successful in subject writing, it is crucial to equip students with the idea of subject-specific genres. The implication for subject teacher training is that, teachers should be prepared for subject-specific literacy so that they could equip students with the ability to express subject concepts in appropriate language.

Over the past few decades, Content and Language Integrated Learning (CLIL) has been developed and past research studies proved effectiveness of the pedagogy in second language learning. The findings of the present study will have important implications for enhancing Non-Chinese Speaking students' mastery of Chinese language of other subjects and offer a new model of content and language integrating learning for Hong Kong and the world.

References

Christie, F. (1984). Young children's writing development: The relationship of written genres to curriculum genres. In B. Bartlett & J. Carr (Eds.), *Language in education conference: A report of proceedings*. Brisbane College of Advanced Education, Mt Gravatt Campus.
Christie, F. (1985). *Language education*. Deakin University Press.
Christie, F. (1996). Geography. *Report of a Research Study into the Pedagogic Discourse of Secondary School Social Sciences*. A study funded by the Australian. Research Council. University of Melbourne.
Christie, F. (2005). *Language education in the primary years*. University of New South Wales Press Ltd.
Christie, F., Gray, P., Gray, B., Macken, M., Martin, J., & Rothery, J. (1990). *Language: A source of meaning- Exploring reports (Teachers' Book)*. Harcourt Brace Jovanich.
Christie, F., Gray, P., Gray, B., Macken, M., Martin, J., & Rothery, J. (1992). *Language: A source of meaning- Exploring explanations (Teachers' Book)*. Harcourt Brace Jovanich.
Curriculum Development Council (CDC) & Hong Kong Examinations and Assessment Authority (HKEAA). (2005). *Proposed New Senior Secondary Curriculum and Assessment Framework – Liberal Studies* 2nd Draft (For Consultation), May 2005.
Derewianka, B., & Christie, F. (2005) Key indicators of development in adolescent writing: a preliminary report. Paper presented at the 32nd International Systemic Functional Congress, 17–22 July 2005, University of Sydney, Australia. Abstract available online: www.asfla.org.au/isfc2005/home.html
Education Bureau. (2021). *Ongoing renewal of the school curriculum*. Education Bureau. https://www.edb.gov.hk/en/curriculum-development/renewal/opt_core_subj.html
Halliday, M. A. K. (1978). *Language as social semiotic: The social interpretation of language and meaning*. Edward Arnold.
Halliday, M. A. K. (1994). *An introduction to functional grammar* (2nd ed.). Edward Arnold.
Halliday, M. A. K., & Mathiessen, C. M. I. M. (2004). *An introduction to functional grammar* (3rd ed.). University Press.
Lemke, J. (1990). *Talking science: Language, learning and values*. Ablex.
Martin, J. R. (1986). Intervening in the process of writing development. In C. Painter & J. R. Martin (Eds.), *Writing to mean: Teaching genre across the curriculum. Occasional Paper No. 9* (pp. 11–43). Applied Linguistics Association of Australia.
Martin, J. R. (1992). *English text: System and structure*. Benjamins.
Martin, J. R. (1999). Mentoring semogenesis: 'Genre-based' literacy pedagogy. In F. Christie (Ed.), *Pedagogy and the shaping of consciousness: Linguistic and social processes*, pp. 123–155. Continuum.
Marton, F., & Booth, S. (1997). *Learning and awareness*. Lawrence Erlbaum.
Rose, D. (2010). Meaning beyond the margins: learning to interact with books. In J. Martin, S. Hood & S.Dreyfus, (eds.) *Semiotic margins: Reclaiming meanings*. Continuum.

Rothery, J. (1994). *Exploring about language in English (write it right: Resources for literacy and learning)*. Metropolitan East Disadvantaged Schools Program.
Shum, M. S. K. (2010). *The functions of language and the teaching of Chinese: Application of systemic functional linguistics to Chinese language teaching* (2nd ed.). Hong Kong University Press.
Shum, M. S. K. (2015). *Subject specific genres of liberal studies and the skills of expression*. Hong Kong Educational Publishing Company.
Shum, M. S. K., Tse, S. K., Ki, W. W., Kwong, W. L., Chan, W. F., & Lo, W. C. (2003a). *Subject specific genres of school chemistry: A resource book*. Support Centre for Teachers Using Chinese as the Medium of Instruction, The University of Hong Kong.
Shum, M. S. K., Tse, S. K., Ki, W. W., Yu, S. K., Chan, M. T., Lai, Y. W., et al. (2003b). *Subject specific genres of school economics: A resource book*. The University of Hong Kong.
Shum, M. S. K., Tse, S. K., Ki, W. W., Chan, W. M., Siu, N. M., Yu, N. S. S., et al. (2004a). *Subject specific genres of school physics: A resource book*. Support Centre for Teachers Using Chinese as the Medium of Instruction, The University of Hong Kong.
Shum, M. S. K., Tse, S. K., Ki, W. W., Chan, C. Y., Yuen, K. C., Yu, N. S. S., et al. (2004b). *Subject specific genres of school biology: A resource book*. Support Centre for Teachers Using Chinese as the Medium of Instruction, The University of Hong Kong.
Shum, M. S. K., Tse, S. K., Ki, W. W., Tung, S. C., Wong, W. K., Pang, Y. W., Chow, S. L., Yu, S. S., & Shi, Y. W. (2006a). *Subject specific genres of school history: A resource book*. Support Centre for Teachers Using Chinese as the Medium of Instruction, The University of Hong Kong.
Shum, M. S. K., Tse, S. K., Ki, W. W., Chan, C. W., Kwan, W. B., & To, W. S. (2006b). *Subject specific genres of school geography: A resource book*. Support Centre for Teachers Using Chinese as the Medium of Instruction, The University of Hong Kong.
Shum, M. S. K., Ki, W. W., & Lam, J. W. I. (2012). *Assessment for learning: Enhancing students' writing ability in Liberal studies by subject specific genre teaching*. Centre for Advancement of Chinese Language Education and Research, the University of Hong Kong.
Street, B. (1984). *Literacy in theory and practice*. Cambridge University Press.
Veel, R. (1997). Learning how to mean – Scientific speaking: Apprenticeship into scientific discourse in the secondary school. In F. Christie & J. R. Martin (Eds.), *Genres and institutions: Social processes in the workplace and school*. Cassell.
Veel, R. & Coffin C. (1996). Learning to think like a historian: The language of secondary school history. In R. Hasan & G. Williams (eds.), *Literacy in society*. Longman.

Part IV
The Language Trajectory: Integrated Language Learning

Sharing Economy in the CSL Classroom: mLang—A New Approach of Using IT to Assist Second Language Learning

Elizabeth Ka Yee Loh

Abstract Chinese as a Second Language (CSL) learners mainly rely on their teachers and pre-designed textbooks to learn the language. However, due to their diversified language proficiency and learning interests, teachers may find it hard to meet each student's needs, stimulate learning motivation, or accelerate learning progress. Inspired by crowdfunding and sharing economy concepts, we created "mLang", an e-learning platform and pedagogy that facilitates CSL teaching and learning by associating students' life experiences and creativity with the learning topics. Students create mLang cards based on the topic they are learning by taking or downloading photos they like, audio-recording their verbal descriptions and writing down vocabulary as homework. After being checked by the teacher with students making necessary corrections, students' mLang cards are "crowdfunded" as co-developed learning materials and "shared" among the class for higher-level learning activities. Research findings revealed that students' learning motivation and CSL proficiency improved significantly after using mLang and related pedagogies for one year. This chapter reports the design of mLang, the implementation of this online learning platform, and how the related pedagogies work.

1 Introduction

Educators and researchers alike have been trying to promote the use of technology (referred to as "digital innovation") in teaching and learning for decades. In 1991, when technological development was rapidly flourishing—not long after the first laptop computer was released, researchers like Garrett (1991) already noticed the potential of applying technology in education. Over the past decades, we have witnessed how technology development keeps scaling new heights; with the use of state-of-the-art technology, the education field is supposed to develop in the same

---

E. K. Y. Loh (✉)
The University of Hong Kong, Pok Fu Lam, Hong Kong
e-mail: ekyloh@hku.hk

manner. This idea is even more salient during the pandemic of COVID-19 from 2020 to 2023, as almost the entire world moved the offices and classrooms online overnight due to large-scale lockdown. While online learning eradicates time and space constraints (Ally, 2008; Cole, 2000), it still leaves us two vital issues of second language learning to deal with, i.e., how to overcome the learning difficulties, and how to enhance learner motivation.

In this chapter, I first discuss the difficulties of CSL learning, review the role and importance of learner motivation, as well as the use of technology in language learning. Then, I introduce the design of a self-initiated online learning platform named "mLang", and prove with data how it helps Chinese as a second language (CSL) learners overcome their learning difficulties by applying CSL learning theories, the economic concepts of "crowdfunding" and "sharing economy", collaborative learning and gamification, to boost their learning motivation, multiple learning outcomes. I further illustrate how all these concepts are applied in the CSL classroom as a pedagogy, report research findings and finally discuss and conclude this chapter.

2 Literature Review

2.1 Difficulties of Learning Chinese as a Second Language

In the past decade, there have been an increasing number of people migrating to Hong Kong from South and Southeast Asian countries, including Pakistan, India, the Philippines, Nepal and the like (Loh et al., 2018). They need to learn the Chinese language to integrate in the community, to pursue further studies or for better career prospect (Loh & Tam, 2016, 2017), particularly after Hong Kong's return to Chinese sovereignty in 1997 (Hong Kong SAR Government, 1997).

However, second language learners can hardly achieve proficiency comparable to their native language (Brown & Miller, 2013). They may be influenced by their mother tongue knowledge and make "language transfer errors" (Hoff, 2014, p. 275) when learning the target language. Such problems would be more severe and fossilized if the linguistic features of these two languages differ significantly, e.g. the first language of the EM learners and the second language, Chinese (please refer to chapter "Chinese Language Learning by Ethnic Minority Students in Hong Kong: Policy and Support" of this book for details).

Another external factor which worsens the situation is that many CSL learners seldom practice or use Chinese in daily life and at home (Sharma, 2018). They have little contact with the ethnic Chinese and prefer using their mother tongues to communicate with the family for convenience, inheriting their own culture, or simply because no one else in the family can speak Chinese. Therefore, school is the only place where they can learn the language. In light of this, CSL learners are at a disadvantageous position when competing with their native-speaking counterparts at schools (Loh & Tam, 2016), as the curriculum is designed for native Chinese students with little consideration for the CSL learners' learning needs.

Common sense tells us that you can still communicate without grammar. But, if you have no words, no communication is possible as "the bedrock of a second language is its vocabulary" (Ellis, 1994, p. 11; Nation, 1990, 2001). Chinese characters are recycled to construct about 90% of the vocabulary for daily usage, and CSL learners need to acquire at least a thousand or more characters to decode and extract information effectively and automatically in text reading (Lundberg & Leong, 1986). However, it is found that many CSL learners have difficulties in character learning, particularly the character-syllable-meaning connection, which restricts their vocabulary growth and hinder their proficiency development (Everson, 1998; Leong et al., 2011; Tse & Loh, 2008, 2009). Their difficulty is partly due to the nature of Chinese language that there is no direct orthophonological rule to decode the sound from the script. The traditional way of vocabulary learning through repeated practice of writing and dictating is laborious, boring, painful and ineffective (Orton, 2016; Scrimgeour, 2014; Tse et al., 2007). They need the strategy to connect the meaning of words, the written form and the pronunciation, so that they know how to read the characters and use the knowledge to draw inference about the meaning of the new vocabulary (Liao et al., 2022; Loh et al., 2021).

In fact, their learning is heavily dependent on and limited to what they are taught by the teachers and the prescribed texts in classroom. Hong Kong teachers primarily use textbooks as their basic teaching materials. These pre-designed materials may not adequately address the diverse needs of individual CSL learners (Yuan & Lo Bianco, 2022). Yet, teachers face a myriad of constraints in adjusting or tailoring materials for their students partly due to heavy workload, and also the highly diverse learning needs in the classroom when both new immigrants without any Chinese language knowledge and fluent Cantonese speakers born in Hong Kong are learning in the same classroom (Loh & Tam, 2016). Furthermore, the Hong Kong Education Bureau (EDB) intentionally allocate CSL learners to over 300 primary and 300 mainstream secondary schools. Most of the Chinese language teachers in these schools have not received any professional training in CSL teaching or have no prior experience in teaching CSL learners (Loh & Tam, 2016; please refer to chapter "Success or Failure: The Important Role of Emotionality for CSL Teachers' Professional Development" of this book for more details).

Low Chinese language proficiency hinder the upward social mobility of EM and consequent on the poverty issues (Hong Kong SAR Government, 2016). There is a pressing need to investigate effective pedagogy to support their learning, overcome the challenges and boost their learning progress. It also demands their effort and persistence over a sustained period in the learning process, so strong self-motivation is an important condition for the learners' success. In the following sections, I will explain the design of "mLang", how it helps CSL learners to overcome the challenges of Chinese language learning themselves, and to become more engaged in the learning process subconsciously with their learning motivation and self-confidence aroused.

2.2 Motivation of Second Language Learners

Previous studies show that students' learning motivation plays a crucial role in second language learning, which affects their persistence and learning behaviours (Hidi & Anderson, 1992), and their willingness to receive input from their teachers (Wu & Miller, 2021). According to Ryan and Deci (2000), motivation refers to "[a person] to be moved to do something" (p. 54), which can be *intrinsic* or *extrinsic* (p.55). The former implies one wants to do something because of their interest (e.g., feel curious or enjoyable), where the latter implies that one wants to pursue another outcome (e.g., parents' approval or a good grade) (Ryan & Deci, 2000). It is believed that intrinsic motivation plays a more vital role in language learning (Pae, 2008) as the learners feel satisfied and fulfilled during the learning process that generates more long-lasting learning persistence (Nicholson, 2015). On the contrary, extrinsic motivation relies on the fear of punishment or extrinsic rewards to keep students motivated and must be upgraded from time to time whenever performance is enhanced (Deci & Ryan, 2004; Nicholson, 2015), which would only stimulate immediate yet short-term effects. Although intrinsic and extrinsic motivations differ in nature, they are not mutually exclusive (Ryan & Deci, 2000) as both are highly influential determinants of students' learning behaviours.

According to Deci and Ryan's (2000, 2004) *Self-Determination Theory (SDT)*, students' basic psychological needs should be fulfilled to drive their learning motivation. These basic psychological needs include competence, autonomy, and relatedness (Nicholson, 2015, p. 4). *Competence* implies that the learners' sense of achievements should be fulfilled, and they would need to build the required knowledge and skills to become competent in mastering the tasks that are important to them. Autonomy implies that the learners should have a sense of control over their learning and the learning behaviours, and be the masters of their destiny. In terms of giving students a sense of control over their CSL learning and related learning behaviours, and enable them to be the masters of their destiny, teachers should allow them the autonomy of learning. Therefore, students should be given the space of learning, so that they can choose what and how much they want to learn at their own pace. Nevertheless, their learning should align with the school curriculum. This might seem impossible as teachers inertially rely on pre-designed textbooks published by the publishers, while the learners are diverse in terms of their CSL proficiency and learning needs. These students often struggle with their learning as their personal needs are hardly addressed, whereas decisions have been made on their behalf, and that they may not have the intellectual ability to be autonomous in a strict sense in CSL learning.

As for *relatedness*, it implies that learners need to have a sense of belonging and connectedness to their classmates, peers and their teachers (Deci & Ryan, 2008). Nevertheless, Deci and Ryan did not go further that the CSL learners and the learning materials should be connected too, as they want to see the "relation" between what they are learning and their personal interests and daily lives. The new teaching design should be flexible enough to address all these issues and build a tripartite connection, i.e., the relationship of the students, their peers and teachers, and the learning materials.

Research findings of SDT show that students who are intrinsically motivated to pursue the sense of "competence" are more willing to learn with higher chances to succeed in school, compared with those who are extrinsically motivated by their significant others, rewards or the grading system. Because of this, teachers should stimulate students' curiosity about what they are learning, challenge their cognitive ability while providing successful learning experiences to promote positive emotions in order to arouse and boost their intrinsic motivation (Yuan & Lo Bianco, 2022).

Enhancing students' sense of self-determination has been shown to result in many positive outcomes (McEown & Oga-Baldwin, 2019; Wehmeyer & Schwartz, 1997). Unfortunately, many CSL learners in Hong Kong are found with low learning motivation or even fear of learning (Loh et al., 2019), due to the lengthy, frustrating and ineffective learning journeys. There is an urgency to speed up their learning progress, rebuild their learning confidence and arouse their learning motivation.

The design of mLang is primarily based on SDT, considering (1) the characteristics and differences between the Chinese language and its phonological counterparts; and (2) the commonly seen learning difficulties among CSL learners, aiming at arousing their learning motivation (both intrinsic and extrinsic motivations), reducing their learning anxiety (Krashen, 1988), rebuilding their learning confidence through generating immediate and long-term learning effects. In the following section, I will further explain why technology should be used to support CSL learning, and how it helps to integrate second language learning theories and motivation theories while overcoming the difficulties of second language teaching and learning that makes it more effective and sustainable.

2.3 Technological Application in Language Learning

In the late twentieth century, Garrett (1991) already noticed the potential of using technology in language learning. Throughout the years, technology has been applied to enhance language learning in different ways. For instance, it allows students to practice the target language (Wu & Miller, 2021) at home through online platforms or mobile apps, even when the family does not use that second language. These are known as "computer-assisted language learning (CALL)" (Higgins, 1983, p. 102) or "mobile-assisted language learning (MALL)" (Wu & Miller, 2021). Therefore, with careful design, technology can provide quasi-real-world situations to simulate the authentic contexts in daily life for second language learners to practice their target language (Hafner & Miller, 2021; Wu & Miller, 2021).

This is especially true in the post-pandemic era (Kukulska-Hulme, 2021). With advanced technology, people have become accustomed to attending virtual classes and enjoying the convenience of real-time online meetings. Students can submit assignments in digital form. Just by changing the format, teachers and students can still see and hear each other. The prevalence of advanced technology in school settings, such as metaverse, Generative Artificial Intelligence (GenAI), may transform school teaching and learning, pedagogical application, and assessment. More importantly, technological application in language learning can also raise one's motivation to learn (e.g., Read & Kukulska-Hulme, 2015; Rico et al., 2015) which would facilitate CSL learners' learning.

Recently, there is an increasing number of research studies on CALL and MALL (Golonka et al., 2014; Miller & Wu, 2021; Nakata, 2011). Researchers use technology to draw students' attention (Wu & Miller, 2021) and provide a more satisfactory learning experience by providing rich media including images, audio tracks, videos (Rico et al., 2015), augmented reality (AR), virtual reality (VR) with mobile console (e.g., Nintendo DS). Results show that both students' motivation and proficiency have improved significantly (e.g. Bicen, 2015; Read & Kukulska-Hulme, 2015; Rico et al., 2015). Even those without any prior learning experience of the target language found it satisfying and motivating (Rico et al., 2015). Some studies showed that the students' motivation and confidence lasted longer—for example, they opted to do interviews in the second language rather than their native language (Bradley, 2015). As discussed in Sect. 2.2, it is crucial to raise the students' motivation because it can facilitate the learning process (Chinnery, 2006; Kukulska-Hulme, 2009; Rico et al., 2015) and maintain persistent learning behaviours. Moreover, only when the students have learning motivation will they have the chance to improve (Wu & Miller, 2021).

Learning activities with the use of technology, particularly those involving games, can achieve immediate learning effects and help students build extrinsic motivation (Figueroa, 2015). The term "gamification" appeared in recent decades, and it keeps gaining popularity since then (Walz & Deterding, 2014). *Gamification* refers to "the use of game elements in non-gaming systems" (Deterding et al., 2011; Lee & Hammer, 2011; Muntean, 2011; Richter et al., 2015, p. 21) to make the experience enjoyable (Richter et al., 2015). Nicholson (2015) suggests six key elements of gamification, namely play, exposition, choice, information, engagement, and reflection (p. 5). This implies on the one hand, the games involved in language learning activities (i.e. the learning tasks) should be play-based where there are rules that can be changed when necessary. On the other hand, the participants (i.e. students) should be in control of the learning process, understand why and how they play the games, and be given the chance allowing them to step back and reflect on their experiences (Nicholson, 2015).

If gamification is successfully implemented, there would be a possibility to turn the students' extrinsic motivation into intrinsic motivation. This is because when students attempt to gain points and achieve levels or badges or higher position on the leaderboard (Nicholson, 2015), they do not only build extrinsic motivation but receive sense of competence, autonomy, and relatedness as well (Muntean, 2011; Richter et al., 2015), which are exactly the three elements of SDT contributing to intrinsic motivation (Deci & Ryan, 2004). Besides, when students achieve the external rewards, they would feel a sense of satisfaction and joy. According to the well-known psychological theory *classical conditioning* by Ivan Pavlov (1955), when a neutral stimulus is paired up with an unconditioned stimulus, it can trigger an involuntary feeling (i.e., the unconditioned response). After conditioning, the neutral stimulus will become conditioned stimulus. The conditioned stimulus alone can trigger the same response, which is now known as the conditioned response—the same response as the unconditioned response (Kalat, 2017). In the case of language learning, it is the neutral stimulus whereas the activity designed with technology and gamification is the unconditioned stimulus. When students attempt to achieve points in the activities, the feeling of joy is triggered. After a certain period of repeated experiences, language learning is paired up with the feeling of joy; hence, the motivation to learn the second language will be converted from extrinsic to intrinsic. This is what mLang aims to provide to our CSL learners.

2.4 Section Summary

In this section, I have looked into the key findings of previous literature regarding second language learning, motivation of second language learners, as well as technological application in language learning. Both internal and external factors are involved in the hindrance of one's learning progress. Internally, learners may be influenced by their mother tongue knowledge and make "language transfer errors" (Hoff, 2014, p. 275); whereas externally, they may lack chances to practice outside the classroom (Sharma, 2018) if no one else in the family speaks that second language.

Technological application in language learning can eradicate the limitations of time and space (Ally, 2008; Cole, 2000). It also provides second language learners with more opportunities to practise, especially in quasi-real-world situations created with technology (Wu & Miller, 2021). The rich media (Rico et al., 2015) can attract students' attention (Wu & Miller, 2021), which in turn enhances their motivation to learn and hence the language proficiency as a result (Rico et al., 2015).

It is crucial to help the second language learners build motivation. Intrinsic motivation plays a more significant role than its extrinsic counterpart in helping the learners to persist in the long term (Deci & Ryan, 2004; Pae, 2008). Nevertheless, with gamification (Nicholson, 2015), it is possible to build students' extrinsic motivation first with external rewards such as points and leaderboard, before turning the extrinsic motivation into intrinsic motivation (Kalat, 2017; Muntean, 2011; Richter et al., 2015). These all provide supporting evidence of applying technology in language learning, which forms the background against which we developed the online learning platform "mLang".

3 The Design of mLang

In this section, I will illustrate the application of SDT, crowdfunding, and sharing economy concepts to the design of mLang, and demonstrate the effectiveness of mLang in enhancing CSL students' learning with reference to the findings of two case studies.

Two Grade 7 classes were recruited from two secondary schools to participate in the project. Ms. C, a CSL teacher at School A, was responsible for teaching a class of 20 CSL students (15 girls and 5 boys; 7 Indians, 5 Pakistani, 5 Nepalese, 1 French, 1 Japanese, and 1 of other nationality). At School B, their CSL teacher Mr. H's class consisted of 17 CSL students (5 girls and 12 boys; 10 Filipino, 2 Pakistani, 1 Indian, 2 British, 1 Thai and 1 American). All students in these two classes could communicate in English, but their Chinese oracy and literacy were considered "emerging". In Mr. H's class, being the lowest in terms of Chinese language proficiency in Grade 7 at School B, four of the students were newly arrived migrants with zero knowledge of Chinese. In both Schools A and B, each student was provided with an iPad for learning purposes.

Both schools adopted the GCSE Chinese (Pearson Edexcel) curriculum which covered five themes, namely (1) identity and culture; (2) local area, holiday and travel; (3) school; (4) future aspirations, study and work; and (5) international and global dimension. The two teachers adopted the mLang pedagogy alongside school-based teaching materials for teaching the first three themes for one academic year.

3.1 Background

"Lang" stands for "language", where "m" carries a number of meanings. First, "m" stands for "*mobile learning*", which refers specifically to the nature of the online platform which allows seamless learning; and "*multimodality*", which refers to the multimodal materials (e.g., texts, pictures and audio tracks) available and being generated by teachers and learners on mLang as teaching examples and language learning outcomes respectively; and also "*multilingual*" and "*multicultural*", referring to how learners from different cultural backgrounds speaking other languages as their mother tongues can learn different languages via mLang together simultaneously; as well as "*motivation*", referring to the design of mLang which is guided by SDT, and determined to offer CSL learners the autonomy to choose what and how much they want to learn, while making the learning materials more relevant to their daily lives for connecting with their peers to (re-)build their sense of competence when completing various mLang tasks. The ultimate goal is to turn students into "*masters of their learning*", with the three aforementioned key elements of SDT (i.e., students' basic psychological needs for effective learning) are adequately covered in their learning process.

3.2 The Design of mLang and CSL Learning Theories

Many teachers complain that their CSL learners are relatively good at speaking and listening but fail to go beyond the beginning stage for word recognition and can hardly develop reading and writing skills (Loh et al., 2019). They were found having difficulties to memorize the combined form, pronunciation and meaning, i.e., the three aspects of Chinese characters, or quickly forget what they have learned (e.g., Loh et al., 2018, 2019; Tse & Loh, 2014). In other words, they are stuck with the beginning stage of "speaking and listening" and have difficulties moving forward along the learning timeline that encompasses the stages "word learning" and "word writing", "reading" and then finally "writing" (Loh & Tse, 2012, p. 177).

Since many CSL students are faced difficulties in linking and memorizing the written form, pronunciation and meaning of Chinese vocabulary (Loh et al., 2018, 2019; Tse & Loh, 2014), mLang features the use of flashcards that show these three essential components simultaneously to strengthen the association. Figure 1 shows an mLang card created by a student uploaded to the platform. In this example, the learning theme is "Classroom Setting". The teacher asked the students to look around their classroom and select one classroom setting they liked by creating an mLang card. The student, i.e., creator of this mLang card, saw the blackboard in his classroom and created an mLang card by taking a photo, entering the written form and recording the pronunciation (lit. 黑板 hak1 baan2). After being checked by the teacher about accuracy, this card was shared among the whole class; students could click to view it and listen to the pronunciation. They were also able to leave comments (see the "dialogue button" on the top-left hand corner of Fig. 1) and show their appreciation by clicking the "like" button (see the "red heart" in the upper left corner). Should amendment be needed, teacher would give verbal or written feedback by clicking the feedback buttons.

The flashcard format was adopted for several reasons. Nation (1982, 2001) points out that, as one of the widely recognized ways to assist vocabulary learning, flashcards as a mobile tool can help learners to master large number of words while enabling the learning not to wear off quickly because it allows CSL students to learn and link up all three aspects of the vocabulary at once easily. The pedagogy behind, nevertheless, is the idea of mental lexicon (Aitchison, 1994) and the principle of SDT (Deci & Ryan, 2008).

CSL learners can master listening and speaking skills relatively easily. Like their native Chinese counterparts, they also have a wealth of life experiences. Therefore, mLang serves as a platform to systematically recall, retrieve, and retain their "mental

Fig. 1 An example of flashcard on mLang platform

lexicon" by themes covered by the teachers. These words reflect their interest, creativity, and their daily lives. They can take photos or download pictures (i.e., meaning of the learning object) from the internet and record audio clips (i.e., the pronunciation, in Chinese or other languages) about their ideas. In this way, the students are making use of multimodal resources to convey ideas about their individual learning interests and needs, and their teachers can teach them how to write the characters (i.e., written form) if they do not know. Teachers can also demonstrate the correct pronunciation in Chinese if the students can only speak English or their mother tongues, or when they have made mistakes. They can integrate and learn the three core components of character on the spot as the learning content is largely based on the learners' own decisions. More importantly, the students do not solely rely on their teachers and the pre-designed materials to learn receptive vocabulary; they generate productive vocabulary (Webb, 2008) that helps to stimulates the whole class even in the beginning stage of their learning.

This has been found to be an effective way to expand students' vocabulary, enrich the learning content by using the Chinese language to share their daily lives, and led to more sustainable learning outcomes. The three core components of SDT are also fulfilled, as the students can choose the words they want to learn (i.e., sense of autonomy) from their life experiences (i.e., sense of relatedness), which they found easy and enjoyable (i.e., sense of competence).

The following are examples collected from the two participating schools that illustrate students' learning outcome reflected in their mLang cards, with elaborations given by the teachers and the research team (see Table 1).

With these authentic learning materials, students were induced to share their real-life personal experiences for social, cultural and communicative exchanges. This enhanced students' learning motivation and sense of ownership in learning, which in turn made learning meaningful.

3.3 Crowdfunding and Shared Economy

Once the students' productive words have been collected, teachers are encouraged to use the "featured" function of mLang to share their flashcards among the whole class to facilitate peer learning as well as for more advanced follow-up learning activities. Such design is thus an example of applying the crowdfunding and sharing economy concepts of economy. *Crowdfunding* refers to raising small contributions of money from a large group of people to launch a new idea (Goran, 2018). In mLang pedagogy, the teachers "crowdfund" their students' knowledge, life experiences and creativity under different learning themes by creating mLang cards. They then share the crowdfunded learning resources among the class by featuring high-quality mLang cards with unique ideas. Everyone in the class can have a full set of learning resources, on top of their own creation, to facilitate higher level language learning, such as sentence making and paragraph writing. This also draws on another economic concept of *sharing economy* that through peer-to-peer sharing, individuals

Table 1 Examples of students bringing life experiences into classroom learning through making mLang cards

Project	Screenshots of Students' mLang Cards	Content Created by Students	Illustration
我是誰 (Who am I)		少民 (Student H)	Teachers observed that students were highly motivated to take selfies with their tablets.
		依撒 (Student I)	
一家人 (Family)		我和我的表妹 (Me and my cousin) (Student L)	Besides selfies, students were also eager to bring the learning task back home and invited family members to participate.
		我的哥哥和他的未婚夫(妻) (lit. My brother and his fiancée) (Student S)	

(continued)

Table 1 (continued)

Project	Screenshots of Students' mLang Cards	Content Created by Students	Illustration
介紹家人的工作 (Family members' jobs)		我的哥哥是一個實習醫生。他先在香港大學讀醫科。 (lit. My brother is a houseman [at a hospital]. He studied medicine at The University of Hong Kong.) (Student C)	
課室的活動 (My lesson)		同學 (lit. Classmates) (Student P)	After studying the texts provided by the schools, students could consolidate what they had learnt within the same context by replacing them with their personal experiences (e.g., photos of their daily lives at school, at home or travelling, etc.). They gained a deep sense of ownership of their collective vocabulary bank.
運動會 (Sports Day)		運動會 (lit. Sports Day) (Student A)	
我的校園 (My school)		在我的學校，我十分愛打排球，所以這個是排球場。 (lit. At my school, I like playing volleyball very much, so this is the volleyball court.) (Student U)	

(continued)

Table 1 (continued)

Project	Screenshots of Students' mLang Cards	Content Created by Students	Illustration
家務 (Housework)		我幫媽媽洗碗。 (lit. I helped mum wash the dishes.) (Student K)	
旅遊行程 (Travel itinerary)		這是我去香港維多利亞公園的花卉市場, 那天非常多人! (lit. I went to the flower market in the Hong Kong Victoria Park, it was very crowded that day!) (Student G)	
我的校園 (My school)		在我的學校有一個好大的籃球場。 (lit. There is a very big basketball court in my school.) (Student F)	Sometimes, teachers were even inspired and enlightened by the students' perspectives. For example, students were asked to take pictures around the school and introduce different facilities. The teacher could never have imagined how much students liked the school toilets, or how talented they were at taking a picture of the basketball court on a rainy day like a professional.
		我的校園有洗手間。我覺得學校的洗手間很乾淨。學校的廁所比公廁更好。 (lit. There are toilets in my school. I think the toilets in my school are very clean. The school toilets are much better than the public toilets.) (Student T)	

(continued)

Table 1 (continued)

Project	Screenshots of Students' mLang Cards	Content Created by Students	Illustration
不同國家的美食 (Multi-national cuisines)		這是巴基斯坦的食物。很好。 (lit. This is Pakistani food. Very good [yummy].) (Student F)	Through different experiential classroom activities, mLang served as a useful tool to generate and curate authentic learning materials. In this unit, students had to learn about different cultures, and they were asked to bring their ethnic dishes to share with each other. Before tasting the food, they would have to take pictures and create mLang cards to introduce what they had prepared.
		這是Momo, 是一個傳統的餃子。 (lit. This is Momo, a traditional dumpling.) (Student G)	
		甜糯米 Suman (Student N)	
難忘時刻 (Unforgettable moments)		我和我的姐姐在花園。 (lit. Me and my sister in the park.) (Student J)	Students were very proud of and willing to share their personal experiences with classmates for better mutual understanding. In this project, the teacher opened the learning space and asked students to share their unforgettable moments. The learning content generated by the students was very diversified as excellent teaching and learning materials, which enabled the teacher to lead more advanced learning activities with the class.

(continued)

Table 1 (continued)

Project	Screenshots of Students' mLang Cards	Content Created by Students	Illustration
		有一天我畢業 (lit. One day I will graduate.) (Student I)	
		我的第一個(隻)倉鼠。 (lit. My first hamster.) (Student Z)	
		在暑假, 我和媽媽到荔園樂園參觀。 (lit. During the summer holiday, I visited Lai Yuen Park with mum.) (Student R)	
		我們節日 (lit. Our festival) (Student I)	

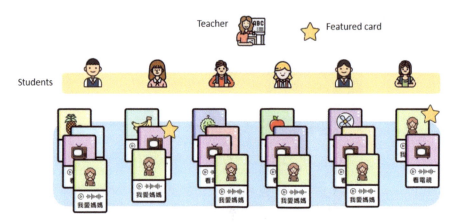

Fig. 2 Sharing featured cards within the class on mLang

could generate income from underutilized assets (Felson & Spaeth, 1978). In mLang, we facilitate students' sharing and fully utilize collective knowledge and creativity. Therefore, mLang is also like a co-constructed resource bank which provides rich content to support more advanced language learning activities.

The whole teaching and learning process is as follows: First, after the students have submitted their assignments as mLang cards, say three vocabulary items regarding the theme "Food around the world", their teachers would mark their work, provide feedback for correction and resubmission, then select the outstanding ones as the "featured" cards and share them with the whole class on the mLang platform. As shown in Fig. 2, the sharing of flashcards allows students to learn more words from each other while accumulating more knowledge related to different learning themes under the curriculum.

Mr. H recounted his own teaching and told us that he gave feedback on the cards, so that individual students could improve their work before sharing with other classmates. Some errors were purposefully kept and brought up for discussion and modification with the whole class. He emphasized participation and creative initiatives and encouraged positive attitude towards collective learning and improvement through errors. During class discussions with the whole class, Mr. H sometimes chose to only play the audio without displaying the corresponding card. The students then became highly attentive, showing eagerness to guess who had recorded the utterances. Some of the quieter students, who had previously been too anxious to speak up, actually did quite well with their recordings. When they discovered that others could understand their recordings, they felt significantly encouraged.

It is also interesting to note that despite being from two different schools, the content created by the students on the same topic was diverse yet closely tied to the learning themes (see Table 2). Students who were more proficient in Chinese typically created longer sentences, while those less fluent often expressed their ideas through words. This allows students to learn at their own pace, and their diverse learning needs were also addressed.

Table 2 Examples of students co-constructing the pool of knowledge on mLang

Project	Screenshots of students' mLang cards[a]	Content created by students	Illustration
孝敬父母的方法 (The way you show filial respect for parents)		我們要努力學習。(lit. We should study hard.) (Student E)	Students were asked to brainstorm and create a card about the behaviours related to filial piety. Great ideas were collected, such as doing housework, taking care of siblings, and studying hard to return the favour to their parents.
		我們能幫父母掃地。(lit. We can help our parents sweep the floor.) (Student O)	

(continued)

Table 2 (continued)

Project	Screenshots of students' mLang cards[a]	Content created by students	Illustration
		我會幫我的哥哥整理他的房間。 (lit. I would help my brother to tidy up his room.) (Student C)	
閱讀 Reading		恐嚇信(Threatening letter) 它是關於一個可怕的信。 (lit. It is about a threatening letter.) (Student D)	In this project, teacher wanted the students to introduce a Chinese book they liked. The teacher said it was a great knowledge exchange activity and it did encourage students to read more Chinese books due to peer or social impact.

	五個小孩的校長是一個感動人的故事 (lit. The "Litter Big Master" is a touching story.) (Student B)
	因為我覺得希臘神話很有趣,所以我看波西傑克森。 (lit. I find Greek mythology very interesting, and therefore I read Percy Jackson.) (Student U)

(continued)

Table 2 (continued)

Project	Screenshots of students' mLang cards[a]		Content created by students		Illustration
黃色 Yellow	芝士 (lit. Cheese)	黃單車 (lit. Yellow bike)	薯條 (lit. French Fries)	檸檬 (lit. Lemon)	Students were divided into small groups. Each group was assigned a colour. They had to create cards of different objects with that specific colour. One could find great variation and the teacher took the opportunity to extend students' semantic network by identifying the contrast and similarity. For example, the mLang cards created by the students could be categorized into foods, transports, clothes, etc. among different projects. Students could "reuse" these cards for sentence writing by reading the "featured" cards from all these different projects.
			英國黃的士 (lit. British yellow cab)	鴨 (lit. Duck)	

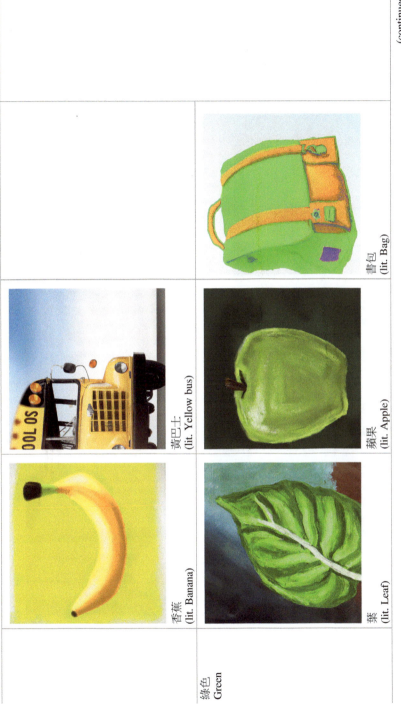

Table 2 (continued)

Project	Screenshots of students' mLang cards[a]		Content created by students		Illustration
中國新年 Chinese New Year	的士 (lit. Taxi)	貼春聯 (lit. Sticking couplets)	草 (lit. Grass)	紅包 (lit. Red packet)	
	青蘋果 (lit. Green apple)		放煙花 (lit. Fireworks)		Everyone could contribute and build a vast pool of knowledge. In this project, a lot of words related to festive celebrations were brought up, which was far beyond the content in the textbook.

aRemark: Considering the copyright issue, the photos students downloaded from the Internet to create their mLang cards have been replaced with imitated paintings generated by "Dall.e"

At the beginning, the cards were organised in terms of the colour. But they could also be grouped according to the same object category. This arrangement allowed for the observation of colour variations within the same category. This brought the students back to the theme of the original text, which was about different colours on national flags and how the colors represented different meanings. The two teachers observed that with the variations and great ideas generated by the students in different cards and projects, every student could contribute and co-develop a vast pool of knowledge (i.e., the idea of crowdsourcing). Given that mobile technology facilitated peer collocation, embracing the concept of sharing economy, teachers found it easier to expand the learning spaces and extend teaching and learning processes, making the learning journey more student-centric.

This pedagogy is effective because students can appreciate their peers' works more easily on mLang platform. It is observed that students are eager to know whose mLang cards are being featured, while being particularly interested in and excited about their peers' audio recordings, viewing the photos they have taken, and knowing more about their thoughts. They are motivated to try harder to impress their teachers and classmates to get their flashcards featured. High achievers' works are good examples which can inspire their peers to perform better. Low achievers or beginning learners can also make contributions by creating unique content, submitting interesting photos and producing quality recordings. By reviewing the featured mLang cards, students receive more input, learn more words and overcome the learning difficulties unintentionally. They are not even aware they are learning Chinese, which is supposed to be one of the most challenging languages in the world. According to our content analysis of the mLang cards submitted by students, about 60% of their outputs are beyond the scope of class, implying impressive learning progress.

Therefore, mLang helps the students to recognise, memorise and accumulate more words quickly and sustainably, and to learn about using the knowledge for meaningful expressions. With the collective effort of the students, a shared yet individualised vocabulary bank is built. Learning can be consolidated through repeatedly reviewing and using the knowledge in different learning activities.

The three core components of SDT are also covered in this case, as the students could choose whose words they wanted to view and learn (i.e., sense of autonomy), while getting to know other students' life experiences (i.e., sense of relatedness). Their determination to impress their teachers and peers with good performance also motivated them to overcome the learning difficulties and enjoy the learning process (i.e., sense of competence).

3.4 Collaborative Learning

The third key pedagogy of the mLang platform is *collaborative learning* (also known as *cooperative learning*) (Ghaith, 2003) that students learning in groups instead of alone (Istifci & Kaya, 2011). Previous literature (e.g. Brown, 2001;

Ghaith, 2003; Ibrahim et al., 2015; Istifci & Kaya, 2011) suggests that collaborative learning is a key factor in facilitating effective learning. Through in-group interactions, students are given opportunities to learn from their peers, which would in turn enrich their own learning experience (Ibrahim et al., 2015). Once the students express their thoughts, their peers may give feedback; meanwhile, upon learning about their peers' points of view, students may learn something they have never thought of, which helps them to come up with more meaningful and creative ideas (Ngeow & Kong, 2004). In addition, students with different language proficiency levels can help each other (Ibrahim et al., 2015), making peer learning within and across groups accessible and possible.

Also, learning in a group instead of alone can enhance students' feelings, as there is a shared goal within the group which generates a sense of belonging. This would prevent the group members from feeling isolated or alienated (Ghaith, 2003; Ibrahim et al., 2015; Johnson, 1979). Moreover, as discussed, it is crucial for second language learners to have ample opportunities to practise. Collaborative learning in second language learning contexts allows the learners to practise the language by using it to interact with their group mates. This, in turn, provides opportunities to participate in learning activities and practise the language actively (Clifford, 1999; Thomson, 1998).

Ms. C commented that mLang lessons had allowed her students to add their own experiences, cultures and personal values into language learning. One particularly exciting example was the mLang activity in relation to the unit on food (see Fig. 3). Students were asked to introduce food in their own ethnic cultures. They cooked the dish, created cards about it and how it was made. They were also asked to bring the food to class for tasting before the lesson, which was considered a lot of fun. After that, students created mLang flashcards by recalling their tasting experiences. They further learnt the names of the food items in their native languages and the Chinese language alike. The most interesting thing was, some cards also showed the students' families who took part in cooking. It was a very delightful discovery that with the use of technology, families can be connected to and learn about the current updates of the class, whereas the class can also be connected to and explore each other's family. The students felt that their cultures were made better understood and respected through Chinese learning.

3.5 Gamification

Aside from vocabulary learning, *gamification* is another key pedagogy of mLang. Kayımbaşıoğlu et al.'s research study (2016) shows that gamification can extend students' attention span and reduce distraction during the learning process. To maximise the learning effectiveness of gamification, six key elements should be included, namely play, exposition, choice, information, engagement, and reflection (Nicholson, 2015, p. 5). These elements served as the guideline for the design of the mLang platform.

Fig. 3 Students introduce the delicious food of their heritage countries they like by creating mLang cards

First, *play* implies that the learning tasks (i.e., the game) should contain play-based elements (Nicholson, 2015, p. 6). Play-based games refer to games where players can decide for themselves the constraints and boundaries of the game. Players of games must follow the rules in general. But they can change the constraints (usually known as "rules") when they find the game is not fun anymore or if they want to make it more fun (Nicholson, 2015, p. 6). Applying the "play" element to the mLang platform, students' online learning is guided by their teachers and the school-based curriculum, yet teachers and students can discuss and decide the constraints (i.e., 'rules') of the games (i.e., learning tasks) they play. For example, when using mLang to assign classwork or homework, teachers can choose a topic based on the students' interests.

While crossing boundaries in game-based learning may lead to the concern of safety, it is safe for students to learn from and to make attempts on the mLang platform. This is because unlike some other online learning platforms where learners learn by themselves, students' learning on mLang is under their teachers' guidance and supervision. Their teachers, as gatekeepers, will mark and assess their work and choose high-quality submissions to share with the whole class. These handpicked flashcards can then become part of the matching games for revision. Teachers and students can then decide together whether the matching game is timed as a quiz or as an exercise. Therefore, it is safe for students to play the "games" on the mLang platform.

The second key component is *exposition*. It refers to the narrative layer presented through the game (Nicholson, 2015) that the players can make meaning, simulate and experience something in authentic contexts that they can apply in the real-world setting (Nicholson, 2015). As for the design of the mLang platform, the learning activities and games simulate learners to retrieve their personal experiences from authentic real-world setting to their school learning. Under the theme of "The food famous in Hong Kong" as an example, CSL students should be able to learn not only about the food but also the culture and traditional practices of the featured city. This in turn can help them integrate into the Hong Kong community.

Third, *choice* implies that players are given options to make choices in games (Nicholson, 2015). This corresponds to the autonomy-related elements in the STD (Deci & Ryan, 2004), where people will have a positive feeling when things are in their control (Nicholson, 2015). According to Krashen's input hypothesis (1985), learners can learn more effectively when they feel entertained and relaxed (Loh et al., 2019). However, only when things are in the learners' control will they feel relaxed and be able to enjoy the fun. As presented above, the design of mLang learning activities is based on discussions between the teacher and the students. In this way, students can feel a sense of autonomy in relation to the learning activities they need to do, as the design is largely based on their opinions and interests. By doing so, they would not feel being forced into doing something they do not like. Besides, regarding the flashcard function presented in Sect. 3.2, aside from teachers, students are encouraged to create the flashcards themselves, which forms the main part of the learning process on the mLang platform. Taking the theme "Famous food in Hong Kong" as the example again, teacher may ask each student to create three flashcards to introduce the food they like the most. They can do research on well-known food items in Hong Kong, take photos of the food items or the restaurants that serves them (i.e., meaning), read aloud to record how they pronounce the words (i.e., pronunciation), and type the item names on the flashcards (i.e., written form) (see Fig. 4). In other words, this activity allows students to choose what they like to include in their assignments, which illustrates how the autonomy offered by mLang for the students to choose what they want to learn and share on the mLang platform (Fig. 4).

Fourth, *information* implies the information the game players should know regarding why they should play the game, as well as how this game helps them in real-world contexts to make meaning to the players (Nicholson, 2015). Therefore, it is necessary to let the players understand how the game connects to the real-world instead of just earning points (Nicholson, 2015). On the mLang platform, teachers can design the themes of learning activities either based on the students' personal interests or the school-based curriculum. This means they can design situations that help the students to connect the learning activities to the real-world contexts, from which they can make meaning as well. By doing so, students can have a taste of the quasi-real-world on mLang. Referring to our example in previous sections, i.e., "Famous food in Hong Kong", if the teacher designs a learning activity about

Fig. 4 Examples of mLang cards made by the CSL students

creating three flashcards of the famous food the students like the most, the students will retrieve their daily experiences or conduct research on that, such as taking photos at local restaurants. After submitting the flashcards, the teacher may carry out other learning activities in class, such as group discussions and/or oral presentations. In this way, students can easily notice how the "games" (in this case the learning tasks) connect to the authentic contexts they have experienced in the real world.

Fifth, *engagement* implies how engaging the game is to the players (Nicholson, 2015). Engagement refers to two senses: (i) how the players engage in the game with others, and this corresponds to the element "relatedness" in the SDT (Deci & Ryan, 2004); and (ii) how much the players can engage in the game considering the flow of the game; in other words, once the level of challenge of the game matches the ability of the players while enhancing the latter's ability, it can be raised adequately to avoid boredom. This way the players can stay entertained when playing the game and continue to engage in it (Nicholson, 2015). Since the mLang platform allows the teacher to design learning activities of any theme and different levels of challenge, the assigned tasks should be able to match the students' ability and language proficiency. Meanwhile, since the mLang platform is designed for students to learn under the teaching and guidance of their teachers, the teachers can monitor the progress (or the "flow") and adjust accordingly. Moreover, the mLang platform allows group activities and sharing of good work within class, which enables students to relate to others and learn from their peers.

Lastly, *reflection* implies offering opportunities for players to stop and step back to reflect (Nicholson, 2015). As discussed, games serve as a means for second language learners to learn the target language. While the games themselves are important, it is also crucial to allocate time for the players to reflect. Thiagarajan (2004) suggests that there are four steps in "reflection", which include: (i) allow players to express how they feel about the game; (ii) look back on what had happened during the game; (iii) think about what they had learned and how they can apply what they learned in new contexts; and (iv) what they intend to do next. These steps form a "ladder" that starts from the most basic one (i.e., to express emotion) to the most advanced one (i.e., what the players have learned and how to apply). In this way, players can have a chance to look back and reflect deeply. Like most social networking platforms, mLang has the "like" and "feedback" buttons whereby students may provide their feedback on others' works based on the assessment criteria provided by the teachers. Besides, teachers can review the learning activities together with the students and ask students to express their thoughts by creating another flashcard. Students may draw, take a picture, record their own voice or write a word. This will help teachers to better understand how their students feel about the learning activities and adjust in the future accordingly. Moreover, as an interaction, the teachers can leave their replies to the students in the same way as how they mark students' work on mLang. This can enhance the relationship between teachers and students while facilitating peer interactions, which in turn makes the learning process more enjoyable.

With all the six key elements of gamification involved, the mLang platform allows students to have fun through the second language learning process, whereby students can build intrinsic motivation. In the long run, they may become persist in learning the target language even without external rewards.

4 Implementation of mLang

Section 3 illustrates the design of the mLang platform and students' learning outcomes with reference to the findings of two case studies, particularly how the mLang platform can be adopted for CSL teaching and learning, and its effectiveness in enhancing the learning experience and language proficiency of the learners.

4.1 Examples of Using mLang for Second Language Teaching

On the mLang platform, teachers can set up themes or topics depending on the learning goals and students' interest. Then, they can assign students tasks like collecting pictures and information for creating flashcards. Upon receipt of student submissions, teachers can mark their work and provide feedback to students for correction and resubmission. Teachers can then select high quality work as featured cards and share them with the whole class, to enrich the students' vocabulary. The collected resources on the mLang platform can further facilitate students to learn the language by participating in different learning activities, which include word reading, listening, speaking, and writing.

When designing learning activities and relevant sequences, teachers can refer to the "4-stage, 3-step" scaffolding cycle as shown in Fig. 5. Stages 1 to 4 refer to the learning of words, sentences, paragraphs, and passages respectively, which involves an increase in levels of complexity and challenge. Each stage involves three steps from which students can learn from the most basic ones (e.g., reading aloud the target vocabulary items provided by their teachers) to the ones involving collaboration work or model writing, before moving on to the most challenging tasks that require students to finish the tasks on their own. In other words, the three steps in each stage move from "dependent" to "independent", and from "fixed" to "expanded" learning content.

The mLang platform supports teachers to easily scaffold CSL students' learning for the attainment of more advanced language proficiency levels through suggested activities for the "4-stage and 3-step" scaffolding cycle. For example, as an introduction, teachers can ask students to create their own flashcards regarding the keywords selected from the text being taught. Once the mLang cards are ready, teachers may instruct students to play language games such as "Bingo" (Loh et al., 2019).

In the present study, Ms. C selected Bingo games for the lesson. She selected some mLang cards and showed them to the class. Students recalled the words, and each student had to choose 9 out of all the cards being shown and write the words on their Bingo worksheets. At the same time, Ms. C walked around the classroom and observed what the more favourable choices were to increase students' chances of winning. Similar to the traditional version of Bingo, students with the chosen vocabulary items lined up on a row, a column or a diagonal will win. On the one

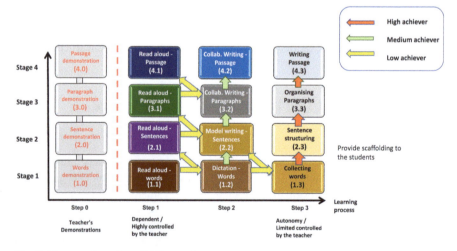

Fig. 5 "4-stage, 3-step" scaffolding cycle

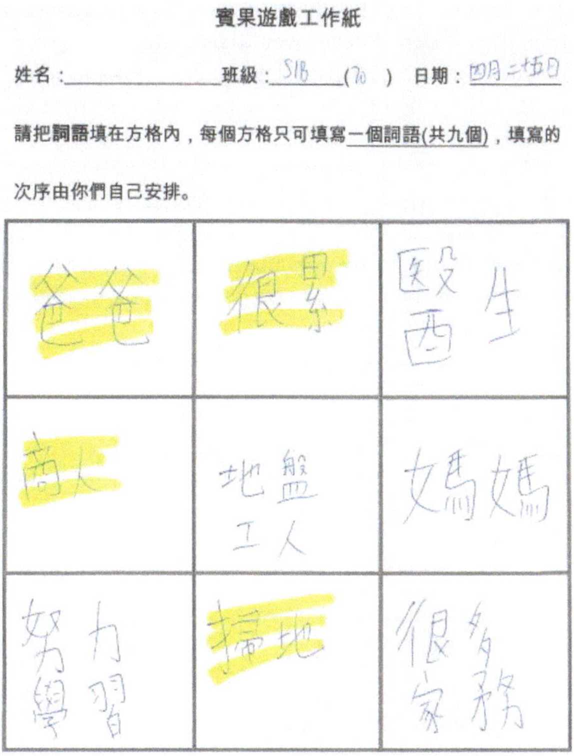

Fig. 6 Sample of CSL student's Bingo worksheet

hand, students with those items on their Bingo sheet would have to correctly pronounce the word or explain the word in English in order to earn points. On the other hand, their peers would have need to confirm the accuracy (see Fig. 6).

In this game, individuals have the choice to guess what would come out as the Bingo-words, which makes the process entertaining and enjoyable. However, the scores of the game are counted on a group basis instead of an individual basis. This encourages students in the same group to help each other, such as checking the words. In the end, each student must hand in their correct word lists in order to score. In general, CSL students do not have a lot of opportunities to read Chinese, but in this game alone, they would have to read the words at least four times (first, one reads and selects the word from the cards; second, one reads to check it against the list being made; third, one rereads it when the word named by the teacher; fourth, one reads to check each other's writing before it is submitted for scoring), which helps consolidate their learning.

In another participating school, Mr. H liked playing the game "Big Television" (Loh et al., 2019) with his students. He would first divide students into small groups, in which each of them would have a student representative nominated by the group members. Mr. H selected words from the mLang platform by lot or by propose. He then showed the cards to the representative of each group in turn, where the representative had to illustrate the chosen vocabulary items to the whole class through gestures. A team would gain additional points if their representative made the guess correctly. This would help students to integrate the meanings, pronunciations, and written forms of vocabulary items effectively in a fun-filled and exciting learning process.

Moving on to the higher levels, Mr. H used mLang to implement more challenging activities (Loh et al., 2019), including teaching grammar points (e.g. 為了 [In order to] …, … 就 [just] …). His students then constructed sentences with the grammar points to by submitting mLang cards (see Fig. 7). Students worked in groups to jointly construct short passages on the online learning platform.

Fig. 7 Samples of sentences made by the CSL students. (*Remark: Considering the copyright issue, the photos students downloaded from the Internet to create their mLang cards have been replaced with the imitated paintings generated by "Dall.e.")

4.2 Effectiveness of Using mLang in CSL Learning

In general, using the mLang platform in CSL teaching and learning is effective in enhancing both the learning attitude and learning performance of the students. Our research has shown that the multimodal materials included on the mLang flashcards help students enhance their language performance in multiple ways (Loh et al., 2018). In terms of productive language skills, students have shown improvement in both speaking and writing. Clearer pronunciation and improved Cantonese tones are noticeable. In terms of writing, students find it pleasurable in learning vocabulary on mLang, through which they can use what they have learnt to write longer and more complex sentences with enriched content. They have also grown more vigilant about their own errors and those of their peers, demonstrating an increased ability to self-correct.

In order to better understand the effectiveness of mLang, we interviewed Ms. C and Mr. H and their students. The two teachers told the research team that using the mLang platform had helped students build good writing habits, enabling them to acquire the ability to problem-solve and learn independently. He also helped his students build an online resource bank on their own in an interesting and funny way—students felt more relaxed when asked to do a writing task because they could use the resources on mLang, which stimulated more ideas for the creative process. Aside from using a larger vocabulary in writing, students also became capable of producing sentences with more complex structures. Besides writing, they also made use of the resources uploaded to mLang platform in other language activities (e.g., debates).

As for student interviewees, they were aware of the changes that they had experienced as well. For instance, when doing the writing exercises, they would refer to mLang, retrieve and try to use the vocabulary they learnt—including more difficult items like idioms. Besides, students felt a sense of autonomy in the learning process, which helped raise their interest in learning Chinese. They also expressed that their classroom experience was significantly more enjoyable with mLang. In conventional classes, textbooks were the primary or only teaching material. However, in classes that incorporated mLang, students had more opportunities for interaction with their teachers and peers, hence allowed for greater participation, enhancing their learning experience in delightful ways. Moreover, the use of the online learning platform aligned better with the students' personal interests, and as a result made Chinese learning more enjoyable.

4.3 Section Summary

In short, in this section I have presented the design of the mLang platform and its supporting theoretical framework. mLang was built based on key pedagogies including CSL learning theories, vocabulary learning, motivation theories, crowdfunding and sharing economy, gamification, and collaborative learning. mLang flashcards allow students to learn from multimodal materials (i.e., pictures for meaning, texts for the written form and audio recordings for pronunciation) and to create their own vocabulary cards (Loh et al., 2018, 2019). Besides, based on the six elements of gamification (Deterding et al., 2011; Lee & Hammer, 2011; Muntean, 2011; Nicholson, 2015; Richter et al., 2015), mLang is designed as the platform for CSL learners to explore with attempts within safe boundaries, and to make meaning from the learning activities in which they participate. The application of "crowdfunding" and "sharing economy" concepts expanded the scope and depth of their learning. In the short term, the play-based gaming environment with points and leaderboards helps to build the students' extrinsic motivation; in the long run, through fun activities and mastering of skills, students can build intrinsic motivation that helps them persist in learning while being willing to pay effort to overcome challenges. Also, mLang allows students to work in groups and to learn from their peers (i.e., collaborative learning) (Brown, 2001; Ghaith, 2003; Ibrahim et al., 2015; Istifci & Kaya, 2011).

Additionally, this section illustrates how mLang can be used to assist and enhance second language teaching and learning. Our earlier research findings (Loh et al., 2018) reveals mLang is effective in enhancing CSL students' motivation, attitude and performance in learning Chinese. With the introduction of the "4-stage, 3-step" scaffolding cycle, the mLang platform allows design of different learning activities, from the most basic ones to the most challenging ones, that cover the second language learning stages of learning words, sentences, paragraphs, and passages (Loh et al., 2019). This pedagogy also helps teachers to scaffold their students from reliance on classroom teaching to becoming independent learners.

5 Discussion and Conclusion

This chapter has looked into why and how the mLang platform is effective in enhancing the teaching and learning of CSL. According to the research literature on second language learning, motivation in second language learning, and technological application in language learning, a well-designed online learning platform and pedagogy should pay attention to the difficulties the learners encountered, be able to improve their motivation, and the adoption of technology in the teaching and learning process should be carefully considered.

The difficulties faced by the CSL learners in Hong Kong including both internal and external factors. Internally, they may make "language transfer errors" being influenced by their first language (Hoff, 2014, p. 275). They also lack ample opportunities to practise outside the classroom (Sharma, 2018) due to the limited exposure of the language in daily life for various reasons.

As for motivation, it is crucial to help CSL learners to build and re-build motivation, especially the intrinsic one, which makes learning more persistent in the long term (Deci & Ryan, 2004; Pae, 2008). With the application of technology, the ideas of crowdfunding, sharing economy, and gamification (Nicholson, 2015) have become more accessible and possible. The scope and depth of learners' learning are expanded; their extrinsic motivation can be built first with external rewards such as points and leaderboard, and later turning the extrinsic motivation into the intrinsic one (Kalat, 2017; Muntean, 2011; Richter et al., 2015).

Technological applications also make seamless language learning (Ally, 2008; Cole, 2000). mLang provides CSL learners more opportunities to practise, especially in quasi-real-world situations (Wu & Miller, 2021). It can attract students' attention (Wu & Miller, 2021), which helps enhance their motivation to learn and perform better (Rico et al., 2015).

With the aim of helping CSL learners to enhance their learning motivation and proficiency, mLang is also built upon key theories of CSL learning. The mLang flashcards allow students to learn all the three aspects of character components, which include the written form, pronunciation, and meaning from multimodal materials (i.e., text, audio recording, and a relevant image) while using multiple languages to express ideas. Students can create their own vocabulary cards (Loh et al., 2018, 2019) to bring individual interest and life experience into their classroom learning.

In addition, the design of mLang is guided by the six elements of gamification (Deterding et al., 2011; Lee & Hammer, 2011; Muntean, 2011; Nicholson, 2015; Richter et al., 2015), so that the learners can make attempts within safe boundaries, and to make meaning from the learning activities in which they participate. By participating in pertinent learning activities within a play-based gaming environment, students can develop their extrinsic motivation, which, over time, can evolve into intrinsic motivation. mLang also allows students to work in groups to learn from their peers (i.e., collaborative learning) (Brown, 2001; Ghaith, 2003; Ibrahim et al., 2015; Istifci & Kaya, 2011).

With the introduction of the "4-stage, 3-step" scaffolding cycle, mLang allows teachers to design different learning activities to scaffold their students from the most basic skills to the most challenging skills encompassing the learning stages of speaking and listening, vocabulary recognition, sentence making, paragraph and passage writing (Loh et al., 2019), as well as from dependent to become independent learners. According to findings of our research studies (Loh et al., 2018), mLang is effective in enhancing CSL learners' attitude and performance. They participated more actively in class while having more fun learning Chinese.

6 Future Directions

In the future, in order to further maximise the effectiveness in enhancing CSL teaching and learning, the mLang platform will be upgraded by means of applying the most advanced technology. Besides the teaching and learning of CSL, we will also investigate the effectiveness of using mLang to support native Chinese speaking students learning English as a second language, as well as to support CSL students learning other subjects in Chinese language.

Acknowledgements I would like to thank the Quality Education Fund (Reference number: 2014/0033), the Language Fund of the Standing Committee on Language Education and Research (Reference Number: 2015-0027), Technology Start-up Support Scheme for Universities (TSSSU@HKU) (Reference Number: TSSSU/HKU/18/05/1), Incu-Tech Programme of Hong Kong Science Park (Reference number: CP-IP/173-2/PM/WC/MC/gm [4320-2018-01]) for their project sponsorship. I also would like to thank the schools and teachers who participated in this study.

Special thanks to Dr. Ki Wing-Wah for his guidance and support and for working with me as a co-founder since 2014; Dr. Lau Kwok Chang for serving as a partner and curriculum development officer to examine, advance and promote mLang; Dr. Shum Shiu-Kee Mark, Miss Kam Wan Man Ava, Ms. Chu Hiu Wai, Ms. Wong Ling Ling, Miss Jessica Choi, Miss Jessica Young and Miss Ankie Ng for their contributions and continued support to my work. Last but not least, my heartfelt gratitude to the school principals, teachers and students for their trust and unwavering support, my technical team, especially Dr. Lau Man Kin Vincent, Mr. Li Kin On, Mr. Jason Fok, Mr. Alan Lam, Mr. Mack Mok and others, who have made my dreams come true.

References

Aitchison, J. (1994). *Words in the mind: An introduction to the mental lexicon*. Blackwell Publishers.
Ally, M. (2008). Foundations of educational theory for online learning. In T. Anderson (Ed.), *The theory and practice of online learning* (2nd ed., pp. 15–44). Athabasca University Press.
Bicen, H. (2015). The role of social learning networks in mobile assisted language learning: Edmodo as a case study. *Journal of Universal Computer Science, 21*(10), 1297–1306.
Bradley, L. (2015). The mobile language learner – Use of technology in language learning. *Journal of Universal Computer Science, 21*(10), 1269–1282.
Brown, B. L. (2001). *Web-based training*. ERIC Digest. Retrieved from http://www.ericdigests.org/2001-2/training.html
Brown, K., & Miller, J. (2013). *The Cambridge dictionary of linguistics*. Cambridge University Press.
Chinnery, G. M. (2006). Going to the MALL: Mobile assisted language learning. *Language Learning & Technology, 10*(1), 9–16.
Clifford, V. A. (1999). The development of autonomous learners in a university setting. *Higher Education Research and Development, 18*(1), 115–128.
Cole, R. A. (2000). *Issues in web-based pedagogy: A critical primer*. Greenwood Press.
Deci, E. L., & Ryan, R. M. (2000). The "what" and "why" of goal pursuits: Human needs and the self-determination of behavior. *Psychological Inquiry, 11*, 227–268.
Deci, E. L., & Ryan, R. M. (2004). *Handbook of self-determination research*. University of Rochester Press.
Deci, E. L., & Ryan, R. M. (2008). Self-determination theory: A macro theory of human motivation, development, and health. *Canadian Psychology/Psychologie Canadienne, 49*, 182–185.
Deterding, S., Sicart, M., Nacke, L., O'Hara, K., & Dixon, D. (2011). Gamification: Using game design elements in non-gaming contexts. In *Proceedings of the 2011 Annual Conference Extended Abstracts on Human Factors in Computing Systems* (pp. 2425–2428). ACM Press.
Ellis, R. (1994). *The study of second language acquisition* (2nd ed.). Oxford University Press.
Everson, M. E. (1998). Word recognition among learners of Chinese as a foreign language: Investigating the relationship between naming and knowing. *The Modern Language Journal, 82*(2), 194–204.

Felson, M., & Spaeth, J. L. (1978). Community structure and collaborative consumption: A routine activity approach. *American Behavioral Scientist, 21*(4), 614–624. https://doi.org/10.1177/000276427802100411

Figueroa, F. J. (2015). Using gamification to enhance second language learning. *Digital Education Review, 27*(21), 32–54.

Garrett, N. (1991). Technology in the service of language learning: Trends and issues. *Modern Language Journal, 75*, 74–101.

Ghaith, G. (2003). Effects of the learning together model of cooperative learning on English as a foreign language reading achievement, academic self-esteem, and feelings of school alienation. *Bilingual Research Journal, 27*(3), 451–474.

Golonka, E. M., Bowles, A. R., Frank, V. M., Richardson, D. L., & Freynik, S. (2014). Technologies for foreign language learning: A review of technology types and their effectiveness. *Computer Assisted Language Learning, 27*(1), 70–105.

Goran, C. (2018). Crowdfunding. In B. Warf (Ed.), *The SAGE encyclopedia of the internet*. SAGE Publications. https://doi.org/10.4135/9781473960367.n40

Hafner, C. A., & Miller, L. (2021). Language learning with technology in the classroom. In L. Miller & J. G. Wu (Eds.), *Language learning with technology: Perspectives from Asia* (pp. 13–30). Springer.

Hidi, S., & Anderson, V. (1992). Situational interest and its impact on reading and expository writing. In K. A. Renninger, S. Hidi, A. Krapp, & A. Renninger (Eds.), *The role of interest in reading and development* (pp. 215–238). Psychology Press. https://doi.org/10.4324/9781315807430

Higgins, J. (1983). Computer assisted language learning. *Language Teaching, 16*(2), 102–114.

Hoff, E. (2014). *Language development* (5th ed.). Cengage.

Hong Kong SAR Government. (1997). *Policy address 1997*. Hong Kong Special Administrative Region Government.

Hong Kong SAR Government. (2016). *Hong Kong ethnic minority poverty situation report 2015*. Financial Secretary, and Census and Statistics Department, Hong Kong Special Administrative Region Government.

Ibrahim, N., Shak, M. S. Y., Mohd, T., Ismail, N. A., Perumal, P. D., Zaidi, A., & Yasin, S. M. A. (2015). The importance of implementing collaborative learning in the English as a second language (ESL) classroom in Malaysia. *Procedia Economics and Finance, 31*, 346–353.

Istifci, I., & Kaya, Z. (2011). Collaborative learning in teaching a second language through the internet. *Turkish Online Journal of Distance Education, 12*(4), 88–96.

Johnson, D. (1979). *Educational psychology*. Prentice Hall.

Kalat, J. W. (2017). *Introduction to psychology* (11th ed.). Cengage Learning.

Kayımbaşıoğlu, D., Oktekin, B., & Hacı, H. (2016). Integration of gamification technology in education. *Procedia Computer Science, 102*, 668–676.

Krashen, S. (1985). *The input hypothesis: Issues and implications*. Longman.

Krashen, S. (1988). *Second language acquisition and second language learning*. Pergamon Press.

Kukulska-Hulme, A. (2009). Will mobile learning change language learning? *ReCALL, 21*(2), 157–165.

Kukulska-Hulme, A. (2021). Moving language teaching and learning from the known to the unknown. In L. Miller & J. G. Wu (Eds.), *Language learning with technology: Perspectives from Asia* (pp. 3–12). Springer.

Lee, J. J., & Hammer, J. (2011). Gamification in education: What, how, why bother? *Academic Exchange Quarterly, 15*(2), 1–5.

Leong, C. K., Tse, S. K., Loh, E. K. Y., & Ki, W. W. (2011). Orthographic knowledge important in comprehending elementary Chinese text by users of alphasyllabaries. *Reading Psychology, 32*(3), 237–271.

Liao, X., Loh, E. K. Y., & Cai, M. (2022). Lexical orthographic knowledge mediates the relationship between character reading and reading comprehension among learners with Chinese as a second language (CSL). *Frontiers in Psychology, 13*. https://doi.org/10.3389/fpsyg.2022.779905

Loh, E. K. Y., & Tam, L. C. W. (2016). Struggling to thrive: The impact of Chinese language assessments on social mobility of Hong Kong ethnic minority youth. *Asia-Pacific Education Researcher, 25*(5–6), 763–770.

Loh, E. K. Y., & Tam, L. C. W. (2017). The role of emotionality in teacher change: The case of Chinese language teachers in Hong Kong. *Teacher Development, 21*(3), 463–479.

Loh, E. K. Y., & Tse, S. K. (2012). An investigation of school-based curriculum design of effective Chinese character learning for non-Chinese speaking kindergartners. *Journal of Han Character Education and Research, 28*, 171–195.

Loh, E. K. Y., Sun, K. W., Ki, W. W., & Lau, K. C. (2018). The building and sharing of knowledge: Mobile app assists students of ethnic minorities to learn Chinese writing. Paper presented at the *International Chinese Practical Writing Research Symposium*, University of Macao.

Loh, E. K. Y., Sun, K. W., Ki, W. W., & Lau, V. M. K. (2019). IT assists Chinese as a second language learners in developing collaborative learning materials: mLang pedagogy. In E. K. Y. Loh, P. W. Y. Chou, M. S. K. Shum, & W. W. Ki (Eds.), *Chinese language education in the multilingual and multicultural contexts: Theories and practice* (pp. 137–150). Hong Kong University Press.

Loh, E. K. Y., Liao, X., Leung, S. O., & Tam, L. C. W. (2021). How do Chinese as a second language (CSL) learners acquire orthographic knowledge: Components, structure and position regularity. *Language Awareness, 30*(3), 297–316. https://doi.org/10.1080/09658416.2021.1972115

Lundberg, I., & Leong, C. K. (1986). Compensation in reading disabilities. *Advances in Psychology, 34*, 171–190. https://doi.org/10.1016/S0166-4115(08)61204-2

McEown, M. S., & Oga-Baldwin, W. L. Q. (2019). Self-determination for all language learners: New applications for formal language education. *System, 86*, 1–11.

Miller, L., & Wu, J. G. (2021). Preface. In L. Miller & J. G. Wu (Eds.), *Language learning with technology: Perspectives from Asia* (pp. v–viii). Springer.

Muntean, C. I. (2011). Raising engagement in e-learning through gamification. In *Proceeding of ICVL 2011: The 6th international conference on virtual learning* (pp. 323–329). University of Bucharest.

Nakata, T. (2011). Computer-assisted second language vocabulary learning in a paired-associate paradigm: A critical investigation of flashcard software. *Computer Assisted Language Learning, 24*(1), 17–38.

Nation, I. S. P. (1982). Beginning to learn foreign vocabulary: A review of the research. *RELC Journal, 13*(1), 14–36.

Nation, I. S. P. (1990). *Teaching and learning vocabulary*. Heinle & Heinle.

Nation, I. S. P. (2001). *Learning vocabulary in another language*. Oxford University Press.

Ngeow, K., & Kong, Y. (2004). *Learning through discussion: Designing tasks for critical inquiry and reflective learning*. ERIC Digest. Retrieved from http://www.ericdigests.org/2004-1/tasks.htm

Nicholson, S. (2015). A RECIPE for meaningful gamification. In T. Reiners & L. C. Wood (Eds.), *Gamification in education and business* (pp. 1–20). Springer.

Orton, J. (2016). Issues in Chinese language teaching in Australian schools. *Chinese Education and Society, 39*(6), 369–375. https://doi.org/10.1080/10611932.2016.1283929

Pae, T. I. (2008). Second language orientation and self-determination theory: A structural analysis of the factors affecting second language achievement. *Journal of Language and Social Psychology, 27*(1), 5–27.

Pavlov, I. (1955). *I. P. Pavlov: Selected works*. Foreign Languages Publishing House.

Read, T., & Kukulska-Hulme, A. (2015). The role of a mobile app for listening comprehension training in distance learning to sustain student motivation. *Journal of Universal Computer Science, 21*(10), 1327–1338.

Richter, G., Raban, D. R., & Rafaeli, S. (2015). Studying gamification: The effect of rewards and incentives on motivation. In T. Reiners & L. C. Wood (Eds.), *Gamification in education and business* (pp. 21–46). Springer.

Rico, M., Agudo, J. E., & Sánchez, H. (2015). Language learning through handheld gaming: A case study of an English course with engineering students. *Journal of Universal Computer Science, 21*(10), 1362–1378.

Ryan, R. M., & Deci, E. L. (2000). Intrinsic and extrinsic motivations: Classic definitions and new directions. *Contemporary Educational Psychology, 25*, 54–67.

Scrimgeour, A. (2014). Dealing with 'Chinese fever': The challenge of Chinese teaching in the Australian classroom. In N. Murray & A. Scarino (Eds.), *Dynamic ecologies* (pp. 151–167). Springer.

Sharma, S. (2018). The difficulties of learning English as a second language. *Deliberate Research, 37*(1), 10–12.

Thiagarajan, S. (2004). *Six phases of debriefing: Play for performance*. Retrieved from http://www.thiagi.com/pfp/IE4H/february2004.html

Thomson, C. K. (1998). Junior teacher internship: Promoting cooperative interaction and learner autonomy in foreign language classrooms. *Foreign Language Annals, 3*(4), 569–583.

Tse, S. K., & Loh, E. K. Y. (2008). *Hong Kong territory-wide system assessment (TSA) 2007: Analyzing the Chinese language performance of P3, P6 & IF ethnic minority students* (in Chinese). Unpublished research report, CACLER, Faculty of Education, The University of Hong Kong.

Tse, S. K., & Loh, E. K. Y. (2009). *Hong Kong territory-wide system assessment (TSA) 2008: Analyzing the Chinese language performance of P3, P6 & F3 ethnic minority students* (in Chinese). Unpublished research report, CACLER, Faculty of Education, The University of Hong Kong.

Tse, S. K., & Loh, E. K. Y. (Eds.). (2014). *Effective teaching and learning of Chinese characters to non-Chinese speaking kindergarten students*. Beijing Normal University Press.

Tse, S. K., Marton, F., Ki, W. W., & Loh, E. K. Y. (2007). An integrative perceptual approach for teaching Chinese characters. *Instructional Science, 35*(5), 375–406.

Walz, S. P., & Deterding, S. (2014). An introduction to the Gameful world. In S. P. Walz & S. Deterding (Eds.), *The Gameful world: Approaches, issues, applications* (pp. 1–14). MIT Press.

Webb, S. (2008). Receptive and productive vocabulary sizes of L2 learners. *Studies in Second Language Acquisition, 30*(1), 79–95.

Wehmeyer, M. L., & Schwartz, M. (1997). Self-determination and positive adult outcomes: A follow-up study of youth with mental retardation or learning disabilities. *Exceptional Children, 63*, 245–255.

Wu, J. G., & Miller, L. (2021). From in-class to out-of-class learning: Mobile-assisted language learning. In L. Miller & J. G. Wu (Eds.), *Language learning with technology: Perspectives from Asia* (pp. 31–48). Springer.

Yuan, C., & Lo Bianco, J. (2022). L2 Chinese teachers' beliefs about engagement strategies for students in Australia: Findings from Q methodology research. *System, 106*, 1–10. https://doi.org/10.1016/j.system.2022.102792

Part V
The Language Trajectory: Learning Motivation

Developing Strategies for Motivating Australian Secondary Students to Learn Chinese

Helena Sit, Haoliang Sun, Shen Chen, Erica Thomas, and Lisa Peterson

Abstract This case study, conducted by an Australian University, at a main-stream school in New South Wales, and a community language school in Victoria, focuses on developing effective strategies for teaching Chinese to native English-speaking secondary school students. With increasing importance of Asian language and literacy in Australian schools, particularly Chinese, it is crucial to address questions regarding student motivation and effective teaching practices. This study aims to understand how to promote non-Chinese heritage-background learners' interest in the Chinese language. The research employed a mixed qualitative method, including classroom observations, in-depth interviews, and student focus groups. Three main findings emerged: intrinsic and extrinsic factors to motivation, the effectiveness of various pedagogies, and the relations between using effective pedagogies and maintaining motivation for learning Chinese. Practical recommendations for motivating secondary students to learn Chinese are proposed and discussed. The study fills a gap in understanding how to motivate monolingual English-speaking Australian secondary students to learn Chinese and has wide implications for teaching and learning Chinese across all levels of educational institutions. It also sheds light on the teaching and learning of various Languages Other Than English (LOTE) in Australia and other English-speaking countries.

H. Sit (✉) · S. Chen
University of Newcastle, Callaghan, NSW, Australia
e-mail: helena.sit@newcastle.edu.au

H. Sun
Xin Jin Shan Chinese Language and Culture School in Melbourne,
Mount Waverley, VIC, Australia

E. Thomas
Kincoppal-Rose Bay, Sydney, NSW, Australia

L. Peterson
Newcastle Grammar School, Newcastle, NSW, Australia

© The Author(s), under exclusive license to Springer Nature Switzerland AG 2024
J. Lo Bianco et al. (eds.), *Supporting the Learning of Chinese as a Second Language: Implications for Language Education Policy*, Language Policy 36,
https://doi.org/10.1007/978-3-031-66135-8_13

1 Introduction

Australia has long been working hard to increase trade and exchanges with Asia, and young Australians are encouraged to learn Asian languages, including Chinese. The motivation to learn Chinese is inextricably linked to Australia's unique geographical advantage and the contribution of new immigrants. According to the census survey released by the Australian Bureau of Statistics (ABS) in 2016, the Asian population in Australia is growing rapidly and is expected to overtake Europeans in the near future, becoming Australia's largest residential group. The Chinese population in Australia is about 1,213,900, accounting for 3.9% of the total population. Therefore, the most commonly used languages in Australia are English (about 17.02 million, accounting for 72.7% of the total population) and Putonghua (about 597,000 Australian residents speak Mandarin at home, accounting for 2.2% of the total population), Arabic (about 322,000 people, accounting for 1.4% of the total population, and Cantonese (about 281,000, accounting for 1.2% of the total population) (ABS, 2016).

In particular, the Melbourne Declaration on Educational Goals for Young Australians emphasises that young Australians need to be "'Asia literate', engaging and building strong relationships with Asia" (p. 4) and able "to relate to and communicate across cultures, especially the cultures and countries of Asia" (Ministerial Council on Education, Employment, Training and Youth Affairs, 2008, p. 9). Over the years, language studies, especially Asian languages, are highly recommended to learn in all years of schooling. Lo Bianco (1987) introduces an overview of the national policy on Languages in Australia and his work has traced the development of the language policy as well as the analysis of some major contributing factors. In a nutshell, the initial Chinese language education entered mainstream schools in Australia. Therefore, Chinese language teaching and learning is greatly promoted in the climate that created the nationally agreed goals for schooling in Australia. Due to the strong financial sponsorship by the federal government, Chinese language as one of the preferred second languages is widely promoted in local primary and secondary schools. McLaren (2011) echoes that Mandarin Chinese has been identified as an essential language for second language (L2) learners from kindergarten to universities, within and beyond the Asia-Pacific region, while White (2014) further points out that Mandarin Chinese is seen as a second must-have language of the business world, due to China's rapid economic development and global spread.

Nevertheless, current research figures show that L2 learning in Australia is in rapid decline and that most students do not choose to study a L2 after Year Ten. Recent figures released by the Australia-China Relations Institute (ACRI) (2015) show a severe decline in L2 Chinese learning in Australia. Only 0.1 percent (or 4149 out of 3,694,101) of Australian secondary students took Year 12 Chinese in 2015, of which, less than 400 were of non-Chinese backgrounds. This claim was firstly promulgated by Dr. Jane Orton (2016), the former director of Chinese teacher training at the University of Melbourne. She reviewed the issues in Chinese language teaching in Australian school in the past 40 years and found of the six most taught languages in schools, Chinese had the smallest number of students. There is an urgent need for Australian schools to boost the number of students learning Chinese, especially learners who are of non-Chinese background. With their teaching background and research interests in this field, the researchers of this paper intend to investigate how Australian secondary teachers teach the Chinese language in an Australian context, and how students respond to this learning.

2 Literature Review

With a history of over 40 years, the teaching of Chinese language was firstly introduced in Australian mainstream schools in the early 1980s, but it did not become widespread until the past two decades (ACARA, 2013; Orton, 2016). Chinese, one of the six most taught languages in school (Japanese, Italian, French, Indonesian, German and Chinese), has the least number of non-heritage students, as shown in the study by Orton (2016). Despite the government's generous financial investment and the great efforts of Australia-wide teachers of Chinese, it has been argued that many Chinese language programmes are insufficiently prepared and poorly taught (White, 2014). Orton (2016) found that a major weakness in the endeavour is the limited specific pedagogical instruction in language teacher training for teaching various languages in school. To date, limited research has been undertaken to promote effective learning strategies for languages other than English (LOTE) that can benefit students, schools and wider communities. There is a lack of indicative data on students' motivations and regarding whether there is sufficient scholarly support from teachers, schools and communities towards Asian language learning in Australian schools. There are several factors contributing to these issues.

Since Chinese language teaching first entered mainstream Australian schools, some studies (e.g., Lo Bianco, 2010; Orton, 2016; Smith et al., 1993) reveal that a critical problem is a lack of appropriate teaching materials for learners with English-speaking backgrounds in LOTE classrooms in mainstream schools. In spite of the fact that a set of widely adopted textbooks for different stages (ranging from elementary, intermediate and advanced levels) were available to mainstream schools in the mid-1980s (Chen, 2021), it is noted that the contents of these textbooks used in both primary and secondary schools did not sufficiently take students' heritage backgrounds or streaming into consideration when being designed and developed (Chen & Sit, 2019). Besides, when the textbooks developed earlier cannot reflect the most up-to-date teaching and learning materials that are aligned with those of today's China, the Chinese language education programme might not be in accordance with the current Australian curriculum for languages (Orton, 2016).

Second, all L2 studies (including Chinese programmes offered in Australian schools) are dependent on each state's curriculum and language syllabus. However, it is compulsory for most secondary school students in mainstream Australian schools to learn a foreign language from the beginning of secondary school (Year

7). Therefore, most secondary schools offer their students some popular languages such as Japanese, French, Indonesian, German, Italian and Chinese to start their L2 learning journey. Orton (2016) explains that there is a common practice for Year 7 students to study two languages sequentially for one semester, and may opt for one of the two in their remaining language study for the rest of the compulsory years till Year 9. Then, students may choose to drop their language study after Year 9, and nationally, less than 12% of students may continue a L2 study in Year 12. As such, the growth in the importance of Chinese is expected to continue but has not translated into growth in the study of the language. As the New South Wales (NSW) Education Standards Authority (NESA) reports, at the senior high school level in Australia, 94% of students learning L2 Chinese drop out by Year 12 (BOSTES, 2012).

It is often claimed that the low uptake of Chinese language learning in secondary schools is due to the high numbers of 'heritage-background speakers' with whom L2 learners have to compete. The teaching of Chinese has thus been complicated by the perception that Chinese teachers are teaching Chinese-heritage students Chinese (Orton, 2016). In New South Wales, secondary schools offering Chinese programmes usually adopt two sets of syllabi of Chinese teaching, including one for K-10 years and the other for Year 11–12 (BOSTES, 2012). Nevertheless, it is argued that the syllabi used for Chinese language teaching was designed under the same curriculum framework of other LOTEs, such as German and French studies, in terms of language learning objectives, learning outcomes and learning hours. Research supports that greater time is needed for an English-speaking learner to master Chinese versus a European language, due to the distinct systems of spoken and written language in Chinese (Chen & Sit, 2019; Smith et al., 1993). The American Foreign Service Institute has also claimed that it takes about three times longer for an English-speaking student to learn Chinese than it does to study a European language such as French or Spanish (Ye, 2011). It is problematic to allocate the same teaching hours to teach Chinese in the hope of achieving a similar proficiency level of a European language as set by the national language policy.

Third, in addition to those studies examining the national language policy, state curriculum and syllabus (e.g. Smith et al., 1993; Sturak & Naughten, 2010), some studies have been conducted on Australian Chinese L2 teaching. For instance, there are comparative research studies towards internationalising the curriculum in Chinese language teacher education programmes in both Australia and China (e.g. Orton, 2016; Wang et al., 2013). Discussions are ongoing on integrating/ dealing with distinctiveness for Chinese development in the Australian curriculum, principles and pedagogical design (e.g. Moloney & Xu, 2015; Orton, 2016; Scrimgeour, 2015). In general, the majority of the studies have found that the pedagogical approaches of teaching Chinese are still undeveloped, on top of insufficient teaching and learning resources (Sit & Guo, 2019). White (2014) asserts that "Chinese is difficult and often poorly taught" (p. 3), supported by Orton (2016) stating that "the field of Chinese teaching is especially weakened by this neglect of direct work on method of teaching Chinese" (p. 373). She further explains that "teachers who have been trained in China to teach the language to foreign students usually have a sound grasp of the nature of the language but have not developed adequate learning principles to support teaching practice" (pp. 373–374). These studies suggest a common challenge for bilingual teachers; that not only should they master the language use for both English and Chinese, but they also ought to better understand L2 pedagogy design and development in teaching Chinese. Currently, the shortage of well-trained or suitably qualified CFL teachers in Australia has appeared to be one of the major reasons that hinders the development of CSL/CFL teaching (Chen & Sit, 2019) and the lack of engagement strategies in the L2 classroom has been reported as one of the greatest challenges for Australian second language teachers (Yuan & Lo Bianco, 2022).

To date, limited studies have systematically investigated teachers' use of teaching practices and strategies in the secondary Chinese education programme. According to Killen (1998, 2016), the use of effective teaching strategies can help teachers translate Australian curriculum guidelines into practice and motivate and engage diverse students to learn. As a result, this current study is a pioneering attempt to explore "what does it take to engage and inspire non-heritage secondary students to learn Chinese?" by setting two research aims: (1) to investigate Australian secondary students' motivations and experiences in Chinese language learning at Australian mainstream schools in New South Wales; and (2) to develop effective strategies to enhance Chinese teaching and learning.

3 Theoretical Framework

To establish a benchmark for the study, effective teaching strategies proposed and developed by Killen (1998, 2016) were adopted as the theoretical framework, to identify their existence and to check their effectiveness in secondary Chinese language teaching. Nine highly recommended teaching strategies are summarised in his latest taxonomy (Killen, 1998, 2016, p. xiii), as Table 1 shows.

Research constantly supports that teaching strategies are teachers' techniques that are used to enhance students' learning (Lee & Ward, 2013; Sit, 2017). The rationale of using this taxonomy is based on a careful literature review. These nine effective teaching strategies are commonly used in Western contexts to facilitate and maximise student learning (Killen, 1998, 2016; Prosser & Trigwell, 2006). It is claimed that each strategy is described and summarised from a reasonably pragmatic viewpoint. There is an assumption that they have universal value and "can be applied in all learning areas, in all phases of education and training, and within the constraints of any curriculum framework" (Killen, 2016, p. xii). To present, few studies evaluate this generic effect on Chinese as a second language (L2) programmes in Australian secondary schools. This study intends to explore to what extent these strategies can be effectively adapted to the Australian L2 educational setting.

The overview of the Australian curriculum on languages shows detailed Year 7–8 and Year 9–10 band descriptions set for the Chinese language learner pathway, in the aspects of the nature of the learners; Chinese language learning and use; contexts of

Table 1 Effective teaching strategy taxonomy

Effective teaching strategies	Definition
1. Direct Instruction	The teacher carefully orchestrates each aspect of the lesson and controls what, when and how students learn.
2. Whole-class discussion	Students are given more opportunities to share their developing understandings but the teacher maintains careful guidance of the direction and progression of the lesson.
3. Small-group work	Groups of students now work together and do not necessarily all engage in the same learning activities or receive the same input from the teacher.
4. Cooperative learning	Group activities are more structured and students are now highly dependent upon one another for their learning.
5. Problem-solving	Learning is specifically focused on developing knowledge and skills though carefully structured problem-solving activities. It usually involves group work but not necessarily cooperative learning.
6. Inquiry	Learners engage in a broader range of activities (not necessarily involving problem solving) with greater scope for pursuing individual interests. Teacher direction is reduced.
7. Case-study	The issues being investigated are now embedded in complex, realistic scenarios, often with ill-defined parameters.
8. Performance activity/ role-play	Learners now engage in realistic activities, rather than simply reading about them and discussing them.
9. Writing	Learning becomes a fully personal activity with teacher guidance but limited direct input from the teacher.

interaction, texts and resources; features of Chinese language use; level of support; and the role of English (used to facilitate explanation and discussion in Chinese language teaching and learning) (ACARA, 2015). In general, the Australian curriculum documents include content descriptors, broad teaching guidelines and achievement standards, but no specific teaching practices and strategies are mandated and/or illustrated to help students learn. For example, the Chinese language learning and use descriptor in the Year 7–8 and Year 9–10 are as below:

> The Australian Curriculum on Languages: Chinese language learning and use
>
> The systems of writing and speaking in Chinese are distinct... Because of the role of character learning and its impact on reading and writing, learners' spoken language use is more advanced than their written language use; therefore, students will be immersed in the sights and sounds of Chinese. They develop oral language through active listening, observing interactions between native speakers, and using the spoken language for purposes such as socialising, transacting and getting things done, sharing information and engaging in imaginative performance... (ACARA, 2015, Year 7–8)
>
> The systems of writing and speaking in Chinese are distinct. Learners analyse how messages are conveyed across languages and apply their skills in mediating between languages and cultures. Classroom discussions focus on exploring and extending learners' understanding of contexts and audiences to enhance their personal communication skills. Students access information and explore texts written in Chinese, developing strategies to interpret meanings where not all characters are known (ACARA, 2015, Year 9–10)

Following the aforementioned absence of specific teaching approaches and practices for individual subjects, such as Chinese as part of a LOTE programme (as pointed out by Killen, 2016), the current study aims to use Killen's (1998, 2016) effective strategy framework to identify and select strategies that are appropriate, useful and effective for the subject content teaching and student learning in Chinese language programmes at secondary schools.

4 Research Methods

This case study was conducted at Newcastle Grammar School (NGS), one of the oldest traditional private schools in New South Wales, Australia. The school follows the Australian and NSW Education Standards Authority (NESA) Curriculum (formerly BOSTES). Since Chinese language teaching and learning are greatly promoted under the Australian national goals for schooling, created in response to the need to encourage and enable Australian citizens to engage with the Asian context, this leading independent coeducational day school began to offer Chinese language classes to its secondary students in 2017. Before 2017, the long-term specialist elective subjects offered were only French and Japanese. Therefore, Chinese is currently one of these three languages available to learn at NGS (2018). Almost all the NGS secondary students learning Chinese are of non-Chinese heritage backgrounds. Thus, this research is timely and needed at NGS, focusing on the strategies required for teaching and motivating secondary students to learn Chinese.

The project involved qualitative data collection and discourse analysis using the technique of ethnographic interviews with teachers, classroom observations and focus group interviews with secondary students. Qualitative investigation is an interpretive inquiry form, enabling researchers to interpret what they see, hear and understand so that a holistic overview of the research context can be captured through observing behaviours and interviewing participants (Creswell, 2012; Punch, 2009). Multiple data collection sources such as interviews, observations and discourse analysis can be included in qualitative data collection.

Firstly, classroom observation, which enables researchers to collect first-hand, on-site experience of teaching and learning (Creswell, 2012), was employed to identify effective strategies commonly used to facilitate students' Chinese learning. Secondly, in-depth interview, widely used in educational research as an instrument to understand individual perspectives (Kayrooz & Trevitt, 2005), was used to investigate and identify teachers' strategies to encourage and support their students in Chinese language learning at NGS. Thirdly, focus groups, which provide interviewees who study in the same learning area with opportunities to share their feelings and opinions together, were adopted as the third instrument to understand students' motivations and experiences in Chinese language learning at school. The group dynamics can stimulate students to openly discuss and generate critical thinking about a topic (Fern, 2001).

Secondary students enrolled in the Chinese programme and their Chinese subject teachers at NGS were invited for an approximately 30-minute focus group interview. All interviews were digitally recorded with the consent of the interviewees and transcribed verbatim. Interview transcripts were imported into NVivo as individual cases and organised for thematic analysis. To ensure validity and reliability, all coding was cross-checked by the researchers. In the meantime, the observational notes from class visits were organised for content analysis, coded following the timeline of the lesson.

5 Study Results

5.1 Classroom Observation

The classroom observation was scheduled based on the school's timetable of Chinese classes for four terms at NGS. Guided by the classroom observation protocol, in total 32 Chinese classes at NGS were visited and observed. The class visit aimed to identify effective teaching methods and strategies to enhance the learning of Chinese at the school. Students' responses towards strategies that were effective for them to learn Chinese were also given close attention. The duration of each lesson was 50 minutes on average. Chinese teaching programmes from Year 7 to Year 10 were covered. Table 2 provides a summary of the number of visited lessons and the general learning topics.

The observation of these Chinese courses at different levels provided the researcher with more opportunities to observe teachers' in-class instructions and students' engaging responses, which were recorded in the classroom observation manual. Teaching activities and strategy use were recorded with the timeline of each lesson.

Table 2 Lessons visited

Grade level	No. of the visited class	General topics
Year 7	4	Expression of greetings; Chinese food; Story telling of Chinese Valentine's Day; Chinese character reading and writing practice; Cultural experience: presentation by exchange teacher from China (student question & answer session included); Making a phone call.
Year 8	21	Transportation; Who is she/he; student's in-class presentation of their self-composed "personal book" in Chinese; Jobs/Occupations; Fruits; Clothing; Chinese traditional festivals; Body parts.
Year 9	5	Sports; Listening & speaking practices; Reading & writing practice; Play card game in Chinese; Sample Chinese essay deconstruction.
Year 10	2	Four language skill practice (listening, speaking, reading and writing).

5.1.1 Effective Teaching Strategies

Based on the observational notes, motivational teaching strategies are characterised by four features:

1. Embedding teaching in narration

Narration was most frequently used by the lecturer in Direct Instruction to assist students in understanding the formation and meaning of Chinese characters, culture-loaded idioms, and sociocultural phenomena taking place in China. Below are three examples extracted from the field-notes on the lesson observation:

> Grade 7, Lesson 8, (9:15–9:25 am): The topic of this lesson was greeting. The teacher introduced new expressions about greeting, e.g. good morning/noon/afternoon/evening, with a focus on the pronunciation, usage, and meaning. Although characters are not the focus for Grade 7, the lecturer illustrated the composition of "早" (morning) as consisting of "日" (sun) and "十" (resembling the horizon), explaining the meaning of the character as the sun has risen above the horizon.
>
> Grade 9, Lesson 13, (11:07–11:12 am): The topic of this lesson was body parts. The teacher firstly depicted each of five students' shape of face; students then pointed out body parts referring to their body as demanded by the lecturer. After this, the lecturer introduced figurative expressions related to "脸" (face), "手"(hand), "脚"(feet), such as 大手大脚(big hand and big feet), 小白脸(little white face), 丢脸(lose face), 三只手(third hand), 大嘴巴 (big mouth).
>
> Grade 8, Lesson 9, (9:55-10:10 am): The topic of this lesson was transportation. The teacher introduced new expressions about different transportation ways, e.g. 坐火车(catch a train), 搭公交车(take a bus), 乘飞机 (take a plane), 坐出租车(take a cab), with a focus on the pronunciation, usage, and meaning. While introducing subway, the lecturer recounted the development of subway in Beijing.

In the first example, students manifested a strong interest in listening to this story-loaded narration. It is reasonable to expect that in incorporating a plot and images, students may be better able to retain the meaning and spelling of this character. In the second case, students were very engaged in the lecturer's narration of these culture-loaded terms. Some of them even initiated efforts to apply expressions such as "大嘴巴" in a joking way to call a classmate.

2. Embedding teaching in performance activity

Performance activity takes a few forms; singing, role playing and presentation. Driving forces embedded in them can be attributed to the pleasurable feeling of singing condition and reinforcement of agency. Some examples are listed below:

> Grade 7, Lesson 3, (8:40–8:53 am): The teacher used two songs to teach students expressions about greeting, one named "How are you?", and the other "What is your name?". Students sang together the songs first after the lecturer; afterwards, they were required to change some parts based on their personal information, and then sang in pairs.
>
> Grade 8, Lesson 4, (9:35-10:20am): This task was in relation to presenting Personal Book. Each student was required to present in front of class a personal book they composed (about their routine life: time to get up, eat, go to school, go to bed, etc.); after each presentation, the teacher invited the audience to answer some questions based on the presentation.

Most students were observed to be very engaged throughout the whole session. Possible reasons are wide-ranging. First, the task was tailored to each individual's personal situation, which may thus give them more agency. As evinced by some students who demonstrated a high level of innovation and originality by either developing the book into a work of fiction or making it aesthetically artistic, this activity typifies a good reinforcement of agency. Second, as there was a public presentation, students might have felt the responsibility to commit themselves more to it, so as to make a good impression.

3. Scaffolding teaching with clues

Thirdly, students' motivation was enhanced by being guided through unravelling a new puzzle or an intricate procedure with either preview or review. Two cases are as follows:

> Grade 8, Lesson 11, (11:45 am–12:05 pm): The topic was job. The teacher explained 班/上班 means 工作(go to work), focusing on character, pronunciation, meaning. The lecturer then asked each student a question: 你爸爸工作吗?(Does your father work?) She then initiated a brief review of a list of occupations learnt previously, such as 工人(worker), 老师(teacher), 商人(businessman), 医生(doctor), 护士(nurse), 牙医(dentist), 农民(farmer). Next, she asked each student a question: 你爸爸做什么工作?(What does your father do?)

Compared to occasions observed where students felt lost and frustrated as a result of their inability to answer questions due to no review being given, it seemed in the example above that a short review helped the students to retrieve relevant information to formulate a better answer. In this case, the teacher assumed a role of facilitator who aided their backward information retrieval, that better situated them in configuring answers based on existing and newly acquired knowledge.

> Grade 9, Lesson 2, (10:50–11:00 am): In this Problem Solving listening task, the teacher briefed the context of the listening material before the practice started. She familiarised the students with the flow of this piece, including some key words and background information.

A short preview as such was evinced to be very helpful and necessary. Throughout the listening practice, most students seemed to concentrate well and the accuracy for the subsequent questions were satisfactory. It manifests that giving clues regarding the topic under discussion is of particular importance in foreign language learning, where listening is one of the harder skills to develop as it deals at speed with unfamiliar sounds, words and structures.

In the above backward and forward clues-giving activities, the teacher scaffolded the teaching process with her guidance. Subsequently, the students were much more stimulated to learn with more confidence and competence. It is indicative of the importance of the teacher's scaffolding role in facilitating students' mastery of knowledge.

5.1.2 Less Effective Teaching Strategies

Based on the observation, non-motivational teaching strategies are characterised by the features of unsuitability to students' cognitive level. The unsuitability of teaching strategies to students' cognitive level was observed to adversely impact on their motivation to learn. Cases in point are below:

> Grade 8, Lesson 12, (9:35–10:10 am): This is a game-based activity on the topic of transportation. Students took turns to present their question pool under different topics (such as plane, boat, train) they chosen for the task. Using Kahoot, a game-based online learning platform, students were required to log in to answer questions; the top three highest score winners stood out once each round finished.

This time Kahoot appeared not to be attractive to the students. Reflecting on the situation, it may have been because many presenters designed a question pool that was constantly beyond the audience's knowledge base. By virtue of that, the result turned out to be purely determined by good luck instead of their repertoire of knowledge. Unsurprisingly, their motivation was hard to be sustained given that the learning context over-demanded engagement that is far beyond their cognitive level.

> Grade 8, Lesson 9, (10:17–10:25 am): This is a game-based activity on the topic of transportation. The teacher wrote down on a whiteboard all characters leant in class today; students in pairs then took turns to proceed to the podium; one pointed at one character while the other covered his/her eyes; then the one covering eyes should guess which character has been chosen by his/her partner by asking all other students "是不是…"(is it…); the audience answered corresponding "是.."(yes, it is…) or "不是…"(no, it is not…).

This activity was proven to be motivational for junior classes. However, this time when used in Grade 9, it seemed that the students were not as interested. The authors' intuition is that this game was not complex enough in terms of its content and structure to sustain their attention and involvement. It manifests that, similar to over-demanding situations, an under-demand on cognition also proves un-motivational for students.

5.2 Teacher Interview

Three teachers volunteered to participate in the one-on-one, face-to-face interview. Two are Chinese subject teachers with Chinese as their mother tongue, and another is the native English-speaking head teacher of the language literacy department. The subject teachers with Chinese as their mother tongue have over ten years' experience of teaching Chinese language in Australian schools, and one of them is in charge of the Chinese teaching programme. The teachers were coded as T1, T2 and T3. Table 3 provides general demographic information of the teachers.

The interview was conducted in English and the interview protocol question was used to elicit how teachers use strategies to encourage and support their students in

Table 3 Teachers interviewed

No. of teachers	Gender	Years of teaching
T1	Female	15
T2	Female	10
T3	Male	15

Chinese language learning. Following the semi-structured interview with open-ended questions, four key areas of interest emerged from the informants' responses: (1) effective strategies used to motivate students to acquire Chinese; (2) challenges of teaching Chinese; (3) school support for the Chinese programme; and (4) teachers' professional development of teaching Chinese language. The findings are presented in the follow sections.

5.2.1 Effective Strategies Use to Motivate Students to Acquire Chinese

To explore the teacher's use of strategies to support teaching and learning, the question "What strategies do you use to motivate students to learn?" encouraged the teacher to discuss what instructional practices they usually employed to incite their students to learn. In general, the teachers expressed that they carefully followed the Australian curriculum and syllabus requirements in teaching Chinese language, however, they also enjoyed the autonomy of designing their own programme and planning the scope of the lesson based on the school syllabus. Since the majority of their language learners are non-heritage learners at NGS, the popular strategies they found that could better promote students' learning interest were integration of crafts and cultural activities in teaching and learning Chinese. Typical examples of this viewpoint was shown as below:

> ...I have the flexibility of designing my own programme and planning this scope and sequence and also the contents of the lessons myself based on the syllabus in New South Wales. And when teaching Year 7–8 which is stage 4 level... I have a lot of crafts and cultural activities in Chinese. Games and stories I bring to the classroom to students at all different levels of academic ability...and for some students they have low learning ability, they easily get the feeling of not able to catch up, but easy activities will make them feel confident and they still feel they can be part of the class. (Interviewee T1)
>
> I think for the high school, they have to follow the syllabus, follow the assessment schedule... So in class you ask them [students] questions, they answer the questions, sometimes have a group of students do a little drawing, on the board, something like that...or listening activities, text, reading and comprehension. (Interviewee T2)

Another set of quotes also explained why focusing on both language and culture was an important strategy to maintain students' interests. Appreciation of culture through language learning was also promoted in this school.

> ...I focus basically 50 and 50 language and culture and to build up students interests and confidence in learning and from stage 5 onwards and then focus on all components: listening, speaking, reading and writing instead of listening and speaking mainly in stage 4. This transition is really important. Otherwise, some students feel scared or discouraged to continue because of the difficulties of writing in Chinese. (Interviewee T1)
>
> ...I think the teacher's Chinese programmes are working quite well. Her [the Chinese subject teacher] engagement with the cultural connections with China within the Newcastle community is very strong. And she uses those connections to motivate students to see that learning a language is not just about vocabulary. It's about an understanding of culture as well... I've been in the classroom visiting Chinese lessons. The materials are strong. They're very well ordered, leading to presentations on the board and learning. I think certainly for Mandarin, the sounds are very, very important. (Interviewee T3)

As shown above, the teachers' use of strategies were not intentionally guided by the instructional practices such as the effective strategy taxonomy, however, some teaching activities and strategies like whole-class discussion, small group work, performance activities (e.g. presentations), skill-based writing, reading and listening comprehension practices were reportedly used for stimulating students to acquire Chinese.

5.2.2 Challenges of Teaching Chinese

The teachers were encouraged to answer the question "what kinds of challenges or difficulties have you experienced in your current Chinese teaching?". They found sustaining students' continued learning motivation could be a challenge. Using effective engaging strategies to encourage students to enjoy this subject would be important, but how to extend/advance the teaching practices would be related to teacher professional development.

> *I think motivation is the most important thing we have to do. We have to engage our students. When they like the subject, they can do better...They try their best ... If they don't like you, or they have a negative feeling about the subject, they can't do it well. I think the most important thing is to have fun in class.* (Interviewee T2)
>
> *It is time to plan or to change the programme to be most suitable for the class. Sometimes if you teach lessons like in a day, you have six lessons and you don't have a free period before you teach the lesson and you will realise that I should have had certain equipment and method and a certain worksheet but you just didn't have time to have that in place. And also activities based on my own personal skills is not going to be enough for students to be learning with me for four years, so I have to repeat some of the activities. So the professional development opportunities is another challenge.* (Interviewee T1)

The other main challenge was described that some students might drop out of the Chinese classes at a later stage (Year 9 or Year 10) because they might have less opportunities to be immersed in listening to, viewing and reading Chinese.

> *Right, that [lack of opportunity to practice Chinese after school] is certainly a factor. Yes, certainly something as well. As I mentioned earlier, for some cultures, some countries where it's much easier to just go visit a different country, and to practice the language. Australia being a little remoted certainly makes it harder to get that daily or weekly practice of a language. It's certainly a challenge.* (Interviewee T3)

5.2.3 School Culture to Support Chinese Education Programme

The third theme was to understand how the school supports the development of the newly introduced Chinese language programmes. All the teachers felt highly supported and encouraged by the school executives in terms of funds and resources. Besides, parents realised the importance of L2 learning like Chinese for their children, so they also had positive influence on the promotion of learning Chinese.

> *At Newcastle Grammar, the support from the head of the school, director of learning and executives are very strong and as a result the whole school knows Chinese has been placed*

at a very important part of the school curriculum and so that makes it easy for me to develop young ones and also related programmes. (Interviewee T1)

Our school, we have a Chinese day, and some exchange students. I think they are a very positive influence for the students. For example, the school has the Light Up, the Chinese New Year activity, so there are culture activities. They're a good reason for students to know Chinese and other cultures. Some parents really like their children to learn Chinese, they know how important the language will be in the future, so some parents have been saying that to their children. They are very good. (Interviewee T2)

Certainly from the school there's a lot of support in terms of, just in terms of funding and introducing the programme entirely. I think the school sees having three languages [Chinese, French and Japanese] to offer as a real bonus. And so that comes through from the top, from the principal. And also I think from the parents' points of views, many parents see China as one of the countries of the future, realizing the power in Chinese economy, and in Chinese nation, that's a factor on encouraging some students. Not all, but some students to learn Chinese as a stepping stone for a career. Maybe not in China, but certainly as a way to have a skill that will be useful in the global environment. (Interviewee T3)

It is also mentioned that involving students in different areas outside of the Chinese language classroom is another useful way to support the Chinese programme. More quotations illustrating this:

…We have sister school students visiting us and I always encourage a student to host and be the school buddy to show their leadership and also parents. They are the great source to encourage students to learn Chinese. (Interviewee T1)

I think with particularly using experiences where students go to China and visit China on excursion or a tour. Those types of things can certainly help, where they see or they're learning and it comes through with exchanges… (Interviewee T3)

5.3 Student Focus Groups

Of the total of 31 students who were invited to participate, 19 non-Chinese heritage students (7 focus groups) volunteered to be involved in the focus group interviews, making the overall response rate 61%. Among them, 5 students (nearly 26%) had just started learning Chinese for less than 3 months, 5 students (nearly 26%) learnt Chinese language for about 1 year, 8 students (about 46%) learnt for 2 years, and only 1 student (around 5%) learnt for 8 years. All of the interviewees, ranging from Year 7 to Year 10, were encouraged to voice their viewpoints on their motivations to learn Chinese and learning experiences of Chinese. Each participant was coded with a number and an abbreviation (i.e., S1) for confidentiality. Table 4 provides the informants' general background information.

All the interviews were conducted in the participants' native language of English. According to the findings, three main themes were summarised from the transcripts: (1) students' motivations to learn Chinese; (2) general learning experiences of Chinese learning; (3) useful strategies to help them learn Chinese.

Developing Strategies for Motivating Australian Secondary Students... 327

Table 4 Student focus group interview

No. of students	Gender	Grade level	During of learning Chinese
S1	Female	Year 7	2 years
S2	Female	Year 7	Less than 3 months
S3	Female	Year 7	2 years
S4	Female	Year 7	2 years
S5	Female	Year 7	Less than 3 months
S6	Female	Year 7	2 years
S7	Male	Year 7	2 years
S8	Male	Year 7	Less than 3 months
S9	Female	Year 7	Less than 3 months
S10	Female	Year 7	Less than 3 months
S11	Female	Year 8	1 year
S12	Female	Year 8	1 year
S13	Female	Year 8	1 year
S14	Male	Year 8	2 years
S15	Male	Year 8	2 years
S16	Female	Year 9	Over a year
S17	Female	Year 9	8 years
S18	Female	Year 10	2 years
S19	Male	Year 10	Over a year

5.3.1 Students' Motivations to Learn Chinese

Almost all the students realised the role of Chinese language in the current context of Australia, when being asked to discuss the reasons why they wanted to learn Chinese as a second language. They thought learning Chinese had become more and more popular in Australian schools. Over half of the participants (n = 12) mentioned that learning Chinese as a future language could help enrich their future career opportunities. A few (n = 5) students expressed that it was cool to be able to speak a second language. Several representative comments are shown as the following:

> Well Mandarin is actually like a really popular language, so I feel like it's something good to learn, but I also really enjoy doing it...I just think languages is interesting because I feel like it's cool some can speak two or more languages and I want to be someone who can do that as well. (Interviewee S11, Year 8)
>
> I think Chinese is good for the future. (Interviewee S14, Year8)
>
> I think that it [Chinese] is just such a good language to know. Like really beneficial for jobs in the future...learning another language is really impressive. But especially Chinese I feel like it's just like ... everyone says the language of the future. (Interviewee S17, Year 9)
>
> To be able to communicate with more people. For me it was more just for fun, like personal benefit, and stuff, so not really for the career side or anything like that. (Interviewee S19, Year 10).

A couple of students doing their Year 9 and Year 10 Chinese language programmes expressed their willingness to go through their Chinese examination in the High

School Certificate (HSC). A notable example was a participant who had learnt Chinese for 8 years, since she had followed her parents to live in an overseas context in which Mandarin Chinese is also regarded as an official language.

> ... I just moved back [to Australia] at the beginning of Year 8... I've been learning Chinese in [place of the country] for my whole life nearly. And when I came here there was no Chinese programme at first, so we kind of inquired into that. And then when we found out they opened the opportunity to learn Chinese I was really excited because I just really want to continue the language and I want to become fluent. (Interviewee S17, Year 9)
>
> I want to continue the second language to my HSE, and hopefully outside, like in university. (Interviewee S18, Year 10)

5.3.2 General Learning Experiences of Learning Chinese

When asked about their general learning experiences of Chinese language at NGS, the students overwhelmingly felt fortunate to be benefitting from their experienced Chinese language teacher who used many motivational strategies, which resulted in more than half (n = 15) of the students being positive about wanting to continue with learning Chinese into the Higher School Certificate. They enjoyed the course because they were learning both language and culture. Here are some typical comments:

> I enjoy the course because we're not just learning the language, we're learning the culture behind the language. (Interviewee S9, Year 7).
>
> I also felt like she [the teacher] gets right to the point and she [the teacher] actually goes into depth to explain cultures. It's really interesting and I also agree with their [focus group peers'] points on how clearly she [the teacher] explains things and it's really good. (Interviewee S5, Year 7)
>
> Ms. [name of the teacher] does include a lot of culture... We do like Chinese New Year, all those celebrations. (Interviewee S14 and S15, Year 8).
>
> I really like it [Chinese learning] because [name of the teacher] makes it really fun. We do interactive activities and also we go out on cultural days, so we get to learn the language and the culture and the background. And the stories behind the characters make it really interesting... (Interviewee S16, Year 9).
>
> I think it's a really good course, especially because we have more attention. Because there's only two of us in the year. We get more time with the teacher, so it's really easy to learn things. If we ever need to revise, the teacher is always there for us. But for me specifically, in [country name], it was a lot harder obviously because it is an Asian country, there was a lot more emphasis on Chinese as a language. Here in Australia, it's a little bit less lessons, less hours, compared to [that Asian country]. (Interviewee S17, Year 9)

The majority of students (n = 12) also commented on how the teacher and school provided them with a supportive, engaging Chinese learning culture. They found that the school's cultural days and the teacher's useful resources offer them good opportunities to be exposed to the Chinese language. Below are widely held viewpoints:

> I think the teachers are obviously very supportive... Our principal, she really likes the fact that we're learning Chinese, and she brought it into the school. So [to] try and promote the language we do a lot of cultural festivals within the school. A lot of language days where

Chinese has been introduced now. To try and spread the word that you can learn Mandarin and that it's a really good language to know. (Interviewee S17, Year 9)

I think they [lessons] are good...I remember sometimes we play games, craft to learn the culture, and just PowerPoints and stuff with slides, could be pretty simple. (Interviewee S3, Year 7).

...not just writing notes off the white board. It's not really a theory lesson, it's more like a practical lesson. We do art. We do craft. It's funnier ways for children to learn and stay engaged with the teacher. (Interviewee S4, Year 7)

All the students felt greatly supported by their School, and that the Principal and Head Teacher have facilitated their LOTE (Languages Other Than English) learning experiences at NGS.

The Chinese classroom has lots of different artworks hung up, and it really ... as soon as you step in, you know it's a Chinese classroom. (Interviewee S2, Year 7)

But I like it when the exchange students came because I actually got to communicate with them, communicate with them with Mandarin, that's pretty fun. (Interviewee S11, Year 8)

I think the teachers are obviously very supportive of Miss Yen as well. Our principal, Miss Thomas, she really likes the fact that we're learning Chinese, and she brought it into the school. (Interviewee S17, Year 9)

5.3.3 Effective Strategies to Help Learn Chinese

The participants were encouraged to discuss what would be the effective strategies to motivate them to learn Chinese. About half of the students (n = 10) expressed the usefulness of strategies such as hands-on activities, culture-related storytelling, group work, performance activities including presentations, visual learning support for characters, and interactive games or apps.

DUOLINGO (a mobile App to learn languages). Just as homework to like practice, like do one lesson every afternoon. (Interviewee S9, Year 7)

Well.. for every topic we learn, for numbers or birthdays and things like that, she always puts together a presentation, a PowerPoint is very helpful. (Interviewee S11, Year 8)

She brings in an iPad and we have visual learning things that we can do on there, which is really helpful to interact. And then she also brought in these VR headset things...I feel like Miss [name of the teacher] is really good with different types of learning materials, learning ways. (Interviewee S17, Year 9)

A couple of students offered suggestions to teachers to incorporate more interactive games and support for the Chinese lessons.

Maybe more class interactive games, so when we're all like working as a group. (7, Yr 7)

I think a good strategy would be for her ... when she [the teacher] explains symbols maybe she could show us a picture behind the symbols because usually symbols make a picture of what they mean. (Interviewee S5, Year 7)

However, several students also commented that the learning activities should be more tailored to cater for student's levels and interests, as the quote below illustrates:

...don't treat children like kids...not interested to always draw pictures, which might be more suitable for younger kids, but could focus more on writing practices... (Interviewee S13, Year 8)

6 Discussions and Recommendations

Following the findings from the methodological triangulation, namely, classroom discussion, teacher interview and student focus groups, four areas of interests emerged for discussion. Followed by the analysis, practical recommendations for the enhancement of motivating English-speaking non-heritage students to learn Chinese as a second or foreign language are also provided accordingly.

First, by and large teaching strategies utilised throughout classes encompass Direct Instruction (narration, storytelling), performance activities/role play (e.g. dress up activity, oral report, presentation), cooperative learning (e.g. hands-on activity, craft in groups), inquiry-based question and answer sharing activities (e.g. food and transportation lessons), game-based learning (e.g. warm-up activity, Kahoot), and problem-solving research activities (e.g. personal book writing and presentation project). With regards to the efficiency of these identified strategies to boost non-heritage students' motivation to learn Chinese, it is counterproductive to summarise a broad-brush claim that any single teaching strategy is superior to others without delineating the full picture of what a teacher did with that strategy and how that strategy was applied. As with many other contexts, content takes precedence over format in language instruction. Killen's (1998, 2016) teaching strategy framework, originating from lessons and practices, is proven to be widely used in L2 Chinese acquisition.

Integration of various teaching strategies is found to be another common strategy, with supporting evidence from the shown data. Didactic teaching together with classroom discussion, small group work and presentation strategies are often seen in the teacher's practice. This finding also supports previous research's claims that small group work, cooperative learning, problem solving, and performance activities/presentations were usually used together as they all support students working towards a common goal (Sit, 2017); and that discussion, role play and presentations, and resolving problems in group work are typical features in a western educational context (Brady, 2006). Below is the first recommendation for an effective strategy for motivating language studies.

6.1 Recommendation One: Innovation Rather Than Mere Repetition

While performance-based activities in most cases are a booster, repetition at short intervals without instilling innovative elements can dampen their attractiveness. To provoke and sustain students' curiosity to learn, there must be a sense of novelty to be appealing to them. There is no 'one-size-fits-all' best teaching strategy to accommodate non-heritage students' motivations of Chinese learning. Integration/selection of teaching strategies should not be arbitrary, but established on a rational basis and used purposefully to maximise students' learning experiences of learning Chinese.

Second, the study reveals that teaching strategies that involved digital humanities in Chinese class greatly encouraged students to develop their better understandings of Chinese culture and traditional festivals, via transmedia in the forms of videos, YouTube, interactive online exercises (Kahoot), and the school intranet board for accessing the teachers' notes and communications. This finding aligns with the current request of the Australian curriculum and new language syllabus, that mandates that in each year, students must study examples of media, multimedia and digital texts which are appropriate to their needs, interests and abilities (NSW Education Standards Authority-NESA, 2024). ICT shows a significant impact on Chinese language teaching and learning when incorporating multimodal and digital media in the classroom. Currently, more and more students do less writing in class but more typing, and students who are learning to speak Chinese are now faced with the problem of not learning it through writing which is also a must of learning. If students are given an opportunity to learn through both written and visual assistance, this could help them in developing their multimodal skills in conjunction with their written and language skills.

Therefore, teachers need to scaffold students' multimodal literacies in Chinese. Other advantages of the digital context for students developing writing skills in L2 is the unlimited access to realia and other resources. One of the important pillars of language learning is the socio-cultural context, which has been vastly opened up in the digital era. Learners are no longer limited to the perspectives of their teachers and static texts, but to the perspectives of native speakers of that target language all around the world. However, the notion of using any ICT in the class is not merely for technology driven and/or ICT integration opportunity; it should be student-centred according to their cognitive levels and used for promoting all possible ways of engaging students to learn in such a digital era. If a learning experience is designed accordingly and can then be enhanced by the use of language, then the use of ICT is beneficial, and meaningful learning can occur. Effective multimedia learning does not necessarily occur just because more than one mode is present (Farías et al., 2007). Designing the instructional practices and strategies to match twenty-first century teaching is vital. Thus, the second recommendation based on the study results comes as the following:

6.2 Recommendation Two: New Possible Ways of Teaching and Scaffolding Comprehensible Input

The current and future states of reading and writing are closely interwoven with the development of digital technologies. Using online and digital resources helps engage students with Chinese language literature to enhance their appreciation of literary styles, and should be highly encouraged as an effective strategy. As evinced earlier in the data presentation section, the suitability to cognitive level is equally important. Ideally, the content and format of teaching activities should neither over-demand nor under-demand students' efforts to achieve an outcome. Tasks should be designed so that students cannot do them on their own, but are able to with enough assistance from teachers or peers. They should enable students to aim for harder tasks slightly beyond the current level of competence of the language learner.

Third, the results further find that hands-on activities like worksheets, singing or drawing are effective strategies to motivate students to learn. Similarly, narrations to the students about Chinese festivals, imparting basic knowledge through storytelling and giving them opportunities to dress up and taste Chinese cuisine are fantastic ways to enhance student learning. The research shows that the students greatly appreciate the level of effort their teacher goes to. For instance, in this case the effectiveness of narration lies in it being funny, engaging and highly entertaining, raising learners' interest in not only listening to culture-loaded terms but also relating them to the lived reality. Another example also demonstrated students' heightened interests in listening to informative narration of a sociocultural phenomenon taking place in China. Given one of their stimuli of learning Chinese is to gain a richer insight into this country and its society, it is not surprising that they were motivated by informative narration as such. As supported by neuroscientists that human minds are biologically wired to best comprehend the world through narrative (Carroll, 2017; Carroll et al., 2017), the preceding examples illuminate that incorporating narration in Direct Instruction was proven to be effective, boasting benefits of enhancing students' interest and facilitating comprehension of sociocultural notions.

The students also appeared to perform best when the teacher created a very lively and interactive lesson and learning environment. Students manifested strong enthusiasm in learning language points delivered in singing. On the one hand, the melodic and rhythmic context is simply more enjoyable than focusing on texts alone. Introducing material in this manner is thus more motivating for students with an integration of lyrics and melody. On the other hand, as they were asked to change lyrics based on personal situation, the expressive requirements bearing on personal relevance were also communicated. Thus, teaching from a culturally relevant perspective should be prioritised in teaching a second language, which is not apparently seen as a key focus in Killen's framework. The third recommendation is made as below:

6.3 Recommendation Three: Integration of Culturally Responsive Pedagogies and Language Learning

The narration of sociocultural anecdotes, folklores, current affairs and literacy practice through songs are helpful to boost students' general interest in a foreign country, into which its native language is a tool to provide a deeper and richer insight. As sociocultural-dependant storytelling or songs are well-suited to the bioecological programming mechanism of humans, the integration of culturally responsive pedagogies and language learning implies a sizeable potentiality to motivate non-heritage students to learn a foreign language, as well as to create a full picture of a country embodied by that language.

Fourth, cooperative learning was fused into the singing and performance activities with information sharing, meaning negotiation, and communicative interaction, which better boosted the students to engage as equal and autonomous learners. This provides confirming evidence on a longstanding social-constructivist view—that cooperative learning helps to foster a team spirit that contributes to motivating students to help each other with reciprocal interaction (e.g. Johnson & Johnson, 1999; Sit, 2017). A high level of activity also prevents boredom and off-task behaviour. Additionally, especially for game-based strategies, a sense of positive competition should be set in motion.

Demonstration and cooperative learning strategies about home and community practices are also considered as an effective motivational strategy. One engaging and successful example was the teacher's demonstration of how to make a Chinese spring roll, and then inviting several groups of students to try their own by following her recipe. It is advocated that "developing curriculum that draws upon students' lives should also include thinking about the resources and knowledge that families use to navigate their daily lives" (Seely-Flint et al., 2017, p. 73). This finding supports the viewpoint that it is a helpful strategy to learn about the home and community literacy practices with the target language.

6.4 Recommendation Four: Juxtaposition of Cooperation and Competition in Literacy Practices

To foster a collaborative learning environment, Chinese language teachers can use cooperative learning strategies such as peer tutoring and group discussions to enhance students' literacy skills both within and beyond the class. In this study, the students showed interest in engaging in group activities to understand Chinese Characters and given worksheets. For example, more group work focused on phonological processing, morphological awareness, and visual-orthographic skills can be designed to develop students' language acquisition. Another effective strategy is to prepare students for competitive school tests and public competitions that rank their performances against peers, which are crucial for academic progression and future opportunities. Therefore, cooperative activities develop students' teamwork and communication skills while competitive scenarios encourage resilience and a drive for excellence. In particular, competition with rewards for good academic performance is beneficial for the reinforcement of students' self-esteem as a competent agent. The efficacy of these collaborative, performing activities relies on the audience not been neglected. By requiring students to answer questions, they were kept alert in presentations. Ostensibly an individual task, it however incorporated engagement of all students. All observations supported that a sense of involvement is essential for a class to remain cohesive.

7 Conclusion and Future Direction

To sum up, Asian language and literacy in Australian secondary schools are becoming increasingly important; in particular, Chinese language acquisition has drawn more and more attention from teachers and academics. The project in this case study answered the question at a micro level of how to develop effective teaching strategies to support English-speaking learners of Chinese at secondary schools. The teaching strategy taxonomy was evaluated as useful for laying a strong foundation in pedagogy and curriculum design, modelling effective teaching practices, and encouraging regular reflections.

Although this study is limited by small participation numbers, proposing these effective data-informed strategies for motivating students have reasonable benefits. A follow-up study with more participants and schools can be considered. More strategies need to be put forward to facilitate and support L2 teaching staff to prepare for their professional development programme. Continuing professional development can better equip teachers with a more holistic approach to specific dimensions of learning and teaching practice undertaken within their normal context of academic practice and provide them with opportunities to extend/enhance their own practice through reflective work.

Despite the limitation, this study is significant as it pinpoints the helpful strategies with practical recommendations to facilitate students to learn Chinese. The results also demonstrate that the school holds a global vision for education and for its students to be aware of the world-wide perspective that is often gained through languages. Since L2 acquisition is a continuing process from childhood to adulthood, a combined research from primary, secondary and tertiary sectors is necessary and urgent if the teachers intend to maintain the students' motivation of learning a second or additional language, and to achieve the maximal learning outcomes. At a macro-level, this study also lays a solid foundation for developing strategies that include: classroom interaction during formative learning in mainstream schools, after-school activities, and continuation of learning at the tertiary level, in order to resolve the national crisis of the historically lowest enrolment level of English-speaking learners of Chinese and discontinuation of choosing Chinese as a second language. The research findings should have both pedagogical and curriculum implications for language education research in Australia.

Acknowledgement This project is sponsored by Xin Jin Shan Chinese Language and Culture School, Melbourne, VIC and Newcastle Grammar School, NSW, Australia. Many thanks to all the research partners, school leaders, teachers, administrators, and student participants for their volunteer involvement and valuable contributions to this project. In particular, we extend our special thanks to Ms. Josie Yan for her tireless efforts and unwavering support of the project.

References

ABS (Australian Bureau of Statistics). (2016). *Census of population and housing: Australia revealed*. Retrieved from http://www.abs.gov.au/ausstats/abs@.nsf/Latestproducts/2024.0 Main%20Features22016?opendocument&tabname=Summary&prodno=2024.0&issue=2016&num=&view,2019-1-29

ACARA (Australian Curriculum Assessment and Reporting Authority). (2013). *Asia and Australia's engagement with Asia*. Retrieved from www.australiancurriculum.edu.au/CrossCurriculumPriorities/Asia-and-Australias-engagement-with-Asia

ACARA (Australian Curriculum, Assessment and Reporting Authority). (2015). *Understand how Chinese works*. NSW, Australia. Retrieved from https://www.australiancurriculum.edu.au

Australia-China Relations Institute. (2015). *Chinese language competency in Australia*. Retrieved from http://www.australiachinarelations.org/content/chinese-language-competency-australia

BOSTES (Board of Studies Teaching and Educational Standards). (2012). *HSC (Chinese) Syllabi*. NSW.

Brady, L. (2006). *Collaborative learning in action*. Pearson, Prentice Hall.

Carroll, J. (2017). Minds and meaning in fictional narratives: an evolutionary perspective. *Review of General Psychology, 22*(2), 135–146.

Carroll, T. J., Taylor, J. L., & Gandevia, S. C. (2017). Recovery of central and peripheral neuromuscular fatigue after exercise. *Journal of Applied Physiology, 122*(5), 1068–1076.

Chen, S. (2021). *Training Teachers of Chinese in Australia: Theoretical Foundations and Practical Applications* (1st ed.). Routledge.

Chen, S., & Sit, H. W. (2019). The impact of Australian language policies on Chinese language teaching. In C. Shei, M. E. McLellan Zikpi, & D.-l. Chao (Eds.), *The Routledge handbook of Chinese language teaching* (pp. 581–592). Taylor & Francis Routledge.

Creswell, J. W. (2012). *Educational research: planning, conducting, and evaluating quantitative and qualitative research* (4th ed.). Pearson.

Farías, M., Obilinovic, K., & Orrego, R. (2007). Implications of multimodal learning models for foreign language teaching and learning. *Colombian Applied Linguistics Journal, 9*, 174–199.

Fern, E. F. (2001). *Advanced focus group research*. Sage.

Johnson, D. W., & Johnson, R. T. (1999). *Learning together and alone: cooperative, competitive and individualistic learning*. Allyn and Bacon.

Kayrooz, C., & Trevitt, C. (2005). *Research in organizations and communities: Tales from the real world*. Allen & Unwin.

Killen, R. (1998). *Effective teaching strategies: lessons from research and practice* (2nd ed.). Social Science Press.

Killen, R. (2016). *Effective teaching strategies: lessons from research and practice* (7th ed.). Cengage Learning.

Lee, M., & Ward, L. (2013). *Collaboration in learning: transcending the classroom walls*. ACER Press.

Lo Bianco, J. (1987). The national policy on languages. *Australian Review of Applied Linguistics., 10*(2), 23–32.

Lo Bianco, J. (2010). Chinese: The gigantic up-and-comer. In L. Tsung & K. Cruickshank (Eds.), *Teaching and learning Chinese in global contexts: CFL worldwide* (pp. xiii–xxiv). Continuum International Publishing.

McLaren, A. (2011) *Asian-Language enrolments in Australian higher education 2008–9* (Report Commissioned by the Asian Studies Association of Australia). ASAA.

Ministerial Council on Education, Employment, Training and youth Affairs. (2008). *Melbourne declaration of educational goals for young Australians*. Retrieved 10th May 2022 from http://www.curriculum.edu.au/verve/_resources/national_declaration_on_the_educational_goals_for_young_australians.pdf

Moloney, R., & Xu, H. L. (2015). Transitioning beliefs in teachers of Chinese as a foreign language: An Australian case study. *Cogent Education, 2*, 1–15. https://doi.org/10.1080/2331186X.2015.1024960

Newcastle Grammar School. (2018). *About us*. Retrieved from https://www.ngs.nsw.edu.au/uploads/files/about-us-pdf-59c4cb6d5d22f.pdf

NSW Education Standards Authority-NESA (2024). *NSW and the Australian curriculum*. Retrieved from https://educationstandards.nsw.edu.au/wps/portal/nesa/k-10/understanding-the-curriculum/curriculum-syllabuses-NSW/nsw-and-the-australian-curriculum

Orton, J. (2016). Issues in Chinese language teaching in Australian schools. *Chinese Education & Society, 49*(6), 369–375.

Prosser, M., & Trigwell, K. (2006). Confirmatory factor analysis of the 'approaches to teaching inventory'. *British Journal of Educational Psychology, 76*(2), 405–419.

Punch, K. F. (2009). *Introduction to research methods in education*. SAGE.

Scrimgeour, A. (2015). Responding to the diversity of Chinese language learners in Australian schools. *Babel, 49*(3), 26–36.

Seely-Flint, A., Kitson, L., Lowe, K., Shaw, K., Humphrey, S., Vicars, M., & Rogers, J. (2017). *Literacy in Australia: Pedagogies for engagement* (3rd ed.). Wiley.

Sit, H. W. (2017). *Inclusive teaching strategies for discipline-based English Studies: enhancing language attainment and classroom interaction in a multicultural learning environment*. Springer.

Sit, H. W., & Guo, S. J. (2019). An exploration of design principles to enhance students' L2 acquisition in a flipped class. In A. Tso (Ed.), *Digital humanities and new ways of teaching* (pp. 111–131). Springer.

Smith, D., Chin, N. B., Louie, K., & Mackerras, C. (1993). *Unlocking Australia's language potential, Chinese volume*. Australian National Languages and Literacy Inst.

Sturak, K., & Naughten, Z. (Eds.). (2010). *The current state of Chinese, Indonesian, Japanese and Korean languages education in Australian school: Four languages, four stories*. Education Services Australia.

Wang, D., Moloney, R., & Li, Z. (2013). Towards internationalising the curriculum: A case study of Chinese language teacher education programs in China and Australia. *Australian Journal of Teacher Education, 38*(9), 116–135.

White, R. (2014). *In with Pinyin: How to improve Chinese language education in Australia*. Australia-China Youth Association. Retrieved from www.acya.org.au/2014/10/pinyin-improve-chinese-language-education-australia/

Ye, L. J. (2011). *Teaching and learning Chinese as a foreign language in the United States: To delay or not to delay the character introduction*. Applied Linguistics and English as a Second Language Dissertations, pp 1–194.

Yuan, C., & Lo Bianco, J. (2022). L2 Chinese teachers' beliefs about engagement strategies for students in Australia: Findings from Q methodology research. *System, 106*, 102792. https://doi.org/10.1016/j.system.2022.102792

"We Are Here to Learn Something Useful": Contextualization of Adult Learners' Motivation

Wenjin Vikki Bo

Abstract There has been an increasing interest to understand students' achievement motivation in foreign language learning, but previous studies primarily relied on quantitative data of questionnaires to generalise students' learning orientations without considering contextual factors. Considering the context-dependent nature of learning motivation, it is necessary to obtain a deeper understanding of motivational developments under various learning contexts. In terms of the research target, while younger students in K-12 education have been the focus, the understanding of adult learners' achievement motivation in foreign language learning is insufficient. To fill in those gaps, the present study examined adult learners' motivational changes under different contexts in a foreign language classroom. An ethnographic multi-case study was adopted, focusing on six students. Findings showed that all the 6 students demonstrated an extrinsic-oriented motivation in the foreign language course that focused primarily on the utility of learning. The reasons shaping such a motivational orientation were observed to be stable among high-achieving students, while fluctuating among low-achieving students due to the change of learning contexts in the classroom, such as the context of peer comparison and the context of high-stake exam. Those context-dependent changes across time could provide pedagogical insights to the instructors with adult learners.

1 Introduction

Despite the critical factor of aptitude in language learning, motivation has been identified for long to significantly go beyond the constraint in language achievements (Gardner & Lambert, 1972). Among all the motivational theories, expectancy-value theory (Eccles et al., 1983) has been influential to understand students' motivational beliefs, motivational behaviours and how their beliefs influenced

W. V. Bo (✉)
Singapore University of Social Sciences, Singapore, Singapore
e-mail: vikkibowj@suss.edu.sg

behaviours in the educational setting. Most of the motivational research under expectancy-value theory focuses on students' annual changes in the long term, by measuring students' self-reported motivation with yearly time points (Musu-Gillette et al., 2015; Wigfield & Eccles, 2000; Wigfield et al., 1997). Those studies are effective to discover a general trend that students' motivational beliefs (task values and ability beliefs) and motivational behaviours (learning engagements) tend to decline across academic grades. However, it was not clear how that change takes place and what factors influence it.

More importantly, considering the dynamic and context-dependent nature of learning motivation, the change of student motivation could occur in a much shorter time than a yearly basis. As Dornyei (2000, p. 523) pointed out, "even within the duration of a single course, most learners experience a fluctuation of their enthusiasm commitment, sometimes on a day-to-day basis". Those changes could be due to a specific lesson or even a particular task in class (Hotho, 2000). Therefore, it is necessary to take a closer look at students' motivational changes within a shorter duration, especially in the classroom context—a formal learning context, which could give direct insights to teachers regarding promoting student motivation. Based on the changes of students' motivational beliefs and behaviours under various learning settings, instructors could make informed pedagogical decisions to meet different students' learning needs.

As for the research participants, expectancy-value theory has been primarily targeting the younger learners in K-12 education (Bong, 2001; Lau, 2009a, b; Lau & Chan, 2001), and the group of adult learners in the context of higher education still needs more research. As a matter of fact, it is suggested that the construct of student's motivational beliefs, especially task values (e.g. intrinsic value, utility value, and attainment value) may vary among different age groups (Wigfield, 1994; Wigfield & Cambria, 2010; Wigfield & Eccles, 1992). For instance, the young children are more likely to choose the tasks based on their personal interest, so intrinsic value may be particularly salient for primary school students' behaviours. In contrast, the usage of the learning activity (utility value) and the importance of good performance (attainment value) would likely emerge in later years when students gain a better understanding of themselves, their career plans, and the relations between their plans and the learning activities (e.g. speak good Chinese to work in China). Accordingly, the behaviours of that age group might be determined by utility value and attainment value instead. To fill in the research gaps mentioned above, the present study aimed to investigate the developments of adult learners' motivational beliefs and behaviours across time in the classroom setting, as well as the contextual factors shaping those developments.

To specify, the research questions are as follows:

1. What are students' motivational beliefs (ability beliefs and perception of task values) in classroom activities at different stages of a language course while learning Chinese as a foreign language?
2. What are students' motivational behaviours (choice of tasks) in classroom activities at different stages of a language course while learning Chinese as a foreign language?

2 Research Method

As discussed above in the introduction, student's motivation is a dynamic, process-oriented and context-dependent construct (Dornyei, 2000). It requires in-depth analysis of learning contexts and people involved, so a qualitative case study fairly serves as the research methodology in a classroom setting, to identify the learning phenomenon and contextual influences upon it.

The nature of qualitative case study enables us to conduct an intensive and deep analysis among a comparatively small sample size (Gomm et al., 2000), like the current study with six cases of research participants. To be specific, the current study focuses on the contextual specificity in class, aiming at identifying the developments of students' motivational beliefs and behaviours at different learning stages. To achieve this, the adoption of case studies can effectively provide a chronological description of incidents in relation to the cases with the focus on individuals and groups of individuals sharing similarities (Cohen et al., 2000). In the current study, research findings were presented in a chronological order throughout the Chinese language course, with the focus on cases who shared similarities in the proficiency levels of Chinese and hence were observed to show similar patterns in their motivational changes in the classroom activities.

2.1 Research Participants

A Chinese as the foreign language class (intermediate level) in a university in Hong Kong was selected as the research site. Among the 16 students in the class, six students were chosen purposefully whose proficiency levels varied from low to high (Table 1). They came from different countries and were at various ages as adult learners. Three were males and three were females; three were university students and three were working professionals.

Table 1 Participant information

Participant	Sex	Nationality	Age	Proficiency level in class	Occupation
Kelly	Female	USA	36	High	Professional
Amy	Female	UK	34	High	Professional
Andrew	Male	Italy	25	Average	Postgraduate
Sam	Male	Korea	21	Average	Undergraduate
Cora	Female	Switzerland	38	Low	Professional
Mike	Male	USA	28	Low	Postgraduate

2.2 Data Collection

To understand students' motivational beliefs and behaviours under various contexts in the classroom, on-going individual interviews, class observations and stimulated recall following the observations were conducted with the six cases of students. Documents such as students' attendance records and worksheets were also collected as supplementary sources of data. The semi-structured interview questions were developed based on the original questionnaires of expectancy-value theory (Wigfield, 1994) with small modifications to adapt to the classroom setting. The observation protocol was developed from the learners' motivated behaviour in MOLT Observation Scheme (Guilloteaux & Dörnyei, 2008), integrating the definitions of motivational behaviours from the expectancy-value theory.

Among all the 20 sessions of the course, 18 instructional sessions were observed and audio-recorded across thirteen weeks. The other 2 sessions were mid-term exam and final exam, respectively. After each class observation, simulated recall was conducted individually with the 6 participants to reflect about their motivational behaviours in the classroom activities, in particular, their choice of task. According to the observed changes of students' motivational behaviours in class, four rounds of interviews were conducted with the individual cases to understand the changes in their motivational beliefs, and how those changes shaped their motivational behaviours accordingly.

2.3 Data Analysis

Qualitative data from individual interviews, field notes from class observations, stimulated recall and relevant documents were analysed inductively based on Miles and Huberman (1994). Descriptive quantitative data from class observations regarding students' choice of tasks were analysed primarily based on the calculation of frequencies and percentages regarding the various classroom activities. According to observational data, six types of tasks were included in the classroom activities, namely grammar, vocabulary, reading, writing, listening and speaking. For instance, if an individual actively chose to participate in 10 tasks during the classroom activities, and 3 choices were in vocabulary, this individual's percentage in the choice of vocabulary would be 30%.

Each case was analysed separately and summarised with a motivational trajectory across time within the Chinese language course. After that, a cross-case analysis was conducted between cases who shared similar motivational trajectories.

3 Findings

Within the course 4 learning stages were identified from the data while tracking students' motivational beliefs (ability beliefs and task values) and behaviours (choice of tasks) in the classroom activities. It is worth mentioning that only the less proficient students (who were below the average level of the class) were indicating evident changes in their motivational trajectory within the course, while the more proficient students (who were around and above the average level) seemed to have relatively stable motivational beliefs and behaviours.

To specify, among the 20 sessions in total, the first stage was the start of the course including the first 4 sessions; the second stage lasted until the mid-term test; the third stage included the 5 sessions following the mid-term test; the fourth stage was the last 5 sessions right before the final exam. This section will describe the findings in chronological order from the first stage to the fourth stage. Within each stage, both participants' motivational beliefs (ability beliefs and task values) and motivational behaviours (choice of task) in class will be presented.

3.1 First Stage: Absence of Social Comparison

3.1.1 Motivational Beliefs: Unestablished Ability Beliefs; Focus on Utility Value

At the start of the course when the students were not yet aware of classmates' proficiency levels, no social comparison was sensed among each other. Hence, none of the six participants clearly expressed their ability beliefs, but simply described themselves as the "average level in the class" during the first round of individual interviews. Their focus was unanimously on "learning Chinese to use it for communication" either in professional settings or social life, demonstrating the perception of utility value. "I want to use what I learn in class." appeared to be the repeating pattern in students' interviews across various participants. They did, however, have different perceptions of which types of learning tasks in class could be more useful. For instance, Sam perceived the tasks of vocabulary and listening to be useful in order to understand people; Mike considered grammar to be useful and explained, "grammar is the essential component to connect all the vocabularies I know, so it is the most useful for me to talk to people".

3.1.2 Choice of Tasks: Shaped by Utility Value

Based on the classroom observations (as shown in Table 2) and subsequent reflective discussions (stimulated recall), all the six participants were choosing to participate in the learning tasks they considered useful, including the ones they might feel

Table 2 Choice of task in class at first stage: Percentage (and frequency) of active participation

	Kelly	Amy	Andrew	Sam	Cora	Mike
Session 1: Top 1 choice	Grammar 70% (7)	Vocabulary 50% (1)	Vocabulary 64% (11)	Vocabulary 38% (6)	Grammar 67% (2)	Grammar 100% (1)
Session 1: Top 2 choice	Vocabulary 30% (3)	Grammar 50% (1)	Grammar/Listening 18% (3)/ 18% (3)	Listening 25% (4)	Vocabulary 33% (1)	None
Session 2: Top 1 choice	Grammar 62.5% (5)	Grammar 50% (2)	Vocabulary 56% (9)	Listening 50% (4)	Grammar 83% (5)	Grammar 100% (4)
Session 2: Top 2 choice	Vocabulary 37.5% (3)	Vocabulary/Reading 25% (1)	Grammar 25% (4)	Vocabulary/Grammar 25% (2)	Vocabulary 17% (1)	None
Session 3: Top 1 choice	Vocabulary 78% (7)	Vocabulary 100% (2)	Vocabulary 60% (12)	Vocabulary 50% (8)	Grammar 60%(3)	Grammar 100% (4)
Session 3: Top 2 choice	Grammar 22% (2)	None	Grammar/Listening 20% (4)	Grammar 44% (7)	Vocabulary/Listening 20% (1)	None
Session 4: Top 1 choice	Grammar 64% (9)	Vocabulary 50% (1)	Vocabulary 65% (15)	Vocabulary 80% (8)	Vocabulary 50% (3)	Grammar 83% (5)
Session 4: Top 2 choice	Vocabulary 36% (5)	Grammar 50% (1)	Grammar 35% (8)	Grammar 20% (2)	Grammar 50% (3)	Vocabulary 17% (1)

Note. In Session 4, no listening tasks were included

incompetent to perform. Taking Amy and Cora as examples, most of their active participations in class were in vocabulary and grammar, although they were both observed to keep making mistakes in those tasks while performing them. In another word, without the sense of social comparison in class, utility value was shaping all the participants' motivational behaviours, regarding their choice of tasks. With the lack of perceived social comparison among students, the common focus seemed to be the usefulness of the learning activities, no matter how competent or incompetent they might be to perform those tasks in class.

3.2 Second Stage: Appearance of Social Comparison

3.2.1 Motivational Beliefs: Ability Beliefs in Hierarchy; Attainment Value in Low-Performing Participants; Utility Value in High-Performing and Average-Performing Participants

Following the first several sessions, students started to be aware of their peers' proficiency levels, which triggered the social comparison in the class. Therefore, all the participants' ability beliefs were gradually established in hierarchy. In another word, the low-performing students (Cora and Mike) realised their proficiency were at the bottom level of the class; high-performing students (Kelly and Amy) noticed their proficiency were at the top level of the class; the average-performing students (Andrew and Sam) perceived their proficiency at the medium level of the class. Due to this difference in the ability beliefs, the six cases' perception of task values began to differ accordingly. To specify, both high-performing and average-performing students still sustained their learning focus on usefulness, indicating utility value; in comparison, the low-performing students' perception of task values began to shift to classroom performance, demonstrating attainment value in the class.

> Cora: "It's absolutely very important to perform well in the class... If I do something, I want to do it at my best. Otherwise, don't do it... But obviously I am not doing it well at all... I hope I am..." (interview at the second Stage)
>
> Mike: "I think there is a range of variation of students' level in the class, and I'm definitely at the bottom. Other people must have felt the same... It is really sad that I am spending lots of time in Chinese but I am not getting any better at it, as you can see in class... Other students were just talking and talking and I am so lost... I cannot keep making mistakes in class" (interview at the second Stage)

This emphasis on performance in class indicated the obvious attainment value Cora and Mike perceived in the learning tasks, which subsequently influence their choice of tasks accordingly. As a result of the emerging social comparison, the participants who had the desire to demonstrate their abilities or the fear to reveal their inabilities in front of their classmates were attaching more value to the attainment of the learning tasks.

3.2.2 Choice of Tasks: Low-Achieving Students' Shaped by Ability Beliefs; High-Achieving and Average-Achieving Students' Shaped by Utility Value

Due to the weakened ability beliefs among the low-achieving participants (Cora and Mike), evident changes were observed in their choice of tasks—their focus gradually shifted to demonstrating abilities and concealing inabilities in the classroom activities. As reflected in Table 3, both Cora and Mike were primarily choosing the types of tasks they perceived able to perform (e.g. vocabulary tasks), and avoided participating in the types of tasks they considered unable to do (e.g. listening tasks). Cora explained such choices in her stimulated recall, "you will never voluntarily participate in the tasks or activities to which you are not completely sure of the answers… It helps me to feel more confident". Mike shared similar reasons for his choice of tasks in class as "a choice to avoid making mistakes".

On the other hand, no evident change was observed among the high-achieving and average-achieving students whose choice of tasks was still dependent on the

Table 3 Choice of task in class at stage 2: Percentage (and frequency) of active participation

	Kelly	Amy	Andrew	Sam	Cora	Mike
Session 5: Top 1 choice	Vocabulary 53% (8)	Grammar 50% (3)	Vocabulary 54% (7)	Listening/Vocabulary 37.5% (3)/ 37.5% (3)	Vocabulary 67% (4)	Vocabulary 67% (2)
Session 5: Top 2 choice	Grammar 40% (6)	Vocabulary 33% (2)	Grammar/Listening 23% (3)/ 23% (3)	Grammar 25% (2)	Grammar/Writing 17% (1)/ 17% (1)	Grammar 33% (1)
Session 6: Top 1 choice	Vocabulary 68% (13)	Vocabulary 62.5% (5)	Vocabulary 54% (7)	Grammar 50% (4)	Vocabulary 67% (4)	Vocabulary 70% (7)
Session 6: Top 2 choice	Grammar 32% (6)	Grammar 37.5% (3)	Grammar 31% (4)	Vocabulary 37.5% (3)	Writing 33% (2)	Grammar 30% (3)
Session 7: Top 1 choice	Vocabulary 53% (8)	Vocabulary 60% (3)	Vocabulary 67% (18)	Listening 42% (5)	Vocabulary 62.5% (5)	Vocabulary/Listening 50% (1)/ 50% (1)
Session 7: Top 2 choice	Grammar 33% (5)	Grammar 40% (2)	Grammar/Listening 15% (4)/ 15% (4)	Vocabulary/Grammar 25%(3)/ 25% (3)	Grammar 25% (2)	None
Session 8: Top 1 choice	Grammar 54% (14)	Vocabulary 60% (3)	Vocabulary 63% (27)	Vocabulary 66% (4)	Vocabulary 75% (6)	Vocabulary 80% (4)
Session 8: Top 2 choice	Vocabulary 35% (9)	Grammar 40% (2)	Grammar 35% (15)	Grammar/Speaking 17% (1)/ 17% (1)	Grammar 25% (2)	Grammar 20% (1)

Note. In Session 6 and Session 8, no listening tasks were included; In session 7, Mike checked the correct answers before all her active participation

usefulness of the activities. For instance, even Sam and Amy kept making mistakes in the grammar tasks, their active participation in the class was still mostly in grammar—the type of tasks they considered useful for Chinese learning. In the reflective discussions (the stimulated recall) after the class observations, they described the classroom activities as "opportunities to practice and learn something useful" and considered the mistakes in the activities as "chances to improve", which indicated the consistent emphasis on the utility value.

3.3 Third Stage: Boost of Social Comparison

3.3.1 Motivational Beliefs: Ability Beliefs Shaped by Mid-Term Test Results; Attainment Value in Low-Performing Participants; Utility Value in High-Performing and Average-Performing Participants

After receiving the results of the mid-term test, the social comparison among the peers reached the peak, which shaped students' ability beliefs accordingly. In another word, the ability beliefs of low-performing students (such as Cora and Mike) continued to be weakened with the low scores, while the ability beliefs of the high-performing students (such as Kelly and Amy) were still maintained at the top level in the class. Interestingly, the average-performing participants (Andrew and Sam) received much higher scores than expected, which substantially strengthened their ability beliefs. As a result, those with low ability beliefs (Cora and Mike) perceived a stronger need to "feel better and more confident in Chinese learning from other ways", as they mentioned in their interviews after the mid-term test, and the classroom activity was described to be the "major source of confidence". Hence, their focus on classroom performance was strengthened at this stage, indicating their perception of attainment value in the classroom activities.

> Cora: "The exam is really hard for our level, so I thought we would all do it badly, but it seems they were not so bad... It seems they were not so bad as expected... I'm really lost... I hope I can do better in the classroom activities so at least I would feel I'm still on the right track..." (Interview at the third Stage)
>
> Mike: "I feel I am really falling behind the class, and sometimes I felt the class was running out of patience in me, so it was really discouraging and embarrassing for me to always get it wrong... You hate to feel like you are wasting other people's time and always get it wrong while the class could have gone faster... I have to do better in class activities than my mid-term test..." (Interview at the third stage)

Different from the low-performing participants, the other four participants received high scores from the mid-term test, which led to a boost of confidence. With the ability beliefs at such a high level, they did not perceive any value to demonstrating good performance or avoiding bad performance, but instead still focused most on "learning something useful", indicating the perception of utility value in learning. Mistakes are still described as "opportunities to learn" and "part of the learning" by the high-performing participants and average-performing participants, since there did not appear to be any desire to demonstrate their competence or any concern of revealing their incompetence at the stage after receiving the results of the mid-term test.

3.3.2 Choice of Tasks: Low-Achieving Students' Shaped by Ability Beliefs; High-Achieving and Average-Achieving Students' Shaped by Utility Value

Similar to the previous stage, ability beliefs continued to shape the choice of low-performing students in the classroom activities, especially with the strengthened social comparison among peers at this stage. According to the observational data (Table 4), Cora and Mike would selectively choose the tasks they felt able to provide the answers (e.g. vocabulary tasks) in class and intentionally avoid the tasks they felt incompetent with (e.g. listening tasks). Mike explained such choices in the classroom activities as "more controllable and easier to do because correct answers could be easily found with dictionaries in advance." In comparison, the high-achieving and average-achieving students maintained their focus on choosing the tasks they considered useful for learning in class, including the ones they kept making mistakes, such as vocabulary tasks. This was the stage when the contrast in the learning focus was the most evident between the low-achieving participants and the remaining four

Table 4 Choice of task in class at stage 3: Percentage (and frequency) of active participation

	Kelly	Amy	Andrew	Sam	Cora	Mike
Session 10: Top 1 choice	Absent	Vocabulary 60% (3)	Vocabulary 73% (19)	Absent	Vocabulary 54% (7)	Absent
Session 10: Top 2 choice	Absent	Listening 40% (2)	Listening 19% (5)	Absent	Listening 38% (5)	Absent
Session 11: Top 1 choice	Absent	Absent	Vocabulary 74% (20)	Absent	Vocabulary 64% (7)	Vocabulary 58% (7)
Session 11: Top 2 choice	Absent	Absent	Grammar 26% (7)	Absent	Grammar 27% (3)	Grammar 42% (5)
Session 12: Top 1 choice	Vocabulary 43% (6)	Vocabulary 62.5% (5)	Vocabulary 76% (26)	Vocabulary 76% (22)	Vocabulary 67% (6)	Vocabulary 100% (1)
Session 12: Top 2 choice	Grammar 36% (5)	Grammar 37.5% (3)	Grammar 15% (5)	Grammar 14% (4)	Writing 22% (2)	None
Session 13: Top 1 choice	Vocabulary 56% (10)	Vocabulary 100% (2)	Vocabulary 74% (17)	Vocabulary 50% (11)	Vocabulary 83% (5)	Vocabulary 100% (1)
Session 13: Top 2 choice	Listening 33% (6)	None	Grammar 22% (5)	Listening 27% (6)	Listening 17% (1)	None
Session 14: Top 1 choice	Vocabulary 100% (3)	Vocabulary 100% (2)	Vocabulary 75% (15)	Vocabulary 100% (7)	Vocabulary 80% (4)	None
Session 14: Top 2 choice	None	None	Grammar 15% (3)	None	Grammar 20% (1)	None

Note. In Session 10 and 11, only three students were attending the class; In Session 11, 12 and 14, no listening tasks were included; In Session 13, Cora checked the right answers before her active participation in listening tasks

participants (average-achieving participants and high-achieving participants) with the impacts of the mid-term test results that intensified the social comparison in class.

3.4 Fourth Stage: Context of High-Stake Exam

3.4.1 Motivational Beliefs: Ability Beliefs Maintained the Same as the Third Stage; Utility Value for Exam in Low-Performing Participants; Utility Value for Practical Use in High-Performing and Average-Performing Participants

Interestingly, the impact of social comparison upon low-performing participants seemed to decrease with the approaching of the final exam—the result of which would determine the students' eligibility to progress to the next level. As a result, in order to prepare for the final exam, the focus of the low-performing participants was changing from classroom performance (either for demonstrating good performance or avoiding bad performance in front of peers) to skills development (getting as many useful skills as possible for the exam preparation). In other words, Cora's and Mike's main focus on classroom activities became how useful the tasks could help them to develop enough skills to pass the final exam, which demonstrated their perception of utility value in the final stage of the semester.

> Cora: "Now my focus is completely on the final exam now, so I can do it as well as I can... I hope the teacher will do more activities in the class that can be useful for our exam preparation... I will try to participate more so I can learn more..." (Interview at the fourth stage)
>
> Mike: "My mid-term test was a disaster, so I would hope to get a better score in the final exam. I am trying to learn as much as I can in the class so that I might get a better chance to pass the exam" (Interview at the fourth stage)

On the other hand, the average-performing and high-performing participants did not demonstrate any concern for the final exam, either the fear to fail or the need to achieve. Consistent with the previous stages, their learning focus in the classroom activities was still on the utility for practical use in work or life, such as "to be able to use it for daily communication", "to use for travelling", "to talk to friends", or "to chat with Chinese colleagues", as described in their individual interviews.

3.4.2 Choice of Tasks: Shaped by Utility Value

Under the context of final exam in the last stage of the semester, the low-performing participants Cora and Mike shifted their focus from performance demonstration in front of peers to skills development for exam preparation. Hence, their choice of tasks in the class was no longer based on whether they felt able to perform, but instead based on whether the activities would be useful to get them prepared for the exam. As reflected in their active participations in the classroom activities (Table 5),

Table 5 Choice of tasks in class at stage 4: Percentage (and frequency) of active participation

	Kelly	Amy	Andrew	Sam	Cora	Mike
Session 15: Top 1 choice	Vocabulary 64% (9)	Vocabulary 71% (5)	Vocabulary 83% (10)	Vocabulary 83% (5)	Vocabulary/Listening 40% (2)/ 40% (2)	Vocabulary/Listening 50% (2)/ 50% (2)
Session 15: Top 2 choice	Grammar/Listening 14% (2)/14% (2)	Grammar 29% (2)	Grammar 17% (2)	Listening 17% (1)	Grammar 20% (1)	None
Session 16: Top 1 choice	Vocabulary 62.5% (5)	Vocabulary/Grammar 50% (1)/50% (1)	Vocabulary 58% (7)	Vocabulary 67% (4)	Vocabulary/Grammar 50% (3)/ 50% (3)	Grammar 100% (2)
Session 16: Top 2 choice	Grammar 25% (2)	None	Grammar 25% (3)	Grammar 33% (2)	None	None
Session 17: Top 1 choice	Grammar 50% (4)	Vocabulary/Grammar 40% (2)/40% (2)	Vocabulary 80% (12)	Vocabulary 40% (4)	Vocabulary/Grammar 37.5% (3)/ 37.5% (3)	Listening 60% (3)
Session 17: Top 2 choice	Vocabulary 37.5% (3)	Listening 20% (1)	Grammar 20% (3)	Grammar/Listening 30% (3)/ 30% (3)	Listening 25% (2)	Vocabulary/Grammar 20% (1)/ 20% (1)
Session 18: Top 1 choice	Vocabulary 58% (7)	Vocabulary/Grammar 50% (1)/50% (1)	Vocabulary 64% (14)	Vocabulary 57% (4)	Vocabulary/Grammar 50% (3)/ 50% (3)	Vocabulary 67% (2)
Session 18: Top 2 choice	Grammar 42% (5)	None	Grammar 27% (6)	Grammar 43% (3)	None	Grammar 33% (1)
Session 19: Top 1 choice	Vocabulary 73% (11)	Absent	Absent	Absent	Vocabulary 50% (4)	Grammar 50% (4)
Session 19: Top 2 choice	Grammar 20% (3)	Absent	Absent	Absent	Grammar 37.5% (3)	Vocabulary/Listening 25% (2)/ 25% (2)

Note. In Session 16 and 18, no listening tasks were included

Cora and Mike were actively choosing to participate in a variety of tasks—not only in vocabulary tasks (the type of tasks they felt more competent to perform), but also in grammar tasks and even listening tasks (the type of tasks they had been feeling unable to do and trying to avoid in the second and third stage of the semester). Cora explained such choices in the simulated recall that "for now I don't care about making mistakes in class anymore, as long as it helps me to learn more for the exam... So I'm trying not to avoid doing it in class just because I might get it wrong now..." Those exam-driving behaviours were also echoed by the other low-performing participant Mike who repeatedly mentioned "passing the final exam is the top priority now" in the stimulated recall. The high-stake exam was forcing the low-achieving students to shift their learning focus from demonstrating performance in front of peers to developing skills to progress in the course.

The other four participants, on the other hand, still maintained the same learning focus as usual—obtaining useful Chinese skills for practical use, either for professional purposes or personal/social purposes outside the classroom. No evident changes were observed due to the final exam in their choice of tasks compared to the previous stages, since there seemed to be "no concern of failing the exam" among those students. In another word, the active participation of the high-achieving students and the average-achieving students in the classroom activities was still primarily based on their perception of utility value in those tasks, but for practice uses in real life rather than for exams (as reflected in the cases of low-performing participants).

4 Discussion

As indicated in the section of findings, the high-achieving as well as average-achieving participants tended to demonstrate stable motivational beliefs and hence motivational behaviours across time in the Chinese language classroom. In comparison, the low-achieving participants' motivation in the class activities was undergoing continuous changes because of two main contextual developments, including (1) non-exam context: social comparison resulting in the weakened ability beliefs and hence the declining motivation, and (2) high-stake exam context: exam preparation resulting in the strengthened task values and hence the increasing motivation.

4.1 Non-exam Context: Students' Classroom Participation

As shown in the findings, when the students become more aware of classmates' proficiency levels, the social comparison among peers would form gradually in the classroom setting, especially among the low-achieving students who would often feel the threat to their self-worth. Hence, with the declining ability beliefs, they would start to only value the tasks that they felt more able to perform. This phenomenon echoes previous research with primary/secondary school students (Jacobs & Eccles, 2000; Jacobs et al., 2002) in that when the level of students' ability beliefs dropped, they would be more likely to value more certain subjects that they felt more competent with (such as language subject versus maths subject). The present research found similar patterns with adult learners, and extends it from the subject-specific level to the task-specific level within one subject (such as vocabulary task versus listening task within Chinese language subject).

Low-achieving students' focus on demonstrating good performance and concealing bad performance in the classroom participation would usually get strengthened when they sense a wider proficiency gap with the classmates and hence a stronger perception of social comparison with peers, such as after receiving feedback from the teacher or tests. As a matter of fact, this reaction after receiving low scores in the test seems to correspond to the previous research, which explained "when students focus on how they are compared with others, their motivation is vulnerable to negative changes when grades are given" (Shim & Ryan, 2005, p. 347). As a result, the low-achieving students would primarily choose to participate in the class activities they feel competent to perform for ability demonstration, and to avoid the class activities they feel incompetent to perform for inability concealment. In stark contrast, the high-achieving students who don't perceive the social comparison in the negative way would tend to focus more on the usefulness of learning activities, and their motivational behaviour (e.g. choice of tasks) seem to remain much more stable across time.

4.2 High-Stake Exam Context: Students' Classroom Participation

It is worth mentioning that the impact of social comparison in shaping low-achieving students' motivation seemed to fade away in the high-stake exam context. Despite the weakened ability beliefs, the low-achieving students' motivational behaviours in the classroom would no longer be dependent on the attainment value of the activities (e.g. demonstrating good performance or avoiding bad performance) in front of peers. Instead, their focus seems to shift to the utility value of classroom activities, although in order to pass the exam—the result of which would decide their eligibility to continue to the next level's course. This drastic change as a result of the high-stake exam in the present study resonates with previous studies (Wise & DeMars, 2005) in that exams would alter students' perception of task values and enhance their motivation; however, the present study tends to specify this impact of high-stake exam is limited to the low-achieving students who feel 'the fear to fail or need to achieve' (Elliot & McGregor, 2001). In other words, even the low-achieving students still perceive the social comparison in the class and hence low ability beliefs in the context of high-stake exam, the focus on exam achievement tends to take precedence. Therefore, their perception of utility value in the tasks would be the prioritised consideration in shaping their active choice of classroom activities.

5 Conclusion

This study explored the dynamic developments of six adult learners' learning motivation within a foreign language course, including their motivational beliefs and motivational behaviours. A particular strength of this study is that it included comprehensive data sources of individual interviews, class observations, stimulated recall and document reviews over an academic semester. Qualitative filed notes integrated with the quantitative data from observation scheme have enabled the study to develop a holistic understanding of the events happening in the classroom of foreign language learning. This is especially efficient to understand the contextualization of learning motivation—a dynamic and context-dependent concept that could vary from week to week or even day to day due to a specific lesson or a particular exam (Hotho, 2000).

In summary, motivational beliefs among the more proficient students (including high-achieving and average-achieving students) seem to be relatively stable. They generally hold high ability beliefs and pay most attention to the utility of classroom activities for external purposes, such as for career or communication. Hence, their active participation in the classroom activities is usually dependent on the perceived usefulness of the tasks. In contrast, the motivation among the less proficient students (low-achieving students) would usually undergo more fluctuations in relation to the change of their ability beliefs. When their ability beliefs are strong, the major focus tends to be the same as the more proficient students—the utility of classroom activities for external purposes (e.g. work/life). To meet the motivational beliefs of students and hence promote their active participation in the classroom, instructors could design certain activities demonstrating the utility value. However, when their ability beliefs are weakened under the impacts of social comparison with peers, their focus would tend to shift to classroom performance, either to demonstrate their competence or to avoid their incompetence in front of peers. To maintain the low-achieving students' engagement in the classroom at this stage, activities covering a wide range of difficulty levels should be designed and instructors are advised to provide feedback focusing on promoting students' ability beliefs. Notably, those impacts of social comparison on low-achieving students appear to fade away under the context of high-stake exams, when the low-achieving students' focus would be prioritised to exam preparation. Therefore, the utility value of classroom activities for exam preparation would take precedence to shape their learning motivation at that particular stage. Classroom activities facilitating students' exam preparation could be integrated in the lesson plan, and instructors could highlight the utility of those tasks to encourage low-achieving students' participation in class.

Notably, no evident intrinsic value (e.g. personal interest) was observed among any of the participants in the present study, whether low-achieving students or high-achieving students. This seems to differ from the previous studies (Eccles & Wigfield, 2002; Linnenbrink, 2005) with K-12 students who usually perceived a variety of task values in learning, including attainment value, utility value and intrinsic value. However, it is worth mentioning that the development of perceived task values among k-12 students has also been identified previously in the literature (Anderman & Maehr, 1994; Lepper et al., 2005) that when students became older and entered higher grades, their intrinsic value in learning tended to decline gradually while the utility value became more evident, particularly when their long-term goals were set along the way. The present study sheds light on the motivational trajectory that intrinsic value in learning might even diminish to the minimum among adult learners, and other extrinsic-oriented values such as attainment value and utility value would become dominant in shaping students' motivation. Those findings should be taken into consideration when language teachers design class activities with the aim to promote students' classroom motivation.

References

Anderman, E. M., & Maehr, M. L. (1994). Motivation and schooling in the middle grades. *Review of Educational Research, 64*(2), 287–309. https://doi.org/10.3102/00346543064002287

Bong, M. (2001). Between-and within-domain relations of academic motivation among middle and high school students: Self-efficacy, task value, and achievement goals. *Journal of Educational Psychology, 93*(1), 23–34.

Cohen, L., Manion, L., & Morrison, K. (2000). *Research methods in education* (Vol. 5). Routledge.

Dornyei, Z. (2000). Motivation in action: Towards a process-oriented conceptualisation of student motivation. *British Journal of Educational Psychology, 70*(4), 519–538.

Eccles, J. S., & Wigfield, A. (2002). Motivational beliefs, values, and goals. *Annual Review of Psychology, 53*(1), 109–132.

Eccles, J. S., Adler, T., Futterman, R., Goff, S., Kaczala, C., Meece, J., & Midgley, C. (1983). Expectancies, values, and academic behaviors. In J. T. Spence (Ed.), *Achievement and achievement motivation* (pp. 75–146). W. H. Freeman.

Elliot, A. J., & McGregor, H. A. (2001). A 2× 2 achievement goal framework. *Journal of Personality and Social Psychology, 80*(3), 501.

Gardner, R. C., & Lambert, W. E. (1972). *Attitudes and motivation in second-language learning.* Newbury House.

Gomm, R., Hammersley, M., & Foster, P. (2000). Case study and generalization. In R. Gomm (Ed.), *Case study method* (pp. 98–116). Sage.

Guilloteaux, M. J., & Dörnyei, Z. (2008). Motivating language learners: A classroom-oriented investigation of the effects of motivational strategies on student motivation. *TESOL Quarterly, 42*(1), 55–77.

Hotho, S. (2000). "Same" or "Different"? A comparative examination of classroom factors in second language settings. *Foreign Language Annals, 33*(3), 320–329.

Jacobs, J. E., & Eccles, J. S. (2000). Parents, task values, and real-life achievement-related choices. In *Intrinsic and extrinsic motivation* (pp. 405–439). Elsevier.

Jacobs, J. E., Lanza, S., Osgood, D. W., Eccles, J. S., & Wigfield, A. (2002). Changes in children's self-competence and values: Gender and domain differences across grades one through twelve. *Child Development, 73*(2), 509–527.

Lau, K. (2009a). Grade differences in reading motivation among Hong Kong primary and secondary students. *British Journal of Educational Psychology, 79*(4), 713–733.

Lau, K. (2009b). Reading motivation, perceptions of reading instruction and reading amount: A comparison of junior and senior secondary students in Hong Kong. *Journal of Research in Reading, 32*(4), 366–382.

Lau, K., & Chan, D. W. (2001). Motivational characteristics of under-achievers in Hong Kong. *Educational Psychology, 21*(4), 417–430.

Lepper, M. R., Corpus, J. H., & Iyengar, S. S. (2005). Intrinsic and extrinsic motivational orientations in the classroom: Age differences and academic correlates. *Journal of Educational Psychology, 97*(2), 184.

Linnenbrink, E. A. (2005). The dilemma of performance-approach goals: The use of multiple goal contexts to promote students' motivation and learning. *Journal of Educational Psychology, 97*(2), 197–213. https://doi.org/10.1037/0022-0663.97.2.197

Miles, M. B., & Huberman, A. M. (1994). *Qualitative data analysis: An expanded sourcebook*. Sage.

Musu-Gillette, L. E., Wigfield, A., Harring, J. R., & Eccles, J. S. (2015). Trajectories of change in students' self-concepts of ability and values in math and college major choice. *Educational Research and Evaluation, 21*(4), 343–370.

Shim, S., & Ryan, A. (2005). Changes in self-efficacy, challenge avoidance, and intrinsic value in response to grades: The role of achievement goals. *The Journal of Experimental Education, 73*(4), 333–349.

Wigfield, A. (1994). Expectancy–value theory of achievement motivation: A developmental perspective. *Educational Psychology Review, 6*(1), 49–78.

Wigfield, A., & Cambria, J. (2010). Students' achievement values, goal orientations, and interest: Definitions, development, and relations to achievement outcomes. *Developmental Review, 30*(1), 1–35.

Wigfield, A., & Eccles, J. S. (1992). The development of achievement task values: A theoretical analysis. *Developmental Review, 12*(3), 265–310.

Wigfield, A., & Eccles, J. S. (2000). Expectancy-value theory of achievement motivation. *Contemporary Educational Psychology, 25*(1), 68–81.

Wigfield, A., Eccles, J. S., Yoon, K. S., Harold, R. D., Arbreton, A. J., Freedman-Doan, C., & Blumenfeld, P. C. (1997). Change in children's competence beliefs and subjective task values across the elementary school years: A 3-year study. *Journal of Educational Psychology, 89*(3), 451.

Wise, S. L., & DeMars, C. E. (2005). Low examinee effort in low-stakes assessment: Problems and potential solutions. *Educational Assessment, 10*(1), 1–17. https://doi.org/10.1207/s15326977ea1001_1

Part VI
Curriculum Design and Learners' Lifeworlds

Planning with Concepts: Creating Opportunities for Rich, Meaningful Language Learning in the Design of Curriculum for the Teaching and Learning of Chinese

Kathy Purvis

Abstract An important element of an intercultural approach to teaching and learning languages in the current Australian context is the central role of concepts in curriculum design. There is a shift from a purely descriptive approach to one in which learning is situated within a broader and deeper conceptual exploration. Concepts such as identity, family, friendship, sustainability, harmony, belonging, celebration not only provide a framework for rich and meaningful language learning within an intercultural orientation, but they also connect language learning with learning across curriculum including Humanities and Social Science, English, and the Arts.

Drawing on my experience of developing Chinese language learning modules for the learning of Chinese both as an additional language and for a bilingual program, in this chapter I explore the value, processes and challenges of working with concepts through a discussion of particular modules written for the project.

1 Introduction

This chapter describes the benefits of working with concepts to design curriculum for the additional language learning of Chinese within the Australian educational context. Using examples of Chinese curriculum modules, it will showcase the ways in which concepts can bring valuable dimensions and perspectives to second language teaching and learning and provide opportunities for creating interdisciplinary connections in language learning. The writing and implementation of modules based on concepts was part of a project to develop curriculum for the first bilingual Chinese

---

K. Purvis died before publication of this work was completed.

K. Purvis (✉)
Chinese Language Teachers' Association of South Australia, Adelaide, Australia
e-mail: j.lobianco@unimelb.edu.au

school in South Australia. The project consisted of two strands: a Chinese strand focussed on building language, and a bilingual strand focussed on content learning through a bilingual approach. Two writing teams were formed which collaborated closely in the writing of curriculum outlines for both parts of the project. As a non-native speaker teacher of Chinese, I was part of the Chinese language writing team with a researcher from the University of South Australia and a Chinese native speaker teacher of Chinese. In this project Chinese was introduced from the first year of primary school and the bilingual program began from Year 3 and continued to the end of Year 6 with both Chinese and English being used to teach Humanities and Social Science (HASS), Arts, and Health and Physical Education. The chapter will also show how an approach to languages education which focuses on concepts and the development of conceptual understanding creates a teaching and learning environment which promotes language learning with personal reflection and intercultural comparison, and which has the potential to greatly enhance and enrich additional language learning.

In the first part of this chapter I briefly describe aspects of the theoretical bases which underpin ways of working with concepts. I give a brief overview of the Australian Curriculum which is the national curriculum for all primary and secondary education in Australian schools and the context within which the modules for the project were written. I describe my experience as a language teacher and reflect upon my work in teacher professional development. I discuss the process of choosing the concepts and give examples of concept maps which were developed to show the way in which the modules were sequenced across the year levels from Reception to Year 6.

In the second part of the chapter I analyse two modules: the first exemplifies the ways in which concepts can reinvigorate language teaching and learning, making it more relevant and connected to students' lives and the second shows how concepts can link language learning with learning in diverse curriculum areas. In the concluding section I consider some of the challenges of implementing a curriculum based on concepts and the implications for the role of English as part of a conceptual and intercultural approach to the teaching and learning of Chinese, particularly in the early years.

2 Background and Context

2.1 The Additional Language Learner, the Role of Concepts and the Intercultural in the Learning Process

The ways in which concepts are realised in the modules which were written for the Chinese strand and which from Year 3 were taught alongside the modules which were developed for the HASS strand of the bilingual program depend upon an understanding of what it means to learn an additional language and to communicate meaningfully with speakers of another language as described in the work of researchers such as Byram and Zarate (1994) and Kramsch and Whiteside (2008).

Byram and Zarate (1994) use the term *"savoirs"* to describe the attitudes and skills required by additional language speakers if they are to communicate successfully across language borders. In a recent work, Byram describes *savoir être* in terms of attitudes: "Curiosity and openness, readiness to suspend disbelief" (2021: 62) and comments that the attitudes that are the precondition for successful intercultural interaction *"need to be not simply positive or tolerant, since even positive prejudice or tolerance can hinder mutual understanding. They need to be attitudes of curiosity and openness, of readiness to suspend disbelief and judgement with respect to others" meanings, beliefs, values and behaviours* (45). In order for students learning an additional language to be able to develop these attitudes of "curiosity and openness" I believe that young learners, especially, need to make a personal connection with the texts in order for them to put aside possible judgemental attitudes and to be open to "others' meanings, beliefs values and behaviours". This approach is evident in the emphasis on personalisation within a conceptual framework in the design of the modules described in this chapter.

In their analysis of multilingual interactions Kramsch and Whiteside (2008: 667–8) describe "complex dynamic systems" and the need for the language learner to develop the ability to *"see him/herself through his/her own embodied history and subjectivity and through the history and subjectivity of others"*. In another article they characterise a language learner as *"someone who not only accrues new linguistic knowledge but who also feels thinks, behaves in new ways, and who puts his or her various languages in relation to one another"* (2007: 918). Here emphasis is placed on the need for a personal commitment to the learning of an additional language. As will be demonstrated in the discussion of the two modules, a conceptual approach provides many opportunities to link language learning with students' own experience of the world, thus encouraging personal engagement. This is the first step in the process whereby students can be supported through learning experiences and well-planned class discussion to reflect on their own culture and way of looking at the world through comparison with different cultural perspectives presented in texts studied, and thus to "see him/herself through his/her own embodied history and subjectivity".

The work of Liddicoat and Scarino (2013) has been influential in developing the idea of the intercultural and what it means for the teaching and learning of languages. They focus on the intercultural and emphasise the role of the language learner in the process of learning an additional language:

> *Language teaching and learning from an intercultural perspective places the learner at the meeting point of languages, cultures, and learning. That is, intercultural understanding is not an abstract, but rather an embodied process. Individual learners, with their own linguistic and cultural positionings and identities, are involved in an encounter with alternate positionings and identities that they need to understand and evaluate. Such a focus on the learner recognizes the multiple roles of the language learner in the act of learning...(2013: 51)*

Scarino and Kohler (2014: 29) bring the intercultural and the conceptual approach taken in this chapter together by describing the central importance of concepts to the development of intercultural capability:

> *A key shift in learning languages through the Australian Curriculum is a shift from language learning as descriptive to language learning as conceptual. In language teaching and learning, especially second language learning, students need to acquire the language as well as to learn how to use it. ......When teaching and learning languages shifts to a conceptual level, there is the opportunity for engaging in the intercultural, comparative work that is likely to capture the interest of students.*

The focus on the experience of the learner provided by Kramsch and Whiteside, and Byram and Zarate, and the importance of the relationship between concepts and the intercultural described by Scarino and Kohler have had a significant influence on the design of the modules presented in this chapter. What the modules aim to show is how the goals of language learning described above can be achieved in practice through the selection, sequencing and design of teaching and learning experiences for the Chinese language strand as part of the bilingual program.

2.2 The Australian Curriculum

The Australian Curriculum has been implemented in schools from 2014. It is the national curriculum for all primary and secondary schools in Australia and it is presented as a

> *progression of learning from Foundation – Year 10 that makes clear to teachers, parents, students and others in the wider community what is to be taught, and the quality of learning expected of young people as they progress through school.* Australian Curriculum and Assessment and Reporting Authority (ACARA) (2014a) *F-10 Curriculum* Understand how F-10 curriculum works

The modules described in this chapter have been written in accordance with the curriculum statement described in the Languages learning area of the Australian Curriculum (AC:L). The design of the AC:L curriculum has been influenced by the theoretical perspectives outlined above as can be seen in the introduction. One of the aims stated is to ensure students "understand language, culture, and learning and their relationship, and thereby develop an intercultural capability in communication" and refers in the key ideas to a focus on "both language and culture, as students learn to communicate meaningfully across linguistic and cultural systems, and different contexts". (Australian Curriculum and Assessment and Reporting Authority (ACARA). (2014b) *Australian Curriculum: Languages* Understand how learning area works Key Ideas)

2.3 My Experience as a Language Teacher

I came to the writing of the modules presented in this chapter from the perspective of a practising teacher. I am an additional language speaker of Chinese while most of my teaching colleagues in South Australia are native speakers of Chinese. I have taught both German and Chinese over many years. I lived in Germany for three years, first as a student and then as an exchange teacher. My experience as an exchange teacher taught me for the first time that the way we teach, and our expectations of students are influenced by our own educational culture. My later experience team teaching in China opened my eyes as to the differences in the value placed on education between our two countries. These experiences have led me to reflect critically on my own teaching practices and what I value as the most important educational experiences that I can provide for my students.

Over the years I have provided professional development to language teachers as Languages faculty leader in several metropolitan secondary schools and through the Chinese Language Teachers Association of South Australia. I have led classroom-based research projects in conjunction with the Research Centre for Languages and Cultures at the University of South Australia and mentored and collaborated with university research students engaged in applied linguistics research projects. It is through this work that I have come to understand the importance of the intercultural in language learning and the value of working with concepts, and authentic texts which provide a rich source for intercultural comparison. These insights have significantly influenced my teaching.

2.4 Working with Concepts

In a study in which she describes the process of designing a university Indonesian course based on concepts with the purpose of developing intercultural language learning, Michelle Kohler (2020: 42–3) characterises concepts in the following way:

> *One of the devices that we have for managing experience is 'concepts', and these help us to reason and abstract our understandings beyond any single instance or experience, to multiple instances and manifestations of phenomena that we experience over time. Concepts therefore are the ideational tools that help us organize the world and interpret our experience in it...Concepts can act as a kind of umbrella for planning, as other dimensions of learning such as textual and linguistic content from different domains, can be addressed as part of fleshing out and exploring the concept...*

She goes on to make the observation:

> *Since concepts can be drawn from any domain, there is a need to consider the basis for their selection, in order to maximise their potential in building connections in learning, within concepts, between concepts, and across conceptual systems.*

Kohler draws attention to the value of concepts in building connections and to the importance of thinking carefully about the choice of concepts in order to maximise these connections. In the Chinese strand of the bilingual program four concepts were chosen for each year level from Reception to Year 6. The first module described in this chapter, "Navigating the Neighbourhood", is the third module in the Year 3 curriculum. It illustrates how the concept of place was chosen to enable students to build personal connections with their community and explore their own personal world in ways which provide the opportunity for learning which goes beyond the learning of just vocabulary and grammatical structures as presented in many Chinese language programs. The second module, "Journey to the West", is an example of a module where a concept was chosen which would enable connections to be created across conceptual systems and curriculum areas. It was designed intentionally to complement a module in the HASS curriculum area and the concept of travel and discovery provided a bridge which facilitated the development of cross curriculum perspectives through its parallel exploration in both the HASS and Chinese contexts. As McTighe and Wiggins (2004: 69) comment in relation to concepts or big ideas:

> *Discrete facts do not transfer. Big Ideas are powerful because they embody transferable ideas, applicable to other topics, inquiries, contexts, issues and problems...*

2.5 Selection and Sequencing of Concepts for Modules for Chinese

The selection and sequencing of concepts in the design of curriculum depend of course on the age and linguistic capabilities of the students and the place and function of the Chinese program within the wider school context. In the bilingual school for which this Chinese program was designed, in the first three years of primary school (Reception, Year 1 and 2) students were introduced to the learning of the Chinese language through one lesson a day of formal Chinese instruction. From Year 3 onwards students continued to study Chinese through a separate language program, but Year 3 was also the first year of the four-year bilingual program.

Particularly in the Chinese programming for the first four years, concepts were chosen and sequenced in a way which allowed students to explore and communicate information about their personal world. and at the same time to develop their knowledge of vocabulary and grammar and characters in a systematic way. These concepts in Reception to Year 3 programs included identity, family, and belonging, and they underpinned modules which were closely connected to and sequenced in a similar way to the material in many traditional Chinese courses for young learners. For each year level a concept map was first created which outlined the key concepts, inquiry questions, inquiry processes and texts both receptive and productive. The Year 3 concept map is included as Appendix 1

Once students have acquired a basic linguistic foundation, there is no longer the need to stick rigidly to a particular plan of sequenced development to ensure continuity of language development as students have sufficient foundation in the language to be able to work with a wider range of texts with unfamiliar vocabulary and grammatical constructions. Byram (2021: 104) comments:

> *In language teaching progression in learning is often thought of as linear and cumulative, with each stage depending on preceding ones, 'a journey or pilgrim's progress, a series of steps up a mountain, a straight and narrow path beset with difficulties and dangers, towards a distant goal which few but the truly devoted ever reach' (Trim, 1978: 5)..., In fact, it is only at the earlier stages of learning that the notion of each step depending on previous ones*

> *is evident. At later stages, the image of climbing a mountain can be replaced by the metaphor of completing a jigsaw puzzle, where the early stages have provided the edges and corners and at later stages learners, sometimes with the help of teachers, gradually complete elements of the whole picture . . . .*

After four years of the Chinese language program, students' linguistic skills were strong enough that concepts could be chosen which were more abstract in nature and which connected language learning to wider cross curriculum perspectives. From Year 4 onwards concepts were increasingly chosen to complement the same concepts which underpinned modules from Strand 2 of the bilingual program, which focussed on content learning. The Year 4 concept map is included as Appendix 2

Unlike the way in which the conceptual development in the Indonesian course described by Kohler was designed in advance, in my understanding the two principles of concept selection and sequencing described above emerged gradually, partly in response to feedback provided by the teachers and classroom observation by the writing team. The selection of concepts provided by the first principle was influenced by the kind of continuity provided by traditional approaches to Chinese curriculum in which each unit builds on preceding ones. The second principle relied to a certain extent on the concept development within the Humanities and Social Science (HASS) curriculum. The close alignment of the Chinese and HASS curriculums meant that the building of connections within and between concepts in the HASS curriculum was able to be reflected in the design of the Chinese curriculum from Year 4 to Year 6. At the same time the ability of the two strands of the bilingual program to achieve a close complementarity with each other was only made possible because concepts "embody transferable ideas applicable to other topics, inquiries, contexts issues and problems".

3 The Modules

The modules described here illustrate the two different ways in which concepts were selected and how they informed the design of the module and therefore the teaching and learning experiences through which the concepts were realised in the classroom.

The first of these, "Navigating the Neighbourhood/Community", provides an example of how the choice of the concept takes the traditional teaching of Chinese language beyond the learning of vocabulary, grammar and characters and creates a rich and deep language learning experience. The module provides a strong example of this process because a comparison with the treatment of a similar theme in a locally used Chinese textbook shows most clearly what a difference a conceptual orientation can make.

While the first module is part of the Year 3 program in which modules focus on and connect with students' personal experience as described above, the second module is an illustration of the deliberate selection of a concept which enables the creation of wider connections that bring language learning together with other fields of learning, enriching both. In the module, "Journey to the West", the stories of imaginary journeys which are an important part of Chinese culture come together with real stories of exploration which were part of the history component of the Australian Humanities and Social Sciences (HASS) curriculum through the design of the module based on the concepts of travel and discovery.

3.1 Example Module 1 "Navigating the Neighbourhood/Community"

My own personal journey in coming to understand the process of working with concepts to inform planning is a good illustration of how concepts can fundamentally change one's approach to curriculum design and transform teaching and learning. My planning for the module began with the idea of teaching directions . "Giving directions" is the title of unit of work in a secondary Chinese textbook entitled *Hanyu for Intermediate Students* by Chang et al. (1994) with which I was familiar. The chapter in the textbook has the following subheadings: 'Asking for and giving directions', 'Expressing 'near' and 'far'', 'Numbers 10 000 to 100 000 000', 'Expressing 'how far'', 'Travelling by bus'. The chapter is focussed on teaching vocabulary and grammatical structures which might prove helpful if students ever find themselves in Beijing. As students in the past have rightly pointed out, however, they probably will never visit China, so they had little personal connection with the topic.

When I began thinking about this module I shared my idea of creating a module based on directions with the curriculum writing team. I was supported to consider a conceptual framework for the module based on the concept of place. Place is a very broad concept and there are many ways in which it can be understood so the next step was to workshop together how to interpret and realise the concept for the Year 3 learners for whom it was intended. We considered two different lines of thinking which then formed the basis for the structure of the module. These were physical place in terms of students' journey to school and the physical features of the neighbourhood, the second was place as community. It is important to appreciate that further lines of thinking would have been possible and that the choice of which lines to develop is somewhat arbitrary. This understanding, however, does not diminish in any way the value of concepts.

When I began writing the module and developing these two lines of thinking it became clear to me how my original idea of asking for and giving directions was now integrated into a much bigger and more meaningful learning framework which allowed students to explore their personal connection with place. This shift to working within a conceptual framework meant that students now not only learnt to give directions from their home to school but were also asked to think about the characteristics of the neighbourhood through which they rode their bike or walked or caught the bus to school. As part of an activity in which they followed teacher directions in Chinese as they walked around the streets surrounding their school they noticed and commented on the local area in which their school was situated. They were then asked to write a short report in Chinese commenting on what they had observed during their walk. Following this activity they were shown some photos of the local area surrounding their sister school in Qingdao and took part in a discussion in English about their impressions of the differences between their own local area and that of the Chinese school. The learning inspired by the concept had its starting point in the idea of giving and following directions in Chinese, but it had acquired a larger purpose because of the immediate rather than deferred relevance to the learners themselves. In the Chinese textbook there was no invitation to students to connect their own personal world with the learning of directions. The conceptual framework encouraged students to think about and reflect on the neighbourhood in which they lived, and it is this eliciting of a personal response which helped to connect and engage students and gave them a sense of the value of their language learning in a larger context. The comparison with the local environment of their Chinese sister school offered them the opportunity to reflect more deeply on their understanding of their own local area through the process of comparing and contrasting it to the local environment of their sister school.

The second part of the module focused on place from the perspective of place as community and we decided to concentrate on the aspect of the different kinds of food and culinary traditions associated with students' own personal lives as members of the class community and as part of their local community. This focus provided an opportunity for the exploration of the intercultural as students learnt about the food cultures of the different cultural groups represented in their class community and compared these food cultures with Chinese food culture and their own. This intercultural learning was scaffolded through the following activities. How they contributed to the development of students' intercultural learning is discussed in the following section:

- Students were asked to carry out a survey in English to gain a picture of the different family backgrounds of their classmates.
- Students learnt to recognise orally the names of the countries represented in Chinese and also to recognise the written form of the names and they created a graph of their survey data in Chinese on their iPad.
- In English students described a typical home cooked meal with their family and through a teacher facilitated discussion they were asked to reflect on their own experience of eating a meal and compare it with the experience of others in the class.
- Students were encouraged to put themselves in the shoes of their classmates of Chinese background and from other cultures and talked about what they would enjoy about sharing a meal with a classmate's family from another cultural background. Depending on the cultures represented in the class questions in Chinese and English included the following:

(continued)

> 你喜欢用筷子吃饭吗?为什么?(Do you enjoy eating with chopsticks? Why)? 你喜欢用手吃饭吗?为什么?(Do you enjoy eating with your fingers? Why?) 你喜欢吃什么?小炒、土豆、米饭、面包、肉，蔬菜? (What kind of food do you like to eat? Stir fries/ potato/ rice/ bread/ meat/ vegetarian dishes? What are the advantages of sharing dishes /eating food served on your own plate?)
>
> - As a fun activity students were given instructions in Chinese on how to eat peanuts with chopsticks and after taking part in a competition to see who could eat the most peanuts in a minute they reflected on that experience.

3.2 Developing Intercultural Understanding

Working with concepts as the major principle of design in this module provided the structure and framework for the development of intercultural understanding as students were invited to connect personally with their learning through activities such as those listed above and challenged to think more deeply about their own cultural practices in relation to those of others. Personalisation, reflection and engagement with authentic texts are important elements of the pedagogical process that bring about the realisation of these goals in the classroom.

Personalisation The intercultural learning that comes from the series of activities in which students learn about, experience and reflect on the food culture of their classmates fits well with Byram's characterisation of *savoir être* as "Curiosity and openness, readiness to suspend disbelief about one's own" (2021: 65) and his formulation of objectives for the realisation of this *savoir*.

> *(b) interest in discovering other perspectives on the interpretation of familiar and unfamiliar phenomena both in the cultures of the social groups to which one belongs and in other cultures and practices*
> - *does not assume that familiar phenomena – cultural practices or products common to themselves and the other – are understood in the same way ....aware that they need to discover the other person's understanding of these, and of phenomena in their own cultures which are not familiar to the other person (Byram, 2021: 84).*

Language learning through an intercultural orientation is a personal journey. In order for students to start this journey each one of them must be encouraged to be personally involved in the activities, the discussion and reflection because without personal engagement that shift in the ability to "discover the other person's understanding" as Byram puts it, and to reflect on their own cultural practices will not happen. In one of the activities described above students were asked to imagine that they were sharing a meal with a classmate from a different cultural background and talk about what they would enjoy in that experience. Students were being asked to step out of their own cultural experience and "discover the other person's understanding" and enjoyment of eating a meal. This "decentring" elicits a personal emotional response from the student which is crucial for the language learning which occurs through personalisation.

Personalisation, or bringing students' personal experiences into the learning process, is a necessary part of developing intercultural sensitivity. In a textbook the material to be taught and the accompanying vocabulary and linguistic structures are set down in advance. In a conceptual approach that foregrounds an intercultural orientation, students' personal experiences form a significant part of the material through which the module is developed. Consequently, the realisation of the concept will necessarily be a little different with each group of learners depending on their contribution, based on their experience and interests, their family background, etc. and that means the vocabulary and character development that accompany the module will not be exactly the same for each group of learners.

Reflection The second important element required for developing intercultural understanding in learners is reflection. Scarino and Kohler (2014) describe the process of reflection in the following way:

> It requires decentring; that is, stepping back from one's own ways of perceiving, knowing and being in the world and seeking to enter into another way of perceiving knowing and being in the world. Learning this process of decentring requires processes of reflection that are also crucial to learning (2014: 9).

Discussion around the experiences of eating a family meal together as contributed by the children was an example of this crucial part of developing intercultural sensitivity. Reflection is the process which helps students to see their own experience *in relation to* the experience of others who do not share the same culture. Eating peanuts with chopsticks was a fun activity but it had a serious intent in providing students with the opportunity to experience for themselves what it feels like to be a Chinese person who eats with chopsticks every day; it gave them insight into another person's everyday world and the opportunity to reflect on their own. This is part of the decentring process.

When students have the opportunity to reflect on the experience through discussion aided by questions such as "What does it feel like to eat with chopsticks? If you don't normally eat with chopsticks, do you think you could get used to eating with chopsticks every day? What is good about eating with chopsticks, compared with eating with a knife and fork or eating with your fingers?" they are encouraged to understand that their own practice of eating a meal is only one way of doing it. There are other ways to eat a meal which work equally well for those who are accustomed to eating in that way.

Use of Authentic Texts Authentic texts can play an important role as a vehicle through which students come to understand a concept and develop intercultural perspectives in ways that are appropriate to their age and level of experience and understanding. Authentic texts bring with them the cultural context in which they were written. Kramsch (1998: 6–7) defines three layers of culture: the social in which "members of a social group use language to meet their social needs", the historical where "the culture of everyday practices draws on the culture of shared history and traditions" and the imaginative. The final part of the module extended the idea of community from the classroom to the local community and the learning activities were designed around an authentic Chinese yum cha menu from a local restaurant. The yum cha menu brought together the social and historical layers of culture. It is a menu for a particularly Chinese social activity of sharing a meal where guests enjoy small baskets of steamed and fried food brought to their table on small trolleys. The menu is written in traditional Chinese characters because this style of eating comes from the south of China where traditional characters are more commonly used than in the north.

The text provided the opportunity to talk about the history of simplified characters and explain why the menu was written in traditional characters. Year 3 students could not of course read the whole menu. They were guided through a sequence of activities to assist them to engage with the text and the practice of eating a yum cha meal in a way which introduced traditional characters and helped them become familiar with the names of some of the dishes. To complete this section of the module students took part in a class excursion to the restaurant where they were able to order and enjoy their own yum cha meal. They were encouraged to use chopsticks to eat their meal and to take photos to record their experience.

This learning experience shifted the place in which the learning occurred from the school to the local community and provided the opportunity for students to connect with an aspect of the cultural life of the local community in which their school was situated. Through direct personal experience of the presentation, tastes, and smells of the food and observation of other diners they discovered that familiar everyday cultural practices such as eating at a restaurant are not the same for everyone in their community. This intercultural learning was reinforced through a follow up activity in which students created a photo story in English and Chinese, explaining what their photos showed and reflecting on their experience. What did they learn? What did they enjoy? What did they find most different or striking about their experience Would they like to take their parents to the restaurant? Why/why not? Is it good to have places like this in their neighbourhood where they can have a little taste of life in another country? Students displayed their stories in the school foyer and took them home to share with their families.

The concept of place in its interpretations as place in the physical sense and in the social sense as place in the community provided a cohesive thread that connected the learning experiences in this module and created the framework for both connecting the Chinese language learning with the real world of students' everyday experience of their local area and also broadening their intercultural understanding of the diversity in their class and local community. These learnings were achieved through learning which was personalized, through working with resources such as the authentic text from the restaurant, and authentic experiences such as the visit to the restaurant and through discussion and questioning which prompted students to reflect on their learning and develop deeper understanding of their own cultural life and that of others.

3.3 Example Module 2: "Journey to the West"

The Year 4 module entitled "Journey to the West", based on the concept of journey and discovery, was designed for students who had acquired a basic linguistic foundation in Chinese. As Kohler (2020) comments, concepts "can act as a kind of umbrella for planning" (42) and in this module the concept of journey and discovery provided the umbrella underneath which the Chinese language module was able to make a connection with the history component of the Australian HASS curriculum and a module entitled "Exploration" created by the bilingual writing team, by bringing together imaginary journeys described in traditional Chinese stories and real journeys of exploration.

The first imaginary story in the Chinese module explored the idea of journey as discovery and personal enrichment through the traditional Chinese story of the *Frog in the Well* 井底之蛙. The Chinese text is difficult and as with all authentic texts the teacher needs to think carefully about how to adapt and scaffold the text so that the students in the class can understand, enjoy the story and then respond to it. This text invited them to question the value of travel and discovery and to reflect on their own identity as a risk taker. To assist students to reflect on what kind of person they are they took part in a class discussion based on the following questions: "Do you think the frog should leave his well and go out into the world?" "What are the advantages and the risks of venturing out of the well?" "Would you rather be the comfortable frog in his well or the well-travelled turtle who has seen the world and the ocean?" After this discussion students were asked to create a bilingual poster illustrating the story in Chinese characters copied from a list provided by the teacher and to write a short reflection in English explaining which character (frog or turtle) they would rather be and why.

In this approach to the story the concept of travel and discovery was explored with students through a personal perspective. What does it mean to travel and what does discovery look like in a personal context? This conceptual orientation gave to that learning a scope for students to explore and reflect on their experiences and learn about themselves in a way which went beyond the context of language learning understood as the acquisition of linguistic code. It provided an added incentive for learners to engage with Chinese. Learning to recognise and write Chinese characters and reading Chinese character texts is a slow, time-consuming process and may be challenging for many learners. If they realise that character learning is not an end in itself but that their developing ability to read Chinese can bring with it the enjoyment of reading and responding personally and imaginatively to interesting stories they are much more likely to engage with their Chinese learning and accept the discipline of character practice.

From the subjective realm of the personal and imaginary in the first part of the module the focus shifts to a factual, historical perspective on discovery in the next section, thus providing the opportunity for the Chinese teacher to plan collaboratively with the HASS teacher teaching the module entitled "Exploration". Both the Chinese module "Journey to the West" and the HASS module "Exploration" taught students factual information about the journeys of discovery of Captain Cook and Zheng He. In the Chinese module students learnt the names, nationalities, countries visited, and the dates of the journeys in Chinese and discussed the reasons for the voyages and what the explorers brought back with them in English.

The text at the centre of the final segment of the module explored the concept of journey and discovery once again through the story of an imaginary journey. It was based on the real adventures of the monk Xuanzhang and is one of the four great classical novels of Chinese literature, 西游记 *Journey to the West*. To gain an understanding and insight into Chinese culture, as Kramsch (1998: 8) points out, it is important to have an appreciation not only of the "**sociocultural context** of language study".

> There is, in addition, a third essential layer to culture, namely, the imagination. Discourse communities are characterized not only by facts and artifacts, but by common dreams, fulfilled and unfulfilled imaginings. These imaginings are mediated through the language, that over the life of the community reflects, shapes and is a metaphor for its cultural reality.

While the historical background of the story was briefly explained to students the main aim of this segment of the module was for students to become familiar with the story, to consider what it means to be a traveller encountering both exciting new experiences and obstacles that must be overcome and to enjoy the story in the same way that young Chinese children do when they first encounter the story. They learnt about the magical character of the Monkey King and followed one part of the Monk's long voyage to India when he crossed the Liu Sha river and had to overcome the river monster in search of the holy Buddhist texts.

Working with an authentic work of this complexity requires a considerable amount of preparation and thought by the teacher to present it to the students in a form that they can understand and enjoy in Chinese. First the teacher needs to decide how much of the text to introduce to students and which section of it will best support an understanding of the concept, giving students a sense of the challenges that arise during a long journey but also appealing to students' imagination. Although the preparation required for working with the story is considerable, this is a major work of Chinese literature, and well worth the effort. In addition, it added another dimension to the realisation of the concept for this module as it focussed on the experience of journeying, and meeting and overcoming the unexpected problems and obstacles that arise when travelling far from home.

The cross-curriculum approach exemplified in this module was developed in the context of a bilingual program, but it has a value and application which go beyond this setting, particularly in the primary school context. In many Australian primary schools language is taught by a specialist teacher for one or two lessons a week. Students and teachers often see these lessons as separate from the learning that takes place with the class teacher. Working with concepts in the design of language curriculum offers a way of creating a bridge so that language learning can add richness and depth to student learning in other areas of the curriculum such as HASS, thus raising the value of languages in the eyes of both students and teachers.

4 Considerations

4.1 The Challenges of Concept-Based Approaches to Content Learning

While there is much value in working with concepts as has been outlined above it is important to also acknowledge some of the issues that arise when planning and teaching curriculum using concepts as an 'umbrella'. An earlier part of this chapter outlined the two principles which guided the selection of concepts for the modules, but the choice of concept is only the first part of the process of developing the module. The second part is to decide how to work with the concept once chosen. One of the advantages of working with concepts is that they are big ideas and so there are many ways of approaching teaching and learning based on them. It must also be recognised that not all approaches to working with a concept can be successfully translated into language teaching and learning experiences for students. Once the concept has been chosen the next step in the realisation of the design of the module is to determine which aspects of the concept are most suitable for development depending on the age, linguistic capability and level of conceptual understanding of the students and to consider the availability of suitable resources.

Ideas for exploring the concepts can come from a number of different sources. For the modules in this project some were suggested by the kinds of linguistic and cultural content that were considered important at a particular stage of students' linguistic and cultural/intercultural development. For some of the modules a Chinese saying related to the concept offered a stimulus for moving forward with the concept. Thinking for the module "Journey to the West" was partly inspired by the saying, 读万卷书不如行万里路 (Travelling a thousand miles is much better than reading a thousand books.) The starting point for another module based on the concept of harmony was the saying: 天人合一 (People and nature in harmony). The particular example of "Journey to the West" drew both concept and some ideas for its development from the HASS curriculum and from the Chinese saying mentioned above.

While the concepts for many modules from the bilingual project draw their inspiration from the HASS curriculum, working with concepts can equally create opportunities for connections with other curriculum areas. In literacy development the concepts in some modules written for this project also enabled connections to be made with English, the Arts, and Health and Physical Education curriculum areas. One of the texts for the Year 3 module entitled "Gardens" based on the concept of harmony mentioned above, for example, was the English language children's picture book *Uno's Garden* (Base, 2013). The teacher incorporated the book into her English program as well as discussing the pictures with her students in Chinese. These kinds of connections which are made possible through a focus on concepts as a design principle open up content areas in languages teaching and learning which are surprising but also inspiring both for teachers and students, as well as cross curriculum opportunities.

4.2 The Role of English

The role of first language instruction in the languages classroom has been controversial in the past (Ostovar-Namaghi, 2015; Yadav, 2014; Cummins, 2007). However, one of the pedagogical implications of working with concepts in the design of curriculum for this project is that English acquires an important role alongside the use of the target language, Chinese, in the teaching and learning process.

Many teachers of languages still believe that it is important to use as much of the target language in class as possible. For most students it is their only opportunity for exposure to the language. They may be willing to accept that the use of students' first language is useful in establishing class relationships, teaching grammar and managing behaviour. The introduction to the Australian Curriculum: Languages makes it clear that the value of English does not reside in its function in classroom organisation and management, but in fact plays an important role in an intercultural orientation to language learning.

> *Learning to communicate involves reflection and analysis, as students move between the new language being learnt and their own existing language(s)...It is not a 'one-plus-one' relationship between two languages and cultures, where each language and culture stays separate and self-contained. Comparison and reference between (at least) two languages and cultures build understanding of how languages 'work', how they relate to each other and how language and culture shape and reflect experience, that is the experience of language using and language learning.* (ACARA, 2014b Australian Curriculum: Languages Introduction)

Kramsch and Whiteside (2008: 667–8) do not mention the role of English but their comments quoted earlier offer a further perspective on "how language and culture shape and reflect experience" when they talk about "complex dynamic systems" and the need for language learners to develop the ability to "*see him/herself through his/her own embodied history and subjectivity and through the history and subjectivity of others*".

In the teaching and learning process concepts are given expression through texts and learning experiences which enable students to explore their own and others understanding of big ideas in ways which are meaningful to them. In concept-based design English performs an important role as part of this meaning making process. This does not mean that the use of the target language is neglected. In a sense it can be said that a concept-based approach works with texts on at least two levels. On one level students need to become familiar with the text so that they can understand the information presented in oral and/or written form and respond to factual questions. At this level the focus is on the use of the target language and the development of the grammar and vocabulary required for them to understand the text. At the next more abstract level students are invited to make comparisons between the Chinese language and culture embodied in the text and their own language and culture, to make connections between the text and the concept that it exemplifies and to reflect on their own personal lives and how their interaction with the text may have contributed to their own way of thinking and being. At this level English becomes an essential part of the learning process.

The Year 5 module "Celebrations and Festivals" offers an example of the use of English in these ways. The module is based on the Mid-Autumn Festival. In the first part students watched a video in Chinese introducing the Mid-Autumn Festival and with the support of written questions in Chinese they wrote a short report in Chinese based on the video. In this section the focus was on developing Chinese language skills and learning factual information about the festival. Students then watched another short video about the symbols associated with Mid-Autumn festival, concentrating particularly on the importance of the homonym 柚子 (yòuzi pomelo) to represent 保佑 (bǎoyòu bless and protect). Homonyms play an important role in the symbols associated with festivals in China. Students were asked to consider why there were many more of these words with double meanings in the Chinese language than in English and therefore why these symbols based on word play might play an important role in Chinese celebrations but not in the celebrations with which they were familiar. These questions provided the scaffolding which supported students to come to an appreciation of one aspect of the difference in the way language functions in Chinese and English and the way language and culture are connected. The focus on homonyms and their importance in shaping the nature of celebrations is an illustration of "how language and culture shape and reflect experience".

The use of English to draw comparisons between languages and cultures , to connect with learners' experience through personalisation and reflection is central to the development of intercultural understanding and deep learning in that it provides the bridge which supports students to connect the concrete factual learning acquired through Chinese language in the texts in the modules with the higher order thinking skills of comparison and reflection which are required for an understanding of the concept and the ability to see one's own culture in a new light.

5   Conclusion

Working with concepts in the design of language curriculum is both challenging and rewarding. Commercially available course materials provide few resources that are suited to concept-based learning and for the teacher finding appropriate resources and adapting them for use in the classroom is a time-consuming process. Also, the rethinking that is required for many teachers in accepting the role of English in some aspects of learning, particularly at earlier phases of learning, in the developing of conceptual thinking can take them out of their comfort zone. This is particularly the case for overseas trained teachers whose personal experience of learning a second language and teacher education courses have contributed to a strong commitment to the use of the target language as much as possible in the classroom. Nevertheless, for the teacher who is willing to embrace these challenges and question their own assumptions about teaching and learning languages, the value of working with concepts within an intercultural orientation is significant.

As has been shown in this chapter curriculum design based on concepts has a solid foundation in applied linguistic research which shows that the ability to communicate meaningfully across language and cultures is a complex dynamic process that requires a lot more than the ability to rote learn vocabulary lists and create grammatically correct sentences. The intercultural orientation which requires a conceptual orientation to curriculum design invites students to explore their own identity and reflect on their own beliefs and values as they engage with the language and culture in the texts with which they interact, not only making them better able to communicate effectively in Chinese but also teaching them about themselves and the world in which they live. Tthis kind of learning is both powerful and engaging.

Working with concepts provides opportunities for teachers to think in different ways about the kinds of content that can be explored in language curricula. Concepts open up fresh perspectives on traditional curriculum design for language learning but also provide pathways for developing new content areas not often explored in languages teaching.

This process of widening the scope of languages curriculum is further enhanced by the usefulness of concepts as big ideas to create connections across curriculum areas. Cross curriculum collaboration creates the opportunity for a common concept to be explored at depth through different subject perspectives, thus enriching both curriculum areas and enhancing the relevance of both subjects to the bigger picture of student learning.

The value of a conceptual orientation to curriculum design in languages within an intercultural orientation lies not only in what it brings to languages learning and learning across the curriculum. In this approach students learn knowledge, understanding and dispositions which have a wider and deeper application to the development of the student as a whole person. Learners develop higher order thinking skills as they engage with quite complex concepts; they understand that knowledge is transferable as they see connections across subjects. They develop empathy through intercultural learning as they come to understand themselves and appreciate the world from the perspective of people who are different from themselves. These understandings make for good language learners who are sensitive to the nuances of language and languages, and beyond that they lay the foundation for those learners to become good future citizens, able to think deeply, draw connections across areas of knowledge , and show empathy and care for people from different linguistic and cultural backgrounds.

Acknowledgement I wish to acknowledge the significant influence of the writing team of which I was a part in the development of the modules. The collaborative environment was a very important factor in guiding my thinking and contributing to the shaping of the modules. I am indebted to Angela Scarino who provided the direction of working with concepts and much of the conceptual framework for the modules. As a non-native teacher of Chinese, it was also important to receive input and advice from a native speaker of Chinese. Lihua (Jenny) Jin who, apart from proofreading the Chinese, also provided me with many valuable insights into Chinese perspectives and ways of thinking which strengthened the intercultural aspects of the modules. Conversations with Kate Loechel who designed Strand 2 of the bilingual curriculum provided me with a deeper understanding of this part of the bilingual program.

Appendices

Appendices 1 and 2 are examples of the concept map of modules created for each year level from Reception to the end of Year 6. They map the four concepts/themes (one each per ten-week school term) which form the building blocks of the curriculum for each year level and together they provide an overview which shows the continuity of development of the curriculum over the 7 years of the program.

Once a concept/theme was proposed inquiry questions were developed which informed the approach taken to working with the concept. The modules were divided into two, or usually three, segments, each with a specific focus. In the module "Journey to the West" for example the three segments were 'Personal journey/story', 'The Monkey King story' and 'Mythological journeys'. The process of deciding upon the segments which provided the next level of structure for the more detailed teaching and learning program went hand in hand with the exploration of the availability of resources to ensure that the concept could be unpacked in a way appropriate to the age level and linguistic ability of the student cohort. Together with the resources, productive and receptive texts were developed and enquiry processes determined to create learning experiences for the students designed to support them to gain an understanding of the concept through the inquiry questions.

The modules highlighted in blue are the modules discussed in this chapter.

Appendix 1: Year 3 Chinese Concept Map

Term	Term 1	Term 2	Term 3	Term 4
Key concepts / themes	Identity	Belonging	Place	Harmony
	• Friends • Daily / weekly activities (and how they reflect identity and values) • A Chinese student's day	• Leisure, hobbies, interests – choices • Participating • Belonging to a group / team	• Navigating the neighbourhood / community • Eating out and at home	• Gardens in Adelaide • Tian ren he yi • The Chinese garden
Inquiry questions	How do our activities reflect identity and values? How does my day at school compare….? [An inquiry into the self, relationships with friends and family, communities, cultures]	What do my interests reflect about me? [An inquiry into the self, interests, choices, and participating in teams]	Where is our school situated? [An inquiry into orientation to place; the interdependence of the individual's situatedness in place and communities / diverse communities / cultural values in communities]	How do people live in their environment? Why do human beings create gardens? [An inquiry into the relationship between nature, design, human beings and aesthetics]
Inquiry processes	noticing identifying recognising listening experimenting comparing questioning	noticing identifying recognising listening experimenting comparing questioning	listening noticing comparing recognising reflecting planning questioning	listening noticing comparing recognising reflecting questioning
Texts (receptive / productive)	description blog presentation (oral)	summary (data / graphic presentation) correspondence (note, text message)	recount (written and oral)	description narrative

Appendix 2: Year 4 Chinese Concept Map

Term	Term 1	Term 2	Term 3	Term 4
Key concepts / themes	Journey to the West *discovery, travel, adventure, science* • Personal journey / story • The Monkey King story • Mythological journeys	People and places *experience, emotion, citizenship* • We are all Australian • Coming to Australia • I am a good citizen	A culinary journey through China *tradition, change* • Food etiquette and traditions • Food and the connection to the land in different parts of China • Food and well-bring	Images of China / Australia *representation, imagination* • In poems / stories • In art works • In our city / community / school • [need titles here]
Inquiry questions	[an inquiry into journeying to discover] What do we gain from travel?	[an inquiry into the diversity of people in diverse landscapes; building citizenship / belonging / identity] What makes me Australian? Why do people move? How do we act as good citizens?	[an inquiry into food / food traditions / influences and how they travel inside and outside China / the meaning of food] Where does our food come from? How does the land make a difference to the food we eat? Why do food traditions travel across the world?	[an inquiry into perceptions – how we see things and experimentation with different modes of expression] What do you see in the image? Do we all see the same things?
Inquiry processes	listening, speaking, reading, writing, expressing preferences, discussing, describing	listening, speaking, reading, writing, recording / tabulating sequencing / ordering summarisings	listening, speaking, reading, writing, explaining comparing describing	listening, speaking, reading, writing, comparing / connecting interpreting representing
Texts	text messages greeting cards discussions	recording / tabulating sequencing / ordering summarising	menus discussions lists class forum	narratives artworks poems class forum

References

Australian Curriculum and Assessment and Reporting Authority (ACARA). (2014a). *F-10 curriculum*. Retrieved from https://www.australiancurriculum.edu.au/f-10-curriculum/. Accessed 2 June 2022.

Australian Curriculum and Assessment and Reporting Authority (ACARA). (2014b). *Australian curriculum: Languages*. Retrieved from https://www.australiancurriculum.edu.au/f-10-curriculum/languages/. Accessed 2 June 2022.

Base, G. (2013). *Uno's garden*. Puffin.

Byram, M. (2021). *Teaching and assessing intercultural communicative competence: Revisited* (2nd ed.). Multilingual Matters.

Byram, M., & Zarate, G. (1994). *Définitions, objectifs et évaluation de la compétence socioculturelle*. Report for the Council of Europe, Strasbourg.

Chang, P., Mackerras, A., & Yu, H.-C. (1994). *Hanyu for intermediate students*. Longman.

Cummins, J. (2007). Rethinking monolingual instructional strategies in multilingual classrooms. *Canadian Journal of Applied Linguistics, 10*(2), 221–240.

Kohler, M. (2020). *Developing intercultural language learning*. Springer Nature.

Kramsch, C. (1998). *Language and culture*. Oxford University Press.

Kramsch, C., & Whiteside, A. (2007). Three fundamental concepts in second language acquisition and their relevance in multilingual contexts. *Modern Language Journal, 91*, 907–922.

Kramsch, C., & Whiteside, A. (2008). Language ecology in multilingual settings: Towards a theory of symbolic competence. *Applied Linguistics, 29*(4), 645–671.

Liddicoat, A. J., & Scarino, A. (2013). *Intercultural language teaching and learning*. Wiley-Blackwell.

McTighe, J., & Wiggins, G. (2004). *Understanding by design: Professional development workbook*. Association for Supervision and Curriculum Development (ASCD).

Ostovar-Namaghi, S. E. (2015). First language use in teaching a foreign Language: Theoretical perspectives and empirical findings. *US-China Foreign Language, 13*(9), 615–622.

SACE Board Strategic Plan 2020–2023. Retrieved from https://www.sace.sa.edu.au/thrive/. Accessed May 2022.

Scarino, A., & Kohler, M., with Benedetti, A. (2014). *Investigating pedagogies for language-and-culture learning*. Project commissioned by the Department for Education and Child Development.

The Shape of the Australian Curriculum: Languages. Retrieved from http://www.acara.edu.au/verve/_resources/the_shape_of_the_australian_curriculum_v4.pdf. Accessed Sept 2022.

Trim, J. L. M. (1978). *Developing a unit/credit scheme of adult language learning*. Pergamon Press.

Yadav, M. K. (2014). Role of mother tongue in second language learning. *International Journal of Research, 1*(11), 572–582.

Chinese Language Education in Australia: Attending to the Lifeworlds of Learners

Angela Scarino and Michelle Kohler

Abstract Given the history of the presence of Chinese in the landscape in Australia it is now one of the languages that presents the greatest variation in learner background in languages education. This diversity of backgrounds is generally understood as a structural and pedagogical challenge (Orton JM. Chin Educ Soc 49:369–375. https://doi.org/10.1080/1061/932.2016.1283939, 2016) with impact on Chinese language learning in schools.

What is less evident is the fundamental difference that pertains to the learners' lifeworlds and their affiliation with Chinese, their perceptions of its value, nature, and the purpose for learning it, and the different personal meanings that Chinese language learning can hold for diverse learners of the language in Australia.

In this chapter, we discuss a case study with a single teacher of Chinese, working with a range of learners of senior secondary Chinese, enacting a curricular intervention designed within a multilingual and intercultural orientation. We illustrate the ways in which the teacher addresses the nature and purpose for learning for diverse learners within the class group. In particular, we consider themes related to the students' lifeworlds, their affiliation with the language and culture and their identity, and the multilingual and intercultural nature and purpose of learning for the diverse learners of this language.

1 Introduction

The teaching and learning of Chinese language and culture in Australian schooling is set in the distinctive context of its dynamic migration history and equally dynamic languages education policy settings. These histories, in turn, reside within a macro socio-political environment marked by globalisation and neoliberal ideologies. The teaching and learning of Chinese in Australia at the present time needs to be

A. Scarino (✉) · M. Kohler
University of South Australia, Adelaide, SA, Australia
e-mail: angela.scarino@unisa.edu.au

understood in relation to the intense politicisation that these ideologies yield. It is now set in a complex world where we see, for example, increasing mobility of people whose presence is not always welcome; xenophobic attitudes, tensions and conflict based on different social and cultural backgrounds and faiths; unpredictable and largely global job markets; inequalities between rich and poor; greater uncertainty for people, and more—all of which influence languages education in marked ways. In addition, there are tensions between the goal of developing proficiency in Chinese for economics and trade and the expanded understandings from the field that support educational, humanistic and aesthetic goals.

In this chapter, firstly, we discuss the place of Chinese language and culture learning in Australian education noting, in particular, the increasing diversity of learners. We discuss the structural ways in which this diversity has been understood and addressed, with related consequences. We then discuss some directions in language education that open up possibilities for reimagining language learning in general, and Chinese language learning in particular. Drawing on a case study with a single teacher of Chinese, working with a range of learners who bring experiences of Chinese language and culture to their learning, we discuss ways in which Chinese language learning might become more meaningful to all these diverse learners. We consider themes related to the lifeworlds, of students of Chinese that offer affordances for meaningful teaching and learning, recognising their diverse affiliations with Chinese language and culture and identity, and the multilingual and intercultural nature and purpose of learning for these diverse learners.

1.1 The Chinese Language and Culture in Australian Society and Education

The Chinese community has had and continues to have a strong presence in Australia across several generations. In the most recent 2021 census (ABS https://www.abs.gov.au/census), China was the second largest country of birth after India. It is the highest in relation to ancestry, highlighting a continuous flow of Chinese migration. It is also the first in the category of languages spoken at home. This migration history means that Chinese language and culture courses are offered from primary through to university levels, as well as through community/heritage language programs.

Provision has also been shaped by policies supporting the learning of Asian languages, following the release of the report prepared for the Council of Australian Governments entitled *Asian Languages and Australia's Economic Future* (COAG, 1994). This policy document recommended targets for the teaching of four Asian languages: Chinese, Japanese, Indonesian and Korean, as priority Asian languages. However, at issue was firstly, that the languages were prioritised according to data from the Department of Foreign Affairs and Trade and thus the policy report foregrounded a largely economic and trade relations rationale which was far removed from the K-12 students' life and language learning reality, and secondly, the fact that the targets in line with the economic agenda, were unrealistic and remained unmet. It would be fair to say that no language has been more strongly linked to socio-political and economic agendas than Chinese. Furthermore, Chinese language and culture programs in Australia post-covid are situated in a highly complex environment where these neoliberal discourses of economics and trade persist and, crucially, do so at a moment when China remains Australia's major trading partner and China-Australia relations have been particularly strained.

Within this complex social and educational environment, Chinese language and culture programs are currently available to an immense diversity of learners with home background in Chinese being the dominant basis for categorisations. Within all groupings of students of Chinese, there are varying degrees of experience and proficiency in Chinese. Students are likely to use the Chinese language in different ways for different purposes, and in diverse contexts across a multilingual, mobile and digital world. The use of Chinese is part of the multiple linguistic and cultural environments in which learners live and learn. They bring to the learning of Chinese, diverse biographies, trajectories of experiences, affiliations and relationships with the Chinese language and culture and often diverse additional languages, expectations and desires and aspirations in relation to learning Chinese. In typical Chinese language learning in Australia, it is likely that there are students who are learning Chinese as an additional language, with or without prior school learning experience of learning Chinese, and with English or diverse home languages (e.g. Vietnamese, Italian); there are also learners who have some home background in Chinese (or dialects), with highly diverse language profiles with respect to literacy and proficiencies in Chinese, but generally well-versed in aspects of cultural life; and there are first language learners of Chinese also a highly diverse group, who use Chinese regularly and who have experienced a part of their education in China. This latter grouping may also include Chinese-speaking international students. In general, Chinese language programs in schools, at least in the K-10 years, are available for all students and, in general, the default arrangement is that they are designed primarily for students with no prior knowledge of Chinese. At senior secondary level, where feasible in terms of the number of students, courses for 'background' learners may be provided. These arrangements serve administrative purposes because the numbers of students do not usually permit the offering of differentiated programs. An assumption is made, on the one hand, that separating the groups would be meaningful for learners where this is possible, and on the other hand, that where differentiated courses cannot be provided, that differentiation will be managed successfully through pedagogy. This means that the learning of those students with Chinese language from their home is not necessarily extended; at the same time, those students without a home background perceive their Chinese background peers to have an 'advantage' and often discontinue their Chinese language learning when they feel that they are competing with their Chinese background peers, and it is just too difficult to do so (Orton, 2016). This situation is a problem at a number of levels. Firstly, it suggests that knowing a language creates 'advantages' for some and 'disadvantages' for others when this kind of discourse of competition is in fact unhelpful to all. Secondly, it foregrounds monolingual proficiency in language use as the dominant goal of learning, when much more learning that is of value can be derived from learning Chinese (see Leung & Scarino, 2016). Thirdly, it indicates the way in which educational systems and language teaching and learning are geared for uniformity in an Australian context that is structured for a monolingual stance towards education and a largely singular approach for all.

To address this phenomenon, which at the present time is more highly marked in Chinese than in any other language in Australian education, educational authorities have, over time, created course structures that seek to represent different levels of Chinese learning. In the Australian Curriculum (ACARA, 2011), for example, the curriculum framework for Chinese has been elaborated at three levels: *second language learners* (for those who are introduced to the Chinese language at school, as an additional language; *background learners* (for those who may use Chinese at home and have knowledge of Chinese to varying degrees); and *fist language learners* (for those who have undertaken at least primary schooling in Chinese). At senior secondary level, where the study of Chinese may be undertaken as part of the senior secondary certificate of education, which marks the end of the secondary cycle of education, and the results of which contribute to scores for entry into university studies, these groupings lead to differentiated assessments, in the interests of 'fairness' to all. (See Elder, 2000a, b, for an extended discussion of the processes, consequences and fairness of these assessments; see also Scarino et al., 2011 for a report on an empirical study undertaken nationally in Australia to investigate learner background in Asian languages, including Chinese). Senior secondary assessment authorities have created 'eligibility criteria' for entry into specific courses, as a mechanism that provides the basis for inclusion and exclusion.

The educational system for Chinese language learning has now been structured around this phenomenon of different groupings. At some level this categorisation reflects one of the dimensions of the diversity of learners, but it also introduces the problems of any categorisation, notably that each category comes to be seen as a firm, distinctive and homogenous grouping. The categorisation also inherits the problem of restricted foci of assessment (that is, assessment of 'proficiency' in Chinese without consideration of additional capabilities that may be derived from learning Chinese). This, in turn, defines the nature and scope of Chinese language learning. The categories do not necessarily fit the needs, desires and aspirations of the learners and do not necessarily permit an expansive view of Chinese language learning which we consider to be necessary in contemporary times. Furthermore, from a learning perspective, the learner 'background' is generally understood as a fixed trait or characteristic and does not recognise the way in which linguistic and cultural background is constitutive of learning (Gutiérrez & Rogoff, 2003; Gutiérrez et al., 2019), that is, that learners come to interpret, understand and learn through the lenses of the language(s) and culture(s) of their primary socialisation. The categories, therefore, ultimately conceal more than they reveal. The prioritising of learners background in Chinese language elides processes of profiling learners in ways that better capture the learners as individuals in all their diversity as a basis for a kind of Chinese language learning that supports their social, emotional, intellectual, aesthetic, and ethical development.

1.2 Learners and Their Lifeworlds

All students of Chinese bring to their learning their own history of experiences, learning, understandings and meaningfulness that come from these experiences. This is their *lifeworld*, that is, all that students bring to their learning and the knowledge and practices that they draw upon as they create new learning. This lifeworld is not static, but rather, it is ever evolving and provides the background through which students come to understand themselves and ideas/knowledge as meaningful (see Gadamer, 2004). What students know and draw upon as they come to know is embedded in a world of meanings and pre-understandings that are socially, culturally, and historically constituted. This world of meanings is culturally grounded. When the reality of students' diverse lifeworlds is taken into account, the classroom becomes a meeting place where students' lifeworlds, including their languages, continue to be shaped intersubjectively through interaction with peers, more knowledgeable others (teachers and other contributors to learning), and resources in the material environment. It is in this sense that the classroom becomes a site of cultural knowledge exchange and cultural formation. Learners use their linguistic and cultural repertoires, as a whole, in the service of meaning making in diverse contexts and learn from the experience of doing so. Kramsch (2002) considers language learners as language *users* whose participation in semiotic (and not just linguistic) interactions creates opportunities for language learning. She sees learning as involving not only one person interacting with another, but rather a whole history of experiences and memories interacting with another history of experiences and memories (Kramsch, 2009).

Liddicoat and Scarino (2013), taking a hermeneutic and multilingual and intercultural perspective, foreground the role of interpretation as students negotiate meanings, their positioning and identities in and through language learning. Any exchange involves interpreting the concepts/ideas being exchanged as well as interpreting self (*intra*culturality), in relation to others (*inter*culturality), and through this, increasingly coming to understand the linguistic and cultural construction of meaning. Within this perspective the learner is understood as *learner*, as *language user* and *as person* (Liddicoat & Scarino, 2013, pp. 51–56), moving between languages and cultures:

> All the languages and cultures the learner encounters play a role in the mediation processes involved in learning, and in this way the learner is positioned in an intercultural space in which multiple languages and cultures are tools through which learning is achieved. For particular groups of learners, the ways in which languages and cultures are distributed across the social contexts of learning varies. (p. 51).

The language learner is also a *user* of the language being learned when the language is used for personal expression. When learners are positioned as language users, the focus turns to who the learners are, and what they bring to the learning of the language. Here, as Liddicoat and Scarino (2013) indicate, it is important to distinguish between a '*legitimate user*', invited to genuinely and authentically interpret and create meanings, and a '*pseudo-user*', invited to provide interpretations and responses which are not personal and therefore meaningful to them. Importantly, the language learner is also *a person*. Each learner has a distinct personal history of languages and cultures that form their identity, and each has a personal relationship with the language being learnt.

Understanding learners in this way, means that they have multiple positions—learners, users, persons—in engaging with languages and cultures. In Chinese language learning the diversity of learners in the Australian educational context has been recognised but this has been in relation to structural 'eligibility' (and the related inclusions and exclusions) more than in relation to the possibilities that come from a productive, generative recognition of the diversity—possibilities of shaping the positions available to students for the interpretation and creation of meaning, and for participation that explores who the learners can be and wish to be in Chinese in the Australian context. Enacting these possibilities requires an expansion of the orientation and goals of learning Chinese.

1.3 Directions in Language Education

The changing, social, cultural, and economic world and the increasing diversities of societies and therefore students, call for an expansion of languages education—its orientation and goals. A major shift in understanding the learning of languages is from a monolingual to a multilingual view of language learning. This has been expressed in diverse ways including 'the multilingual turn' (May, 2014), 'metrolingualism' (Pennycook & Otsjui, 2015), 'translanguaging' (García & Li, 2014), and 'translingual practices' (Canagarajah, 2013), among other formulations. This includes the notion that languages in use are blended and combined in holistic, flexible, multimodal ways to render meanings. The 'multilingual turn' recognises that learning an additional language is in itself a multilingual and intercultural act where the focal language being learnt interacts with the languages that learners bring to language learning.

An important orientation advanced in the body of work of Claire Kramsch (see Kramsch, 2009, 2011), Michael Byram (2021) among others, is an intercultural orientation. This orientation, as elaborated by Liddicoat and Scarino (2013) (c.f. Kohler, 2020; Scarino, 2014), sees intercultural capability as a reciprocal, interpretive process of making sense of the ideas/concepts being exchanged and the person. Within this orientation, language learning begins with the linguistic and cultural profile of the learners that comes from their lifeworlds, and the recognition of the mediating role of languages and cultures in the act of learning (see Leung and Scarino (2016) for a discussion of expanded goals). It seeks to enact a richer view of the languages learning that goes beyond an instrumental view that has characterised Asian language learning in Australia, including the learning of Chinese. As McNamara (2019) has stated:

> Defining the goals and meaning of language learning in purely functional, communicative terms ignores the role of language learning in the subjective experience of the learner as an individual with a history, both personal and cultural… erases all historical and cultural

differences among languages and learners in their specific socio-cultural and historical contexts as determining influences on the motivation to learn languages. (p.116)

To this foregrounding of the personal, subjective dimension of language learning, Pennycook (2019) includes critical and activist dimensions; he states:

A central goal of language education is surely the development of critical and resourceful language users who have good access to a range of linguistic resources, are good at shifting between styles, discourses, registers and genres and whose developing language practices aim not just at personal but also social change." (p. 171)

These perspectives invite an expanded view of language learning in which language is an object or system as well as action and interpretation. Furthermore, it is not only something that people use but it is also recognised that people are 'at home' in their language and culture (Gadamer, 2004) and that it is through language in interaction that people come to establish understanding. It invites gearing teaching and learning towards making meaning, enhancing experience and developing identity (Creese & Blackledge, 2015).

Intercultural language learning offers an expanded construct where there is a shift from monolingual communication within a singular language and culture to communication as interlinguistic and intercultural; from communicative competence to symbolic competence (Kramsch, 2011); and learning to communicate as interpretive, reflective and reflexive (Liddicoat & Scarino, 2013). It is intended to develop the capability of students to integrate into communication an understanding of themselves as already situated in languages and cultures, recognizes the same for others.

It is an experimentation with the positioning of diverse learners and their lifeworlds at the centre of learning and this multilingual and intercultural orientation that shaped the work of the teacher of Chinese in the case study which we now discuss. In presenting this case study, we signal that we were the research team in this praxis-oriented study and facilitated the experimentation with the multilingual and intercultural orientation as discussed. In the analysis that we present, we focus on the need to draw upon the diverse lifeworlds of students in the classroom to add value to the learning of all students. Our focus here is on the way in which the teacher incorporated her understanding of the lifeworlds of her students; Chinese-speaking researchers would also be able to offer further analysis of the students' language use and languaging practices.

2 The Case Study: A Unit on the Concept of 'Leisure'

2.1 Background to the Study

The case study outlined in this chapter was part of a larger collective case study conducted over a 6-month period with 5 experienced teachers of different languages across primary and secondary schools. The study was intended as a curricular and assessment intervention based upon the teacher's program and class context. Each teacher was asked to plan and enact a unit of work designed within a multilingual and intercultural orientation and provide an accompanying explanation as to their rationale for inclusion of particular aspects in order to capture their intentions and understandings of this orientation. Following the initial design, the research team provided feedback on the unit, and the teachers enacted it with their classes, gathering evidence of students' learning throughout, and participating in a debriefing session on completion of the unit.

The purpose of the case study was to consider the development of learners' multilingual and intercultural capability. As such, initial discussions between the research team and the teacher participants highlighted the need to incorporate from the outset design features of a multilingual and intercultural language learning orientation into the program of study.

Teachers were invited to consider how to design their teaching and learning programs within a multilingual and intercultural language teaching and learning orientation (Liddicoat & Scarino, 2013). Discussions foregrounded the need to attend to learners' lifeworlds and to provide rich conceptual content as a basis for intercultural and multilingual comparison and reflection. Furthermore, the notion of learning experiences as something that impacts and remains with learners, as distinct from tasks that learners 'do', with potentially limited personal meaningfulness and transformative impact.

2.2 Profile of the Class

The class was comprised of 17 students in their second to last year of secondary school, in Australia, Year 11. The students were a mixture of students with some 'heritage' in Chinese, having been born in China or a Chinese-speaking country, some having been born in Australia and speaking Mandarin or Cantonese in the home, and some students with no prior learning, with a range of backgrounds including Australian-Canadian, Cambodian, Indian, Malaysian and Vietnamese. All students were experiencing schooling through English as the dominant language of Australian education.

The teacher was born and completed her schooling and undergraduate degree in Mainland China. Following her migration to Australia, she completed a postgraduate Masters in Languages Education at an Australian university. The teacher is a highly experienced teacher of Chinese background learners, having taught in an International Baccalaureate (IB) Diploma school for many years, and having taught the full range of learners from beginners through to composite classes for background students. She is comfortable with both the culture of teaching languages in China and in Australia, as well as being confident in moving between Australian and Chinese contexts more broadly.

2.3 Principles of Design for Multilingual and Intercultural Language Learning

In designing the teaching and learning program, the teacher of Chinese sought to apply a set of principles of a multilingual and intercultural language learning orientation (Scarino & Kohler, 2022; c.f. Kohler & Scarino, 2024; Liddicoat & Scarino, 2013), as follows:

- *multiplicity* [foregrounding multiple languages, modes, perspectives, representations]
- *personalisation and embodiment* [foregrounding the learner and their lifeworlds and affect]
- *conceptual* [foregrounding abstracting and connecting knowledge]
- *interactive* [foregrounding the role of mediation]
- *reflective and reflexive* [foregrounding decentring, recognising situatedness]; and
- *developmental*; [foregrounding the dynamic and iterative nature of such learning].

These principles provide a means for considering how the teacher of Chinese in this case, planned and enacted her teaching with the diverse group of learners.

The intention of the unit was to invite students to explore multilingual and intercultural perspectives on 'leisure' as a concept and phenomenon. The teacher wanted students to consider how language and culture, and in particular age and gender, shape ideas such as the concept of leisure and related cultural practices. She was particularly interested in students expanding their understanding of generational change and what constitutes 'leisure' through intercultural comparison and reflection, on the phenomenon and on themselves. Teachers were invited to consider three facets of intercultural language learning: experience or participation, analysis and reflection (on the phenomenon in general) and reflexivity (that is, self-reflection) (Liddicoat & Scarino, 2013). In this way, the teacher was seeking to develop students' language and cultural awareness as an integral part of language learning for all students. Through the three facets, students work in a multilayered manner, engaging both in the experience and stepping back from the experience to consider the phenomenon in the context of diversity.

The teacher of Chinese worked closely with the research team to open up possibilities for attending to learners' lifeworlds through designing a teaching and learning program within a multilingual and intercultural orientation. The result was a unit of work based on the concept of 'leisure'. Working with concepts was familiar to the teacher in the sense that she was operating within the IB program which is framed around the use of core concepts. The teacher sought to be responsive to the diversity of learners in her class by sourcing concepts and related texts in line with ideas that students care about.

The reason for framing the unit through the concept of 'leisure' is related to the value of conceptual learning for an intercultural orientation to language learning.

Table 1 Pre-knowledge survey questions (Scarino et al., 2023:160)

Questions provided to students	Translation (not in original)
1. 你平时在学校参加什么课外活动 (kewai huodong, extra curriculum activities)?	What extra-curricular activity do you normally participate in?
2. 你平时的休闲(xiuxian, leisure)娱乐(yule, entertainment)活动有哪些?	What are your typical recreational activities?
3. 你的家人(父母和祖父母)通常有什么休闲娱乐活动?	What are typically your family's (parents and grandparents) recreational activities?
4. 你认为休闲生活方式(fangshi, style)给人们带来了什么好处?为什么?	What benefits do you think a casual lifestyle provides? Why?
5. 你认为哪些休闲娱乐活动是男生或者女生专有的 (zhuanyoude, exclusively/particularly)?	What casual activities do you think are exclusive to males or females?
6. 你认为为什么男生和女生有专有休闲娱乐活动?	Why do you think there are gender exclusive activities?
7. 你觉得什么影响了你对休闲娱乐活动的选择 (xuanze, choice/choose)?	What do you think affects your choice of recreational activities?

Liddicoat and Scarino (2013) outline how concepts provide fertile ground for exploration of diverse knowledges and intercultural perspectives:

> Concepts in intercultural language teaching and learning are not necessarily specifically linguistic, rather they orient to broader points of intersection between language, culture, and learning, which allows the relationship between languages and cultures to be explored. A concept therefore may represent a level of abstraction beyond language. (Liddicoat & Scarino, 2013: 152)

Concepts therefore provide a basis for intercultural comparison and reflection, as students make observations, analyse, and draw the ideas back to their own experiences and linguistic and cultural frameworks. Through this intercultural comparison and intracultural reflection, students expand their conceptual, linguistic and cultural frameworks.

The unit was organised through a teaching and learning sequence designed around a series of texts and tasks/learning experiences (Liddicoat & Scarino, 2013). The sequence began with what the teacher referred to as a 'pre-knowledge survey' (Table 1) in which she sought their preliminary views about the idea of 'leisure' and their own experiences of it.

2.3.1 Pre-knowledge Survey

The teacher indicated that she had not previously conducted a diagnostic survey of this kind. By developing the survey, she aimed to learn more about her students' lifeworlds and to discover what views students already held about leisure. In particular, she wanted to draw their attention to the gendered and generational aspects of the concept. As she explained,

> I want to direct them to think about the diversity of the choices over leisure between males and females as well as among different age groups – middle school students, their parents and grandparents.

The survey was designed to move students from simple description of their activities, through to more reflective thinking about family influence, and then gender stereotypes. In this way, the survey enabled students to personalise their learning in diverse ways, to relate it to their immediate world of experience, and then to move from an individual perspective to a broader societal perspective, by considering the generational and gendered nature of leisure. The final question returned to students' own experiences and invited them to decentre from these, to reflect on the role of age and gender in shaping their own views and practices.

Following the survey, students shared their responses and were further invited to consider the broader range of responses across the class group. They were asked to comment on any similarities and differences between their own leisure activities and those of classmates, and to try to explain these. This invited students to draw connections and consider the diversity of experiences and views of their group in sharing their perspectives. In sharing them, several students commented on the role of one's enculturation. For example, one student noted:

> There is a lot of difference between my classmates and I, as there are different influences and environmental factors. These influences include family, parents, friends and social media. The way someone is brought up and raised can play a major role in how they spend their leisure and what they find entertaining.[Student born in Australia with Chinese-Malay parents who migrated to Australia for their undergraduate university education]

Finally, students were invited to reflect on the survey itself, to consider why they had been given such a task. Not only was the teacher seeking feedback about the value of diagnostic surveying, but she wanted students to develop their criticality. Students commented on the underlying purpose, noting that the questions were designed to *'get us to think more widely and requires our deep thoughts and understanding. It also aids us to communicate and think in groups, with discussions about global understanding'*. One student noted that the gender question was difficult to answer, *'not because we don't know what is stereotypically masculine and feminine, but because we have to ask ourselves just how much we believe in these stereotypes'*. Another student noted that the questions overall had made them *'aware of the way we think'* and raised their self-awareness about their own perspectives and how they are influenced by culture.

Following the pre-knowledge survey, the students engaged in critical analysis of a series of texts related to leisure in China. The sequence began with an autobiographical recount generated by the teacher.

2.3.2 Teacher Recount Text

The first text provided for critical analysis was an autobiographical piece prepared by the teacher in which she recounted her childhood 'leisure life' in China, as she described it, particularly her learning of calligraphy (Fig. 1).

The text was particularly designed to present students with a dilemma (in line with the principle of *personalisation*). She built in two points aimed at provoking a

Fig. 1 Extracts from teacher recount text (Scarino et al., 2023:161)

response from students, firstly, describing the expectations of family in influencing leisure pursuits, and secondly, the impact of work/study commitments on pastimes. Through the recount, the teacher revealed aspects of her own lifeworld to her students as a way of building rapport and modelling the intercultural process of considering one's own enculturation through childhood/adolescence. In the process, she also reveals her own values as reflected in her choices about work/study and leisure ('*I had to give up all my hobbies for study*', she explained).

In this way, the teacher invited her students to consider matters of situatedness in time, place and cultural framings, through her own story. The task asked them to consider her choices and provide advice to her, and in doing so, to *decentre* from the position taken, revealing their own linguistic and cultural framework in the process. The teacher explained the task as follows:

> In the article 'My Leisure Life', I carried out practicing Chinese calligraphy at home for years as my father and grandfather believed it would be good for me, and during high school, I had to give up all my hobbies to focus on my studies due to the heavy workload. Students are asked to comment on my decision to practice calligraphy and give up hobbies if they were in the same situation.

The following are three extracts from students' responses which were written in Chinese and translated by the students themselves into English (for the purposes of the research). The extracts reveal a diverse range of views amongst the students, varying from the idea that young people should adhere to parental and grandparental expectations, through to a more individualistic ideology of personal choice:

> (a) *Although listening to your parents' advice and following their requests is quite common throughout all cultures, the associated 'Chinese ideology' may stem from each generation's past experience which influences the upbringing of their own offspring. This may be in order to improve their children's living conditions or to avoid repeating the same mistakes. In my opinion, children who are still of primary school age should be*

> disciplined enough that they follow their parents' instructions and wishes. Thus Ms X should continue to practise Chinese calligraphy. The male figures in her family wish for her to practise this skill and the reasons behind this may be to improve the 'social status of her upbringing' or to fulfil what society may expect of them. However, as Ms X matures and understands more about the society and starts to develop her own opinions and beliefs about certain activities, it is not justified that her opinion is denied.
>
> [Student (a) born in Australia with Chinese-born parents, lived in China for 4 years, speaks Chinese at home, English is the stronger language]

Extract (a) indicates the student's view that there is an underlying 'Chinese' ideology that has its origins in societal pressure related to improving one's life prospects. There is also nuance in the student's position, recognising that age influences choices and behaviours, with greater independence from family developing with age. The student is making connections between family, age, gender with a sense of this being a dynamic relationship that changes with time.

The next extract reveals quite a different view, one that affirms a sense of obligation to family elders. The student also makes a connection between certain behaviours and their social capital, recognising that these are related to values such as respect.

> (b) *Ms X should obey her parents because they are older than her and know more. She should respect her elders. Ms X needs this calligraphy training because her parents believe that handwriting determines someone's character. When people see her calligraphy skills, they will respect her more.*
>
> [Student (b) born in Australia with Malaysian-born parents]

In the next extract, another student articulates a more individualistic perspective, noting that while respecting elders is important, one also has to consider one's own desires.

> (c) *I think when Ms X was little, she should refuse to write calligraphy everyday, not only because she doesn't like it, also because she had many other hobbies. She really liked her other hobbies, therefore she should have focused on improving those skills. Listening to your elders is important, but it is more important to listen to one's self. Her Grandfather and Father want her to practice calligraphy, because they think beautiful writing represents quality upbringing and character. I think this thinking is very old-fashioned, because many other attributes also represent good character, such as patience and kindness. Small Ms X should have at least talked to her grandfather and father to negotiate how often she practices calligraphy. She should most importantly participate in activities that make her the most happy.*
>
> [Student (c) Born in Australia with Australian-born English speaking parents]

These brief extracts are reflective of the range of responses from students, which go someway towards understanding the origin of their perspective, however, there needs to be a caution against notions of cultural determinism which students also need to appreciate. What it does show is that the lifeworlds of the students, do come into play in important ways in formulating their perceptions. The teacher enabled students to not only *personalise* their learning, through offering their own interpretations of the situation, but also to then see the diversity of views among their group as an opportunity to develop awareness of *multiplicity* of perspectives as a norm.

2.3.3 Analysing Authentic Texts About Cultural Practices

The next phase of the unit involved students analysing two authentic texts related to contemporary leisure practices in China. The first of these texts focused on the emergent phenomenon at the time of 'binge-watching'. The teacher's rationale for choosing this text was:

> Binge-watching TV dramas has become the leisure activity for most of the Chinese people in recent years. I want the students to know about the trend and understand the reasons behind it through researching to investigate what makes so many Chinese people watching TV dramas as their leisure, after work, during commuting, and on the weekends. And this popular trend has impacted on people's life and health in what way. Some students in class also are big fans of TV dramas, so it will be interesting to see how they reveal what makes them follow the dramas, and what the impact of their leisure life on their study, hobbies and health might be.

Again, the teacher foregrounds her desire to connect with students' lifeworlds, to enable them to personally relate to and consider their own views about phenomena such as this and draw intercultural comparisons between diverse Chinese contexts and Australia. She wanted them to think through why such activities are changing in modern China and where such influences come from, ultimately relating this back to themselves.

Students analysed the text on 'binge watching' of television programs and were asked a series of questions including *What is the impact of this phenomenon in China? Why does it happen in Australia? What are your thoughts?* (Fig. 2)

In this task, students were invited to consider both the phenomenon as it occurs in China and to turn their gaze to their own cultural context to consider how it plays out in Australia. The teachers' questions therefore enabled students to take a

Fig. 2 Extract from informational text: binge watching (Scarino et al., 2023:163)

comparative perspective, to consider each cultural context in its own terms, and relate it back to their own lifeworlds. The principle of *multiplicity* is evident through the bringing together of (primarily) two cultural contexts, as well as the principle of reflection and reflexivity as students consider their own cultural context and behaviours. The students needed to draw on their linguistic and cultural experiences and frameworks related to both Chinese and Australian culture to complete the task. They need to mediate diverse linguistic and cultural frameworks to make sense of the text and also stand back from their immediate reality, to *reflect* on what this practice might mean for them.

Following one further task, analysing another informational text related to the cultural practice of public dancing in China, the teacher designed a final task to bring together all of students' intercultural learning and Chinese language development. The final task was for students to prepare an interview script as though they were a reporter interviewing a person in Chinese about their leisure life. The teacher explained that her intention was to expand students' *conceptual understanding* of leisure and recognise how it changes according to time and place, and how these changes impact on people's lives. Furthermore, students were asked to explain their choice of questions for the interview, why these were important to them and how these related to their own perspectives and cultural values. In this way, the final question invited a *reflection* on the overall learning and *development* that students had made through the unit. They had drawn upon their diverse multilingual repertoires to engage in the learning experiences, as well as the intercultural analysis and reflection, and at the same time considering their perspectives in relation to the multiple perspectives offered by others.

3 Conclusion

The unit of work on 'leisure' was intended to provide opportunities for diverse learners of Chinese to develop their multilingual and intercultural capabilities. In designing the unit, the teacher aimed to build in features that would develop such learning, such as planning the sequence around multiple texts that presented diverse perspectives that would prompt personal and critical interpretations, and that enabled subsequent reflection on the multiplicity of perspectives within the class itself. Personalisation was particularly strong throughout the unit, with students being invited to consider their own views and values, drawing on their multiple linguistic and cultural worlds to do so. A limitation of the study, however, is that class discussions were not recorded and yet it is through these that the teacher mediates learning for the diverse learners, not just in terms of their ability but also in terms of the cultural dimensions that come into play for different learners. It is in interaction, that teachers cater for learner diversity, knowing where to pitch the learning and how to mediate it for specific learners, through taking account of who they are.

Throughout the unit, students in their diversity, were positioned as central, active participants, contributing their experiences, critical perspectives and reflections rather than as passive receivers of fixed forms and ideas. Through experiences such as these, students become increasingly aware of language variation, the role of culture in exchanging meanings, and their own and each others' perspectives or phenomena in the world and about learning Chinese and what it means for them—differently. For 'background' learners, it builds understanding that their lived experience of learning Chinese in Australia is valued and extended—in multilingual and intercultural ways—and for 'second language' learners, they come to appreciate wider matters related to learning Chinese in Australia, for themselves and others. The experiences and trajectories of diverse learners are different but participation in experiences and building meta-awareness holds for all learners. It is through this orientation that Chinese language learning can be transformative for all learners, both in relation to their Chinese language learning and development, and to their identity formation.

Acknowledgements We wish to acknowledge the teacher who participated in this study for her thoughtful work and willingness to experiment. We are grateful also for the teacher's translations of the recount and informational texts from Chinese into English, given that neither author is a speaker of Chinese.

References

Australian Curriculum, Assessment and Reporting Authority (ACARA). (2011). *Shape of the Australian Curriculum: Languages.* Australian Curriculum, Assessment and Reporting Authority. Retrieved from https://docs.acara.edu.au/resources/Languages_-_Shape_of_the_Australian_Curriculum.pdf

Byram, M. (2021). *Teaching and assessing intercultural communicative competence: Revisited* (2nd ed.). Multilingual Matters.

Canagarajah, S. (2013). *Translingual practice. Global Englishes and cosmopolitan relations.* Routledge.

Council of Australian Government. (1994). *Asian Languages and Australia's economic future.*

Creese, A., & Blackledge, A. (2015). Translanguaging and identity in educational settings. *Annual Review of Applied Lingustics, 35*, 20–35.

Elder, C. (2000a). Learner diversity and its implications for outcomes-based assessment. In C. Elder (Ed.). Defining standards and monitoring progress in languages other than English. *Australian Review of Applied Linguistics, 23*(2), 36–61.

Elder, C. (2000b). Outing the 'native speaker'. The problem of diverse learner backgrounds in foreign language classrooms. *Language, Curriculum and Cultures, 13*(1), 86–108.

Gadamer, H.-G. (2004). *Truth and method* (2nd ed.) (J. Weinsheimer & D. G. Marshall, Trans.). Continuum.

García, O., & Li, W. (2014). Translanguaging: Language, bilingualism and education. *Palgrave Macmillan.* https://doi.org/10.1057/9781137385765

Gutiérrez, K. D., & Rogoff, B. (2003). Cultural ways of learning: Individual traits or repertoires of practice. *Educational Researcher, 32*(5), 19–25.

Gutiérrez, K. D., et al. (2019). Youth as historical actors in the production of possible futures. *Mind, Culture and Activity, 26*(4), 1–18.

Kohler, M. (2020). *Developing intercultural language learning.* Palgrave.

Kohler, M., & Scarino, A. (2024). A principled pedagogy for a multilingual and intercultural orientation to learning for diverse (language) learners. In L. Veliz (Ed.), *Multiculturalism and multilingualism in education: Implications for curriculum, teacher preparation and pedagogical practice*. BRILL.

Kramsch, C. (2002). Introduction. 'How can we tell the dancer from the dance?'. In C. Kramsch (Ed.), *Language acquisition and language socialization* (pp. 1–30). Continuum.

Kramsch, C. (2009). *The multilingual subject*. Oxford University Press.

Kramsch, C. (2011). The symbolic dimensions of the intercultural. *Language Teaching, 44*(3), 354–367.

Leung, C., & Scarino, A. (2016). Reconceptualiszing the nature of goals and outcomes in language/s education. *The Modern Language Journal, 100*, 81–95.

Liddicoat, A. J., & Scarino, A. (2013). *Intercultural language teaching and learning*. Wiley-Blackwell.

May, S. (Ed.). (2014). Introducing the multilingual turn. In *Implications for SLA, TESOL and bilingual education*. Routledge.

McNamara, T. (2019). *Language and subjectivity*. Cambridge University Press.

Orton, J. M. (2016). Issues in Chinese language teaching in Australian schools. *Chinese Education and Society., 49*, 369–375. https://doi.org/10.1080/1061/932.2016.1283939

Pennycook, A. (2019). From translanguaging to translingual activism. In D. Macaro (Ed.), *Decolonizing foreign language education: The misteaching of English and other colonial languages* (pp. 167–185). Routledge.

Pennycook, A., & Otsjui, E. (2015). *Metrolingualism. Language in the city*. Routledge.

Scarino, A. (2014). Learning as reciprocal, interpretive meaning-making. A view from collaborative research into the professional learning of teachers of languages. *Modern Language Journal (Special Issue), 98*, 386–401. https://doi.org/10.1111/j.1540-4781.2014.12068.x

Scarino, A., & Kohler, M. (2022). 11 assessing intercultural capability: Insights from processes of eliciting and judging student learning. In T. McConachy, I. Golubeva, & M. Wagner (Eds.), *Intercultural learning in language education and beyond: Evolving concepts, perspectives and practices* (pp. 188–206). Multilingual Matters. https://doi.org/10.21832/9781800412613-018

Scarino, A., Elder, C., Iwashita, N., Kim, S. H. O., Kohler, M., & Scrimgeour, A. (2011). *Student Achievement in Asian Languages Education (SAALE) project*. Report commissioned by the Department of Education, Employment and Workplace Relations. Retrieved from https://saale.unisa.edu.au/

Scarino, A., Kohler, M., & Liddicoat, A. J. (2023). Assessing intercultural mediation in language learning and teaching: A focus on interpretation, reflection and reflexivity. In A. J. Liddicoat, D. M. Plard, G. Alao, J. Breugnot, D. Chan, W. Meng, S. Chan, J. Guiza, M. Himeta, N. Iwasaki, S. Klayklueng, M. Kohler, B. Pizziconi, Y. Saito, A. Scarino, E. Suzuki, & G. Zarate (Eds.), *La Médiation interculturelle en didactique des langues et des cultures [Intercultural mediation in teaching and learning languages and cultures]* (pp. 155–168). University of Bourdeax.

Part VII
Teachers as the Changing Agents

Success or Failure: The Important Role of Emotionality for CSL Teachers' Professional Development

Elizabeth Ka Yee Loh and Loretta Chung Wing Tam

Abstract Over the past decade, many Chinese language teachers in Hong Kong have experienced many new challenges. They are expected to design and implement their own school-based curricula and adopt innovative pedagogies and customised materials for students learning CSL. The current literature suggests that some teachers are not ready for or even resist changes (e.g. Richardson V. How teachers change: what will lead to change that most benefits student learning? Focus on Basics, 2(C). National Center for the Study of Adult Learning and Literacy. Retrieved from http://www.ncsall.net/index.html@id=395.html, 1998), amid new challenges and paradigm shifts. Based on Guskey's (Educ Res 15(5):5–12, 1986) Model of Teacher Change, Hall et al.'s (A developmental conceptualization of the adoption process within education institutions. Research and Development Center for Teacher Education, University of Texas at Austin, 1973) Concerns-Based Adoption Model, and Bennett's (Toward ethnorelativism: a developmental model of intercultural sensitivity. In Paige RM (ed) Education for the intercultural experience. Intercultural Press, pp 21–71, 1993) Developmental Model of Intercultural Sensitivity, this case study highlights the role of emotionality as a key factor for successful teachers' change and revisits the sequences of the progressive stages when teachers facing change or innovations. Research findings suggested that an integrated model with inclusive support of collective lesson preparation and teaching demonstrations/ practical sessions in professional development programs is a key element that helps the facilitation of CSL teachers' change, provides them with experiential learning opportunities for the enhancement of their confidence and reduction of anxiety, leading to their voluntary adoption of the new pedagogical approach, and gradual change in their beliefs and attitudes after witnessing the feasibility and effectiveness of the newly introduced concepts. Taking reference from such findings, the adaptation and modification of these three classical models is then proposed. Implications and suggestions for the design of CSL teachers' professional development programs are discussed.

E. K. Y. Loh (✉) · L. C. W. Tam
The University of Hong Kong, Pok Fu Lam, Hong Kong
e-mail: ekyloh@hku.hk; lcwtam@hku.hk

1 Introduction

Teacher professional development (TPD) plays a pivotal role at all levels of education. Teachers, pre-service and in-service alike, are exposed to and familiarized with concepts, theories, and practical strategies new to them for the improvement of teaching and learning. The "tipping point" lies in the changes taking place during the process that motivate teachers to accept and adopt the newly acquired knowledge, beliefs, and practices in their daily classroom teaching.

This chapter aims to offer an overview of three classical models of change that encompass the pedagogical, social, and psychological aspects of teacher professional development, and to argue that the "catalyst" for teacher change in the highly complex situation of Hong Kong Chinese as a second language (CSL) education is collective lesson preparation and teaching demonstrations/practical sessions within school contexts. Drawing upon the original Guskey's (1986) model of teacher change, the Concerns-Based Adoption Model (Hall et al., 1973), the Developmental Model of Intercultural Sensitivity (Bennett, 1993), and their adaptation and modification for L1 Chinese language teachers in Hong Kong (Loh & Tam, 2017), stages of teachers' concerns about and responses to the new curricula/pedagogies are outlined and examined for illustrating the proposed integrated model based on the case of teacher change among CSL teachers in mainstream secondary schools.

2 Teacher Professional Development: For the Profession, For the Professionals

TPD takes root in the professional growth a teacher achieves as a result of gaining increased experience and examining his or her teaching systematically (Glattenhorn, 1995), while being offered to both pre-service and in-service teachers (Dos Santos, 2019) at different developmental stages of a teacher (Dreyfus & Dreyfus, 1986). After decades of existence, there has been a paradigm shift from ad hoc information workshops and seminars to systematically planned, regular events to promote professional development and growth (Villegas-Reimers, 2003). The North American-European divide between the terms "professional development" and "teacher development" (Johnston, 2003, p. 95) has thus been narrowed, and "teacher professional development" or "teachers' professional development" has been widely adopted in education and academia.

Another change that comes with the paradigm shift was the emergence of the bottom-up approach (Opfer & Pedder, 2011), which is featured by its integration into teachers' daily work and context specificity (Bergmark, 2020), contrary to its top-down counterpart that does not necessarily align with the actual issues and concerns of the participating teachers while emphasizing the lack of knowledge and skills of the teachers (Clarke & Hollingsworth, 2002). In Hong Kong, according to the recommendation of the Advisory Committee on Teacher Education and

Qualifications (ACTEQ) (2003), every teacher should accumulate 150 hours of continuing professional development (CPD) over a three-year cycle. CPD in Hong Kong for teachers, in other words, is a form of TPD offered in line with both the bottom-up and top-down approaches, offering a wide range of learning activities and educational events including workshops, seminars, in-service teacher education courses, school-based consultancy services, and university-school partnerships (ACTEQ, 2006, 2009) for teaching professionals in different roles along their career ladder. The objective of providing more systematic and focused professional development opportunities is to be achieved with the provision of training programs for newly-joined teachers, enhanced training for in-service teachers, and the enhancement of training requirements for promotion (Education Bureau of HKSAR, 2020).

The success or failure of teacher change lies in the effectiveness of TPD, with one of the major evaluation criteria being the resulting teacher change. According to Fullan's educational change theory (1982, 1991, 2007), there are three broad phases in the change process, namely initiation, implementation, and continuation. Characteristics of change, including need, clarity, complexity, as well as quality and practicality, affect implementation (Fullan & Stiegelbauer, 1991). All successful strategies are socially based and action oriented (Fullan, 2007). Numerous studies revealed that many TPD programs were not exactly effective (Cohen & Hill, 1998, 2000; Kennedy, 1998; Wang et al., 1999), given that the relationship of teachers' professional learning and student learning further relates to wider questions concerning teachers' identity, self-efficacy, and expertise (Forde & McMahon, 2019). This leads to the next question regarding TPD for Chinese language teachers in Hong Kong: What makes for the success or failure of teacher change in the Hong Kong CSL context? Does emotionality, which has long been considered a key part in teaching and learning (Hargreaves, 1998; Schutz et al., 2006) particularly in L2/FL education (Gabryś-Barker, 2018), play a part in the process?

3 Research Background and Design

Considering the development and effectiveness of teacher professional development in Hong Kong, there are a number of region-specific issues that require special attention. Pre-tertiary education in Hong Kong has long been considered difficult and stressful (Wong & Pennington, 1993), contributed by social, economic and education development (Pang, 2012) in a system based on high-stakes testing (Cho & Chan, 2020), making the adoption of innovative curricula/pedagogies a challenge to both the in-service teachers and the teacher trainers.

This follow-up study, in the light of the above, aims to answer the following research questions:

1. Do L1 and CSL TPD share the same key elements to facilitating change in frontline teachers and their teaching?
2. What is the role of emotionality in the facilitation of change in CSL teachers?

3. Is it possible to adapt and integrate the three classical models to illustrate the process and mechanism of teacher change in the Hong Kong CSL context?

As an interview-based case study, this chapter aims to present an analysis of ethnographic data from semi-structured, in-depth individual and focus group interviews with the participating CSL teachers and their TPD instructors. Three innovative pedagogies were introduced to the frontline teachers of 8 local secondary schools for a university-school partnership project over a two-year period, including Reading to Learn, Drama in Education, and mobile-assisted CSL Learning.

The first author was the principal investigator of the project, in which 6 subject experts joined the projects as demonstrators and TPD instructors (5 male, 1 female, with an average of 28.5 years of teaching experience). A total of 38 secondary school teachers were selected by their schools to participate in the project (13 male, 25 female). Centered on the aforementioned research questions, all the interviews were conducted in Cantonese, i.e., the predominant spoken variant of the Chinese language in Hong Kong. The interview data presented in this chapter were first transcribed into Traditional Chinese by a native-speaking research assistant, before being translated into English by an experienced linguist. Minimal changes were made to preserve the tone of the original texts as well as the contexts.

4 Classical Models of Change: Applicability and Beyond

To identify the key elements and various stages of teachers' concerns and responses about innovative curricula/pedagogies in the local educational context, three models immediately relevant to the research questions are adopted as the major frameworks of reference for the new Model of Teacher Change for CSL Teachers, namely Guskey's (1986) Model of Teacher Change, The Concerns-Based Adoption Model (Hall et al., 1973), and the Developmental Model of Intercultural Sensitivity (Bennett, 1993).

In this first model, as illustrated in Fig. 1, professional development would induce change in teachers' classroom practices. As pointed out by Guskey (2002), "[the teachers] believe it works because they have seen it work, and that experience shapes their attitudes and beliefs" (p. 383). In other words, significant change in teachers' beliefs and attitudes would only take place once evidence of change in student learning outcomes had been disclosed and noticed. The third and final stages in

Fig. 1 Guskey's (1986) model of teacher change

the model, on which the debate has been centered, require adaptation with reference to the current CSL context in Hong Kong. How TPD can possibly be related to the change of teachers' classroom practice, as well as the stages to be covered and their sequence, are our major concerns as to whether the existing model truly reflects the situation in Hong Kong CSL classrooms.

4.1 The Concerns-Based Adoption Model (Hall et al. 1973)

Developed in the 1970s through 1990s, the Concerns-Based Adoption Model (CBAM) (Hall et al., 1973) has been well-received globally for teacher PD at different levels. Focusing on the psychological aspect while identifying different stages of teachers' concerns about change, the most commonly adopted parts of the model are Types of Concern (ToC) and Stages of Concern (SoC) which refer to the perceptions and attitudes of staff (Anderson, 1997) (see Tables 1 and 2).

According to CBAM, an educator would experience seven Stages of Concern (SoC) when facing change or innovations (see Table 1). This model assumes that change is a process to be accomplished by individuals and possibly facilitated by interventions. It is highly personal experience that involves developmental growth (Anderson, 1997). With reference to the situation in Hong Kong, CSL teachers' concerns, like their counterparts teaching Chinese as a first language, vary from the original CBAM in terms of the stages of concern due to differences in beliefs and practices. A modified version (see Table 3), therefore, was developed for illustrating the different stages of Chinese language teachers' concerns through the course of change (Loh & Tam, 2017).

In this modified version, Stages 1–2 in the original model are juxtaposed under the umbrella of 'Self Concerns', in which the focus lies in the teachers' informational and personal concerns. Stage 3 (Consequence), students' performances are taken into consideration by the teachers with reference to class instruction and lesson planning during demonstrations. Further, in Stage 4 (Operational Procedure), teachers consider the management issues in terms of operation, e.g. class instruction during demonstrations. In the final stages 5–6 (Collaboration and Refocusing) respectively, teachers focus on the classes or school administration to relate their own actions and decisions to what their fellow teachers or even supervisors are doing, while attempting to improvise according to readily accessible theories, strategies, and resources. Given the outcome-based teacher appraisal system of CSL teachers in Hong Kong, who are often well-experienced in teaching native-speaking students, tend to be more concerned or even worried about the Consequence than Operational Procedure given the performance-oriented workplace culture. The sequence of the aforementioned stages in the modified model, therefore, has been reversed to better illustrate the case (see Table 4).

Table 1 The concerns-based adoption model (CBAM)—Stages of concern (Hall et al., 1973)

Types of concern	Unrelated concerns	Self concerns		Task concerns	Impact concerns		
Stages	0	1	2	3	4	5	6
Name	Awareness	Informational	Personal	Management	Consequence	Collaboration	Refocusing

Table 2 Typical behaviors and expressions of concern corresponding to the different Stages of Concern among teachers

Stages of concern	Typical behaviors	Expression of concern
6 Refocusing	Teachers attempt to explore more from the innovative curriculum/pedagogy, including modifications and adjustments, or change to use another more effective one instead. Teachers have a clear personal idea of the new curriculum/pedagogy.	I have some ideas about something that would work even better.
5 Collaboration	Teachers focus on how to cooperate with peers and coordinate the innovative curriculum/pedagogy with reference to other projects and pedagogies.	How can I relate what I am doing to what others are doing?
4 Consequence	Teachers focus on the actual processes and tasks of the innovative curriculum/pedagogy, and the best ways of using information and resources. The issues of concern include the effectiveness of the innovative curriculum/pedagogy, organization, management, schedule and time planning.	How is my use affecting learners? How can I refine it to have more impact?
3 Management	Teachers focus on the impacts of innovative curriculum/pedagogy on students, in particular the relevance and appropriateness of the innovative curriculum/pedagogy on students, assessment of student learning, as well as the necessary changes for enhancing student learning.	I seem to be spending all my time getting materials ready.
2 Personal	Teachers are not sure about their role and the requirements of the innovative curriculum/pedagogy, and their capabilities of such requirements.	How will using it affect me?
1 Informational	Teachers have a superficial understanding of the innovative curriculum/pedagogy and are interested in further details. Teachers do not care about their relationship with the innovation curriculum/pedagogy, but characteristics, impacts and requirements of the latter.	I would like to know more about it.
0 Awareness	Teachers is hardly involved in the innovative curriculum/pedagogy.	I am not concerned about it.

After Hord et al. (1987)

4.2 Developmental Model of Intercultural Sensitivity (Bennett, 1993)

Teachers, in contemporary school settings, are often tasked with intra-team and inter-team collaborations, especially when it comes to curriculum planning and professional development. According to Hargreaves (1995), cultures of teaching

Table 3 A local adaptation of the concerns-based adoption model for Hong Kong Chinese language teachers

Types of concern	Unrelated concerns	Self concerns		Impact concerns	Task concerns	Administrative concerns	
Stages	0	1	2	3	4	5	6
Name	Awareness	Informational	Personal	Consequence	Operational Procedure	Collaboration	Refocusing

After Hall et al. (1973)

Table 4 Typical behaviors and expressions of concern corresponding to the different stages of concern among Hong Kong teachers (Loh & Tam, 2017)

Stages of concern	Typical behaviors	Expression of concern
5 & 6 Refocusing & Collaboration	Teachers focus on how to cooperate with peers and coordinate the innovative curriculum/pedagogy with reference to other projects and pedagogies. Teachers attempt to explore more from the innovative curriculum/pedagogy, including modifications and adjustments, or change to use another more effective one instead. Teachers now have a clear personal idea of the new curriculum/pedagogy.	Refocusing: Will it be better if I… Informational: How do I ask my others colleagues to…
4 Operational Procedure	With increasing understanding of the theories and rationales behind the innovative curriculum/pedagogy, the focus of teachers' concern now moves to the actual practices in their own classroom. They are keen to look at the actual processes, tasks of the innovative curriculum/pedagogy and the best ways of using information and resources.	Why do I seem to be spending all my time getting materials ready? Should I…in class? What should I do if my students…?
3 Consequence	When teachers witness changes in students' learning outcome, they become eager to understand the reasons and theories behind the innovative curriculum/pedagogy, and the impacts of the innovative curriculum/pedagogy on students.	Why did my students do that? How will it help my students?
1 & 2 Personal & Informational	Teachers have informational and personal concerns, as they are observing their student performance and other teachers' instruction and lesson planning during demonstration. The concerns are generally simultaneous.	(The concerns being simultaneous) Personal: How will using it affect me? Our school… Informational: I don't know too much about it. Give me some information.
	At this stage, in terms of informational and personal concerns, teachers have a superficial understanding of the innovative curriculum/pedagogy and are interested in further details. Anyhow, they are not sure about their role and the requirements of the innovative curriculum/pedagogy, and their capabilities of such requirements. They tend to analyze their role in the structure and the school policies, and consider the impacts on and possible conflicts between the existing school organization/personal commitment and the innovation curriculum/pedagogy.	
0 Awareness	Teachers are hardly involved in the innovative curriculum/pedagogy.	I heard of it and that's all I know. I am not concerned about it.

Table 5 Bennett's (1993) developmental model of intercultural sensitivity

Denial	Defense	Minimization	Acceptance	Adaptation	Integration

are formed by teachers' relations with other colleagues, through which the former are realised, reproduced and redefined. The use of innovative pedagogies is strongly recommended or even promoted as part of a so-called 'team (school) culture' in line with a regional or ethnic culture. To examine Hong Kong teachers' sociopsychological responses to the use of innovative pedagogies, and the role of emotionality in teacher change, the authors adapted the Developmental Model of Intercultural Sensitivity (Bennett, 1993) (also known as DMIS or "the Bennett Scale", see Table 5) towards a Model of Teacher Change in Hong Kong for Chinese language teachers for better illustration of the local scenarios (Loh & Tam, 2017), on which the integrated model proposed in this chapter is based.

The first one amongst the six progressive stages, Denial, as the inability to acknowledge and understand cultural differences, is often displayed in superficial observations and statements of tolerance. The attribution of deficiency in intelligence or personality to culturally deviant behavior, or even dehumanization of outsiders, may accompany such behaviors according to Bennett (1993). The second stage, Defense, refers to the "recognition of cultural difference coupled with negative evaluation of most variations from native culture". It is featured by the "we/they" thinking and overt negative stereotyping, which are at times accompanied by sociocultural proselytizing of "underdeveloped" cultures as well.

Minimization, as the third stage, refers to "how superficial cultural differences are recognized and appreciated while one still holds on to their original ideology, and emphasizes the similarity of people and commonality of basic values in universal terms", sometimes in ethnocentric forms. The fourth stage, Acceptance, refers to "how cultural differences are recognized and appreciated in terms of behavior and value, and seen as viable alternative solutions to the organization of human existence". Ability to analyze and understand different phenomena within one's own contexts, as well as substantial elaboration of differences are observed at this point.

Adaptation, the fifth stage, points to "the development of communication skills that enable intercultural communication". Effective use of empathy or frame of reference shifting for understanding and being understood across cultural boundaries is observed in this stage. As for the sixth and final stage, Integration, which refers to "the internalization of bicultural or multicultural frames of reference", one sees themselves as "in process" while maintaining a definition of identity being marginal to any particular culture. As mentioned earlier in this section, the authors attempted to adapt DMIS for illustrating how teachers in Hong Kong react to changes, in particular the use of innovative pedagogies being promoted or strongly recommended. In the modified version (Table 6), it is characterized by non-unilinearity. Defense (Stage 2) and Minimization (Stage 3) have been merged as one, i.e. a new Stage 2.

In Stage 1 (Denial), teachers are not motivated and/or fail to construe the differences between the curricula/pedagogies they are currently using, and those

Table 6 A local adaptation of developmental model of intercultural sensitivity for illustrating teacher change in Hong Kong amongst Chinese language teachers (Loh & Tam, 2017)

Denial	Defense & Minimization	Acceptance	Adaptation	Integration

new ones being introduced in various contexts (e.g. PD programs). After that, as they move on to Stage 2 (Defense and Minimization), teachers are informed about issues or problems with the current situation, although they tend to maintain their own views and highlight the superiority of old curricula/pedagogies to the new ones. Besides, they are inclined to minimize the differences with doubts about the effectiveness of the newly introduced curricula/pedagogies.

Stage 3 (Acceptance) marks a key turning point from negative views to positive feedback. Through personal witness of how effective the new curricula/pedagogies are, teachers give them their recognition and begin to accept them as viable means to help students learn. Teachers begin to show behavioral changes in Stage 4 (Adaptation) by taking initiatives to implement the new curricula/pedagogies in their own classes. Through the course of experiencing the actual procedures, they identify specific traits and issues or concerns regarding the students and their learning.

Towards the final stage (Integration), teachers integrate the new pedagogies/ curricula into their daily teaching while developing adaptations for their own classrooms, based on the class settings, their teaching styles, and the students' needs. In the next section, we will look into how the modified models can possibly be combined as an adaptation for CSL, with ethnographic evidence from Hong Kong in which CSL has been introduced in recent decades for the increasing diversity in the composition of the student population.

5 Adapting the Models for CSL: Evidence from the Field

Bringing together the three modified models detailed in earlier sections, we come up with a multi-dimensional model of teacher change for CSL teachers that explains the interrelations between different components, incorporating our 2017 local adaptation of Guskey's (1986) Model of Teacher Change for Hong Kong Chinese Language teachers (see Fig. 2).

5.1 Rationales Behind the Developmental Concern-Based Intercultural Sensitivity Model of Teacher Change for CSL

With special reference to the teaching and learning of CSL in Hong Kong, the overall sequence has been modified with two additional stages to illustrate the transition from TPD to change in teachers' classroom practice. "Demonstration of

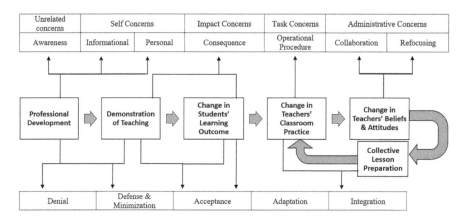

Fig. 2 A developmental concern-based intercultural sensitivity model of teacher change for CSL

Teaching" highlights the importance of demonstration and its positive impact on the student learning outcome, echoing with Guskey's (1986) "seeing it work" argument and filling the research gap about the relationship between PD and teacher change in terms of teachers' emotionality. It is based on our observations in the 2017 and current studies on how CSL teachers in general, like their teaching Chinese as a first language counterparts, tended to change their practices only when change in students' performance was observed.

The sequence of stages in this integrated model for CSL is further altered by moving "Change in Student Learning Outcome" forward to align with the aforementioned teacher change process in Hong Kong (Loh & Tam, 2017). The second addition to the original model, "Collective Lesson Preparation", emphasizes the importance of group work and peer review in collective lesson preparation and feedback after teaching demonstrations. Being another key bridging element, Collective Lesson Preparation is another medium through which motivated teachers' willingness to facilitate changes in their classroom practices while displaying new attitudes and behaviors.

In the above model, professional development is introduced in an attempt to arouse teachers' self-concerns towards implementing innovations in their own classrooms. As one moves on to the demonstration/practical sessions, Denial, Defense and Minimization arising from the informational and personal concerns are gradually replaced by Acceptance, as the impact of new pedagogies are thoroughly considered and classroom procedures understood while witnessing changes in students' learning outcome. The new curricula/pedagogies might as well be adapted by these teachers as actual changes in teachers' classroom practices, which at the same time motivate the teachers to change their beliefs and attitudes via consolidation activities such as professional support and part of TPD (in the form of Collective Lesson Preparation), while focusing on the administrative concerns, i.e. Collaboration and Refocusing. In other words, they are given the opportunity to reflect on their own pedagogical practices by considering an array of variables (e.g. school requirements, characteristics of their current students) in such Collective Lesson Preparation sessions. Through time, teachers would be able to integrate the innovative pedagogies into their daily teaching.

As detailed in the previous section, the proposed model of teacher change finds its roots in three classical models, namely Guskey's (1986) Model of Teacher Change, Hall et al.'s (1973) Concerns-Based Adoption Model (CBAM), and Bennett's (1993) Developmental Model of Intercultural Sensitivity (DMIS). The resulting model, covering pedagogical, social, and psychological aspects, is characterized by adaptations based on the local situation in relation to the key role of emotionality. In the forthcoming sub-sections, supporting evidence for this multi-dimensional model, drawn from the ethnographic data collected during the course of the project, is presented and analyzed to further illustrate the rationales for the local adaptations for CSL.

5.2 From the Overt to the Covert

Guskey's (1986) Model of Teacher Change pinpointed teachers' change of beliefs and attitudes should come after change in student learning outcomes, which was a breakthrough from the traditional framework claiming vice versa. The modified version, as proposed earlier in this paper, suggests that the stimulant, or catalyst, of teacher change in the case of Hong Kong lies in demonstration/practical sessions. Up to this point an immediate question arises: what makes demonstration/practical sessions the key to the success of teacher change, and what are the roots of the socio-psychological mechanisms as featured by the local model?

To answer this question, it is worth looking into what makes for the specific, if not unique, socio-psychological concerns and responses of teachers regarding teacher change in the Hong Kong setting. The juxtaposition of multiple concerns for Stage 1 (i.e. Informational and Personal, Consequence, and Management) in the adapted CBAM and responses for adapted DMIS (i.e. Denial, Defense and Minimization) reflect the intricacy of teachers' decision-making process when facing changes. To account for such differences between the original and the adapted models, three main factors are identified: the determining role of school management, the impacts of outcome-based culture on in-service teachers, and the "experimental" nature of innovation promotion in Hong Kong's CSL TPD.

5.2.1 The Determining Role of School Management

Like their L1 counterparts, school management (including the principals, vice-principals, and assistant principals, who are major decision-makers) often plays a crucial role in the choice of TPD programs and innovative curricula/pedagogies to be promoted or adopted for CSL. Reports from informants, including a subject panel head, revealed that they had played a rather passive and submissive role in their participation of TPD which promoted the "Drama in Education" pedagogy (Loh et al., 2019; Kan & Loh, 2023):

#1

> This way, I'll let them (less experienced teachers) know the advantages of teaching CSL through drama (innovative pedagogy), such as motivating the students to take actions, making the content more memorable, learning with fun...in other words, making learning more interesting for the students. I'd also tell them though there are different parameters to be controlled, such as classroom disciplines. The students could make a lot of noise in class, and support from the school management, or school management's understanding, has to be sought...
>
> – Teacher K,
> Participant with 25+ years of teaching experience

#2

> I haven't been informed yet, honestly. They told me application for the Chinese one (university-school support program) had been submitted, for which they had given their endorsement. However, when the results were out, I was told it's not the case [...] and then informed the opportunity (to join the university-school support program) was given to the English Panel instead of the Chinese Panel. Well, we used to have a meeting together at the Principal's Office to discuss the needs of different subjects. I'm not sure why there's no such meeting this year.
>
> – Teacher U,
> Participant with 20+ years of teaching experience

Opportunities to learn about and to try out innovative curricula/pedagogies are, on the one hand, considered "a personal choice" from the school management's point of view at one end of the spectrum, and the teachers involved would feel the urge to justify for their adoption of an innovative curricula/pedagogies already endorsed by the school management. At another end of the spectrum though, the "choice" itself might not always be available and voluntary, especially when there are competitions within the same school for external TPD resources. Their concerns, therefore, encompass the informational level (the new teachers who might need extra information about the new curricula/pedagogies), the personal level (what changes they would expect), the consequences (how their students would benefit from the new curricula/pedagogies, and how their efforts would be evaluated by the school management), and the management issues (how they would manage the preparation, facilitation, and resource distribution). As change was well-expected and the stress level at work was high, the teachers tended to be cautious, if not always reserved, when given a choice to adopt new curricula/pedagogies in their daily CSL teaching.

5.2.2 Impacts of the Outcome-Based Culture on CSL Teachers

The second issue related to the juxtaposition of multiple concerns and responses in the adapted Guskey's model, CBAM and DMIS is the outcome-based culture in Hong Kong and its impacts on the CSL teachers. When the authors interviewed the informants about their thoughts about using innovative curricula/pedagogies in their classrooms, there had been recurring narratives like the below on the contesting views and priorities in their workplaces:

#3

To be frank, we should let the teachers to try it out first. I'm more inclined towards the "take it easy" approach, i.e. trial and error. It's okay to retry if the first attempts do not work. But some teachers would be sad if they couldn't achieve their objectives in those 45 minutes...

– Teacher U,
Participant with 20+ years of teaching experience

#4

Recommend drama for CSL teaching? But I'm not sure if they (Teacher K's fellow CSL teachers) would accept that, as we all know drama in education gives an impression of being time-consuming. A waste of time, I mean...so...

[Also] Firstly, I'm not very familiar with my colleagues [CSL teachers] though we are in the same department, which means [I] won't...novice teachers?...Teachers new to CSL?... Do you mean individual, new...so you meant not those from our school. I would share with them the benefits and weaknesses, as I don't think there's one ideal, flawless solution. For example, we had to handle the classroom management issues, the noise...whoa, I really didn't know what to do in the very beginning. Or the conflicts between students, I mean sometimes they really don't bother to respond to us. We've been there...I think we did experience these challenges...that's true...[but] I got what you meant.

– Teacher K,
Participant with 25+ years of teaching experience

Like their L1 counterparts, the informants displayed a contradictory mix of defensive yet understanding behaviors, as featured in the proposed integrated model with the adapted DMIS highlighted. The lack of confidence and even learned helplessness might as well be related to the challenges they had been facing when switching from L1 teaching to L2 teaching, especially in the case of experienced teachers who were assigned to teach or to lead CSL programs after the policy changes in Chinese language education upon Hong Kong's return to Chinese sovereignty. In Hong Kong mainstream schools, CSL teaching was mainly introduced to cater for the needs of the academically- and culturally-diverse ethnic minority students, which had posed yet another challenge for the participating teachers in the predominantly outcome-based culture. Therefore, the teachers tended to find themselves with a myriad of concerns about the new curricula/pedagogies, which in turn echoes with the adapted CBAM.

5.2.3 The "Experimental" Nature of Innovative Promotion in TPD

The third issue regarding juxtaposition of multiple concerns and responses in the modified CBAM and the adapted DMIS remains the "experimental" nature of new curricula/pedagogies in terms of actual implementation. Temporariness of the innovation promotion and flexibility helped to explain the intertwined pedagogical concerns and psychological responses of the teachers.

Less experienced informants, when being asked by the first author to reflect on the use of new curricula/pedagogies, tended to respond with uncertainty and uneasiness about introducing innovative practices to their CSL classrooms. Here below are a couple of such examples:

#5

> And, when the expert visited us, I thought we were less anxious the first time. I was, in turn, being more playful and flexible. The students got anxious when they saw the expert, and so did I…
>
> – Teacher Q,
> Participant with 3+ years of teaching experience

#6

> We all have different personalities. Some of our colleagues might prefer following certain procedures and not exactly suitable facilitators for teaching Chinese through Drama. I'm more "laid back" and not into detailed planning of my lessons, and ready for whatever comes to me in class. My ultimate goal is achieving the objectives, and flexibility is important to me. Therefore, drama would be more suitable for me, as I find it more fun to come up with "impromptu" elicitations and responses…
>
> – Teacher W,
> Participant with 15+ years of experience

The informants' responses take root in their unfamiliarity to the innovative curricula/pedagogies and witness of how other "less flexible" teachers were demotivated in the workplace. This third issue, like the case of L1 Chinese language teaching, activates the teachers' concerns and their defense mechanism. As few innovations would sustain in mainstream school settings, teachers tend to focus on the consequence, such as the effectiveness of the newly introduced curricula/pedagogies, and how these would affect their students' learning.

5.3 Why Do the Extra Steps Work?

Given that roots of juxtaposition in the adapted models for Hong Kong lie in the three factors as illustrated above, the processes having been added to the adapted Guskey's (1986) Model of Teacher Change, i.e. teaching demonstration/practical sessions and collective lesson preparation, shows us the key to the success of teacher change in the Hong Kong CSL context. The extra steps, namely teaching demonstration/practical sessions and collective lesson preparation, are highly significant through the process of teacher change due to their experiential, interactive nature. Again, like their L1 counterparts, both the CSL subject experts/demonstrators and participants interviewed in this study suggested that teaching demonstrations/practical sessions outperform traditional workshop seminars. Workshop seminars, which are often a combination of lectures and Q&A sessions, require the participants to listen to the theories and explanations in a quiet room. Relying on uni-directional way of dissemination, there is minimal interaction, making them less effective in helping the in-service teachers to advance their skills while grasping new concepts.

Teaching demonstration/practical sessions, plays the role as a stimulant or even catalyst that arouses teachers' interest and motivations in innovative curricula/ pedagogies, while enhancing the effectiveness of TPD for frontline CSL teachers. Through hands-on tasks and authentic scenarios, teachers are often surprised at how much easier it is to grasp the new concepts and theoretical constructs behind the innovative curricula/pedagogies, as well as to acquire the skills necessary for flexible adaptation for classroom use in different streaming and student groupings.

Also, traditional workshop seminars often fails to offer solutions to real-life problems in actual settings, especially the often academically- and culturally-diverse CSL classrooms. On-site professional support with both collective lesson preparation and teaching demonstration/practical sessions would be pivotal to motivating teachers to try—or to try even harder. Two participants shared their personal experiences and feelings about the two extra steps:

#7

For example, your drama expert visited us twice. [...] For example, the first time was a huge surprise for me, that is, wow, how did they manage that so well?

– Teacher U,
Participant with 20+ years of teaching experience

#8

Your team [...] provided many teaching exemplars for our reference. Like what (another interviewee) said, we weren't sure what to do in the very beginning. We're supposed to teach the students something when the classroom management hadn't been in place. What we tried ourselves were...I thought I learned quite a lot in the first year, such as "role play, still image, and hot seating" which I personally found quite interesting. I didn't expect it to be so challenging. When the students managed "still image" and wanted something new [...] then next (activity/skill), and that's it. They're really into this (change of activity).

– Teacher Q,
Participant with 3+ years of teaching experience

According to the above informants, the customized on-site skill sharing, step-by-step mentoring, and "space of learning" were additional advantages of teaching demonstrations/practical sessions. Being involved in the process as either presenters or peer reviewers, empowered teachers were able to gain first-hand experience in the actual operational procedures in an authentic setting, while making sure their initial attempts were on the right track.

Demonstration/practical sessions, to our informants, are effective and right to the point. Nevertheless, there are also a number of limitations as in the case of L1 Chinese language teaching, namely time constraint, adaptability concern, and suitability concern:

#9 Time Constraint

Yes, time is really limited. If she (one of the participating teachers experiencing difficulty in keeping up with her progress on the program) has to "digest" the knowledge we acquired, such as after our meetings, I don't think she has enough time for it.

– Teacher U,
Participant with 20+ years of teaching experience

#10 Adaptability Concern

We'll have to assess if introduction of "Reading to Learn" (another innovative pedagogy) would become a constraint for the participating teacher. We hope that the teachers would be independent and flexible, that is, taking "Reading to Learn" as a tool, instead of the other way round. So, if you're able to keep using the pedagogy in our daily teaching, it implies you're making appropriate adjustment to your teaching, and that's what we're glad to see.

– Teacher P,
Subject Expert/Demonstrator

#11 Suitability Concern

So what is the constraint? I'd say the culture, such as the cultural background of the set text, and the area of the teaching venue. These are pivotal to the success of the intervention in a particular class. If it's an "inclusive" class with a minority of NCS students, the teacher would need a lot of energy to motivate 30+ students in that same class to perform the assigned tasks. [...] For the new teachers, or teachers less familiar with the innovative pedagogy, it would be a challenge. In turn, if you put the NCS students in a separate class, you'll have different concerns as you're supposed to provide even more effective support to the students. [...] As for cross-grade ability grouping, I've given it a try and the challenge lies in the differences between Form 2 and Form 3 in terms of Chinese language proficiency, mentality, and school expectations. It's important for the [teacher] to provide level-appropriate input, so that the Form 3 students won't find the content silly whereas their Form 2 counterpart would find it too difficult. Balance is key and that's what I can come up with for now.

– Teacher U,
Participant with 20+ years of teaching experience

In view of the above concerns and constraints, collective lesson preparation and teaching demonstration/practical sessions serve as key elements in TPD programs for relieving teachers' stress, doubts, and anxiety. With feedback and advice from subject experts/demonstrators tailored to the participants' needs, collective lesson preparation is pivotal to the success of their first attempts to apply the innovative pedagogies to their own classes. According to one of the informants:

#12

That means I'm relatively lucky to have this "lifesaver" (the subject expert/demonstrator), whom I could consult from time to time whenever I came up with questions like "is this considered drama in education?" Once you've tried a few times (adopting an innovative pedagogy), you would figure out where the boundaries are. Actually, when you've come to a right scenario or level, you'd be able to create an extra lesson with reference to the existing framework.

– Teacher W,
Participant with 20+ years of teaching experience

Besides input from the subject experts/demonstrators, the participating teachers are also able to benefit from the peer responses and self-reflections through collective lesson preparation and teaching demonstrations/practical sessions. Revisiting one's existing practices and comparing them with the newly-acquired concepts and skills, the teachers are likely to come up with ways to improvise or improve their methods and curricula, particularly for those of them who have been struggling to switch to CSL and flipped classroom:

#13

> Firstly, I have a better understanding of the app [a mobile language learning app being introduced in the program in relation to mobile-assisted CSL pedagogy] now, which means my teaching methods won't be limited to Chinese-English and English-Chinese translations. I would be able to come up with many different teaching activities for the purpose. Secondly, I've come to realize that the pedagogy is not to be "used for using's sake". That's my old mentality, like I'd like to try this [app], adopt it in my classes and perhaps my students would be interested. This year though, I gave this app a try and found that the progress had improved and saved us a lot of time. Back in those days when we had little IT support, we'd have to use less direct or effective methods. [...] I talked to my colleagues at the Chinese Panel, and they shared the same mentality of "using it for using's sake". Actually, NCS students need information input like how Chinese-speaking students learning English. When you teach them about fruit, you shouldn't just upload the names of 15 types of fruit. It's better for them to look for the terms themselves instead of having you "spoon-feed" them. Learning a second language should be based on what they already know about daily life – what they are lacking is the language (instead of the general knowledge).
>
> – Teacher N,
> Participant with 15+ years of teaching experience

6 Conclusion

Evidenced by the positive classroom atmosphere and enhanced interactions between teachers and students, collective lesson preparation and teaching demonstrations/ practical sessions are valuable additions to CSL TPD programs. The provision of pedagogical diagnoses and practical advice, they empower and motivate teachers who have gained skills and self-confidence to implement innovative curricula/ pedagogies in their own classrooms. As in the case of L1 Chinese language teachers, CSL teachers also benefit from the discussions with the subject experts/demonstrators and fellow participants, especially from each other's feedback and experience sharing. The two extra steps offer opportunities to talk about one's needs and concerns, and serves as sources of teaching tips, classroom management strategies, timely and succinct solutions to student-specific issues and other challenges in daily teaching.

In view of the above, one would need to recognize the important role of emotionality in TPD, which is highly relevant to teacher's professional and personal growth in a time of transition and innovation. To better prepare teachers for the ever-changing profession, refresh their teaching skills and enhance student learning, it is essential to provide teachers with clear guidance in the form of experiential learning, so that they can apply the knowledge and skills acquired from TPD into their classroom teaching. These, in turn, would serve well as the practical implications of the current study. The findings should be an updated reference for the teacher trainers, especially those who are motivated to revise their current TPD practices for a greater impact on TPD itself and perceptual change.

Participation in teaching demonstrations/practical sessions and collective lesson preparation offers teachers a sense of security and serves as an aid for improving their self-efficacy. Frontline educators, especially those who are new to CSL and struggling to master the practical skills for successful CSL teaching and learning (such as and the application of the theories and adaptation of innovative curricula/pedagogies for their own classroom setting), are essential change agents in the present-day collaborative school culture. By comparing and contrasting the findings with the classic Teacher Change models and the authors' earlier adaptation for L1 Chinese language teachers, this study has presented a new adapted model for CSL teachers with reference to the psychosocial stages of professional development, and identified key factors leading to perceptual changes in TPD and university-school support projects. Future research is required to provide more evidence of the applicability of the proposed integrated model at different levels of education, as well as other variables that might affect the feasibility.

Notes Pseudonyms are randomly assigned to informants to safeguard their identities.

Acknowledgements The authors would like to thank the Standing Committee on Language Education and Research (SCOLAR) of the Hong Kong Special Administrative Region (HKSAR) for their project sponsorship (Project Reference: EDB(LE)/P&R/EL/164/8), as well as the schools, teachers and students who participated in this study. Their appreciation also extends to Dr. M. S. K. Shum, Dr. W. W. Ki, Mr. K. W. Sun and Mr. F. K. L. Tang for assisting in the focus group interviews, and Mr. Nixon T. H. Leung, Ms. Jenny Zeng, Ms. Sophia Liu, Ms. Karen Jiaxin Song, and Ms. Jasmine Shum for their research assistance.

References

Advisory Committee on Teacher Education Qualifications (ACTEQ). (2003). *Towards a learning profession: The teacher competencies framework and the continuing professional development of teachers*. ACTEQ.
Advisory Committee on Teacher Education Qualifications (ACTEQ). (2006). *Towards A learning profession: Interim report on teachers' continuing professional development*. ACTEQ.
Advisory Committee on Teacher Education Qualifications (ACTEQ). (2009). *Towards a learning profession: Third report on teachers' continuing professional development*. ACTEQ.
Anderson, S. (1997). Understanding teaching change: Revisiting the concerns-based adoption model. *Curriculum Inquiry, 27*(3), 331–367.
Bennett, M. J. (1993). Toward ethnorelativism: A developmental model of intercultural sensitivity. In R. M. Paige (Ed.), *Education for the intercultural experience* (pp. 21–71). Intercultural Press.

Bergmark, U. (2020). Teachers' professional learning when building a research-based education: Context-specific, collaborative and teacher driven professional development. *Professional Development in Education, 49*(2), 210–224. https://doi.org/10.1080/19415257.2020.1827011

Cho, E., & Chan, T. (2020). Children's wellbeing in a high-stakes testing environment: The case of Hong Kong. *Children and Youth Services Review, 109*, Article 104694.

Clarke, D., & Hollingsworth, H. (2002). Elaborating a model of teacher professional growth. *Teaching and Teacher Education, 18*(8), 947–967.

Cohen, D. K., & Hill, H. C. (1998). *State policy and classroom performance: Mathematics reform in California* (CPRE Policy Briefs (RB-23-May)). Consortium for Policy Research in Education.

Cohen, D. K., & Hill, H. C. (2000). Instructional policy and classroom performance: The mathematics reform in California. *Teachers College Record, 102*(2), 294–343.

Dos Santos, L. (2019). Pre-service teachers professional development through four-step problem-solving model: A seminar method. *International Journal of Education and Practice, 7*(3), 146–157.

Dreyfus, H. L., & Dreyfus, S. E. (1986). *Mind over machine: The power of human intuition and expertise in the era of the computer.* Basil Blackwell.

Education Bureau of HKSAR. (2020). Education Bureau Circular No. 6/2020 Implementation of the recommendations of the task force on professional development of teachers.

Forde, C., & McMahon, M. (2019). *Teacher quality, professional learning and policy: Recognising, rewarding and developing teacher expertise.* Springer.

Fullan, M. (1982). *The meaning of educational change.* Teachers College Press.

Fullan, M. (1991). *The new meaning of educational change.* Teachers College Press.

Fullan, M. (2007). *The new meaning of educational change* (4th ed.). Teachers College Press.

Fullan, M., & Stiegelbauer, S. (1991). *The new meaning of educational change* (2nd ed.). Teachers College Press.

Gabryś-Barker, D. (2018). Emotionality in L2 teacher discourse: Implications for teacher education and future research directions. In J. D. M. Agudo (Ed.), *Emotions in second language teaching: Theory, research and teacher education* (pp. 301–321). Springer.

Glattenhorn, A. (1995). Teacher development. In L. W. Anderson (Ed.), *International Encyclopedia of Teaching and Teacher Education* (2nd ed., pp. 41–45). Pergamon.

Guskey, T. R. (1986). Staff development and the process of teacher change. *Educational Researcher, 15*(5), 5–12.

Guskey, T. R. (2002). Professional development and teacher change. *Teachers and Teaching, 8*(3), 381–391. https://doi.org/10.1080/135406002100000512

Hall, G. E., Wallace, R. C., & Dossett, W. F. (1973). *A developmental conceptualization of the adoption process within education institutions.* Research and Development Center for Teacher Education, University of Texas at Austin.

Hargreaves, D. H. (1995). School culture, School effectiveness and school improvement. *School Effectiveness and School Improvement, 6*(1), 23–46. https://doi.org/10.1080/0924345950060102

Hargreaves, A. (1998). Emotional politics of teaching and teacher development: With implications for educational leadership. *International Journal of Leadership in Education, 1*(4), 315–336.

Hord, S. M., Rutherford, W. L., Huling-Austin, L., & Hall, G. E. (1987). *Taking charge of change.* Association for Supervision and Curriculum Development.

Johnston, B. (2003). *Values in English language teaching.* Lawrence Erlbaum.

Kan, Z. W. N., & Loh, E. K. Y. (2023). Teaching modern Chinese literature to second-language Chinese students through the use of drama. In L. Li & D. Zhang (Eds.), *Reading in Chinese as an additional language: Learners' development, instruction and assessment* (pp. 217–245). Routledge.

Kennedy, M. (1998). *Form and substance in teacher in-service education* (Research Monograph No. 13). National Institute for Science Education, University of Wisconsin Madison.

Loh, E. K. Y., & Tam, L. C. W. (2017). The role of emotionality in teacher change: The case of Chinese language teachers in Hong Kong. *Teacher Development, 21*(3), 462–479.

Loh, E. K. Y., Woo, J. P. S., Ki, W. W., & Tang, F. K. L. (2019). Drama in education pedagogy assists students in learning Chinese as a second language: Theories and research. In E. K. Y. Loh, P. W. Y. Chou, M. S. K. Shum, & W. W. Ki (Eds.), *Chinese language education in the multilingual and multicultural contexts: Theories and practice* (pp. 87–102). Hong Kong University Press.

Opfer, V. D., & Pedder, D. (2011). Conceptualizing teacher professional learning. *Review of Educational Research, 81*(3), 376–407.

Pang, I. W. (2012). Teacher stress in working with challenging students in Hong Kong. *Education Research for Policy and Practice, 11*, 119–139.

Richardson, V. (1998). *How teachers change: What will lead to change that most benefits student learning?* (Focus on Basics, 2(C)). National Center for the Study of Adult Learning and Literacy. Retrieved from http://www.ncsall.net/index.html@id=395.html

Schutz, P. A., Hong, J. Y., Cross, D. I., & Osbon, J. N. (2006). Reflections on investigating emotion in educational activity settings. *Educational Psychology Review, 18*, 343–360.

Villegas-Reimers, E. (2003). *Teacher professional development: An international review of the literature*. UNESCO International Institute for Educational Planning.

Wang, H. A., Thompson, P., Shuler, C., & Harvey, L. (1999). Problem-based learning approach for science teachers' professional development. Paper presented at the Annual Meeting of the Association for the Education of Teachers in Science.

Wong, M., & Pennington, M. C. (1993). *Are resource class English teachers in Hong Kong satisfied with their work?* (Research Report No. 31). English Department, City Polytechnic of Hong Kong.

Index

A

Academic success, x, 77, 165
Acculturation, 24
Achievement, viii, xiv, 10, 11, 34, 48, 165, 166, 171, 172, 175, 176, 183, 246, 274, 337, 350
Achievers, xii, 169, 171–175, 183, 186, 199, 253, 262, 266, 294
Acting system, 202, 203
Adaptability, 415, 416
Adaptation, 39, 180, 400, 403, 406, 408, 409, 411, 415, 418
Additional language learning, 357
Adjectival predicates, xi, 125–157
Affiliation, xvi, 380, 381
Alternative CSL learning pathway, absence of, 44
Anti-racial Discrimination Ordinance, exemptions in, 25
Applicability, 231, 402, 418
Application, x, xiv, 20, 33, 99–121, 126, 128, 171, 180, 183–186, 188, 189, 197, 198, 202, 246, 264, 275–277, 305, 370, 374, 412, 418
Applied Learning (Chinese) Programme, 22, 23
Appraisal, 166, 167, 169–171, 173, 175, 190–195, 259, 403
Asian languages, 11, 314, 380, 382
Assessment, xi, 7, 21, 22, 27, 38, 40, 44, 47, 63, 83, 85, 86, 164–167, 175, 184, 185, 191, 193, 195, 231, 240, 247, 251, 253, 276, 299, 324, 360, 382, 385, 405
Assimilation, 24

Attainment, ix, 44, 45, 300, 338, 343, 345, 350, 352
Australian curriculum, 315–318, 324, 331, 358, 360, 372, 382
Australian secondary students, xiv, 313, 314, 317, 319, 321, 323, 325, 327, 329, 331, 333
Australian secondary teachers, 315
Authentic text, 361, 366–369, 392
Auto ethnographic study, 41
Autonomy, 32, 37, 105, 274, 276, 278, 280, 294, 297, 303, 324

B

Background, xi, xiii, xiv, xvi, 4, 5, 15, 34, 35, 38, 40, 44, 62, 77, 81, 82, 92–94, 105, 113, 126, 131, 135, 138, 151, 155, 157, 184, 204, 210, 215, 216, 226, 277, 278, 313–316, 322, 326, 328, 358, 365–367, 370, 374, 380–383, 385, 386, 394, 401, 416
Benchmarking, 20, 44
Bicultural orientations, compartmentalised/harmonious, 30
Bifurcation of Chinese and English MOI, 27, 43
Bilingual approach, 358
Bilingual education, 43
Biliterate and Trilingual Language Policy, 17, 45
Body movements, 60, 61, 71, 215
Building connections, 361

© The Editor(s) (if applicable) and The Author(s), under exclusive license to Springer Nature Switzerland AG 2024
J. Lo Bianco et al. (eds.), *Supporting the Learning of Chinese as a Second Language: Implications for Language Education Policy*, Language Policy 36,
https://doi.org/10.1007/978-3-031-66135-8

C

Capability, 5, 7, 8, 11, 36, 42, 165, 180, 181, 359, 360, 371, 384–386
Case study, xi–xvi, 50, 99, 105, 114, 117–121, 179, 183, 198, 201–223, 225–237, 313, 318, 319, 334, 337, 339, 379, 380, 385–386, 399, 402
Catalyst, 400, 411, 415
Causal explanation, 244
Character configuration, 56, 62, 63, 65–71
Character identification, 57, 62, 71, 72
Character meaning, x, 55, 56, 58, 61–71
Character-meaning identification, 68, 71
China, x, 3, 6–8, 10–12, 15–17, 28, 32, 37, 42, 77, 78, 83, 94, 105, 163, 180, 205, 264, 314–316, 320, 321, 324, 326, 332, 338, 361, 364, 368, 373, 377, 380, 381, 386, 389, 391–393
  knowledge, 7
Chinese, 3, 16, 55, 77, 100, 126, 163, 180, 202, 225, 240, 272, 314, 338, 357, 379, 400
Chinese as a first/native language, x–xvii, 77–94, 244, 247, 403, 410
Chinese as a Second Language (CSL), viii–xvii, 19, 20, 55, 77, 99, 100, 125, 164, 179, 271, 400
Chinese characters, x, 32, 55–62, 67, 69, 71, 72, 78–80, 84, 105, 136, 169, 171, 174, 175, 180, 191, 279, 321, 368, 369
Chinese culture, 21, 331, 364, 370
Chinese language education, viii, ix, xv, 6, 8, 13, 15, 18, 164, 314, 315, 379–394
Chinese language learning, viii, xii, xv–xvii, 15–49, 93, 163, 165, 184, 225, 227, 272, 273, 316–319, 324, 357, 368, 379–382, 394
Chinese language programmes, 19, 315, 325, 327
Chinese language teacher education, 336
Chinese language teaching, 8, 28, 314–316, 319, 331, 414, 415
Chinese literacy, 32, 55, 58, 59, 69, 77, 171
Chinese reading comprehension, 77–94, 244
Chinese subject teachers, 323
Circumstances, 3, 204, 206–210, 213–217, 222, 234
Classroom, xi–xv, 9, 15, 17, 28, 35, 36, 38, 43, 55, 60, 61, 72, 99, 101–103, 107–109, 111–112, 116–117, 119–120, 126, 127, 142, 169, 179, 181, 183, 184, 199, 210, 211, 220, 230, 243–245, 266, 271–307, 313, 315, 317–320, 324, 326, 329–331, 334, 337–352, 361, 363, 366, 368, 372, 373, 383, 385, 400, 402–405, 407, 409–418
  observation, xii, xiv, 211, 313, 319, 320, 341, 363
Code-mixing, 43
Cognitive
  perspective, 60, 227
  skill, 81, 82, 91, 93
  writing strategies, 232, 234, 235
Cognitive-based curriculum, 55–73, 241, 296, 297
Cognitive processing-based, x, 56, 61, 68
Collaborative
  learning, 294–296, 304, 305, 333
  school culture, 418
  teaching, 234–236
Collective lesson preparation, xvi, 399, 400, 410, 414, 416, 417
Comparison, xv, 33, 60, 81, 83, 86, 88, 104, 113, 131, 139, 169, 171, 185, 189–191, 193–195, 199, 208, 244, 253, 266, 337, 341, 343, 345–347, 349–351, 358, 359, 361, 363, 365, 372, 373, 386–388
Competence, 7, 17, 31, 37, 48, 55, 56, 72, 113, 130, 274–276, 278, 280, 294, 322, 332, 345, 351, 385
Competency, 23, 180, 181
Competent, 17, 37, 101, 274, 333, 343, 349, 350
Complication, 166, 168, 170, 171, 219
Component knowledge, 56, 58, 60, 69
Composition, 59, 80, 109, 111, 116, 120, 165–167, 169, 170, 173, 175, 180, 183, 186, 232, 321, 409
Computer-Assisted Language Learning (CALL), 275
Concepts, xv, xvii, 25, 29, 39, 103, 104, 180, 236, 240, 241, 267, 271, 272, 277, 280, 304, 357–377, 383, 384, 387, 388, 399, 400, 415, 417
Conceptual reflection, 386, 388
Conceptual understanding, 358, 371, 393
Concerns-Based Adoption Model (CBAM), xvi, 400, 402–404, 406, 411
Confirmatory factor analysis, 89, 90
Conjunctions, 167, 169, 171, 175, 191, 193, 195, 197, 254, 256, 257, 260
Conscience alley, 37, 102, 106–108, 111
Consequential explanation, 244, 248, 257–259, 262, 266
Constituent components, 56–59, 64
Content and Language Integrated Learning, 267

Index

Context, 4, 5, 13, 15, 25, 26, 33, 39, 49, 61, 63, 71, 78, 84, 110, 111, 113, 164, 166, 167, 173, 181, 185, 186, 189–191, 193, 195, 196, 201, 206, 209, 216, 217, 225, 232, 234, 235, 244, 245, 282, 315, 319, 322, 323, 327, 328, 330–332, 334, 337–339, 347, 349–351, 357, 358, 362, 365, 367, 369, 370, 379, 382, 384, 385, 387, 392, 393, 400–403, 414
Contextual, xv, 136, 167, 173, 192, 194, 337–339, 349
'Continuum of actions', 8, 48
Contrast(ing), 6, 26, 33, 83, 92, 103, 110, 118, 119, 128, 134, 139, 186, 256, 259, 266, 290, 338, 346, 350, 351, 365, 418
Correlation analyses, 86
Critical features, 104, 105, 110, 121
Cross-curriculum approach, 370
Crowdfunding, 271, 272, 277, 280, 304
Cultural activities, 324
Cultural context, 209, 331, 344, 367, 392, 393
Cultural identity development, 28
Culturally responsive teaching, 34
Curriculum, vii, x, xi, xiii, xv, 4, 5, 8, 9, 19–21, 24, 30, 31, 38, 44–48, 55, 56, 59–63, 65, 67, 69, 71–73, 78, 85, 93, 94, 105, 125–127, 165, 166, 180, 182, 198, 199, 237, 239–244, 247, 253, 272, 274, 278, 286, 296, 297, 307, 315–319, 324, 326, 331, 333, 334, 357–377, 382, 388, 405, 407, 418
Curriculum and syllabus, 316, 324
Curriculum closure, 247, 253
Curriculum design, xv, 55, 237, 334, 357, 364, 374
Curriculum initiation, 247
Curriculum negotiation, 247

D

Data analysis, 231, 340
Deconstruction, 34, 181, 244, 248, 262, 265, 320
Description, 151, 157, 166, 185, 206, 207, 244, 339, 376, 389
Designated schools, and its abolishment, 43
Detailed reading, 34, 183, 187–189, 196–198
Developmental, 55, 56, 61, 67, 72, 80, 118, 387, 399, 400, 402, 403, 405, 408–411
Developmental Concern-based Intercultural Sensitivity Model of Teacher Change for CSL, 410

Developmental Model of Intercultural Sensitivity (DMIS), 402, 405, 408, 409, 411
Diaspora, viii, 3, 8, 9, 12
Discernment, 59, 104, 110, 118, 121
Discourse, 12, 101, 132, 164, 166, 167, 171, 173, 175, 185, 186, 189, 191, 193, 195, 197, 241, 242, 319, 370, 381
Discussion, xv, xvii, 4, 17, 28, 41, 43, 48, 68, 90, 102, 117, 118, 127, 132, 138, 151, 153, 155, 157, 166, 181, 186, 187, 189, 198, 201–203, 211, 242, 244, 253, 264, 265, 286, 304, 318, 322, 325, 330, 349, 357, 359, 365–369, 382, 384
Dominant languages, 4, 226, 230, 386
  constellation, 42
Drama and writing, 202–203
Drama convention, 37, 120
Drama-in-education (DiE), 202

E

Education, 4, 16, 78, 100, 126, 164, 198, 223, 225, 240, 271, 314, 338, 358, 379, 400
Educational needs, 86
Effectiveness, vii, xii, xiv, xvii, 7, 8, 12, 23, 45, 56, 61, 65, 68–70, 100–103, 118, 131, 134, 180, 184, 185, 189, 198, 201, 210, 231–236, 253, 267, 277, 295, 303, 305, 313, 317, 332, 399, 401, 405, 414, 415
Emotionality, 103, 273, 399–418
Emotion memory, 204, 213, 214, 217, 222, 223
Empower, 417
Engagement, 7, 12, 60, 61, 102, 164, 171, 175, 276, 295, 298, 317, 323, 324, 351, 359, 366
English, viii, xiv, xv, 3, 5–7, 10, 12, 13, 17–19, 21, 22, 26–31, 34, 35, 42–46, 48, 62, 78, 81, 102, 105, 126, 128–130, 133, 170–175, 180, 182, 186, 194–196, 199, 226, 230, 233, 240, 242, 246, 248, 251, 278, 280, 301, 305, 313–318, 323, 326, 329, 330, 334, 357, 358, 365, 368–373, 381, 386, 390, 391, 394, 402, 412, 417
  value of, viii, xiv, xv, 26, 28, 372
Equity, 16, 18
Ethnic minority(ies) (EM), x, 4, 12, 15–49, 61–63, 77–78, 99, 100, 125, 163–165, 172, 180, 201, 202, 272, 413
Exam, xv, 20, 44, 45, 114, 118, 126, 130, 337, 340, 341, 345, 347, 349–351
Executive function (EF), 77, 78, 81, 82, 85

Expectancy, 337, 338, 340
Experienced policy, 9
Experiential learning, xvi, 399, 418
Experimental, xi, xii, 121, 125, 130, 134–136, 138–141, 202, 246, 411, 413
Explanation(s), xii, xiii, 17, 43, 70, 91, 92, 113, 164–175, 179–199, 208, 209, 239, 242–266, 318, 386, 414
   genre, xii, xiii, 179–199, 239, 245, 247, 248, 251, 253, 256, 259, 262–266
Exploratory factor analysis, 88
Exposition, 166, 242, 244, 276, 295, 297
Extrinsic, xiv, xv, 31, 37, 274–277, 305, 306, 313, 337, 352
   motivation, 31, 37, 274–277, 304, 305, 313, 337, 352

F
Factorial explanation, 239, 244–266
Feasibility, xvii, 5, 399, 418
Feedback, 8, 9, 36, 48, 111, 120, 214–216, 229, 279, 286, 295, 299, 350, 351, 363, 386, 389, 409, 410, 416, 417
Field, 164, 166, 167, 169–171, 175, 198, 199, 201, 206, 217, 225, 227, 229, 236, 240, 271, 315, 316, 321, 340, 380, 409
First foreign language, 10
First language instruction, 372
Focus group interviews, 166, 319, 326
Foreign, vii–ix, xv, 4, 10, 26, 100, 126, 135, 180, 226, 229, 315, 316, 322, 330, 332, 337–339, 351
Forms, 5, 18, 25, 36, 46, 59, 61, 63, 81, 99, 104, 105, 110, 121, 131, 135, 165, 166, 169, 205, 206, 208, 222, 241, 244, 277, 297, 302, 321, 331, 394, 408
4-stage, 3-step pedagogy, 300, 304
French, 6, 10, 180, 249, 278, 290, 315, 316, 319, 326
Frontline educators, 418
Function(s), 64, 80, 128, 133, 165, 166, 173, 181, 190, 193, 196, 197, 206, 241, 244, 266, 373
   words, 262
Functional grammar, 201, 202, 205, 209–211, 221–223, 239
Functional model, 181
Functional structure, 185
Fusion, 103, 104

G
Gamification, 272, 276, 277, 295, 299, 304, 305
Generalisation, 103, 104, 143

Generation, 226
Genre-based approach, 164, 180, 181, 244
Genre-based literacy, 165, 166, 239, 243, 244
Genre-based pedagogy, 34, 181–183, 244–247, 266
Genres, xiii, 34, 164–167, 175, 181, 206, 239, 242–248, 262, 266, 385
Genre theory, 239, 242
Geopolitical, 10
German, 10, 315, 316, 361
Given circumstances, 204, 209, 213–217, 222
Goal-oriented, 181
Grammar, xi, xii, 4, 28, 118, 125–127, 129–133, 136–143, 166, 167, 185, 189, 190, 194, 201, 202, 205, 209–211, 214, 217, 221–223, 239, 242, 273, 302, 319, 325, 334, 340–346, 348, 349, 362, 363, 372, 373
   teaching, 130, 131
Graphic features, 164, 166, 171, 185, 189

H
Halliday, xii, 4, 181, 197, 201–223, 239, 241, 242
Heritage languages, 17, 100
Hong Kong, 12, 16, 56, 83, 100, 125, 163, 179, 202, 226, 240, 272, 339, 400
Hong-Kong-er identity, 16

I
IBDP Chinese B, 225, 230, 231
ICT integration, 331
Identity, xv, xvi, 4, 11, 12, 26, 28–31, 36, 48, 113, 209, 226, 252, 278, 357, 362, 369, 374, 376, 377, 379, 380, 384, 385, 394, 401, 408
'Identity text', 36
Ideographic script, 32
IGCSE (0547), 125, 126, 135, 226
Implemented policy, viii, xvi, 8, 9, 48
Improvement, xi, xiv, 8, 22, 26, 36, 48, 65, 69, 70, 120, 125, 139, 165, 169, 175, 190, 202, 210–212, 223, 230, 234, 235, 259, 262, 264–266, 304, 400
Independent construction, 181, 244, 253, 263, 265
Individual rewriting, 183
Inductive learning, 4
Inhibitory control, x, 77–94, 244, 247
Inner action, 205, 213, 215–217
Innovative pedagogies, xvi, 399, 408, 411
Input processing, xi, 125, 129–131, 133, 136
In-role-reading, 114

Index

In-role-writing, 106, 107, 109
Integration, viii, xii, 15, 16, 18, 24–26, 56, 78, 82, 83, 100, 179, 198, 324, 330–332, 400, 408, 409
Integrative perceptual approach (IPA), 32
Intended policy, 9, 11
Interactive, xii, xiii, 111, 197, 201, 202, 217, 225, 236, 242, 328, 329, 331, 332, 387, 414
Intercultural, xv, xvi, 5, 11, 19, 21, 24, 38–41, 48, 357–361, 365–368, 371–375, 379, 380, 383–394, 399, 400, 402, 405, 408–411
  approach, xv, 357, 358
  comparison, 361, 387, 388
  sensitivity, xvi, 39, 48, 367, 399, 400, 402, 405, 408–411
  understanding, 5, 21, 359, 366, 368, 373
Interpersonal, 4, 181, 206, 217, 227, 264
Interpretation, 45, 243, 244, 366, 383–385
Interview, xi, 7, 117, 138, 142, 163, 172, 184, 186, 197, 198, 203, 211, 230, 263, 265, 319, 320, 323, 324, 327, 330, 340, 343, 345, 347, 393, 402
Intrinsic, xiv, 10, 31, 37, 274–277, 299, 304, 305, 313, 338, 351, 352
  motivation, 31, 37, 274–277, 299, 304
Invariance, 99, 104, 105, 110–113, 118–120
Italian, 8, 315, 316, 381

J

Japanese, 8, 10, 11, 126, 278, 315, 316, 319, 326, 380
Joint construction, 181, 183, 187–189, 196–198, 244
Joint rewriting, 183, 196, 197

K

Krashen, S., xi, xii, 126, 129–132, 202, 214, 275, 297

L

Language
  acquisition, xi, 5, 43, 126, 127, 129–130, 132, 142, 164, 170, 181, 202, 214, 226, 228, 333, 334
  arrangements, 11
  education policy, vii–xvii, 11, 41, 45–48
  identity and investment, 29
  ideologies, 25–29
  input, xii, 129, 130, 133, 142
  learning, xii–xv, 6, 13, 26, 31, 35, 37, 44, 45, 92, 93, 118, 163, 164, 176, 182, 211, 227, 228, 237, 244, 267, 271–307, 316, 324, 331–333, 337, 351, 357–377, 380, 381, 383–387, 417
  learning strategies, 228
  output, 126, 127, 129, 130
  syllabus, 135, 315, 331
Language selves, ought-to language self and ideal language self, 31
Languages Other Than English (LOTE), 315, 329
Learner
  diversity, 38, 393
  pathway, 5, 317
Learning
  of Chinese, viii–xvii, 4, 5, 8, 17–19, 21, 27, 31, 43, 57–58, 60, 93, 94, 100–103, 105, 125–157, 163–176, 180, 201, 211, 225, 239, 271, 295, 304, 305, 314, 319, 324–330, 332, 338, 341, 345, 357–377, 381, 382, 384, 394
  motivation, vii, x, xiv–xv, 26, 31, 71, 101, 103, 105, 118, 197, 248, 272–277, 280, 304, 305, 325, 337, 338, 351
  needs, xi–xiii, 5, 18, 164, 166, 172, 175, 176, 183, 272–274, 338
Less skilled students, xiii, 232, 234–236
Lexicogrammatical features, 183
Liberal studies (LS), xiii, 165, 239–267
Lifeworlds, xv, 379–394
Linguistic level writing strategies, 232
Literacy
  development, ix, 5, 69, 72, 73, 166, 242, 371
  practices, 333
  tasks, 164–166, 169, 173, 176, 181
Local immersion, 4
Low socio-economic status, 180

M

Magic If, 101, 102, 205, 213–217
Mainstream schools, 17, 18, 100, 314, 315, 317, 334, 414
Make-believe play, 120
Mandarin Chinese, 126, 135, 314, 328
Mandarin songs, xi, 125–157
Mandatory subject, Chinese as, 21
Marginalization, 24

Meaningfulness, 383, 386
Medium of instruction (MoI), 17, 18, 25, 27, 28, 43, 46, 62, 105, 180, 266
Mentoring, 415
Metacognitive writing strategies, 232, 234, 235
Meta-function, 181
Mitigative measures, 23
mLang, xiii, xiv, 36–38, 271–305
    pedagogy, 36, 278, 280
Mnemonic(s), 60–63, 69–73
Mobile-Assisted Language Learning (MALL), 275
Mode, xiv, 119, 166, 167, 175, 197, 206, 210, 217, 249, 250, 331
Model of Teacher Change, xvi, 402, 408–411, 414
More skilled students, xiii, 232, 234, 235
Morphological awareness, 80–83, 333
Motivate, xiv, 9, 30, 199, 294, 317, 324–325, 329, 332, 333, 400, 410, 416, 417
Motivation, xiv, xv, 26, 30, 31, 37, 40, 102, 103, 112, 114, 127, 130, 174, 198, 205, 251, 272, 274–278, 299, 304, 305, 314, 322, 323, 325, 330, 334, 349–352
Multilingual, xvi, 26, 32, 36, 42, 278, 359, 380, 381, 383–393
Multimodal, 36, 59, 62, 118, 206, 278, 280, 303, 305, 331, 384

N

Narration, 164–171, 173, 175, 183, 321, 330, 332
Narrative writing, xii, 166–168, 202, 203, 210, 211, 213, 216, 221–223
New senior secondary (NSS) curriculum, 240, 243
Non-Chinese heritage-background learners, xiv, 319
Non-Chinese Speaking Students (NCS), xii, 165, 174, 179–199, 239–267
Non-native Chinese speaking, 105, 202, 210

O

Observation, xii–xiv, 24, 58, 183–185, 198, 211, 213–216, 231, 235, 265, 319–323, 333, 340, 341, 345, 346, 351, 361, 363, 368, 388, 408, 410
1.5 Chinese learners, 226, 227, 230, 235, 237
Orientation, xv, xvi, 24, 30, 34, 166, 168, 170, 171, 215–218, 222, 242, 363, 366, 367, 369, 374, 376, 384–387, 394

Orthographic awareness, x, 56, 58–59, 61–65, 67–73
Orthographic knowledge, 56, 58, 60–62, 65, 67, 71, 72, 78–80, 82–84
Overuse of 是 (is), 126–129, 142

P

Pedagogic intervention, xi, 164, 165
Pedagogical approaches, xvi, 69, 119, 316
Pedagogy, x–xiii, 5, 32–36, 38, 101, 103, 112–119, 121, 126, 131–133, 163, 164, 179–199, 202, 210, 236, 243–247, 264, 266, 267, 272, 273, 278–280, 294, 295, 304, 317, 334, 381, 405, 407, 412, 416, 417
Perceptual change, 121, 418
Performance, xii, xiii, 7, 17, 78, 81, 91, 92, 106, 109, 111, 120, 121, 164–167, 169, 171–173, 175, 176, 180, 183, 185, 196–197, 199, 202, 209, 211, 212, 214, 228, 232, 236, 245–247, 251, 253, 262–263, 265, 274, 294, 303–306, 318, 321, 325, 329, 330, 333, 338, 343, 345, 347, 349–351, 403, 407, 410
Personalisation, 359, 366, 367, 373, 387, 389, 393
(Personal) reflection, 358
Perspectives, 11, 25–31, 56, 105, 114, 137, 208, 227, 240, 241, 244, 254, 283, 319, 331, 357, 359, 360, 362, 363, 366, 367, 374, 375, 385, 387, 389, 391, 393, 394
Phenomenography, x, 99–121
    theory, 59, 103, 112
Phenomenon, xi, 33, 43, 104, 127, 132, 133, 136, 138, 140, 141, 166, 168–171, 185, 186, 189–196, 207, 210, 229, 244, 249, 252, 254–261, 332, 339, 350, 382, 387, 392
Phonetic radical, 64, 72
Physical action, 205, 209, 213–216, 218–222
Planning, viii, xv, 8, 13, 45–48, 119–120, 210, 227, 231–235, 324, 357–377, 393, 403, 405, 407, 414
Pop songs, xi, 133
Positional constraints, 56, 70
Positional knowledge, 56, 80
Positional regularity/regularities, 70, 72, 79, 80
Post-test, xiii, xiv, 63, 65, 66, 70, 135, 138, 139, 141, 142, 183–185, 189–197, 199, 210, 211, 245, 253, 254, 256, 257, 259, 260, 262–266
Practical sessions, 400, 410, 411, 414–418

Index 427

Pragmatic level writing strategies, 232, 234
Pre-test, xi, 63, 65, 66, 70, 135, 137–139, 141, 165, 167, 169, 171, 172, 183–187, 189–197, 199, 210, 211, 245–248, 253, 254, 256, 257, 259–264, 266
Principles, 11, 23, 56, 57, 104, 132, 133, 136, 137, 316, 317, 371, 387–393
Process, 4, 18, 56, 78, 101, 129, 169, 181, 203, 227, 242, 273, 322, 358, 382, 400
Professional development, xvi, xvii, 8, 43, 273, 324, 325, 334, 358, 361, 399–418
Proficiency, xiv, 5, 8, 11, 12, 20, 22, 27, 29–31, 59, 78, 92–94, 100, 101, 103, 117, 121, 130, 131, 138, 164, 170, 171, 173, 175, 180, 181, 184, 189, 196, 198, 203, 226, 229, 230, 246, 272–274, 276–278, 295, 298–300, 305, 316, 339, 341, 343, 349, 350, 380–382, 416
Profiles, 381
Psychology, 227
Psychosocial stages of professional development, 418
Public esteem, 9

Q

Qualitative, 110, 118, 183, 229, 230, 319, 339, 340, 351
Qualitative case study, 183, 339

R

Radical awareness, x, 58, 63–68, 70–73
Radical knowledge, 58, 71
Reading comprehension, ix, x, 77–94, 244
Reading to Learn, Learning to Write (R2L) pedagogy, xi, xii, 34, 179–199, 244, 264
Recommendation, 143, 244, 248, 260–262, 266, 330–334, 400
Reflexive, 385, 387
Regression analysis, 65, 67–68, 87–88
Relatedness, 31, 37, 274, 276, 280, 294, 298
Resolution, 20, 166, 168–171, 215–217, 220, 222
Revising, 47, 111, 232–235
Russian, 10

S

Scaffolding, 183, 221–223, 322, 331–332, 373
Schooling, ix, 5, 164, 165, 167, 246, 314, 319, 379, 382, 386
Second language (L2) acquisition, 126, 127, 129–130, 142, 202, 228
writing, xii, 202
Secondary school, x, xi, xiv, 22, 27, 28, 31, 39, 43, 83, 85, 91, 102, 125–157, 165, 180, 202, 210, 223, 241, 243, 245, 246, 251, 252, 315, 350, 402
Segregated, 16
Selection, 85, 232, 246, 250, 251, 330, 360–363, 371
Self-determination theory (SDT), 31, 274
Self-determination theory of learning motivation, 31
Self-efficacy, 401, 418
Semantic information, 56, 57, 61, 69, 72
Semantic radical, 64, 72
Semi-structured interview, 138, 184, 230, 324, 340
Sense memory, 204, 213–216, 222
Sentence level, 175, 183, 199
Sentence making, 183, 188, 189, 197, 280, 305
Sentence writing, 183, 197, 290
Separation, 24, 103, 104
Sequencing, 360, 362–363, 377
SFL theory, 181
Shared economy, 280–294
Sharing economy, xiii, xiv, 271–307
Simultaneity, 104, 105
Skill sharing, 415
Social context, 26, 181, 349
Socio-cultural environment, 4
Sociocultural perspective, 229
Sociolinguistic, vii, 181
Song-Stuck-In-My-Head Phenomenon, xi
South Asian ethnic minorities, 164, 165
Space of learning, x, 99–121, 415
Spelling, 56, 166, 183, 187–189, 198, 321
Spoken or written texts, 181, 186, 211, 264, 318
Staged, 181, 242
Stanislavski, xii, 201–223
Stanislavski's system, xii, 201–204, 209–217, 221, 222
Stimulated recall, xiii, 230–231, 340, 341, 344, 345, 349
Structural equation modelling, 89–90
Structural knowledge, 56, 58, 68–71
Structured input activities, 127, 131–134, 137–139, 141–143
Subject-specific genre, 165, 243, 266
Subject-specific literacy, 242, 267
Suitability, 331, 416
Systemic functional linguistics, 4, 181, 184, 205–206

T

Taxonomy of genres, 165, 181
Teacher change, xvi, 400–402, 408–411, 414, 418
Teacher education, 198, 199, 316, 374, 400, 401
Teacher professional development (TPD), 325, 358, 399–418
Teacher-in-role, 102, 106–108, 113, 117, 119, 121, 203
Teachers, Intercultural Development and Emotional Challenge of, 38–41
Teacher's concerns, 400, 402, 403, 407, 414
Teaching
   context, 228, 234, 235, 237
   demonstration, xvi, 400, 410, 414–418
   practices, xiv, 106, 230, 317, 318, 325, 334, 361
   strategies, 133, 183, 198, 199, 317, 318, 321–323, 330, 331, 334
Teaching and learning cycle, 181–183, 244, 245, 266
Teaching of Chinese, ix, 6, 9, 32, 210, 315, 316, 323–325, 363
Technology driven, 331
Tenor, 166, 167, 175, 206, 217
Text analysis, xii, 172, 175, 196, 198, 210, 231
Textual level writing strategies, 232
Theoretical underpinning, xii
Think aloud, xiii, 230–231
Third space, 4, 6, 7, 11–13
Topic sentence, 191, 193, 195, 197, 248–252, 256, 259, 262, 263, 265, 266
Trade and diplomacy, 11
Traditional teaching, 59, 130, 234–236, 363
Trajectories, 340, 381, 394
Transformative, 32, 386, 394
Transforming, 232, 234, 235
Transitivity, 202, 206, 210–213, 221, 222
Translanguaging, 43, 93, 384
Transnational, 12, 49
Tripartite structure, 181

U

UNESCO, 8
University, xiv, xvii, 6, 17–19, 22, 25, 28, 31, 32, 34, 44, 47, 180, 184, 205, 220, 240, 242, 246, 251, 252, 282, 314, 328, 339, 358, 361, 380, 382, 386, 389, 401, 402, 412, 418

University-school partnership, 19, 401, 402
Utility, xv, 338, 341–352

V

Value of concepts, 361, 364, 367
VanPatten's theory, 131, 151, 153, 155, 157
Variation, xv, 24, 28, 34, 110–120, 173–176, 194, 251, 266, 290, 294, 343, 394, 408
Variation theory, 33, 34, 110, 112–117, 266
Variation theory of learning, 32, 34, 103–105
Visual and spatial
   aspects, 65
   information, 69, 70
Vocabulary, xi, 36, 40, 59, 62, 86, 104, 130, 131, 133, 174–175, 180, 186, 194, 196, 197, 199, 215–217, 232–234, 256, 259, 262, 265, 273, 279, 280, 282, 286, 294, 295, 300, 302, 303, 305, 340–344, 346, 348, 349, 362–364, 367, 373, 374
Vocabulary and phrases, 256, 259, 262, 265

W

Whole text level, 175, 199, 266
Word level, 175, 194, 266
Writing, ix, xiii, 3, 21, 28, 36, 48, 57, 63, 105–107, 109, 116, 132, 164, 165, 167, 171, 173–175, 180, 181, 186, 188, 191, 202, 206, 210, 211, 217–221, 227, 230, 231, 244, 264, 265, 273, 279, 280, 297, 302, 305, 316, 318, 331, 358, 360, 365, 368, 371, 373, 376, 390
   ability, xii, 196
   assessment criteria, 185, 251, 253
   performance, xii, xiii, 166, 167, 169, 171, 172, 175, 183, 184, 196, 197, 199, 202, 210–212, 223, 232, 236, 245, 246, 253, 262–263
   process, 215, 216, 227, 228, 230–234
   skills, xiii, 172, 173, 175, 180, 184, 202, 203, 227, 237, 239–267, 278, 331
   strategies, xiii, 225–237
   strategy effectiveness, 231, 235
   system, ix, 58, 79, 80, 82

Y

Young CSL learners, 56–73, 241, 247

Printed by Libri Plureos GmbH
in Hamburg, Germany